A filmmaker like no other, Ken Russell remains one of cinema's extraordinary talents, a creator of masterpieces such as *The Devils*, *Tommy* and *The Music Lovers*, and a body of work that flies from the pastoral, Romantic lyricism of *Delius: Song of Summer* and *Elgar* to the wild extremes of *Lisztomania*, *Altered States* and *Mahler*.

This book explores all of Ken Russell's key movies and television productions, his themes and symbols, his filmic style and direction, and his use of music and visuals.

MEDIA, FEMINISM, CULTURAL STUDIES

*The Sacred Cinema of Andrei Tarkovsky*
by Jeremy Mark Robinson

*Jean-Luc Godard: The Passion of Cinema/ Le Passion de Cinéma*
by Jeremy Mark Robinson

*Liv Tyler: Star In Ascendance*
by Thomas A. Christie

*Mel Brooks: Genius and Loving It!*
by Thomas A. Christie

*John Hughes and Eighties Cinema*
by Thomas A. Christie

*Stepping Forward: Essays, Lectures and Interviews*
by Wolfgang Iser

*Wild Zones: Pornography, Art and Feminism*
by Kelly Ives

*'Cosmo Woman': The World of Women's Magazines*
by Oliver Whitehorne

*Andrea Dworkin*
by Jeremy Mark Robinson

*Cixous, Irigaray, Kristeva: The Jouissance of French Feminism*
by Kelly Ives

*Sex in Art: Pornography and Pleasure in the History of Art*
by Cassidy Hughes

*The Cinema of Richard Linklater*
by Thomas A. Christie

*The Christmas Movie Book*
by Thomas A. Christie

*The Erotic Object: Sexuality in Sculpture
From Prehistory to the Present Day*
by Susan Quinnell

*Women in Pop Music*
by Helen Challis

*Detonation Britain: Nuclear War in the UK*
by Jeremy Mark Robinson

*Luce Irigaray: Lips, Kissing, and the Politics of Sexual Difference*
by Kelly Ives

*Helene Cixous I Love You: The* **Jouissance** *of Writing*
by Kelly Ives

*Julia Kristeva: Art, Love, Melancholy, Philosophy, Semiotics*
by Kelly Ives

*Feminism and Shakespeare*
by B.D. Barnacle


FORTHCOMING CINEMA BOOKS

*Akira: The Movie and the Manga*
*Ghost In the Shell*
*Legend of the Overfiend*
*Fullmetal Alchemist*
*Tim Burton*
*George Lucas*
*Francis Coppola*
*Orson Welles*
*Pier Paolo Pasolini*
*Ingmar Bergman*
*Contempt*
*Pierrot le Fou*
*The Pirates of the Caribbean Movies*
*The Twilight Saga*
*The Harry Potter Movies*

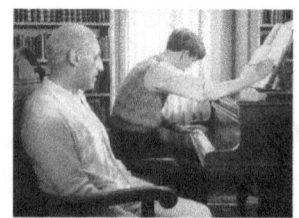

# Jeremy Mark Robinson's Book

## On

# Ken Russell

### England's Great Visionary Film Director and Music Lover

CRESCENT MOON

First published 2015. © Jeremy Mark Robinson 2015.

Printed and bound in the U.S.A.
Set in Book Antiqua, 10 on 14pt.
Designed by Radiance Graphics.

The right of Jeremy Robinson to be identified as the author of this book has been asserted generally in accordance with sections 77 and 78 of the Copyright, Designs and Patents Act 1988.

All rights reserved. No part of this book may be reprinted or reproduced, stored in a retrieval system, or transmitted, in any form or by any means, electronic, mechanical, photocopying, recording or otherwise, without permission from the publisher.

*British Library Cataloguing in Publication data available for this title.*

*ISBN-13 9781861712318*
*ISBN-13 9781861715081*
*ISBN-13 9781861714920*

*Crescent Moon Publishing*
*P.O. Box 1312*
*Maidstone, Kent*
*ME14 5XU, Great Britain*
*www.crmoon.com*

CONTENTS

Acknowledgements   9
Picture Credits   9
Abbreviations   10

Foreword by Sammi Davis   21
Introduction   24

PART ONE: KEN RUSSELL

1   Ken Russell: England's Great Visionary Filmmaker   34

PART TWO: THE WORKS

1   *The Debussy Film*   132
2   *Isadora Duncan*   152
3   *Billion Dollar Brain*   166
4   *Dante's Inferno*   179
5   *Delius: Song of Summer*   217
6   *The Dance of the Seven Veils*   225
7   *Women In Love*   237
8   *The Music Lovers*   289
9   *The Devils*   344
10   *The Boy Friend*   399
11   *Savage Messiah*   417
12   *Mahler*   434
13   *Tommy*   464
14   *Lisztomania*   535
15   *Valentino*   579

16 *Altered States* 597
17 *Crimes of Passion* 616
18 *Gothic* 629
19 *Salome's Last Dance* 643
20 *The Lair of the White Worm* 653
21 *The Rainbow* 668
22 *Prisoner of Honor* 685
23 *Whore* 688
24 *The Mystery of Dr Martinu* 699
25 *Lady Chatterley* 6705
26 *Dogboys* 726
27 Other Movies and Projects 729
28 Unmade Movies 741
29 The Cinema of Ken Russell: Some Conclusons 760

Appendices
   A Summary of Ken Russell's Movie Career 769
   Some Finest Moments in Ken Russell's Movies 773
   Quotes By Ken Russell 774
   Video and DVD: Availability 775
   'Figs' By D.H. Lawrence 776
   *Salomé's Last Dance* by Oscar Wilde 779
   The Who 781
   *Quadrophenia* 796
   Fans on Ken Russell 801
Filmography 803
Bibliography 806

ACKNOWLEDGEMENTS

Thanks to Ken Russell.
Thanks to Sammi Davis for her foreword.
Thanks to John Baxter.

To the copyright holders of the illustrations.
To authors quoted and their publishers.

PICTURE CREDITS

Ken Russell. MGM. United Artists. Warner Bros. Vestron. Virgin Vision. Trimark Pictures. Major Motion Pictures. New World Pictures. Goodtimes Enterprises. BBC. Columbia. Associated British Picture Corporation. Channel 4 Films. London Films. RM Asociates. HBO. RBT Stigwood Productions. Hemdale. British Film Institute.

British pounds have been converted to US dollars at a rate of 1:1.6.

## ABBREVIATIONS

BP   *A British Picture* by Ken Russell
DL   *Directing Film* by Ken Russell
Bax  *An Appalling Talent* by John Baxter
G    *Ken Russell* by Joseph Gomez
PF   *Phallic Frenzy* by Joseph Lanza
WL  *Women In Love* by D.H. Lawrence
RC  *Reel Conversations* edited by G. Hickenlooper

*For Sam*

*All absolute sensation is religious.*

Novalis

*Art is never expressing anything but itself.*

Osar Wilde

Alan BATES  Oliver REED  Glenda JACKSON  Jennie LINDEN

# Women in Love

"Sensuous. Appealing. An intensely romantic love story."

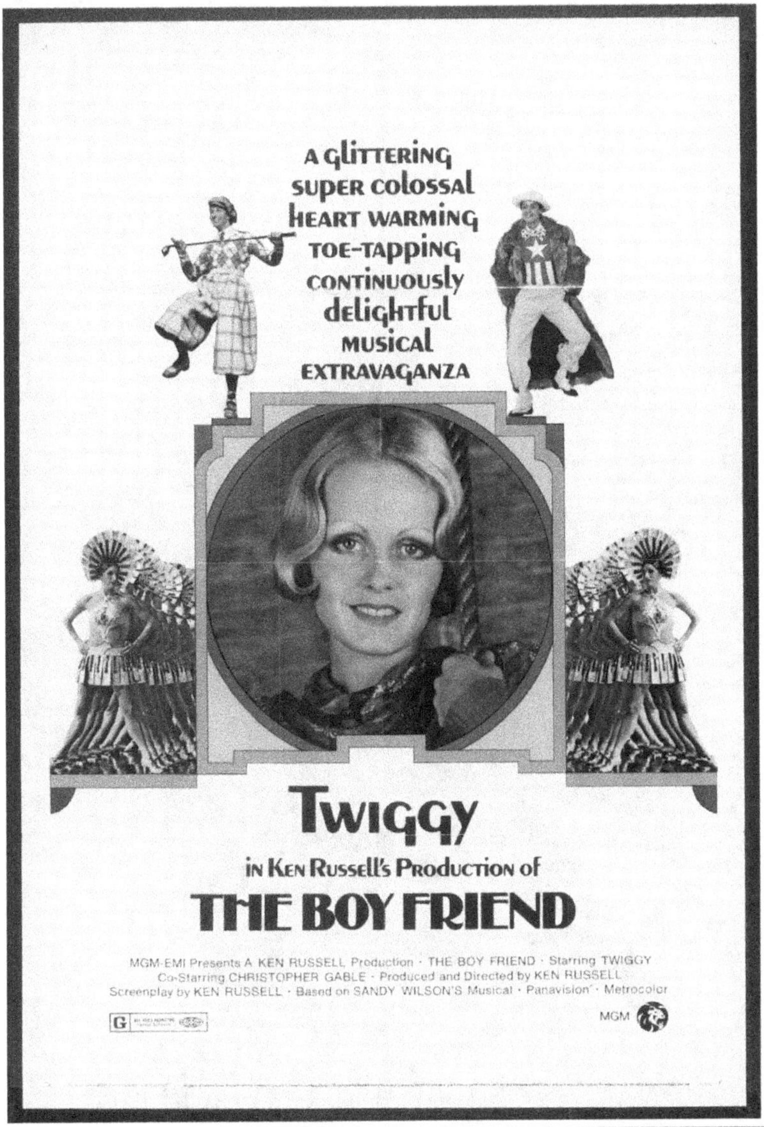
A GLITTERING
SUPER COLOSSAL
HEART WARMING
TOE-TAPPING
CONTINUOUSLY
DELIGHTFUL
MUSICAL
EXTRAVAGANZA
TWIGGY
in KEN RUSSELL's PRODUCTION of
THE BOY FRIEND
MGM-EMI Presents A KEN RUSSELL Production · THE BOY FRIEND · Starring TWIGGY
Co-Starring CHRISTOPHER GABLE · Produced and Directed by KEN RUSSELL
Screenplay by KEN RUSSELL · Based on SANDY WILSON'S Musical · Panavision · Metrocolor
G
MGM

EMI - MGM PRESENTS KEN RUSSELL's PRODUCTION OF
THE
BOY
FRIEND
STARRING
TWIGGY
A KEN RUSSELL PRODUCTION
THE BOY FRIEND
TWIGGY
CHRISTOPHER GABLE
KEN RUSSELL
SANDY WILSON'S
KEN RUSSELL

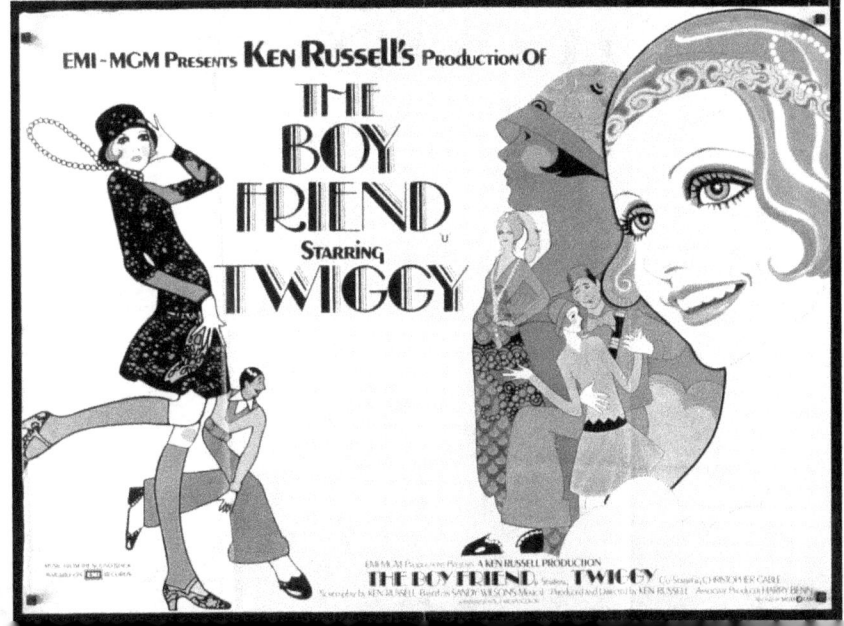

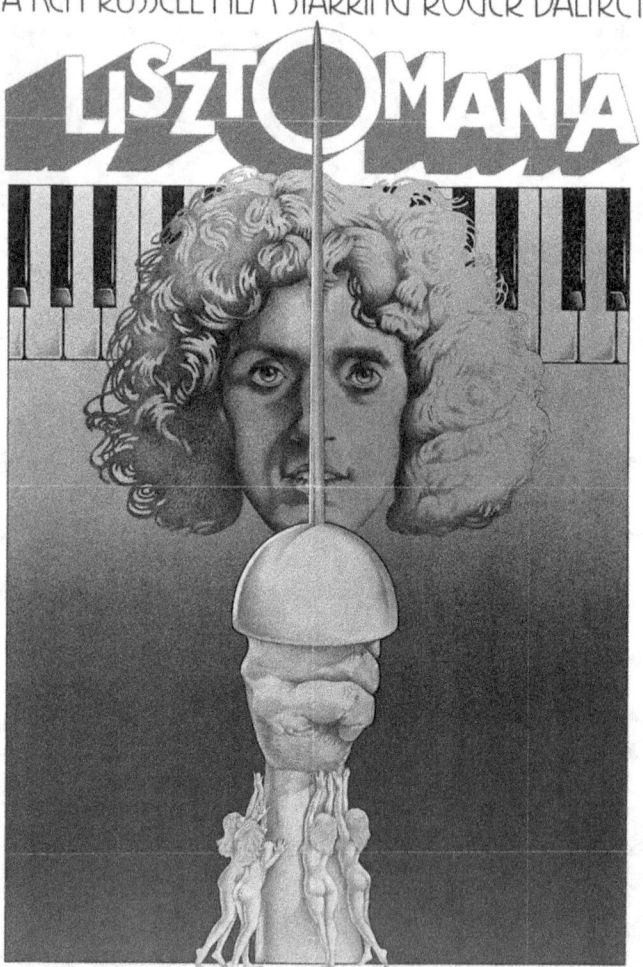

# AU-DELA DU RÉEL
## "ALTERED STATES"

**L'expérience la plus terrifiante de l'histoire de la science échappe à tout contrôle...**

"AU-DELA DU RÉEL" avec WILLIAM HURT · BLAIR BROWN · BOB BALABAN · CHARLES HAID
DANIEL MELNICK · JOHN CORIGLIANO · SIDNEY AARON · PADDY CHAYEFSKY
HOWARD GOTTFRIED · KEN RUSSELL

# FOREWORD

by Sammi Davis
(Actress in *The Lair of the White Worm* and *The Rainbow*)

Ken Russell appeared in my life one bright autumn afternoon in 1986. I had a fifteen minute appointment with him at his London apartment about a role in his now cult classic film, *The Lair of the White Worm*. My first memory of Ken is the vision of a king, a wild-white-haired jovial king. His smile then and now is one of the brightest and most earnest smiles I have ever seen. We chatted happily, the meeting was brief. Twenty minutes after our goodbye, I arrived at my agent's office, Ken had already called to offer me the role.

A man of outrageously creative vision, a man of intuition and passion for his craft, Ken in his red woollen bobble hat and giant winter coat made me laugh and leap like a child throughout the filming of *The Lair*. Full of energy with no tolerance for laziness, he was at times declared a tyrant by grumbling members of the crew; he is no such thing, he lives in a world of enthusiasm and readiness, eager to realize his vision, the reflection of which can be seen so vividly and enjoyably in each of his films; the pace, the passion, leaping from moment to moment.

One day towards the end of *The Lair of the White Worm*, Ken wandered up to me with a manila envelope in his hand and mumbled something about how I might like his new script. A part of him is bold, a part of him is shy, in either respect he has no pretensions. This script was *The Rainbow* which we began shooting a month or so later. We were a team, a team of actors most of whom had worked with Ken before, including Amanda Donohoe and the wonderful Glenda Jackson. I felt an incredible sense of privilege to be chosen as part of the continuance of Ken's repertoire.

Whilst shooting a scene one morning in which I was riding an old bicycle down a hill, I hit a stone, flew into the air and landed smack on my face knocking myself out for several minutes. As I came to, I opened my eyes to the sight of Ken, towering God-like above me and holding out a glass of Champagne to ease my pain. I have to wonder if there is any connection to the fact that Champagne is now my favourite choice of drink…

Later in the shoot, Ken, with a giggle, put a stone in my boot, this time to increase my pain, for a scene in which I had to limp. He always made me laugh with his sparkly eyes and mischievous nature.

This is a man whom I adore, a genius, a joyful leader of uniqueness and fun adventures in the world of film making. I thank Ken Russell for his unequalled visual imagination, his loyalty and care towards his actors, his inspirational quirkiness, and for his dear friendship.

Sammi Davis

# PART ONE
✸
# KEN RUSSELL

# INTRODUCTION

*For me, Ken Russell is the greatest living filmmaker in Britain. Even though he died on November 27, 2011, he's still somehow very much alive. After the death of Michael Powell in 1990, who else was there? As an image-maker, Russell is not only a total natural, he has very few peers among filmmakers — not only in Britain, but also around the globe. Russell's inventiveness seems to know no bounds, and his films are cascades of images, so much so that it can't all be taken in on the first viewing of a picture. Russell does everything a great director and a great artist should do, and then he does so much more.*

Thanks to Ken Russell for his encouragement in writing this book.[1] When I told him I was writing a book on his cinema, his first question was, when will it be finished? Well, it's taken me a lot longer than I anticipated; I've been working on it for years, adding to it, again and again, and rewriting it. Russell is a colossus, incredibly prolific. But Russell was encouraging, and I always hoped he would be able to read it.

---

1 We corresponded (but didn't meet).

## WHY DO I LOVE KEN RUSSELL?

Why do I love Ken Russell's movies so much? For many reasons: the spirituality, such a rare commodity in recent British cinema: Russell's films are not afraid of addressing spiritual issues. ♣ The poetry. ♣ The music – no other filmmaker of the same era in Britain has been such a tireless and enthusiastic promoter of music. ♣ The dancing – no other British film director has included so much dance in their output (and *very few* directors anywhere!).[2] ♣ The British popular culture elements. ♣ The English landscape.[3] ♣ The romance and romantic sensibility. ♣ His stories of artists and creativity. ♣ His interviews and public persona, appearing on everything from websites and YouTube to silliness like British TV's *Big Brother*. ♣ His encouragement of young filmmakers and his teaching.[4]

England… Britain… Wouldn't it be wonderful if British or English movies could be made about England or Britain that were as awe-inspiring as recent Japanese movies made about Japan, like *Princess Mononoke* or *Spirited Away*? Or wild, flamboyant, enormously imaginative *anime* series such as *Fullmetal Alchemist*, *Escaflowne*, *Ghost In the Shell: Stand Alone Complex*, *Moribito: Guardian of the Spirit* or *Mushishi*? Instead, what do we get? Crappy heritage movies, horrible and vicious gangster movies, smug, self-satisfied rom-coms, and dull-as-shit soap operas!

Where are the great filmmakers who can make mythical, visionary works about Britain?

Ken Russell has got closer than most.

• Why isn't there a Ken Russell Film Festival every year? (in the New Forest or Southampton, naturally – come as your favourite Ken Russell character! Dress up as a nun or a Nazi or a hooker or a WW1 soldier or a Decadent dandy!).

• Why aren't the BAFTAs re-named the Russells?

• Why isn't the Royal Albert Hall re-dubbed the Imperial Russell Palace of Music?

• Why isn't there a Ken Russell chain of cinemas, showing German Expressionist masterpieces, British naval WW2 pictures,

---

[2] Yep, there ain't a lotta dancing in the flicks of James Cameron, Ridley Scott, Michael Bay, Jerry Bruckheimer, Wolfgang Petersen, Roland Emmerich *et al*.
[3] Ken Russell's Britain is much more *England* than it is Scotland, Ireland of Wales.
[4] Ken Russell has contributed to many educational courses and film courses. He has been happy to give lectures or help out with workshops. He has been a visiting tutor at Newport Film School and the University of Southampton.

MGM musicals and Charlie Chaplin shorts?
- Why isn't there a Ken Russell radio station, playing Russell's beloved classical composers and folk songs (but without the inane blather of BBC Radio 3 and Classic FM)?

Ken Russell has been dubbed 'the *enfant terrible* of British cinema', 'the Wild Man of the BBC' and 'a fish and chips Fellini' (no, no, it's vice versa – Fellini is a 'pasta and pizza Russell'!). I've been calling him The Greatest Living British Filmmaker for ages.[5]

We all have our favourites. For me, Ken Russell's cinema ranges from the completely stupendous and spell-binding – *The Devils, Tommy, The Music Lovers, Dante's Inferno, The Debussy Film, Delius: Song of Summer, Isadora Duncan, The Dance of the Seven Veils* – to the sheer fun – *Crimes of Passion, Women In Love, Billion Dollar Brain* – to the flawed but majestic – *Lisztomania, Altered States* – to the flawed and disappointing – *The Rainbow, Lady Chatterley, Gothic, Valentino, The Lair of the White Worm* – to pieces I just find flat – *Always On Sunday* and *The Fall of the Louse of Usher*.

Part of problem of assessing the works of Ken Russell is availability and accessibility (a topic we will return to). If you mention Ken Russell, many people will have seen *Women In Love* and *Tommy* and maybe one or two other flicks, such as *The Music Lovers* or *Billion Dollar Brain* (but they likely won't realize that *Billion Dollar Brain* was directed by Russell). If they're older, they might have seen some of the pieces for television, including the *Monitor* programmes, and will talk fondly of *Elgar*. But that's about it.

Which's better than some filmmakers – at least many viewers will have some idea who Ken Russell is, or they will link Ken Russell to particular movies or TV shows. Most film directors don't have that kind of recognition: *very* few film directors have a high profile media image, and are recognized by the general public (even so-called 'major' film directors still get sold as 'from the director of' on the trailers and ads, rather than being referred to by name).

But beyond that, I would guess that the general viewing public (whoever the hell they are) wouldn't have seen or know

---

[5] One of the only other people to agree with me is critic Mark Kermode: 'Russell is Britain's greatest living director', Kermode asserted in *Hatchet Job* (34).

much about Ken Russell's many, many other projects.

And that is in Britain. Outside of the green, sceptred isle, Ken Russell's star will fade rapidly, I would imagine. For instance, he would be known in parts of the United States of America, and in France (where they love movies and filmmakers more than anyone), but not much beyond that. However, many more movies directed by Russell are available in the U.S.A. – not least because he directed most of his movies for North American producers and studios.[6]

Ingmar Bergman, Andrei Tarkovsky, Rainer Werner Fassbinder, Luis Buñuel, Hitch – these are European filmmakers revered by the film *cognoscenti*, but Ken Russell's name would not be placed among that company by many film critics. As Russell himself remarked, if he'd been called 'Russellini' he might be more accepted in movie circles.[7] (But no, it's the *other way around*: Federico Fellini is 'the Italian Ken Russell'!).[8]

In a way, it doesn't matter... but it does if you've evaluating cinema and a particular filmmaker. There are whole books, for instance, on over-rated filmmakers who have only made three or four movies! Quentin Tarantino, Peter Jackson, Steven Soderbergh, Terry Malick, etc. By comparison with them, Russell is a major filmmaker with an incredible body of work.

Yet to fully appreciate Ken Russell's cinema, you need to have seen films such as *The Devils* and *Savage Messiah* and *Mahler* and *Delius: Song of Summer* and *Crimes of Passion* and *The Rainbow* and so on. You also need to have caught a good proportion of Russell's TV work. Russell's output is truly staggering and mind-boggling: in television and cinema, he has produced a huge number of pieces.

For instance, if you think that Ken Russell turns out brash, vulgar, self-consciously excessive and dumb movies, you must see *Delius: Song of Summer* or *Savage Messiah* or *Prisoner of Honor*.[9]

---

[6] However, filmmakers with an encyclopedic understanding of cinema, such as Martin Scorsese, wrongly believed that more of Russell's BBC work was available in Britain than the U.S.A.

[7] Sometimes Russell is 'Russellini', often he's 'Russellstein' (Eisenstein) and 'Russellelles' (Welles), and sometimes he's 'Russell-lin' (Chaplin).

[8] M. Kermode, 2013, 34.

[9] Journos still trot out total misrepresentations of Russell's art. For ex, Sally Vincent in a 1999 piece *The Guardian* summarized Russell's movies as a 'relentless battering of desperately joyless sexual images... It is all so pointlessly energetic: frantic masturbations, mountings, jerkings, throbbings, pumpings, suckings, gruntings, stocking tops and brassieres, stiletto heels heels and suspender belts and crotches and yoghurt-smeared lippy', etc etc. What crap! What was Vincent watching?!

The problem is, only a handful of Russell movies are broadcast on TV, and most of Russell's TV programmes have hardly been seen at all since their original air date.[10] It's true that *Elgar* was repeated a number of times in the 1960s, but that's a film that doesn't represent Russell's work properly, and is regarded as a white-wash and PR job[11] by the director.[12] It's more about what the audience wants to see about Edward Elgar (1857-1934). 'It's me hero-worshipping him, and it's what everyone wanted him to be like, what *I* wanted him to be like,' admitted Russell (in G, 45).[13]

It's true that most TV shows aren't usually repeated anyway.[14] Some are, but it's a tiny proportion of the whole output of television – even of a small country like Britain. It's also true that TV shows are very rarely exported. So viewers in Italy, say, or South Africa, will probably never have seen a TV show directed by Ken Russell. Similarly, most theatrical films are *not* shown outside of their country of origin. A Jean-Luc Godard movie or an Ingmar Bergman movie might travel to other European countries, or to the U.S.A., but only because they are well-known film-makers with a very high critical standing. But most movies made in, say, Poland, will only ever be seen in Poland, and only ever on Polish TV (if they are lucky enough to be broadcast at all).

So a full appreciation of an important filmmaker such as Ken Russell cannot take place unless viewers have seen most of his major works. I discovered this when recently writing books on Jean-Luc Godard and Walerian Borowczyk. Andrei Tarkovsky

10 The BBC's newer cable channel, BBC Four, has re-broadcast some of the early Russell works.
11 Certainly it led to an increase in sales of Edward Elgar's music, and altered the public reception of Elgar in Blighty.
12 It's just 'all too lovely, like a TV commercial for the Malvern Hills!' It was too uncritical, Russell said, taking the composer's music at face value, and not seeing what was behind it, what Edward Elgar was really like. If he was to remake the *Elgar* show, Russell said in 1989, he would include 3 elements that didn't fit with the current view of Elgar: his dalliances; his relationship with his music publisher and friend, Jaeger; and his preoccupation with suicide. Russell put some of those elements into his re-visit to Elgar in 2002: *Elgar: Fantasy of a Composer on a Bicycle*.
13 However, there was some ironic commentary on Elgar's music – for instance, when one of his most famous pieces was played, the *Pomp and Circumstance March*, which has become one of England's unofficial national anthems, and about as pro-British, pro-establishment and nationalistic as music can get, the *Monitor* programme included images of the First World War, taken from the archives at the Imperial War Museum in London.
14 One aspect of television that Ken Russell liked was that shows were repeated, whereas movies were released, did the rounds of the theatres, then disappeared. Sometimes they might pop up on TV. As he remarked in 1973: 'if I could feel that films I did for television were shown all over the world at frequent intervals I'd probably never make a so-called feature film again' (Bax, 138). Those views were expressed before home video and DVD, which Russell embraced, and before the rise of the internet, which Russell also embraced wholeheartedly.

was easy – he only helmed seven feature films, all of which are available. But many of the movies of Godard and Borowczyk (including key works) are *not* available, not on video or DVD. The advent of video, and later DVD, has certainly made many works obtainable, but even then often only in particular territories or in sub-standard versions.

With Ken Russell, you'd think that, in Britain at least, his films would be readily available. Many are, but many are not. There are numerous reasons for this – to do with money and sales, obviously – but also legal issues, who owns what, etc. It's probably true that if Warners or MGM or United Artists or the BBC or whoever found out that a Ken Russell movie might sell 30 million units on DVD, it would be in Wal-Mart or Tesco's this afternoon.

Some filmmakers never produce audio commentaries to DVD versions of their movies, and one wishes they would: Woody Allen, Ingmar Bergman and Steven Spielberg, for example, are some filmmakers I really wish would provide commentaries. Happily, Ken Russell does, and I highly recommend buying the DVD versions of his films for the commentaries alone. Russell is a wonderful commentator on his own movies, offering all sorts of priceless stories and snippets about the productions.[15]

The American DVD release of some of Ken Russell's 1960s BBC films (*Ken Russell At the BBC*) is absolutely indispensable: the box set includes *The Debussy Film, Isadora Duncan, Dante's Inferno* and *Delius: Song of Summer*. If you haven't seen some of these masterpieces, get this box of DVDs. You won't believe your eyes.

I have been amazed many times in writing this book about Ken Russell's cinema. He's astonishing, as we all know, but until only recently have I realized just how astonishing. *Delius: Song of Summer* has been available for some time, and it's one of Russell's finest works. But I hadn't seen three of the 1960s TV films, *The Debussy Film, Isadora Duncan* and *Dante's Inferno*, before (collected on the BBC Video DVD).

OMG, this man is a genius! I simply can't believe how Ken Russell achieved it all. The level of imagination and flair is just astounding. Russell proves for all to see that with a group of dedicated actors and film crew, a masterpiece can be attained on a tiny budget (and you need a ton of ideas, a strong screenplay and

---

15 On the internet, the Savage Messiah site is a good place to start: iainfisher.com/Russell.

lots of food – plus a tipple or two).

Ken Russell has never been establishment as a film director like, say, Alfred Hitchcock, David Lean, Carol Reed or Michael Powell, some of the film directors continually wheeled out as the best of British talent. However, one of Russell's films made it into the Top 100 British movies collated by the guardians of Brit film culture, British Film Institute, in 1999 (guess which one? Yeah, *Women in Love*. Let's ignore the fact that the studio was North American (United Artists), that the money was American, that the co-writer and producer and originator of the project (Larry Kramer) was also American.)

But, as this book insists, Ken Russell as a filmmaker is every bit as fascinating, as talented, as stylish, or as crazy as Hitch, Lean, Reed or Powell & Pressburger. And his pictures are just as extraordinary.

Quite a few film critics as well as film fans criticize Ken Russell's later work in the light of his earlier work. It's unfair, but it's difficult not to do it. Thus, *Mindbender* or *Dogboys* will be compared with *The Devils* or *Tommy*. It's unfair because the context and conditions of each project are different: the production of, say, *Altered States*, was pretty tough, and *Women in Love*, for instance, was produced in a different cultural as well as cinematic context from, say, *Prisoner of Honor* or *The Fall of the Louse of Usher*.

And we should always remember that it's *extremely difficult* to make films as good as the finest of Ken Russell's movies – *The Devils*, *Tommy*, or *The Music Lovers*. To demonstrate that, you could have a go yourself. Assuming you can raise the finance for a movie about nuns and priests in Loudun or a classical composer, you'd have to tackle by far the toughest task on any movie: developing a script that did everything you wanted to do (also within a particular budget, also satisfying your backers, also something filmable).

Which's why some movies – including the best of Ken Russell – seem miraculous. How did they get the money and resources and actors to produce *The Devils*?! Or other filmmakers' work, like *The Wind Rises*?! Or *Chimes At Midnight*?! Or *Ran*?! It's completely remarkable.

The best movies seem as if they have always already existed.

As if they came from nowhere but should always have been there. As if you have always known them, to the point where you seem a part of them (almost as if you had made them yourself).

But not every movie can be that miraculous (if only!). And so not every Ken Russell picture can be *Savage Messiah* or *Mahler* or *Delius*.

The vitriol that Ken Russell has personally attracted from critics is striking, as if he's become the whipping boy for whatever is pissing off the critics. But a large number of 'major' film directors have produced turkeys.

Recent duds include:

Steven Spielberg, *Tin-Tin* (some would add *Hook* and *1941*)

Ridley Scott, *Hannibal*,[16] *Kingdom of Heaven, G.I. Jane, Black Hawk Down*

Peter Greenaway, *8 1/2 Women*     Alan Parker, *Evita*

Peter Jackson, *The Hobbit, King Kong, The Frighteners*

Brian de Palma, *The Bonfire of the Vanities, Snake Eyes, Mission To Mars*

Terry Gilliam, *The Brothers Grimm, Fear and Loathing In Las Vegas*

Quentin Tarantino, *Kill Bill*     Sam Raimi, *Spider-man 3*

Paul Thomas Anderson, *Punch-Drunk Love*

(Of course, one wouldn't class Jackson, Raimi, de Palma, Parker, Tarantino, etc, as 'major' film directors).

And how about these total bombs? –

*The Lion, the Witch and The Wardrobe* (cost: $180m), *Prince Caspian* (cost: $200m), *Voyage of the Dawn Treader, Spider-man 3* (cost: $300 million), *Home On the Range* (cost $110 million), *Snow White and the Huntsman* (cost: $170 million!), the *Bourne* series, *Quantum of Solace, Casino Royale, The Hunger Games, Batman Begins, The Beach, 8MM, Alien vs. Predator, Chocolat, Vanilla Sky, Amélie, About a Boy, Billy Elliot, The Hulk, Oceans 11,* the *Charlie's*

---

[16] *Hannibal* (2001), part of the *Silence of the Lambs/* Thomas Harris franchise, was overseen by film legend Dino de Laurentiis (1919-2010). *Hannibal* was a pitifully bad thriller, woefully misjudged in tone and substance. It's difficult to believe that Ridley Scott directed it, and that David Mamet and Steve Zallian worked on the screenplay (*Steve Zallian!* He wrote *Schindler's List!* Much-celebrated playwright *David Mamet!*). Some critics agree with me: 'very likely the worst film of this year and quite possibly the next', commented Charles Taylor in Salon.com, while Ella Taylor in *L.A. Weekly* called it 'the flabbiest of cop-outs'. Mick LaSalle in the *San Francisco Chronicle* found *Hannibal* 'wilfully gross, fundamentally stupid and in no way worth the discomfit of watching it.'
According to Wikipedia, the budget for *Hannibal* was $87 million. 87,000,000 bucks! You have GOT to be kidding! For a routine thriller that would cost less than a million on TV! And what could Ken Russell have done with $87 million?!

*Angels* movies, *Unbreakable*, *Jungle Book 2*, *Lemony Snicket*, *Sin City*, *Lara Croft*, *King Arthur*, *The Village*, *X-Men Origins: Wolverine*, the *Bridget Jones* films and *Where the Wild Things Are*.

So, sure, Ken Russell has directed some financial flops, and some very disappointing pictures, but many of the bombs I've noted above (there are *plenty* more!) are shockingly inept and misconceived (and *very* expensive): *Snow White and the Huntsman*, a travesty of a movie,[17] *Casino Royale*, the 2006 *James Bond* re-boot which had the sophisticated, world-weary super-spy acting like a ditzy, love-sick teenager, *Where the Wild Things Are*, Universal's cretinous movie-as-psychotherapy, offensive on every possible level, *Alien vs. Predator*, a shocking devaluation of a once-entertaining horror franchise, *The Hulk*, simply awful and woefully misjudged (despite the high-calibre talent involved), *X-Men Origins: Wolverine*, a deeply disturbing cesspit of a movie, and *Chocolat*, a gruelling two hours of insipid shit.[18]

Some of those movies are truly abysmal (some are even offensively bad, with their insidious pro-military, pro-war, pro-American ideology). And the sum total of the budgets and P & A and marketing of just this handful of movies amounts to – $4 billion? $5 billion? $10 billion? (Just *one* of those crappy movies would've paid for *all* of Ken Russell's unmade projects! Ack!).

※

In one respect Ken Russell is far ahead of the critics, and that is in the realm of music. No *major* film critic, alive or dead, has the anything like the knowledge that Russell has about music. Thus, they simply *can't* assess the depictions of music and composers accurately. (Music critics, tho', have taken Russell to task for his representations of composers and music, particularly, of course, the assassinations. But even they would also have to (grudgingly) admit that Russell contributed towards the dissemination of classical music in popular culture).

I have refrained from quoting too many critics who dislike Ken Russell's cinema: you know who they are, and you know

---

17 A complete flop, *Snow White and the Huntsman* (Universal, 2012), was… a series of empty shots, a fairy tale eviscerated of all magic. There's literally *nothing here*, nothing going on. I wait and wait for *something* to happen. But it doesn't.
What a waste of money! *Snow White* isn't 'bloated' or over-done or OTT (some of the usual accusations against current blockbuster flicks), it's not 'done' at all (it's uncooked). It's just empty. There really is nothing there at all. And it cost $170 million!!
18 Despite starring two gorgeous actors, Johnny Depp and Juliette Binoche.

what they've written. There's no point really in bringing those complaints and attacks back to life. Russell's films polarize people as few other British filmmakers' works do. It does seem that people either love his movies or hate 'em.

If you've bought this book or are reading it, I'm guessing you like Ken Russell's films a lot. So we don't need to spend time going over what Pauline Kael or Vincent Canby or Judith Crist or Alexander Walker said about this or that Russell movie.

Besides, Ken Russell himself has found the sheer number of critics who have come out against him daunting and upsetting. In his review of Joseph Lanza's 2008 study of himself, Russell said that when Lanza piles up so many negative reviews, it has the effect of depressing the hell out of the director. And Russell wondered if the sheer number of bad reviews might influence the undiscerning reader.[19]

I'm reminded of England's greatest painter, J.M.W. Turner. *Every* major art critic of the day came out against Turner's art: William Hazlitt, John Taylor, James Boaden, Richard Westmacott, William Thackeray, Leigh Hunt, *The Times*, *The Athenaeum*, *Tatler*, etc. It deeply distressed the painter (though he was a tough character, a working class Cockney).

But all of the critics of Joseph William Mallord Turner were *wrong*. WRONG. And no one remembers what Hazlitt or Thackeray said (except the animosity between, say, James Whistler and Turner). But no one can forget Turner's extraordinary paintings. I've been to exhibitions in New York City of Turner's art which have been packed with punters, and lectures on Turner which fill a giant auditorium at the Met.

J.M.W. Turner's art lives on... But the critics fade into *utter oblivion*.

✻

I admit I have not been able to finish this book – it remains a work in progress. Why? Because there is simply too much to say about Ken Russell and his cinema, and too much still to say.

Jeremy Robinson

Los Angeles and Kent, England

---

19 Ken Russell stated in the London *Times* in 2008: 'But because Lanza feels compelled to reprint the worst of every bad review my films have received as a coda to each chapter, I can only surmise that I'm damned on every page. It has taken some nerve for me just to keep reading. More than once the temptation to retire to bed with the covers over my head reared up like a phantom holiday in the park. Did I do that? Did I say that? And more to the point, did they say that?'

# 1

# KEN RUSSELL: ENGLAND'S GREAT VISIONARY FILMMAKER

> We do live on a magic island, without doubt, but so far as British films are concerned there is precious little evidence of this. By and large, contemporary filmmakers seem to revel in squalor, glorify ignorance and extol violence. There is another kind of life outside of this which many people in this country would like to celebrate, if only they were given the opportunity and not made to feel guilty about it. It has nothing to do with religion; it is to do with the spirit of the land in which we live, that elusive quality touched on by the music of VW (Vaughan Williams) and his contemporaries such as Arnold Bax, Frank Bridge and John Ireland: music expressing the majesty of nature, forgotten rituals, pagan goddesses and ancient heroes.
>
> Ken Russell, *A British Picture* (238-8)

ENGLAND'S GREATEST LIVING FILMMAKER.

Ken Russell is England's greatest living filmmaker; I've been saying this for years, and even now he's staging musicals featuring angels and great artists on heavenly clouds,[20] it's still true. Russell seemed to have always been around.

After the deaths of Michael Powell and David Lean, Ken Russell was The Man.

---

[20] Nothing's changed there then! – Ken Russell would be right at home in heaven (chatting with his favourite classical composers, for instance) – but he'd probably ask for a transfer to somewhere hotter and wilder!

Who else was there? Oh, yes, there are many other British film directors who have become more successful, commercially, than Ken Russell: Ridley Scott, Tony Scott, Alan Parker, Adrian Lyne, Mike Newell, *et al*. And there are the 'important' or 'serious' Brit filmmakers, like Mike Leigh or Ken Loach or Alan Clarke. And the mavericks, like Peter Greenaway and Derek Jarman.

It's true that filmmakers like the Scotts, the Parkers, the Hudsons and the Lynes can make big, glossy movies with tons of action and pretty people and all, and it's true that I love many of the films of the above film directors...

...But there's something about Ken Russell's films that makes him, ultimately, a more fascinating filmmaker than pretty much *all* other British filmmakers of recent times. It's do with, I think, the subjects that he's chosen and how his movies seem to be reaching for something. Often they don't reach it; often they don't deliver on their promise or their goals. That happened more with the later pieces... But the group of movies that Ken Russell produced from the late 1960s to the end of the 1970s are remarkable on so many levels. Part of it is to with the sheer *joy* of making cinema, which the films of that period are full of. And then there is the enormous *ambition* of those subjects (even more extraordinary bearing in mind that these works were mainly made for low budgets). And there's the way that Russell tackled those subjects and themes and stories. Visually, they are stunning. The muse of music has no superior in British cinema. And there are some outstanding performances.[21] It's all quite remarkable.

☆

Henry Kenneth Alfred Russell was born in Southampton in Southern England on July 3, 1927;[22] he grew up in Southampton. He died in Lymington, Hampshire, on November 27, 2011. As well as being associated with Southern England, where he lived (in the New Forest), and where many of his movies have been filmed (all along the South Coast), and with London and the Home Counties (where Britain's film production is centred), Russell also has strong links to the Lake District in Northern

---

[21] For a film director often derided for emphasizing visuals and spectacle too much (unfairly and mistakenly, I think), Russell managed to provide the creative context on set for numerous great performances in his movies.

[22] Ken Russell is of the generation of Stanley Kubrick (b. 1928), Jean-Luc Godard (b. 1930), Bryan Forbes (b. 1926), Kenneth Anger (b. 1927), Andrzej Wajda (b. 1927) and Andy Warhol (b. 1928).

England.[23]

☆

Ken Russell studied at Pangbourne, as a cadet at the Royal Naval College, from 1941; and later at Walthamstow (the Technical College and School of Art, where he met Shirley Kingdon, his first wife). He spent time in the Merchant Navy[24] and the Royal Air Force. He worked in an art gallery (Lefèvre Art Gallery) in Bond Street, London. In the 1950s, he was a stills photographer, for magazines such as *Picture Post* and *Illustrated*. He became fascinated by ballet, and studied evenings in Hampstead, at the International Ballet School.[25] He toured with dance companies (both photography and choreography would feature prominently in his movies).[26] By the late 1950s, Russell was working for the BBC, making arts documentaries (the first was in 1959 – having impressed the BBC with his home-made movies).

Ken Russell was married four times – to Shirley Kingdon (married between 1956-78), Vivian Jolly (1983-91),[27] Hetty Baynes (1992-99) and Elize Tribble (2001-2011). Jolly, Russell's second wife, was a film student and assistant on *Savage Messiah*. Russell met his fourth wife, actress Baynes, when he was casting a *South Bank Show* documentary. Russell met his fourth wife Tribble when she answered a lonely hearts ad he placed in *The Times*: 'Unbankable film director Ken Russell seeks soul mate – mad about movies, music, and Moët and Chandon champagne'.

Every biography, autobiography, interview and study of Ken Russell agrees that in his youth movies played a huge role. Russell consumed thousands and thousands of movies in his childhood. He has cited so many cinematic influences, so many film icons he worshipped, so many movies he saw, some repeatedly: William Boyd Westerns... *The Fleet's Inn* ('drooling over Dorothy Lamour' a dozen times)... Betty Grable in *Spring-time In*

---

[23] For many years Russell had a place in the New Forest, and also a bungalow near the ocean. A fire in recent years burnt up numerous belongings. Russell has also lived in his beloved Lake District, and in London.

[24] He left the Navy, according to Joseph Gomez, due to a nervous breakdown (1976, 18).

[25] Russell acknowledged that he wasn't the greatest of dancers, and dancers were some of his (many) heroes.

[26] Ken Russell has written at length in his autobiographies and interviews of his time in the Merchant Navy, his tours with dance companies, and his early attempts at amateur filmmaking.

[27] Anthony Perkins officiated at Russell's wedding to Vivian Jolly – the ceremony took place on the *Queen Mary*, included extracts from Thomas Hardy and William Wordsworth, and doubled as a wrap party for *Crimes of Passion*.

*the Rockies* ('lots of Grable musicals')... giant, German Expressionist epics like *Metropolis* and *Die Niebelungen* and of course the crazy, abstract *Cabinet of Dr Caligari*... Andy Clyde, Old Mother Reilly... *The Secret of the Loch*... *Citizen Kane*... Mickey Mouse... Charlie Chaplin... Felix the Cat... Snub Pollard... Betty Boop... *Of Mice and Men*... *The Westerner*... and 'almost every Warner Brothers film'...

Going to the movies was not just every week, but several times a week for Ken Russell (often with his mom or aunts or relatives). Sometimes 2 or 3 times a day. As he recalled: even when he was stationed out of town in the military, he 'still managed to see almost every film released in the early Forties', and sometimes would bicycle 30 miles to Salisbury to catch a movie (which gives an idea of his passion for cinema, which never left him).

CLASSIC RUSSELL.

The two periods of 'classic' Ken Russell work would be the TV documentaries of the early-to-late 1960s (with 1962's *Elgar* as the highpoint that everyone remembers), and the feature films of the late 1960s to late 1970s (with *Women in Love* and *Tommy* being the high watermarks among audiences if not critics).

Certainly, it's with *Women in Love*[28] that Ken Russell begins that extraordinary run of feature-length movies: *Women In Love* thus helped Russell's career enormously: *Women in Love* was followed by *The Music Lovers* (his favourite movie), which was followed by *The Devils*, which was followed by *The Boy Friend*, which was followed by *Savage Messiah*, which was followed by *Mahler*, which was followed by *Tommy*, which was followed by *Lisztomania*. That's a run of eight amazing movies. You could add *Valentino* and *Altered States* (many wouldn't).

'OUTRAGEOUS', 'VULGAR', 'ENFANT TERRIBLE'.

Over the course of his film career, Ken Russell has been asked the same questions again and again. Like Alfred Hitchcock or Charlie Chaplin, Russell is one of the very few film directors that the general public might have heard of and who also has a recognizable media persona. As he put it in *A British Picture*:

---

[28] D.H. Lawrence himself had not been opposed to the idea of making *Women in Love* into a movie, when it was suggested back in the 1920s.

Am I difficult to work with? Do I hate actors? Am I a misogynist? Do I set out to shock just for the sake of it? Do I distort facts? Does it bother me that many of my films are flops? Is it true that I never go to the cinema? What does it feel like to be the oldest *enfant terrible* in the business? (BP, 161)

In short, people – film critics too, who should know better – believe and endorse the legend (and Ken Russell, like Orson Welles or Werner Herzog or Michael Powell, certainly helps along the legend with his anecdotes and chat show stories).[29] But maybe he recounts those stories because it's expected of him, and it's what people want, and it's easier than sitting in silence.

Ken Russell was known as an 'outrageous' filmmaker, delighting in 'shock' tactics – as Joe Gomez succinctly put it in his excellent mid-1970s study of Russellini: 'his films are outstanding examples of the 'kick 'em in the crotch' school of overstatement' (1976, 70) – including extremes of sex,[30] temperament, behaviour and violence;[31] his style employed flamboyant camerawork, rapid cutting, anti-naturalism, and extravagance; he preferred out-size acting, often camp[32] and self-mocking; his themes were art, sex, death and the individual (usually the artist) in society; his films seemed to be apolitical, far more interested in depicting the many strands of an artist's life than social comment or ideology. If Russell had any political views, they were formed in the middle of the 20th century (Existentialism, bohemia, the artist as rebel, psychoanalysis, and a profound 18-19th century Romanticism), and rounded off by the hippy ideals of the 1960s. Russell's one overriding theme or driving philosophy was Romanticism, and the myth of the Romantic artist informed most of his work (meaning Romanticism in the 18th and 19th centuries, with its tenets of infinity, going to extremes, the sublime, subjectivity, emotionalism, ecstasy, paganism, mythology, poetry and art, mysticism and spirituality, unity, idealism, the individual over/ against society, and so on). 'He's a very romantic man', Glenda

---

29 Ken Russell is the film director as 'Mr De Thrill', the director in *The Boy Friend*.
30 Glenda Jackson defended the depiction of sex in a Ken Russell movie: it wasn't exploitative, she affirmed, it was part of the characters and the drama. And eroticism is so personal anyway.
31 Later filmmakers, such as Peter Greenaway or Derek Jarman, were sometimes dubbed 'controversial' by the media. But how tame the works of Greenaway and Jarman appear beside those of Ken Russell!
32 Ken Russell is so camp he out-camps many gay filmmakers, as Raymond Murray pointed out in his guide to gay and lesbian cinema. Critics have noticed that homosexuality is sometimes sent up or denounced in Russell's cinema. This campest and gayest of heterosexual filmmakers often portrays homosexuality negatively.

Jackson said (1972).

The psychology that Ken Russell employs in his cinema is of the Freudian school, as if Russell picked up a book on Sigmund Freud in the 1950s, and applied it to everything he did after that. Russell's philosophy and approach is very much of the mid-20th century, of the 1940s and the 1950s, *not* the 1960s (he was 33 when the Sixties began). That is the mid-20th century of Existential philosophy (with its emphasis on outsiderness, alienation and the individual), the Parisian *avant garde,* Surrealism, psychoanalysis, the American Beat Generation, jazz and early rock 'n' roll (tho' classical music has always been Uncle Ken's rock music). Over that all, World War Two dominates.

Ken Russell's films were just as often set in rural landscapes, including the wild reaches of Cumbria, as in towns and cities; his pictures were not London or Home Counties-biased, like so much of British cinema; Russell's cinema enshrined the myth and dream of England/ Britain, like the work of Derek Jarman, John Boorman and Michael Powell, a place rich in history, poetry, art and culture.

What is a filmmaker, in the realm of commercial, entertainment cinema? A storyteller. *A filmmaker is a storyteller* (among many other things). And I guess I like the stories that Ken Russell tells, and I like most of his characters. It ain't the same with many contemporary filmmakers – I don't like (or want, or need) their stories or their characters.

Yes, the *way* that Ken Russell tells his stories and presents his characters is wild, unusual, flamboyant, colourful – and sometimes crude and hysterical. But I still much prefer his stories and characters to so many of contemporary Western cinema's stories and characters. Who cares about violent gangsters and drug dealers and the banal, stupid, smug, arrogant, vain white heroes and heroines of so many contemporary Hollywood or British movies? Not I.

Luis Buñuel is a useful comparison in terms of the critical reception with Ken Russell: quite a few of Buñuel's movies were satires and comedies about religious or social topics (often with Catholicism as the target). Yet although Buñuel is revered by many critics, some of his satires aren't particularly funny, and certainly not as successful as some of Russell's satires. A late 'comedy' of Buñuel's like *The Milky Way* (1969), for instance, is a series of feeble anti-clerical skits (and filmed in a flabby, indifferent manner, too). And not a patch on *Dance of the Seven Veils*, which Russell directed (and wrote) a year later.

Anti-Russell critics are many; some critics just can't get on with Ken Russell's form of cinema. British critics especially don't seem to know what to make of him. David Shipman said in *The Story of Cinema* that while Russell is 'capable of spectacular and *outré* images on the screen... he has no gift for character, situation, pacing, rhythm, tension or tone' (1130). That is *rubbish!*

Critics saw Russell's cinema as self-indulgent, excessive, pretentious, boorish, coarse, and simplistic. D.H. Lawrence's champion, the (over-rated but influential) critic F.R. Leavis, hated Russell's interpretation of Lawrence (*Women in Love*), calling it an outrage and 'an obscene undertaking'. Russell's movies are not what critics expect, or want: and they don't offer a pretext for the things that critics like to write about. As Jack Fisher put it, 'the critics, confronted with work which doesn't stimulate what they are prepared to say, flounder and react negatively'.[33]

'The cult of Ken Russell really depends on an act of faith, a willingness to believe in the master's integrity in what he does,' remarked Peter Webb in *The Erotic Arts* (290). That applies to virtually any artist. You have to go along with what they're doing. Otherwise there's no exchange at all.

Asked about the notion of being 'indulgent' in movies, a critique often hurled at Ken Russell, the filmmaker replied:

> Films are hard to make and I think the word indulge really leads one to believe that it's an easy sort of business and it's really extremely difficult. You'll be standing out there in the rain thinking that it's not an easy job being a film director. But the director is the director and if he feels for whatever reason, perhaps under great delusion, that he wants that scene and he can get away with it even though it might be questionable in terms of taste then he should be allowed to do it. It's his movie. But if the committee steps in and says you can't do that because we're going to cut it out then it's a waste of time.

Excessive? Well, *duh*, <u>of course</u> Ken Russell's cinema can be excessive. As Michael Gallagher pointed out, in reference to *The Devils* and *Lisztomania* (in the *Catholic Film Newsletter* of all places), 'to accuse Russell of excess when he is working in this area, however, is very much like accusing Rubens of sensuality'.[34] Yes

---
[33] J. Fisher, in T. Atkins, 40.
[34] Quoted in PF, 7.

– being excessive is what Russell does for a living.

Like Federico Fellini and Kenneth Anger, Ken Russell's is a pagan, earthy, visionary form of cinema: Camille Paglia in *Sexual Personae* calls Hollywood the modern Rome, with its depictions of

> pagan sex and violence that have flowered so vividly in our mass media. The camera has unbound daemonic western imagination. Cinema is a *sexual showing*, a pagan flaunting. Plot and dialogue are obsolete word-baggage. Cinema, the most eye-intense of genres, has restored pagan antiquity's cultic exhibitionism. Spectacle is a pagan cult of the eye. (33)

Huw Wheldon on Ken Russell:

> Ken needs a strong producer or a strong script-writer, or both, because without them his own powers of invention and imagination are so enormous that he's like a bird being driven along on a huge gale. It was this gale that made him such a marvellous colleague. Most of my colleagues in those days were drivers but Ken was like a team of stallions. He had a leaping imagination and, as frequently happens with people of this kind, great tenacity and determination. He would go through a stone wall to get the proper location. If it's necessary to be on the 54th floor then you go to the 54th floor, and *certainly* you walk up the stairs. (Bax, 123)

Entertainment came first in movie-making for Ken Russell: 'to entertain first, and the preaching comes second. Most of my films are based on that premise'. Russell said that he made his films for himself, and hoped that someone else was entertained (RC, 247).

There are times when you're watching a Ken Russell work and you think, oh crap, he's not going to do *that*! And he does. Yep, Russell delights in delivering some really simplistic symbolism or gestures, stuff that a fifth grader or 14 year-old kid getting hold of a video camera might think was really cool.

Ken Russell's public persona was also larger-than-life, and often threatened to undermine the attention given to his movies. He had run-ins with censors and film critics (famously attacking Alexander Walker with a newspaper on television in 1971 on the late night discussion programme *24 Hours*); he was a regular (and entertaining) guest on TV chat shows and documentaries (talking about Oliver Reed, for instance, or Keith Moon, or the current state of the British film industry). He was on TV and radio and in print so often his stories, such as one about how the naked wrestling scene was shot in *Women in Love*, became very familiar (Russell has discussed that scene so many times, it would make a movie longer than ten *Women In Loves*). He often appeared in his films (*Lady Chatterley, Whore, Gothic, Valentino, Tommy*, and so on), and presented TV documentaries (part of Russell's personality is definitely the frustrated actor).

Approaching someone from the outside as a subject for a movie, from the media, from books and magazines and newspapers, would all be lies, Ken Russell asserted: he didn't want the everyday facts about someone, what time they woke up, but the spirit of their work: 'the spirit of music, the spirit of Mahler, the spirit of D.H. Lawrence, that's what I'm into. That's the truth, the artistic truth' (RC, 245).

No one had really got to grips with the real Ken Russell, the director complained: 'nobody knows the real me and I've never seen the real me written about' (RC, 245).

His reputation as the Bad Boy of British Cinema, a rebel, an iconoclast, etc, was ill-founded, said Ken Russell. In person, he said he was quite mild-mannered and shy, which disappointed and upset people when they met him (BP, 156). That Russell is shy and quiet is attested by numerous colleagues: Huw Wheldon recalled that when he met Russell in the late 1950s, he was 'shy and quiet... A little watchful, but silent and extremely modest' (in PF, 36). The abrasive Russell emerged after he left the Beeb, Wheldon remarked: but although 'singularly quiet, gentle and modest', Russell was also very confident from the beginning, knew what he wanted, and would walk through walls to get it (Bax, 121). Of course: only someone with incredible drive, energy and ambition could've produced that huge amount of work. You don't make movies and TV shows by sitting on your ass at home complaining that nobody returns your calls or reads your scripts! Russell is the classic filmmaker as self-taught artist, where the philosophy is: *fuck it, let's grab a camera and go do it already!*

The more flamboyant, dandy and outspoken aspects of Ken Russell's media persona developed in the late 1960s. Before that, Russell was often seen as introvert: as his stature increased with the successes of *Women in Love* and *The Music Lovers*, the familiar Ken Russell – camp, loud, OTT – came to the fore in media appearances. In John Baxter's priceless book *An Appalling Talent*, Russell is described thus:

> He is wearing a grey flannel suit, additions to which include a black sweater decorated with a jewelled semiquaver, a lapel badge of a ferret with the caption "Deviate Today", silver rings showing on one an Egyptian *ankh* and on the other Mickey Mouse, black shoes with white kid tops and a blue cloth cap whose badge is embossed with a double-decker tram and the word "Leeds". (Bax, 95)

And when Joseph Gomez visited the set of *Tommy*, he found Russell:

> Sporting an unkempt silver-grey beard, longish hair, sunglasses, and a candy-striped suit and resembling a cross between Sam Peckinpah and Edmund Gwenn (Kris Kringle in *Miracle On 34th Street*). (1976, 91)

As well as shy and reserved, Ken Russell has also been described as temperamental and mercurial, occasionally given to outbursts of anger on set. But also very generous, and a lot of fun – there can be a lot of laughs on a Russell set.

John Baxter described Ken Russell in the familiar terms of an emotional, volatile personality: those whom he discovers to be enemies are resented, but loyalty and friendship and devotion are rewarded – with loyalty, friendship and devotion (Bax, 124).

Despite occasionally falling out with some people on his crews, and one or two actors, and the odd writer or producer, during the most successful times of his career, Ken Russell had plenty of people eager to work on his movies. There was a regular bunch of filmmakers and actors, for instance, who would turn up to work on each subsequent production. If a Ken Russell movie really was a tough experience, with the director overly demanding and given to prima donna outbursts, and the hours long, and the pay low (and the food terrible), many performers and crew wouldn't come back. But they did.

One thing was sure with a Ken Russell movie: you got to do stuff, in front of or behind the camera, that you hardly did anywhere else. (There are things that actors have done on a Russell movie/ TV show that they will only have done that once: running along a field waving the Czech flag while naked, dressing up as a combination of Wagner, Hitler and a storm-trooper and mowing down Jews in the street with a machine gun, and of course wrestling in the nude!).

THE FILM CAREER.

Writing this book, I am struck again and again by the sheer amount of work that Ken Russell has produced, by the quality of it, by the breadth of subjects in it, by the number of genres he has tackled, and by the torrent of images he has created. 'Putting pictures to music has always been a pleasure,' Russell wrote, 'like being paid to screw your favourite film star' (BP, 268-9).

Simply to consider Ken Russell's television work would require a hefty book in itself. Russell is probably always thought of a film director first, but he has actually produced many more TV shows than feature films.

In 2000, Ken Russell (aged 73) ventured into the world of very low budget filmmaking, a return to home movies, based in his New Forest home, edited on computers, with friends and helpers working for next-to-nothing (Russell embarked on an ambitious interpretation of *The Fall of the House of Usher*, and hoped to sell his movies on the internet). Other short films of the 2000s included *A Kitten for Hitler* (2007), *Hot Pants* (2006) and *Boudicca Bites Back* (2009). *Hot Pants* comprised 'three sexy shorts': *Revenge of the Elephant Man* (2004), *The Mystery of Mata Hari* (2004) and *The Good Ship Venus* (2005). That Russell couldn't obtain backing for his later projects was awful, Glenda Jackson complained after his death, for a filmmaker with his incredible talent and body of work.

The 23 feature films directed by Ken Russell and released theatrically are:

*French Dressing*
*Billion Dollar Brain*
*Women In Love*
*The Music Lovers*
*The Devils*
*The Boy Friend*
*Savage Messiah*
*Mahler*
*Tommy*
*Lisztomania*
*Valentino*
*Altered States*
*Crimes of Passion*
*Gothic*
*Aria* (segment)
*Salome's Last Dance*
*The Lair of the White Worm*

*The Rainbow*
*Whore*
*Mindbender*
*The Lion's Mouth*
*The Fall of the Louse of Usher*
*Hot Pants*

The films directed for television include:

*Isadora Duncan*
*Dante's Inferno*
*The Debussy Film*
*Delius: Song of Summer*
*The Dance of the Seven Veils*
*Clouds of Glory*
*The Planets*
*A British Picture*
*Road to Mandalay*
*The Strange Affliction of Anton Bruckner*
*The Insatiable Mrs Kirsch* (from *Tales of Erotica*)
*The Mystery of Dr Martinu*
*The Secret Life of Arnold Bax*
*Prisoner of Honor*
*Lady Chatterley*
*Ken Russell's Treasure Island*
*Alice in Russialand*
*Classic Widows*
*In Search of the English Folk Song*
*Dogboys*
*Elgar: Fantasy of a Composer On a Bicycle*
*Brighton Belles*

Ken Russell favoured films about classical composers (Tchaikovsky, Mahler, Strauss, Prokofiev, Debussy, Delius, Elgar, Liszt, Sir Arnold Bax, Bruckner), and artists (Gaudier-Brzeska, Byron, Shelley, Wordsworth, Coleridge, Rossetti, Valentino),[35] and literary adaptions and allusions (D.H. Lawrence, Lord Byron, Percy Bysshe Shelley, Oscar Wilde, Dr Polidori, Aldous Huxley, H.S. Ede, Bram Stoker, Edgar Allan Poe and Len Deighton). Most of Russell's films have been based on novels or biographies[36] (as with many film directors, including the greats): *The Music Lovers, Savage Messiah, The Lair of the White Worm, Valentino, The Rainbow, Women in Love* and *Lady Chatterley*. Plays have also been favoured

---
35 Ken Russell said he might like and revere artists, but he also recognized that they were people too, and he saw their flaws (RC, 246).
36 The biopic is one of Russell's key forms – but fictionalized, highly theatrical versions of biographies.

by Russell: *Whore, Salomé's Last Dance, The Devils, The Boy Friend,* and the musical *Tommy*. Ken Russell filmed three D.H. Lawrence novels (*Women in Love, The Rainbow* and *Lady Chatterley's Lover*) – something, I think, no other director has done.

The most celebrated of Ken Russell's early films, made for the BBC (where his mentor was Huw Wheldon), were about classical composers (Edward Elgar, Claude Debussy, Sergei Prokofiev, Béla Bartók, Richard Strauss, Frederick Delius). He also directed films about Antonio Gaudi, James Lloyd, Dante Gabriel Rossetti, Lotte Lenya, Isadora Duncan, Marie Rambert, Shelagh Delaney, Gordon Jacob, and painters Robert McBryde and Robert Coquhoun.

Ken Russell called his film on Richard Strauss, *The Dance of the Seven Veils,* 'an irreverent comic strip, as lurid as his music' (1993, 101). Russell wanted to pop Strauss's pompous ego, but the resultant film was controversial, with questions being asked in the House of Commons. Russell noted that he wasn't employed by the BBC after the Strauss film for 21 years (until *Lady Chatterley*). It was only screened once, and never since. What a shame! It's *wild*!

An early trip to Haworth, centre of the Brontë cult, when Ken and Shirley Russell were newly-weds in 1957, resulted in a series of b/w photographs of Kingdon impersonating the Brontë sisters in costumes she'd made. For Russell, it was

> the beginning of a lot of things I still attempt on films. I still enjoy location, for instance. The recce trip is one of the most enjoyable things about filmmaking. And the do-it-yourself approach has carried on. We still beg, borrow and steal props and make do and mend and improvize a lot. It might be rough and ready but it pays off in a kind of intangible authenticity. (Bax, 92)

Ken Russell's *Monitor* and *Omnibus* documentaries of the late 1950s and 1960s included *Bartók, London Moods, Mr Chester's Traction Engines, Old Battersea House, Architecture of Entertainment, Cranks At Work, The Light Fantastic, Marie Rambert Remembers, The Miner's Picnic, Shelagh Delaney's Salford, Gordon Jacob, Guitar Craze, McBryde and Coquhoun: Two Scottish Painters, Poet's London, Portrait of a Goon, Variations On a Mechanical Theme, The Debussy Film, Elgar, Lotte Lenya Sings Kurt Weill, Dante's Inferno, Always On Sunday, Diary of a Nobody, The Dotty World of James Lloyd, Lonely Shore, Watch the Birdie, Pop Goes the Easel, Preservation Man, Antonio*

*Gaudi, Don't Shoot the Composer, Song of Summer* and *Dance of the Seven Veils.* (Remember that many of the *Monitor* and TV pieces were only ten or fifteen minutes long).

Ken Russell had a long-standing friendship with Melvyn Bragg, presenter of ITV's *South Bank Show* in England. Russell made a few documentaries for *South Bank Show*, and other TV slots, in the 1980s and 1990s. Bragg (b. 1939 – now Lord Bragg) is one of Russell's most important collaborators – not only has he been one of Russell's strongest supporters, he has, with the London Weekend Televison/ *South Bank Show* team, given Russell many opportunities to present documentaries and film essays on national television.

And Melvyn Bragg[37] wrote one of Ken Russell's most significant movies: *The Music Lovers,* the one Russell regards as a masterpiece, a long-cherished project which he wouldn't change at all. And Bragg also co-wrote TV films such as *Always On Sunday,*[38] *Clouds of Glory,* and *The Debussy Film.* (It must be significant, too, that Bragg shares with Russell a passion for British Romantic poets and artists, and also for the Lake District – for a while they were neighbours up in Cumbria).[39] Following his early film scripts, Bragg worked chiefly in televison and radio (a pity, because his movie scripts are excellent).

Ken Russell produced a documentary on Georges Delerue in 1966, who had scored his first feature film, *French Dressing* (and went on to compose the music for *Women In Love).* Delerue (1924-92), along with Henry Mancini and Michel Legrand, was one of the chief composers of the French New Wave films (he wrote the scores for *Don't Shoot the Piano Player, Contempt, Hiroshima Mon Amour, La Peu Douce, Day For Night, The Conformist, Anne and Muriel, A Man For All Seasons* and *Anne of the Thousand Days,* for example. Many of those movies are regarded as classics).

Joseph Gomez identified two traditions of filmmaking that were forerunners of Ken Russell's cinema: the film biography, such as those about Émile Zola or Louis Pasteur or Abraham Lincoln or Glenn Miller or General George Patton or Sir Thomas Becket. Russell has made the biopic his own genre. Russell's films

---

[37] Bragg's movie credits include *Jesus Christ Superstar, The Music Lovers, Isadora, Play Dirty, Orion* and *A Time To Dance.*
[38] With Melvyn Bragg, Ken Russell wrote a portrait of the French painter Henri Rousseau, the misunderstood 'primitivist' – *Always On Sunday* (1965).
[39] Bragg has included the Lakes in his fiction, with Thomas Hardy as an obvious touchstone.

draw on the biographical filmic tradition but depart from it radically. They might begin with research and facts, but they don't bother with historical contextualization,[40] for instance, or with a chronology.[41] And they reserve the right to veer off into fantasy, nightmare, dream and more fantasy: Russell has never let anything hold him back when he wants to explore the inner life of his subjects. If they're hankering after sex, or fame, or spiritual oneness in their dreams, Russell will show that, rather than have 'em talk about it to someone else, or muse wistfully in voiceover.

The other tradition is the British documentary – first on film, then, from the 1950s onwards, for television. But the British documentary tradition is closely linked with socialist-realist approaches, of which the 'kitchen sink' dramas of the 1960s are an off-shoot. Ken Russell, needless to say, is *not* part of the left-wing or left-liberal political school of filmmaking in Britain, the Mike Leighs and Ken Loachs. (For instance, altho' Russell has included scenes of hard labour such as mining (in *Women In Love*), or scraping a living in poverty (in *Savage Messiah*), it is not in the naturalistic/ realistic mode of the 'kitchen sink' brigade).

Focussing on an individual in the biopics cleverly combines two strands in Ken Russell's œuvre: documentary/ history and fantasy/ fiction. A point that Russell has made time and time again is that reality is always more fantastical and unbelievable than fantasy. It's true: real life is *far stranger* than anything anyone can imagine. Any time critics or studio executives have questioned whether this or that crazy event really occurred, Russell has responded with photographs and written evidence to say, yes, that crazee stuff *did* happen. 'People are always saying my films are bizarre,' Russell said, 'but they pale beside reality'.[42]

Ken Russell is among the most accomplished filmmakers at stretching budgets.[43] Many of his films were made in the region of $400,000-$1,500,000. And, considering many were historical films, that meant that Russell and his production team had to find all manner of ways of enhancing the movie within strict limits.

---

[40] But the first question for everybody (cast and crew) in the team would be: *'what year is this?'*
[41] Some of Ken Russell's historical films simply dispense with many of the conventions of the genre. For instance, bustling street scenes or long shots or cities, to set the scene. There are none at all in *Lisztomania*, and very few in *Mahler*.
[42] Quoted in J. Baxter, 1976, 22
[43] Ken Russell enjoyed having a high budget on *Altered States* – his biggest (RC, 249).

Working in the same arena of historical films on very low budgets (and in the same era) were filmmakers such as Werner Herzog, Luis Buñuel and Pier Paolo Pasolini.

Although Ken Russell disliked historical films for their romanticized, nostalgic look, he wasn't against doing lots of historical research. For pictures such as *The Devils* and *Savage Messiah*, Russell said he conducted tons of research. Russell remarked that it was impossible to use every bit of information that research turned up, 'so you may as well use the ones that suit your concept best' (Bax, 223). Russell smarted from critics attacking his historical films for something that was actually accurate (often it was the things that seemed the more ludicrous that were actually true).

One of Ken Russell's notions was a kind of cinematic simulacrum, a re-animation of the dead and of the past: to use the real locations if possible,[44] and to use the dialogue that people really said, and to cast actors who looked like the originals. Then 'there is a chance that one will get some resonance, capture the elusive, ghostly moment when it all happened' (Bax, 134). At the same time, Russell also acknowledges that the idea of dressing modern actors up in old costumes and having them pretend to be real, historical people was also bogus – and he sent up that way of making documentaries in his wild, OTT *The Dance of the Seven Veils*.

One could extend the study of Ken Russell's films into areas like Russell's cinema in the international marketplace, and how they have fared at the box office. If Russell's films had been huge hits, he probably would've been given more money to spend on his films. At the same time, there would have more studio (and producer) interference. One of the advantages of low budget filmmaking is the independence. It's all about balances: even with their modest budgets, Russell had many run-ins with studios and producers who disagreed with how he'd put his movies together.

Part of the context of Ken Russell's work of the late 1960s and early 1970s, for instance, which's the golden age of Russell's cinema, is that North American studios were still investing in European (and British) film production (that is, timing played a

---

[44] Over the course of his career, Ken Russell must've filmed in more of Britain's country mansions and churches, as well as 100s of picturesque spots in the landscape, than almost any other film director.

significant role in Russell's career: had he entered feature film production 7-10 years later, it would have been a different story).[45]

Sometimes the American film studios got more than they bargained for from some of their British productions (such as *Performance*, *The Devils* and *The Music Lovers*). Ken Russell remarked that American studios wanted to have it both ways: they wanted to come to Great Britain and produce movies – which they did more of in the 1960s than any other time (and the British film industry never really recovered when they pulled out) – but they also wanted them to conform to their conservative values. And when they saw the more out-there movies they'd paid for, such as *The Devils* or *Performance* (both funded by Warners), they reacted badly.

And when Hollywood pulled out of Albion, partly due to its own crisis, around 1970-71, bang went the backing of studios like United Artists and Warner Brothers. For some commentators, including me, the British film industry has never really recovered from that collapse.[46] It was certainly much more of a struggle for many British filmmakers after the early Seventies, including Ken Russell. His films *Mahler* and *Savage Messiah*, for instance, were made on much smaller budgets ($268,000) than *The Devils*, *Women in Love* or *The Music Lovers*, which were backed by Warners and UA.

One of the striking things is that, although most of his productions were financed with North American money, the casts were usually all-Brits (one or two Americans were cast in the earlier movies, such as *Billion Dollar Brain,* and increasingly from *Tommy* onwards; but Ken Russell's movies avoid token Americans or international casts). Not only that, but many of the key roles were taken up by relatively unknown British actors: nobody in the U.S.A. would've heard of Dudley Sutton, Georgina Hale, Christ-opher Gable, Judith Paris, Max Adrian or others in the Russell Repertory Company). If *The Devils* or *The Music Lovers* or another historical movie of the 1960s and 1970s were made today, roles such as Count Chiluvsky in *The Music Lovers* or Baron de

---

[45] For instance, you can only make a series of stupendous movies like those of Ken Russell's if you have decent financial backing, the resources of a fully-equipped studio, a terrific crew, amazing performers, and talented collaborators.

[46] Yeah – when was the last time you saw a British movie about a British subject in a first-run British movie house? I don't mean *James Bond, Harry Potter* or something filmed in Britain, or using British actors and crew, and I don't mean on television, DVD, Blu-ray, video or online, I mean a properly, fully *British* theme and subject in a British cinema.

Laubardemont and Father Barré in *The Devils*, would definitely be cast using prominent American or international performers.

Ken Russell had a deal with the small, North American company Vestron in the 1980s which allowed him to make lower budget films without interference (Dan Ireland, Vice President at Vestron in acquisitions, was a big fan of Russell's work).[47] The budgets were very low – 'so tight it hurts', complained Russell (BP, 274). However, Russell was a wayward talent, and even when he was given free rein, he still occasionally produced low quality films. His movies of this 1980s period – *The Rainbow*, *Gothic*, *The Lair of the White Worm* and *Salomé's Last Dance* were for some critics low-power pictures. Many had literary origins (Bram Stoker, John Polidori, Mary Shelley, Oscar Wilde and D.H. Lawrence).

I have to admit, each of the four pictures of 1986-1989, from *Gothic* to *The Rainbow*, failed to amaze me in the same way as *Tommy* or *The Music Lovers* or *The Devils* did. They are not in the same class, I reckon. However, repeated viewings uncover all sorts of treasures in those four movies: the most significant aspects are that they are all about *British* subjects, they were based on material that was British, they were made in Britain, they were produced by a (mainly) British cast and crew, they were directed by a Brit, and, perhaps most importantly, they were in a *British* style of filmmaking (OK, the finance was North American – but the money is American for most of the 'British' movies you've seen or heard of. And, sad to say, any movie that appears to be 'British' that you've seen in a first-run theatre will be backed by American or foreign money).

Disregarding the $$$$$, this is the 'British picture' of Ken Russell's ideal philosophy: movies made about British subjects. But they weren't bleedin' gangsters in white Jags, not silly heritage melodramas, and not 'realistic' dramas about miserable lives on housing estates.

COMMERCIALS AND CAPITALISM.

Selling your soul to commercial television, commercials made for television, is one of Ken Russell's *bête noires*. He reckoned he

---

[47] The Vestron deal of 3 movies came about partly due to the success on video of *Gothic* (released in the U.S.A. on Vestron Video), according to Joseph Lanza (PF, 272).

produced about 20[48] in the early to mid 1960s:

> Black Magic chocolates; that was a bad one. Half a dozen for Galaxy chocolate bars, all slow-motion things shot in Rome. I did Horlicks, baked beans, though I drew the line at cancer-killing cigarettes. But I thought that even the apparently harmless ones were immoral and doing me as much harm as everyone else, so I stopped. (Bax)

Everybody remembers the famous and amazing scene in *Tommy* where Ann-Margret rolls around in a sea of baked beans, washing powder and chocolate (it was altered form its original conception in the script). It's a send-up of mass advertizing, which is a recurring theme in Ken Russell's cinema: he distrusts the idealizations of advertizing, and reckons that they create gulfs between desire and attainment in Western society. The ad men show one thing, but the consumer can never attain it.

Commercials for Ken Russell are

> fantasies on life which promise a romantic solution but which can only lead to disillusionment, disappointment – death! To me, commercials are the twentieth century's greatest crime against man. I hate the insidious brain-washing effect they are having on our society. (Bax, 192)

The flood of chocolate and soap powder out of the television set in *Tommy* is also an ironic comment upon Ken Russell's own work within the advertizing industry. Like many of his contemporaries, Russell has made some TV commercials. That bitterness was originally going to be stronger in *Tommy* – in the script, Nora wouldn't have enjoyed it so much, and there would have been an ironic compilation of music from Peter Tchaikovsky, Sergei Rachmaninoff and Liberace.(Even so, the scene is still over-the-top, but it works partly because of the intense anger fuelling it).

For Ken Russell, the core of *The Music Lovers* was really the 'destructive force of dreams', how dreaming can disrupt lives, rather than simply a story about Peter Tchaikovsky. *The Music Lovers* was 'a black comedy about the decadence of romanticism'. Russell linked this to the rapacious consumerism of a late capitalist society:

---

[48] Meanwhile, Ridley Scott was happy to boast that he had made about 2,000 commercials before he went into features.

The television adman's trick of passing off his dream as an attainable and desirable reality is to my mind the great tragedy of our age.

## HUMOUR AND SATIRE.

There is a *lot more* satire and irony and send-up, some of it vicious and unmerciful, in Ken Russell's cinema than many critics as well as many audiences realize. There is an anger, too, especially in the films of the 1968-1975 period (I am reminded of friends of Jean-Luc Godard, including Anna Karina, who were shocked sometimes by just how angry Godard was – at everything, not only America and capitalism – but most of all at himself. The rage erupted in movies such as *Weekend, La Chinoise* and *Masculine Feminine*). Ken Russell's cinema is sometimes as caustic and vitriolic as Godard's: *The Devils,* most especially, but also *The Music Lovers, Women in Love, Savage Messiah* and *Mahler*. The anger certainly gives those pictures a tremendous energy, as with Godard's work. (Anger is also a key element in the work of Ingmar Bergman, Oliver Stone and Hayao Miyazaki).

American painter Ad Reinhardt remarked:

> The ugliest spectacle is that of artists selling themselves. Art as a commodity is an ugly idea… The artist as businessman is uglier than the businessman as artist.

The *Monty Python* team satirized Ken Russell's films a number of times (their famous TV shows were first broadcast between 1969 and 1974, the time of Russell's 'golden age' of filmmaking). In one send-up, entitled *Ken Russell's Garden Club, 1958* (1971), a bunch of people in silly costumes (including a pantomime goose), a Gumby and a naked woman cavort in a tangle of bodies on a flower bed (part of the Pythons' series 3, programme 1, *The Money Programme*). In another sketch (in series 3, programme 9, *The All-England Summarize Proust Competition*), a group of language students (wearing headphones, in booths) do a dance routine, Sandy Wilson's version of *The Devils*. And in the blindingly brilliant comedy *Monty Python and the Holy Grail*, they took on the plague scenes in *The Devils* – 'bring out your dead!'

Ken Russell's kind of cinema has always been easy to parody, because it's extravagant, over-the-top and ambitious (and *distinctive*, which makes it easier to parody). Actually, it's *already* parodying itself. No one can out-Russell Russell, because his movies satirize their subjects ruthlessly. (Really, it wasn't the Pythons spoofing Russell's movies so much as loving that kind of filmmaking themselves – the Pythons weren't averse to having people dressed in animal costumes or doing silly dances in their sketches).

## KEN RUSSELL AND BRITISH CINEMA

Art is never expressing anything but itself.

Oscar Wilde, *The Decay of Lying*

Ken Russell isn't usually placed with the European New Wave filmmakers by critics. Some filmmakers working in Blighty, such as Dick Lester, Lindsay Anderson and Ken Loach, had consciously taken up some of the French New Wave's techniques. You can see the influence of the New Wave on Russell's films, though. And there are direct links to the French *nouvelle vague*: Russell had Georges Delerue compose the music for *French Dressing* and *Women in Love* (he scored New Wave classics like *Jules et Jim, Shoot the Pianist, Hiroshima Mon Amour* and *Contempt*); and Jeanne Moreau was Russell's first choice for *Savage Messiah*.

*British cinema* – both François Truffaut and Jean-Luc Godard denounced British cinema, claiming that it didn't even exist. Those bastards! Well, OK, they do have a point. But to counter their oh-so French sneering, their oh-so arrogant denunciations, I would put forward some names:

Alfred Hitchcock
Charlie Chaplin
David Lean
Michael Powell
and Ken Russell

Oh, for certain, Truffaut and Godard (and all of the Parisian film *cogniscenti*) would dismiss David Lean as lightweight and populist, and Michael Powell as too fey, arch, self-conscious and pretentious, but they couldn't ignore Alfred Hitchcock or Charlie Chaplin – oh no, they are two filmmakers that French ciné culture absolutely reveres (along with Tsui Hark, Jerry Lewis, Woody Allen *et al*). And, *no,* Hitchcock was *not* American, even though many of his most famous and celebrated movies were made (and set and financed) in the Land of the Free. Nope, Hitch is *British* through and through (and he didn't even go to make movies in the U.S. of A. until he was 40!).

I've added Ken Russell to that list. Why not?

In the 1960s and the 1970s, when Ken Russell was at the height of his power as a filmmaker in the theatrical release arena, his series of films (and TV shows) could certainly hold up well against *anything* that continental Europe or North America was turning out. True, Godard, Rohmer, Chabrol, Truffaut and their ilk in the Nouvelle Vague have been the darlings of film critics, and Russell has never had a similar solid, gushing critical following.

Of all the countries of the world, it is *Italian* filmmakers that I think of most often in connection with Ken Russell. And three Italian filmmakers in particular: Federico Fellini,[49] Luchino Visconti and Pier Paolo Pasolini (you can certainly spot the influence of Fellini on Russell, though Russell is virtually anti-Pasolinian; yet the poetics of cinema, which Pasolini continually evoked, are fundamental to Russell's movies). Closely followed by Germans such as Fritz Lang and F.W. Murnau (there are 100s of links between Russell's cinema and the great German film-makers – but that's also true of just about anybody, as their influence has been almost universal). And of course Hollywood: Vincente Minnelli, Gene Kelly and MGM musicals, but also Busby Berkeley musicals of the 1930s, and RKO Fred Astaire musicals of the 1930s and 1940s. Orson Welles, always (*Citizen Kane* in particular). Among fellow Brits, Michael Powell above all, but also Charlie Chaplin, and maybe a little Alfred Hitchcock from time to time (but not much).

But although Ken Russell is one of the very few international filmmakers who evoke an authentic 'British' culture and society, who has been devoted to aspects of art and culture in Britain, he is not really a 'British' filmmaker. Neither is he American, or international: he is his own genre and category: Russellian. Just

---

[49] Ken Russell liked Federico Fellini's movies, and wrote in 2007 in praise of Fellini's classic 1954 picture *La Strada*, which 'features the director's wife, Giulietta Masina, in a heartrending performance as a female clown, Gelsomina, who partners a hard-hearted strongman in his act after her mother sells her to a carnival'. In turn, Fellini enjoyed *The Devils*.

like Orson Welles or Alfred Hitchcock created their own niches within world cinema – watch two or three successive shots from Hitch or Welles, and you can tell it's them, out of 1000s of movies. It's the same with Russell.

In short, Ken Russell has always been an outsider figure (a maverick, an oddball, an individualist, an eccentric even), in many respects.[50] From the kind of movies (the subjects, the approach) he makes… to the way of working.

> Maybe I was born in the wrong country. I'm not into small-time no-hopers and the dull and boring things that seem to interest English film directors. I don't see any point in making films about people painting electricity pylons in northern England. It's ludicrous, and that's the British film industry. (2009)

Similarly, within the British film industry, Ken Russell has not been one of the establishment figures: in 2009 he commented:

> I don't really consider myself part of the industry here, and never have, because all my films but one have been financed by Americans.

That's a point worth considering, but it's true of many of the most celebrated filmmakers in Britain or born in Britain: many of their movies are financed by North American companies (certainly that's true of filmmakers like Ridley and Tony Scott, Mike Newell, Alan Parker, Paul S. Anderson, etc).[51]

Often thought of as a *British* film director making *British* movies about *British* subjects, Ken Russell has actually directed most of his movies for North American film studios and North American film producers, with, crucially, *North American* money, and most of his feature-length movies have been about non-British subjects.

It's not just about finance, though: take *Harry Potter* and *James Bond*, two of the most well-known and financially successful movie franchises associated with the United Kingdom. Put aside that those films are American-financed (which includes marketing, PR, distribution, etc, as well as the negative cost and the rights); the *form* of the *Harry Potter* and *James Bond* movies is entirely

---

[50] 'I've never played the game. I have my own game and I'm very happy playing that', Ken Russell said in 2009.
[51] That most of Ken Russell's features are North American-financed is part of the reason why his movies are much more available in the Land of the Free than in many other territories. As Russell says, there are shelves devoted to his films in the U.S.A., but not in Blighty.

American.

Even though *Harry Potter* and *James Bond* contain British characters and settings, are made or based in Britain, and include British crews and performers, they are wholly *American* movies.[52]

## MICHAEL POWELL AND KEN RUSSELL.

In *Fire Over England*, Ken Russell expressed his admiration for Michael Powell's movies, such as *The Red Shoes* ('the best film on classical ballet ever made'), *I Know Where I'm Going!* ('the most magical romantic comedy ever made in England'), *Black Narcissus, A Canterbury Tale* and others. Russell said he saw *The Red Shoes* twice at the Odeon, Haymarket, when it opened in 1946;[53] although *The Red Shoes* was melodramatic, with the sets looking like 'chocolate box surrealism', the ballet had 'many imaginative touches' (1993, 33). Russell admired Powell's talent for bringing out the British landscape, in films such as *Gone To Earth, I Know Where I'm Going!* and *A Canterbury Tale* (Powell and Pressburger were very unusual in this respect, among the very few to get to grips with what the world of Britain really was).

But Ken Russell also makes some waspish swipes at Mickey Powell, such as the comment that the last time he saw Powell the elder director was working as a teaboy for Francis Coppola at Zeotrope in the early 1980s (not true of course).[54] Russell was dismissive of *Peeping Tom*[55] (along with many critics and audiences – at the time, but since then the 1960 picture has been re-evaluated as a cult classic. However, Powell didn't write

---

[52] It's the same with *Star Wars* and *Indiana Jones*: although they were based in film studios in Britain, employed many people from Britain in the crew, and in front of the camera, no one thinks of them as 'British'.
[53] Where I saw Russell's own *Crimes of Passion* in its first run, forty years later.
[54] Powell was working at Zeotrope Studios, which Coppola had relocated from 'Frisco to Hollywood General Studios (where, incidentally, part of *The Thief of Bagdad* had been filmed, which Powell had co-directed).
[55] Ken Russell was bemused by Powell's decision to make *Peeping Tom*, in which 'he engineered his own suicide... Has any other director in the history of the cinema been buried by one of his own movies?' (1993). I don't agree with Uncle Ken: and if it was 'suicide', it was a helluva way to go! It was more complicated, more ambiguous than that.

*Peeping Tom* – Leo Marks did).[56]

It's ironic seeing Ken Russell lay into Michael Powell, because Russell has made his fair share of turkeys in his time – or what crrritics have perceived as turkeys (*Whore, The Lair of the White Worm, Gothic, Lady Chatterley*, etc). Also, Russell had only one film that has definitely entered 'classic' status as far as movie critics and film fans are concerned (*Women in Love*, though *The Devils, The Music Lovers* and *Tommy* are definitely masterpieces, and *Delius: Song of Summer* and *The Dance of the Seven Veils* are very high quality works, not to mention *Lisztomania* or *Mahler* or *Savage Messiah*), while Powell had at least four accepted masterworks (*The Red Shoes, A Matter of Life and Death, Colonel Blimp* and *Black Narcissus*; many would also include *Gone To Earth, I Know Where I'm Going!, Tales of Hoffman* and *Peeping Tom*).

Mickey Powell and Ken Russell share many things in common: both absolutely *love* dance and movement; they tend to prefer using cinema visually, not verbally; they love to cut to music (cinema as a multi-media form); they love excess – in performance, *mise-en-scène*, melodrama, sets, costumes, lighting; they use literary sources, and employ many high cultural allusions; they operated at times as mavericks, on the edges of the British film industry; they had problematic relations with the studios; they fiercely fought for their independent status; they have been much misunderstood, slated by critics, and controversial; they are Romantic poets of cinema, deeply conscious of British literary history, the Romantics, nature poetry, and the inspiration of the British landscape. And both found it difficult to get the films they wanted to make off the ground in their later years: Powell's last decades were especially sad in terms of high quality film production (*viz*. the longed-for interpretation of *The Tempest*, the one 'lost' Powell project many would dearly love to see, like Orson Welles' unmade but much discussed version of *King Lear*), while Russell hadn't done anything really significant in years and years, since the 1980s.

56 *Peeping Tom* has rightly been reconsidered and reinstated as a Powell classic after its initial critical drubbing (whereas many films deserve to die a thousand deaths). And *Peeping Tom* was bound to be appreciated by filmmakers and critics, especially the late modernists and postmodernists. Like *Psycho*, *Peeping Tom* lends itself well to a rigorous filmic deconstruction with its dramatic exploration of the relation between desire and looking, desire and death, desire and women, desire and cinema, desire and art. *Peeping Tom* is one of those films that becomes an endlessly discussed 'text' in critical cinema studies, a film almost tailor-made for critics to bring in Sigmund Freud, Jacques Lacan, voyeurism, scopophilia, the mirror image, narcissism and intertextuality.

## KEN RUSSELL THE *AUTEUR*

Is Ken Russell an *auteur*? I don't know for sure, but I bet he doesn't like the term or the concept – and I don't know of *any* major filmmaker who does. It's entirely an idea cooked up by film critics, many of whom haven't much of a clue about what really goes into making a movie (indeed, film critics, who are presumably *professional* writers, have very poor knowledge about movie production, marketing and distribution. For example, they continually emphasize dialogue, the easiest thing to put into a film review (like the lyrics of a pop song – you just quote them), and also the easiest thing to denigrate. But all major filmmakers stress that dialogue is a very small part of the overall scheme and impact of a movie).

To the extent of conceiving, writing, producing and directing his own films, Ken Russell is only partially an *auteur*; he does not write all of his own films, for instance. But in the sense of exercising a huge amount of control over most of the stages of production, yes (down to operating the camera (those distinctive tilted, kinetic, handheld camera moves come directly from the way that Russell wields the camera),[57] sometimes lighting scenes, and being closely involved with all of the other principal aspects of filmmaking).

In the sense of producing *as well as* directing his films – yes (and that is absolutely vital: Orson Welles, for instance, also acted as a producer on most of his twelve completed feature films he directed, and that makes a huge difference). Being his own producer meant that Russell was able to exercise more control over the pre-production – such as casting, and commissioning writers to create a script. (However, Russell, like just about *all* major filmmakers, has rarely had final cut on his films, and has also had to trim back movies due to censorship – for instance, *The Devils* and *Crimes of Passion*).

In the sense of having particular themes, concerns, and even images, Ken Russell is definitely an *auteur*. At the level of the æsthetic, the visual, the aural, and the technical, Russell is most definitely an *auteur*, a filmmaker whose imprint is all over his films. Let's face it, there are *very few filmmakers* that you can look

---

[57] Ken Russell likes to operate the camera on his films (unions and DPs permitting),. Like filmmakers such as David Lean, Steven Spielberg and Walerian Borowczyk, Russell works very closely with the cinematographers of his films.

at and say, yep, that was definitely made by so-and-so. And you can do that with A Ken Russell Film – and you can recognize A Ken Russell Picture from very early on in the proceedings, too. Very few filmmakers would begin a film with a scene of a man kissing a woman's tits back-and-forth, faster and faster, speeding up a metronome and music, and following it rapidly by a semi-naked sword fight (and without a title, credits or explanation).

Ken Russell explained in 1973 how he worked with screen-writers:

> I usually tell [writers] how I would like the story. We discuss it; they will say why they don't like something or how they think something can be improved or come up with their own idea. They read it to me, and we revise as we go along. Usually, when I'm shooting, I revise yet again according to the necessities of the day. I believe in using what is available, and when I've changed my mind, I rewrite the whole thing.[58]

It's very significant that Ken Russell has co-written many of his movies and TV programmes, and has also had sole writing credit on many of them. Although the general view seems to be that film directors do everything on a movie – it's the *auteur* theory plus laziness (it's just easier to talk about one artist instead of 100s) – most directors do *not* write their movies (and I maintain that the writing, the concept, the creation of the characters, and the structure, are things the *screenwriter* does, *not* the director, the producer, the studio executives or the second unit clapper loader).

Ken Russell acknowledged that he couldn't write as well as his writers, certainly when it came to dialogue.[59] But I'd say when it comes to getting across ideas in written form so they can be translated into images and sounds and music, Russell did just fine.

Alain Robbe-Grillet's comments (made at the time of 1962's *Last Year At Marienbad*) summarize the position of Ken Russell perfectly:

> I don't think either the cinema or the novel is for explaining the world. Some people believe there's a certain definite reality and all that a work of art has to do is pursue it and try to describe it... I don't think believe a work of art has reference to anything outside itself. In

---
58 In T. Fox, 102.
59 In J. Walker, 1974.

a film there's no reality except that of the film, no time except that of the film... The only reality is the film's, and as for the criterion of that reality, for the author it's his vision, what he feels. For the spectator, the only test is whether he accepts.[60]

Movies, as Josef von Sternberg explained in *The Parade's Gone By,* are about making stuff up:

> When I made *Underworld* I was not a gangster, nor did I know anything about gangsters. I knew nothing about China when I made *Shanghai Express*. These are not authentic. I do not value fetish for authenticity. I have no regard for it.[61]

## KEN RUSSELL AND THE CENSORS

It's tempting to get into a lengthy discussion of movie censorship and ratings, but there are good studies elsewhere which do so.[62] Ken Russell is one of those film directors who have become well-known for their run-ins with the film censors (and not only censors, but also media watchdogs, such as the National Viewers and Listeners Association and the Festival of Light in Great Britain (and their most prominent spokesman, Mary Whitehouse), and right-wing and religious groups in North America).

The number of filmmakers whose works were censored, banned or shelved is vast. In the postwar-1975 period, they include Andrej Wajda, Pier Paolo Pasolini, Bernardo Bertolucci, Robert Aldrich, Bob Rafelson, Stanley Kubrick, John Huston, Orson Welles, Sam Peckinpah, Arthur Penn, Frank Perry, René Clement, François Truffaut, Joseph Losey and of course Ken Russell.

As well as run-ins with the censors on movies such as *The Devils* and *Crimes of Passion* (or the British government with *Dance of the Seven Veils*), some of Ken Russell's films have been re-cut by the studios: *The Boy Friend* had fifteen minutes taken out of it for

---

60 A. Robbe-Grillet, *The Observer*, Nov 18, 1962.
61 *The Parade's Gone By*, New York, 1968.
62 M. Barker, 1984, M. Barker & J. Petley, 1997, E. De Grazia & R.K. Newman. *Banned Films: Movies, Censors and the First Amendment*, Bowker, New York, NY, 1982, T. Matthews, 1994, P. Keough, 1995, G. Phelps, 1975, and J. Lewis, 2000.

the U.S.A. release by the studio (MGM). And Warners re-cut *The Devils*, and that was after the parts had been lopped off it by the censors.

On the Hollywood practice of re-editing movies after the filmmakers have delivered them to the studio, Ken Russell hated the butchery:

> They're handed over to some Hollywood "cutter" who does a quick hatchet job on something I've slaved long and lovingly over for months. One company who didn't have an editor actually got their lawyer and the projectionist to cut one of my movies. (BP, 103-4)

Very few filmmakers have 'final cut', even among film directors one would regard as masters, and even among film directors who have helped generate billions. Once a movie's been shot, control over it is given over to studios and executives (a movie, for example, will be edited on the studio lot). And it's the *studios* who *own* the film – a director might write and direct (and co-produce) a movie, but it's the studio who owns it and its rights.

One of the chief benefits of making movies on a low budget is that the filmmaker can retain (more) control of the project throughout its production. And filmmakers such as Ken Russell are so individual and unusual, it requires a good deal of sensitivity to re-cut their movies. They are simply not your average factory products churned out by mainstream, commercial film industries. So to cut a Ken Russell movie, you really have to be in tune with what the filmmakers were trying to achieve. And clearly some film studios weren't. (Film editors are thus sometimes caught in the middle of a struggle between the film directors, the producers, the censors and the studios. No wonder that many film studios take away a movie from the producers and director, and assign their own editors to projects. Some studio editors are loathed by filmmakers because they're butchering their babies).

Ken Russell's movies have often been positioned on the borders of the 'X' classification, particularly in the early 1970s. It's where Russell likes to operate – in the 'R' or 'X' zone. Adopting the 'R' rating and moving away from the 'X' classification, which occurred in the early 1970s, helped Hollywood reposition itself in the marketplace (distancing itself from the negative connotations of the 'X' certificate); it also meant that those who were criticizing

Hollywood for turning out sleaze, violence or porn could be assured that Hollywood was producing fewer 'X' rated films.

The new 'NC-17' rating of the early 1990s was intended (again) to diffuse the stigma attached to 'X' rated movies: it was meant for movies which went beyond 'R' but which wouldn't be classed as porn (or 'R-18'). However, the entire ratings system is all about money: it's about categorizing movies for the marketplace: who pays for the MPAA (Motion Picture Association of America) and the ratings and censorship boards around the world? The film studios do. (At this time, in the 1990s and after, the members of the MPAA were seven: Sony, MGM, Universal, Paramount, Fox, Warners and Disney).

*Henry and June* (Philip Kaufman, 1990) – an art movie with sex scenes released by Universal, exploring similar territory of love, sex, art and relationships in the mid-20th century of *Women in Love* and *The Music Lovers* – was the first film to be awarded an NC-17 rating from the MPAA's Classification and Ratings Administration.[63] When 1991's *Whore* was given an 'NC-17' rating, Ken Russell protested, and compared his movie to the previous year's Disney blockbuster *Pretty Woman*, which he insisted glorified prostitution (*Whore* was partly an answer to *Pretty Woman*).

For some critics, the 'NC-17' rating was effectively a form of censorship. It was a kind of economic censorship, because a studio wouldn't promote an 'NC-17' rated film the same way they would an 'R' rated picture (the studios, anyway, demand an 'R' rated product in the contract. Agreeing on a movie's rating is absolutely essential in positioning it in the marketplace). Indeed, between 1990 and 2002, the major Hollywood distributors had only released two American movies with an 'NC-17' rating: *Henry and June* and *Showgirls* (foreign movies were occasionally distributed under 'NC-17').[64]

The line between an 'R' rating and an 'X' or 'NC-17' rating is continually changing, but it has to be seen as a fixed boundary as far as the industry, the distributors and exhibitors were

---

[63] On *Henry and June*, see J. Matthews: "Henry Miller Meets the MPAA", *Los Angeles Times*, 27 Aug, 1990 and "Sell-Out Crowds for *Henry and June*", *Los Angeles Times*, 8 Oct, 1990; L. Rother: "A 'No Children' Category to Replace the 'X' Rating", *New York Times*, 27 Sept, 1990; J. Voland: "Valenti: *Henry* Ban Like 'Dark Ages'", *Hollywood Reporter*, 8 Oct, 1990; S. Farber: "A Major Studio Plans to Test the Rating System", *New York Times*, 4 Sept, 1990; D. Kissinger: "X-Rated *June* Could Ignite Major Revolt Against MPAA", *Variety*, 10 Sept, 1990.
[64]

concerned. The line between 'R' and 'NC-17' had to be formalized by everyone in the industry so that business could be conducted without the threat of films being perceived as 'pornography' or 'offensive'. Hence the decision across Hollywood to move away from the problematic 'NC-17' rating (and the old 'X' rating). With the rise of DVD, laser discs and home video, different versions of a film could be released, as well as the theatrical version and the broadcast version. Unrated cuts and 'director's cuts' could be found alongside the approved studio cuts. Even so, some of Ken Russell's movies, such as *The Devils*, had not been released in the version the filmmakers intended (in Russell's lifetime).

ACTING AND PERFORMANCES

> He's not doing it, thinking, "This'll bring 'em in, this'll make more money." He's exorcising demons of some kind.
>
> Glenda Jackson (1972)

Ken Russell isn't known as an 'actor's director' like Ingmar Bergman or Robert Altman. But he sure did coax some great performances from his cast: Ann-Margret was nominated for an Oscar for *Tommy*, Glenda Jackson won an Oscar for *Women In Love*, and Oliver Reed delivered his career best in *The Devils* (and was also incredible in *The Debussy Film*, *Women In Love* and *Dante's Inferno*). There are sensational performances throughout Russell's work: Christopher Gable in the Richard Strauss satire, Kathleen Turner and Anthony Perkins in *Crimes of Passion*, Vanessa Redgrave in *The Devils*, Scott Anthony in *Savage Messiah*, Roger Daltrey in *Lisztomania* and *Tommy*, Twiggy in *The Boy Friend*, Stratford Johns in *Salome's Last Dance*, Amanda Donohue in *The Lair of the White Worm*, Robert Powell in *Mahler*, Max Adrian in, well, everything (but *Delius* especially), and of course an astonishing, incendiary performance by Richard Chamberlain (and Jackson again) in *The Music Lovers*.

Ken Russell acknowledged that he wasn't an 'actor's director', and didn't really know how to direct actors (I think he was being too modest). Instead, he said, he aimed to cast the film as well as he could, and to establish a creative atmosphere[65] on set. Many directors have said similar things:

> I don't know how to direct actors. I can talk to them and tell them what *I* think it's all about but I can't *make* them act and I'm not interested in doing so. That's up to them. What I *can* do is choose people and put them in an atmosphere that brings something out of them they didn't think they had. (Bax, 189)

Ken Russell could create a wonderful environment on the set, Richard Chamberlain said, in which actors were encouraged to experiment. Alan Bates remarked: 'I don't think Ken would listen to anything an actor said'. Glenda Jackson maintained that Russell could not direct actors much; instead, he would focus all his attention on some minor visual detail. Certainly Russell found working with Jackson 'a very great experience'. He discovered that she was so good he didn't need to say much to her about direction (Bax, 189).

What Ken Russell did best, Glenda Jackson remarked, was 'intensely emotional scenes', and for those he would create a strong atmosphere for the actors (1972). Rather than great acting, Russell said he was often after atmospheres. It wasn't about great speeches or dramatic ability. He has remarked that the initial discussion with an actor is where it all happens, is the really crucial meeting, where he lays out the story and the character.

The performances in Ken Russell's films have the appearance of improvization and spontaneity. But no: as with many another film director (Jean-Luc Godard, Ingmar Bergman and Francis Coppola come to mind), it's all actually carefully orchestrated. There might be suggestions from the actors, but the moves, the lines, the gestures, the blocking and so on are all worked out beforehand (and then rehearsed). The result may *look* effortless and spontaneous, and to viewers and to (too many) critics it can *look* as if it's 'just happening' there and then, but that's great art.

Sammi Davis, the star of *The Rainbow*, told me:

---

[65] 'In a lot of my films it's the atmosphere I'm after and acting ability doesn't have a lot to do with that', Russell remarked (Bax, 190). Sometimes Russell would deliberately deflect attention from the scene or the actors or ramp up the tension by focussing on some minor detail, like a chair, or a costume, in order to 'create a tension, an atmosphere, a charge of electricity' (Bax, 189).

Mostly if a scene didn't flow, Ken would say, 'Do it better', and I would say, 'You're right, I'll do it better'. He was fun to me in that way, he just said it like it was. In the film business there are many ways to inspire or gain a reaction or connection. With Ken, his ability to always just be himself is his key form of inspiration.[66]

I don't know for sure,[67] but I imagine that being an actor in a Ken Russell movie means throwing yourself into it wholeheartedly and trusting the director. If he tells you to take off your clothes and roll around in the grass, you do it. I bet Russell isn't the kind of director who's going to get into a two-hour discussion about your motivations for being nude in this particular scene.[68]

> I don't talk to my actors too much. I explain as much as I can to them but life isn't to do with explaining or manipulating. There's a danger of killing an instinct by analysing it. (Bax, 128)

And again, Ken Russell explained that often it was on his first meeting that everything about the character was laid out for the actor:

> I really direct an actor's performance during that first hour when I explode my concept of the character into his head for good and all. That is the moment of the creation of the character – the rest is rhubarb. (Bax, 184)

If Ken Russell has a reputation for being tough sometimes on his performers, so have other directors: Stanley Kubrick, Jean-Luc Godard and Federico Fellini, among many others, are also known for pushing their actors.

Ken Russell could be 'very demanding', 'very headstrong' and 'emotionally exhausting to work with', remarked DP Billy Williams.[69] Dorothy Tutin commented, as many actors have done, on Russell's eagle eye for detail, for the visuals.

> Somehow Ken was the eye. He worked like a sculptor, using film as his material. The crew felt this too. I've never known a crew so on the ball. They had to be. Ken has an eye like a hawk. (Bax, 196)

---

66 S. Davis, letter to the author, 2007.
67 But I have chatted to Sammi Davis about it.
68 Actress Diana Laurie (in *The Lion's Mouth*) remarked of working with Ken Russell: 'He is a mix, he's such a mix of generous and stingy, relaxed and control freak, warm and then at times quite suspicious or untrusting of you, and comfortable and uncomfortable with himself.'
69 B. Williams, in D. Schaefer, 1984, 271.

And Dorothy Tutin also recalled, *pace Savage Messiah*, that the actors felt like they were performing not for the camera, but for the director. It's a common attitude among actors: they love to get a response from directors, to make them laugh or cry.

> He knows *exactly* what the film will be like, and we weren't doing it for the camera – we were doing it for *him*. It was often a question of catching up with Ken and his conception of the film. (Bax, 196)

Ken Russell has said he can talk to the actors about the characters and the story, but after that it's up to them. Sometimes he will deliberately keep an actor uninformed about aspects of a role (a common tactic).

Ken Russell has also employed psychological techniques that some would regard as harsh, tactics where a director will secretly manipulate a performer in order to obtain a particular result. For instance, not allowing Dorothy Tutin to have pins in her hat on a windy day, and also telling the crew that nobody was to help with her hat. Or making actors wear under-garments even if they won't show up on camera (a common gripe among actors). And you would have to accept that, going in, knowing it was a Ken Russell movie.

In *An Appalling Talent,* Ken Russell was very critical of the extras on some of his movies – on *The Music Lovers, The Devils* and *The Boy Friend*, for instance, some of the extras mocked the principal performers during takes, asked for more money, disrupted filming, and behaved badly in the rape of Christ scenes (Bax, 208f). There was a dispute between Equity and Russell's production over the use of extras. (Subsequent Russell productions had run-ins with Equity: *Valentino* and *Moll Flanders*).

SEX AND NUDITY.

I'm sure that many actors would have not even bothered to go to a casting session if a role was advertized in the trade papers thus: 'this role will require full nudity'. And in Hollywood there are clauses in some actors' contracts about which bits of the body can be shown. That can be worked out by agents and producers months beforehand – much better than getting cold feet the day before filming.

But there's a starchy, British nervousness about nudity and sex in cinema, isn't there? Somehow, it's OK for Jean-Luc Godard or Pier Paolo Pasolini to ask for actors to go nude or simulate tupping in their movies, 'cos they are masters of the Euro art film, right? They're bleedin' *French* and *Italian*, ain't they? Intellectual and arty and oh-so sophisticated.

But for a British film director, it seems, well, just not done, old boy. Fine for porn, or stag reels, or a saucy seaside postcard (one of many bizarre British traditions), but not for a movie that you and your maiden aunt might go and see at the local fleapit of a Friday evenin'.

But a Ken Russell movie doesn't think like that – it's not that Russell was setting out to upset or shock the bourgeoisie (though there is an element of flaunting bad taste in his movies) – rather, it's what was required for the piece. I'm sure it was not the filmmakers thinking along the lines of, 'shit, this is going to really *annoy* people, isn't it?', but, 'you get your clothes off for this scene, dear.'[70]

That's all it is. It's a body, it's a bit of fooling around, it's people fucking (like they have to do for there to be people at all: no sex = no humans). As Spike Milligan put it: 'People like to fuck'. The fuss about sex and nudity and 'bad language' and 'bad taste' comes from film critics, media watchdogs, broadcasters, and one or two irate people who live in Tunbridge Wells in England and read the *Times* (i.e., arch conservatives, who usually happen to be white and middle-aged and middle-class, too).

There's plenty of gay and lesbian material in Ken Russell's cinema too, from lesbianism in *The Rainbow* and *Dante's Inferno* (but cut from the final show), to homosexuality in *The Music Lovers*, *Women In Love,* and *Salomé's Last Dance.* Russell has also worked with gay writers such as Barry Sandler and Larry Kramer. As Russell has quipped, maybe he is gay. 'I don't think anyone knows themselves. We can all pretend, but I have no idea what I am. I'm me!'

RUSSELL'S WOMEN.

Ken Russell's cinema is full of beautiful women – so many amazing people have appeared in his movies and TV shows, including models Gala Mitchell and Twiggy, and actresses Fiona

---

[70] Rick Wakeman relates an amusing anecdote about the filming of the Rheingold scene in *Lisztomania* with its naked maidens: it was supposed to be a closed set with a minimal crew for the actresses who would be nude, but on the day the stage was heaving with 300 guys, hardly any of which had anything to do with the movie (2010, 113).

Lewis, Annette Robertson, Kathleen Turner, Françoise Dorléac, Ann-Margret, Tina Turner, Michelle Phillips, Nell Campbell, Blair Brown, Leslie Caron, Sammi Davis, Amanda Donohue, Helen Mirren, Theresa Russell, Vanessa Redgrave, Natasha and Joely Richardson.

Compared to all of his contemporaries, Ken Russell's cinema has offered more significant roles for women. The above list is just a small selection of the actresses who have worked for Russell. And let's recall again that Russell's works feature once-in-a-lifetime roles for actors: *Dante's Inferno, The Debussy Film, Isadora Duncan, The Dance of the Seven Veils, Delius: Song of Summer, Women in Love, The Devils, The Music Lovers, Savage Messiah, Mahler, Tommy, Lisztomania, Valentino, Altered States, Crimes of Passion, The Rainbow,* and *Lady Chatterley*. Those kind of ultra-challenging star roles don't come along very often.

OLIVER REED.

If there's an actor who's most associated with playing Ken Russell's alter-egos on film, it is probably Oliver Reed (1938-99).[71] An actor with a dark, bullish, glowering look[72] (like a British Brando), and a cult following, Reed has appeared in leading roles in *The Debussy Film, Dante's Inferno, The Devils, Women In Love* and *Tommy* (as well as having cameos in other Russell movies, such as *Lisztomania, Mahler* and *Prisoner of Honor*.[73] Some filmmakers have actors who act as lucky charms in their movies, and they like to include them in every film, if they can; Reed in one of those lucky charms for Russell). Reed was an instinctive actor, who took his work seriously, and learnt his lines,[74] and who preferred to capture scenes in one or two takes.

Meeting Ken Russell was a turning-point in his career, Oliver Reed acknowledged. 'Working with Russell nearly always produced Ollie's best acting, and the reason for that was simple: Ollie believed in Ken' (R. Sellers, 288). Russell was very important to Reed's career. They liked each other, shared a similar sense of

---

[71] One of Ollie Reed's nicknames for Ken Russell was Jesus – Russell often wore sandals, had a beard and long hair.
[72] Oliver Reed's voice was not a loud, shouty voice, but soft and often a whisper ('the whispering giant', he was called). When Reed played villains, he did it with a low, quiet voice, because a bad guy didn't have to storm about and shout.
[73] Ollie was paid in bottles of champagne, apparently (three Dom Perignon for *Mahler* [R. Sellers, 281]).
[74] Many have attested to Ollie's drunken nights, only for him to turn up on set sober and well-prepared.

humour (and a taste for recklessness). As Glenda Jackson put it, 'there was real affection and real respect, I think, on both sides. Oliver would have done anything for Ken, absolutely anything'.[75]

Stories about Oliver Reed are many, some legendary, and many humourous. Ken Russell has often told the story of visiting Reed and getting into a drunken sword fight (Reed had wanted to do a film about Sir Thomas Becket, and launched into a rehearsal at his home with real swords). And everybody knows the show biz story of preparing for and filming the nude wrestling scene in *Women In Love*. Really good parts for Reed dried up in his later career (*Castaway*, 1987, was a notable role, tho' a weedy movie), and in the 1970s and 1980s he appeared in many, many truly dreadful movies (purely for the $$$$$). Reed famously made a great come-back with *Gladiator* (2000), as the gladiator manager Proximo, but he died during the last part of filming (and even his demise – arm-wrestling with a bunch of sailors in Malta – became part of the Ollie Legend).[76]

As well as being a well-known 'hell-raiser' and drinker, the Oliver Reed Legend also included flashing: he 'would take little persuading to produce his penis', according to biographer Cliff Goodwin.[77] Sometimes Reed's desperate need to play, to perform pranks and tricks on victims, seems not only childish but pathetic and occasionally violent (even more so when he teamed up with Keith Moon, another prankster who wore everyone out with his restless need to act the clown).

※

CHRISTOPHR GABLE.

Much less revered than Oliver Reed, and without his star status, but also important for Ken Russell's cinema, was Christopher Gable (1940-98) – Russell's dancing alter-ego, you might say (Gable can dance on screen what Russell would love to be able to do). Gable appeared in *Delius: Song of Summer*, *The Music Lovers*, *Women In Love*, *The Boy Friend*,[78] *The Dance of the Seven Veils*, and *The Rainbow*. Certainly in a piece such as *Dance of the Seven Veils*, Gable is absolutely wonderful: it's a star part, of course, but only one which could have been performed by a

---

75 Quoted in R. Sellers, 180.
76 As was the rewriting of the Proximo character, and the use of doubles and even digital visual effects to complete Reed's role.
77 C. Goodwin, 2001.
78 Twiggy might get all of the press attention for her role in *The Boy Friend*, but Gable is an essential part of the mix. And he can *really* dance!

professional dancer. Gable throws himself wholeheartedly into this once-in-a-lifetime role – where else would you get to play a god, a famous classical composer (from youth to old age), stumble thru a WW1 battlefield, enjoy an Alpine picnic, drink champagne from a lady's shoe, be teased by a dominatrix, and cavort with Nazis, carrying Adolf Hitler on your shoulders? – Only in a Ken Russell movie!

Other regular actors in Ken Russell's films and TV shows were members of the 'Russell Repertory Company': they included: Georgina Hale, Vladek Sheybal, Judith Paris, Catherine Wilmer, Iza Teller, Ben Aris, Max Adrian, Glenda Jackson, John Justin, Fiona Lewis, Andrew Reilly, Antonia Ellis, David Collings, Peter Vaughan, Imogen Claire, Ken Colley, Murray Melvin, Dudley Sutton and Andrew Faulds. And most of his children have appeared in many of his films (as well as working on them as crew – Victoria, Xavier, Alex, James, Toby, etc).

Sammi Davis told me about a time making *The Lair of the White Worm* when she wanted some hints at her characterization:

> I asked him one day on the set of *The Lair of the White Worm* what I was meant to be thinking whilst peering into the mirror to check out a big wound on my neck. He said something like, 'Well obviously, you're feeling quite sad having just found you're missing mother, realising she has turned into a vampire and then shocking you by taking a huge chomp on your neck'. That did the trick, very simple, nothing more needed![79]

---

[79] S. Davis, letter to the author, 2007.

Ken Russell on set (this page and following pages).

Filming The Rainbow

Filming Mahler (above).
Savage Messiah (below).

(Photos on this page and over are by Sérgio Leemann)

Filming The Boy Friend

Filming Tommy (above).
Filming Lisztomania (below)

Filming Crimes of Passion

# KEN RUSSELL AND THE CRITICS

> Pay no attention to what the critics say. No statue has ever been put up to a critic.
>
> Jean Sibelius

Ken Russell has been well served by the writers who've written book-length studies of his cinema: John Baxter, Joseph Gomez, Ken Hanke, and Gene Phillips. All excellent, all highly recommended. Other supporters of Russell's cinema include Stephen Farber, Mark Kermode and Paul Joyce. (More recent books include: Kevin Flanagan, Joseph Lanza, and Richard Crouse).

The first full-length study of Ken Russell was by John Baxter (it appeared in 1973).[79] Highly recommended (like Baxter's other books), it is an invaluable portrait of Russell at work, and includes many of his views and comments. It was held back from being published because producer Harry Saltzman threatened the book with a lawsuit.[80]

Ken Russell has written books about cinema – *Fire Over England: The British Cinema Comes Under Friendly Fire*[81] and *Directing Film* – as well as his memoirs. His autobiography – essential reading – is *A British Picture* (a.k.a. *Altered States*). Russell's books are to be treasured, even if some folk might disagree about how he remembered some of the famous stories. What comes over strongly is his passion for movies (note, for instance, how many movies he cites seeing in his childhood, and where, and when. Like Jean-Luc Godard, Ingmar Bergman and Martin Scorsese, Russell has an insatiable love of cinema).

Joseph Gomez in his 1970s book study has suggested that Ken Russell's films have a 'tripartite structure', which incorporates: (1) facts, research, history; (2) the characters' view of themselves; and (3) Russell's own views of the subject (205). For Gomez, Russell's films combine these three elements in varying degrees, so that a

---

[79] Unfortunately, John Baxter's book is out of print. I engaged in lengthy discussions about re-publishing it, but sadly the project fizzled out. I'm not sure why.
[80] Extracts from the earlier manuscript of John Baxter's book are included in Joseph Gomez's study. But the book is still critical of Saltzman – particularly his treatment of filmmakers.
[81] *Fire Over England* (a.k.a. *The Lion Roars*, 1993) is another idiosyncratic installment of Ken Russell's view of the movies mixed with autobiography (which rehashes most of the material from Russell's *A British Picture*), and skips over films of Russell's such as *Altered States*, *Crimes of Passion* and *Whore* (his three Hollywood films).

film such as *Delius: Song of Summer* sticks closely to the facts and research (such as Eric Fenby's account of living with Delius), and minimizes Russell's and his team's views of Delius.

But movies like *Mahler* or *The Music Lovers* contain much more of the subjects' self-image, as well as much more of Ken Russell's interpretations of these people and their work. Which makes them confusing to viewers expecting a regular biopic of the composers.

The biopics helmed by Ken Russell are not your average biographical movie. They don't take the same approach as the usual biopic, so can't really be judged in the same manner. They are also dealing with highly creative people, artists, not ordinary people, or 'ordinary people in extraordinary circumstances' (the Steven Spielberg model). Which means their approach is different again.

One of the ways in which the different approach is indicated is by the opening sequences: Ken Russell's films announce from the beginning that they are *not* going to be traditional movies, with conventional narratives and dramaturgy. They are not going to move from A to B to C methodically, or chronologically, or with full motivations for each character and event. They are not going to contain regular characters or characterizations. They are not going to adhere to traditional conventions of realism, naturalism, believability, etc. And they are not always going to take themselves so seriously, or their subjects so seriously (they will thus simultaneously mock and celebrate their characters).

The viewer needs to take all of that into consideration, and mustn't apply all of the usual conventions of cinema to the movies of Ken Russell. And that is where so many of the misunderstandings occur: viewers come to Russell's films expecting, say, a conventional biopic of a classical music composer, but Russell and his team don't want to deliver that.

And so much of the negative criticism of Ken Russell's movies is about these conflicting expectations: the critics want one thing, but Russell and his team deliver another thing. If you want a conventional narrative and regular characters and a traditional movie, look elsewhere. There are plenty of movies around like that. Russell simply doesn't want to do that, and it frustrates some viewers and critics who only want that.

I'm reminded of Jean-Luc Godard, who said that he couldn't make an ordinary film; he tried, he said, but he just couldn't do it. Somehow, his movies always came out like Godard movies, with unconventional narrative structures, characters that stop and turn to the camera and declaim on Marxist politics, with self-consciously silly moments, and montages of flashing, word game captions.

Entries on Ken Russell appear in most of the main film reference books. Nearly always critics assess Russell by praising some of his finer moments, but they always end by stressing his limitations, his deficiencies, and his vulgarities. A typical critical view occurs in *The Oxford Companion To Film*:

> Russell's flair for deliberate sensationalism has perhaps obscured his considerable originality and flair. His excursions into the psychology of artists have become increasingly exaggerated: at the same time his work provides acute comments on the cruelties arising from sexual inadequacies. (L. Bawden, 610)

*Halliwell's Film and Video Guide*, one of the standard film guides in Britain, denigrates most of Ken Russell's movies. But what does *Halliwell's Guide* know? Here's what Leslie Halliwell said about *Summer With Monika*, one of the sexiest, most sublimely wonderful movies ever made: 'Probably truthful but rather glum and unsophisticated drama of young love; not among Bergman's most interesting films.' (2000) 'Unsophisticated'?! Ingmar Bergman?! Bergman's about the most sophisticated filmmaker ever! Culturally, artistically, technically, cinematically, politically, socially, and definitely psychologically!

I would guess that pretty much every major critic in Europe and North America came out *against* Ken Russell at some time or other. There are bad reviews of his films by Judith Crist, Vincent Canby, Charles Champlin, William Wolf, Paul Zimmerman, Richard Schickel, George Melly, Robert Hughes, Gary Arnold, Alexander Walker and Pauline Kael (no surprise there).

Both Alexander Walker and Pauline Kael, two of the most prominent critics in the U.K. and the U.S. of A., were well-known for their dislike of Ken Russell's movies. Kael was sometimes extreme in her vitriol. The feelings were usually mutual: Russell called Kael a 'shrilling, screaming gossip', and famously whacked Walker with a newspaper on TV.[82] Kael attacked *Savage Messiah* savagely (why didn't Kael drink a case of champagne before

---
[82] Russell came out better from the fracas with Walker, in terms of public perception.

reviewing Russell?!):

> now it's all random buffoonery... [he] is always turning something from the artists' lives into something else – a whopping irony, a phallic joke, a plushy big scene.[83]

I don't know if that affected Ken Russell, but he has referred from time to time to the negative responses his films have garnered. It's got to rankle just a little when you've spent a long time working away at something and along come some newspaper people and rip it to shreds. (However, I'm sure after a swig of champagne and a shrug, Russell just got on with living and working).[84]

But Ken Russell's pictures have attracted much more violent negative reviews than those of many another filmmaker (and very few among British directors). Russell, it seems, became one of those filmmakers that critics love to hate – like Michael Winner or James Cameron. A punchbag for journos: 'let's beat up Russell again'... 'yeah, why not?!'

In short, Ken Russell has never had the glowing adoration of film critics that Akira Kurosawa or Billy Wilder or François Truffaut have enjoyed. He has never been the darling of movie criticism.

Not that it means anything – far more significant, as far as the film industry itself goes, is ticket sales. And in that respect, Ken Russell has not had the mega-hits of contemporaries such as Ridley Scott or Paul Verhoeven. But box office counts for nothing for film viewers – who cares what a film cost to make or generated on its release? Box office receipts are routinely employed in marketing these days – '*Sluts of the Caribbean – On Acid! In 3-D!* grossed $100m in its first week!', as *Variety* puts it – but it's a numbers game, pure business, capitalism and more capitalism.

In 2008 (in the London *Times*), Ken Russell said:

> Although I've read all the critics' best shots in their time, I must reiterate, with all the fervour of a novice's vow, that not one word of criticism written has ever altered in any way my scripts or my next project. I believe in what I'm doing wholeheartedly, passionately, and

[83] P. Kael, "Hyperbole and Narcissus", 1972.
[84] Mark Kermode noted in 2013 that 'there's no indication that Russell was ever hampered or confined by the snipings of those who accused him of being an unruly and excessive filmmaker; such claims merely seemed to light a fire under him, encouraging him to be more adventurous, more risk taking, even more contrary' (60).

what's more, I simply go about my business. I suppose such a thing can be annoying to some people.

I don't think that Ken Russell's cinema has been served well by critics. Of course, his films have had their admirers, but when it comes to full-length critical studies, there are far fewer than one would expect (or hope for). And most of those books are out of print. Compared to contemporaries such as David Lean or Jean-Luc Godard, Russell has not only received far less excellent critical attention, he has also been widely mis-understood and misinterpreted.

Some critics may have found it difficult to write about Ken Russell's cinema because so much of it is exploring a world beyond words and beyond stories. It's about music, and images, and movements. It's cinema coming close to the condition of music.

Ever tried to describe music?

I mean, what music *actually is*? What music *is* as a sound, and as an experience? I don't mean who composed it, who performed it, what the musicians looked like. I don't mean the friggin' lyrics, what sappy story the lyrics tell. I mean the *actual sounds* of the music. Not the instruments. Not the technology involved in creating it or recording it.

The music itself.

Not easy. It's the same with Ken Russell's cinema – or any of the great filmmakers. How can you describe the sight and sound and experience of Pier Paolo Pasolini's mother Susanna kneeling on the ground and weeping as she plays the aged Virgin Mary at the climax of *The Gospel According To Matthew* (1964), to the sound of Johann Sebastian Bach? You can't.

As Thomas Atkins put it:

> Russell's complex, combustible mixture of sacred and profane elements, high and low art, makes his films popular with audiences but difficult to analyze verbally or categorize. His best work combines the graphic immediacy and simplicity of the comic strip with the subtlety and suggestiveness of music. (1976, xi)

## KEN RUSSELL'S CINEMATIC STYLE

> The whole idea of making art is to be open, to be generous, and absorb the viewer and absorb yourself, to let them go into it. I have to go into all those places in order to make it work.
>
> Frank Stella

THE CAMERA.
When it comes to shooting a scene, in terms of camera angles and movement, Ken Russell in his audio commentary to *Delius: Song of Summer* said there was only one way to shoot a scene, and he never had any hesitation about it. Steven Spielberg and Orson Welles have made the same remarks: they just *know* where to put the camera, and how to move it. Stanley Kubrick commented that choosing the camera angles and such like was relatively easy compared to the rehearsals.

Thus, Ken Russell does not walk onto the set and run through the standard master shot, medium shot, close-up, over-the-shoulder shot, etc, that film students are taught and that so many filmmakers persist in employing. Instead, Russell tended to shoot in single master shots, covering a scene from one, main viewpoint, sometimes adding close-ups or reaction shots. Of course, if a scene required a simple set-up of two close-ups or two medium shots, of two actors, Russell would do that (and some of Russell's later work for TV does resort to conventional shooting, partly no doubt because the schedules for TV are *much* tighter than for movies. You won't find a television production shoot running a 100 days for a two-hour movie! Or 18 months for 1980's *The Shining* and even more for 1963's *Cleopatra*! Shit, TV would've nailed *Heaven's Gate* in three weeks!).

At its best, though, Ken Russell's cinema is not a jog through standard camera angles and movements. Russell used the comparison with choreography – if the actors weren't moving, then the camera would be.

This has an effect on the editing, of course: it means that many scenes in Ken Russell's pictures are not shots of three or four seconds in a standard shot-reverse-shot pattern. It means that scenes are often broken down into single, mobile shots, sometimes peppered with reaction shots or insert shots. Although sometimes Russell and his editors will employ rapidfire montages, much more often they will allow the master shots to run on, so that some shots are quite long.

Actors love that, allowing them time and space to get into a scene, instead of lots of short shots (but they have to be good actors to concentrate over a lengthy take). However, Ken Russell's cinema is not known for *very* long takes, such as the films of Andrei Tarkovsky, Orson Welles, Jean-Luc Godard or Theo Angelopoulos.[85]

Ken Russell enjoys actors looking into the camera, in particular moments where actors turn to wink at the camera or glance at it in fun. Another aspect of Russell's style is self-conscious anachronisms, particularly the ones which pop out of the screen in the historical movies. Some viewers find them jarring, taking them out of the moment. For instance, while he found the anachronisms in *Dante's Inferno* jarring and in dubious taste, critic Richard Schickel also praised Russell for trying to push the medium of television.[86]

EDITING.

Ken Russell likened editing to composing music, inevitably. It was a case of mixing scenes with different tempos and moods, so the result was like a classical symphony, moving through a variety of moods. Getting the flow of scenes right, and the structure of a film, was very important for Russell. Editing is always an aspect of filmmaking that film critics tend to miss. With a filmmaker of eye-popping visuals, as with Oliver Stone or Pier Paolo Pasolini or whoever, it's easy to be distracted by the other technical aspects of the filmmaking. But it's clear with Russell, as with Stone or Pasolini or whoever, that editing is absolutely central. Because if the editing is wrong, the other elements won't work so well either.

I have drawn attention to editing many times in this study of Ken Russell's cinema, because it is *so important*. Yes, the visuals are extraordinary, and the sets, the costumes, the performances, and all the rest. But it's editing that puts all of this together. 'I like editing,' admitted Russell; 'it's very much a hands-on process'

---

[85] What would happen if Russell had filmed in long, ten-minute takes, like Theo Angelopoulos, or Hitch's *Rope*? Instead of people meandering and staring forlornly into space, as in Angelopoulos's eternally downbeat, Euro-Greek cinema, actors wouldn't be able to stop themselves breaking out into a Busby Berkeley dance routine, or getting freaky.

[86] R. Schickel, "Great Lives On TV", *Harper's*, Jan, 1971.

(DF, 98).

Like Orson Welles, Ken Russell doesn't like to hang about: his movies cut rapidly from one scene to another, once the point has been made. Welles hated those s-l-o-w movies (i.e., Michelangelo Antonioni), which showed someone walking right to the end of a road. No. Welles would *cut, cut, cut*! Dorothy Tutin remarked of *Savage Messiah* that it would have benefitted from a slower, quieter scene (which she was expecting to be in there somewhere), but perhaps was better without it: 'with Ken the instant an impression's made, it's off; gone. He never dwells on *anything* and I think that's right' (Bax, 195).

PUTTING ON A SHOW.

Many of Ken Russell's films contain scenes of theatricality and putting on a show. You could hire Russell to stage the Oscars or Grammy's, for instance, and I bet it'd be fab television (there would be *loads* of dancing, for example, and glittery costumes, and at least two or three orchestras on stage as well as in the pit, and the climax would involve four hundred naked performers doing the tango with live snakes).

There are shows-within-shows too, and films-within-films. *Valentino*, for instance, contains numerous examples, ranging from informal dances to big, theatrical performances, plus screenings of films for a couple of people or a theatre full of women. *The Devils* opens with the King of France camping it up as the Goddess Venus in a theatre. Characters dance for one person or put on shows for guests (as in *Women in Love*). Sometimes whole movies involve putting on a show (*Salomé's Last Dance* and *The Boy Friend*). Russell's movies portray backstage dramas, recreations of silent films, and plenty of painting and photography, too. Voyeurism is a constant theme, particularly the eroticism of looking, of scopophilia ('we are all voyeurs', Russell says).

MEN AND WOMEN.

Generally, the main characters in the films of Ken Russell have been men – in common with the vast majority of films, written or directed by men or women. However, some of Russell's films have featured women in the lead roles: *The Boy Friend, Whore, The Devils, Crimes of Passion* and *Women In Love*, for instance, as well as TV work such as *Isadora Duncan, Lady*

*Chatterley* and *Shelagh Delaney's Salford*.

Ken Russell would not be regarded as a leading light in feminism, however, and sometimes his movies have been criticized for being sexist, chauvinistic or even misogynist. One could counter that the objectification of women in his films is also applied to men as many times, and there is plenty of male nudity (though more female nudity, I guess). Another defence would be that many of Russell's films are set in periods going back to the Middle Ages (in *The Devils*).

TIME AND HISTORY.

Ken Russell is very fond of using framing devices and multiple narrative layers in his movies.[87] They occur in, for instance, *The Debussy Film, Salomé's Last Dance, The Boy Friend, Valentino,* and *Mahler*. Russell explores the self-conscious, modernist device of one layer of narrative (a theatre company in *The Boy Friend* or a group of amateurs in *Salomé's Last Dance* putting on a play), commenting upon and reflecting the content of the play itself (belying the view that Russell's works are narratively simplistic).

As to time periods, Ken Russell's films long favoured the 19th century and early 20th century. That's partly because so many of his films are about classical composers: Mahler, Wagner, Martinu, Tchaikovsky, Liszt, Bartók, Debussy, Strauss, Elgar, Prokofiev, etc. *Women In Love* is set in 1920; *Savage Messiah* and *The Rainbow* in a similar First World War period; *The Boy Friend* in the 1920s; *Lady Chatterley* in the late 1920s; *Delius Song of Summer* in the 1920s; and *Gothic* in the early 1800s. *Prisoner of Honor* goes back to the late 19th century and early 20th century. *The Devils* goes furtherest back, to 1623-34 (altho' the setting might also be regarded as the High Middle Ages – and Sister Jeanne's erotic fantasies go back to the era of Christ).

The movies set in the present day include *Altered States*,[88] *Crimes of Passion, Mindbender, French Dressing, Whore, The Lair of the White Worm, Dogboys* and *The Fall of the Louse of Usher*. This means that Ken Russell is very at home in the 19th and early 20th centuries: that is his time period.[89] It has freed his imagination,

---

[87] Russell self-consciously aped the narrative structure of *Citizen Kane* a few times.
[88] In *Altered States*, tho', Edward Jessup goes back to the dawn of time!
[89] Other filmmakers have gone back to the early part of the 20th century repeatedly: Woody Allen and Francis Coppola come to mind.

perhaps, to be able to go back to the mid-19th century or to the period of the Great War. It also means, from a production point of view, that most of his films have been historical pieces, requiring period costumes, props, sets, vehicles, and all the rest. That also means they are going to cost a little more than films set in the contemporary world.

Ken Russell – despite the look and feel of some of his films, with their Pop Art and pop culture visuals and references, their pop promo and MTV-like montages – is not a fan of pop music. His passion is classical music. For instance, although Russell agreed to direct the Who's rock opera *Tommy*, he didn't like the music, and didn't like it after the film was made.[90] Russell is not, for example, a baby boomer, or of the hippy generation: he is a generation older than baby boomers (his formative years were the 1930s and 1940s: he was out of his teens by 1947, and was 33 in 1960). Russell didn't make documentaries about pop musicians, for instance (tho' I wish he had! – he was ideally placed in the boom in British music in the 1960s to produce documentaries on the Beatles, the Stones, the Kinks, the Who, etc), but about classical music (with the odd foray into folk).[91]

But Ken Russell has become associated with rock music – not least because he directed one of the great rock operas, *Tommy*. He has also helmed some pop promos (for acts such as Elton John, Sarah Brightman, Cliff Richard and Bryan Adams; the music videos were made mainly between 1985 and 1993).[92] And Russell's form of rapid montage cut to music certainly foreshadows MTV and music videos of the 1980s (that is, he films classical music like rock music – and if you've heard Ludwig van Beethoven, Dimitri Shostakovitch or Guiseppe Verdi, you'll know that classical music can be *way* heavier, *more* violent, *more* intense and *more* visceral than Led Zep, Black Sabbath, Napalm Death or the hardest of hardcore, the deadliest of death metal, or the scariest of speed metal music).

---

90 D. Sterritt, 1975.
91 However, some of his documentaries contain pop music – *Pop Goes the Easel*, for instance.
92 Pop promos were easy money for someone like Russell, and meant only one or two days for shooting (like commercials! Unlike commercials, tho', music videos were based around music, Russell's undying passion).

ROMANTIC STYLE.

A recurring motif in Ken Russell's approach to the natural world is to put a single figure in amongst the sublime beauty of the world and completely dwarf them. Often Russell will instruct his camera operator to frame the figure at the end of the zoom, then zoom out slowly. An apparently simple technique, yes, but immensely effective. It crops up in *Dante's Inferno*, in *Tommy*, in *The Dance of the Seven Veils*, in *The Devils*, in *The Debussy Film*, and in many Russell works. In *The Debussy Film*, there's a memorable scene where the camera frames the composer swimming in the English Channel and holds it for a long time: the human figure is a tiny speck in the immensity of the natural world. In *Dante's Inferno*, the camera begins on William Morris in Iceland (actually the Lake District), and pulls back and back, revealing the epic scenery of mountains and lakes, dwarfing the figure. The memorable climax to *Women In Love* features Gerald Crich trudging off into a wilderness of snow and ice (a one-take shot).

The concept clearly draws on the Romantic artists, on British artists such as John Martin and J.M.W. Turner, and on German artist Caspar David Friedrich. It's about Romantic ideas such as the Sublime, the Transcendent, the Infinite, and Nature. Ken Russell's images are direct inheritors of Romanticism (and some of his images are celluloid versions of a Friedrich painting).

VISUAL EFFECTS.

With so many fire, smoke and water effects, plus explosions and stunts, Ken Russell's movies are very much visual effects movies. Oh, they don't have spaceships and light sabres and Godzilla monsters, so they don't seem to be special effects movies, but they are: fire, smoke, rain and water effects, for instance, are classed as special effects or practical effects, and require a dedicated team to deal with them. And Russell likes lots of fire – bombed-out areas lit with fire, or flaming torches, or fields on fire, for instance. Fire, water, fog, steam and smoke all add texture, which filmmakers love, and all drive up the budget, as producers know. (The special effects crew on Russell's films included famous technicians such as John Richardson and Dick Smith, people who've worked on, well, *everything*).

Many of Ken Russell's movies are stuffed with visual effects –

from the opticals in *Tommy* and *Altered States* to the fire, smoke and special make-up in *The Devils* or *The Music Lovers*. Russell also loves trick shots and gimmicky shots – he is very much of the Géorges Méliès school of cinema, where a movie is a magical performance.

OVER THE TOP.

I've mentioned how exotic and weird some of Ken Russell's movies can be, but there were many films made in the 1960s through 1980s which were just as Out There – I mean those films labelled 'mondo cinema', or 'exploitation cinema', or 'sexploitation', or 'underground cinema', or 'horror cinema' (movies which developed cult status, and had re-runs at midnight screenings, and later came back from the dead (like re-animated zombies) on video cassette, and yet again on DVD and Blu-ray).

Spoofing Catholic themes and imagery is a big part of those European mondo/ exploitation/ horror flicks (understandable, being as many were made in Italy, France and Spain, and even lapsed Catholics or anti-Catholics still lerrve to exploit the imagery). There are films about Dracula, Frankenstein, monsters, vampires, occultism, horror, Satanism, the Devil, nuns, and on and on, in 100s of pictures made in Europe between the 1960s and the 1980s, the era when Ken Russell was directing his best-known feature films. And Russell's films, with their eroticized nuns, their sex scenes and nudity and flashcuts and all, are very much part of low budget, European filmmaking of the 1960s-70s, part of the clutch of horror, sex, exploitation and *fantastique* films – the vampires, aliens, serial killers, babes and freaks.

Part of the reason is that horror, thriller and occult flicks are cheap to make. And that's also why so many of those films include nudity – all you have to do is get people to take off their clothes: instant special effects! (Even better if they possess super-gorgeous bodies). You don't have to build vast sets or have costly costumes. It's the same with porno films (and also why porn often takes up horror or sci-fi or occult genres).

So although we exalt filmmakers such as Ken Russell or Pier Paolo Pasolini or Walerian Borowczyk or whoever – because they are 'serious' filmmakers, filmmakers who've made some 'serious' work which can be properly called 'art' – there are hundreds of other filmmakers and films of that period which contain just as much outrageous imagery. I mean filmmakers like José Bénazéraf, Jess Franco, Jean Rollin, José Larraz, Massimo Pupillo, etc. Or maybe it's because, somehow, the works of filmmakers like Pier Paolo Pasolini, Alain Robbe-Grillet and Ken Russell have survived, while so many others have been forgotten.

### CATHOLIC STYLE.

Ken Russell's pictures are awash in Catholic imagery,[93] so much so it constitutes a style of its own (no other British filmmaker has produced so much Catholic and Christian material – tho' European ones have). If there's an opportunity for putting in a reference to Catholicism, Russell will take it. If there *isn't* a chance, Russell will invent one! Russell's Catholic style tends towards the extreme end of Catholicism, where sex and the sacred, sin and spirit, merge: lusty nuns (*The Devils*), randy, insane priests (*Crimes of Passion*), Nazi stormtroopers writhing in front of crucifixes (*Mahler*), Christ figures kissing nuns (*The Devils*), phallic worms sliding over crosses (*The Lair of the White Worm*), Satanic goats (*Altered States*), and so on. *The Devils* is a summary of Catholicism.

In *Tommy*, for instance, Marilyn Monroe replaced the Blessed Virgin Mary as a deity for veneration in a church: Catholicism informs everything about how that scene was staged and shot – because the scene is a religious healing rite. In an animated sequence in *Tommy*, rows of RAF bombers standing on end were turned into cemetery crosses. Robert Powell's Captain Walker was crucified on the shape of a bomber plane. (And Ann-Margret writhed around in baked beans and soap suds and rode a giant, sausage-shaped cushion between her legs. Nothing to do with Catholicism as such, but not the kind of thing a caring, nurturing mom usually did in movies).

### NAZISM.

World War Two is the spectre that haunts so much of Ken Russell's cinema, and also the rise of fascism, in particular National Socialism (Russell was 12 in 1939). Russell has attacked Nazism and anti-semitism many times in his movies (anti-fascism is a very potent ingredient in the cinema of Orson Welles, too). And the classical composers who became associated with the Nazis

---

[93] 'All my films have been Catholic films, films about love, faith, sin, forgiveness, redemption', except for *The Boy Friend*, Ken Russell remarked.

– Richard Wagner and Richard Strauss – were the object of some of Russell's angriest attacks.

Ken Russell was not alone in sending up Nazism in movies, and deploying the imagery of fascism to comic and satirical effect. Two major, American Jewish filmmakers have often done the same thing: Woody Allen and Mel Brooks. The number of times that Brooks sends up Germany, German culture, Germans and in particular the Nazis is striking – not only most famously in *The Producers*, but also in films such as *Blazing Saddles, Spaceballs* and *Robin Hood*.

And critics have attacked Mel Brooks' films the same way they have attacked Ken Russell's pictures: for being too crude, too silly, and for taking on serious topics, such as Nazism, in a glib, superficial and vulgar fashion. And there are definite stylistic affinities between the way that Russell and Brooks send up Nazism – they can't resist to portray exaggerated Nazi salutes, or satirize the swastika or the German soldier's helmet, or produce grotesque satires on the fate of Jews in Nazi Germany.


## THE KEN RUSSELL SCHOOL OF FILMMAKING: RUSSELL'S COLLABORATORS

Ken Russell's films, like those of Francis Coppola or Orson Welles, were somewhat family affairs: for many years his costume designer was his wife Shirley Kingdon. His children (by Kingdon) appeared in and worked on many films (Victoria (b. 1963), Alex (b. 1959), James (b. 1958), Toby (b. 1964), Xavier (b. 1957), and Victoria and Xavier were part of the crew on later productions (as well as her dad's movies, Victoria Russell has also designed the costumes for *Color Me Kubrick*).[94] Molly has acted in US TV shows. Alex is a painter.

Ken Russell's son Xavier has cut (or helped to cut) many of his later TV and film projects, including *A British Picture, Ralph Vaughan Williams, The Secret Life of Arnold Bax, The Insatiable Mrs Kirsch, The Mystery of Dr Martinu, Lady Chatterley, Ken Russell's*

---

[94] Most memorably, Victoria appeared as Sally Simpson in *Tommy*. Ken Russell's other children – Alex, Molly, Rupert, etc – have also appeared in his movies.

*Treasure Island, Alice In Russialand, Classic Widows,* etc.

Among the most important collaborators on Ken Russell's films were his producers – Roy Baird and Harry Benn and Ronaldo Vasconcellos and Dan Ireland (and also Sandy Lieberson and David Puttnam). Baird acted as producer, with Benn often doing production manager duties.

SHIRLEY KINGDON.

The influence of Ken Russell's wife Shirley Ann Kingdon (1935-2002)[95] should not be under-estimated: presumably they would have discussed Russell's projects in great detail, with Shirley contributing all sorts of suggestions.[96]

And the importance of costume in Ken Russell's movies cannot be over-stressed: *all* of his movies are costume movies – not only in the usual sense of being historical films – but because they emphasize costume in every single shot (Russell described *Lisztomania,* for instance, as a costume film, a movie in which costume assumed prime significance). Taken as a whole, Russell's movies constitute some of the most impressive expressions of costume design in film history.

In their incredible book *Film Art,* one of *the* standard texts on cinema, David Bordwell and Kristin Thompson use the costumes and design in *Women In Love* to illustrate a good example of storytelling with colour:

> Ken Russell's *Women In Love* affords a clear example of how costume and setting can coordinate and contribute to a film's overall narrative progression. The opening scenes portray the character's shallow middle-class life by means of highly saturated primary and complementary colors in costume and setting. In the middle portions of the film, as the characters discover love on a country estate, pale pastels predominate. The last section of *Women In Love* takes place around the Matterhorn, and the character's ardor has cooled. Now the colors have become even paler, dominated by pure black and white. By integrating itself with setting, costume may function to reinforce the film's narrative and thematic patterns. (163)

And while we are mentioning *costume*, it's vital to include *hair* and *make-up* too: George Blacker and Peter Robb-King (make-up) and Joyce James (hair) on *Tommy,* for instance, or Charles Parker

---
[95] I have referred to Shirley Russell as Shirley Kingdon in this study to differentiate her from Russell when using just the surname.
[96] John Baxter remarked that Kingdon was in on every stage in a production, and a vital member of Russell's coterie (Bax, 56).

(makeup) and Ramon Gow (hair) on *The Devils*. That is, as well as being *costume* films, Ken Russell's films are also *hair* films, and *make-up* films. The importance of make-up (and special effects make-up) on a movie such as *The Devils* or *Altered States*, for instance, hardly needs to be stressed, while hairdressing is central to any costume movie.

Although he questioned the practicality and tensions of a husband and wife working together professionally (it's still very rare in cinema), there's no doubt that Ken Russell appreciated the enormous contribution that his wife Shirley Kingdon made to his movies. She was known as 'Second Hand Rose', someone who could find treasures in second hand (used) stores. In *A British Picture*, Russell writes:

> Undoubtedly, one of her greatest talents was the ability to sort through mountains of old clothes and unearth a Fortuni dress – the equivalent of coming across a Stradivarius in a junk shop. In fact, some of our happiest moments together were spent in junk shops with me as her willing assistant. And one has only to look at *Savage Messiah*, *The Music Lovers* and *The Boy Friend* to see that it all paid off. (BP, 95)

VIVIAN JOLLY.

Ken Russell's second wife, Vivian Jolly (they were married between 1983 and 1991), was an American working in England; she had been an assistant on *Savage Messiah*, and later studied film at Boston University. Russell met Jolly again when she filmed a documentary on the making of *Valentino*. Jolly became a key associate in the Ken Russell School of Filmmaking – collaborating on scripts, discussing projects in detail, and helping with productions (Jolly has a co-writing credit on *The Rainbow*).

STUART BAIRD.

One of the regulars on Ken Russell's production team was editor Stuart Baird (*Savage Messiah, Tommy, Valentino, Lisztomania, Altered States* and *The Devils*), one of the superstar editors in the British film industry. Baird is certainly one of the great editors of action movies: Baird went on to edit *Ladyhawke, Demolition Man, Maverick, Casino Royale, Outland, Superman 1* and *2, Gorillas In the Mist, New Jack City, Robin Hood: Prince of Thieves, The Omen, Revolution, Die Hard 2* and the first two *Lethal Weapon* flicks. Baird eventually turned to directing (*Executive Decision, US Marshalls,* and my favourite of the *Star Trek* pictures, *Star Trek: Nemesis* [2002]).

The influence of editor Stuart Baird on Ken Russell's cinema should not be under-estimated. Baird and his editing team really punched up the rapidity of the imagery of movies such as *Tommy, Valentino* and *Lisztomania,* and made sure that the famous, Russell 'shock' cuts were really rammed home.

MICHAEL BRADSELL.

Prior to *Tommy,* Ken Russell's regular editor had been Michael Bradsell: he had cut *The Devils, Women In Love, The Music Lovers, The Boy Friend, Mahler* and *Savage Messiah.* And Bradsell cut later movies such as *Gothic, Aria* and *Hot Pants.* Which makes Bradsell one of the absolutely vital contributors to Russell's cinema, because editing is a particularly important ingredient in Russell's filmic style. It's Bradsell and his team who would have worked out in detail the counter-pointing that Russell likes to employ, where one section or scene is played against another, and the editing techniques such as the famous, Russellian shock cuts.

Other regular editors included Peter Davies (*The Lair of the White Worm, The Rainbow, Lady Chatterley*), and Brian Tagg (*Crimes of Passion, Whore, Prisoner of Honor* and *The Strange Affliction of Anton Bruckner*). Terry Rawlings, Maurice Askew and Brian Simmons worked on the sound of Russell's films. Allan Tryer edited many of the early TV documentaries. (It's worth noting that Russell's movies have been pioneers in the realm of sound: *Tommy* was the first production to use the quintaphonic system; and *Lisztomania* was the first Dolby Stereo show).

DEREK JARMAN.

Derek Jarman (1942-1994) worked with Ken Russell in the early 1970s (on *The Devils* and *Savage Messiah*), and Russell's love of flamboyance and rich imagery is easily spotted in Jarman's cinema (think of the very Russellian *Caravaggio,* or films such as *Jubilee, The Garden* or *The Last of England*). While Jarman might have hated working out at Pinewood on Russell's films, his time with the older filmmaker was clearly crucial. Both artists employed 'shock' tactics; shared similar themes (the artist in society, religion, British traditions); both had highly idiosyncratic cinematic styles; both were rebels; both often worked on the margins of the industry; both were ostracized by film critics; both exalted British art (such as the Romantics, and early modernism); both loved the British landscape (Jarman's Dorset, London and Dungenness, Russell's beloved Lake District and the South Coast); both loved classical music (Jarman made a film of Benjamin Britten's *War Requiem*, while Russell was well-known for his classical composer biopics); and both enshrined the artistic calling.

'There was no better director to learn from', Derek Jarman said in *Dancing Ledge* of Ken Russell, 'as he would always take the adventurous path even at the expense of coherence' (105).

Although Derek Jarman became a cult icon in some circles, and his movies were lauded critically (but not by everybody – some loathed them as much as they loathed Russell's work), his movies now seem very minor compared to the output of giants like Ken Russell (or any of filmmakers that Jarman revered, such as Pier Paolo Pasolini). Jarman is not, in the end, a 'British Pasolini', or a worthy or significant successor to Russell. There's a fatal desperation to be trendy in Jarman's work, to be 'cool', to be self-consciously ironic and arch, which hampers his movies in particular, whereas Russell couldn't give a shit about all that. You always felt that Jarman yearned to be taken as seriously as Pasolini or Michelangelo Antonioni, but he didn't have the chops in cinema to achieve that. Jarman's sub-Kenneth Anger/ sub-Andy Warhol, trashy effects are over-worked and ill-conceived, his pop culture references are laboured, and he has little to no feeling for staging decent drama.

Christopher Hobbs, Derek Jarman's regular production designer (he worked on *Jubilee, Caravaggio, The Last of England, The Garden* and *Edward II*), also designed a number of Ken Russell films (like Jarman himself), including *Savage Messiah, The Devils, Salomé's Last Dance*[97] and *Gothic*.

♣

Among the actresses who appeared in Ken Russell's movies, the stars receive the most comment – Glenda Jackson, Vanessa Redgrave, Ann-Margret, Kathleen Turner, etc. But there's a group of actresses who have been essential to the success of Russell's cinema – such as Georgina Hale, Judith Paris, Imogen Claire, and Fiona Lewis. They are less well-known or praised, but

---

97 And Michael Buchanan was production designer on both *Caravaggio* and *Salomé's Last Dance*.

they form a key group in Russell's work.

Some among Ken Russell's regular actors were first dancers: Christopher Gable was a dancer with the Royal Ballet (and apparently gave up his dance career to appear in Russell's films), Hannah King and Judith Paris. And of course the biggest diva in the dance world starred in *Valentino*.

Ken Russell has often taken cameos in his movies, sometimes reluctantly, when no one else was available (or the actor cast turned out to be unsuitable or unco-operative, as in *Valentino*),[98] and sometimes joyfully, as in *Lady Chatterley*. And in the more recent, low budget movies, such as *Hot Pants* and *The Fall of the Louse of Usher*, Russell seems to be enjoying himself hamming it up in front of the camera (as well as behind it).

Ken Russell has also appeared in other people's films – in *The Russia House* (1990) and *Brothers of the Head* (2006). And on TV shows such as *Marple, Color Me Kubrick, Waking the Dead, Celebrity Naked Ambition, Big Brother, Open House, Carry On Darkly, Legends, Great Composers, Light Lunch, A History of British Art, Masterchef, Denton, Without Walls, The Last Resort*, and numerous news shows, chat shows and documentaries.[99]

THE OPENING SCENE

One of Ken Russell's specialities is the strong opening sequence. Many filmmakers, such as Orson Welles and George Lucas, have also cultivated the technique. It's the opposite of employing a s-l-o-w opening sequence which takes five minutes to get into the narrative. Not for Russell a montage of fifteen 2nd unit shots of the principal setting of the story, for example, accompanied by slow, depressing music. Or lengthy quotes or captions. Or a lot of exposition upfront. Russell gets right into it.

Orson Welles said that a movie should open powerfully, because the screen was dead, the thing was just film projected onto a screen. Theatre could get away with slower openings, as

---

98 One of Russell's best cameos was as the legendary film director Rex Ingram in *Valentino*, shooting in the California desert.
99 Such as documentaries on censorship: *X-Rated* and *Empire of the Censors*.

the audience settled into their seats. But a movie had to grab the audience right from the beginning – the 'riderless horse' must enter the scene, as Welles put it. Hence the beginning of *Othello* (1952), with that extraordinary funeral on the battlements, or the unbeatable start of *Citizen Kane*.

The Big Beginning was a lesson that Ken Russell learnt from his television days,[100] when his documentaries for *Monitor* were broadcast in a Sunday evening slot after a movie. As Russell explained:

> I gradually learned that as we followed the main feature film on Sunday night when anyone saw *Monitor*, the average viewer would take x number of seconds to get up and turn it off, so if I had a film on we would drop the logo thing at the beginning and put it at the end and I would devise an opening sequence for my films which would stop them turning off.

So *Lisztomania* starts with composer Franz Liszt and one of his lovers fucking (swiftly followed by a comic duel with swords); *The Debussy Film* (1965) has a beautiful woman being shot with arrows, in a St Sebastian skit; *Mahler* opens with a building by a lake exploding; *Tommy* starts with a man silhouetted against a mighty, orange sun; and *The Devils* launches with a high camp musical number. Russell also acknowledged that viewers tended to be desensitized by so much television viewing. They'd be talking while the news was on, or eating supper while watching a movie. Hence the shock effects, to wake up the audience.


SOME OF KEN RUSSELL'S INFLUENCES

SYMBOLIST ART.
An important influence on the cinema of Ken Russell is late 19th century literary and artistic culture in Europe, including, in Britain, Oscar Wilde,[101] Aubrey Beardsley, and the Pre-

---

[100] The device comes from television, where it's called the 'short hook', typically a murder, car crash, or explosion, designed to stop people changing channels (A. Block, 433).

[101] Oscar Wilde became enamoured of French Symbolism, and employed its influences (Moreau, Huysmans, Louÿs), in his *Salomé*.

Raphaelites. Wilde and his play *Salomé* and the figure of Salomé herself (particularly as enshrined by Beardsley), crop up in many places in Russell's output (even in unlikely places, such as a Michael Caine *Harry Palmer* movie).

### SALOMÉ.

Direct references to Salomé can be found in *Delius: Song of Summer, Salomé's Last Dance, Billion Dollar Brain* and *Isadora Duncan*. Salomé is of course one of the key female figures of Symbolist and Decadent art. She is the *femme fatale* type who symbolically melds sex and death, desire and fear, contact and loss, for the (male) artist. *Femme fatales* are aplenty in Ken Russell's cinema (to cite just a few obvious examples: China Blue in *Crimes of Passion*, Lady Sylvia in *The Lair of the White Worm*, Nina Milyukova in *The Music Lovers*, Life in *Delius: Song of Summer*, etc). In Symbolism, the *femme fatale* is Medusa, Salomé, Delilah, Jezebel, the Queen of Sheba, Judith, Lilith, Ninuë (the lover of Merlin), Venus, Helen of Troy, the Mona Lisa, and Cleopatra. She's there in literary and poetic women such as Salammbô (in Gustave Flaubert), La Belle Dame Sans Merci (in John Keats' poem), Carmen (in P. Mérimée), Cécily (in the *Mystère de Paris* by Eugène Sue), Conchita (in Pierre Louÿs), Matilda (in M.G. Lewis) and Eustacia Vye (in Thomas Hardy's *The Return of the Native*). But the artist who completely made Salomé his own was the French Symbolist painter Gustave Moreau: Salomé dominates Moreau's art (and it was Moreau and his *Salomé* that Des Esseintes enthused over in the *Bible* of the Symbolist and Decadent period, J.-K. Huysmans' *À Rebours*).

### SURREALISM.

Ken Russell was a fan of Surrealism, and wanted to make a film about Salvador Dali. Jean Cocteau was another big influence on Russell's cinema, and it's easy to spot Cocteau's heightened, theatrical and fantastical elements in his films.[102]

Jean Cocteau's influence can be discerned all over the place – in the work of Jean-Luc Godard, Donald Cammell, Derek Jarman, Orson Welles, Francis Coppola, Kenneth Anger, and of course the Walt Disney Studios, who updated *Beauty and the Beast* in 1991 (as

---

[102] 'His films (*La Belle et La Bete, Orpheus*) made a big impact on me. The third amateur movie I made, *Amelia and the Angel* was heavily influenced by Cocteau. It was the one that got me into the BBC', Russell later said.

a Broadway musical). It's probably impossible to watch *La Belle et la Bête* or *Blood of a Poet* or one of Cocteau's *Orpheus* films and *not* be influenced. They are so beautiful and enchanting, they can't help but throw a spell over you.[103]

Dancers such as Vaslav Nijinsky[104] and Isadora Duncan were heroes for Ken Russell, and are directly referenced in films such as *Women in Love*, *Valentino* and *Isadora Duncan*. Not only did Russell make or plan films about two of the most famous dancers of modern times – Duncan and Nijinsky – he also had the most famous classical dancer of the era – Rudolf Nureyev – star in *Valentino*.[105]

THE LAKE DISTRICT.

The Lake District was used many times by Ken Russell: his beloved Skiddaw, Castle Crag, Derwent Water and Borrowdale Valley (Russell first visited the Lakes in 1965, looking for locations for his Dante Gabriel Rossetti documentary, and later lived there for over 20 years). Cumbria was used for the crag Roger Daltrey climbed at the end of *Tommy* (and the opening picnic scene); Robert Powell's lakeside retreat in *Mahler*; Oliver Reed solemnly consecrates Mass in the mountains and lakes in *The Devils*; and the waterfall where Sammi Davis and Paul McGann made out in *The Rainbow* (and where Reed as Dante Gabriel Rossetti contemplated suicide in Russell's *Monitor* programme about the Pre-Raphaelites).

The Lakes also featured in *Dance of the Seven Veils*, *Dante's Inferno*, *Song of Summer*, *A British Picture* and films on Wordsworth and Coleridge. The area stood in for Norway, Iceland, Bavaria and France. In *A British Picture*, Ken Russell described his first sight of the mountain Skiddaw:

> I jumped out of bed, pulled the curtains and froze. My heart pounded, my blood raced, I caught my breath, my eyes widened, my hair stood on end, an unseen orchestra played a tremendous chord. Only clichés can describe what no one has ever been able to portray – a vision of God. (BP, 130-1)

---

103 *The Red Balloon* (Albert Lamorisse, 1956) was also an inspiration for the young Ken Russell.
104 In *Valentino*, Rudolf Nureyev dresses up as Vaslav Nijinsky, in body paint, as the ballet dancer appeared as the faun in Claude Debussy's *L'Après-midi d'un Faune*.
105 Even tho' by some accounts they didn't get on so well (Nureyev commented waspishly on filming *Valentino*, for instance), Russell must've had some admiration for the sheer brilliance of Nureyev as a dancer.

It's striking how much of Ken Russell's cinema deals with France and French culture: *The Devils, Always On Sunday, The Debussy Film, Don't Shoot the Composer, Delius: Song of Summer* and *Prisoner of Honor*, are either set in France or are about French art and culture. Meanwhile, French scenes appear in *Savage Messiah, Isadora Duncan,* and *Lisztomania*.[106]

Russia and Russian culture is found in many places in Ken Russell's cinema (as well as pro-Soviet politics): in *The Music Lovers*, obviously, which takes on a Russian musical icon. Also: *Isadora Duncan, Billion Dollar Brain*, the unmade *Nijinsky*, and *Valentino* starred a famous, Russian ballet dancer. Germany and German society and art is another element in Russell's movies, from *Mahler* and *Lisztomania* to *Lotte Lenya Sings Kurt Weill* and *Dance of the Seven Veils*. And of course there are numerous references to German music (Beethoven, Wagner, Strauss) in Russell's cinema.

FILM INFLUENCES.

Ken Russell said in *A British Picture* that he consumed movies by the ton when he was young. Like Ingmar Bergman, Russell had his own film projectors, and played Fritz Lang, Leni Reifenstahl, Harold Lloyd, Charlie Chaplin, Felix the Cat, Mickey Mouse, Snub Pollard, Betty Boop, and, later, Jean Cocteau, René Clair, Jean Vigo and Orson Welles. The visionary epics *Die Niebelungen* (1924) and *Metropolis* (1926) were some of Russell's most beloved early influences. 'I'd seen thousands of films by then but never any that excited me as much as these', Russell recalled in 1973 (Bax, 62). *The Secret of the Loch* was another favourite. At the local flea pit he saw *Flash Gordon*, Felix the Cat, Betty Boop and Old Mother Reilley; later, he devoured F.W. Murnau, Jean Vigo, G.W. Pabst, Sergei Eisenstein, Jean Renoir and Jean Cocteau (BP, 16-17). Orson Welles was another inspiration for Russell:

> Orson Welles had that magic as well. I still think *Citizen Kane* is a masterpiece. There's nothing like that ever made in English cinema, not with that style and flair.[107]

---

106 But very few of Russell's Francophone flicks were filmed in France.
107 Ken Russell has cribbed the beginning of *Citizen Kane* a number of times – consciously, of course. At the beginning of *Isadora Duncan*, for instance, or in *The Debussy Film*, or the multiple viewpoint form of *Valentino*.

There's so much one can say about *Citizen Kane,* of course, but here I'll emphasize one aspect in relation to the cinema of Ken Russell, and that's the feeling of *play,* of experimentation, of trying all sorts of stuff out in a movie. In short, the utter *joy* of making movies. Orson Welles had that, and Russell has it in spades. And it never leaves him (just as it never left Welles: Welles simply *adored* making movies).

The *sheer joy* of making cinema bounces out of *Citizen Kane,* and it does in Ken Russell's finest work. It's the pleasure of putting sounds and music and images together, which's an important aspect of the some of the best movies – you can see it in *An American In Paris* or *Contempt* or *Porco Rosso* or *Once Upon a Time In China.* The filmmakers' enjoyment undoubtedly helps to keep these movies alive in the very crowded world of cinema.

And in Ken Russell's movies and TV shows, you can see that he and the production teams were having a ball. True, there were productions that were fraught with problems, but you don't make as many movies and TV shows as Russell has unless you're crazy about the whole process.

The Marx Brothers were favourites of Ken Russell's – who doesn't like the Marx Brothers? In 2007, Russell wrote in the London *Times* of his favourite male character in movies:

> that man for all seasons, Rufus T. Firefly, from *Duck Soup* – alias Captain Spaulding, the African explorer ("Did someone call me schnorrer?"), from *Animal Crackers* – played by Groucho Marx. That painted-on moustache, that crouching walk (like an inept private eye), that unlit cheap cigar (from which he continually flicks nonexistent ash), that knowing glance at the audience that lets us in on the gag, have kept me chuckling for more than 50 years.

In his films, Ken Russell, like many another filmmaker, would create conscious nods to some of his favourite filmmakers: silent comedy *à la* Harold Lloyd or Charlie Chaplin (in *Tommy*);[108] a slice of epic action from Sergei Eisenstein[109] (in *Billion Dollar Brain*); the Surrealism and dreamy fantasy of Jeans Cocteau and Vigo; or the deep focus, black-and-white cinematography of Orson Welles and Ingmar Bergman (in *Delius: Song of Summer* and *Dante's Inferno*), plus plenty of Bergman's penchant for angst and

---

108 Ken Russell adores the silent comedy classics, and has references to Charlie Chaplin, Laurel and Hardy, Harold Lloyd, and Buster Keaton in numerous places in his movies.
109 There's quite a bit of Eisenstein in Russell's *œuvre.*

intensity.

It's clear that Ken Russell would've flourished in the early days of Hollywood, for instance – working alongside giants like D.W. Griffith or Cecil B. DeMille, or turning out knockabout comedy for Mack Sennett or Charlie Chaplin. Indeed, the melodrama and spectacle of Griffith's cinema has so many affinities with Russell's – such as *Intolerance,* with its grandiose sets, its extravagant costumes, its parallel stories, its incredible climaxes, its eye-popping action, and the screen teeming with details and life.

In fact, silent comedy is an *enormous* influence on Ken Russell's cinema, and scenes filmed in a silent comedy manner can be found everywhere in his work. Silent comedy is one of Russell's default modes of filmmaking; it's something he can do as naturally as anything else. A *major* fan, a *passionate* fan of all of silent cinema – there are references to it in every single one of Russell's movies and TV shows.

Ken Russell would've been quite at home in the Germany of the 1920s, too, in amongst great productions such as *The Last Laugh, Nosferatu, Metropolis* or *Die Niebelungen.* The silent cinema era features prominently in *Mahler, Tommy, Lisztomania, Isadora Duncan, Dante's Inferno, The Dance of the Seven Veils, The Boy Friend,* and the whole of *Valentino.*

When considering Ken Russell's influences from the history of cinema, it's striking just how many were French and German: Fritz Lang, F.W. Murnau, Jean Vigo, René Clair, G.W. Pabst, Jean Renoir, Leni Reifenstahl, Jean-Luc Godard and two Jeans (Vigo and Cocteau). So as well as consuming the usual North American and British movies (Disney, Chaplin, Lloyd, *Betty Boop, Fritz the Cat,* etc), Russell was very into European cinema.

# SYMBOLS AND MOTIFS

> You can't shake your own sensibility. No matter what the concept is, the artist's eye decides when it's right... which is a notion of sensibility.
>
> Kenneth Noland

Among the numerous recurring symbols or motifs that Ken Russell employs are circles, the sun, mountains, mirrors, fire, water (lakes, rivers, waterfalls), the colour red, symmetry, trains, and crosses (and anything Catholic or Christian). Russell loves circular motifs, and they appear throughout his work; there are circular windows, circular staircases, circular mirrors, close-ups of mouths and eyes; and course buildings and rooms.

Linked to circles is Ken Russell's use of the spinning camera – when a scene gets really intense, the camera rotates wildly (and there are many upside-down shots too). There are circular dances (like around the Maypole penis in *Lisztomania*); carousels; and spinning pianos (also in *Lisztomania*, and in *The Music Lovers*).

Mountains and spectacular landscapes such as lakes and rivers and the ocean are in Ken Russell's cinema embodiments of romantic, pantheistic, lyrical, life-affirming feelings. Russell becomes a late addition to the roster of Romantic poets: Tommy standing in the sun; Ursula and Skrebensky running around naked on the hills in *The Rainbow*; Edward Elgar on the Malvern Hills; Grandier communing by the lake in *The Devils*; Henri Gaudier at the Isle of Portland in *Savage Messiah*.

Often there's a character standing with their arms outstretched, embracing the natural world and fusing with it, in *Tommy, Savage Messiah, Delius: Song of Summer, The Devils, Women In Love, Dante's Inferno*, etc. As Ken Russell describes Tommy's act at the end of *Tommy* in the shooting script: it is 'an affirmation of Man's eternal divinity. Tommy raises his arms as if to embrace the life giving sun' (the image was put on Russell's coffin at his funeral).

Fire would typically connote chaos and destruction (as in *Mahler, The Devils* and *The Music Lovers*): no one can forget the startling image of the burning fields in *The Music Lovers*, when Peter Tchaikovsky returns to his country estate to find himself locked out by Madame von Meck (after Count Chiluvsky has told von Meck that Tchaikovsky is gay).

Symmetry is a favourite visual motif: so often, Ken Russell and his cinematographers will place a character or subject of a scene dead centre. And Russell likes a frontal, *tableau* approach too, as part of his stylization of cinema (like Sergei Paradjanov or Pier Paolo Pasolini). That is, very often scenes will be staged with the characters, props and scenery arranged along lines at right angles to the direction of the camera. However, although the *tableau* approach can produce rather static cinema, Russell's films contain so much dynamism in other areas they are seldom static.

Although he began by making black-and-white movies (as so many have done), and some of his finest pieces, such as *Delius: Song of Summer* and *The Debussy Film*, are in black-and-white, Ken Russell is certainly a remarkable director of *colour* movies. From his first major colour movie – *Billion Dollar Brain* – onwards, Russell has devoted plenty of energy to colour. His techniques include highlighting a particular colour (with red as a favourite, as with Jean-Luc Godard in the Sixties), and also by selective colour, draining all of the colours out of a scene except for one (such as the '1812 Overture' fantasy in *The Music Lovers*, where the scene's reduced to the grey of Peter Tchaikovsky's statue).[110] (Yet the five masterpieces Ken Russell made for television in the late 1960s – *Delius: Song of Summer*, *The Dance of the Seven Veils*, *Dante's Inferno*, *Isadora Duncan* and *The Debussy Film* – are all in black-and-white. And that's partly a cost issue, because the BBC wanted to keep costs low. Thankfully, they were filmed on 35mm film stock, because 16mm from that era looks horrible).

DEATH.

Examining the narratives of many of Ken Russell's movies, and the paths they pursue, reveals unusual results. Take the topic of death, for example. In the action-adventure movies and formula dramas, such as *Billion Dollar Brain* and *Dogboys*, one expects the bad guys to die. But many characters die in Russell's other movies, underlining the themes of tragedy, toxic personalities and self-destruction.

At the end of *Women in Love*, Gerald Crich stalks off into the

---

[110] Jack Fisher wrote of the colours in *Women in Love*: 'Ranging from the dark, suffocating browns, through red-golds, through the lush warm exteriors, to the green-white of the snow, the colors constantly reaffirm Russell's visual attitude to the events' (1976, 43).

snowy mountains to die. Peter Tchaikovsky dies at the end of *The Music Lovers* (and his mother at the beginning). So does Gustav Mahler, and Henri Gaudier, and Rudolph Valentino, and Frederick Delius, and Franz Liszt. Tommy's parents are killed in front of him. Urbain Grandier in *The Devils* has the lengthiest and most gruesome demise, in a movie literally littered with corpses. 'The emphasis on death and violence in my films could be a reaction against death being hushed up', Russell mused in 1973 (Bax, 200).

Clearly, for his artist characters, Ken Russell uses death as the means of closing the piece dramatically *and* thematically. And these deaths are not tacked on to the piece, to give it some serious import, as lesser filmmakers do, they are signalled throughout the piece (with their death drives, their suicidal tendencies, their corrosive personalities which affect everyone around them).

We're not talking in terms of some viewers in the audience knowing that Gustav Mahler or Henri Gaudier-Brzeska died before their time. We're talking about *movie* logic. And by that same dramatic logic, other characters should really die – for instance, after that feverish night in 1987's *Gothic,* one of those crazy writers and poets should die (Lord Byron definitely, and perhaps Percy Bysshe Shelley, too). That would ram home the cost of creativity in the Russellian manner (of course, *Gothic does* end with a corpse – the dead baby, with its Frankensteinian features).

## KEN RUSSELL'S INFLUENCE

You don't think of Ken Russell as an influential filmmaker, like, say, Orson Welles or D.W. Griffith, Stanley Kubrick or Jean-Luc Godard, filmmakers who have certainly influenced many, many filmmakers. But Russell has definitely had an impact on cinema, and not only in Blighty. Anyhoo, a filmmaker with such a strong style is bound to influence somebody.

For instance, when he was shooting what is perhaps the greatest war movie, *Apocalypse Now* (1979), Francis Coppola said he was directing it like a Ken Russell movie, operatic, with coloured flares. And Coppola again took up the Ken Russell approach when he adapted *Dracula* for the screen in 1992 (as critics such as Ken Gelder have pointed out in *New Vampire Cinema*).[111]

As well as Francis Coppola, you can detect Ken Russell's impact in the films of Oliver Stone (*The Doors*), Baz Luhrmann (*Romeo + Juliet, Moulin Rouge*), Rob Marshall (*Chicago*), Peter Jackson (*The Lord of the Rings*), Derek Jarman (*The Tempest, Caravaggio*), Peter Greenaway, Franc Roddam (*Quadrophenia*), Milos Forman (*Amadeus*), Alan Parker (*Pink Floyd: The Wall, Evita*), Bob Fosse (*All That Jazz*)[112] and Michelangelo Antonioni (*Blow Up*).

The 1963 documentary *Watch the Birdie*, about the photographer David Hurn, apparently influenced Italian director Michelangelo Antonioni when he came to direct *Blow Up* in Londinium (according to Ken Russell [G, 44]). Antonioni used it for research into Swinging London.

Rainer Werner Fassbinder was also influenced by Ken Russell, according to Joseph Lanza (who discerns Russell's impact on *Berlin Alexanderplatz*; it's easy to spot the affinities between Fassbinder and Russell!). 2001's *Moulin Rouge* is a Ken Russell movie in all but name (but not as good), as are *Amadeus* and *Shine*.

Sometimes filmmakers – and film critics – have used Ken Russell as an example of the kind of filmmaking they *don't* want to produce or to see more of. The socialist-realist school, those filmmakers who derive from the British 'kitchen sink', the 'Angry Young Men' and the documentary tradition, sometimes use Russell as the sort of filmmaking they want to avoid (even though Russell has of course produced many documentaries, and he also emerged from the documentary tradition in Britain of the early 1960s which also helped to form prominent filmmakers such as Ken Loach, Mike Leigh, Lindsay Anderson and Karel Reisz).

References to Ken Russell crop up all over the place. For example, in *The Complete Anime Guide*, the cult *film noir* series *Wicked City* (1987) is described as possessing 'the noir feel of Raymond Chandler, combined with the rollercoaster horror thrill

---

111 'The vision of scarlet blood splashing over Lucy's bed – as well as Lucy's writhing body, etc – probably owes something to the 'symphonic', camp/ apocalyptic set pieces found in the lurid horror films of Ken Russell, particularly *Gothic* and *The Lair of the White Worm*' (2012, 6).
112 The fantastic biopic/ auto-biopic *All That Jazz* (1980), for instance, is gleefully Russellesque (as well as, as critics noted, Felliniesque, being yet another version of *8 1/2* from a contemporary filmmaker).

of John Carpenter and the sordid thrill of Ken Russell'.[113]

There's no doubt that in the realm of acting and performance, Ken Russell has had an influence. Russell has coaxed out some marvellous and memorable performances from his casts. For someone who says he doesn't really know how to direct actors, the performances mentioned below (there are many more) are proof that Russell must've been doing something right: Oliver Reed and Vanessa Redgrave in *The Devils,* Reed and Judith Paris in *Dante's Inferno,* Alan Bates, Glenda Jackson and Reed in *Women in Love,* Max Adrian in *Delius,* Richard Chamberlain and Jackson in *The Music Lovers,* Ann-Margret in *Tommy,* Robert Powell in *Mahler,* Roger Daltrey in *Lisztomania* and *Tommy,* Christopher Gable in *Dance of the Seven Veils* and Amanda Donohue in *The Lair of the White Worm*.

CLASSICAL MUSIC

> The combination of pictures and music has always been my favourite form of expression – surmounting all language barriers.
>
> Ken Russell (BP, 209)

Music ♪, for Ken Russell, is perhaps

> the most incredible event in human history.[114]

I love that remark!

Ken Russell has never lost that sense of awe of music, and the ecstatic pleasure it gives. I totally agree with him:

I could not live without music.

Many times Ken Russell has employed music on set to get his actors (and crew) into a mood: for the 'rape of Christ' scene in *The Devils,* Russell

> found the most barbaric bit of *The Rite of Spring*, the music to which I

---

113 T. Ledoux & D. Ranney. *The Complete Animé Guide*, Tiger Mountain Press, Washington, DC, 1997, 57.
114 L. Langley, 1971.

had danced naked myself in my parents' house, and played it flat out. Without it the nuns were simply unable to cope: they were totally inhibited. There's a liberating force in music which, even if they don't appreciate the music as such, people can't help responding to, being primitive creatures at heart. If you let it take you over, as Glenda did, you can do anything you like. (Bax, 188-9)

The number of classical composers that Ken Russell made films about is very impressive:

Peter Tchaikovsky
Gustav Mahler
Richard Wagner
Franz Liszt
Sergei Prokofiev
Claude Debussy
Frederick Delius
Richard Strauss
Edward Elgar (twice)
Ralph Vaughan Williams
Sir Arnold Bax
Anton Bruckner
Béla Bartók
Boshuslav Martinu
Gustav Holst

Extraordinarily, although most of those studies of classic composers were made for television, the first four were feature films (Wagner and Liszt appeared in *Lisztomania*).

And he staged operas by Igor Stravinsky (*The Rake's Progress*, 1982), Giacomo Puccini (*Madame Butterfly*, 1983 and *La Bohéme*, 1984), Gioacchino Rossini (*The Italian Woman In Algiers*, 1984), Bernd-Alois Zimmermann (*Die Soldaten*, 1984), Charles Gounod (*Faust*, 1985), Arrigo Boito (*Méphistophélès*, 1989),[115] Gilbert & Sullivan (*Princess Ida*, 1992) and Richard Strauss (*Salomé*, 1993).[116] This's one reason why there were fewer movies in Russell's later years – he was working in live opera.

Ken Russell directed operas, but he could've had a career directing stage musicals for Broadway and the West End. His flair

---
[115] This was filmed by Valiant SRL.
[116] Ken Russell's approach to opera was to deliver a new interpretation – rather than a traditional take (BP, 227), and that sometimes led to controversy. In his autobiography, he waxes lyrical about particular singers.

for combining images, sets, costumes, colours, lighting, movement, dance and dialogue with music is simply extraordinary (and *timing*, too: Russell has a showman's sense of timing, rhythm and pace, of knowing just when to slow a movie down, and when to ramp up the energy. He is also a master of the sudden reveal and the surprising jolt, the equal of Alfred Hitchcock or D.W. Griffith).

Then there was a documentary called *Classic Widows* (1995) about the wives of William Walton, Benjamin Frankel, Humphrey Searle and Bernard Stevens, a revisit to Edward Elgar on TV in 2002, a documentary about folk songs (*In Search of the English Folk Song*, 1998),[117] and a guide to British music (1988).

And more recently, in the 2000s, Ken Russell embarked upon some fictionalized accounts of classical composers: essentially, they are novelizations of his movies (such as Frederick Delius, Ludwig van Beethoven, Johannes Brahms and Edward Elgar), focussing (inevitably) on their erotic relationships, in book form (and also as e-books).

In books such as *Elgar: The Erotic Variations, Delius: A Moment With Venus, Brahms Gets Laid* and *Beethoven Confidential*, Ken Russell was able to rework the research carried out for movies and TV documentaries into fiction. Viewers of Russell's films and TV shows will recognize many of the events in the books (some of these projects were unmade – publishing them in book form was a way for Russell to recycle material, which he, like everyone else, did all the time).

Ken Russell's books about famous composers were marketed in part by emphasizing their erotic elements.[118] But these were not 'sex lives of famous artists' stories. Rather, they were irreverent, witty, and entertaining. For Russell, they allowed him to include numerous details from the composers' lives that he hadn't been able to squeeze into the films and TV shows.

A novel followed, called *Violation* (2001), a self-conscious attempt at offence, involving Adolf Hitler, Eva Braun and a

---

[117] Ken Russell's exploration of the British folk song included performances by a roll call of many big names of the time, including: Waterson Carthy, Eliza Carthy, June Tabor, Osibisa, the Albion Band, the Percy Grainger Chamber Orchestra, Donovan, and Fairport Convention.
[118] The book covers of the British editions were by Paul Dufficey, the art director on movies such as *Lisztomania* and *Tommy*.

Jewish boy.[119] And a futuristic rewriting of the *Bible*, in *Mike and Gaby's Space Gospel* (1999).

Ken Russell has also produced radio plays – for example, *The Death of Alexander Scriabin*, which was broadcast on BBC Radio 3 in 1995, and featured James Wilby and Oliver Reed.

Over the years, Ken Russell worked with many composers and conductors who were important figures in the British (and international) classical music scene: Peter Maxwell Davies, Richard Rodney Bennett, André Previn and Carl Davis. Russell also collaborated with some of the big names in British pop music: the Who, Elton John, Eric Clapton (*Tommy*), Rick Wakeman (*Lisztomania* and *Crimes of Passion*), and Thomas Dolby (*Gothic*).

Presumably Ken Russell could have continued with films and TV shows about composers – moving onto Ludwig von Beethoven,[120] Alexander Scriabin,[121] Giuseppe Verdi, Robert Schumann, etc.

No other filmmaker I can think of has made such a passionate and lengthy exploration of classical music and composers (except Tony Palmer).[122] As to feature-length biographies, you can count the number on one hand. No, that's not true, there *have* been some biopics of composers, including some from the Classical Hollywood era and from more recent times: on Richard Strauss (*The Great Waltz*, 1938 and 1972, and *The Waltz King*, 1963), on Giuseppe Verdi (*The Life of Verdi*, 1984), a TV series, on Richard Wagner (*Wagner*, 1984), on Ludwig van Beethoven (*Immortal Beloved*, 1994), on Frédéric Chopin (*A Song To Remember*, 1945, and a 2002 film), on Giacomo Puccini (1953 and 2001), on Robert Schumann (and Clara, of course): *Spring Symphony* (1983, and *Song of Love*, 1947), and on Alma Mahler (*Bride of the Wind*, 2001).

Probably the most famous (and certainly one of the most celebrated) of recent movies about a classical composer was *Amadeus* (1983), a film which clearly drew upon Ken Russell's

---

119 'It's a satire on Spielberg,' Ken Russell explained in 2000, 'a satire on concentration camps, a satire on schmaltz, a satire on Christmas, a satire on war movies, a satire on everything'.
120 Ken Russell got very close to shooting *The Beethoven Secret* when the finances dematerialized.
121 Ken Russell had written a script about Alexander Scriabin, but couldn't find any backers.
122 Among British directors, Tony Palmer (b. 1941) has produced many documentaries about composers, including for the BBC. Palmer has covered Mozart, Rachmaninov, Dvorak, Handel, and Stravinsky, as well as pop acts like Tangerine Dream, Cream and a history of pop. Palmer was keen to work with Ken Russell in the 1960s, when he was starting out, and eventually helped Russell on the TV *Isadora Duncan*.

landmark classical music and artists' biopics (that was Russell's Oscar really, not Saul Zaentz's or Peter Schaffer's).

And more recent movies about performers, such as *Shine* (1996), about David Helfgott, and *Hilary and Jackie* (1998), about Jacqueline du Pré and her sister Hilary.

There was also a Russian biopic on Peter Tchaikovsky, released a year after Ken Russell's own movie *The Music Lovers*, 1971.[123] And Liszt had been the subject of a 1960 movie starring Dirk Bogarde (*Song Without End*).

However, *very* few biographies of classical music composers have taken an irreverent approach, like Ken Russell's. The opposite is the norm: total awe at the creative process (though the messy private lives are explored in some biopics). Russell's *ir*reverence is still unusual: that sort of attack on a Great Artist is still seen as disrespectful.

When he takes on a classical composer, it is the *music* that is primary for Ken Russell, not only the biography of the composer. *The music.*[124] This cannot be over-stated enough, but it's one of the main reasons for the misunderstandings that Russell's films lead to. He is *not* producing a 'realistic' film or even a standard documentary piece about an artist. He is looking at their *art*, and is regarding music (perhaps incorrectly) as expressing something of the inner life of the subject. As he explains about his approach to the 1974 movie *Mahler*: he 'searched for the soul of the man in his music' (BP, 141). That sums it up neatly: films such as *Mahler*, *The Music Lovers*, *Lisztomania*, *Delius: Song of Summer* and *The Debussy Film* are searches for the soul of the man in his music.

If it was possible, Ken Russell said he liked to start with the soundtrack first:

> I try to start with the soundtrack first – you see, that's the most difficult part. Because once you have the soundtrack, you have the movie. Music is architecture to me so I always try to get a musical or architectural sense for the film. (RC, 252)

Ingmar Bergman has said the same thing:

---

[123] Ken Russell dismissed the rival Russian film. 'About the only thing our films had in common was the humble silver birch. [Dimitri] Tiomkin's version with its brash Hollywood score and Sovexport scenario was as phoney as an official tour of the Tchaikovsky Museum at Kiln,' Russell complained waspishly in his autobiography (BP, 55).
[124] The title itself – *The Music Lovers* – is clearly deeply personal for Ken Russell.

> When we experience a film, we consciously prime ourselves for illusion. Putting aside will and intellect, we make way for it in our imagination. The sequence of pictures plays directly on our feelings. Music works in the same fashion; I would say that there is no art form that has so much in common with film as music. Both affect our emotions directly, not via the intellect. And film is mainly rhythm; it is inhalation and exhalation in continuous sequence. Ever since childhood, music has been my great source of recreation and stimulation, and I often experience a film or play musically.[125]

Ken Russell also clearly *understands* music in depth – very few film directors possess that level of understanding and knowledge (many, many famous film directors knew absolutely nothing about music, and weren't able to communicate with their composers beyond simple suggestions. Many of the celebrated directors today can't get beyond statements such as: 'I like the music'). Even when he is being outrageous and conjuring out-size imagery and scenes, you can still tell that Russell understands the music in his movies in an incredibly detailed manner.[126]

Ken Russell's classical music movies and TV shows also depict plenty of musicians at work: composers are seen composing, writing on manuscripts, playing at the piano, conducting, performing live, singing, etc. The trappings of classical music are everywhere, too: musical manuscript paper, the conductor's baton, the metronome, the brass band, the violin, the piano (the props guys must've humped 100s of pianos on and off sets for Russell's movies).

Ken Russell remarked that raising finance for films about classical music composers was difficult. I should say nearly impossible. Many of Russell's films were about artists, and very few biopics about artists cross over into the mainstream and become big hits. You need big stars and a fantastic script and a really sexy subject for your biopic. Films about movie stars or rock stars, well, that's different (*The Doors, Ray, Rock Star, Almost Famous, Dreamgirls*).

But even then, biographical flicks rarely hit the big time, in terms of box office rentals (like musicals nowadays. They can revered by critics and the Academy of Motion Picture Arts and Sciences – such as *Bird* (about Charlie Parker), *Walk the Line, Sid &*

---

125 "Introduction", *Four Screenplays*, 1960.
126 However, Russell wasn't a musician. But being so knowledgeable about music no doubt made it so much easier for his composers to talk with him about film scoring.

*Nancy* (about Sid Vicious and Nancy Spungen), *What's Love Got To Do With It?* (about Ike and Tina Turner), *Shine, Amadeus, Almost Famous, Nashville, A Hard Day's Night, The Doors* and *Ray* (about Ray Charles). But few do really big business. The incredible thing is that Ken Russell and his producers managed to persuade United Artists to put money into a film about a classical music composer. We know the famous story about how Russell pitched it to UA: 'a story about a homosexual who fell in love with a nymphomaniac'. But there was clearly more to the pitch than that.

Even so, movies about classical music composers – that has to be a minority interest from the get-go (imagine it today: in a multiplex in New Jersey, what're audiences gonna see: a movie about a tortured, depressed artist set in Berlin in the 1840s or the latest popcorn, Summer blockbuster about superheroes protecting the White House from aliens?). Which's why most of Ken Russell's films about classical music composers have been television-based productions, *not* movies. It's part of public service broadcasting (at least in Britain) that television should explore all of the arts, not just, if left to its own devices and the rampant commercialism of a capitalist social system, pop music and movies and fashion and celebrity gossip (with the occasional prestige drama rehashing Jane Austen or Charles Dickens yet again).

Or to put it another way: in Britain, public service television and radio (i.e., the BBC) is funded by the British tax payer. Everyone owning a television set must have by law a TV licence. And that pays for the British Brainwashing Corporation (there are other streams of revenue for the Beeb, of course, including rampant capitalism). And part of that deal between the BBC and the British government is that the BBC is beholden to broadcast all sorts of things a commercial broadcaster would not bother with. A classical music radio station (BBC Radio 3), for instance, or hundreds of hours of television programming on all sorts of minority interest topics, including most of the arts.

So Ken Russell's TV documentaries about classical music composers or architects or poets or painters came about very much because of the public service broadcasting tradition in Britain. Without that support from the British tax payer, those sorts of TV programmes would dwindle to a very small audience or a minor TV channel (in the age of cable and satellite TV).

And what's incredible about Ken Russell is that he attempted to continue the public service broadcasting tradition of little, old Britain into the cut-throat world of internationally-distributed movies. And without television finance (which was the way to go in many cases from the 1980s onwards). That is, *The Music Lovers* and *Mahler* and *Savage Messiah* were conceived and produced in the era *before* video cassettes and DVDs (which would have brought in essential revenue), and also without backing from TV companies.

Or to put it another way: *The Music Lovers,* a biopic about a Russian, classical music composer, was paid for by a North American movie studio not a British broadcaster. However, United Artists had some provisos (if not guarantees) that at least some elements that would be included to encourage them to greenlight the project: first, two stars, Richard Chamberlain and Glenda Jackson (and Jackson had recently won as Oscar). And a hot director. And a script that would promise to be talked-about if nothing else.

In recognition that the interest among the movie-going public will be small, many of Ken Russell's projects, in the dog-eat-dog world of global movie distribution, have been made with small budgets: *Savage Messiah*, *Mahler*, *The Rainbow*, *The Lair of the White Worm*, etc.

# MORE ABOUT MUSIC

> No other art can so sublimely arouse human sentiments in the innnermost heart of man. No other art can paint to the eyes of the soul the splendours of nature, the delights of contemplation, the character of nations, the tumult of their passions, and the languor of their sufferings as music can. Regret, hope, terror, meditation, consternation, enthusiasm, faith, glory, tranquillity, all these and more are given to us and taken from us thanks to her genius and according to the bent of our own.
>
> George Sand, *Consuelo* (1843)

One of Ken Russell's great passions is classical music. His memoirs abound with references to Tchaikovsky, Mahler, Strauss, Elgar, Liszt, Prokofiev, Beethoven, and Bach. 'My imagery comes from listening to music,' Russell asserted (BP, 156). He is a 'slave of music', as Percy Bysshe Shelley put it.

In 1997, US chiildren's author Maurice Sendak remarked:

> To me, the best of all art forms is music and perhaps opera is my favourite, and the best best best of all that is Mozart.

'I was mad on music, and would rush out like a starving man and get all the records I could afford,' Ken Russell recalled of his youth. 'I couldn't get enough of it' (Bax, 82-83). Well, we know that!: music saturates Russell's entire work, in movies, television, books, newspaper articles, and photography. For Russell, music was like oxygen (Bax, 102).

The affinities between cinema and music are countless, and filmmakers have been exploiting them since the birth of cinema. The notion of all the arts moving towards the condition of one art (or as Walter Pater famously put it, towards music), developed in the age of Romanticism. German poet Novalis spoke of 'painting, plastic art are therefore nothing but figurative music. Painting, plastic art – objective music. Music – subjective music or painting'.

Huw Wheldon and *Monitor* was instrumental in getting Ken Russell's ideas for biopics on great composers made – building on the *Monitor* TV programmes, Russell continued with feature films on musicians. Russell noted that there have very few films on composers, apart from his own *The Music Lovers* and Tony Palmer's *Testimony* (presumably he means *his* sort of films about composers). 'What I've always been after is the spirit of the composer as manifest in his music' (1993, 75).

Ken Russell's work for BBC's *Monitor* was vital in launching his career, and enabling him to explore classical music via celluloid. The *Monitor* shows included *Pop Goes the Easel* (about four young Pop artists), a biopic of Douanier Rousseau, *Two Scottish Painters, The Biggest Dancer in the World* (on Isadora Duncan), and *Dante's Inferno* (about Dante Gabriel Rossetti and the Pre-Raphaelites). The *Monitor* programme on Edward Elgar was a Russell success: it used the Malvern Hills in Worcestershire as the backbone to a portrait of Elgar (famous shots included Elgar staring out towards Wales, kite-flying and horse-riding on the Hills).

Ken Russell said that he sent his three amateur films (*Peepshow, Lourdes* and *Amelia and the Angel*) to the Beeb, which resulted in his being employed by *Monitor*. In *A British Picture*, Russell asserted that Edward Elgar had 'captured the spirit of England, past, present and future, more convincingly than any other artist, living or dead' (BP, 27).

Ken Russell's preference for making films about real people was seen as problematic for the BBC, who weren't sure about the ethics of this kind of dramatized documentary (it became widely adopted from the 1980s onwards). Russell said he learnt much from Huw Wheldon and *Monitor*, including how to stretch a budget, how to improvize within financial limits. Russell claimed that his talks with Wheldon were 'the only time I've been able to talk with someone about my work and really get something of fantastic value out of it' (Bax, 112-3).

Ken Russell spoke nostalgically of the discussions in the *Red Lion* pub near the BBC – '[t]hat was the most rewarding drinking I ever did... It was thrilling, believe it or not, and bloody instructive at the same time' (ib., 113). Russell called Huw Wheldon the 'guiding genius' of 'the one and only English experimental film school ever' (ibid.). For his part, Wheldon remarked that Russell had enormous powers of invention and imagination that required a strong producer or scriptwriter to rein them in (ib., 123). 'He had a leaping imagination and, as frequently happens with people of this kind, great tenacity and determination'.

BIOPICS.

Many of Ken Russell's films are drawn from biographies of real people – most obviously, classical composers. Some of those biopics are based on books, and some on extensive research. For the rest of his output, Russell has used, like almost all filmmakers, books and plays: literary works such as *The Rainbow, Women In Love, Lady Chatterley's Lover, Billion Dollar Brain, Altered States, The Fall of the House of Usher, The Lair of the White Worm, The Devils of Loudun,* or plays such as *The Boy Friend, The Devils, Salome's Last Dance* and *Whore*.

So most of Ken Russell's films are not original screenplays in the sense of original stories featuring characters that haven't been seen before. There is plenty of research in a Ken Russell movie. Like Francis Coppola and Stanley Kubrick, Russell enjoys that part of the preparation for a project. But that doesn't mean that the research will end up on screen undiluted by Russell's vision and style.

Before he begins a biopic, Ken Russell said he immersed himself in the

> iconography of the period, the photography, the painting, the literature. I absorb it like a piece of blotting paper and then I just go and do the film. (In F. Robbins, 1973)

For *Savage Messiah*, Ken Russell said he did an extensive amount of research, which included visiting Paris, seeing the library where he met Sophie Brzeska, explored Henri Gaudier's London, talked to people who knew him, read Brzeska's letters and art histories, etc (Bax, 222). And there's a point where all of that research snowballs into madness, and you say, no more! Enough! OK, I know *everything* about this guy. Then you move beyond it all, and start making the movie.

But that doesn't mean that the film is a straight translation of research to the screen (how could it be?). Indeed, like all filmmakers, Ken Russell constantly changes contexts, times, places, characters, etc: dialogue from one context or time is put into another time or context,[127] characters are combined, and if the budget won't allow it, some events have to be reduced to a much cheaper equivalent event.

---

[127] Ken Russell likes to use the actual things that real people said, or real quotes from novels, in his movies. Although the meanings and contexts may be different, sometimes whole scenes would be made up of real quotes (G, 112).

Ken Russell's first biopic was of a classical music composer, naturally – Sergei Prokofiev (*Portrait of a Soviet Composer*, 1961). Many of Russell's programmes for television were about music: *The Miner's Picnic* (brass bands), *Portrait of a Soviet Composer* (Sergei Prokofiev), *Variations On a Mechanical Theme* (mechanical instruments), *Guitar Craze, Lotte Lenya Sings Kurt Weill, Elgar, Bartók, The Debussy Film, Don't Shoot the Composer* (Georges Delerue), *The Dance of the Seven Veils* (Richard Strauss) and *Delius: Song of Summer*.

Two of Russell's early TV films were about dance: *Marie Rambert* (1959) was about the Ballet Rambert company, and *The Light Fantastic* (1960) was about dancing in England. And *Isadora Duncan* was of course about one of Russell's favourite artists (Duncan also influenced Gudrun's dancing style in *Women In Love*, and 'Gosh' Smith-Boyle in *Savage Messiah*).

Then there were shows on painters (*Pop Goes the Easel, McBryde and Colquhoun*, the Pre-Raphaelite Museum in Battersea, Dante Gabriel Rossetti, Henri Rousseau), poets (John Betjeman, and, later, William Wordsworth and Samuel Taylor Coleridge), and architecture (*Antonio Gaudi*).

Ken Russell said he was trying to do what music composers do – to express something inexpressible, to reach an area of divine mystery.[128] You could put it another way: Russell's movies tend towards the condition of music. Or that he is trying to explore the same realms as music.

Life is a mystery for Ken Russell – and one reason why artists were important was because 'artists somehow make mysteries concrete, make them more tangible. They interpret the ineffable for the rest of us' (RC, 246).

For Richard Eder (1976), Ken Russell's biopics are really about Russell himself: they reveal more about the director than they do about Mahler or Tchaikovsky or Liszt.

> As far as the audience is concerned, it is almost as if Tchaikovsky, Liszt and Mahler had taken turns making films about Mr Russell.

You may not notice a significant omission from many of Ken Russell's films and biographies about classical music composers, and this is the standard *contextualization* of documentaries and biographies. In Russell's TV shows and films about composers

---

[128] J. Walker, "Ken Russell's New Enigma", *The Observer*, Sept 8, 1974.

(and artists), there is no introductory segment outlining the politics and key events of the period, no images of kings and queens and politicians and big events such as wars or coups or revolutions or assassinations or whatever. There are few dates, too, saying what year it was that, say, Frederick Delius contracted syphilis (it was 1922), or what year Franz Liszt first met Richard Wagner (it was in 1849), or when Gustav Mahler composed his *Ninth Symphony* (it was in 1908-09).

All of that is simply left aside in Ken Russell's TV shows and movies – all of that pedagogical stuff which public service broadcasters such as the BBC and PBS put into their documentaries. Russell's films and television programmes don't lecture their audience, don't assume the role of a teacher or a nanny. (If you want that info, you can look it up in your own time – the movie or TV show won't do it for you).

Instead, the shows go straight for explorations of the artist themselves and their work. And they also assume that their viewers are fairly intelligent, and already know quite a bit about European history from 1800 to the present.

The BBC mandate to 'inform, educate and entertain', the Reithian mantra of the early days of the Beeb, are simply put to one side in Ken Russell's documentaries and biopics. Oh, you can learn plenty, and the films and TV shows are teaching you plenty, if you want to see it like that. And, yes, there is a huge amount of historical research in the films and shows. But these shows and movies are *not* historical lectures, they are not homework, their aims are quite different.

So many of the films and TV programmes of Ken Russell hope that the audience is going to do quite a bit of work themselves. As Joseph Gomez pointed out, re. *The Music Lovers*, if the viewer isn't willing to unravel the complexities of the movie, it can lead to misunderstandings (G, 98).

DANCE.

Another Ken Russell passion was dance (at one time he had trained in ballet). He performed with the British Dance Theatre and the London Theatre Ballet, including going on tours, and also with the Norwegian Ballet (including a visit to Oslo). Russell has written of his times with touring dance companies in his autobiographies.

There was an enormous amount of dancing in *The Boy Friend*; Glenda Jackson cavorted in front of the cattle in *Women in Love* (plus Hermione's dance, and the dance in Switzerland); Rudolf Nureyev, probably the world's foremost ballet dancer of the period, starred in *Valentino*; characters in *The Music Lovers*, and *Mahler*, and *Savage Messiah*, and *The Debussy Film*, and many others move choreographically; dance runs throughout *Isadora Duncan* and *The Dance of the Seven Veils*, movies which're wholly dance-oriented. If there's a chance to squeeze in a dance number into a film, Russell will do it. In fact, it'd be quicker to cite movies and TV shows directed by Russell which *don't* contain any dancing. (And there's plenty of ballet dancing, as well as more popular dancing in Russell's movies; films featuring ballet are a sub-genre of the dance genre. Some are records of performances, like *Swan Lake, A Midsummer Night's Dream* and *The Nutcracker Suite*, or ballet companies such as the Bolshoi Ballet. Russell contributed with ballet documentaries; and one of his key performers, Christopher Gable, was with the Royal Ballet).

'When you're dancing, you're really alive'.

So says Isadora Duncan in Ken Russell's and Sewell Stokes' 1966 BBC movie *Isadora Duncan*. It's certainly one of Russell's credos. No other British filmmaker, and probably no other filmmaker in the history of cinema, even including great dance directors such as Bob Fosse, Gene Kelly or Vincente Minnelli, has included so much dancing in their works. (Fosse, for instance, directed far fewer movies than Russell, and although Minnelli made more musicals than Russell, including some of the classics, Russell includes choreography even in straight melodramas. If Russell had directed a biopic of Vincent van Gogh, he would've been dancing thru the wheatfields).

In other movies, Ken Russell often favours physical acting, rather than verbal dexterity. Russell advocated a cinema of visual spectacle, not people sitting around talking. Like Michael Powell, Russell had admired Vaslav Nijinsky (he had planned a film on the Russian dancer, while *The Red Shoes* (1948) had a Sergei Diaghilev figure). Nijinsky and Duncan were touchstones for Russell, even tho' they died before his time. One can imagine that if a time machine were available, Russell would certainly have gone to see them dance, as well as met heroes of the classical music world, such as Ludwig van Beethoven, Gustav Mahler and

Peter Tchaikovsky (and wherever Russell is now, maybe he's chatted with some of his heroes!).

## RELIGION

✟

One aspect of Ken Russell's cinema is so potent and pervasive it's impossible to miss, but it's not uppermost in many appraisals of his output by critics and viewers: *religion*.

What are the major themes in Ken Russell's cinema?

Art and artists, yes.

Classical music, yes.

19th and 20th century culture, yes.

Sex and love and relationships, yes.

Nature and pantheism, yes.

Death, suicide, loss, yes.

And a stylistic approach which's typically parodic or camp as well as reverential – an approach that simultaneously sends up and celebrates its subject matter, yes.

But there is one theme that often pushes aside all of those themes: religion.

Religion is a major component of the following pieces: *The Dance of the Seven Veils* (Richard Strauss's Catholicism), *Mahler* (Gustav Mahler's conversion to Catholicism), *Lisztomania* (in which the superstar composer lives in Rome (in/ near the Vatican), and hobnobs with the Pope, and Nazism as a new religion), the operas *Faust* and *Méphistophélès* (bargains with the Devil), *Salomé* (Strauss's opera, and Oscar Wilde's play), *Tommy* (a rock messiah with a cult of followers), *Altered States* (religious guilt and drug-taking as self-transcendence), *The Lair of the White Worm* (all about an ancient snake cult), *Crimes of Passion* (featuring a manic priest), and of course *The Devils*. There are many other examples.

No other major British filmmaker in the history of British cinema has put religion to the forefront in so many films and TV shows. It's a concern so fundamental to Ken Russell's cinema, it places him in the same company as Ingmar Bergman, Pier Paolo

Pasolini, Andrei Tarkovsky and Carl-Theodor Dreyer.[129]

And *no* other filmmaker in recent times has staged so many crucifixions. Not Martin Scorsese, not Piero Paolo Pasolini, not Abel Ferrara, not Paul Verhoeven, not even the many directors of made-for-TV religious specials and mini-series.[130]

Nope, when it comes to crucifixions, Ken Russell is king: they occur in *The Lair of the White Worm*, *The Dance of the Seven Veils*, *Mahler*, *Altered States*, *The Debussy Film* and of course *The Devils* (there may be others I've forgotten about). So many crucifixions! – to the point where it must have become routine for Russell's film crews:

> 1st A.D.: 'What're we filming today, boss?'
> Russell: 'A crucifixion'.
> 1st A.D. 'Right you are, guv. Bill! Fetch the dummy nails[131] and the blood!'

☦

Ken Russell converted to Catholicism around the time he was making his first film, *Peepshow,* in 1956. As Russell told it in 1973:

> During a lunch break one day on *Peepshow* I had been talking with this North Country friend of mine [Norman Dewhurst] about the Mass. He mentioned the phrase "Take of my body and eat", and I suddenly realized that, as far as he was concerned, it was the living body of Christ he ate in the communion service. That was the most mind-shattering thing that had ever struck me. I don't think I ever thought of anything again in quite the same way. I was ripe for conversion. (Bax, 101)

Catholicism fed most of Ken Russell's subsequent movies, and his movies wouldn't be the same without his conversion:

> All my films have been Catholic films, films about love, faith, sin, guilt, forgiveness, redemption. Films that could only have been made by a Catholic.[132]

---

129 Needless to say, Ken Russell did not like *The Passion of the Christ*; he felt that Mel Gibson and co. had misinterpreted the *Bible*.
130 Had Ken Russell been born thirty years earlier, and had be gone to Hollywood, he might have been one of the great filmmakers of religious epics in the Cecil B. De Mille and William Wyler manner in the 1950s and 1960s.
131 Director Norman Jewison recalled that when they shot the Crucifixion scene in *Jesus Christ Superstar*, an extra playing one of the soldiers was going to hammer a real nail through Ted Neeley's palm b4 someone stopped him.
132 And the conversion to Catholicism helped his addiction to snuff, Ken Russell admitted. He was taking snuff (Dr Rumney's Mentholyptus) to the point where it became a problem (PF, 31). Being Catholic added a new irony to his worldview, Russell said, and helped to get rid of easy sentimentality – because Catholicism taught him that there was no easy way out.

What are the views expressed about religion in Ken Russell's cinema? They are very easy to see:

☦ organized religion has its uses, can be æsthetically pretty, but is all too often corrupt and dangerous.

☦ individual spiritual feeling and transcendence can occur within organized religions, but often flourishes best outside of them.

☦ the means to self-transcendence and spirituality are many: in Russell's cinema, they might include:

(1) art,
(2) sex and love,
(3) drugs,
(4) music,
(5) nature mysticism.

MADNESS.

There are more disturbing images of madness in Ken Russell's films than in the work of many a filmmaker. Nina Milyukova at the end of *The Music Lovers,* for instance, or the nuns in *The Devils* and the composer in *Delius: Song of Summer.* And not only insanity, but also hysteria. Richard Wagner at the end of *Liszto-mania,* for instance, or the poets in *Gothic.* So many images, one wonders if there is some biographical reason for it. While the costs of being an artist for some dramatists might be death, in Russell's cinema it can lead to madness (a living death).

And in drama and cinema, the living death of madness can be much more disturbing than death itself. While death might give a character's story a tragic or noble or melancholy ending, insanity, like a severely disabling illness, is much more of a punishment (it sure ain't spiritual transcendence or an upward move into martyrdom). At the end of a Hollywood movie a character might end up heroically sacrificing themselves and dying, and saving the world in the process. But to have that same heroic figure becoming insane is very different.

And suicide is a recurring theme, too: characters take their life, or try to, in *The Music Lovers, Women In Love, The Debussy Film, Isadora Duncan, Dante's Inferno* and *The Devils.* And often those suicides are linked to the central characters, to the artists: they can't take anymore, so they find a way out.

MAKE YOUR OWN KEN RUSSELL MOVIE.

A do-it-yourself kit for a Ken Russell movie would require the following items:

♣ a piano
♣ candles
♣ smoke and fire
♣ 19th century costumes
♣ spangly modern costumes
♣ S/M gear
♣ Nazi uniforms
♣ nun costumes
♣ a horse (and maybe a carriage)
♣ crucifixes
♣ swastikas
♣ a whip
♣ a conductor's baton
♣ swords
♣ a banana,[133] bottle or other phallic totem
♣ a brass band
♣ masks & feathers
♣ a train
♣ a mirror
♣ a theatre
♣ a church
♣ an asylum
♣ a lake
♣ mountains
♣ a forest
♣ champagne
♣ a CD player or i-Pod plus giant speakers & amp (for music playback)

---

[133] Bananas! In a Jean-Luc Godard movie, when actors are at a loss of what to do in a scene, they light a cigarette (again and again in French movies!). In a Ken Russell movie, when an actor asked, 'what shall I do here, Ken?', the maestro probably replied, 'well, I dunno, how about eating a banana?' And if the actor retorted, 'I did that in the last movie, Ken!', the exasperated director might have replied, 'phooey, love, no one will notice! Terry! Where's my champagne?!'

A few of Ken Russell's film influences: clockwise from top right:
Betty Grable. Leni Riefenstahl. Metropolis. The Fleet's In.
The Cabinet of Dr Caligari. Die Nibelungen.

Some of Ken Russell's favourite composers: clockwise from top right: Claude Debussy. Franz Liszt. Dimitri Shostakovitch. Ralph Vaughan Williams. Gustav Mahler. Igor Stravinsky.

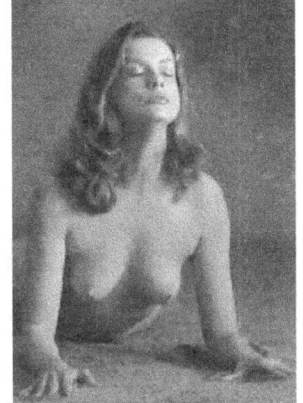

Russell's Women: from top right, clockwise:
Gala Mitchell. Sammi Davis & Amanda
Donohue. Helen Mirren. Ann-Margret.
Glenda Jackson. Annette Robertson.
Georgina Hale. Françoise Dorléac.
Theresa Russell. Blair Brown.

Vaslav Nijinsky (in Scheherazade, c. 1912), one of Russell's heroes.

One of the landscapes of the soul for Ken Russell, Derwentwater, as photographed by Roger Fenton in 1860

Ken Russell on location for The Rainbow
in his beloved Lake District

# PART TWO
## THE WORKS

# 1

# THE DEBUSSY FILM

Why do love affairs always end miserably?

Pierre Louÿs

Once again, as I look at some of Ken Russell's work from the 1960s, like *Isadora Duncan* or *The Debussy Film* or *Dante's Inferno*, I am stunned by just how much Russell achieved before becoming well-known and fêted as a feature film director, from the time of *Women In Love* (1969) onwards. If you completely ignore the theatrical movies, for instance, and the work in other areas, like opera or publishing or newspapers, Russell's achievement in one medium – television – is simply stupendous.

*The Debussy Film* contained all of the usual Ken Russell ingredients: plenty of dancing, late 19th century/ Art Nouveau settings, the natural world (the ocean, beaches, rain, trees, sunlight, gardens), films-within-films, swimming, nudity, sex, violence, painting, visual effects from commercials (backlighting, slow motion, sunshine), appearances by his family,[1] and of course plenty of music.

### CAST AND CREW.

1965's *The Debussy Film* (tx 1965.5.18) was made at the Beeb, but it was originally intended to be a feature movie (tho' it

---

[1] Victoria Russell appears as the toddler Chou-Chou, Claude Debussy's daughter, who died at 13.

would've made a fairly esoteric movie).[2] It was co-written by Ken Russell and Melvyn Bragg, edited by Alan Tyrer, the DPs were Ken Westbury and John McGlashan, sound by Stan Morcom, costumes by Velma Buckle and make-up by Maureen Winslade. Russell is also credited as producer. The cast included Oliver Reed, Vladek Sheybal, Annette Robertson, Penny Service, Iza Teller, Vernon Dobtcheff, Verity Edmett, Stephanie Randall and Jane Lumb.

Many in *The Debussy Film*, on both sides of the camera, were Ken Russell regulars. This needs to be stressed: one of the reasons that Russell was able to produce such a formidable body of work in TV and cinema was due to the talented team he gathered around himself.

The casting in *The Debussy Film* is spot-on: and while Oliver Reed and Vladek Sheybal rightly received much of the attention, Annette Robertson[3] (b. 1940) was absolutely stunning as Gabrielle (Gaby) Dupont, Claude Debussy's lover. Tiny, sexy, large, dark eyes made up heavily with kohl, Robertson had to do a ton of work in *The Debussy Film*, playing both the Actor's girlfriend and Debussy's lover. There's no doubt that *The Debussy Film* is partly in love with Robertson, which works on every level.

Like many of Ken Russell's movies, there are some attractive people in *The Debussy Film*, such as Annette Robertson, Stephanie Randall, Jane Lumb, Verity Edmett and Penny Service (you'll find many of these actresses in TV shows of the period such as *The Saint* and *The Prisoner*). Well, it *was* the 1960s, so beautiful, blonde women wandering about seems *de rigeur*. Yeah, it's indulgent, it's sexist, it's — wait a minute! This is *Ken Russell* we're talking about here!

DUAL STRUCTURE.

*The Debussy Film* was intended to be a satirical look at the ambiguous status of the television documentary, using a multiple-level narrative approach, in which Oliver Reed and Vladek Sheybal (two actors) played both an actor and a TV director and

---

[2] Russell said in 1973 that he had offered the project to producer David Deutsch, and later to Harry Saltzman.
[3] Annette Robertson had appeared in *A Kind of Loving* and *The Young Ones*, and later in numerous British television shows (*Dr Who, Angels, Boon, The Woodlanders*, etc). She was married to John Hurt in the early 1960s.

the characters of Claude Debussy[4] (August 22, 1862 - March 25, 1918) and writer Pierre Louÿs (1870-1925), who were in turn real people.[5] The dramatic device fulfilled many functions:

(1) It allowed a ton of exposition about the life of Claude Debussy and his music to be delivered to the audience (much of it given by the Director). As Ken Russell explained in 1973, a question-and-answer format was one way of doing the piece, and a director and an actor were a good couple of characters for questions and answers.[6]

(2) It allowed numerous parallels between the lives of the performers and those of their characters, thus offering a familiar entry-point (of 1960s characters) into the historical drama for the television audience (variations on the time travel approach are common in historical stories and movies. In many stories, it's sometimes a distraction, and not really necessary. In *The Debussy Film*, it's a focus of the whole project).

(3) It allowed for introductions to each piece of music by Claude Debussy, to set them up dramatically and emotionally: and by putting the exposition into the Director's voiceover, it didn't come across as a dry, academic, TV narration.

(4) It included an exploration of the documentary format, and by extension of the media itself, and the relation of cinema and television to history, and to real people.

And there were further levels to the dramatic device of *The Debussy Film*'s film-within-a-film: the voiceover, which was largely by Director, also included the Director as Pierre Louÿs, *and* it included the Actor as Claude Debussy, and the Actress as Gaby Dupont. And at the top of the show, a narrator (Melvyn Bragg) introduced the major characters.

> Claude Debussy, born in poverty in 1862; died friendless in 1918. A film based on incidents in his life, his own words, and his relations with Gabrielle Dupont, attempted suicide; Lily Rosalie Texier,

---

[4] There are links to Ken Russell's later works: there are direct connections between Claude Debussy and Frédéric Chopin, for instance (his piano teacher), which the movie mentions, and Peter Tchaikovsky (Debussy was music tutor to Nadezhda von Meck's children). Debussy completed one opera, *Pelléas et Mélisande* (1902).
[5] While critics admired Harold Pinter's adaption of *The French Lieutenant's Woman* (because, well, it was scripted by Harold Pinter!), Ken Russell had got there first. (Actually, film-within-film narratives and dramatic doublings go back a long way – *Singin' In the Rain*, for instance, is a marvellous example).
[6] 'I thought the time had come to ask questions, and the natural way for me to ask questions was to have a film director talking to an actor, because an actor always asks questions about the character he's playing and the director usually had to answer them, or try to, often just to keep him happy' (Bax, 128).

attempted suicide; 'Chou-Chou', died at the age of 13; Madame Bardac, wife of a wealthy banker, and the man who took most of these pictures, Pierre Louÿs, pornographer, novelist, photographer.

Yet another level or narration was the play-within-the-film, in which three actors on a stage (filmed at Tollard Royal),[7] re-played a scene from Claude Debussy's life in which the discovery of adultery was the theme. And while that was playing on stage, the Actor playing Debussy had slipped into a nearby room for some more fooling around, only to be discovered. (Ken Russell returned to this device many times, so there's an emotional feedback loop created, with art imitating life, and life imitating art, and the same scenarios are repeated again and again).

The actors're playing scenes from Claude Debussy's life in modern dress, but the costumes and settings don't matter, because the film has established the links between then and now so strongly. (The costumes in the 1960s scenes, by Velma Buckle, concentrated on white, a colour that crops up in many of Ken Russell's movies of the period).

*The Debussy Film* is thus a sophisticated piece of screen-writing, keeping a number of juggling balls in the air at the same time, as well as delivering a public service broadcasting show which educates and informs the audience.

What is history? is a question that Ken Russell has asked many times. What is a historical fact? What is important in history, and what is superfluous? What was life like in 1890 or 1910? How can you recreate it or suggest it using actors and costumes and cameras and dialogue and actions?

These issues face the movie-maker of historical pictures every time they attempt a new movie. Ken Russell has come up with a variety of solutions – but early on in his career he was questioning notions of history, of documentary, of fact. Thus, by 1965, Russell was already in the process of dismantling the notion of documentary and history, and documenting history, by employing the dramatic device of a multi-layered narrative. *The Debussy Film* doesn't take anything from history at face value, for instance, but dismantles it. Although the Director's authority on history isn't questioned (partly because he is a film director!), *The Debussy Film* does show that history has to be *interpreted*, that it isn't simply a question of translating a bunch of facts to the screen.

---

7 Tollard Royal, near Cranbourne Chase, was a favourite Russell location.

(Can you believe it, Ken Russell gets in another performance of Richard Wagner's *Ride of the Valkries* in *The Debussy Film*. Actually, being 1965, this must be the first time he used it – and it's no surprise that he can't take Wagner seriously for a minute: the so-famous music is played thru a scene where the actors playing Maurice Maeterlinck (Vernon Dobtcheff) and Claude Debussy fight using a broom and a walking stick as swords in a mock manner around a big manor house. It's a send-up of Ye Olde Hollywoode Sworde Fighte Scene (looking forward to the even sillier spoof that opens *Lisztomania*). And of course, during it all, the actors playing the Actors are delivering pages of information about the Debussy-Maeterlinck relationship. Russell has never been able to stage a straight-faced sword fight!)

HOW TO MAKE A KEN RUSSELL MOVIE.

The opening shot of *The Debussy Film* shows the Cinema Circus Coming To Town: trucks, a hearse on a trailer, props, actors in costume, extras, a fire truck and firemen (for rain), and loads of cars arrive at a location next to an old building.[8] It announces the film-within-a-film element from the off, and simply but effectively expresses the craziness of filmmaking, which has been described many times as a hundred people, tons of equipment, and loads of trucks – all for a scene of two people talking. If you've driven or walked past a film crew at work, you might think, with all that gear, they're filming a Napoleonic battle with a cast of thousands. But no, it's just a typical film crew shooting two people talking in a room (it's a bit of a more elaborate sequence here, tho' – it's Claude Debussy's funeral, featuring a few mourners, a carriage, a coffin and the obligatory rainfall. So we see the hoses and paraphernalia of filming a rain scene. Also, yet again, Russell begins a movie in the form of *Citizen Kane*, with the death of the protagonist).

*The Debussy Film* is also an insight into the making of a movie, Ken Russell-style. Yes, there were scenes where the Director was shown explaining about the historical people for the benefit of his actors (and also laying the groundwork for motivations and the like, as in the scene on the beach, where the

---

8 Ken Russell is heard in voiceover as an assistant director or production manager, yelling at people to get things moving. Of course, the director and his assistant have a white Citroen (flashy – and *French*),which stands out (and nearly crashes into a truck).

Actor asks about Debussy's relationship, with Madame Bardac).

But that is not Ken Russell's directorial manner, however – sitting patiently explaining motivations to his performers. I like to think of the scene where the Director and his crew are filming the religious procession on the beach in Sussex at night[9] as much more typical of Russell's directing style: here the Director was depicted running ahead of the procession, encouraging them gleefully, revelling in the chaos of filmmaking. Around him technicians are running with lights, cameras, smoke machines, etc (and Russell has been filmed at work like that. As actor Julian Sands put it during the making of *Gothic*, Russell 'is a big-game hunter filming in the middle of a rhino charge).

Of course, there are countless elements of filmmaking that are noticeably absent from *The Debussy Film* – not least producers and money people (and no lawyers in sight!). There is no discussion of money (or contracts) anywhere in *The Debussy Film* (though the Film Director does look at his watch, as film directors have always done, every single day of shooting, since the invention of cinema in 1895).

And no discussion of any technical problem, personal problem, production problem, or organizational problem, etc (which all movies are full of, contrary to those happy, smiling publicity featurettes). Instead, *The Debussy Film* reduces the filmmaking team down to the Film Director and his secretary (the crew are merely glimpsed in the background). But it works beautifully, because using a film director as the mouthpiece of the whole cinematic shebang in *The Debussy Film* is a simple but effective dramatic device of compression (and it also plays into what audiences would expect a filmmaker to do or to be, and into the *auteur* theory. Russell & co. are sending up film directors too, of course – as they did in *Valentino* – but there is perhaps something of Russell in the personality of the Film Director).

And the Actor pretty much goes along with whatever the Film Director suggests. Only in the beach scene in *The Debussy Film*, where he, the Director, and the Madame Bardac-Actress (Iza Teller) discuss Claude Debussy's later life and new relationship, does the Actor seriously question the Film Director's take on things (we know, for instance, that Ollie Reed wasn't always like

---

[9] In the night scenes, you can see the lighting crew struggling to illuminate a big area like a beach on a minuscule BBC budget! Hence the people carrying flares and flaming torches.

that with Ken Russell!). There are moments of boredom, where the Actor's had enough of hearing about Debussy and his travails (like during the play in the park), but, generally, the Actor's a good, dutiful soldier, and does what he's told. (The Actresses, meanwhile, don't have anything like the on-going dialogue with the Film Director. The Actress is often portrayed as wearying of the endless discussions between the Film Director and his disciple).

Inevitably, some critics compared *The Debussy Film* to *8 1/2* (Federico Fellini, 1963), a favourite with movie critics as a meditation upon films and filmmaking. However, all of Ken Russell's movies about creative artists are versions of *8 1/2*.

1963's *Contempt* might be another reference point: the merging of a film with a film-with-a-film, relationships falling apart, a movie crew on location by the sea, beautiful women, discussions about historical periods, about art, about cinema, etc.

Certainly there's a conscious move towards a European style of filmmaking in *The Debussy Film*, and a turning-the-back-on English/ British cinema/ television (*The Debussy Film* looks like nothing on British television in the mid-1960s – or since). With *The Debussy Film*, Ken Russell asserts himself as an international filmmaker, not a 'British' filmmaker at all. Although you can see numerous minor details of Englishness or Britishness in *The Debussy Film*, in fact the movie is decidedly *not* 'English' or 'British'.

EARLY SCENES.

One of Ken Russell's famous opening scenes occurs at the beginning of *The Debussy Film*, the kind that crrritics call 'camp'/ 'shock'/ 'vulgar'.[10] It featured the blonde Jane Lumb as St Sebastian in a white Tee shirt having arrows shot into her by a bunch of other pretty blondes in Russell's take on the music[11] that Claude Debussy wrote for Gabriel D'Annunzio's *The Martyrdom of St Sebastian* (St Sebastian is always good for some titillation and nudity, as painters (and their patrons) from the Renaissance onwards have known).

But it adds another layer of complexity to the proceedings,

---

10 The scene doesn't occur right at the top of *The Debussy Film*, however, but about four minutes in, after some exposition scenes.
11 It's striking that there isn't a major musical sequence in *The Debussy Film* until around seven minutes into the piece.

because the scene is being filmed in modern dress by the Film Director. However, the Claude Debussy documentary that the Film Director and his crew are producing is in period costume. So why is this scene being shot in contemporary clothes, and in such a ridiculous fashion? Because the rest of the way that the Film Director shoots his piece on Debussy – no matter what he may *say*, or what he *tells* the Actor playing Debussy in conversations – is in a conventional docu-drama manner.

Well, perhaps the Film Director is producing a satire on the television documentary, just like Ken Russell and co. are doing with *The Debussy Film* itself. In which case, this makes *The Debussy Film* even more complicated structurally: it is now a satire on a TV documentary and a film about the making of a documentary which also contains parts which are being filmed as satire.

Hell, if this 1965 movie was coming out of Hollywood these days – helmed by whoever is the latest Quentin Tarantino clone or hot-shot, trendy director – it would be fêted by film critics as a masterpiece (just like critics went ga-ga over *Pulp Fiction*, while those of us who know Jean-Luc Godard found it all so *passé*).

Up on the cliff during lunch break is a key scene in *The Debussy Film*, where the Film Director introduces some of the main characters – and he introduces them as the *characters*, not as So-and-so who's playing Claude Debussy or Gaby Dupont or whoever (maintaining the dual focus). It's another question-and-answer session, with a local news reporter (who's interest is teased by the promise of nudity – and journalists're the same decades on). Recognize the steal in this scene? It's from *Citizen Kane*, again (Ken Russell sure loves that movie! But who doesn't?).

❦

On a technical level, *The Debussy Film* is incredible[12] – and how the hell Ken Russell and his production team managed it on a 1960s British Broadcasting Corporation budget is beyond belief (which still today can look shoddy when they try to stage

---

12 *The Debussy Film* employs once again symmetrical compositions, but also uses the whole frame of the 4:3 television ratio (shooting close-ups with the Actor framed very low, for instance, or far off on the right side). The symmetry extends to the circular structure of *The Debussy Film*, which ends as it began, with Debussy's funeral in the rain.

ambitious scenes).[13] *The Debussy Film* demonstrates Russell at the height of his powers, with an inventiveness that seems without limit. One wonders how much of *The Debussy Film* was altered when it became a public service television documentary instead of a feature film, but for sure Ken Russell and co. squeeze a huge amount of material into *The Debussy Film*.

*The Debussy Film* is another example of the genius of Ken Russell and his collaborators in turning the limitations of making a movie in Eastbourne and Sussex (and many other English locations) to their advantage, instead of going to Paris.[14] The invention of the dual dramatic focus of *The Debussy Film* leads to one of the most complex narratives in Russell's *œuvre*. So the limitations of money brings about a re-think of the screenplay and in this case the filmmakers come up with a inspired solution. (But when Russell and co. had the $$$$$ for a really big, historical, city scene – in *The Music Lovers* – they went overboard with it, opening the movie with a giant scene on a giant, backlot set).

Thank God for Ken Russell, I say – when you consider all of those stodgy, solemn, po-faced literary adaptions and TV series churned out by the BBC, ITV, HBO, cable channels, all of that dreck spewing out of Burbank, Vancouver, Berlin, Rome, London, Sydney, and film and TV centres the world over.

All of those s---l---o---w, those let's-be-*serious* TV adaptions of Charles Dickens or Jane Austen or Leo Tolstoy or Edith Wharton… Oh, Ken Russell is just delightful!

SEX, LOVE, RELATIONSHIPS.

*The Debussy Film* was subtitled *Impressions of the French Composer*, but it might also be subtitled *Debussy and His Women* (as with some of Ken Russell's other movies about artists and composers). Or maybe 'The Music Lovers' is an accurate generic title for the way that Russell approaches his movies about classical composers.

One thing's for sure, Ken Russell and his co-writers hone in on emotional and sexual relationships before anything else in a biopic. Everyone can relate to those relationship issues, of sex, separation, betrayal, loss, death: they are eternally-recurring,

---

13 Only one technical element distracts in *The Debussy Film*, and that's the looping, which, given the television budget, is not as effective as in theatrical releases of the time. It really shows up in the volatile, argumentative scenes, scenes which really do require the live sound of the actors on the set performing them.
14 Part of *The Debussy Film* was shot in Chalon-sur-Saône in France.

have been around since forever.

But while the audience is locked into the drama of the erotic, romantic and psychological issues of the biography of the artist or composer, the filmmakers are in fact exploring other elements as well. And they are also delivering tons of information about the artists to the audience, but the audience won't always realize it. (A lesbian sub-plot was cut from *The Debussy Film* (and also from *The Boy Friend*). Huw Wheldon wanted to cut it, and it was.)

### THE FILM DIRECTOR.

The Film Director in *The Debussy Film* takes on the personality of the French artist Pierre Louÿs, a man who liked women. A lot of women. Young women, too, as the Film Director explains earlier. Thus, when the newspaper reporter interviews him, the Film Director is more concerned with the pretty, blonde Lili-Actress sitting next to him in a bikini.

And it's no surprise that the Film Director himself has a strikingly attractive assistant (played by Stephanie Randall). In this movie, the Film Director created by the film director Ken Russell is surrounded by beautiful women. But, yes, film directors are often surrounded by beautiful women (many of them actresses), but also scuzzy, ageing character actors, scruffy, unshaven sparks, beefy, working class drivers and teamsters, fussy, neurotic agents (glued to their cell), and faceless suits from the studio or TV station (also glued to their cells).

There are also hints in *The Debussy Film* (though not too strong) of a relationship between Pierre Louÿs and Gaby Dupont. Notice too that the Film Director is playing svengali to his actors, and also a tempter – he seems to be deliberately stirring up tension between his players, so it will help his movie, something directors do (including Ken Russell). It seems as if he introduces the Lili-Actress to the cast when she's topless on purpose – knowing the effect it will have on the Actor (who looks her over), but also, crucially, on the Actress.

The Film Director in *The Debussy Film* is precisely the kind of filmmaker who will manipulate the psychological dynamics of his cast and crew to get the best results on celluloid.

PIERRE LOUŸS.

The works of Pierre Louÿs (1870-1925) led to some classic, revered movies: for instance, his book *La femme et le pantin* was adapted as the Josef von Sternberg-Marlene Dietrich movie *The Devil Is a Woman* (1935) and the last film of Luis Buñuel, *That Obscure Object of Desire* (1977). *La femme et le pantin* was also the basis of a 1992 TV movie, a 2007 TV movie, and movies in 1920, 1929 and 1946.

Other pictures based on Pierre Louÿs' work include: *Bilitis* (1977), *A Woman Like Satan* (1959), *Aphrodite* (1982), *Les filles de leur mère* (1985), *The Adventures of King Pausole* (1933), *Take Me Naked* (1966) and *The Merry Monarch* (1933).

Pierre Louÿs' erotic poetry included *Astarte* (1891) and *Songs of Bilitis* (1894),[15] novels such as *Aphrodite* (1896) and *La femme et le pantin* (1898), and erotic works such as *Les Aventures du roi Pausole* (1901), *Pervigilium Mortis* (1916), and *Manuel de civilité pour les petites filles à l'usage des maisons d'éducation* (1917).

Pierre Louÿs also took lots of photographs (the 1965 movie uses some of them at the top of the show), including plenty of erotica (one of Louÿs' books was a study of women's asses, entitled *La cul de la femme* – it's a volume of curvy, round butts pointed at the viewer).

THE LOVE TRIANGLE.

One of the intriguing sequences in *The Debussy Film* occurred *chez* Pierre Louÿs (a place many æsthetes and dandies today would love to visit), evoking the erotic triangle between Claude Debussy, Louÿs and Gaby Dupont. The French's love of Oriental culture (especially in this *fin-de-siècle* era) was introduced, too, with Zohra (Verity Edmett) in a belly dancer costume slinking thru the scene (presumably one of Louÿs' lovers). Two men, two women – the 1965 movie played with sexual mirrors (in one moment, Debussy leans over to kiss Gaby, not Zhora).

In the midst of this sequence, and halfway thru the *Danse Sacré* scene, Claude Debussy descends into dreams (with no drugs to be seen! Instead, he's sitting by some windows, or looking up at the trees in a hammock, or wandering around Pierre Louÿs' menagerie). Here, as often in Ken Russell's cinema, there's an attempt to suggest some of the experiences the artist has that may

---

[15] Claude Debussy set some of the *Chansons de Bilitis* to music in 1898.

have inspired his work, rather than depicting the artist at work. (Debussy isn't shown working much. Debussy, rather like Dante Gabriel Rossetti in the TV film two years later, was a bit of a lazy slob, and took a long time to complete some of his works, such as *La Mer*).

YOUNG LOVERS.

To send up the characters and scenes, Ken Russell and his team once again employed the visual style culled from television commercials, including slow motion, backlighting, shooting through rain, over-exposure, etc. The scene where Gaby Dupont fools around with a white balloon (to the strains of Claude Debussy's popular 1894 piece *Prelude To the Afternoon of a Faun*[16] – she's the faun) in some trees and sunlight was typical[17] (as was the quip from the Film Director that, yes, they did play with balloons, we checked – a direct quote from Ken Russell, one would imagine. And when the Actor asks where did Debussy gets his kicks, the Director retorts, 'in his music'. That is pure Russellian philosophy: one can imagine Russell replying similarly: 'in my movies').

Every Ken Russell piece has to have a scene of young love. And, do you know what?, so few movies can get away with this kind of scene. But, somehow, Russell and his team get away with it every time! I mean, when a typical Hollywood movie tries to depict young love, it becomes vomitable very quickly (outside of a Disney flick, maybe. Or maybe not). And it's a scene that is very long.

But Ken Russell and his cohorts somehow manage to make new love between young lovers work. It might be the self-consciously artsy and fake, TV advertizing approach which diffuses the topple into bathos and sentiment. It is also the narration, which provides context and distantiation. And it's that very often the scenes of young love are viewed in retrospect, thru the lens of old age's tired, sad eyes. And *humour* is a key ingredient – never playing the bliss of young love straight.[18] And it's also that you know it ain't gonna last. Oh no, baby, it sure

---
16 *L'Après midi d'un faune* was based on the poem by Stéphane Mallarmé.
17 It's classic Ken Russell also to have the costumes at this point in the movie pristine white. Not virginal white, no, but the white of youth untrammelled yet by the vicissitudes of life.
18 For instance, in the scene in the greenhouse and gardens in the rain (lots and lots of rain!), the lovers are fooling around chasing each other.

ain't!

And in the scene in *The Debussy Film*, it is more layered and complex than that: it is part of a rough cut which the Film Director is showing to his team in a hotel room: and the film cuts from the lovers kissing on screen to the Actor and the Actress kissing.

IN THE TATE GALLERY.

For British viewers, or those familiar with the British scene, *The Debussy Film* had added pleasures – like seeing Eastbourne and Beachy Head in a movie.[19] And the lengthy episode filmed in Tate Britain, or the Tate Gallery as it was back then, in the old Pre-Raphaelite galleries at Millbank. The art gallery episode was an opportunity for the filmmakers to slip in some art history lessons – about the Pre-Raphaelites (with cuts to paintings by John Everett Millais, Edward Burne-Jones, Dante Gabriel Rossetti,[20] and others). Here the BBC's Reithian agenda of educating, informing and entertaining the general public was marvellously embodied. Indeed, the BBC never had a better entertainer making shows for it than Ken Russell.[21]

All of that discussion about the Pre-Raphaelites would of course flower two years later in *Dante's Inferno* (and with Oliver Reed also in the title role – and by then Reed was a more matured actor).

But even though the Tate Gallery sequence is nought more than one person telling another person about 19th century British art, there were other things going on. This is a tribute to Ken Russell's genius with delivering complex historical material to an audience. Because we have all probably seen dry-as-death documentaries about art on television, in which some pompous jerk speechifies to camera in a museum. I know I have, and only a *very few people* can be riveting in this kind of public service television.

But *The Debussy Film* gets away with a ten minute lecture on art history because it has already established a web of dramatic relationships, and these are doubled, by the dual time frame. So

---

19 Beachy Head is a famous landmark (and an infamous suicide spot – which's apt, being as suicide is one of the themes of *The Debussy Film*), seen at the end of *Quadrophenia*, the follow-up to *Tommy*, for instance. And Kevin Costner lands not far away, at the Seven Sisters, in *Robin Hood* (1991).
20 Soon to follow was Ken Russell's movie about Rossetti (1967), and Debussy in 1888 wrote *Blessed Damozel*, from Rossetti.
21 But the Beeb didn't go for *The Debussy Film*: it wasn't what they wanted (although they did broadcast it again).

when the filmmakers add the Actress (Annette Robertson playing the Actress playing Gaby Dupont) getting bored in the background and wanting to go (and pleading with the Actor), it stands in for the audience. Can we go now? Enough with the art history already!

And the Tate Gallery episode also works because of the way it's filmed and performed. You just can't help following Vladek Sheybal's charismatic, sophisticated Film Director explaining about Debussy being inspired by the Pre-Raphaelites, and by J.M.W. Turner, and James Whistler (and this is when one wishes that *The Debussy Film* was filmed in colour).

The Tate Gallery sequence bears directly on Claude Debussy's life and art, of course, because, as the Film Director explains, many (or most) of Debussy's works were inspired by painting or poetry or some cultural source. Because as well as William Turner, James Whistler, the Pre-Raphaelites and other painters, Debussy also drew deeply on poets, and the movie mentions Stéphane Mallarmé and Paul Verlaine, among others.[22] (Charles Baudelaire is quoted aloud in the Tate Gallery scene).

*The Debussy Film* was another of the loving recreations of a vanished but beloved era of Ken Russell – the late 19th century and the 20th century up to the First World War, an epoch he has explored numerous times (like Hayao Miyazaki and Walerian Borowczyk, and modern, British authors like Michael Moorcock and Philip Pullman). *The Debussy Film* was stuffed with historical and cultural allusions to Art Nouveau, *fin-de-siècle* art, the Pre-Raphaelites, and to music, all of these were favourites of Russell. So… a ton of work for the production designers and the props guys, and the DPs to light it all. But it pays off (and also fulfills the BBC's 'let's educate Britain!' remit). *The Debussy Film* is *crammed* with information.

There are numerous *objets d'art* in *The Debussy Film*, for instance (vases, statuary, carafes), some of which Claude Debussy contemplates as his music plays – they are some of the ingredients of Debussy's dream world. Martin Battersby was credited as art historical consultant, and the *objets d'art* are placed within the frame with the reverence of a museum curator. It works, because

---

22 There is also plenty of talk of Paris and Parisian cultural life, because of course this movie does not go to Paris, and it really, really should. It's only two hundred miles over the English Channel from Eastbourne. I reckon *The Debussy Film* might've benefitted from some newsreel footage of Paris, to evoke the epoch. Maybe even some Géorges Méliès movies.

Oliver Reed is in included in the frame, looking at these beautiful things, in the same shot: that is, the film doesn't cut away to the artworks, shot at a different time. It places them into the web of the movie.

THE *SACRED DANCE* SCENE.

Another stand-out sequence had the actors dancing in what was presumably a disco or bar (the Film Director says it's Soho), but throughout the music was by Claude Debussy. The Director and the Actor discuss Debussy in the foreground, while the other actors dance in the background. The scene had a Godardian flavour to it, with the local sound, presumably of some mid-Sixties pop music, being replaced with Debussy's music. It's very effective, in contrasting the popular music of the 1960s and the classical music of the late 1800s. (And it's as if Russell insists in getting in some more dance sequences).

At times it seems as if Method acting is taking over the production: at a party which further explores the tense, erotic relationships in Claude Debussy's life, the Actor takes off the Kinks' classic mid-Sixties pop single 'You Really Got Me', which everyone at the party is dancing to, and wants to put on some of Debussy's music. An argument at the record player about what to play at the party is probably a familiar scene at parties the world over.[23]

The screenwriting by Melvyn Bragg and Ken Russell cleverly blends both the Actor and the Actress, and the characters they play – Claude Debussy and Gaby Dupont. The Actress describes the music as crap, but the Actor replies not as the Actor (in many scenes the Actor appears as if he's not really bothered about Debussy or his music at all), but as Debussy.

The blurring of realities works perfectly. The Actor gets his way, and puts on Claude Debussy's *Danse Sacré et Danse Profane* (1904) – a slow, moody piece – and the total opposite of what you'd play at a party. To wind up the Actor, the Actress stands on a table and performs a striptease (much to the appreciation of the party-goers).

---

23 Again, this is Godardian: in the same year, 1965, Jean-Luc Godard had made *Masculine Feminine*, in which Jean-Pierre Léaud's character Paul plays classical music on a record player, while the young women around him (including his girlfriend, emerging pop star Chantal Goya) prefer pop music (the same conflicts occurred in *Pierro le Fou* between Anna Karina (pop) and Jean-Paul Bemondo (classical).

> That was a specific example of where one was able to take a piece of music [Russell explained], do something totally different with it than Debussy intended but make a point about the public attitude to his work. I think it's one of the best examples I've done of an exposition of an idea in music.

Annette Robertson is superb here – not because she's cute and sexy (although she is), but the way she effortlessly mocks the Actor, who of course can do nought but stare at her moodily (Oliver Reed's 'Moody Three', as Ken Russell would put it). Gaby Dupont 'ridicules both the man and his music', because she thinks he's being perverse, Russell commented: but the scene's also about how listeners are too reverential about classical music, how they stop talking and dancing and 'listen to the music with a mixture of duty and piety, which is all too often the case' (Bax, 129). (The sound editors add off-screen calls and whoops from the party-goers, who're enjoying the way the scene's heading – a striptease).

It's a re-play of a familiar scene in Ken Russell's cinema: the artist's lover using his own art to get back at him. Yes, the Actor might wanna play Claude Debussy's *Danse Sacré et Danse Profane* and become the ultimate party-pooper,[24] but the Actress is gonna turn the tables with a striptease (and the movie makes sure the audience understands that the Actress has gone 'all the way', down to nudity, by having the Actress take off her panties and twirl them wildly in Debussy's face. The Actress is also playing Gabby here, of course).[25]

THE KITCHEN SINK SCENE.

The scene where Gaby Dupont blows up and launches herself at Claude Debussy,[26] berating him for being lazy, and how she hates their garret existence, is a recurring scene in Ken Russell's biopics, and also in other biopics of this kind. It wasn't the best example of a domestic blow-out, however (the dodgy looping didn't help), but it was dramatically essential. As was the scene where Debussy's new lover, dressmaker Lili Rosalie Texier

---

24 'But artists are dogmatic and pig-headed, and they over-ride people', Russell commented about this scene (Bax, 129).
25 No doubt Ken Russell and co. would've gone further in terms of sex and nudity in *The Debussy Film*, but this was the BBC in 1965.
26 In the argument scene, the Film Director's heard off-screen explaining a ton of background information and motivational detail to the Actress. The sophistication of the multiple narrative levels in *The Debussy Film* enables this shift in viewpoint and address to occur.

(Penny Service) has simply replaced Gaby as Debussy's cook and cleaner[27] (yes, *The Debussy Film* does have Lili doing some ironing, a worn-out, housewifely cliché – well, this *was* the 1960s. She is also seen making clothes).

But at the end of the scene, when Pierre Louÿs turns up at the garret, and tries to diffuse the situation, the 1965 film itself does that, by having the Film Director as Louÿs say 'cut', and it's back to actors and a film crew making a movie. Yet the then-and-now conflation of epochs continues, when the Actress spits at and shakes the actress playing Lili (while Claude Debussy convulses with laughter).

The romantic-erotic relationships among the cast are further echoing those of the characters they're playing to a striking degree in *The Debussy Film*. For instance, look at the way that Lili is introduced: the Lili-Actress (Penny Service) is deliberately brought into the 1965 BBC movie in an eroticized manner, swimming topless in the hotel swimming pool at night. The Film Director introduces her to both the Actor and the Actress (and his assistant, though of course they would've already met – there are hints of the erotic entanglements surrounding the Film Director here).

Thus, while some reviewers (even today) have seen the topless swimming pool scene as gratuitous nudity, it is actually serving a dramatic purpose, deliberately eroticizing the Lili-Actress, so that from the off she will be attracting the Actor (and Claude Debussy), and causing friction between the Actor and the Actress, and between Debussy and Gaby.

Also, the Lili-Actress is carefully presented as virtually wordless; she is more a foreboding feeling than a real person, hanging around on the periphery of the cast and crew, waiting for her chance to steal the leading man, the Actor. *The Debussy Film* orchestrates an enormous number of big close-ups (remember, this was made for television, which thrives on close-ups). The striptease at the party scene, for instance, mainly comprises big C.U.s.

Also, the crudity and clichés of the domestic blow-up between Claude Debussy and Gaby Dupont – which looks (and sounds) like an kitchen sink drama of the early 1960s – can also be justified because it isn't Ken Russell directing this, but Russell

---

[27] They married in 1899.

directing it as if it were being directed by the Film Director. In which case, it's a satire of a satire of a historical scene done in a particular form, the British socialist-realist drama of the early 1960s. And if you add in the industrial conditions of this production – a television show of the middle Sixties made for a British broadcaster on a small budget – you have many layers of narrative and dramatic complexity.

✞

Towards the end of *The Debussy Film,* the Film Director notes that Debussy was getting into all sorts of projects (partly for the dough). One of the more intriguing commissions was music for movies: *The Debussy Film* included a scene in a film studio with the Film Director making notes into a tape recorder while Debussy lurked up in the gantries (yet more shades of *Citizen Kane* – in particular, the Chicago opera house sequence). *The Debussy Film* included some footage from a silent movie, as the Film Director discussed the music that Debussy composed.

There are also evocations in the latter half of *The Debussy Film* of: the war music that Claude Debussy composed (playing over images of soldiers in gas masks wading thru water in heavy smoke – imagery that Ken Russell will reprise many times in his career); and the music for his daughter Chou-Chou (playing over shots of Debussy and the child).

ART, CREATIVITY, MADNESS, SUICIDE, DEATH.
- get too close to an artist and you will be burnt;
- you won't have much to eat or much money;
- you will do most of the housework;
- you will have to spend time hanging around boring museums;
- you will have to put up with the artist's weirdo friends;
- you will have to deal with the artist's mood swings and womanizing.

It's all there in *The Debussy Film*. As the narrator tells us at the top of the show, some of the people involved with Claude Debussy attempted suicide. The movie shows that, in sequences which play both as the reality of the film-within-a-film, and as dreams.

Yes, this is a movie where the lovers of the main character try to kill themselves! That tells you all you need to know about him!

Fifty years later, Claude Debussy would be Jim Morrison of the Doors. He's lazy, promiscuous, self-absorbed, stupid, boorish, pompous, stubborn, indulgent. A typical man. A typical artist. (Tho' his fatal flaw, according to this movie, is that he's a dreamer).

The film-with-a-film structure of *The Debussy Film* also suggests that these emotional events are repeating themselves all the time. For instance, there's a scene where the Actor dressed as Claude Debussy stands on the balcony of the Grand Hotel in Eastbourne, but when the camera tilts down and zooms in, it reveals the Actress in the swimming pool, in her polka dot bikini (not in late 19th century costume).

*La Mer*, one of Claude Debussy's signature pieces, and one of Ken Russell's favourites amongst Debussy's works, featured prominently in *The Debussy Film*. Indeed, Debussy had been in England when he was working on *La Mer*, hence the decision to shoot *The Debussy Film* in Eastbourne and Sussex. In keeping with the theme of the ocean, there are numerous scenes in or around water: Debussy swims on his own (and is framed in a lengthy zoom out shot so he's dwarfed by the ocean); the Actor fools around in the sea with his girlfriend, the Actress; actors swim in the hotel pool (the actresses are in bikinis or topless – why waste an opportunity for nudity?); and there are many scenes on the beach in Sussex (including religious processions, the Actress looking for the Actor; intense discussions about motivation between the Actor and the Director; Debussy and his new lover, Madame Bardac, wandering on the rocks while his old flames lie as if dead in the sun – they are the lovers who attempted suicide). In *The Debussy Film*, the ocean is both life-giving and death-dealing, both a source of nourishment and birth, and of isolation and suffering.

*The Debussy Film* is a classic example of Ken Russell's approach to documentary and historical drama: cast actors who look like the originals, dress them up in authentic costumes, take them back to the places where the events really happened, and have them speak the lines that have been recorded. Then, by the magic of movies, a kind of historical metamorphosis will occur. And it works in *The Debussy Film*: the scenes where Claude Debussy's *La Mer* is playing on the soundtrack and the visuals show Debussy with his lovers or swimming alone are very effective.

Certainly, *The Debussy Film* is always not on Claude Debussy's side (though feminists could easily deconstruct the 1965 movie and find it coming out much more on the composer's side than on that of the women in his life). Debussy is an ambiguous figure for Ken Russell and Melvyn Bragg: indeed, *The Debussy Film* can be regarded as another movie among thousands and thousands in which masculinity is under threat (have a look at any of hundreds of recent Hollywood movies, for instance). Debussy, for instance, isn't sure about taking up with the rich Madame Bardac, who becomes his new benefactor (some of the doubts are expressed by the Actor to the Director in the scene on the beach). The same ambivalence will crop up again in films like *The Music Lovers* and *Lisztomania*.

In Ken Russell's cinema, the relation between artists and patrons is problematic *at best*, and even more so when the patron is a woman and the artist is sexually involved with her. Then it can become painful to the point of suicide.

THE ENDING.

The ending of *The Debussy Film* (1965) was intended to be another portrayal of the costs of artistic endeavour, as Ken Russell explained:

> The end of the film, the music from his unfinished opera *The Fall of the House of Usher*, with Debussy alone in the castle and his ghostly mistresses – whom he drove to attempted suicide – rising up, was an analogy of the lost romantic idea he had destroyed by his disregard for people. You can be an egomaniac up to a point, but in the end it can destroy you, or your work, or both. (Bax, 129)

The Edgar Allan Poe sequence was another of Ken Russell's ventures into the Gothic, with Orson Welles playing Charlie Foster Kane at the end of his life in the 1941 RKO movie as an inspiration (the images of Kane walking through the vast halls of Xanadu, for instance, in that slow, shell-shocked, straight-backed manner, staring rigidly ahead). The narration tells us that Claude Debussy became obsessed with Rodney in *The Fall of the House of Usher* (Russell will revisit similar territory in *Dante's Inferno*, *Gothic*, *Lisztomania* and of course *The Fall of the Louse of Usher*).

The ending of *The Debussy Film* displays one of Ken Russell's chief themes: the costs of artistic creation, the Faustian pact of being an artist. The sequence vividly embodied the artist as an ultimate loner, left with nobody around him at the end of his life, wandering in a Gothic castle that was the visual and spatial expression of his empty soul[28] (meanwhile, he is haunted by dead lovers: Gaby, for instance, walks up to him at a climactic moment in an enormous, empty corridor, and re-enacts her suicide, collapsing before him to his horror. Here, Debussy is playing the role of the haunted, melancholy Rodney, who's tormented by his past, including his mistresses, such as Gaby Dupont).

---

[28] He walks about giant rooms, closing windows one by one, so the screen turns dark.

# 2

# ISADORA DUNCAN

I have discovered the dance. I have discovered the art which has been lost for two thousand years.

Isadora Duncan

It seems inevitable that Ken Russell would have made a movie about Isadora Duncan (1877-1927) at some time or other (his project on Vaslav Nijinsky being the other movie about a modern dancer which he cherished). Unfortunately, a feature film based on the life of Isadora Duncan was being made (by Universal, with direction by Karel Reisz, and Vanessa Redgrave in the title role), around the same time, so Russell and his team were unable to use much of the material, which had been bought up by the Hakim brothers (Raymond and Robert, who were paying for the feature production). It was the feature movie that Russell *should have* made, of course (and Melvyn Bragg, who was already working with Russell, co-scripted the rival *Isadora* production).

But despite the limitations of the television budget (which Ken Russell strained against all of the time – 'the Hakim project and our own tiny budget caused endless troubles,' Russell said [G, 46]), *Isadora Duncan: The Biggest Dancer In the World* (tx 1966.9.22) was a documentary that Russell very much wanted to make – because he was such a big fan of Isadora Duncan. 'I think she is one of my favourite artists', Russell remarked (ib., 36). Although the budget was small, *Isadora Duncan* is yet another of Russell's *totally remarkable* feats of filmmaking: because *Isadora Duncan* contains a *huge* number of different locations (many of them real locations), and a *huge* number of actors and extras (including many speaking parts). And Russell's on-fire invention and imagination.

Talk about *ambitious*: *Isadora Duncan* is a *giant* of a movie made on a lillputian British Broadcasting Corporation 1960s budget. And, just as remarkable, it's about a *dancer*! And it stars a relative unknown (Vivien Pickles)! And the main character is a woman! (yes, folks, that's *still* unusual!). And much of the movie concerns a woman teaching young women and girls how to dance!

There is so much that is remarkable about *Isadora Duncan* from a production point-of-view. Such as: the imaginative use of locations; the skilful integration of newsreel and library footage into the narrative; the immense *energy* of the performances and the staging (this show *never* keeps still for long); and the orchestration of the voiceover and the scenes.

And *Isadora Duncan* evokes a thoroughly *feminine* world: the images of Isadora Duncan building beds from planks o' wood for her pupils (in Russia), and putting them to bed, and training them, struggling to keep her ballet schools afloat,[29] are *very rare* in television and cinema. In *Isadora Duncan,* Duncan comes across as a mother figure to an extended family of young girls, a Greek deity like Athena or Artemis or Diana, a mother-protector: in short, she's a Goddess (who, ironically, lost her own children in an accident as bizarre as her own death).

While the reality was somewhat down-at-heel and shabby and drunk, and *Isadora Duncan* didn't stint on depicting that (and would've gone further had it not been a British Broadcasting Corporation production of the mid-1960s), the idealizations were compelling: especially the images of Duncan in her floaty, white dresses running around the world's stages or ballet schools.

Born Angela Isadora Duncan in San Francisco on May 27, 1877, she lived most of her adult life in Europe and Russia. She was famous for her bohemian lifestyle, her many affairs (with men and women), her new, modernist form of dance, and her grotesque death at the age of 50. Duncan was the perfect subject for Ken Russell, as Susan Au noted in *Ballet and Modern Dance:*

---

[29] Duncan's first school was in Grünewald in Germany.

> Isadora Duncan was arguably more than a dancer: she was the symbol of female longings, well-hidden or perhaps even unconscious, for emancipation from the traditional roles of wife and mother, for sexual freedom and personal fulfilment. Her life was of a piece with her dancing in that both placed natural instincts above the dictates of convention. (89)

Isadora Duncan has also been the subject of plays (1991), musicals (2008), and a 1981 ballet. There are schools and dancers around the world who keep the Duncan free-flowing style of dance alive. For instance, there is an Isadora Duncan Dance Foundation, an Isadora Duncan International Institute, the Isadora Duncan Dance Group and an Isadora Duncan Heritage Society.[30] Six of Duncan's older students, Irma, Anna, Maria-Theresa, Lisa, Erica and Margot, continued her work after her death (they were known as the 'Isadorables').

Among Isadora Duncan's dances were *Primavera* (from Sandro Botticelli's painting), the *Marceillaise* (1915), the *Marche Slave* (1916), *Narcissus* by Ethelbert Nevin, *Iphigenia In Aulis* by Christoph Gluck, and *Ave Maria* (1914) by Franz Schubert (where she played the Madonna).

Another aspect of Isadora Duncan's art endeared itself to Ken Russell: she drew on many classical composers, such as Frédéric Chopin, Christoph Gluck, Ludwig van Beethoven, Johann Sebastian Bach, Franz Schubert, Peter Tchaikovsky and Johannes Brahms.

The rival production, *Isadora* (a.k.a. *The Loves of Isadora,* 1968) was written by Melvyn Bragg, Clive Exton and Margaret Drabble, produced by Raymond and Robert Hakim, distributed by Universal, directed by Karel Reisz, and starred Vanessa Redgrave, James Fox, John Fraser and Jason Robards. *Isadora* is certainly a movie that aligns itself *very closely* with the Russell approach: in a way, Russell didn't need to direct *Isadora*, because the movie looks as if he did! (Right down to the *rondo* flashback form, which was one o' Russell's favourite devices). But the *Isadora* movie is *far* less entertaining, and is much more of your standard movie biopic, all very reverential and tame.

However, the BBC *Isadora Duncan* was broadcast in 1966 (on September 22, 1966, around the time of the anniversary of Duncan's death), while the Universal *Isadora* movie wasn't released until 1968 (and the Beeb documentary was repeated a

---

[30] You can find plenty o' Isadora Duncan info online.

couple of times: in 1967 and 1969). It was also the first documentary directed by Ken Russell to be shown in the U.S.A.[31]

The crew on *Isadora Duncan* included Luciana Arrighi, production design, Joyce Hammond, costumes, DPs Dick Bush and Brian Tufano, editors Michael Bradsell and Roger Crittenden, and even Leni Riefensthal is in the credits, for the Greek sequence (it's a quote from Riefenstahl's Olympic film). Among the cast were many Ken Russell regulars, and included Vivien Pickles, Peter Bowles, Alexei Jawdokimov, Murray Melvin, Jeanne Le Bars, Alita Naughton and Sandor Elès, plus Russell's family, and 100s of extras (and cameos from Russell).

One of the key collaborators was the choreographer, Bice Bellairs (who brought along dancers from her school of dancing, who acted as the numerous young girls in Isadora Duncan's many dance schools – dubbed the 'Isadorables'). No need to spell out how significant Bellairs' contribution was to the success of *Isadora Duncan*. In a movie like this, the choreographer is so vital; but in Ken Russell you had a film director who was totally sympathetic to the rigorous demands of good choreography. You had to believe that Duncan really was a great dancer, really was that free spirit, that rule-breaker in dance. (It has to be said that Vivien Pickles was not a professional dancer, and that, at 35, she was older than many producers would've preferred, had *Isadora Duncan* been a commercial production. They would also want a name, if possible. But casting Duncan is *very* tough – to get the look, the persona, the tone and the dancing right).

Isadora Duncan's biographer (and friend), Sewell Stokes, was instrumental too in this British Broadcasting Corporation production: Stokes' book *Isadora, an Intimate Portrait*, was drawn on (and Duncan's autobiography, *My Life*, 1927), and Stokes appeared at the top of the movie, sitting in a Chelsea church graveyard and talking about Duncan. That gave the *Isadora Duncan* a different slant from the usual Ken Russell documentary: Eric Fenby might've appeared in *Delius: Song of Summer*, for instance (but clearly he wouldn't want to). Stokes lends *Isadora Duncan* the air of authority, because, as he tells the viewer, he knew Duncan.

For actress Vivien Pickles (b. 1931), Isadora Duncan is the role of a lifetime – and even more so when it's a Ken Russell movie of

---
[31] Critic Andrew Sarris compared it favourably to the Universal movie.

Duncan's life! And Pickles throws herself into it whole-heartedly (can you perform Duncan by holding back? And what would be the point?). And it's terrific too that Pickles isn't the svelte figure of the usual dancer in movies (which Duncan wasn't, as Russell insisted), but an ample lady (note the sub-title, 'the biggest dancer in the world').

Ken Russell's Isadora Duncan is the kind of personality he likes to portray often: ballsy and outspoken, a larger-than-life character who won't be quiet and respectful. Someone's who fun to be with, always the centre of attention, but also ridiculous and over-bearing (and exhausting).

Vivien Pickles captures the brassy, in-your-face aspects of Isadora Duncan's personality, her mercurial changes of direction, her desperate bids for success, and her descents into hedonism. Her sensuality, her idealism, her sorrows, her agonies. Her energy and tireless attempts at making a go of things. And her joy of being alive – as she says, dancing means being alive: when you're dancing, you are alive, a notion that Ken Russell endorses throughout his cinema.

Like professional dancers everywhere, Vivian Pickles' Isadora Duncan *smiles* a lot. No matter what professional dancers have to do when they're performing, whether it's topless dancing in Las Vegas or a high class ballet in St Petersburg, they have to smile.

The interpretation that Ken Russell and company take is that although Isadora Duncan may have been a bit pretentious and crass, exasperating and demanding, capricious and moody, she was also wonderful: 'she was just a great person and *that* was her art', as Russell put it:

> Isadora seemed to embody the best and worst of an artist. She had genuine talent, some mystical insight, but she was a bit bogus as well. She had that touch of vulgarity which I think art and people connected with it could profit by. Although she put it there as much as anyone by her work and life, she negated the esoteric of Art because she couldn't help but give it her own humanity. And though she was usually drunk or broke or shacked up with some ne'er-do-well, she always survived. She was just a great person and *that* was her art. (Bax, 129-130)

That's what comes across in the 1966 BBC TV show – the irrepressible energy of Isadora Duncan, even when she's having a terrible time. Her struggles are remarkable, but the movie is so in love with Duncan as a personality, the failures somehow don't matter, or at least, don't hurt so much.

❉

The British Broadcasting Corporation film *Isadora Duncan* contains all of the key ingredients of Isadora Duncan's life, from her modern form of choreography (rejecting the traditions of ballet and classical dance, free-flowing costumes, going barefoot (called 'barefoot dancing'), and long hair), to her many relationships (such as her marriage to the Russian poet Sergei Yesenin, 18 years younger than her, or to the sewing machine magnate's son Paris Singer), her travels to Brazil, Russia, Nice, Paris, and Berlin, and the death of her young children in an accident (when the car they were riding in rolled into the River Seine in 1913).

That sequence involves ironic parallel cutting with dissolves from a dance scene involving Isadora Duncan and her children, to the children travelling in the car (while mom continues to dance, as the room darkens to nightfall), culminating in images of bodies underwater, and a children's doll in water (the doll's the equivalent of a news photographer placing a teddy bear in a bombed house to play upon readers' emotions). Needless to say, the low, BBC budget doesn't stretch to the vital scene of the car actually rolling into the River Seine.

Other relationships of Isadora Duncan's included the Italian sculptor Romano Romanelli, and Gordon Craig, a theatre designer (he appears in a brief, early scene). Duncan also had romantic liaisons with women – such as the poet Mercedes de Acosta, and possibly with the actress Eleonora Duse (these were not depicted – but if Ken Russell had filmed a biography of Duncan later, and outside of the BBC, you can be sure they would be in there).

The lesbian relationships that Isadora Duncan had[32] one might have expected to take up more room in a Ken Russell version of Duncan's life, but maybe the backers – the BBC in 1966 – might not have gone for that (after all, Huw Wheldon had excised a lesbian sub-plot from Russell's *The Debussy Film,* made a year

---

[32] For instance, there are erotic letters written between Isadora Duncan and de Acosta during their long affair, which attest to its intensity (such as this extract from a letter to de Acosta: 'A slender body, hands soft and white, for the service of my delight, two sprouting breasts round and sweet, invite my hungry mouth to eat, from whence two nipples firm and pink, persuade my thirsty soul to drink, and lower still a secret place where I'd fain hide my loving face'.)

earlier).³³

✞

*Isadora Duncan* is very strong on the attempts of Isadora Duncan to work outside of convention and social norms and to found and develop her schools of dance. Of course it's easy to relate these ventures to the lot of the filmmaker, begging for money from potential backers (or, as Duncan does a few times, from a stage in a theatre, to the point where she is berating the audience for financial support). But that is the lot of the creative artist, and it's a recurring theme in Russell's cinema – and it's a staple of all artists' biographies. Unless you make bargains with Popes or kings, millionaires or tycoons, how do you survive as an artist if you're relying solely on sales, on drumming up interest from the public?

*Isadora Duncan* was also vivid in its depictions of Isadora Duncan's form of dancing, which drew on ancient Greek models (wearing her 'little Greek tunic'), on folk dance, on social dances, on nature, and on sports. The skipping, jumping and running, the free movements, using the belly and torso, all based on the natural movement of the body. ('Her dances were characterized by simplicity and economy of means, qualities that applied not only to her choreography but to her themes, scenery and costumes… Her subject was the soul: universal emotions, responses and aspirations', remarked Susan Au in *Ballet and Modern Dance* [89]).

SET-PIECES AND STYLE.

The full arsenal of Russellian cinematic effects and tricks was employed in *Isadora Duncan*, pretty universally to immense effect. Shock cuts, slow motion, back-lighting, rapid editing, giant close-ups, handheld camera following dancers, and symmetrical compositions, etc. However, the choreography wasn't quite captured every time in a wholly satisfying manner, with the 1966 movie sometimes relying too much on rapid cutting, rather than allowing the body to breathe in full-body shots. In subsequent movies Russell and the teams would become more adept at filming dance. (How to film dance is a much-debated topic: like Woody Allen, I favour full body shots, in the manner of Gene Kelly, Vincente Minnelli and Bob Fosse, and not relying on

---

33 Though Russell said that Wheldon liked *Isadora Duncan*.

impressionistic shooting and rapid cutting.)

Trains, old cars, Art Nouveau, photo sessions, cameras, artists, bohemia, the sea, beaches, swimming, elegant hotels, OTT costumes, broad humour, vulgarity, sex, nudity... oh, and heaps of music and heaps of dance – all of the usual Ken Russell ingredients were in full effect in *Isadora Duncan*. And comedy: *Isadora Duncan* needed comedy, Russell said, to lighten the mood, because 'Isadora's life was so pathetic and tragic'.

The set-pieces come thick and fast in *Isadora Duncan*. The pace is frenetic. The level of imagination and invention from Ken Russell, Sewell Stokes, Bice Bellairs and the team, is dazzling. They unashamedly took the *March of Time* sequence from *Citizen Kane* for the potted biography of Isadora Duncan that played at the start of the 1966 documentary on the dancer (and reprised the technique in *Valentino*, Russell's most *Citizen Kane*-like movie).[34] Thus, *Isadora Duncan* opened in true Ken Russell style with a naked woman on stage dancing, as Duncan throws off her costume, b4 being carried off by a cop. And from that in-your-face opening, *Isadora Duncan* never lets up.

As with *The Debussy Film* and *Dante's Inferno*, the affinities between *Isadora Duncan* and Orson Welles and *Citizen Kane* were self-conscious, and were noted by critics. The scenes in Paris Singer's (Peter Bowles) mansion in South Devon, for instance, seem intended to echo those in the halls of Xanadu, where Kane and Susan converse across empty reaches, utterly separate from each other emotionally, socially, and personally. In *Isadora Duncan*, Singer's indulges Duncan like a plaything: she's a trophy wife.

The scene where neurotic, hypochondriac, playboy Paris Singer gives Isadora Duncan a giant, shiny box of a gift is pure Ken Russell: inside are six, female harpists (they would crop up at the end of *Lisztomania*). However, more important is how Duncan insists on dancing to the harp players – and dancing non-stop, through the night: it shows how Duncan could exhaust everyone else around her. (The images of the moon and sunrise show just how long Duncan kept up that dance!).

There're also some fun recreations of moments from a crazy lifestyle that would chime with the antics of rock supergroups (Led Zeppelin, the Who, the Rolling Stones) in the 1970s: such as

---

[34] But the footage is often speeded-up, to cram more in, but also to satirize the newsreel biography.

pushing a grand piano out of a hotel room, or dancing on a piano, or dancing in a brothel.

Another set-piece has Isadora Duncan and a faithful disciple arriving in the Soviet Union to a zero welcome at a grim, dark railroad station. The following scene, where Duncan feeds multitudes of hungry waifs from her Selfridges hamper isn't meant to be taken literally, and neither is the subsequent scene of Duncan leading the Russian mites in a musical dance number across the platforms and railroad tracks to the strains of John Philip Sousa's *Stars and Stripes Forever*. Dancing along the platforms, riding on a trolley, laughing and smiling, waving their arms, it's another exuberant, Russellian sequence which's about an attitude, a mood, an ambition, rather than something to be seen literally or seriously.

How the mighty are fallen: *Isadora Duncan* charts a continuous decline and fall. One of the most bitingly satirical scenes occurs towards the end, when Isadora Duncan attends a dance performance in her honour, and finds the whole thing ghastly. A dance troupe of young women clad in floaty, white, Greek costumes flounces about to *Narcissus* by Ethelbert Nevin. (The detail where Duncan waves away a cup of tea from the waitress in favour of a bottle of champagne is pure Ken Russell. Although by many accounts Duncan was often drunk and dissipated in later life, *Isadora Duncan* thankfully doesn't labour that aspect of her life: it's too easy, and too dull, to portray a character perpetually soused or druggy).

The ending of *Isadora Duncan* is one of Ken Russell's famous set-pieces: it totally works: it intercuts the truly horrible death of Isadora Duncan in September, 1927 in Nice, France (in that automobile accident with the scarf, with Bugatti (Sandor Eles) at the wheel), with a posthumous dream or idealized sequence in which she dances with 500 young girls in white dresses, on a hillside, to the strains of Ludwig van Beethoven's *Ninth Symphony*.[35] (A similar ploy was used to climax *Savage Messiah*).

The *gap* between an artist's dreams and ideas and the reality is something that Ken Russell is a genius at portraying (and *Ode To Joy* fits perfectly). It's not that his artists over-reach, it's that they can never attain their dreams. But they are continually

---

[35] There is some amusing footage of Russell and co. filming this scene, and Russell complaining that it didn't look like much of anything, until he incorporated slow motion footage with the music.

reaching for them. Russell's artists are real troupers, battling on against all odds. Which's something that viewers can readily identify with, whether or not they're an artist.

A PORTRAIT OF THE ARTIST.

Isadora Duncan was another portrait of the kind of artist that Ken Russell loves to focus on: a free spirit, someone who tries to do their own thing, who flouts convention and breaks rules, someone who struggles to find their place in the world, who battles to get ventures off the ground and to find financial backing, someone who's at odds with the modern world, and doesn't fit in, someone who seems to come from a different era, someone who's not afraid to be out-spoken, to say what she really thinks, someone who knows lots of artists, and someone who likes the high life (including drinking champagne, her one luxury she won't give up, and which Russell enjoys).

There's no doubt that Ken Russell identifies with Isadora Duncan, and that comes across in the 1966 movie. It enhances the production. *Isadora Duncan,* for instance, celebrates both the vulgarity and the sophistication of Duncan; it's in love with her portentous pronouncements on art and dance, and of course it worships her dances, but it also sends her up.

The remark (an accusation by her poet husband Sergei Yesenin, played by Alexei Jawdokimov) that her art will die when she dies has been refuted many times over, because Isadora Duncan's form of dance has been passed down the generations (meanwhile, who reads Yesenin's poetry? He committed suicide at age 30 in 1925).

Once again, as in quite a few other portraits of artists by Ken Russell, suicide looms large over *Isadora Duncan:* there's a suicide attempt in the ocean, for instance (where Russell has a cameo as the one-legged guy who saves her, done in speeded-up, silent comedy style, and filmed on yet another cold, wet, windy British beach), and Duncan also discusses suicide. There's the suicide of her husband Sergei Yesenin (complete with a C.U. of the suicide note written in his blood, and a shot of his boots spinning in the air).

MUSIC.

*Isadora Duncan* also contains a *ton* of music – all kinds of music, from pop music to classical music to folk music. *Isadora Duncan* is *stuffed* with music, to the point where barely a minute goes by without a new piece of music coming along. The music performs many narrative functions in *Isadora Duncan,* from live piano accompaniment to dance lessons (Erik Satie), to orchestras in the pit at concerts, to people singing, to many early gramophones set up for picnics or for background music at parties.

No, *no one else* in the history of British cinema has employed *so much music,* and pretty much *any* filmmaker in the whole history o' cinema. Music, music, music. It really is extraordinary, the all-encompassing emphasis on music in Ken Russell's cinema. And it's very beautiful. The soundtracks to his movies simply *sing,* they are so alive (and it's no wonder, either, that Russell is so picky about getting the sound mixes and sound editing spot on, to the point where soundtracks will be ditched even though they're finished, and then they're started over).[36]

The soundtrack for *Isadora Duncan* includes 'Bye, Bye, Blackbird', Erik Satie's *Three Gymnopedies*, Peter Tchaikovsky's *March Slav,* Ludwig van Beethoven's *9th Symphony,* John Philip Sousa's *Stars and Stripes Forever,* Ethelbert Nevin's *Narcissus,* Richard Wagner's *Tristan and Isolde,* and 'The Sewing Machine' by Betty Hutton.

As well as music, *Isadora Duncan* contains more voiceover than most Ken Russell's movies: it comes mainly from Sewell Stokes (presumably derived from his biography), but there is also voiceover from Duncan herself, and a little from Russell himself.

Thus, once again, although *Isadora Duncan* is a *tour-de-force* visually, and in terms of performance and choreography, it is the invisible elements of editing and sound that do so much of the work: the editing (by Michael Bradsell and Roger Crittenden), to bring together so many elements, the sound editing (by Stan Morcom, John Murphy and Brian Simmons), to cut together the voiceover, dialogue, sound effects and music, the music editing amd supervision, to put all of that music together, and the sound mixing and dubbing, to make it all work. *Isadora Duncan* is a technical marvel, a rival for Orson Welles – yes, even for the great genius of North American cinema. Go back and look at *Isadora Duncan* again, but this time *listen* to that soundtrack, how

---

36 John Baxter described Russell and co. mixing the soundtrack for *Savage Messiah* (at De Lane Lea in London), then worrying over it, and remixing it 'with an absorption close to fury' (Bax, 143).

the editors and mixers are weaving in the voiceover and the dialogue, the music and sound effects (even more remarkable when you consider how short the post-production schedule was for television in the 1960s, and still is today).

POLITICS.

*Isadora Duncan* sends up La Duncan continually, but it also plays along with some of her crazier moments and schemes. Some of the more amusing are the scenes where Duncan faces off against global politics – either espousing her pro-Communist or pro-Russian ideology back in the Land of the Free to an audience of the bourgeoisie, or attacking a bunch of Russian aristos in Moscow who're acting like crude, American capitalists. And the scenes of the poet Sergei Yesenin hanging out red flags from parapets in New York City or Duncan on stage with her red scarves are terrific (these scenes are played at full throttle, and in silent comedy style, with Yesenin declaiming Soviet propaganda from several London buildings (including the Albert Hall), while the police chase him across the rooftops, in the manner of the Keystone Kops).

Remember that *Isadora Duncan* was produced at the height of the Cold War, the mid-1960s, when the paranoia over Russia and Communism seemed to be at its height in the West. Ken Russell would do the same thing in *Billion Dollar Brain* the following year, giving American capitalism the finger by waving red flags in its face.

To Ken Russell and the team, it seems as if the loud expressions of ideology on either side of the Cold War are simply silly, whether it's Soviet propaganda (there are images and footage of Vladimir Lenin and Joseph Stalin), or American con-sumerism (the diet Isadora Duncan survives on in Russia, potatoes *and* champagne, is another joke on East-West politics, simple but effective swipes at life in Communist Russia being close to poverty – and not forgetting that Duncan went to Russia (in 1921) partly because she wasn't getting anywhere in the West. Russell – and all filmmakers and artists – can certainly identify with that quest for a place where one can work, where one is appreciated, and where one can get a decent meal!).

There are scenes where Isadora Duncan appears on stage in North America (in Boston), and talks about her revolutionary and

Communist sympathies (including baring her breasts), to the outrage of the bourgeois, Yank audience, and they work in the context of the 1920s but also the 1960s: nothing has changed in the West between the 1920s and the 1960s: indeed, the reactionary fear of the Red Invasion, especially in America, was far fiercer in the Sixties than it was in the Twenties (and xenophobia is still alive and well everywhere on Earth).

In fact, the more you think about it, the more sophisticated and enjoyable the political commentary is in *Isadora Duncan*. It's about a brash, loud-mouthed Yank, yes, it's about a dancer and bohemian free spirit, yes, and, true, Ken Russell's not known for being a political filmmaker, but *Isadora Duncan* engages with superpower politics in a comicbook, bold fashion. Look at the way that Russell and his editors Michael Bradsell and Roger Crittenden cleverly and wittily intercut their own footage with still photos and library footage, of Lenin, of Stalin, of workers, and of post-WW2 Russia.

*Isadora Duncan* is a portrait of a modern artist, yes, but it's also a commentary on modern life and politics, from the late 1800s to the late 1920s. And it's intelligent, too: it assumes a good deal of historical knowledge in its audience. True, the narration by Sewell Stokes *et al* fills in some background information, but the 1966 movie assumes that the audience knows plenty about Leningrad/ St Petersburg and Moscow in the revolutionary period and afterwards.

The editing of the newsreels with the 1966 British movie is impressive: the editors have trawled the film libraries at length for images of St Petersburg in the snow, riots in New York, Atlantic liners, Lenin, Stalin, poverty on the streets, Rio de Janiero, etc. It's one of the best and cheapest ways of achieving a broader, historical scope to a movie. *Isadora Duncan* benefits from the large amount of existing footage, I reckon, but Ken Russell would abandon this approach for later documentaries and movies (a pity, I think: at times some of his movies would be enhanced with a few newsreel scenes. However, *Isadora Duncan* probably contains a little too many). Instead, Russell's films rely on the audience knowing plenty already about 20th century history. (And of course, if you use a lot of newsreel images, it means less time for your own images).

# 3

# *BILLION DOLLAR BRAIN*

*Billion Dollar Brain* (1967) was one of many 1960s spy films; it was the third in the *Harry Palmer* trilogy by Len Deighton, which starred Michael Caine as British spy Harry Palmer (the previous two movies were *The Ipcress File*, 1965, and *Funeral In Berlin*, 1966).[37] *Billion Dollar Brain* was produced by Harry Saltzman and André de Toth[38] for United Artists (Saltzman and UA were best known at the time for the *James Bond* movies, of course). John McGrath wrote the script.[39]

On the production team of *Billion Dollar Brain* were Syd Cain (production design), Bert Davey (art direction), Alan Obiston (editing), Billy Williams (DP), Jack Causey (AD), Shirley Kingdon and John Brady (costumes), Eva Monley (production manager), John Mitchell (sound), Joan Smallwood and Freddie Williamson (make-up), and Richard Rodney Bennett (music). Some of those would become Russell regulars.

Ken Russell's helming of a genre picture was solid and assured. In *Billion Dollar Brain,* Russell managed to work in some of his familiar motifs: churches, trains, paintings, classical music,

---

[37] There's a website dedicated to the *Harry Palmer* movies, at keesstam.tripod.com.
[38] André De Toth was a legend of cinema, working with the Kordas (as AD on *The Thief of Bagdad* and *The Four Feathers,* for instance), and Michael Powell. Married to Veronica Lake, de Toth was best-known for directing Westerns; his movies included *House of Wax, Crime Wave, Monkey On My Back, The Indian Fighter, The Bounty Hunter, Man In the Saddle,* etc.
[39] Ken Russell complained that Len Deighton's book was 'totally illogical. The reasons people did things, went places and said things had no rationality whatsoever… It was just a hotch-potch of ideas the author had strung together and strung together rather badly' (Bax, 154).

sex and nudity, and colour schemes based on red (very noticeable in *Billion Dollar Brain*).

The one-time BBC TV *Monitor* director managed to squeeze in some high art allusions into *Billion Dollar Brain*: there was a scene at a classical concert, the *femme fatale* plays a cello (!), and the camera panned over many paintings and murals (there was a Paolo Uccello mural in the background of the computer set, Art Nouveau paintings of semi-naked women in a couple of locations, and another mural at the church/ monastery location. Plus Russian ikons).

Syd Cain, Bert Davey and their team in the art department did a terrific job in *Billion Dollar Brain* of delivering an off-kilter, Middle European setting, with many Ken Russell flourishes. It's heightened, it's out-size, and although the genre elements – the big super-computer room, the villain's lair – are predictable, they work very well.

Yes, *Billion Dollar Brain* is a 'PG' picture, but it's also a Ken Russell movie, and Russell manages to pack in some nudity. How does he do it? He and his art department (headed by Syd Cain and Bert Davey) prefer to use visual art: there are Aubrey Beardsleyesque nude murals, for instance. But when Karl Malden and his beau Anya (Françoise Dorléac) appear in a sauna, the familiar, decorous camera framing is employed (Malden's dropout, American agent Leon Newbegin is one of the oddities of *Billion Dollar Brain* – taking up the bohemian lifestyle in late middle-age. It doesn't quite convince, but it certainly enhances this strange movie).

The bigger-than-usual budget for Ken Russell of *Billion Dollar Brain* meant that the movie was partially shot on location in Finland (instead of Russell's beloved Lake District or Hampshire standing in for several parts of Europe). However, there were holes in the budget (RAF Canberra jets, for example, stood in for Russian MIG fighters).

*Billion Dollar Brain* was shot in London and Finland (in Helsinki and the port of Turku). Filming in Finland certainly gave the movie welcome production values: *Billion Dollar Brain* is a great snow movie, with many scenes set in the snow and the lakes.[40]

The *Harry Palmer* flick also receives a lavish Maurice Binder-

---

[40] *The Third Man*'s alluded to when Harry Palmer arrives in Finland, although the big wheel is quite a bit smaller!

designed titles sequence (Binder created the famous opening titles for the *James Bond* movies), a classic of late 1960s design (taking computers and numbers as a key motif). The budget for the titles alone was probably more than five of Ken Russell's BBC documentaries put together.

Ken Russell's visual flair in *Billion Dollar Brain* extended to reworking of the famous horses on the ice scene from *Alexander Nevsky* (1938),[41] this time with snow buggies and oil tankers.[42] This was a huge, complex and dangerous sequence involving stunts, practical gags, fire, smoke and water.[43] Russell could've had a career as an action director-for-hire if he'd wanted (tho' he soon loses interest in action for action's sake).

At the climax of *Billion Dollar Brain*, there's a convoy of oil trucks hurtling across a frozen lake, armed with missiles and troops (filmed on a snow-covered airfield).[44] It's wonderfully bonkers, and brilliantly staged. The action is as big and crazy as a *James Bond* movie or one of those high budget comedies of the period, like *Those Daring Young Men In Their Jaunty Jalopies* (a.k.a. *Monte Carlo or Bust,* 1969) or *Those Magnificent Men In Their Flying Machines* (1965).

Don't you wish that United Artists and Eon Productions had let Ken Russell direct a *James Bond* movie? After all, Russell directed *Billion Dollar Brain* for Harry Saltzman. They must've discussed the possibility. Come on, how could it hurt? It surely couldn't be worse than the utterly dreadful *James Bond* flicks of the 2000s (*Casino Royale* and *Quantum of Crap*).

Michael Caine was superb, as usual, as Harry Palmer: it was a star vehicle role, with the actor in almost every scene. However, Palmer's a rather under-written role, and it's the kooks and megalomaniacs that Palmer comes into contact with that provide

---

[41] The *Alexander Nevsky* climax of *Billion Dollar Brain* is accompanied by the *Leningrad Symphony* of Dimitri Shostakovitch.

[42] Ken Russell wasn't the only filmmaker to be thrilled by *Alexander Nevsky*: the young Stanley Kubrick went nuts for it. His friend Alex Singer, who helped Kubrick shoot his first film, *Day of the Fight,* exposed Kubrick to different sorts of films: 'I take him to *Alexander Nevsky* and we hear Prokofiev's score for the battle on the ice and Stanley never gets over that. He bought a record of it and played it until he drove his kid sister Barbara right around the bend. He played it over and over and over again and she broke the record in absolute rage. Stanley is – I think the word 'obsessive' is not unfair'. (Quoted in V. LoBrutto, *Stanley Kubrick*, Faber, London, 1997, 56)

[43] Just watching it you know it was hell to shoot.

[44] Originally, the plan was to use models. But getting the ten-foot miniatures to look good riding over salt standing in for snow didn't work. So the airfield was salted, polystyrene was used for the blocks of ice, and ramps were built for the tankers to run into the water.

much of the fun. *Fun* – yes, *Billion Dollar Brain* is meant to be nothing more than an entertainment movie. And it is hugely entertaining. Of course, some similar movies of the 1960s were bigger and flashier, but *Billion Dollar Brain* has a charm of its own.

Michael Caine said Ken Russell wasn't always helpful when it came to the direction of actors. 'As an actor, you rely on the director to tell you where you are,' Caine recounted.

> With Ken you'd suddenly be standing in six feet of snow and you'd say, "Where are we at?" And he'd say, "Standing in six feet of snow." Then you're in trouble.[45]

No one is taking themselves seriously in this 1967 movie, they all know it's a bit of Cold War, campy, spy adventure candy, and some of the people – like actors Ed Begley and Oscar Homolka – look like they're having a great time.

Story-wise, *Billion Dollar Brain* was familiar 1960s spy stuff: a super-computer, Communism, spies, betrayals, missiles, and the usual conflicts of America vs. Russia, capitalism vs. Communism, West vs. East, etc. World War Two inevitably looms behind much of the Cold War politics of *Billion Dollar Brain*. However, the United Artists movie is more sympathetic to Russia and Communism than some North American films of the period.[46] And Russia would of course be the setting for one of Russell's most important films, his own favourite, and his first *personal* feature film, *The Music Lovers* (*Billion Dollar Brain,* fun as it is, is in no way a personal movie: Russell is very much a director for hire on this outing; it's a packaged, agented, producer-dominated genre flick).

The 1967 picture contains numerous genre elements: for instance, from the detective fiction and crime genre there's Harry Palmer's squalid, private eye's office,[47] the visit from a former boss, the hero reluctant to accept any assignments, the beautiful, cool agent (Françoise Dorléac (1942-67), sister of Catherine Deneuve), who turns out to be a *femme fatale*, with dubious

---
[45] J. Crist, 1991, 436.
[46] Ken Russell called *Billion Dollar Brain* 'the first anti-American spy film ever' (Bax, 154) – and compared Latvia to Vietnam, and the anti-American feelings of the period, during the Vietnam War.
[47] There's even a 'red bus shot', establishing the setting of Palmer's office in central London.

motives and goals.

Later, *Billion Dollar Brain* shifts into familiar *James Bond* territory, with a crazy villain, General Midwinter, played with gusto by Ed Begley (chewing up the scenery):[48] a mad Texan who wants to rid the world of Communism by destabilzing a Soviet country with a privately-funded invasion. Every cliché is delightfully trotted out (as well as spoofed): Midwinter's lair, for instance, is built on oil (of course), and sports a shooting range and plenty of guns.

*Billion Dollar Brain* wasn't the happiest shoot for Ken Russell, and was another movie where some in the crew disliked Russell's methods and attitude. Later, Russell recalled: 'making the film was such a struggle and its reception so dispiriting that for years after I automatically ran it down to everyone' (Bax, 160). But when he saw it on TV he found some of it pretty good – 'quite stunning in parts' – particularly the Midwinter section. I also liked the Russian general's speech about Lenin in the hotel bedroom'.

But in terms of his career, *Billion Dollar Brain* was a big step, a crucial shift into A-list features. *Billion Dollar Brain* was vital in allowing Russell to move on to directing *Women In Love*, and the success of that picture led to his finest work, *The Music Lovers* and *The Devils*.

---

[48] As well as Ed Begley, Oscar Homolka is terrific as the Soviet counterpart, Colonel Stok, a blustery portrait of old Russia.

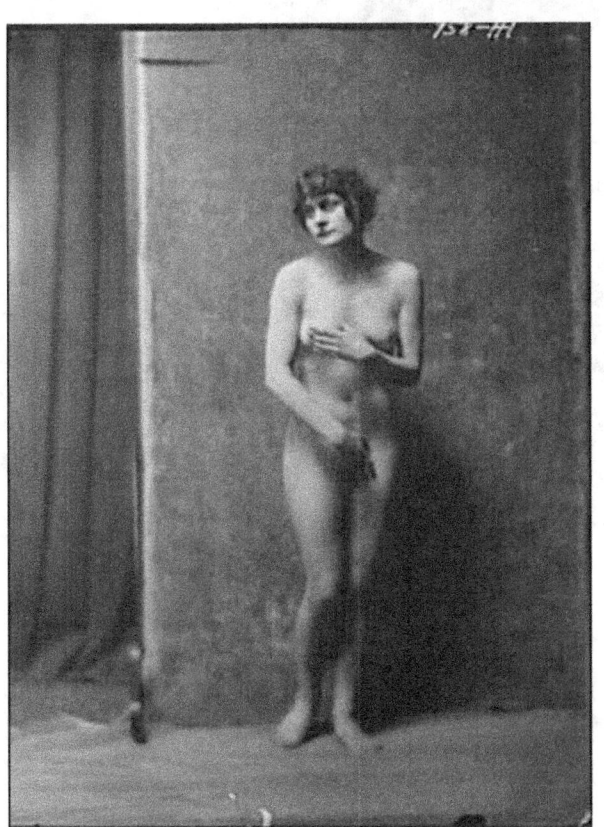

Russell on set with
Vivian Pickles (above).
Isadora Duncan (left,
photographer unknown).

Isadora Duncan (left).

Ken Russell's film on Isadora Duncan (below).

The Debussy Film (1965)

Billion Dollar Brain, the 1967 entry in the Harry Palmer series

One of the most celebrated of Ken Russell's BBC works, the Elgar documentary from the early 1960s

# 4

# *DANTE'S INFERNO*

I don't think any honest artist sets out to make art. You love art. You live art. You are art. But you're just doing something. You're just doing what no one can stop you from doing.

Robert Rauschenberg, 1978

INTRO.
There has been no film like *Dante's Inferno* (tx 1967.12.22), and certainly nothing like it before or since broadcast on television. It is one of Ken Russell's masterpieces, a film with a unique atmosphere and texture, and one of the most extraordinary soundtracks ever assembled from library music.

*Dante's Inferno* is classic Ken Russell: the central role by Oliver Reed, late Victorian setting, an artistic *milieu* (arty and bohemian and very English), and a host of Russell regulars behind and in front of the camera (Luciana Arrighi was production designer, Shirley Kingdon was wardrobe, Shirley Boakes was make-up, Nat Crosby was DP, Sandy MacRae recorded the sound, Stan Morcom was dubbing mixer, Marc Wolloff was production manager, Mike Bradsell and Roger Crittenden were editors). Tim Braine and M. Meagher were executive producers, and Russell was producer. Austin Frazer is a significant collaborator on *Dante's Inferno*, providing the narration and co-writing the script.[1]

---

[1] Joseph Gomez reckons that the book that Austin Frazer and Ken Russell drew on mainly for *Dante's Inferno* was Oswald Doughty's 1949 study.

According to Ken Russell, it was director Bryan Forbes who suggested doing something on Dante Gabriel Rossetti: he handed Austin Frazer's script to Russell saying he couldn't make it commercial. Russell's response was:

> why he thought it wouldn't be commercial I just could not understand. A man digging up his wife's remains to get a book he buried with her? It *screams* 'Commercial'. (Bax, 132)

But of course, not everyone sees things the same way as Ken Russell!

Unfortunately, *Dante's Inferno* was not one of Ken Russell's happiest shoots. The biggest set-back was losing ten days of principal photography – and on the tiny British Broadcasting Corporation budget,[2] that was absolutely critical.[3] It was because of film stock – to cut back, films were shot on 16mm, but it was gradually realized that the rushes were out of focus (and we have to be thankful today that *Dante's Inferno* was filmed on 35mm).

Other problems included the cast: Ken Russell said they were 'probably the worst lot of actors I ever had in a film'. But it doesn't really show (thanks, Russell said, to editing – by Mike Bradsell and Roger Crittenden).[4] A 'bolshy sound man' was fired (B, 134). The cinematographer (Nat Crosby) took too long to light scenes (yes, but the results were superb).[5]

Oliver Reed had to undergo some tough acting tasks – in his attempted suicide scene, he crashes through a door into the back garden, stumbling around caged birds[6] (the symbolism is both intuitive and crushingly obvious – but it works), falling to the ground and having a snake crawl on his face (on *his face*, with his eyes open – there are not many actors who would do that! Would

---

[2] However, Russell would've acknowledged that this was the kinda material that movie financers would be reluctant to back (it's way too esoteric for mainstream cinema). TV was the only place to get the thing produced.

[3] There are scenes which aren't quite what they would be with more time. There's a scene where Lizzie and Gabriel return from a night's carousing. It should be a night scene, but it's filmed in full daylight (the sky's cropped out, but the scene doesn't use day-for-night).

[4] There are moments in *Dante's Inferno* when one would expect to hear more from, say, Holman Hunt, or Edward Burne-Jones, but one doesn't really notice them. Partly because there is so much else going on, and partly because the two leads are so strong.

[5] And Russell is a director who certainly appreciates intricate lighting. Trouble was, this was a television schedule, not movies.

[6] In Cheyne Walk in Chelsea, Rossetti did have animals in the bachelor pad he shared with Algernon Swinburne. The birds are white doves, and 'Dove' was one of Rossetti's names for Siddal.

you let a real, live snake crawl over your face? No, nor me! And neither would Ken Russell – he hates snakes).

And those challenges were in addition to the usual physical rigours of a Ken Russell shoot: clambering over rocks, being doused under freezing waterfalls, being dunked in the sea and floating in a river (for Judith Paris), and of course nudity (for Gala Mitchell). (And you know, this being a low budget BBC production of the 1960s, that the cast and crew did not have luxurious trailers, or limos or helicopters to take them to the set).

☦

THE PRE-RAPHAELITES.

The Pre-Raphaelites are a big part of modern British art history, like the Symbolists are in France or the Expressionists in Germany or the Futurists in Italy. You'll see a lot of their art if you visit many of the big museums in Britain, and they are heavily merchandized in birthday cards, calendars, posters, tea towels and all that other crap (yep, and the original artists, some of whom struggled with poverty, don't get *a cent*).

In *Dante's Inferno*,[7] Ken Russell, Austin Frazer and the BBC team took on the Pre-Raphaelites with a full-blooded account focussing on the poet and painter Dante Gabriel Rossetti (1828-1882).[8] Rossetti had Italian parents, a poet sister Christina, and lived and studied mainly in London (at Sass's art school, then the Royal Academy). He met Lizzie Siddal (1829-62) in 1850, idolizing her in many works until her death in 1862 from a laudanum overdose. Their odd, uneasy relationship is central to *Dante's Inferno* (Russell, as we know, loves quirky, unusual relationships – his cinema's full of them – especially ones that subvert the classic, erotic couple of a man and a woman).[9] Rossetti's subsequent relationship with the Pre-Raphaelites' pin-up and Muse, the enigmatic 17 year-old from Oxford, Jane Burden, forms the latter part of *Dante's Inferno* (but the ghost of Lizzie Siddal, of course, never leaves Rossetti: this is a film about a supremely haunted man – tortured by his insecurities, his weaknesses, his addictions, his failures and his ambitions. *Dante's Inferno* is very much a

---
7 It was broadcast on December 22, 1967.
8 A good online research website is: rossettiarchive.org.
9 The narrator quips that although Rossetti and Siddal had been together in some form for five years, she was still a virgin. In one scene, to illustrate the nervy, shaky erotic relationship, Rossetti stands behind Siddal, reaching down to touch her breasts, and she flies back, wielding a sewing needle, which she subsequently scratches across his chest. It is one of the first of many arguments they have.

portrait of the artist as a tortured soul who canna find peace anywhere. Not in the arms of mistresses or hookers, nor in drink, nor in chloral, nor even, in the end, in art or in poetry).

All of the Pre-Raphaelites and their associates are here in 1967's *Dante's Inferno*: Ford Maddox Ford, Edward Burne-Jones, William 'Topsy' Morris, Holman Hunt, John Ruskin, Algernon Swinburne, John Everett Millais, and assorted wives, girlfriends, sisters, brothers, whores and models (Annie Miller, Janey Burden, Fanny Cornforth, William Rossetti, and Emma Brown). They're not *all* portrayed as assholes, but some of 'em are (they are blighted by too much education, too much self-aggrandizement, too much ego, and too much self-absorption).

Of the Pre-Raphaelites and that notion of nostalgically evoking the past, and preferring it to the present, Ken Russell remarked:

> All these people started out with great ideals, then sold out. They thought that by returning to the past they could beat the present, but you can't do that. You've got to transcend the present somehow, beat the system, not opt out of it. (Bax, 134)

Ken Russell reckoned 'we got closer to the Victorian Decadent romantics than anything I ever did, or indeed I've ever seen on film before or since' (B, 135). He's right: they did. The combination of this cast, this film crew, this production set-up, this era of the late 1960s, and this target audience of TV viewers, it all seemed to coalesce so well for Russell and co. at this time. In British cinema and television, I can't think of a show which better captured the era of the Pre-Raphaelites, and also the Decadent and *fin-de-siècle* era, the period of the Symbolists and the Decadents in Europe (even tho' it *begs* to be in colour, or at least to have colour inserts of the artworks). *Dante's Inferno* works also as a poetic account of the world of artists such as the French Symbolists, such as poets like Paul Verlaine, Charles Baudelaire, Arthur Rimbaud, Gérard de Nerval, Tristan Corbière, Stéphane Mallarmé, Paul Valéry and Lautréamont, or Northern European Symbolist painters such as Gustave Moreau (above all), Edvard Munch, Félicien Rops, Odilon Redon, Jean Delville and Franz von Stuck. *Dante's Inferno* isn't the only film about the Rossetti-Siddal relationship: there was *The Love School* (1975), with Patricia

Quinn as Siddal, and *Desperate Romantics* (2009),[10] a BBC TV mini-series, with Amy Manson as Siddal.

☦

Dante Gabriel Rossetti had many of the attributes of the artists that Ken Russell has seized upon in many films and shows: troubled relationships with women; uneasy relationships with patrons (in *Dante's Inferno*, it's John Ruskin); he drank and took drugs (he became addicted to chloral for insomnia); lassitude; idealism; and he attempted suicide in 1872.

The Pre-Raphaelite Brotherhood was formed in 1848 by Dante Gabriel Rossetti, Holman Hunt, John Everett Millais, and Rossetti's brother William, and others. A second Brotherhood coalesced around Rossetti, and included younger artists such as Edward Burne-Jones and William Morris (Oxford graduates).

The Pre-Raphaelite Brotherhood's art was marked by a veneration of the Early Renaissance artists and the Early Netherlandish painters (Fra Filippo Lippi, Fra Angelico, the van Eycks, etc), visually flattened spaces, bright colour, historical, religious or moral subjects (mainly Christian, and many Arthurian), plenty of poetic influences (Giovanni Boccaccio, William Shakespeare, John Keats, Lord Tennyson), and a nostalgic, conservative and curiously English outlook.

☦

PRODUCTION.

There are two sensational performances at the heart of *Dante's Inferno*: Oliver Reed in the title role, and Judith Paris[11] as his doomed lover, model and later wife, Lizzie Siddal.[12] Both were roles of a lifetime, gifts to an actor to grab them and run to the stars with them. And Reed and Paris threw themselves into the 1967 movie completely.

Oliver Reed is not merely stunning to look at and brilliant at

---

10 So the BBC delivered a 6-part mini-series in 2009 about the Pre-Raphaelites. It was wholly predictable (good-lookin' young cast, jokey, childish approach, an eye on international sales), full of padding and tedious repeitions (even in the first show), and the only advantage over *Dante's Inferno* was being filmed in colour (tho' in ugly, murky video). I just about got thru the first episode (by fast-forwarding the DVD), but the *smugness* of the cast and the filmmakers is just irritating. Watching a great actor like Tom Hollander (as John Ruskin) is enjoyable, but if I see yet another scene of po-faced Brit actors taking tea and sitting in embarrassed silence I will FUCKING SCREAM!!

11 Judith Paris appeared in many Ken Russell works, including *The Devils*, *Lady Chatterley* and *Savage Messiah*.

12 Dante Gabriel Rossetti's later relationships included model Fanny Cornforth, Holman Hunt's wife, and William Morris's wife Janey (there were other women, of course: once again, it is an artist and his women).

playing moody, tortured souls, he is also acting up a storm in each of his leading roles for Ken Russell. Indeed, as Dante Gabriel Rossetti, there are very actors of the time who could've been so effective as Reed (Alan Bates, of course, and maybe David Hemmings, but not many others).

And although Ollie Reed rightly receives much of the attention in Ken Russell's cinema, Paris is just superb in a complex role that demands a host of emotions and scenarios (angry, hurt, sulky, seductive, wistful, scheming, sad, ill, embarrassed, awkward, impatient and shy – and that's all in the first scene!). Paris also has to run the whole gamut of physical performance that a Russell picture demands.

The supporting performers in *Dante's Inferno* are very strong, one of most impressive group in Ken Russell's cinema (despite Russell's complaints about the cast).[13] Very fine is Andrew Faulds as William Morris (1834-96). It's not a movie about Kelmscott Manor, the Arts and Crafts movement (and Art Nouveau), Augustus Pugin, and Morris's socialism (all faves with art critics), but *Dante's Inferno* does contain plenty of insights into Morris's world[14] (including a scene where Morris heads off into the mountains of Iceland[15] for an obscure, chivalric, mediæval adventure with horses and sheepskins and grand scenery – very Arthurian and Wagnerian. Morris's there 'to write the longest saga ever known', as Russell put it [B, 132]. And the lengthy quote by Morris about Siegfried and the dragon Fafnir is an allusion of course to one of Russell's favourite movies, the German *Niebelungen*).

Andrew Faulds captures William Morris's tendency to recite poetry or declaim at every opportunity (was he really like that?). Norman Dewhurst was Burne-Jones; Derek Boshier was Millais; Clive Goodwin was Ruskin; Douglas Gray was Hunt; Iza Teller was Rossetti's sister Christina; Caroline Coon played Annie Miller;[16] and Janet Deuters was Emma Brown.

Algernon Swinburne was played by Ken Russell regular Christopher Logue as a lecherous, cynical, intellectual hedonist, a

---

13 Some in the cast were friends or people the filmmakers knew, and some were artists themselves.
14 There are scenes at Morris's famous Red House, for instance, and later at Kelmscott Manor.
15 Filmed guess where?! Yup, the Lakes!
16 Caroline Coon, a journalist and artist, managed The Clash for a time (see her book *1988: The New Wave Punk Rock Explosion*).

classic *fin-de-siècle* æsthete, a dandy who's stepped right out of J.-K. Huysman's *Against Nature*. Swinburne (who's never shown at work), is a party animal who an eye for anything in a skirt (and if a living being isn't around, he'll smooch a stone effigy!). Logue would appear in his biggest role in Russell's work not long after this in *The Devils*.

Pat Ashton played Fanny Cornforth, another of Dante Gabriel Rossetti's lovers, as a ballsy, no-bullshit lover and helpmate. She is one of Rossetti's mistresses, and later his housekeeper, tidying up after he's had another night of drink and chloral. Cornforth plays an important role in the movie in representing something like ordinary life or regular people, a necessary counterpoint to the crazy, self-indulgent bohemian artists (Ashton might've stepped out of South Kensington tube station of 1967 into the movie).

Jane Burden/ Morris (1840-1914) was played by *Vogue* model Gala Mitchell (a favourite with Ossie Clark),[17] whose incredible face and magnetic eyes eat up the screen (Mitchell's a gift to a cinematographer, and *Dante's Inferno* exploits her beauty to the maximum). She's first introduced as an æthereal angel (Burden was 17) who beguiles the second Pre-Raphaelite Brotherhood (Morris, Burne-Jones, Swinburne, Rossetti) in Oxford into a slack-jawed, erotic stupor. One woman, four men (but it's William Morris who wins her).

A glowing, shadowy close-up worthy of Marlene Dietrich in a Josef von Sternberg movie introduces Gala Mitchell's Jane Burden, sitting in a pew in a church. The church setting is perfect for the Pre-Raphaelites and their Anglicized Christianity (but churches are some of Ken Russell's favourite locations, of course). And the guys can't take their eyes off her. The editors create a panoply of looks of erotic desire, with Burden at the centre – but the staging also brings in artworks, stained glass, and Christian symbols. Love In A Church is a scenario that Russell will revisit many times.

For Joseph Gomez, Janey Morris's portrayed by the film-makers as a 'beautiful, bored, mindless woman' (1976, 52). No, I don't think Burden is mindless, but at times bored, yes: it's more that Burden can't fit in (and doesn't want to fit in) with these crazy bohemians, these English aristos with their mad notions and

---

[17] Mitchell now works in complimentary therapies in California.

schoolboy antics. She finds them bemusing and silly, and all too easy to manipulate because they are salivating over her extreme beauty.[18] (Gala Mitchell's inexperience as an actor, and her rather flat delivery of dialogue, fits the character and her role in *Dante's Inferno*).

The point, also, is that Janey Burden-Morris's beauty and presence is multi-faceted, and can be interpreted any way you like. She's there to suggest the attractions as well as the dangers of artistic creation. She is a muse but also a mask, she is a princess tied to a cliff to be rescued by a Perseus or a Roger but also a harpy or *femme fatale* who can destroy men with a casual flick of a knife.

Janey Morris is what the artists want, but what they shouldn't have. She is their desire, but also their death. This is a recurring motif in Ken Russell's cinema, but it also very much a part of the Romantic-Symbolist form of art, where what you want to need or crave – drugs, drink, tobacco, food, sex, money, fame – is portrayed as an out-of-reach *femme fatale*. And we never really know what Morris is thinking or feeling.

In the latter scenes of *Dante's Inferno*, set in the 1870s, the characters are aged up, with make-up and greyed hair – all except Gala Mitchell: it's quite right that Jane Burden should appear as (maddeningly) youthful and angelic as when the P.R.B. first met her.

Both Judith Paris and Gala Mitchell captured the idealizations of women at the heart of the Pre-Raphaelite Brotherhood's art – and how when men idealize and objectify women like this in art, it can lead to brilliant works of art, but is potentially damaging in real life. Paris's Siddall and Mitchell's Janey Morris have the look down to a 'T', courtesy of make-up by Shirley Boakes and costumes by Shirley Kingdon. And they also portray the negative, dangerous aspects of the idealized woman in late 19th century art, when women were portrayed as *femme fatales*.

*Dante's Inferno* depicts Lizzie Siddal as out of her depth many times – the working class girl in amongst this group of crazy bohemian and middle-class artists. Christina Rossetti dislikes her from the beginning (illustrated in the tried and tested scene of the English taking tea. And Iza Teller as Rossetti's sister can convey

---

[18] Accounts differ as to Jane Burden's personality, some calling her smarter than Morris (Theodore Watts-Dunton), and others finding her shy, retiring and a bit silly (George Bernard Shaw). (J. Gomez, 1976, 74).

disdain with one look).[19]

*Dante's Inferno* also explores the world of 19th century prostitution (there are scenes in Cranbourne Alley in London, a back street with the milliner's store where Lizzie Siddall worked at the end of it, where whores hang out),[20] and the notion of the 'fallen woman', an artistic subject which crops up a lot in Pre-Raphaelite art.[21] Indeed, one of D.G.R.'s key works is entitled *Found*: a man and a fallen woman in a London street.[22] The links between prostitution and art (and between being a prostitute and being an artist's model), have been made before, of course (and many times since). We return to Cranbourne Alley twice – in the first scene, Siddal hysterically refers to her time hooking; in the second, Gabriel Rossetti's haunted by the spectre of Siddal, reflected in a window, as two prostitutes wonder if he'd like some company.

I was never a big fan of Dante Gabriel Rossetti's painting, finding it too self-conscious, too fey, too self-absorbed, too pompous, and a little crude. *Dante's Inferno* persuades me that there is more to it. Yes, it *is* fey, self-conscious, self-absorbed and very pompous, but when you know much more about the artist, in this case it definitely enriches the art (that's not always the case).

✞

STYLE.

*Dante's Inferno* has a classic Ken Russell opening, pure Universal-era horror movies (1930s), and pure German Expressionist cinema, *à la Nosferatu* or *Caligari* (1920s): a coffin being raised from a grave (at night, naturally), the lid being prised back, a hand pulling back a veil to reveal a skeleton and taking out a book – all done in one, overhead shot.[23] Classic Russell, as was the scene following the title card of rebellious artists gleefully pitching old-fashioned art onto a bonfire (at night, naturally),

---

[19] Later in the piece, Christina R. seems more sympathetic towards Siddal, tho' her comment about Siddal losing a child seems designed to wound her.
[20] Swinburne in the voiceover points out the difference between working for a few hours on the street or all day in a shop.
[21] Siddal harangues Rossetti about the exploitation of labour, linking it to prostitution, towards the end, when she is ill, the men are drunk, and the self-loathing overcomes the couple.
[22] Begun in 1853, he worked on it off and on until his death, but never finished it. The models for it were Fanny Cornforth and Annie Miller.
[23] Ken Russell loved the idea that Dante Gabriel Rossetti had raided his beloved's grave for the book of poems, so he could make some money. Indeed: it is a scene tailor-made for Russell.

filmed in the classic, Russell manner of handheld camerawork and rapid editing. (The event pinpointed the start of this poetic docu-drama: the revolutionary year 1848, when our Gabriel was 20 years-old. Thus, *Dante's Inferno* takes in a long period, from 1848 to the late 1870s or even near Rossetti's death in 1882: 30 or so years. The evocation of creative revolution no doubt also reflects the period when *Dante's Inferno* was produced – 1967).

The prologue, though, isn't explained for some time. Who's hand?[24] Whose corpse? What book? And *why*? But the Gothic horror image of the raising of the casket and the filching of the book is a very strong opening to the piece; it establishes the tone; and introduces one of the key themes of this and all of Ken Russell's work: D-E-A-T-H. (The answer, tho', is provided right after the title card, when the hero of the piece leaps towards the camera into close-up, yelling. That is classic movie-making: introduce your star as soon as possible).

The raising-the-dead prologue also sets the television show apart from the stream of shit that most television is. Like other famous Ken Russell opening scenes to TV shows, it makes it clear that this ain't the another dreary sit-com or a Val Doonican or Cliff Richard variety show or the friggin' news.

☨

*Dante's Inferno* displays once again Ken Russell's genius with location scouting and improvizing a minuscule BBC budget into something lavish and decadent (as well as boho and low-life. It's handy, for instance, that so many of Russell's subjects were starving artists, so the TV shows and movies didn't always require palaces and five-star restaurants – back alleys and garrets would do). But there are a vast number of props required, including canvases, sketches, frames, paints, easels, statues, music boxes, armour, etc. And a *lot* of locations.

As for the famous, Ken Russell, flamboyant style, startling images and shock cuts, *Dante's Inferno* contains them all, floods of them, including one of the first appearances of the Lake District, which Russell made completely his own, as no other filmmaker has.

*Dante's Inferno* employs the full pirate's treasure chest of Ken Russell flourishes, including slow motion, backlight, rapid montage, parallel action, shock cuts, extreme close-ups, crash zooms,

---

24 Only later is it revealed that it was Rossetti's art dealer, Charles Augustus Howell, who organized the exhumation at Highgate Cemetery.

anachronisms, ironic music, etc. (Water imagery is all over *Dante's Inferno*, with many scenes in or beside the sea, on rivers, beside rivers, in baths, next to lakes... And, of course, lots of fire imagery.)

Like *Delius* and *Isadora Duncan*, *Dante's Inferno* was filmed at the height of Ken Russell's absorption in the cinema of Ingmar Bergman. There are numerous links to Bergman's movies in *Dante's Inferno* (such as the silhouette of the dead tree that closes the movie, or the giant, Gothic close-ups). You can intercut scenes from Bergman's 1950s-1960s movies and Russell's late 1960s movies and they would blend together seamlessly.

The naughty Victorian club where Dante Gabriel Rossetti, Algernon Swinburne and the gang hang out with assorted prostitutes and bohemians (the Grand Turkish Rooms), is classic Ken Russell – he will re-visit this kind of kinky, decadent watering hole many times in his movies and TV shows. The woman in a gold mask performing as an automata playing a zither lying back on a couch was an exemplary piece of E.T.A. Hoffmann via Powell & Pressburger (Russell would revisit the same territory in *Gothic*, though not so successfully).

There is a dramatic editing cut in *Dante's Inferno* which Ken Russell revived to great effect in *Women In Love*: the editors (Mike Bradsell and Roger Crittenden) cut from Dante Gabriel Rossetti and a new lover (Holman Hunt's wife) about to get freaky in some ferns[25] to Lizzie Siddal ill, lying on her bed.[26] It's another example of Russell's Eisensteinian montage, using simple but emotionally explosive contrasts – slamming together love and death, sex and guilt. That is, while someone is enjoying some outdoor sex in the sunny countryside, their beloved is home alone and declining.

As a flow of images, *Dante's Inferno* is simply remarkable: it's shot (by DP Nat Crosby) in the crisp black-and-white style which draws on Ken Russell's favourites, including: German Expressionism, Universal 1930s horror classics, and the intense chamber pieces of Swedish genius Ingmar Bergman. (This is one movie which really *should* be in colour to show off the hyper-saturated colouration the Pre-Raphs favoured. B/W reproductions simply

---

[25] There's also a Russell favourite trope – lovers on fairground swings, where the push-and-pull, the rapid cutting, and the smiling, radiant faces are all stand-ins for sex. Russell reprised the motif in *The Rainbow*.
[26] And also to Siddal undergoing a cure in France, being dunked in the briny. Finally, she lies exhausted on the sand in the surf.

don't capture their art).

✝

THEMES.

The story is familiar in *Dante's Inferno* – 'the private life of a poet and painter', as the subtitle has it – but not the approach of Ken Russell and his co-writer Austin Frazer. It contains numerous clichés about an artist's life, from the love affairs, the adultery and betrayals, the rise (gradual) to fame and (monetary) success, the pompous declarations of principals and ambitions,[27] the silly, bohemian friends, and the slide into self-loathing, self-delusion, and self-destructive behaviour. Yet none of *Dante's Inferno* appears clichéd at all, but absolutely riveting drama. Russell will tell this story again and again, yet each time you can feel the strong empathy of the filmmakers with the artist, the fascination with what makes artists tick, with how they operate – socially and politically as well as privately and emotionally and sexually.

*Dante's Inferno* is about the recurring theme in Ken Russell's cinema of the costs of being a creative person. It is about the crushing guilt[28] that the artist feels about those around them that he hurts, that he can't help hurting, no matter what he does (witness the scene near the end of *Dante's Inferno* where Dante Gabriel Rossetti rushes away from the ailing Lizzie Siddal, lying ill in bed, running down the gloomy staircases and stopping to hear her cries of 'DON'T LEAVE ME! DON'T GO!', then he hurries on, then he stops again, moving into a shadowy close-up. Guilt <-> selfishness <-> guilt <-> remorse <-> guilt <-> escape <-> guilt <-> flight: *Dante's Inferno* illustrates this cycle of emotion vividly. It's a guilt trip story, and guilt, you have to admit, is one of Russell's primary themes).

Well, one can relate the enormous emphasis on guilt in *Dante's Inferno* (and the rest of Ken Russell's cinema) to Catholicism, and to the director's own life and beliefs. But it plays beyond the religious dimension, to become a major dramatization of moral and ethical issues.

Suicide is once again a recurring motif in *Dante's Inferno*, as in so many of Ken Russell's works. As if life is simply too painful to bear when one is an artist or lives close to an artist, as if artists

---

[27] *Dante's Inferno* also captures the pretentiousness of these artists, and their sometimes tiresome penchant for expounding philosophically, or for reciting poetry.
[28] In his study of Rossetti, Evelyn Waugh called him a 'Catholic without the discipline or consolation of the Church' (*Rossetti*, Dod, Mead & Co, New York, 1928, 13).

somehow open themselves up to life so much they leave nothing behind that can be protected, as if they expose everything inside them, like a quivering, little animal, and there are no defences left against the stones and shocks of life, so when something happens, they are knocked sideways.

In Ken Russell's cinema, artists are simply too selfish on the one hand and too sensitive on the other. Too needy and clingy on the one hand, and too domineering and manipulative on the other. Too open to the universe and the sublime and the gods on the one hand and too blinkered and narrow-minded and conservative on the other.

Ken Russell's artists reveal the ambivalences, the hypocrisies, the stupidities of being a person, of being alive. The forces surging around inside Russell's artists are immense, continually threatening to break the bounds of their selves, their bodies. His artists are promiscuous but demand unswerving loyalty and dedication. They are intellectually sophisticated but they are also people with the emotional ages of children or babies. They need to be hugged and consoled as well as admired and praised. They want to be the centre of attention, the life and soul of the party, but they also crave isolation and solitude.

MARRIAGE.

The marriage between Lizzie Siddal and Dante Gabriel Rossetti has a Thomas Hardyan feel to it ('weddings be funerals', as an old crone in *Jude the Obscure* puts it). That is, for Hardy,[29] the equivalence between weddings and wakes is not strange at all. In *Dante's Inferno*, they emerge from the church at the end of a rapid montage of weddings (Ruskin and Macdonald, Morris and Janey) to find... nobody there to throw confetti (Russell, like Hardy, can't play a wedding ceremony straight, without incident. There has to be twist on it, something that goes wrong).

The subsequent scene on the beach, as the newly-weds walk 'side the surf, is another slice of British Gloom (we Brits are good at Gloom – Misery is our speciality, from Thomas Hardy to Joy Division and the Smiths), and the poetry recited comes from 'Even So':

---

[29] But if Ken Russell had taken on Thomas Hardy, it would've been much more dynamic than the usual po-faced actors filmed against pretty landscapes.

> Seemed it so to us
> When I was thine and thou wast mine,
> And all these things were thus,
> But all our world in us?
>
> Could we be so now?
> Not if all beneath heaven's pall
> Lay dead but I and thou,
> Could we be so now?

And the 1967 film complicates the quotation of poetry by having it occur in between dialogue and over step-motion. Very effective in a stylized, lyrical way.

The use of poetry quoted in voiceover opens up the gulfs between life and desire, life and need, and even life and art: because poetry (art) reminds the poet (the artist) what life lacks. Poetry simultaneously balms and bruises, it soothes over wounds even as it opens them up again.

Ouch!... Poetry *hurts*.

Oh yes it does, it really does. (As poets, this is something we know *a lot* about, having studied it for centuries). And you can bet a priceless book of newly-discovered poetry written in William Shakespeare's own hand, that many poets from history would love *Dante's Inferno*, if they'd been able to see it: Francesco Petrarch... Dante Alighieri... the *stil novisti*... the troubadours... Sappho... Emily Dickinson... Thomas Hardy (of course! it's pure Hardy)... and Shakespeare.

Or put it this way: artists are their own worst enemies. As we all are. Who can damage us, wind us up, annoy us, stupefy us, and scare the living shit out of us better than... *us*? And, as Ken Russell and his production teams have demonstrated in numerous movies and TV shows, artists create their own hells. And they can't help it: they can't help themselves doing what they do, even when they know the consequences.

Artists want *that* drug, *that* girl, *that* boy, *that* success, *that* fame, *that* praise...

• Even better if the lovely body they want is married to someone else; they'll still pursue 'em.

• Even better if they know that drink and drugs taste like shit and send them spinning into oblivion.

• Even better if they recognize that fame and success mean absolutely *fuck all*.

SUICIDE.

There are so many outstanding scenes in *Dante's Inferno*, beginning with the opening sequence of the coffin and the book of poems (replayed subsequently in a variety of forms). Later, *Dante's Inferno* moves into a pure sound and music form, Ken Russell's favourite mode, with Russell and his team conjuring mediæval mystery play imagery of coffins, corpses that come alive, tortured souls, set amongst rivers and boulders in the wilderness. It's right out of German Expressionist cinema and Ingmar Bergman's Cinema of Angst, and it works brilliantly.

The suicide overdose scene is one of those lengthy, master shots that Ken Russell employs numerous times: Lizzie Siddal lies back in her bed, clad in angelic white, harshly lit from above. She has a glass and some laudanum: at first she takes a drop or two, but hesitates, b4 swallowing the whole lot. The detail of Siddal drawing on a white shift is marvellous, as she prepares for the end (she has been often clad in white, as if she remained virginal to the last). But there are other things going on here – the camera zooms in slowly, for instance, then pulls out; Judith Paris is acting to the max; and finally there is some voiceover from Paris.

She recites her death-bed poem (which she has been writing):

> I am gazing upwards to the sun,
> Lord, Lord, remembering my lost one.
>   O Lord, remember me!
> How is it in the unknown land?
> Do the dead wander hand in hand?
> Do we clasp dead hands, and quiver
> With an endless joy forever?
> Is the air filled with the sound
> Of spirits circling round and round?
> Are there lakes of endless song,
> To rest our tired eyes upon?
> Do tall angels gaze and wend
> Along the banks where lilies bend?[30]

One of the fascinating elements in *Dante's Inferno* is the structure. Because for the first half of its 90 minute running time, it is a somewhat familiar rags-to-riches tale (well, no, never riches, of course: although the commissions eventually flow in, Dante Gabriel Rossetti seems pretty down at heel throughout, despite

---
[30] Quoted in O. Doughty, 298.

the aid of folk like John Ruskin).

But around the time that Elizabeth Siddal is deteriorating, *Dante's Inferno* moves into more internal, dream-laden territory. You think it's going to close fairly soon with Siddal's suicide (aged 33), followed by Dante Gabriel Rossetti's descent into morbid self-loathing (Rossetti died at the age of 54). It's going to be the drinks-and-drugs decline we've seen so often.

But *Dante's Inferno* doesn't stop there. It continues.

All sorts of intriguing events and elements are introduced, such as dream sequences, fantasies, flashbacks to D.G. Rossetti and L. Siddal in happier times, and the move into a new Pre-Raphaelite Brotherhood, the trip to Oxford (to paint the Oxford Union), and the new romance with William Morris's wife Jane. Gala Mitchell's extraordinary face and presence haunts this part of *Dante's Inferno*: she is the perfect cinematic presentation of the artist's muse and model, the embodiment of beauty, desire, idealism, but also something unreachable, unattainable, unworldly, yet also someone who is a real person, a real mother seen with her children[31] in the garden.[32]

☦

ART AND LIFE.

*Dante's Inferno* is one of the most successful films I think of linking art and life in this particular group of artists. Production designer Luciana Arrighi covers the walls and floor of Dante Gabriel Rossetti's home with paintings and drawings, which's expected in this kind of artist biopic (there are shots of walls plastered with drawings, when John Ruskin visits Rossetti; and Ruskin's place is dense with art on the walls). And you need that, all of that visual material, to remind you where you are, culturally (just to source and reproduce all of the art on display is a major undertaking).

But that's not what I mean: *Dante's Inferno* folds together the artist's pursuit of ideals and beauty and radiance in art and the artist's real life, with its endless complications and set-backs. Art is not life – or, rather, life is not art: that is, life is not as refined and controllable as art. *Dante's Inferno* explores the psychological fall-out stemming from the gulf between art and life – very elegantly,

---

31 Played, yet again, by Russell's kids.
32 The tactic of limiting Jane Burden's dialogue, so she appears more mysterious, more like an æthereal presence than a real person, has been used many times – because it works.

I think, and very convincingly.

A large number of films and TV shows have tried to explore the same territory, but only a few are really convincing. *Dante's Inferno* is one of them (but not all of Ken Russell's works are as good as this). Certainly, in the late 1960s, Russell seemed to possess an uncanny and incredibly imaginative insight into art and artists which produced *five* television masterpieces: *Delius: Song of Summer*, *Dante's Inferno*, *The Dance of the Seven Veils*, *The Debussy Film* and *Isadora Duncan*. Five!

The man was on fire!

Yes, because there's no doubt that *Delius: Song of Summer* is one of the great movies about music and composing. And that *Isadora Duncan* is one of the great movies about dance. And that *Dante's Inferno* is the greatest film about the Pre-Raphaelites.

☦

Stuffed into the multi-layered wedding cake of *Dante's Inferno* is plenty of poetry and voiceover. Pretty much everyone gets to speak in voiceover, or from poems, including Dante Gabriel Rossetti's poet sister Christina (Iza Teller), William Morris, Algernon Swinburne, Lizzie Siddal, John Ruskin and Rossetti himself. And there's plenty of narration from Swinburne, knitting the story of Rossetti's private life together. (That Swinburne is the narrator gives the events in *Dante's Inferno* a particular slant: this is a seen-it-all-before narrator, someone who's not surprised by any of the crazy goings-on).

By the end of *Dante's Inferno* you know a good deal about Dante Gabriel Rossetti, about his art, his poetry, his artistic *milieu*, and his inner life. And it's remarkable, because not *once* does *Dante's Inferno* feel like it's lecturing its audience, or patronizing its audience, or dragging them along. A *ton* of information is delivered in *Dante's Inferno* about Rossetti and his circle and love life, but it never feels as though the filmmakers are descending to the level of boring communicators of information.

The invisible elements of *Dante's Inferno* are superbly handled, with the sound editing of the multiple voiceovers being particularly strong. *Dante's Inferno* has an aural density which Orson Welles would be proud of: and, yes, I have put Welles and Russell together in the same sentence! Go look at *Dante's Inferno* again, and *listen* to how the editors (Mike Bradsell and Roger Crittenden) and the sound editors (Stan Morcom and Sandy

MacRae) are fusing images with many voices.

And the *levels* of narration are important, too: it's not simply one kind of voiceover, from, say, a TV documentary narrator telling the audience about people, places and dates. And the addressees also change. Some of it is from letters. Some of it is interior monologue. Some of it is interior monologue in the form of poetry. Some of it is from other people's poesie which is shifted so now it's about Rossetti or Siddal. And, folks, that poetry isn't straightforward 'the cat sat on the mat' kinda poetry.

We're talking about a very intelligent script, which assumes that audiences can get to grips with late 19th century poetry, and very highly stylized poetry (with a vocabulary not in use today).

And the music: what a soundtrack *Dante's Inferno* has! Some of the music is really unexpected and unusual,[33] including cheesy 1960s organ music, 'Cuando, Cuando, Cuando' (the kind you might've heard during the interval in a cinema). But also a strident, classical organ piece which surges underneath the footage. Also in the soundtrack is 'There's No Business Like Show Business' (by Irving Berlin), 'I Want To Be Happy', 'In a Persian Market' by Albert Ketèlbey (from the 1920s), 'Ma, He's Making Eyes At Me', a s-l-o-w version of the *Wedding March*, music box tinklings, a slow, haunting choral cue for the final scenes, John Ireland, Alban Berg's *Wozzeck* (1922), Sergei Prokofiev's *Third Symphony* and extracts from Gustav Holst's *The Planets*.

Or to put it another way, it's another highly eclectic soundtrack from Ken Russell, which further separates *Dante's Inferno* from all of British TV in the 1960s. Or put it like this: there is no film or TV show in the history of cinema with a soundtrack like that. *Dante's Inferno* probably contains the finest mixture of library music in Russell's *œuvre*.

☥

The self-consciously over-the-top fantasy sequence in *Dante's Inferno* with the knights in armour fighting an unseen dragon which's merely tons of smoke beautifully satirizes the obsession of the Pre-Raphaelites and their ilk with all things mediæval and Arthurian[34] (you can still see that fascination today, in J.R.R.

---

33 For instance, 'There's No Business Like Show Business' is played under a scene of Rossetti and Cornforth cavorting and running about amongst farm animals in a field. That famous piece of music has never been used like that, b4 or since.
34 Apparently, they – calling themselves the Jovial Campaign – did used to do stuff like this.

Tolkien,[35] the *Lord of the Rings* movies, British fantasy, etc). And you gotta love Ollie Reed riding an old bicycle as a knight in armour wielding a lance, and the shift from dragons to a steam engine (done with sound effects, because no train and no dragon appear). Even without Algernon Swinburne's cynical mocking of the scene in the voiceover (and to camera) – the Brotherhood are battling against Progress in the form of a railroad engine – it works. It shows what a silly bunch of white, English, aristocratic toffs these guys were.

✝

Looking at *Dante's Inferno* today, you wonder what British television audiences made of it back in the Sixties, because Ken Russell and his team were operating at such a high level of sophistication and intelligence. This is not only culturally advanced material to begin with, dealing with high art, it is also a very dense and intense kind of filmmaking, which expects the viewer to keep up all the way.

Jean-Luc Godard remarked that you give 10% of yourself to the average Hollywood movie. They are often no-brainer stuff, dumb stuff; you can flick round ten different Hollywood movies on TV and follow the story in each one. They don't tax the brain none. But to his movies, Godard said people gave a lot more of themselves, 90%.

Well, Ken Russell's works also require a lot of the audience's attention and mind. You get out what you put in, to a degree. And if you launch yourself into Russell's movies, there is so much there, so much going on, so much packed into the corners and spaces.

✝

For Ken Russell, *Dante's Inferno* was about 'the dream of the idyllic life or love that doesn't exist'. And it's about guilt: 'all Rossetti's poems are full of guilt' (B, 132). The film relates most of that guilt to Rossetti's love affairs, in particular with Lizzie Siddal. And it was about death:

> about death, about physical and moral decay. The Pre-Raphaelites cut themselves off and tried to create something from the decay of the industrial revolution, and they only succeeded in doing what Debussy did, incarcerating themselves in an atmosphere of nightmare which destroyed them.

---

35 Tolkien was of course influenced by William Morris.

Dante Gabriel Rossetti valued his painting less than his poetry towards the end of his life, it seems. 'I wish one could live by writing poetry. I think I'd see painting d—d if one could', he wrote in 1871 to Ford Maddox Ford. It's the recurring motif in Ken Russell's cinema too of the artist struggling to survive financially in the world. Yeah, but no one thrives on poetry alone. There b'ain't be no money in it, see? Poets have always had to do other things to make ends meet.

☥

The recreations of some of the famous Pre-Raphaelite works (including how they were produced) are delightful. Especially when the filmmakers put a twist on them. There's Holman Hunt's famous *The Light of the World* (1854, Keble College, Oxford), for instance – Jesus holding a lantern – but the model for Christ is a woman wearing a beard. Yes, a woman dressed as Jesus is still a rare thing to see in movies (imagine the controversy if Elizabeth Taylor instead of Max von Sydow had played Jesus in *The Greatest Story Ever Told* of 2 years earlier!).

*Ophelia* (1852) by John Everett Millais (Derek Boshier), an iconic Pre-Raphaelite image, is cited many times, including the scene where Lizzie Siddal posed for Millais in the bath (for the first time Gabriel Rossetti and Siddal meet). Later, when D.G. Rossetti is haunted by her death, *Dante's Inferno* recreates *Ophelia* in a fantasy sequence.[36]

*Dante's Inferno* does show artists at work many, many times. Dante Gabriel Rossetti is writing poetry, he's drawing, he's painting. Some of the best scenes in Ken Russell's cinema of artists at work occur in the Oxford Union sequence, with Jane Burden standing on a plank between two ladders, as she poses for Guinevere, playing with a yo-yo (she modelled for both Rossetti and William Morris). And the artists (Rossetti, Burne-Jones, Morris) sit high on ladders, painting and gossiping and fooling around. And, as if they're all Harpo Marx confronted with a raving beauty, they all stand and stare dumbly at Burden. It's just marvellous.

The scene of the four artists and their Muse punting on the River Isis is a thoroughly classic, English scene. They are all stare

---

[36] There's plenty of physical acting for Oliver Reed and Judith Paris in *Dante's Inferno* – they are clambering over boulders and wading through freezing streams in the Lake District – which every Russell actor had to do – and Paris is floating in cold rivers, and also in the sea. And I bet they didn't have wet suits.

at Jane Burden, Gabriel Rossetti plays with her hair, and of course William Morris recites poetry. It's striking just how effortlessly Ken Russell and his team seem able to stage scenes such as this.

Of course, the cultural allusions to the very well-known Arthurian legends – which constitute Britain's own alternative mythology to Christianity – chime here with the love triangle between Arthur, Lancelot and Guinevere (and also Isolde, Tristan and King Mark), and Morris, Rossetti and Janey (the editors cut to close-ups of the principals, so we link them to the figures from mythology). The murals of 1857, which were never finished, were inspired by *Morte d'Arthur*. (Notice that Lizzie Siddal arrives, and has the meaning of the frescoes explained to her).

*Dante's Inferno* is steeped in Pre-Raphaelite art and culture, with countless references to famous works. The filmmakers' research is stuffed into every available space in *Dante's Inferno*. It's really a series of ten art history lectures, or a complete Open University or online art history course: *British Art, 1860-1890*.

Some of the most effective recreations of Pre-Raphaelite art occur in the fantasy and dream sequences, in which the filmmakers make a movie in the style of Pre-Raphaelite art. For instance, the stunning footage of Gala Mitchell's Jane Burden in the boat on the lake (Derwentwater Lake). There's a very effective moment where the boat's pushed away from the camera, and Burden (somehow managing to stay upright) has her arms raised in a gesture of farewell (or supplication?), and Rossetti's heard in voiceover crying, 'don't leave me!'[37] It's the mirror image of the scene where Rossetti walks away from the ailing Lizzie Siddal, who also called out to him. But Rossetti of course imagines the departing lover as a grand vision in a spectacular wilderness.

There are also scenes shot as if with the light employed in a Pre-Raphaelite painting: that is, the soft glow in dark Victorian interiors, as if reflected from the wings of an angel flying into a sunset. (Emulating the lighting in famous paintings is the kinda challenge cinematographers enjoy, but it takes time to set up the lamps).

Lizzie Siddal appears as Joan of Arc in the stunning opening scenes: she is a vision glimpsed on the other side of the revolutionary bonfire of 1848, right out of the cinema of Fritz Lang or F.W. Murnau, clad in shiny armour, wielding a giant sword, at

---

[37] A smash cut, right after Rossetti and Burden are in bed discussing Rossetti having children.

night, with flames writhing below her. Wow! What an entrance! (Images that good are of course reprised later on).

And the scene – of Dante Gabriel Rossetti staring at her, and Lizzie Siddal staring back at him – perfectly embodies the relationship of the artist and Muse, the artist and lover, the artist and woman, the artist and pure mystery, the artist and life itself.

☥

*Dante's Inferno* could've explored the Pre-Raphaelites much further, of course: their story of artists and models and wives and lovers is one of Britain's art history soap operas (John Millais, married John Ruskin's ex-wife, for instance – they are glimpsed hurtling thru a forest in delight, presumably eloping).

There is plenty of comedy, too, in *Dante's Inferno* – the scene where Lizzie Siddal returns from her health treatment in France, for instance, is played for broad farce: Siddal throws out Fanny Cornforth from Rossetti's rooms, and, soon after that, Holman Hunt's wife; meanwhile, on the street below, Rossetti's family (sister, brother and mother) are coming to see him. Cornforth, in high spirits at the silliness of it all, and partially clothed, rushes past loudly; the scene closes with the OTT gag, right out of *Laurel and Hardy*, of the three Rossettis being smothered in heaps of the ivory dust that John Ruskin gave to Siddal.

☥

There's something mysterious and compelling about Ken Russell's finest TV shows and movies about Britain and British cultural life. They reach aspects of British life which do not appear in *any* other filmmaker's work. It is something to do with the landscape. It is something to do with a romantic, nostalgic view of life. It is something deeply, deeply poetic. It is something distinctly *British* – and, even more, distinctly *English*.

You can see it in *Dante's Inferno*, in *Savage Messiah*, in *Women In Love*, and in *Tommy*. Yes, and even the movies set in France, Germany, Russia, Austria, such as *Delius: Song of Summer*, *Isadora Duncan*, *Mahler*, *Lisztomania* and *The Dance of the Seven Veils*, it's there (but not, alas, in *The Rainbow* or *Gothic* or *The Lair of the White Worm* or *Lady Chatterley*).

*Dante's Inferno* also evokes an atmosphere that is convincing at every level – what do filmmakers trying to be 'contemporary' sometimes call it? – 'immersive' (but *all* good storytelling in *any* medium is 'immersive'!). *Dante's Inferno* immerses the viewer in a beautifully realized world of London and Oxford and the coast and the lakes, of eccentric artists and their crazy ideas and luxurious paintings, and an erotic tangle of lovers, wives, and husbands.

There's also the uneasy relationship between an artist and his benefactors, one of Ken Russell's recurring themes. Here, it's Rossetti and the ascetic æsthete John Ruskin (Clive Goodwin), who's later replaced by his art dealer, Charles Augustus Howell, played with cool disdain by David Jones (the touch of Howell carrying a lizard is inspired: Howell is a much more sinister fish than Ruskin: it's Howell who brings Rossetti the film's MacGuffin, the book of poems, and forces Rossetti to confront it).

ECHOES.

There are numerous repetitions and echoes, of whole scenes, of visual emblems, of lines of poetry in *Dante's Inferno*. For instance: the opening scene of the coffin is replayed, but with variations, later on, when it becomes the centrepiece of a fantasy sequence after Lizzie Siddal's death. • There are two scenes where lovers desert their partners (Rossetti leaving Siddal; Janey leaving Rossetti). • There are two scenes where a man watches behind some trees as the object of his desire is with another man (Rossetti watches Morris and Janey, later Morris takes his place, spying on Rossetti and his wife Janey). • There are two scenes on the hillside overlooking the lake with a dead tree (this forms the closing image of the piece – it was also the setting for the much happier times of courtship between Rossetti and Siddal).[38] • The coffin and the bath are visually rhymed, as well as the theme of suicide – in a bed, in a bath, and in a river, as Ophelia). • There are two scenes where a man wanders alone in the wilderness in a kind of self-imposed exile (Morris in Iceland, Rossetti by the river). • There are two scenes where a woman plays outside on a see-saw and a swing just before Rossetti starts an affair with them (Annie Miller, left by Holman Hunt (Douglas Gray) in Rossetti's care, b4 leaving for the Middle East, and Topsy Morris b4 he goes to Iceland).

As well as numerous repetitions and parallel scenes, there are pairs which are continually compared: two women, for instance: Siddal and Miller, Siddal and Burden, Siddal and Cornforth,

---

[38] Happier – but Rossetti is irritated that Siddal doesn't really understand his poetry.

Siddal and Christina Rossetti, Burden and Cornforth.

POETRY.

There are numerous quotations from poetry by D.G.R., his sister Christina, Lizzie Siddal, William Morris, etc. There is probably more poetry in *Dante's Inferno* than in any of Ken Russell's other films, and more than in most movies (even those about poets). Joseph Gomez has studied the use of poetry in *Dante's Inferno*. The Rossetti quotes include 'Beauty and the Bird', 'Valentine To Lizzie Siddal', 'The House of Life', 'Alas, So Long', and 'Even So'.

The quotations of poetry run from adolescent love poetry to the wistful, nostalgic reminiscences of old age. Time and death and how they work on love and life are the recurring themes. For the courtship scene, sitting in Russell Land's central zone – the hills of the Lake District – D.G. Rossetti entertains Lizzie Siddal with lines from "I looked and saw your eyes":

> I looked and saw your eyes
>     In the shadow of your hair,
> As the traveller sees the stream
>     In the shadow of the wood...

By the end of *Dante's Inferno*, when Lizzie Siddal is long gone and the 1967 movie enters some of the most fascinating and lyrical dream-fantasy-imagined sequences in Ken Russell's cinema, the poetry is classic High Victorian regret and remorse: Dante Gabriel Rossetti recites from 'Alas, So Long' in the final scene, when he's beaten, worn-out, at the end of life:

> Ah! dear one, you've been dead so long, –
>     How long until we meet again,
> Where hours may never lose their song
>     Nor flowers forget the rain
> In glad moonlight that never shall wane?
>         Alas, so long!
>     Ah, shall it then Spring weather,
>     And ah! shall we be young together?

But the poetry is complexly interwoven with the images; and it also includes Lizzie Siddal, now dead, speaking some of the lines. It's a moving evocation of regret, nostalgia, loss and romantic desire.

Christina Rossetti wrote a poem about the Rossetti-Siddal relationship, which's quoted in the film:

> One face looks out from all his canvases,
> One selfsame figure sits or walks or leans:
> We found her hidden just behind those screens,
> That mirror gave back all her loveliness.
> A queen in opal or in ruby dress,
> A nameless girl in freshest summer-greens,
> A saint, an angel – every canvas means
> The same one meaning, neither more nor less.
> He feeds upon her face by day and night,
> And she with true kind eyes looks back on him,
> Fair as the moon and joyful as the light:
> Not wan with waiting, not with sorrow dim;
> Not as she is, but was when hope shone bright;
> Not as she is, but as she fills his dream.

As a movie about a poet as well as a painter, *Dante's Inferno* is sensationally good. Compare it with the more recent biopic about John Keats, *Bright Star* (2009). In this well-meaning, modest but ultimately dull movie, John Keats (Ben Whishaw) comes across as a rather insensitive drip (there's no indication whatsoever that he is capable of writing great poetry), and Fanny Brawne (Abbie Cornish), who adored Keats, comes over as a passionate woman disastrously attached to a wash-out and a loser. *Bright Star* is hopelessly reverential to its subject – to Keats, but also to Brawne, and also their love affair. And at 119 minutes, *Bright Star* is one of the *longest* and *slowest* and *dullest* movies ever. (How did any viewer make it to the end of *Bright Shit*? Always hoping it would improve – it *didn't*! I can't remember how I got thru it – must've been the laudanum or opium).

THE DECLINE AND FALL.

Edgar Allan Poe's influence is in there, once again, as it was in *The Debussy Film*: the scenes where Dante Gabriel Rossetti is declining into drink-and-drug-induced self-loathing in the rooms in Chelsea are filmed in a Gothic, Romantic manner: Rossetti glowers up at his portrait of Lizzie Siddal on the wall, eternally haunted. Her voice's heard on the soundtrack, and in scenes that might be dreams, or flash-forwards, or real life, Rossetti reaches for the chloral or laudanum in a cupboard as he rehearses his suicide.

Long stretches of the latter part of *Dante's Inferno* are wordless, with ominous classical cues providing the soundtrack to streams of hallucinatory images. This is Ken Russell in his favourite film-making mode, interweaving life, dream-life, fantasy-life and the past. There is so much poetry, so much music, and the atmosphere conjured up here is like nothing else in television or cinema. It's simply a marvellous piece of work.

Dante's Inferno (aired December 22, 1967)

Dante Gabriel Rossetti and his women,
in 1967's Dante's Inferno

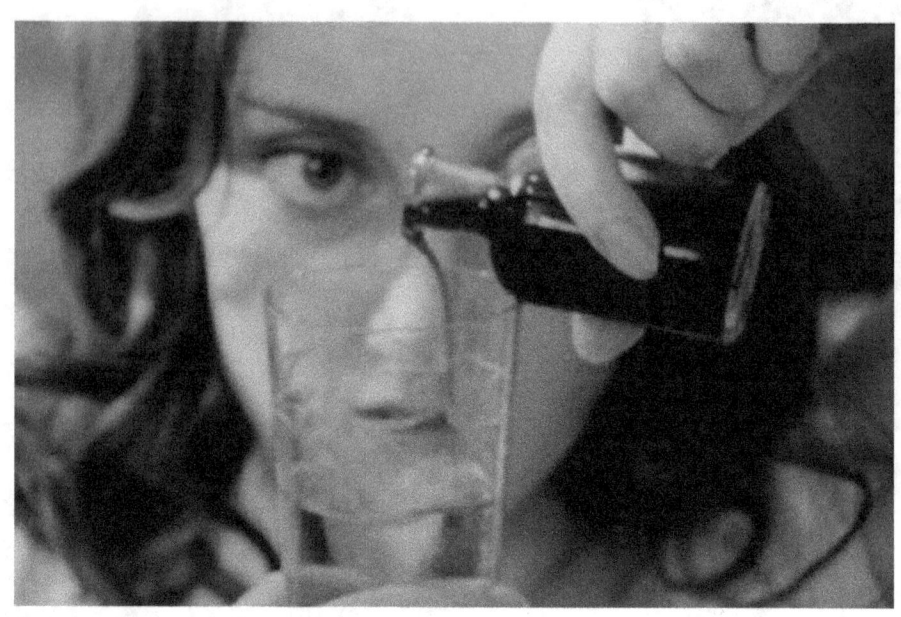

Death, suicide - the recurring theme in Ken Russell's art of the artist haunted by death and the people around him who suffer. Images from Dante's Inferno (1967), recreating John Everett Millais' iconic Ophelia, with Rossetti's lover Lizzie Siddal as Ophelia (above). And another dose of The Cabinet of Dr Caligari (below).

John Everett Millais, Ophelia.
An icon of Pre-Raphaelite art,
quoted in Dante's Inferno

Dante Gabriel Rossetti, Dante's Dream At the Time of the Death of Beatrice, 1871, Walker Art Gallery

Dante Gabriel Rossetti, Self-Portrait (right), and Beata Beatrix (above).

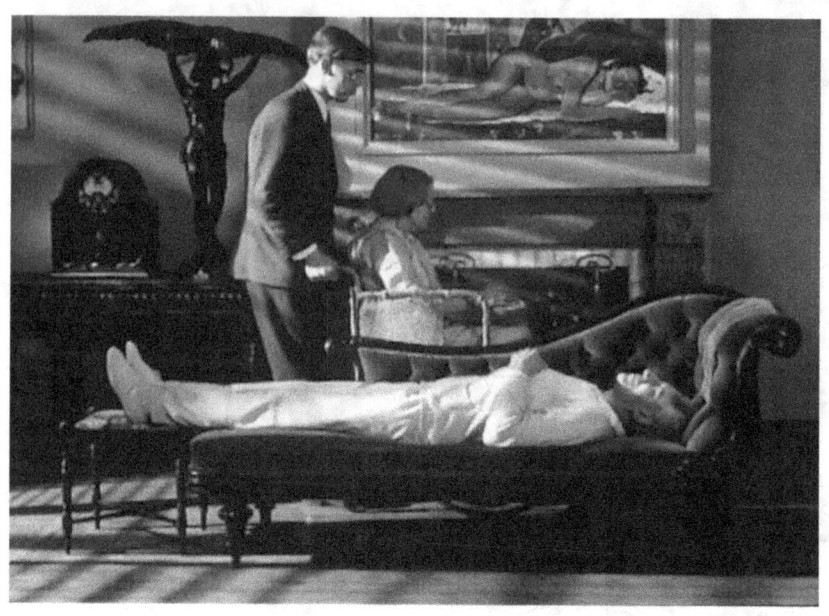

Thsi page over: images from Delius: Song of Summer

A masterful depiction of artistic creation at work
in Delius: Song of Summer

# 5

# *DELIUS: SONG OF SUMMER*

> Most of the people in my films are taken a bit by surprise, like Isadora and Delius. They're out of step with their times and their society, but nevertheless manage to produce rather extraordinary changes in attitudes and events.
>
> Ken Russell, *An Appalling Talent* (205)

1968's *Delius: Song of Summer* (tx 1968.9.15) is a superb piece of early Russellania. It starred Max Adrian, Maureen Pryor and Christopher Gable (this was Gable's first lead role in a movie). Essentially, it was a modest, small-scale drama documentary made for BBC television about the last years of the classical music composer Frederick Delius's life, when he managed to create despite being blind and disabled. The film was seen through the eyes of Eric Fenby, a young Brit who visits Delius in Grez-sur-Loing in France. Most of the film boiled down to two or three people in a house (which's many movies), but the subject matter – the artist, artistic creation, and in particular music – was as expansive as ever in Ken Russell's cinema.

Frederick Delius (January 29, 1862 - June 10, 1934) was English, but of German parentage (he was born in Bradford in Yorkshire), taught in North America, studied in Leipzig, and settled in Grez-sur-Loing near Fountainbleau in Northern France. Delius's works include *Songs of Sunset, Requiem, A Song of the High Hills, Over the Hills and Far Away, Paris, Summer Night On the River, The Magic Fountain* and *Fenninmore and Gerda.*

The 1968 *Delius* movie takes in most of the facts about Frederick Delius's life, which're noted in dialogue or images: his time in Paris, in Florida (where he was taught by Thomas Ward, an organist in Jacksonville, in 1884), in Leipzig (at the Conservatoire in 1886), teaching in the U.S.A., friendship with Edvard Grieg in Norway, and with Percy Grainger, marriage to Jelka Rosen (in 1897), the concerts of his works in England (in 1907-1909), his contraction of syphilis in 1922 (and subsequent paralysis and blindness), his visit from Eric Fenby in 1928, and his wife Jelka Rosen being a German painter (there are many paintings in the house, including by Edvard Munch and Paul Gauguin – Rosen was of Danish descent).

*Delius: Song of Summer* is not in the front rank of Ken Russell's films, among most critics, but for me it is, because it is a very fine piece of work, and is one of the maestro's films which is all the better for being modest and not as flamboyant as more well-known pieces. If you go back and have a look at *Delius: Song of Summer*, you'll discover a delightful gem of a film. It is one of Russell's favourites among his movies: 'it's one of the my favourite films, and perhaps the truest, because I was able to get the story and the atmosphere at first hand' (Bax, 136).[1]

*Delius: Song of Summer* was shot in crisp black-and-white by regular Ken Russell cameraman Dick Bush (in high contrast, too – very white walls, and deep blacks), and even by today's standards, the narrative moves along at a rapid pace (Russell's films don't date in terms of editing and pace). Roger Crittenden cut the movie, Shirley Kingdon was costumier, make-up was by Eileen Mair, sound by Stan Morcom and John Murphy, and production design by Judy Steel.

The idea, Ken Russell explained, was to develop a style which would offer a filmic correlative of Delius the man: 'we shot the film with very high contrast. Delius was a hard character who talked in very black and white terms. Everything was good or everything was bad, so the environment had to be very contrasty' (quoted in G, 66). The influence of the cinematography of both Ingmar Bergman and Orson Welles is obvious.

The 1968 BBC movie presents figures isolated against white backgrounds, Ken Russell said, which emphasizes their loneli-

---
[1] Among the film's fans is pop star Kate Bush; she wrote a song inspired by the movie.

ness. *Delius: Song of Summer* also includes many close-ups: the viewer is right in there amongst the characters.

Ken Russell said he had written a script about Frederick Delius some time before *Delius: Song of Summer*, but 'it was really a rather boring story'. Delius *plus* Eric Fenby, however, was a different story: it's a love affair and a death affair; it's one personality feeding on another and being destroyed for his trouble' (PF, 85). Delius becomes the vampire sucking the life out of Fenby, a Count Dracula to his Jonathan Harker. Fenby described Delius as 'hard, stern, proud, cynical, godless, completely self-absorbed'.

Ken Russell spent a lot of time with Eric Fenby, and absorbed all he could from him about Frederick Delius. The film was based on Fenby's book, *Delius As I Knew Him*, but Russell was also able to talk to Fenby at length about Delius, even down to pieces of dialogue that Fenby remembered:

> I'd ask Fenby about a particular event and he'd just tell me the dialogue for it. It was the most immediate impression I've ever had of any person I've filmed. (Bax, 137)

Eric Fenby also discussed the film with the actors, including advising Max Adrian on how Frederick Delius spoke. Fenby lived with Frederick and Jelka Delius in Grez-sur-Loing from 1928 to mid-1933, and returned to Germany when Delius was dying, in 1934.

The central relationship of *Delius: Song of Summer* was the familiar one of father and son, great artist and disciple, teacher and student, rendered endlessly interesting by the two strong performances from Max Adrian and Christopher Gable (this is Adrian's show, tho', and he makes sure everyone knows it!), superb support from Maureen Pryor, and a script by Ken Russell and Eric Fenby which tackled artistic creation from a number of angles (Fenby's account of his time with Delius, *Delius As I Knew Him*, had been published in 1936).

There are a couple of minor characters in the house – the maid (played by Elizabeth Ercy) and Bruder (Roger Worrod).[2] They are also involved in the round-the-clock reading aloud from books.

Max Adrian (1903-73) was a veteran of theatre, including

---

[2] Ken Russell thought it would have been good if Fenby'd had an affair with the maid, but no, he didn't (Russell also mused that the actress was attractive enough to be the next Brigitte Bardot).

spells at the Old Vic; in Gotham in the 1930s; with John Gielgud's rep company in the 1940s; as a founder member with the Royal Shakespeare Company (in 1960); and the National Theatre (from 1963). His famous roles included Feste in *Twelfth Night*, the Cardinal in *The Duchess of Malfi*, Serebryakov in *Uncle Vanya*, and the Inquisitor in *Saint Joan*. Adrian specialized in revue shows (in the 1940s), and performed his one-man shows about Gilbert & Sullivan and George Bernard Shaw in the 1960s.

Without doubt the most impressive sequences in *Delius: Song of Summer* were those involving musical composition. With Eric Fenby at the piano[3] and Frederick Delius sitting straight-backed and frozen beside him, the film beautifully depicted Delius composing and Fenby taking down the compositions, as well as commenting upon them and altering them.

In his later novelization of the life of Frederick Delius, *Delius: A Moment With Venus*, Ken Russell described the scene thus:

> And so for many months, with Eric at the piano and Delius seated by his side, they fought to give life to something of real potential that might well have remained stillborn. It was a battle of wills, with Delius calling out the notes and instrumentation and Eric illustrating them on the piano and occasionally suggesting alternatives and thoughts of his own. (2007, 169)

There were detailed musical elements, too – an A sharp here, a D major there. At these times, when *Delius* shifted into lyrical montage mode, Ken Russell and the team delivered memorable equivalents for the mysterious act of creation (in particular a montage sequence illustrating the music with images of the sea and seagulls).[4] And the scenes of composition demonstrated Russell's belief that art is 'basically hard work with only about five per cent inspiration', as Joseph Gomez pointed out (65).

This was what *Delius: Song of Summer* was really about, for Ken Russell: musical creation. To depict the hard work of artistic creation, how it took a good deal effort to drag the music out of Frederick Delius's head, as Russell put it (like the carving-the-sculpture scene in *Savage Messiah*).

And it was also about the *costs* of artistic creation, how artists are selfish (because they have to be, said Ken Russell), and how

---
3 It does appear that Christopher Gable is really playing those notes, too – very impressive (Ken Russell recalled that the notes and dialogue was written down on the manuscript in front of Gable).
4 The sea and cliffs scenes where filmed near Scarborough.

that affects the people around them. That is, Eric Fenby sacrifices his own art and his own life for Frederick Delius (the people around an artist make the sacrifices willingly, Russell reckoned).

As an exploration of the artistic process and the costs to the artist and those around them of creativity, *Delius: Song of Summer* is as good as any movie I can think of in British cinema. And certainly in Ken Russell's cinema it hasn't been bettered (for instance, the depiction of creating art isn't spoilt by awe or sentimentality; it's actually very straightforward – in theory, at least).

And *Delius: Song of Summer* found time to sit and listen to music, too (as we often do in a Ken Russell movie), as the composer, his wife Jelka and Eric Fenby listened to Frederick Delius's own compositions or African American spirituals on a wind-up gramophone.[5]

So that *Delius: Song of Summer* didn't become too claustrophobic and interior-based, there were many excursions to places outside that hothouse: walks in the woods to collect flowers or vegetables, a flashback to the misty mountains, walks along the road, a visit from Percy Grainger[6] (which included running in the forest), and early scenes of Eric Fenby beside the ocean.

Essentially a chamber piece, with a single location (the house at Grez-sur-Loing), those exterior scenes were a welcome relief from the sometimes intense dramas unfolding inside the house. It helped too that there were filmed in burnished black-and-white.

There's also a scene where Eric Fenby, who can't stand the pressure anymore, rushes outside and onto some railway tracks, perhaps with a view to killing himself (which Fenby said really happened).

The BBC drama documentary didn't need to undelrine everything, either: Eric Fenby remained a mystery, and it wasn't explained why he stayed with Frederick Delius for so many years (especially since Delius wasn't the easiest guy to get along with!). The film wasn't interested in Fenby so much as his relationship with Delius. And Delius was of course the diva at the heart of the piece.

There were all sorts of narrative branches in *Delius: Song of*

---

5 It was Frederick Delius's own gramophone, Ken Russell said, which had been given to Eric Fenby. The film depicted a scene where Fenby is given a brass pocket watch – all he gets, Russell quipped, for four years' work.
6 Accompanied by some of Percy Grainger's music.

*Summer* which could have been explored – Eric Fenby's relation to his family back home, for instance, or exactly what Frederick Delius was like in his younger days (that was suggested in the scene where Fenby meets a neighbour, which Ken Russell and the team kept deliberately mysterious, with the actor (Geraldine Sherman) shrouded by leaves).[7]

Ken Russell said there was lots more he could've put into the film about Frederick Delius, and about his past. But the 1968 movie concentrated on Delius in old age,[8] with Eric Fenby as the observer figure for the audience to identify with: Fenby was the way-in for the audience, so his own story was suppressed.

Once again, in *Delius: Song of Summer* Ken Russell demonstrated his genius for exploiting a low budget and using locations to the maximum. Most memorable were the excursions into the mountains – it was the Lakes in Northern Britain yet again, of course. A snowy trek in flashback over the mountains in Norway to see the sun setting, with Frederick Delius being carted around in a chair on poles by a Norwegian guy and Percy Grainger, was marvellous. This was Russell's interpretation of Delius's *A Song of the High Hills*, which described in his novelization of *The Dance of the Seven Veils*:

> With the help of a burly Norwegian guide they had strapped Fred to a chair, lashed it to a couple of poles and lugged him all the way up to the top of a hill in a freezing mist, which miraculously cleared to reveal a most glorious sunset. (2007, 173-4)

The sequence (reminiscent of Leni Riefenstahl and German mountaineering films) is one of Ken Russell's finest, and sweeps aside yet again any doubts about Russell as a monumentally talented filmmaker. It's about art and the artist, and about transcendence and beauty, of course, and about the Romantic Sublime (J.M.W. Turner would've loved it), but it was also about the costs of such ambitious enterprises on the people around the artist.

Part of the reason that the filmmakers shot this scene early in the schedule was according to Ken Russell to humble the actors and 'show them they're at the mercy of the elements, and of me'

---

[7] That encounter is meant to be enigmatic, and it isn't wholly convincing the way it's staged, where Eric Fenby just meets her in the bushes.
[8] Ken Russell had considered filming Frederick Delius and other characters at a younger age. He also thought of illustrating some of Delius's music with fantasies inspired by the music, but decided that the film didn't need that.

(PF, 87). It was also because he liked to do the physical tough stuff and the location work early on, as many filmmakers do (before everybody gets knackered).

Much of *Delius: Song of Summer* was also about caring for someone who's ill – all done with a patience and sensitivity that belied Ken Russell's reputation as a director of somewhat emotionally cold films. The tenderness with which the people in Frederick Delius's life care for him was palpable – and that despite his irascible and often downright obnoxious behaviour (Russell wondered if he could have stood up to Delius. Two divas in one room?! No!). Just as much as the music, *Delius: Song of Summer* is about people caring for someone who's slowly dying. (As such, the film had an inevitable slide towards gloom, lightened by the rapturous quality of Delius's music).⁹

And *Delius: Song of Summer* contained some archetypal Russellisms: Frederick Delius in his garden worshipping the sun; the snowy mountain trek; the musical composition scenes; and the sudden appearance of composer Percy Grainger, dashing through the house to catch a tennis ball.

The sun-worshipping scene in *Delius: Song of Summer* occurs when Frederick Delius mentions that he can understand the ancient Persians worshipping the sun – a classic piece of Russellian dialogue (and Delius's impatient moans about wanting the sun to come out of course mirror the film director beaten by the elements time and again, as the crew wait for the light).

At times Bergmanesque,¹⁰ *Delius: Song of Summer* hints at repressed sexuality in a number of ways, from the *mise-en-scène* of the paintings by Edvard Munch (Munch one of the kings of angst-ridden, sex-obsessed, European Expressionism) and Paul Gauguin, to the allusions to syphilis and adultery. The repression of erotic desire is in Eric Fenby too, of course, but is subtly brought out by the filmmakers (subtly, that is, compared to some of Ken Russell's later works!). And as Frederick Delius advises Fenby, 'an artist should never marry', with suggestions of chastity, and sublimating sexuality in the Nietzschean manner,¹¹

---

9 One of the final images is of Frederick Delius on his couch, dead, with Eric Fenby and Rosen behind him, strewing white flowers over his body – staged in a *tableau*-style, like a painting.
10 I wonder if Ken Russell and his team were inspired by the films of Ingmar Bergman: movies such as *Persona*, *The Silence* and *Through a Glass Darkly*, intense and intimate dramas shot in crisp black-and-white, seem to be models of *Delius: Song of Summer* (Russell was certainly a big Bergman fan).
11 There's a portrait of Friedrich Nietzsche on the wall.

but also perhaps keeping mistresses and not being tied to one woman.

◉

Ken Russell was very fond of *Delius: Song of Summer*, and it remained one of his favourite films. Despite concentrating on only three people in a house, it explored some very important themes – particularly artistic creation, how art is made, and also artistic collaboration. And how those living with an artist are affected. Russell said that Benjamin Britten and Igor Stravinsky had liked it.

Ken Russell was delighted that Eric Fenby himself had said the BBC movie was an accurate depiction of his time with Frederick Delius. Russell recalled that one time when Fenby visited the set he wept – it was all coming back to him.[12]

The odd relationship between Frederick Delius and Eric Fenby fascinated Ken Russell, and that kind of relationship would crop up in later works, such as *Lisztomania*. As Russell put it in *A British Picture*, Fenby was 'sometimes willing, sometimes reluctant, his love of the music overriding his distaste for the man' (BP, 3).

---

[12] Although some might think that crying is bad, or not a good response to a movie, it's flattering to a filmmaker when they can move an audience like that.

# 6

# *DANCE OF THE SEVEN VEILS*

> It was meant to be an upsetting film, insofar as it's an upsetting subject. It's the artist just throwing his responsibility to the winds, and going along with the establishment... Strauss sold everyone down the river very fast. He was *a Fascist composer*. Everything he did, I think, was a glorification of the Master Race... he had the possibility of affecting the lives of the nation. I don't think it's putting it too strongly to say that. He could have done a lot, and prevented a lot of suffering.
>
> Ken Russell[13]

*Dance of the Seven Veils: A Comic Strip In Seven Episodes On the Life of Richard Strauss, 1864-1949* is a truly extraordinary film. No other filmmaker in Great Britain has produced anything like it – but nor has any filmmaker in the history of cinema. Although there were important collaborators – not least the British Broadcasting Corporation in commissioning the production and paying for it, and co-writer Henry Reed, *Dance of the Seven Veils* is completely a Ken Russell movie, through and through.

Only Ken Russell could have made it.

And only Ken Russell *would* have made it.

Forty-plus years on, *Dance of the Seven Veils* is still startling, and contains material that's still very rare to see in film, television or on the web. And no, it wouldn't get made today.

*Dance of the Seven Veils* is an assassination job, similar to the

---

[13] Quoted in G, 68-69, from the original typescript of John Baxter's book.

one undertaken in *Lisztomania* of Richard Wagner. It draws, according to Joseph Gomez (G, 67), on *Richard Strauss: The Life of a Non-Hero* by George Marek, and also Strauss's letters (some of which are quoted verbatim).[14]

❧

*Dance of the Seven Veils* is among Ken Russell's most controversial productions. It has only been broadcast once – on February 15, 1970, by the British Broadcasting Corporation (the people who commissioned it).[15] And that led to the film being denounced by twenty members of the Conservative Party in the British government (politicians attack movies or TV from time to time – an easy target. It should be remembered, though, that television in Great Britain is paid for by the tax-payer: the BBC is funded by the television licence, which's enforced by law.) 'There was a *huge* rumpus', Russell recalled, 'especially from those who hadn't seen it' (Bax, 141).

Not only wouldn't the British Broadcasting Corporation be showing *Dance of the Seven Veils* any time soon following its February, 1970 broadcast (yeah, and they haven't shown it since), the music was withheld by Richard Strauss's son. Ken Russell did include extracts from *Dance of the Seven Veils* in his autobiography for the *South Bank Show*, but used Johann Strauss instead.

Indeed, the filmmakers knew that *Dance of the Seven Veils* might only be seen once – they knew they wouldn't be able to get permission from Richard Strauss's music publishers, Boosey & Hawkes, for instance, and there was no way they would submit a script to the Strauss family for approval.

In a typical move of the We Want To Please Everybody liberal approach of the BBC, the corporation put on a talk show following the *Seven Veils* broadcast in which a range of pundits, musicians and composers had their say.[16]

And Mary Whitehouse, inevitably, tried to sue the BBC, found she couldn't, then had a go at the Post Office (because they ran the means of communication, the cables and all that). That

---

[14] One of Powell and Pressburger's unrealized projects was a biopic of Richard Strauss, *The Golden Years* (it was offered to Columbia, who declined, perhaps due to Strauss's links to Nazism).

[15] And is in limbo apparently until 2019 – to do with copyright, rights, death and the copyright that lasts after death – 70 years – in this case, Richard Strauss himself, who died in 1949.

[16] And there was a disclaimer at the beginning, where dear, old Auntie Beeb announced: 'it has been described as a harsh and at times violent caricature of the life of the composer'.

backfired too.

❖

*Dance of the Seven Veils* was co-written, directed and produced by Ken Russell for the BBC, with Henry Reed co-writing. Terry Gilbert was choreographer, Dave King was editor, Derek Dodds was designer, Shirley Kingdon did the costumes, and Peter Hall was DP. *Dance of the Seven Veils* starred Christopher Gable in the performance of his career, an absolutely outstanding star turn as the composer Richard Strauss, with the wonderful Judith Paris as his wife Pauline de Ahna, Ken Colley as Adolf Hitler, Vladek Sheybal as Joseph Goebbels, James Mellor as Hermann Goering, Sally Bryant as Life (i.e., the spirit of life), Imogen Claire and Rita Webb both playing Salomé (large and small), and a host of performers playing dancers, nuns, critics, Jews, monks, and Nazis (only in Ken Russell movie – or perhaps a Mel Brooks picture – are extras called upon to play nuns one minute and Nazis the next!).

The locations in the *Richard Strauss* movie are the familiar Ken Russell ones of the Lake District – of woods and hills and lakes and waterfalls and rivers and stone bridges and castles. The mountains of Northern England once again stand in for the Alps (in the 'Alpine Symphony'), the forests of Germany, the slate quarries for Wagnerian fantasies, waterfalls and rocky streams for Nietzschean Supermen and nature mysticism, and Macbeth's castle of Dunsinane in Scotland for the *Macbeth* skit.

Many of the aspects of *Dance of the Seven Veils* are familiar Ken Russell themes or motifs: there's yet another evocation of the First World War and the trenches, for instance… there are nuns and Virgin Marys and Catholic imagery… and Nazis and Hitlers… rapid montages and crash zooms and shock cuts… and tons of dancing and lashings of music.

'All his bitterness was poured out on Richard Strauss', John Baxter remarked (1976, 35). *The Dance of the Seven Veils* is also a send-up of the po-faced, reverential, respectful, 'civil service' way of producing TV documentaries.[17]

---

[17] In *Dance of the Seven Veils*, Ken Russell and the team were sending up the documentary form, which Russell had helped to develop at the Beeb. He wanted to take apart the civil service, somewhat pompous or academic approach to documentary (Bax, 138). A satire on all of those clichés (which Ken Russell had helped to develop for television, of course). Russell wanted to 'dress people up in old clothes and do it in a totally *un*real way, and thus make it more real than ever' (Bax, 138).

♣

There are a number of Strausses in classical music, including Johann Strauss (1804-1849), his son Johann Strauss (1825-1899), Josef Strauss (1827-1870) and Eduard Strauss (1835-1916). But Richard Strauss (1864-1949) is not part of the group of related Strausses. Our Strauss studied at Munich and Berlin; he conducted at Meiningen, Berlin and Weimar. He married singer Pauline de Ahna in 1894. Strauss's influences included Franz Liszt, Hector Berlioz and Richard Wagner.

Richard Strauss worked with librettists such as Hugo von Hofmannstahl and Stefan Zweig, and also used Johann Wolfgang von Goethe, William Shakespeare and Friedrich Hölderlin for songs. Strauss's works include *Salomé, Intermezzo, Daphne, Die Liebe der Danaë, Capricio, Elektra, Don Juan, Macbeth, Don Quixote*, and symphonies, military marches, serenades, string quartets, concertos, and song cycles. His most famous pieces are probably *Also Sprach Zarathustra* and *Der Rosenkavalier*. Strauss was linked to the Nazi regime: for instance, he composed the music for the Berlin Olympic Games.

In *Dance of the Seven Veils,* the *Macbeth* skit draws on Richard Strauss's first symphonic poem (1889). The *Salomé* sketch uses Strauss's 1905 opera (Ken Russell directed this on stage in 1993 in Bonn).[18] The *Don Quixote* spoof employs Strauss's 1898 piece, while the Alpine picnic is taken from the *Alpine Symphony*.

*Also Sprach Zarathustra* is deployed in *Dance of the Seven Veils* a number of times, including the opening sequence, with the young Richard Strauss conducting and also appearing as Zarathustra himself. Then ironically, in the Hitler rally and speech; and triumphantly, when Strauss conducts it and turns back time to his youth. (*Also Sprach Zarathustra* had been popularized two years before, in the 1968 MGM movie *2001: A Space Odyssey*).

The images of Richard Strauss silhouetted on the conductor's podium come of course from the Disney Studios' *Fantasia* (in which Leopold Stokowski was silhouetted at the beginning of the animated classic on a podium): the design of the shot is consciously mirrored in the scenes of Adolf Hitler addressing the faithful at a political rally.

---

18 So altho' Russell denounced Strauss in 1970, he wasn't averse to directing an opera by Strauss in 1993.

The level of imagination and invention in *The Dance of the Seven Veils* is staggering. It really is a classic of its kind (as well as being the only one of its kind).

The sub-title of *Dance of the Seven Veils* is accurate – *A Comic Strip In Seven Episodes On the Life of Richard Strauss*. It draws attention to the episodic nature of this astounding piece of television: it is structured in a series of *tableaux* or episodes (and mini-episodes within some episodes).

The sub-title calls *Dance of the Seven Veils* a <u>comic</u> <u>strip</u>. If you don't get that, you miss the point entirely. Actually, as well as comic books, *Dance of the Seven Veils* is also a dance film, and a musical film, and a comedy. Certainly it is not a documentary in any accepted sense, but neither is it a film essay or personal essay (the kind that Jean-Luc Godard or Werner Herzog made, for instance). It's 'painted colours, bold colours, and it's superman comics,' Russell insisted.[19]

*Dance of the Seven Veils* breaks down all genres, and is impossible to classify. It is, in short, its own genre, which is of course A Ken Russell Movie. It's Russellania, or Russellanian, or Russellesque. To repeat: there is nothing else like *Dance of the Seven Veils* in all of British cinema or world cinema.

A dance film would certainly capture the genre of *Dance of the Seven Veils* to an extent, because there is dancing throughout this 1970 television piece. And a musical, because not many feet of celluloid whizz through the projector without some music being played. And a comedy – that cannot be emphasized enough. A dance-musical-comedy, then.[20]

WOW! Just look at what Ken Russell and his team were doing – and on a BBC TV budget of 1970! Budgets of TV documentaries then were relatively smaller than more recently, especially those prestige shows aimed at the international market. How the hell did Russell & co. create such a stupendous movie on such a small budget (a public service television budget!), and a *costume* piece too, and with *so many* locations, and so many *different* locations, and with such a large cast?!

It's mind-boggling.

Forget the frickin' *Blair Witch Project* or the latest trendy

---

19 Quoted in J. Gomez (1976, 76), from the typescript of J. Baxter's book.
20 There is some voiceover from Richard Strauss, and short explanations to camera, but words and dialogue are not the point of *Dance of the Seven Veils* at all.

Sundance/ Raindance/ film festival 'indie' shit. Look at *Dance of the Seven Veils*. A masterpiece of low budget filmmaking. Ken Russell is a genius.[21]

◈

In *Dance of the Seven Veils,* the filmmaking is at full throttle and Ken Russell is at the height of his powers: this is the Grand Russell of *The Devils* and *The Music Lovers,* a director whose facility for staging elaborate and meticulously choreographed scenes involving a host of actors and dancers and props and sets and costumes seems limitless. He is Britain's very own Vincente Minnelli or Busby Berkeley. And he went *beyond* even them!

The *energy* coming off the screen is in full force, like a waterfall.

*Dance of the Seven Veils* opens with an extended dance sequence played out on the lakesides and waterfalls and streams of Northern England, with Richard Strauss in his guise as a bleach-blond, white-tuniced god or hero[22] or Orpheus (or the spirit of music), dancing among his sprites and water nymphs. Oh, and nuns, of course (there are plenty of nuns in this forerunner of *The Devils*). And, typically, the choreography runs from graceful, classical ballet movements (very Isadora Duncan) to crazed hysteria, from musical hall play-acting to Marx Brothers and silent comedy, as Ken Russell, Terry Gilbert and co. stage another of Russell's bacchanalias or Dionysian orgies.

The filmmaking here is outstanding, with a genius feeling for framing and staging – for instance, for slow reveals via zoom outs, or startling match cuts. The fusion of choreography with camerawork is sensational – look at the way that Ken Russell and the team employ the terrain, putting their dancers atop rocks and cliffs, for example, or next to rushing streams.

Much of the credit for brilliance of *Dance of the Seven Veils* must go to Terry Gilbert, Ken Russell's regular choreographer, who created some exciting dance routines in amongst the natural splendour of the Lakes, in woods, in fields, beside water, in theatres, etc. The opening scenes of *Dance of the Seven Veils* were simply marvellous, some of the best dance numbers that Russell has put on screen.

---

21 'In my opinion Ken Russell is a genius, by which I mean that his films are extraordinary, unique, and provide a view of the world that is new and profound,' remarked Jack Fisher (67).

22 Why couldn't he be a hero? Richard Strauss wondered, and compared himself to Napoleon Buonaparte and Alexander the Great in a letter.

♣

Among the extraordinary sequences in *Dance of the Seven Veils* were: a nun writhing on top of Richard Strauss, surrounded by ecstatic nuns. *Also Sprach Zarathustra* appeared in a scene of Adolf Hitler addressing the multitudes at a Nazi rally, the familiar gestures in time with the music. If it hadn't gone further, that scene might have been accepted as comedy (but not by every viewer). But Ken Russell and his team went further: evoking anti-semitism, the desecration of Christian symbols (a statue of the Virgin Mary is thrown down by Hitler and stamped on, and Christ on the Cross is hurled onto the ground and becomes a swastika in a jump cut, which's then held aloft). The nuns, wailing over the toppled Madonna, are now transformed into worshipful Hitler Youth.

In these jump cuts – from Christ to a swastika, from a swastika to a Star of David – *Dance of the Seven Veils* ups the ante in stirring up controversy. But there's more, including the sacrifice of a cow, conducted by a rabbi, with a group of Jews nodding their heads in grotesque caricatures.[23] The sacrificial knife dripping with blood held up by the rabbi in front of the Star of David is one of numerous memorable images in this outrageous sequence. As Ken Russell insisted: '*It was meant to be an upsetting film*, insofar as it's an upsetting subject' (my italics).

♦

One of the most amusing scenes in *Dance of the Seven Veils* had Richard Strauss and an orchestra attacking the crrrritics. It was a scene where Ken Russell got back at the critics, who were already launching their attacks on his work (but the vitriol would continue far beyond 1970).[24]

The assault on the critics began with a scene in a theatre, with the critics assembled in a theatre box, costumed in black coats and top hats, and giggling inanely at the performance of *Don Juan* (not unlike the two old coots in *The Muppet* show). Richard Strauss appears as an Erich Von Stroheim character making love to a woman in a box (drinking champagne from a boot, a kinky, Russellian bit of business – champagne and foot fetishism).

When the scene in *Dance of the Seven Veils* shifted to some woodland, it became crazier, as the critics were set upon in a

---

23 The filmmakers had a corpse on stand-by – the BBC might not have gone for the on-screen slaughter of an animal (though they will in their wildlife documentaries).
24 The Harrogate Operatic Players were some of the extras.

number of silent movie gags and slapstick: menaced by sliding trombones, lying on the ground with their heads in drums, running the gauntlet through ranks of musicians, and so on (accompanied by Richard Strauss's *The Hero's Battlefield*). The staging was again as a Busby Berkeley dance number, with symmetry and rows and patterns created for the camera.

It might have been harmless fun, but there was no disguising the 1970 film's contempt for critics, and the dim view the movie took of the tense, parasitical and potentially damaging relationship between an artist and his/ her critics. Strauss's quips too are employed to attack critics and criticism. Another scene involved a stripper (appearing as Potiphar's wife, from *Joseph-Legende*) showering Strauss with gold coins.

Movie-making is sent up a number of times too in *Dance of the Seven Veils* – for instance, the spoof of a silent, romantic comedy, or the old man mask and bald pate that Pauline thrusts onto Richard Strauss's head, a poignant moment, economically expressing how old age suddenly catches up on Strauss ('cos by this time – the Second World War – he should be in his seventies, not the hand-some, blond youth he's been all the way through). But the old man make-up is employed to make another satirical, ideological point,[25] when the elderly Strauss, appearing in London to conduct (what else but *Also Sprach Zarathustra*?), tears off the mask to reveal the youthful, blond Strauss underneath: he has never changed (cue: applause from the audience).[26]

A scene of a hymn to Richard Strauss's Muses in *Dance of the Seven Veils* includes Salomé, Clytemnestra and Potiphar's wife (with more dancing, partial nudity, wild costumes, and Salomé portrayed as a both a regular ballet dancer and flabby, middle-aged woman). In this sequence, Strauss introduces his three Muses by opening the doors of a giant wardrobe while sleepwalking (yes – it's a Ken Russell Movie!). And of course they're in revealing stage clothes (the scene cuts to *Salomé* being performed in a theatre, with the Salomés being interchanged behind a throne). And of course there's the essential Russell scene of the Muse as a dominatrix, in fetish gear (but true to the historical period), teasing Strauss on a bed.

---

25 When your piece is this OTT and satirical, you don't need complex (and costly) old man make-up – the rubber Hallowe'en mask is perfect.
26 He has friends among the Brits, Strauss notes.

To the strains of *Domestic Symphony*, *Dance of the Seven Veils* portrays Richard Strauss and his wife Pauline de Ahna fucking on a bed right in front of an orchestra (there's an amusing cameo from Ken Russell as a white-haired conductor, glancing behind at the newly-wedded couple on the bed). Pretty wild for a BBC documentary – but the film also includes Strauss encouraging the conductor to time the climaxes in the music with his orgasm (one orgasm isn't enough for Russell!).

Richard Strauss runs into the smoke and crossfire of World War One: here the 1970 movie becomes gruesome, with blood and gore. In an outrageous sequence, Strauss is held by soldiers, with his dead son on his lap, while another group of soldiers rapes his wife nearby, as he watches, powerless to help her. Even more controversial is that the film shows Pauline enjoying the rape (constituting further insults to Strauss and his masculinity).

That alone, without all of the other episodes in *Dance of the Seven Veils*, is enough to render the piece unbroadcastable. Not just the rape, which has appeared in other films (though carefully monitored by the censors – *Straw Dogs, The Accused, Deliverance*), but the moments showing Judith Paris's orgasmic face as Pauline de Ahna enjoys the assault (rape as pleasure is simply too much for the censors, especially British censors, who are particularly strong on the linking of sex and violence). And showing Strauss waking up and, oh, it was all a dream, doesn't soften or lessen the impact of the previous sequence.

For Ken Russell, the torture and rape scene was included:

> in order to get across the fact that Richard Strauss was uninterested in the Second World War because it didn't touch him personally. I presented a dream sequence in which Strauss is forced to watch his wife raped and his child murdered by the Nazis. (PF, 88)

There's a lengthy and elaborate silent movie parody in *Dance of the Seven Veils* – a romantic comedy in 18th century trappings, *Der Rosenkavalier* (featuring Richard Strauss's wife Pauline and a crossdressing woman as the man). It's included in a scene in a cinema, where Strauss conducts an orchestra accompanying the movie.

But if you were fooled into thinking, well, this isn't too bad, the sequence shifts into virulent anti-semitism among the audience, as an elderly Jewish couple are set upon, culminating with the man having the Star of David cut in blood on his chest, and the woman's eyes maimed.[27] Richard Strauss's response is to encourage his orchestra to play louder.

By contrast with the above craziness, some of the other skits in this assault on Richard Strauss were more conventional: Strauss as Macbeth, with his wife playing Lady Macbeth, stabbing King Duncan in time with Strauss's *Macbeth*. A *Don Quixote* sketch, with a religious procession out of *The Seventh Seal* (Strauss plays Miguel de Cervantes' eternal knight, of course). Quixote is flattened by a giant cross.

The Alpine picnic in *Dance of the Seven Veils* inevitably evokes *The Sound of Music*, but you know that Ken Russell would shoot idyllic scenes like that whether Julie Andrews and Christopher Plummer had sung in the mountains or not, because sending up Hollywood schmaltz and saccharine advertizing imagery is one of his recurring motifs. As Russell pointed out, *The Dance of the Seven Veils* was 'highly coloured, schmaltzy and crude... because I wished to reflect those elements in his music' (Bax, 141).

A further skit in *Dance of the Seven Veils* had a group of Nazi officials, led by everyone's favourite movie demagogue, Satan Himself – Adolf Hitler (played by Ken Russell regular Ken Colley). Goering (James Mellor), Goebbels (Vladek Sheybal) and a woman that might be Leni Riefenstahl visit Strauss and his wife for a jolly luncheon done over as a Charlie Chaplin dance and silent comedy routine.

It's completely bonkers, and mad and wild and silly and fun, and contains memorable images such as Adolf Hitler sitting on Richard Strauss's shoulders, with them both playing the violin, Strauss dancing on a grand piano which Hitler plays, the group stepping in time out of the car (on a red carpet), and the troupe exchanging gifts and photos and awards (and vinyl records on the Swastika record label, a classic Russell touch).

It's quite mad, and I think we've got the point by now, Mr Russell!

---

27 Cueing yet another nod to *Battleship Potemkin*.

The Dance of the Seven Veils, Ken Russell's seldom seen BBC exploration of Richard Strauss, one of the most extraordinary television shows ever made. Broadcast once (in 1970), and never again!

Scenes from Dance of the Seven Veils, a TV show
that no one else would have made apart from Ken Russell
– and a TV show that no one else could have made.

# 7

# WOMEN IN LOVE

> People come up to me and say, 'I loved your *Women In Love*.' Well, to me, it was one of the worst films I ever made. But it was romantic, and that's what people like.
>
> Ken Russell

Ken Russell reluctantly admitted that people always mentioned *Women In Love* (1969) as their favourite Ken Russell film. Russell complained that he has made better films than *Women In Love*, his third feature as director, but recognized that it seemed to chime with the public. Russell is right there: *The Devils*, *Savage Messiah*, and *The Music Lovers* are better movies cinematically, but it's *Women In Love* that people remember more than those three pictures. *Women In Love* was included in the British Film Institute's Top 100 British movies (of course, a lot of those top 100 movies aren't 'British' at all, and some of them don't deserve to be in the top 100).[1]

*Women In Love* was one of the first Ken Russell movies I saw (on TV around 1981, I think).[2] It's a film guaranteed to make an impression. Who can forget Alan Bates talking about figs as vulvas, or the haunting water party shot at magic hour, or Glenda

---

[1] For example, *Four Weddings and a Funeral*, *My Name Is Joe*, *Life Is Sweet*, *Secrets and Lies* and *Mona Lisa*. Gimme a break!

[2] For some reason, *Women In Love* is linked in my memory to romances – in particular, Alison Dunworth. *Women In Love* and *Far From the Madding Crowd* (and *Doctor Zhivago*): emotional stuff in the English Midlands *circa* 1981.

Jackson dancing with the cattle? And the scene everyone remembers: Ollie Reed and Alan Bates wrestling nude?

It certainly helped Ken Russell's career to have made *Women In Love* – it did good business, first of all, and it won an Oscar for Glenda Jackson[3] and was also nominated for the best director,[4] screenplay[5] and cinematography[6] Oscars (good going for a third feature!).[7] It helped too that *Women In Love* contained scenes which had people talking – primarily, that nude wrestling scene. It wouldn't have the same impact today, probably. Or maybe it would: Mel Gibson and Arnold Schwarzenegger completely nude would be sure to get people talking (yep, there are still numerous actors who wouldn't do that scene. In fact, most of the big stars).

The wrestling scene[8] also provided Ken Russell with oft-told anecdotes for chat shows and interviews – about how Ollie Reed had persuaded Russell to change the setting from a moonlit, riverbank scene[9] – 'all in slow motion like a pouffy commercial', Reed complained to Russell (BP, 59);[10] about how Reed and Alan Bates were very reluctant to do the scene[11] but went out drinking the night before and decided to do it; how Russell had an alternative scene planned in case they chickened out; how Reed retired to the toilets to encourage his dick to grow,[12] and so on.

As Ken Russell explained:

> as the day came closer we looked forward to it less and less. Firstly, I knew it was going to be very difficult to shoot. Secondly, I knew it was going to be a tough lighting job, seemingly lit just by the glow of the log fire. And thirdly, I knew neither actor particularly wanted to

---

3 Beating Jane Alexander, Ali MacGraw, Sarah Miles and Carrie Snodgrass.
4 Russell was up against Federico Fellini, Robert Altman, Arthur Hiller and Franklin Schaffer. Not bad company.
5 Competing with *Mash, Airport, I Never Sang For My Father and Lovers* and *Other Strangers*.
6 Against Freddie Young (*Ryan's Daughter* – which won), Fred J. Koenekamp (*Patton*), Ernest Laszlo (*Airport*) and Osami Furuya, Sinsaku Himeda, Masamichi Satoh and Charles F. Wheeler (*Tora! Tora! Tora!*).
7 This was the year that *Patton* cleaned up at the Oscars.
8 The nude wrestling scene was filmed at Evanston Castle near Derby, which had a billiards room done out as an Arthurian hall featuring a huge fireplace (the film-makers decided to use real fire, which made the room very hot.
9 It was to appear in the film with the scenes of Birkin fishing or bathing in the mill stream. Gerald would've discovered him, and joined him in the stream, and they'd be larking about in the water, leading to a wrestling match. The splashing water would've aided in covering up the bodies, of course (Bax, 177).
10 Oliver Reed showed Ken Russell and his wife Shirley how the scene could be played in a drawing room, in one of Russell's regular anecdotes.
11 'I was scared stiff,' Ollie confessed.
12 On that point, there are tricks that could've been employed: body doubles, for a start, for close-ups; a prosthetic penis, as in *Salò* (1975), or 1997's *Boogie Nights*; or even the good, old elastic band, a trick used in porn flicks.

do it, and Oliver in particular wished he'd never got so drunk as to come round and suggest the wretched thing. (Bax, 178)

Ken Russell said he had turned down *Women In Love* at first, but then he'd read the 1920 novel and decided to do it. But it wasn't Russell's pet project, it wasn't a film he'd been nurturing for years to make: he was a hired director, and it was the producer and screenwriter, Larry Kramer (b. 1935), who was one of the key personnel behind the project.[13] Kramer is known today as a gay rights activist (he was the co-founder of ACT-UP and Gay Men's Health Crisis), his work against AIDS, the author of plays such as *The Normal Heart,* and the script for 1973's *Lost Horizon.*

So although I'm sure many people regard *Women In Love* as 'a Ken Russell film', it's actually more of 'a Larry Kramer film'. And that's also because the script is absolutely vital on a literary adaption, and D.H. Lawrence's fiction is especially difficult to adapt.

Ken Russell wasn't the first film director associated with *Women In Love:* other directors (including Silvio Nazzizano, Peter Brook, Jack Clayton and Stanley Kubrick), had been approached by the Hollywood studio United Artists to direct *Women In Love* before David Picker at UA tried Ken Russell. American writer Larry Kramer had written the adaption. Silvio Narrizano had worked with Kramer on a script. Only United Artists among the studios wanted to make the film, apparently, and they didn't like the idea of Narrizano (*Georgy Girl, Blue*) directing it. It was Picker and David Chasman at UA who suggested to Kramer that Russell might be suitable for the project.

Ken Russell's regular producers, Roy Baird and Harry Benn, were vital in the production of *Women In Love,* and liaising between the filmmakers and Martin Rosen and Larry Kramer. According to Russell, though, the first *Women In Love* script was 'a tawdry piece of sensationalism' which missed out some of the best scenes in Lorenzo's novel, including the Switzerland episode, and Kramer and Silvio Narrizano had added scenes, such as Gudrun and Gerald tupping in a mine, and the couple riding off into the sunset on Gerald's white stallion (G, 80). Kramer told Russell,

---

[13] Larry Kramer wanted more involvement in the day-to-day shooting of *Women In Love,* he wanted to be around for the filming, rewriting scenes, etc (Bax, 180). But Ken Russell (like many film directors) didn't work like that. Many directors aren't keen on having the screenwriter(s) on set, for a number of reasons (however, Russell did have Christopher Logue on set for some of his later movies).

'don't blame me. I did it for Silvio and just wrote it the way he wanted it' (Bax, 169).

Ken Russell said that he and Larry Kramer worked on the script together, with each putting into it what they thought would work from the novel. Russell would visit Kramer at his place with his notes and ideas for the adaption, and Kramer would type them up (Bax, 169). The second script was revised so much that only two or three scenes survived, remembered Russell. These included:

(1) the market scene at night (which Larry Kramer had expanded from the novel);

(2) the classroom scene;

(3) Hermione Roddice's party (though Ken Russell added the ballet, which's pure Russellania – what other screenwriter would add a ballet in the middle of a dramatic scene?!);

(4) Ursula and Greek mythology;

and (5) the early scenes establishing the town.

Ken Russell said he added some dialogue, to link scenes which he wanted to include from D.H. Lawrence's novel, and that Larry Kramer had written some good dialogue (Russell has acknowledged that dialogue isn't his strongest point – and *Women In Love* does contain some terrific crystallizations of Lorenzo's famous speeches).

So, to emphasize yet again: it was Larry Kramer who conceived the idea of doing *Women In Love* (he had optioned the 1920 novel, for instance), and who had written the first script, and much of the second script (in collaboration with Ken Russell). Or, to put it another way, if Davids Picker and Chasman at United Artists hadn't suggested having Russell direct the film, Russell would not have done *Women In Love* as his next project. And also, he had plenty of other things he wanted to make, including more biopics of classical music composers.

Ken Russell admitted that his film of *Women In Love* had 'failed to do the novel full justice', and wondered whether 'the esteemed author would have been satisfied with my best efforts to bring two of his masterpieces to the screen' (DF, 37). Knowing D.H. Lawrence and his work very well, I would say, no, Lorenzo would probably have loathed 99% of Russell's adaptions of his work! Partly due to time constraints, so much is left out (Larry Kramer and Russell cut the book down drastically). And the film comes out episodic, without the sequential flow of Bertie Lawrence's novel.

But even more importantly, the 1969 production of *Women In Love* fails to capture the unique substance of the 1920 book, which means not only what happens and the characters and all that, but D.H. Lawrence's prose, its rhythmic, repetitive and musical evocations of sexual love and loving sex and the struggles between men and women.

However, despite its faults, *Women In Love* has become *the* D.H. Lawrence film, the one by which all subsequent adaptions will be judged (though there were adaptions prior to that, and Lawrence himself was not averse to a film adaption of his book. Lawrence had considered a movie of *Women In Love* in the 1920s, according to Harry T. Moore. Tho' what Lorenzo would've made of the 1969 United Artists picture is anybody's guess! He wasn't a big fan of movies (deriding them in *The Lost Girl*), being a more traditional guy in his some of his cultural tastes).

*Women In Love* ran to 131 minutes. It was released in September, 1969 (G.B), and May 25, 1970 (U.S.A.). Colour was by Deluxe Laboratory (in Hollywood). It was filmed in 35mm in the regular aspect ratio of 1: 1.85. The budget was estimated at $1.25 million or $1.6 million. Rated: 'R'.

Larry Kramer, Martin Rosen and Roy Baird were producers; United Artists and Brandywine produced;[14] Billy Williams was DP; Michael Bradsell was editor; Kenneth Jones was art director; Luciana Arrighi was set designer; Harry Cordwell was set dresser; Shirley Russell was costume designer; George Ball was prop master; Georges Delerue was composer; Jonathan Benson was AD; Charles E. Parker was makeup artist; A.G. Scott was hairdresser; Neville C. Thompson was unit manager; Lee Bolon was location manager; Brian Simmons was sound recordist; David Harcourt was camera operator; and Terry Gilbert was choreographer.

THE SCRIPT.

After agreeing to direct the film, Ken Russell collaborated with Larry Kramer on producing a new script. Russell added many scenes, including the Crichs' picnic (knowing that would be a pricey sequence), and Gudrun Brangwen and the cattle. Russell

---

[14] Brandywine was involved with *Women In Love* – best known for the *Alien* series.

also invented some new scenes, such as the fig scene (which Russell said he found in one of Lawrence's poems), and Gudrun and Loerke fooling around to Peter Tchaikovsky's *Pathétique Symphony* in the Swiss chalet.15

Ken Russell ditched many of Larry Kramer's scenes, including the invented ones like Gudrun Brangwen and Gerald Crich having sex in a mine (but he kept Gudrun and Ursula at the market). Other scenes dropped from D.H. Lawrence's book included the rabbit scene (this was shot but left out of the final cut – Russell thought that the movie had already covered similar themes of violence and animals in the scene with the horse and the train).16 Russell later remarked (in 1973) that much of *Women In Love* was repetitious and pretentious:

> Lawrence simply repeated his theme about the separate-yet-united philosophy of love 8 times over in different guises. I thought twice would be enough in the film for most people to get it. (Bax, 175-6)

Ken Russell and Larry Kramer argued over the screen credit: Russell wanted a co-credit, because he said he had written much of the script himself. Kramer wanted – and got – sole credit. That would've meant an Oscar nomination for Russell. Russell did not share the same vision of the book as Kramer, or the other producer, Martin Rosen, and he often argued with them about it – during shooting, and through the editing process (which can't have helped).)

And when they viewed the finished movie, Martin Rosen and Larry Kramer were not happy with it. It was too long. They didn't like the ending or the beginning. Ken Russell agreed with some of their comments, and re-edited the movie before showing it to United Artists. *Women In Love* had originally opened with a long scene in the classroom, full of exposition, involving Rupert Birkin, Ursula Brangwen and Hermione Roddice. It took a few weeks for a solution to present itself: to cut the classroom scene with a

---

15 There're some in-jokes or self-advertizing here, as Ken Russell's next movie would be about Peter Tchaikovsky, of course, and it would star Glenda Jackson as Nina. For some critics, including that scene was going too far – a self-conscious advert for the director's next movie (but how many in the general audience woulda noticed?).

16 However, the rabbit (a big, black-and-white one) does appear, in the scenes where Gudrun visits the Crichs' place (to teach his sister Winifred), and Winifred talks about the rabbit – but the dialogue is not about Winifred or the rabbit at all – instead, it's really evoking the nascent Gerald-Gudrun relationship (it's cleverly laid over images of Gudrun and Gerald staring longingly at each other. A simple editing technique, but very effective).

different scene, involving the two women going to the Crich wedding. The classroom scene would then be sliced up, with the vital parts retained, but inserted into a montage, so it became essentially a flashback. That's one standard method of presenting exposition at the top of a movie, by integrating it into a montage, so the audience doesn't get bored sitting through a single, long-winded scene.

Routinely derided by many critics for his flamboyance and vulgarity, or the simplicity of his narratives, Ken Russell in *Women In Love* delivers a relationships movie and a love 'n' romance movie every bit as nuanced and detailed as many classics of the genre. The script by Larry Kramer and Russell expertly charts the two relationships from courtship to consummation to dissolution. And Russell is particularly good at depicting relationships in trouble, and relationships that are falling apart.

'I don't know Lawrence's work well enough to say how close the film is to its spirit,' Russell admitted in 1973 (Bax, 175). And when shooting began, Russell purposely didn't read of D.H. Lawrence's novels (apart from a couple of biographies).

ADAPTING D.H. LAWRENCE'S FICTION.

In a way, an adaption of D.H. Lawrence's art is doomed to failure, because so much of his fiction occurs in a psychosexual realm, in characters' minds, which exist beyond the reach of most of cinema. A closer look at the 1920 novel reveals how difficult Lawrence's fiction is to adapt for the screen. (The nature poetry aspect is probably the easiest to portray, and Ken Russell succeeds here, having a similar, Romantic love of the natural world, and being the most accomplished British director at putting that nature mysticism onto celluloid).

Part of the problem of adaption D.H. Lawrence's fiction is that, as Ken Russell put it, his characters are 'metaphysical characters enacting some symbolic drama in his own mind, rather like Wagner's *Ring* in music' (Bax, 176).

The battle between the sexes is at its most fierce in *Women In Love*, in all D.H. Lawrence's fiction. All arguments are extended up to death. Things are not just bad, they're deathly. When something goes wrong, it's not painful, it means death. The men are death – both Birkin and Gerald are obsessed by it.

The 1920 novel plays out the age-old connection of love and

death. The thing that connects them is sex. Sex and the body are the locations of the fierce duel between love and death. The book is decadent, in its depictions of sex, death, anality, excrement, war, violence, control – this is very much a novel about male obsessions. It explores the male domain of pornography.

*Women In Love* is static, while *The Rainbow* is cyclic, in motion. *Women In Love* is full of restlessness, but this movement pivots around a single point, the meeting of men and women. *The Rainbow* moves through three generations, but *Women In Love* stays with one generation. It squashes everything together. And D.H. Lawrence splits up the protagonist, Ursula Brangwen, into two, the two sisters, and does likewise with the man. The result is the classic foursome, the Jungian quaternity. Forward motion is suspended in favour of an intense, spatial dialogue. The novel opens with a dialogue, getting straight down to the metaphysics of sex. The sexes are polarized ('the man makes it impossible', says Glenda Jackson's Gudrun early on in the film, as the sisters watch the wedding).

The women in *Women In Love* are seen together, in a sisterhood, in a female bonding. Later, D.H. Lawrence will note that when the sisters were together, they 'were quite complete in a perfect world of their own' (*Women In Love*, 230). Two sisters and two brothers, the latter are later joined by a blood-oath and rite. Lawrence goes down to the most basic fusion, which for him is not vaginal or of the womb, but anal. The anal connection is alchemical, Faustian, at the foundation of organic matter, beyond and below spirit, where atoms fuse and excrement turns into Freudian gold. (The 1969 movie, like the 1993 *Lady Chatterley*, avoids the anal mysticism).

Ursula destroys Birkin in the chapter "Excurse" in *Women In Love*, but not sexually, as she did with Anton Skrebensky in "The Bitterness of Ecstasy" chapter in *The Rainbow*, but verbally. She flattens him, calls him perverse and death-eating (389). Then comes the famous scene of bowels and loins being caressed. Dark floods of passion are released. For literary critic Jeffrey Meyers, D.H. Lawrence employed Biblical language here 'in order to disguise and ennoble unacceptable acts'.[17] Some critics have noted that this scene really consists of Ursula sucking Birkin's penis while she puts a finger in his ass.[18] But it's got to be more than

---

17 J. Meyers, *D.H. Lawrence*, Knopf, NY, 1990, 221.
18 C. Wilson. *The Sexual Misfits: A Study of Sexual Outsiders*, Collins, London, 1989.

fellatio with anal frills surely? Lawrence writes:

> She closed her hands over the full, rounded body of his loins, as he stooped over her, she seemed to touch the quick of the mystery of darkness that was bodily him. (396)

This is not just a blowjob, it's far more than that. D.H. Lawrence could have used the unsubtle style of pornography.[19] It's not simply that Lawrence couldn't write *cock* and *cunt* in a novel published around 1916 and 1920 (he could have written it but would have known it wouldn't be published; he waited until *Lady Chatterley's Lover* a few years later, to do that., But he still published it privately). Rather, the language of *Women In Love* is 'mysterious, ritualistic, and contemplative, and cannot be decoded for the details of actual sexual behaviour', remarked John Worthen in 1991.[20]

D.H. Lawrence's aiming for a transcendence to a state of being beyond sex. Touch is the means, but the end is not orgasm, but transformation of being. Sodomy and death and darkness are tied up together in Lawrence's fiction. He uses anal sex to get to the essence of things. For him the essence is of the *body*, based in the *body*, before and after the spirit. A transformation that excludes the body is for Lawrence invalid. The body is the site of the mystery. So start with the body. Sex is one way of getting in touch with the body, but only one of many ways.

The chief means is *touch* – pure touch. David Herbert Lawrence is a priest of touch, not sex. The body is the site of mystery, religion, spirit. If Lawrence describes his characters at all, it is always as *bodies*, as presences, as flesh and blood. There is always get a great sense of physicality in Lawrence's fiction, of people's physical bodies, their physical surroundings. As Gerald Doherty wrote in 1994: '[i]n an astonishing revision, the anus becomes the dynamic source of transcendence'.[21]

Focussing on the anus rather than the womb or clitoris or phallus revises traditional sexual configurations. Instead of being associated with dirt, death and the Kristevan abject, the anus becomes metaphorized as the site of mysticality and transcend-

---
19 Porn is full of blowjob scenes: this one might be written thus: 'she grabbed his balls and licked his cock until he pumped his come down her throat'.
20 J. Worthen, *D.H. Lawrence*, Arnold, London, 1991, 51.
21 G. Doherty. "Death and the Rhetoric of Representation in D.H. Lawrence's *Women In Love*", *Mosaic*, 27, 1, 1994, 69.

ence. From death to 'riches', as Ursula calls it.

The chapter "Excurse" in *Women In Love* presents perhaps D.H. Lawrence's most concentrated description of sex (up to that point). The emotions are fierce, tragic, painfully poignant. The language goes to extremes:

> Then a hot passion of tenderness for her filled his heart. He stood up and looked into her face. It was new and oh, so delicate in its luminous wonder and fear… "My love!" she cried, lifting her face and looking with frightened, gentle wonder of bliss… Kneeling on the hearth-rug before him, she put her arms round his loins, and put her face against his thighs. Riches! Riches! She was overwhelmed with a sense of a heavenful of riches. "We love each other," she said in delight… Her face was now one dazzle of released, golden light, as she looked up at him, and laid her hands full on his thighs, behind, as he stood before her. He looked down at her with a rich bright bow like a diadem above his eyes. She was beautiful as a new marvellous flower opened at his knees, a paradisal flower she was, beyond womanhood, such a flower of luminousness… She had established a rich new circuit, a new current of passional electric energy, between the two of them, released from the darkest poles of the body and established in perfect circuit. It was a dark fire of electricity that rushed from him to her, and flooded them both with rich peace, satisfaction. "My love," she cried, lifting her face to him, her eyes, her mouth open in transport… It was a perfect passing away for both of them, and at the same time the most intolerable accession into being, the marvellous fullness of immediate gratification, overwhelming, outflooding from the source of the deepest life-force, the darkest, deepest, strangest life-source of the human body, at the back and base of the loins. (*Women In Love*, 392-6)

The challenge for the filmmaker is: how the hell are you going to film that?! Larry Kramer and Ken Russell, Martin Rosen, Roy Baird and their team devised a number of correlatives or equivalences in the film of *Women In Love*, but I don't think the movie captured what D.H. Lawrence was evoking here (and certainly not the elements of anal-sexual mysticism).[22] Again, it

---

[22] *Last Tango In Paris* (1972) was a film which played around with anal sex, the transgressive aspects of it. The scene where Marlon Brando buggers Maria Schneider on the floor of the apartment, using butter as a lubricant, all the while ranting about the family was 'the most famous sex scene in the history of the cinema', remarked Tom Matthews (211-2). It was the sodomy scene that the British Board of Film Censors objected to (as well as the dialogue); there were arguments between the producers and the BBFC, with the BBFC demanding cuts to the scene and the filmakers standing fast. But *Last Tango in Paris* had already played well in France and the U.S.A., so the scene was kept in – with a compromise, half of what the BBFC asked for. Some 50 local councils in Britain banned *Last Tango in Paris*. Pressure groups such as the Festival of Light and the Union of Catholic Mothers campaigned against the film.

must be stressed that the 'fault' is not with the direction, which pretty much everyone agrees was superb, but the adaption.

Ken Russell, Larry Kramer and the production team of *Women In Love* have a go at depicting Ursula Brangwen and Rupert Birkin making love in front of the fire for this scene: the blocking of the scene has Jennie Linden kneeling before Alan Bates, then a match cut of Birkin walking, with the camera on its side, so Birkin leaning over to Ursula matches with Birkin walking.

The sideways-shot love scene is filmed in Ken Russell's TV commercial style, deliberately ironic: heavily backlit, with a pinky-gold cast, and in slow motion. The lovers, naked (well, topless), walk towards each other, smiling, hands outstretched. It's meant to be clichéd and sickly sweet (and sure as hell ain't meant to be taken seriously!). That works within the context of the film, but all of that ecstatic prose in 1920 Lawrence's 1920 novel is lost. No sense in the 1969 film of *Women In Love* of Birkin's loins and darkness, and Ursula's awareness of establishing 'a rich new circuit, a new current of passional electric energy, between the two of them'. Sometimes Lorenzo is being ironic and distanced, commenting upon his characters, but more often he's deadly serious (indeed, for some critics and readers, Lawrence's too serious and too po-faced too much of the time. Yep, he really means it!).

The anal mysticism here relates to 'burning out the deepest shames' in *Lady Chatterley's Lover* (1928), where Connie Chatterley is sodomized by Oliver Mellors in an ecstatic, transformative experience. Of Ursula, for example, the narrator says

> She wanted unspeakable intimacies. She wanted to have him, utterly, finally to have him as her own, oh, so unspeakably, in intimacy. (*Women In Love*, 343)

However, Ken Russell, Larry Kramer, Martin Rosen and the production team were not about to depict a woman receiving a spiritual awakening via buggery (it would be another twenty years before Russell tackled *Lady Chatterley's Lover*, but again anal sex was not portrayed – or suggested).

In the novel of *Women In Love*, the physicality is male. It's women in love one reads of, but men's bodies that are foregrounded. Women are decentred, psychologically. Birkin and Gerald are described fully, but Hermione Roddice's body is hardly described at all, and Ursula's and Gudrun's bodies are only described occasionally. Men's bodies are portrayed in detail, often through women's eyes. When Gerald stalks into Gudrun's house like a supernatural being, his body dominates the scene. He moves from the death-bed of his father through darkness to the love-bed of his beloved. He feels transformed – it is ecstasy, a miracle, a marvel (430). But Gudrun lies awake, for hours. This is a superb piece of realization – the woman lying awake, holding her man who is in another world as the hours slide by. The woman dies, inside, while the man replenishes himself in sleep. As American feminist Mary Daly writes of Gudrun's state:

> …it is the dull aching state of one who has sold her body and soul and will continue to do so. It is a state of perfectly false consciousness.[23]

In the United Artists version, Ken Russell and Larry Kramer spend much time building up Gerald Crich's approach to Gudrun Brangwen's house, and his quiet exploration of it, until he comes to Gudrun's room. However, the film can only indicate the sense of time passing for Gudrun as she lies beneath the sleeping Gerald, with some chiming on the music soundtrack, and some Hollywood montage (lap dissolves). Oliver Reed, superb as Gerald, does convey a sense of weighty, unavoidable physicality (and the detail of putting his hand into the mud of his father's grave, then pressing his soiled hands over Gudrun's breasts is effective).

THE DIALOGUE.

Many of the lines of dialogue[24] in the 1969 film of *Women In Love* are taken from the book – but don't let that fool you that this 'captures' the book or is a 'faithful' adaption of the book. But some of Lorenzo's dialogue is too memorable – or too silly – not to use from time to time.

Of course, nobody speaks like a D.H. Lawrence character in 'real life', in that pontificating, self-conscious, highly intellectual and desperate-to-be-poetic manner. Sure, but nobody speaks like characters out of the works of Alexandre Dumas, Thomas Hardy or Dante Alighieri, either! (Go to Spike Milligan for his wonderful

---

[23] M. Daly, *Gyn/Ecology: The Metaethics of Radical Feminism*, Women's Press, London, 1979, 364.
[24] Unfortunately, some of the lines are ropily looped.

send-ups of Lawrencean lingo).

But Bertie Lawrence just couldn't stop himself: he *had* to say what he wanted to say! He knew he was being ridiculous some of the time, but he went ahead anyway. Just look at his letters! Page after page of rants and complaints (as well as all the other usual domestic, everyday stuff you find in letters). Lawrence must've been a pain to live with at times, and the 1969 United Artists movie captures that in Alan Bates' performance of the priggish, preachy side of Lorenzo. When you want to say, oh shut up, you jerk! As people no doubt did to Lawrence when he went too far.

CHARACTERIZATION.

The filmmakers took a somewhat biographical approach to some of the characters in *Women In Love*, partly because they knew that some of them were drawn on people that Bertie Lawrence knew (understandable in a movie, because you have to start somewhere with a visualization of a character, but it's critically dubious at best). Lawrence's friends John Middleton Murry and Katherine Mansfield were apparently inspirations for Gerald Crich and Gudrun Brangwen (though some critics have suggested that Gerald's appearance (down to the moustache Gerald sports) drew on Sir Thomas Philip Barber, a Nottinghamshire mine owner, and the owner of Lamb Close House (which was Shortlands in the novel). Quite a few critics reckon that Rupert Birkin shared characteristics with Lawrence, which the movie exploited.)

A famous example of this biographical approach in *Women In Love* was Hermione Roddice, who's loosely based on Lady Ottoline Morrell. There's plenty of biographical and literary criticism of the Morrell social scene (where people such as Aldous Huxley, Bertrand Russell, John Middleton Murry, Katherine Mansfield, Mark Gertler, Siegfried Sassoon, Lytton Strachey and others were visitors to Morrell's home at Garsington Manor, Oxfordshire), so there's no need to repeat it here.

What counts, though, is that Ken Russell and the filmmakers took a *satirical* approach to some of these characters.[25] Russell said he'd read biographies of D.H. Lawrence, and reckoned that Lawrence didn't like Lady Morrell much, but found her 'a

---

25 That *Women In Love* is satirizing the characters leads to some confusion about Russell's cinema: are his movies investing in the charas seriously, or sending them up? Well, it's both – throughout Russell's cinema.

pretentious, selfish woman'. So although *Women In Love* was a piece of fiction, Russell recalled that he had used some of the people that Lawrence drew on in his depiction of them in the movie (Bax, 169). The fact, for instance, that Rupert Birkin shares some of Lawrence's own views: but the filmmakers took this to a literal extreme, and had Birkin look almost exactly like Lawrence himself, complete with the familiar Lawrencean beard and hair, the pale, crumpled suits, the intense way of speaking, the lyrical flights about figs and catkins, and all the rest.

### SOME OF THE DELETIONS AND ALTERATIONS.

*Women In Love* explored sexual relations intimately, Ken Russell said, 'as few movies had before, but I can take scant credit for that. I was only putting on the screen what D.H. Lawrence had written half a century before' (1993, 72-73). Russell admitted that it was 'impossible to film a 600-page novel and be true to the author's vision' (ibid.).[26] Glenda Jackson said Russell respected the book, and handed out copies of it during discussions about the adaption. Russell was not a dictator, Jackson said, but was quite open to ideas and collaboration.[27]

The London scenes, when the Brangwens join the bohemians at the Café Royale, were left out (and the many characters too, such as Halliday and Possum). This was the kind of imagery that Ken Russell would have greatly enjoyed filming (you can get an idea of what they might have been like from the Vorticist club scenes in *Savage Messiah*). For Glenda Jackson, Ken Russell's talent was in creating detailed backgrounds, the 'minute details that really reveal the interior landscape of a human being' (B. McFarlane, 314).

We could explore in detail the many alterations to the novel, the numerous deletions, and the numerous additions. But if you know the novel, you'll know what was left out, and what was added and altered. A 'faithful' adaption of a novel is impossible for lots of reasons. But even if the 1969 movie of *Women In Love* departed greatly from the 1920 novel, it has come to be accepted as a 'faithful' adaption, as well as being *the* D.H. Lawrence movie.

---

26 Ken Russell admitted that *Women In Love* 'had some very good performances in it and it was very outspoken about relationships', but you couldn't cram a 600-page novel into a 2-hour movie (RC, 250).

27 However, some aspects of the production Glenda Jackson wasn't so happy with, such as Ken Russell having her below Oliver Reed for the rape scene, hiding the fact that she was pregnant, and contending with some of Reed's bad habits.

Besides, the 1969 United Artists production did include some fundamental narrative elements of *Women In Love*, such as Birkin's relationship with Hermione Roddice, Birkin leaving Hermione for Ursula, but also wanting Gerald. As Ken Russell noted, Lorenzo explored his theme repeatedly, going round in circles, and the movie didn't have time for all of the variations that Lawrence loved to put into his books.

UGLY ENGLAND.

There are other themes and elements in the novel of *Women In Love* that the 1969 interpretation did not feature, such as: the search for identity in the modern world; philosophizing on just what life is, and what constitutes a good or useful life (how to *be*); the importance of work or having something significant to *do*; and the ugliness of modern existence (a recurring theme in D.H. Lawrence's fiction, and surely one of the reasons why he left England and went wandering for much of his life). *Women In Love* isn't only about finding fulfilment in love and sex and relationships, it's also about counteracting boredom with a range of activities.

D.H. Lawrence wrote incisively and unapologetically of the horrible, industrial Midlands (in *The Rainbow, Lady Chatterley's Lover* and *Women In Love*, for example). Lawrence was not afraid of severely criticizing his surroundings. 'The weather's awful and we simply hate it up here', Lawrence griped from the Midlands in 1925.[28] He laid into his homeland of Nottinghamshire in many books – the writing reflects his love and hatred of the place. He wrote of the 'ugly winter-grey of houses [that look] like a vision of hell that is cold and angular' in *Women In Love* (450). Lawrence described the modern world of suburban vapidity. Near the beginning of *Lady Chatterley's Lover*, Lawrence's narrator describes the mining village of Tevershall in unambiguous terms:

> ...a village which began almost at the park gates, and trailed in utter hopeless ugliness for a long and gruesome mile: houses, rows of wretched, small, begrimed, brick houses, with black slate roofs for lids, sharp angles and wilful, blank dreariness. (14)

Of a visit to his homeland of late 1926, which helped with the research for *Lady Chatterley's Lover*, Bertie Lawrence described the

---
28 In H. Moore, 1976, 516.

miners, strikes and policemen in a letter as depressing: 'they've pushed the spear through the side of *my* England' (1934, 674).

In his 1926 essay about his hometown, Eastwood in Nottinghamshire, "Return to Bestwood", Lawrence described the familiar feelings of nostalgia and revulsion that many a homecoming has initiated in people of all ages and countries: 'I feel at once a devouring nostalgia and an infinite repulsion'.[29] Lawrence felt bitter about it, about the mess into which the homeland's slipped. In his essay "Nottingham and the Mining Countryside", Lawrence wrote: '[t]he real tragedy of England, as I see it, is the tragedy of ugliness. The country is so lovely: the man-made England is so vile'.[30] Many would agree with him.

THE PRODUCTION OF *WOMEN IN LOVE*.

Location scouting was 'always the most exciting part of a film to me', Ken Russell remarked, describing scouting for locations on *Women In Love* in England in the late 1960s:

> ...finding the locations, conceiving the action to go with them, linking one colour to another and probably just discovering England which, all things considered, is still the most undiscovered country in the world. You might know bits but you can never know it all. We looked for country mansions, water mills, forests, fields, mines and rivers. We'd pencil around all the stately homes, which are naturally marked on that wonderful work of art, the ordnance survey map, and just whip up the drive in a fast car, zip once around the house and be out again before they could shoot at us. (Bax, 170)

A huge number of locations can be found for a movie within a few miles of any point. I know, I've tried it, on my adaption of D.H. Lawrence's *The Horse-Dealer's Daughter*: pick a town in Britain, and within a radius of ten miles you can find cliffs, rivers, lakes, hills, forests, country houses, roads, castles, caves, quarries, etc.

In the novel of *Women In Love*, the settings included Beldover, perhaps based on Quorn or Eastwood, or a variety of towns in Leicestershire and Nottinghamshire. The famous Garsington (in Oxfordshire) probably inspired the depiction of Breadalby, though D.H. Lawrence may have drawn on Kedleston Hall.[31]

*Women In Love* was shot in D.H. Lawrence's homeland of

---

[29] In *A Selection From Phoenix*, 146.
[30] *A Selection From Phoenix*, 108.
[31] See K. Sagar, *A D.H. Lawrence Handbook*, Manchester University Press, 1982, 263f.

Nottinghamshire, and also Cheshire, Derbyshire, Durham, Northumberland, Yorkshire (Denaby, Sheffield, etc), Sherwood Forest in Nottinghamshire, Zermatt in Switzerland and Bray Studios. Kedleston Hall near Derby was Hermione Roddice's house (the Neo-classical Robert Adam interiors are particularly fine and instantly recognizable as the work of Adam – the movie ensures there's a shot of the ceiling. The Russian ballet dance was staged in the circular saloon, based on a Roman temple). The Swiss inn was the Riffelberg Inn in Zermatt. The church (and Brangwens' house) was in Matlock, Derbyshire. The war memorial was in Derby. The funeral was in Belper, Derbyshire. Gerald's home of Shortlands was shot at Elvaston Castle, near Derby. Newcastle's back streets stood in for the mining environment and the market (in both South and North Shields, with Gateshead used for Gudrun on the streets). Also, a school in Sheffield. (Ordnance Survey maps of Blighty were used, as ever on a Ken Russell picture – or any British movie, and also the Royal Commission of Historic Monuments).

*Women In Love* began filming on September 25, 1968. Exteriors were shot first (as is often customary), with the scene with Gudrun and the cattle being among the earliest.

CASTING AND ACTING.

Casting was tricky on *Women In Love*, Ken Russell said; not finding Oliver Reed and Alan Bates, but finding the right female leads. In 1973, Russell admitted that Jennie Linden (b. December 8, 1939) was 'too 'pert", and played Ursula too young. And the actor chosen to play the Brangwen sisters' father hadn't worked out, and Russell and the producers fired him after a week (which producers are very reluctant to do), and hired the ever-dependable, always-excellent Michael Gough.

Ken Russell set the picture in 1920, seven years b4 he was born (*Women In Love* was published privately in late 1920), although it had been written from 1913 onwards (it was conceived as a giant epic that continued the story of *The Rainbow*). The slight shift in years gave the movie a slightly different historical perspective, making it a post-WW1 piece (with quite a few references to the Great War).

The acting in *Women In Love* was strong, on the whole, though Jennie Linden was too often weak and unconvincing as the amazing Ursula Brangwen.[32] Certainly Linden is by far the least convincing among the principal actors. Linden looked a little too late 1960s, too (though the whole film does too, just as any movie looks exactly like the year it was made).[33]

Ursula Brangwen is one of the great characters in modern fiction – a rebellious, polemical, mercurial, passionate woman. She's got to be on fire at times, a walking tornado of emotions, but that's the last thing you get from Jennie Linden, unfortunately. Linden is an uninspiring actress, which might be OK for soap opera on TV or a lightweight rom-com, but for D.H. Lawrence's fiction, you need actors who've got everything, and then some. And they *must* catch fire when needed. And they *must* be able to suggest depths and layers. (Ken Russell did express some reservations about Linden later).[34] And, as the film is about four characters in two couples, one weak performance affects all of the others.

Ursula Brangwen is way too meek in the 1969 movie of *Women In Love*: she is only really allowed to let rip against Rupert Birkin once (in the scene where her jealousy over Hermione Roddice explodes – beautifully staged by the filmmakers, in a classic Lawrencean setting of fields and trees). In the two novels, *The Rainbow* and *Women In Love*, Ursula is far fiercer – she's one of the most fascinating and powerful characters in modern literature. In the United Artists movie, she opposes Birkin, yes, but also demurs to him too often.

It might have been possible to lose Jennie Linden and re-cast the part, although from experience I know that it's very difficult and wrecks schedules. I would imagine that Ken Russell has had to fire actors over the course of a long career in film and television, but it's something everyone tries to avoid if possible.

Glenda Jackson was superb, as one would expect (and she rightly won an Oscar).[35] Jackson (b. 1936) is an unusual star, with unconventional looks. She is one of England's major actresses, and she can act up a storm. As Ken Russell put it, 'sometimes she

---

32 And following *Women In Love*, Jennie Linden did not achieve much, acting-wise, although she did appear in Russell's *Valentino*.

33 Besides, that is partly down to the costume designer, the hair and make-up department, who have used a very late 1960s look.

34 Two of the actresses that Russell had passed on but had since worked with might have been better, he thought (Bax, 172). Russell also remarked that he let Linden see the rushes, which the actress said had altered her performance: she opted to play Ursula younger than agreed.

35 I would say that both Alan Bates and Oliver Reed also delivered Oscar-worthy performances.

looked plain ugly, sometimes just plain, and then, sometimes, the most beautiful creature one had ever seen' (L, 71). Jackson was 32 when *Women In Love* was made: she was mainly known as a stage actress, in *Marat/ Sade* (1964-65, her big breakthrough), *Three Sisters, Henry VI, Hamlet, Collaborators, The Maids, The White Devil, Stevie, Antony and Cleopatra* and *Hedda Gabler*.

Glenda Jackson had appeared prior to *Women In Love* in movies such as *This Sporting Life, Marat/ Sade* and *Negatives*. After *Women In Love* and *The Music Lovers*, Jackson acted in *Sunday Bloody Sunday*, the BBC's *Elizabeth R* (one of her famous roles, which she also did in *Mary, Queen of Scots*), *A Touch of Class, The Tempest, Hedda, House Calls, Stevie, Return of the Soldier, Turtle Diary* and a couple of later Russell outings, *Salomé's Last Dance* and *The Rainbow*. Jackson later went into politics, and was elected a Labour MP in 1992 at the General Election.

Oliver Reed[36] was dark and troubled as Gerald Crich, smouldering under English sexual repression, giving a convincing impression of someone who desires something, but doesn't know exactly what it is (all of these characters are searching, questioning, examining). Certainly Gerald comes from a troubled family – his mother (played by Ken Russell regular Catherine Wilmer) is portrayed as mad (setting the hounds on miners coming to the house, for instance, or dropping a shovel on her husband's coffin at his funeral), his sister Laura kills herself and new husband, Tibby Lupton, in the lake, and his father dies soon after.

Glenda Jackson and Oliver Reed were very different people, and they did not socialize off-camera in *Women In Love*.[37] As with Vanessa Redgrave in *The Devils*, Jackson was another strong woman that Reed couldn't dominate (and in their subsequent appearances in the same movies, Jackson and Reed continued to be chalk and cheese; but Jackson admired Reed's abilities as an actor).

It's called *Women In Love*, but there are quite a few deaths on-screen – and two suicides, no less – and all of them are within the Crich family. This is a tormented, dysfunctional family: one daughter simultaneously kills herself and murders her new

---

36 Ken Russell had wanted Michael Caine for the role of Gerald Crich, but Caine wouldn't do the nudity.
37 Reed had been a little intimidated by Jackson, as she was a celebrated stage actress by this time. But he found that Jackson was down-to-earth and not the snobby theatrical actress at all.

husband; the mother is insane; the father loses his will to live after his daughter's death; and the son kills himself.

All of this's featured in *Women In Love* partly to set up the finale of the movie – Gerald Crich walking off into the snow to die.[38] The suicide has to be convincing – because Gerald is a powerful character, a strong man, now the head of his family, a tyro in the local community (and wealthy), and he's played by Oliver Reed, an actor with a commanding presence. You have to show, in *Women In Love*, how a character embodied by Reed would do something like that. And it works – you never question that Gerald's suicide seems unbelievable, or out of kilter with the rest of the movie, or added on, or false.

Indeed, it's more ironic that Gerald Crich's played by Oliver Reed as a physically confident, energetic man, but is brought low by the torment of a relationship with a strong-willed woman (and the family curse of insanity). Real strength is inside.[39]

Top-billing in *Women In Love* went to Alan Bates (1934-2003), who's one of those actors who's always wonderful (Larry Kramer had cast Bates before Ken Russell's involvement, and Russell agreed with Kramer that Bates would be great). Prior to *Women In Love*, Bates had appeared in some British and American classics, such as *A Kind of Loving, Whistle Down the Wind, Far From the Madding Crowd, The Caretaker, Zorba the Greek* and *Georgy Girl*. After *Women In Love*, Bates was in *The Go-Between, The Shout, The Rose, Quartet, Britannia Hospital, An Englishman Abroad, A Prayer For the Dying, Hamlet* and *Nijinsky* (a movie Russell wanted to make). An immensely charismatic actor, I remember him vividly in Peter Schaffer's play *Yonadab* (1985) at the National Theatre.

Alan Bates gave a satisfying Lorenzo impression (complete with Lawrencean beard, hair, hat, tie and crumpled suit). Indeed, it's still *the* definitive Lawrence on screen. The costume designer (Russell's wife, Shirley Kingdon), had clearly studied archive photos of Lawrence to emulate the whole look. It made sense, although it was a little obvious, to base Birkin's appearance on Lawrence himself. Looking at *Women In Love* again, the three leads are really excellent, their performances include all sorts of

---

38 DP Billy Williams: 'We were underneath the Matterhorn, it was very deep snow, it was quite a long sequence, and he walks a long way. And of course it could only be done in one take because there was no hope of ever doing another one. Everything was perfect, the lights, the camera, the performance, it was a great moment' (R. Sellers, 179).
39 Even Gerald's suicide becomes a big physical act, however.

nuances.

Alan Bates' Rupert Birkin had most of speeches in the 1969 picture (along with Glenda Jackson's feisty, independent Gudrun), though the endless debates on male-female relations became tiresome (as the tendency in D.H. Lawrence's fiction to produce lengthy diatribes and soap-box lectures can be). Even so, Bates' Birkin is sent up by the film itself, as well as some of the characters. And Bates was terrific at delivering some of that complex dialogue.

And plenty of the dialogue was authentic, Lawrencean stuff, even though it was rewritten. Rare are the movies, for instance, in which the hero virulently denounces love and marriage as sordid and demeaning and a lie (Rupert Birkin rants walking through the crowd at the war memorial service, for instance, and in his conversations with Gerald, and when he and Ursula visit a street market). At these moments, D.H. Lawrence's voice came through – in its ferocity, but also its mistaken insistence on absolutes, its preachiness, and its occasional silliness.

Alan Bates also captures the way that Bertie Lawrence enjoyed playing the trickster and teaser – how, although he might have believed most of what he wrote and said, he also knew he was deliberately winding people up. Lawrence knew he was a pain in the ass at times, and the movie recognizes that.

Alan Bates' Rupert Birkin became the classic depiction of a Lawrence-like character on screen; lit'ry critics tend to identify D.H. Lawrence with Birkin, although if you're going to do that kind of author-character identification, there's much more of Lawrence in Ursula and Gudrun (who are the stars of both *The Rainbow* and *Women In Love*). But I guess some literary critics find it easier to think that a male author has equivalents with a male character, although these two novels, like *The Plumed Serpent, The Fox, The Virgin and the Gipsy* and *Lady Chatterley's Lover*, among others, are centred on women.

The ensemble acting of the central two couples gave the United Artists film much of its power. Yes there was some sex and nudity in *Women In Love* (though not as much as one might expect from Ken Russell). Fundamentally, no film could translate the exact descriptions that D.H. Lawrence offers of sexual relations. Watching actors entwine and pant, from the outside, no matter how good they are, cannot be a translation (or even an equivalent) for Lawrence's amazing prose. (Maybe Orson Welles was right: there are two things you can't film, for Welles: sex and prayer).

For actors, *Women In Love* offered plenty of challenges – not only sex scenes but also other nude scenes (swimming nude, for instance, or cavorting in nature). And dancing. And plenty of dramatic emoting and confrontation. One thing's for sure, you got to do a lot in a Ken Russell movie if you were an actor!

### THE LOOK AND STYLE OF *WOMEN IN LOVE*.

Billy Williams,[40] who photographed *Women In Love*, said it was a 'very sumptuous looking film, very rich and colourful. It was very much a cameraman's film'. The photography in *Women In Love* is very beautiful; it has a lovely *quality* to it, a *texture* which's sadly lacking from some of the later works directed by Ken Russell (and most video photography simply can't compete).

Billy Williams said that Ken Russell was prepared to experiment (we knew that!). There were handheld Arriflex shots, zooms, slow motion, the camera on its side, and so on. Russell and Williams also experimented with a range of lighting conditions – soft, Summer light, dusk, candlelight, firelight.[41] *Women In Love* offered many opportunities for cinematography, Williams said, in terms of colour, different lighting effects, day-for-night, night-for-night, candlelight, firelight, twilight, dawn and snow scenes. 'It had everything going for it, all the opportunities'.[42] That's true of so many Ken Russell movies – a DP for Russell has to able to shoot in very low level conditions, or in firelight, or candlelight, or dawn, or magic hour, or night. (Indeed, one of the things that attracts cinematographers to historical movies is the opportunity to explore lighting that doesn't crop up so much in contemporary-set films – candlelight, firelight, etc).

The most memorable lighting effect in *Women In Love* occurred in the most famous scene in the 1969 movie, probably the scene most people associate with Ken Russell more than any other: the nude wrestling between Oliver Reed and Alan Bates in the pool room, in front of a huge, log fire. As often in his films, Russell, Williams and the camera crew moved from medium shots

---

[40] As well as shooting *Women In Love* and *Billion Dollar Brain*, Billy Williams also shot *Sunday Bloody Sunday*, *The Wind and the Lion*, *Saturn 3* and *The Devil's Advocate*. He received an Oscar for *Gandhi*, and a nomination for *On Golden Pond*.
[41] D. Petrie, 1996, 155.
[42] B. Williams, in D. Schaefer, 1984, 271.

to handheld close-ups (using two Arriflexes), as the action intensified.

In the scene in *Women In Love* where Gudrun Brangwen dances with the cattle (one of the first scenes filmed), the film-makers used handheld camera, intercut with images of Rupert Birkin dancing in front of Ursula and singing 'Oh, You Beautiful Doll'. Both Gudrun and Birkin seduce their partners by dancing, with Gudrun's dance having a much more elemental and animalistic aspect to it, emphasized by the way she dances with the cows then in front of Gerald (choreography was by Russell regular Terry Gilbert. Some of the scene was shot by Russell himself – you can spot the way that Russell handles the camera a mile off. So he was dancing in amongst his actors – that inter-relationship of the director, the camera and the actors is a key ingredient in Russell's cinema. Russell is not the kind of director who huddles behind the video monitors in a tent).

Ken Russell recalled that the physical aspects of the scene contributed to its impact: Glenda Jackson hated the cows and the cold and the mud, didn't get on with Oliver Reed, it was late in the day with the light going,[43] and she had the director operating the camera himself (Bax, 174). All of which added to the pressure – exactly the kind of thing that Russell thrives on.

*Women In Love* also contains perhaps Ken Russell's most extravagant mirror scene, in the duologue between Gerald and Birkin, which employs mirrors extensively for its close-ups, as well as the (inevitable) infinity mirror shot, famous from *Citizen Kane*. And, like all mirror shots in movies, it can mean anything, from the two men's lives or personalities being fragmented at that point onwards, to the multiplicity of selves that everyone possesses, to any psychological or psychoanalytical interpretation you fancy. Mirror scenes make film theorists go ga-ga, so we'll leave it to them to scrutinize the scene with their nerdy toothpicks and laser-guided spectacles.

Many of the costumes in *Women In Love* are taken from the book (like Gudrun's dark blue dress), but what *was* Jennie Linden wearing in that first scene? With that hat and colourful coat she might have just wandered out of the Biba store or Carnaby Street (it had bugger all to do with the character in D.H. Lawrence's 1920 story). Later on, Ursula sports a bright orange outfit, and

---

43 Directors and cameramen love magic hour photography, but everyone else is knackered at the end of the day, and feels the pressure to get the scenes done.

Gerald has a jacket with orange and brown stripes (a nice touch has Birkin wearing the tie that goes with Gerald's jacket, suggesting the intimacy between the men). Orange, gold and brown form the colour scheme of the 1969 production, particularly in relation to the Brangwen sisters (Gudrun's bedroom, for instance, is gold and orange, and she wears a gold outfit). And often the two women are clad in bright colours (such as orange or blue) to contrast with the miners in black and grey or the grimy town, emphasizing their individuality and exoticism. Later, the palette shifts into blacks and whites, reflecting moral absolutes.

Every costume drama says as much about the time it was produced as about the intended historical period, of course, and *Women In Love* is no exception. *Women In Love* is *very* Sixties, and very *late* Sixties. The characters could walk onto the set of *Blow-Up* or *The Magical Mystery Tour* or *Performance* and would blend in perfectly. Times change, fashions change, and by the 1990s and after for costume dramas, the wardrobe was much more restrained and muted, colour-wise, with blacks, greys, dark blues and creams predominating (in films such as *Sense and Sensibility, Emma, Wings of a Dove, Oliver Twist,* etc). Meanwhile, *every* friggin' movie and trailer and poster in the 21st century seems to be coloured in steely greys, blues and blacks, as if the warm end of the spectrum has vanished and left the planet.

THE WEDDING SCENE.

The first big scene in the 1969 adaption of *Women In Love* was the wedding of Gerald Crich's sister, Laura (Sharon Gurney) to Tibs (Christopher Gable). Some scene-setting was employed as Gudrun and Ursula walk through the streets of Beldover (cue images of a Lawrencean mining town), and ride on a tram (when they arrive and walk through the streets, there are further environmental scenes of shops and extras). These scenes establish the 'women in love' of the title, two of the principal characters (and, importantly, also the lead actors), the setting, their relationship, and some of their desires. But already the film was shifting into different forms of narration (the dialogue between Gudrun and Ursula isn't heard – instead, there's George Delerue's music).[44]

---

[44] There's a lot less music in *Women In Love* than one might imagine for a Ken Russell movie, and there are more popular songs than usual in a period movie about love and relationships. Delerue provides some terrific music cues, however.

And when the 1969 film of *Women In Love* reaches the church, a montage form of editing is employed to depict some of the back stories of the characters (such as the scenes of Rupert Birkin's school inspector visiting Ursula Brangwen, and the introduction of Hermione Roddice – beautifully and extravagantly played with arch artifice by Eleanor Bron). Such montages were likely developed during the editing period, as they often do. The producers didn't like the opening, and asked for a re-edit. (Ken Russell and Mike Bradsell would employ the technique again and again – most famously and imaginatively in the *First Piano Concerto* sequence in *The Music Lovers*, a *tour-de-force* of exposition and editing). The montage form of editing is also a way of getting across exposition and back-story but keeping it lively (by not staying with one scene too long).

The wedding at the top of *Women In Love* is a big scene allowing the introduction of a bunch of characters, including the two men, Rupert Birkin and Gerald Crich (just like one of the most famous wedding scenes in movies – *The Godfather*). And, unusually, the 1969 movie constructs a sequence of women looking with erotic desire at men (the other way around is the norm in cinema). Indeed, *Women In Love* announces from its opening scene that it's going to be, in part, a 'woman's film'. Ken Russell making a 'women's picture'?! You bet: because the first two, major characters introduced here are Ursula and Gudrun. And the title has two terms linked to the 'feminine' and to 'women's films' – 'women' and 'love'.

Strategically, this was a good move for Ken Russell, at that stage in his career, because a movie titled *Women In Love* is probably going to bring in a female audience (the opposite of *Billion Dollar Brain*). Strategically good, because it meant that Russell wasn't typed as only producing male-oriented movies early on in his career (many movie directors, including many of the biggest names, rarely if ever include women in the title roles or main roles, and they would *never* produce a movie with the title *Women In Love!*).

*Women In Love* also announces early on that it's going to be about *relationships*. It is a 'relationship movie', without a doubt. What is the battleground of *Women In Love*? It's not war, or heroes vs. villains, or cowboys, or car chases in Paris, or samurai in Edo period Japan, it's about *relationships*. The first big scene, for instance, is (very ironically) a wedding (thus, it doesn't *end* with a wedding, like a conventional romantic yarn), with the four main characters discussing or thinking about erotic relationships (and set against the wildly enthusiastic lovers – Tibby Lupton races up the church path to embrace his bride and kiss her (she hares off up the path to escape him), and in subsequent scenes they are always shown madly in love, kissing and the like – which makes Laura Crich's desire to kill herself and her new husband even more tragic – and inexplicable).

Before the dinner party under the trees, there's a scene of Rupert Birkin and Hermione Roddice by a pool, which depicts their uncomfortable relationship (when Birkin spills his drink, and Hermione begins to lick it off, the awkward embrace/ kiss demonstrates clearly that the erotic aspect of their relationship is very dead – the movie also mocks Hermione, as well as the other characters, reinforcing the portrayal of her an eccentric and unfeeling soul). Ursula and Gudrun are invited to Hermione's place for a meal.

THE FIG SCENE.

If you don't think that Ken Russell is a good screenwriter, the fig scene proves otherwise (Russell and Larry Kramer co-wrote the script, but the fig scene seems to have been Russell's idea). It's good scriptwriting, because it's doing a bunch of things simultaneously (just as Russell said of D.H. Lawrence's poem): the fig scene shows:

(1) Rupert Birkin's unusual views, including the emphasis on sex and sensuality;

(2) Birkin's tendency to lecture his audience, and to be a bit of jerk when he's doing it;

(3) Gerald's bemused reaction (he's probably seen Rupert going on like this many times – we all have friends like that!);

(4) Ursula's fascination with Birkin, particularly the unspoken erotic link between them;

(5) the power games between Birkin and Hermione (and how their relationship is past its use-by date);

(6) and, lastly, it's pure D.H. Lawrence.

The poem that Ken Russell found is quoted in full in the appendix. This is the first part:

The proper way to eat a fig, in society,
Is to split it in four, holding it by the stump,
And open it, so that it is a glittering, rosy, moist, honied, heavy-
                    petalled four-petalled flower.

Then you throw away the skin
Which is just like a four-sepalled calyx,
After you have taken off the blossom, with your lips.

But the vulgar way
Is just to put your mouth to the crack, and take out the flesh in one bite.

You can see that Ken Russell and Larry Kramer took many lines from the poem and put them into the 1969 movie. Seems simple, doesn't it? You get D.H. Lawrence to write your script for you. Yeah, but you can only do this if (1) you know how to put it in the movie, (2) it fits with the character and the story (and the theme), (3) you rewrite it so it doesn't sound like poetry, and (4) you have very good actors who can deliver this sort of material (trust me, not every actor could do this scene as excellently as Alan Bates. He makes it look effortless – because he is a *very* good actor).

The fig scene came from Bertie Lawrence's poetry, Ken Russell said: it was typical of Russell's approach to adapting books that he would take dialogue or ideas from an author's other works and incorporate them into the film. The dialogue about the fig works partly because the Birkin in the *movie* is closely modelled on Lawrence himself (and Lawrence's voice comes through loud and clear in his poems. There's a refrain in the scene where Birkin talks about catkins).

*Women In Love* is what you could call a 'subtext film' – a movie in which everything really significant is played as subtext. What is the subtext of the fig scene (which Ken Russell added to the script)? Well, Birkin makes the subtext the centrepiece of the scene, it's not hidden at all: it's about women, sex, erotic relationships, etc. It's the kind of speech that has driven feminists nuts about D.H. Lawrence. Looking at the United Artists film again, Birkin comes across as a bit of a tit, and a pretentious tit, too (but quite a few of Lawrence's characters are twerps). And it's one of those odd scenes where a bunch of characters listen quietly to one character going on and on, and no one stops him and tells him he's a dick (you try delivering that speech at the next dinner party you go to!). But Alan Bates plays it beautifully.

Meanwhile, the editing is creating another network of reaction shots, to actors Jennie Linden, Oliver Reed, Glenda Jackson and others, and further hinting at the erotic attraction between the two couples. And there is another subtext, which's the dissatisfying erotic relationship between Birkin and Hermione.

Look at the 1969 movie of *Women In Love* again, and you'll see just how much the *editing* is contributing towards the piece (courtesy of Mike Bradsell and his team). Of course, the visuals are ravishing at times, and Ken Russell has always been known for being a master at creating intoxicating visuals. But it's the *editing* that is doing so much of the storytelling, especially in this movie about subtexts and relationships.

Thus, while the dialogue is doing one thing, and the actions within a scene are doing another (plus the *mise-en-scène*, costumes, sets, etc), it's actually the editing that is controlling the meanings and subtexts and emotions of the movie. D.H. Lawrence does spoil his novels sometimes by being way too obvious and insistent in his dialogue – continually, Lorenzo's characters tell each other how they're feeling, how they're reacting to the other person, what they want, what they don't want, etc.

That can work in a movie (or a stage play), but often it can also be too on the nose. Filmmakers like to *show* not tell (well, the good ones do, and especially the visual filmmakers). In *Women In Love*, it's the editing that is doing so much of the telling, although there is Lawrencean dialogue too (especially from Ursula and Birkin).

THE MASQUE.

In the novel of *Women In Love*, the masque in the style of the then fashionable Russian ballet (Vaslav Nijinsky and Sergei Diaghilev) takes up not much more'n a page. In the 1969 interpretation, it becomes a major set-piece (Ken Russell was a big fan of Nijinsky (1890-1950), and planned a film about him). Russell & co. manage to stage a lengthy music and dance number in a literary adaption (maybe Russell was thinking, well, if Harry Saltzman isn't going to produce my Nijinsky movie, I'll just squeeze in a ballet scene in *Women In Love*!).

The episode is a battle of wills between Hermione Roddice and Rupert Birkin: Hermione is leading the scene, but Birkin takes over (much to Hermione's ire). *Dramatically*, it's that simple. *Cinematically*, it's more complex, and includes many beats and bits of business. Piano music pounds throughout (like an audition for *The Boy Friend*), as Hermione leads the Brangwen sisters, Gudrun and Ursula, in a mythological dance, while the men watch. One can imagine that Ken Russell would be quite happy to make a whole film like this. Forget the dialogue – move into music and movement and dance: *Women In Love* as a ballet, or a musical, or an opera. Russell once joked that it might have been better to turn *Women In Love* into a musical – certainly music and dance play far more important roles here than in any other adaption of D.H. Lawrence's fiction.

As Joseph Gomez pointed out, the influence of Isadora Duncan, one of Ken Russell's heroes in dance, influenced the 1969 movie, particularly in the Greek ballet sequence at Hermione Roddice's, and also in the scene where Gudrun dances before the cattle (G, 82). Russell reckoned that Lawrence must've drawn on Duncan's elemental approach to dance: 'Gudrun would have liked to be Isadora, but a bit more intellectual with it… [Duncan] was the first woman to be aware of the elemental sense around her and respond to it. Lawrence must have been conscious of this'. (Bax, 174)

Halfway through, with Rupert Birkin's encouragement, the scene became a semi-drunken dance to modern music. Hermione Roddice's rage is carefully repressed (she's a little like a movie director who's furious when the organized chaos of the film set becomes disorganized chaos, and the actors are jiving to jazz or thrash metal or garage when they should be swanning around smoothly to Peter Tchaikovsky or Sergei Rachmaninov).

♣

COMMUNING WITH NATURE.

The nude wrestling scene gets all the press coverage, but there is much more male nudity in *Women In Love* than that: Alan Bates goes nude in the previous sequence, where he communes in Lorzeno-style with the natural world. Hmmm; it's kinda D.H. Lawrence, but not really (it's a modern (or rather, a late 1960s) interpretation of what a Lawrencean character Communing With

Nature might do).⁴⁵ The scene is effective in its deployment of sound effects, however – the soft brushing sounds of walking through grass and bushes, with some nighttime sounds added. (Alan Bates rubs himself on a pine tree – surely an oak tree or a beech tree would be softer?! But maybe there wasn't an oak or beech nearby. He also lies down in the grass – classic images of a soul uniting with nature). And Ollie Reed also appears nude – when he dives into the lake (once again while Gudrun and Ursula look on). So this movie sets up the male nudity early on – and it's unusual in that it's the guys who disrobe first (and that they are looked at by women, and women who are becoming attracted to them).

*Women In Love* captured a particular quality of the British landscape, John Baxter reckoned, which could also be found in the art of Charles Dickens, H.G. Wells, John Constable and especially J.M.W. Turner. Quaint, romantic, pastoral, but also 'a little threatening, a little absurd' (Bax, 142-3).

Then follows a scene which conjures classic images of the Brits being Brits: war and religion, a priest, hymns, and a war memorial. Rupert Birkin rails against it all, of course. This is more Lawrencean – or, at least, the didactic D.H. Lawrence who never missed an opportunity to lecture his readers, and give his five cents – well, three thousand dollars – of thoughts on the state of the world (Birkin can come across as a whinger, as many Lawrencean figures do – nothing is good enough, society is going to pot, the government are idiots, there's nothing and no one worth loving, etc etc etc).

*Women In Love*'s coal-mining scene is very impressive, a big scene with plenty of extras; it has an earthy feeling of the hard labour that goes into hauling material out from the planet. Of course, a D.H. Lawrence adaption *has* have a coal mining scene, and *Women In Love* has one of the best (similarly the streets in the town, with its miners, alleys and pubs, are vividly depicted). There's a stunning high angle, long shot of the miners walking home at the end of the work day, with a steam engine thundering by, clouds of steam, and Gerald and his father in their white car

---

45 Or maybe rolling around in the grass and rubbing branches over his body was the kind of thing that Ken Russell got up to in the Lake District! What was Russell's direction to Alan Bates as they filmed that scene? 'Err, have a go at getting closer to nature, love, you know, roll in the grass for a bit!'

moving through the workers.[46] (I'm not sure where it was filmed, but it looked like a plant that was still functioning; thirty years later, film companies in the U.K. had to go to coal mines that had been turned into heritage centres, places with that plasticky, cleaned-up, theme park look. In *Women In Love*, the scenes are authentically gritty and non-glossy).[47]

GUDRUN DANCES BEFORE THE CATTLE.

The water-party scenes lay the groundwork for three of the most memorable scenes in *Women In Love*: the drowning of Laura and Tibs; Gudrun dancing with the cattle; and the parallel romances of Gerald and Gudrun and Birkin and Ursula. These are genuinely cinematic scenes, not talky, not dialogue-led, not 'filmed theatre', not television. Ken Russell put down *Women In Love* continually, and insisted he'd done better work elsewhere, but these are all very fine scenes. (And he finally has a decent enough budget to mount a large-scale version of the historical scenes he'd filmed in *Dante's Inferno* and *The Debussy Film* Altho', at $1.25-1.6 million, the budget for *Women In Love* is still tiny).

We're in the middle of the 1969 film, with a series of scenes that seem idyllic and lyrical – Gudrun and Ursula Brangwen go swimming nude (there has to be a nude, bathing scene in a D.H. Lawrence film); they have a picnic; and Gudrun decides to dance. Yes, Ken Russell has squeezed in *another* dance scene into the movie! It's one of his best, partly because of the way it's staged and choreographed, the way it's shot and cut (largely with the lake in the background, under some huge trees in full leaf), partly due to the superb way that Glenda Jackson plays it, and partly because it doesn't have strident music accompanying it (instead, it's Ursula singing 'I'm Forever Blowing Bubbles'. which's faded quietly into reverb). 'All my films are choreography. The camera moves and the people move', Russell remarked (Bax, 190).

It's a very effective scene, playing to that non-verbal, musical-movement realm which's Ken Russell's specialty. Indeed, this might be the most successful sequence in the 1969 film of *Women In Love*, this group of scenes – the shift from the picnic, to Ursula

---

[46] The image of the big posh car in amongst the throng of exhausted coal-miners going homeward was an old but effective commentary on the power relations between owners and workers. Steven Spielberg and David Lean – they've all used that scene.
[47] Such as the utterly abysmal adaption Britain's ITV made of *Sons and Lovers*.

dancing, to the confrontation with the cattle, to Gerald's approach, to the colloquy between Gudrun and Gerald.[48]

When Gudrun Brangwen faces the cattle, and dances before them, the episode is a genuine piece of D.H. Lawrence's fiction – more so, perhaps, than the anguished lovemaking or the nude wrestling. The United Artists picture shifts from the lyrical images of Gudrun making shapes against the lake to much looser, handheld images and rapid cutting. And when Gerald arrives (running, more dynamic than his arrival with Birkin in the book), the film shifts its style of narration yet again, with lap dissolves between the shots.

THE WATER-PARTY SCENE.

The biggest scene in *Women In Love*, in terms of extras, costumes and budget, illustrated the novel's chapter XIV, "Water-Party", where rowing boats lit by paper lanterns floated on a lake at twilight (shot over three successive dusks,[49] at the 'magic hour', beloved of cameramen, because of the soft light it creates, making everyone look great, and hated by line producers, because it only lasts ten minutes). The water-party also featured details like fairground rides, miners drinking beer, and introduced Mrs Crich (Ken Russell is very fond of festival or masquerade scenes – anything with plenty of chaos and movement and colour).

As Joseph A. Gomez said of Ken Russell: he

> is consumed by images, and his entire career could be analyzed in terms of his attempts to transform other people's words into his unique images. (1981, 249)

One of the most memorable images from *Women In Love* was the brilliantly-executed cut between the nude bodies of the drowned couple, Tibby and Laura Lupton, on the mud at the bottom of the lake, after the boating party, to the figures of Ursula Brangwen and Rupert Birkin after they have made love (lying in very similar positions). The cut suggested the Lawrencean (Western) preoccupations with sex and death, with death-in-love

---

[48] As well as 'I'm Forever Blowing Bubbles', *Women In Love* also employs other popular and folk songs, and includes brass bands, and a rendition of 'Jerusalem' by William Blake and Sir Hubert Parry (1848-1918) at the war memorial ('Jerusalem' is an alternative, British national anthem).

[49] 'With this being so long and complex it took three evenings to shoot it,' recalled DP Billy Williams. And Olly Reed and the other actors had to swim in the cold water time after time.

and love-in-death. That was when the 1969 movie came close to the spirit of the 1920 novel, or at least found images which seemed to be striking equivalents for what happens in the book.

Why include the death of the newly-weds, Laura and Tibby Lupton? They are a sub-plot and minor characters, but their story relates directly to the main plot of love and sex and relationships. We see Laura getting married to Tibby at the opening of *Women In Love*, and they seem madly in love with each other. Giggingly, laughingly in love. And in subsequent scenes (such as at the Russian dance), they are still all over each other.

Then, during the water party, the couple are still the happy, young lovers, fooling about on the water, and going skinny-dipping (creeping into the lake when they're naked). So when Laura calls to Tibs, chuckling, then disappears under the water and Tibby's splashing about in trouble, like Susan Backlinie at the beginning of *Jaws* when the shark attacks her, and yelling for help, the flipside of love – tragedy, destruction, death – is vividly revealed. The cut from the dead lovers in the mud to Ursula and Birkin after their clinch rams home the point.

So the sub-plot of Laura and Tibby Lupton in *Women In Love* – like a mini *Romeo and Juliet* play, with its doomed, young lovers – is included to throw light on the twin relationships of Gerald-Gudrun and Birkin-Ursula. The death of Laura and Tibby is all the more shocking, in dramatic terms, because they seemed so wildly in love, and, even more extraordinary, it was a suicide. It's also important that the 1969 film deliberately *doesn't* explain their death, or psychologize it. (But we note that it is the *woman* who drags the man underwater, further developing the theme of the predatory woman established in the fig scene; also, one of Laura's first acts is to rush away from Tibs at the church, encouraging him to pursue her, like Daphne and Apollo in Greek mythology. And in that legend, Apollo was torn to shreds! We also note that in the previous scene, we saw the mentally ill Mrs Crich, suggesting that insanity is in the family– and, in true Lawrencean style, it's on the mother's side).

And the death and suicide of Laura and Tibby's included for another important reason: how it relates to Gerald Crich. Who is it who walks through the mud in the drained lake and stands over the drowned lovers? It's Gerald. Why? Because the picture has to set up that Gerald is going to kill himself too by the end of the story (*Women In Love* contains two suicides, no less).

### BIRKIN AND URSULA MAKE LOVE.

Another memorable effect in *Women In Love* was the tilted camera – putting the camera on one side when filming the long lens close-ups of Ursula Brangwen and Rupert Birkin meeting in an overgrown field, accompanied by over-sumptuous (i.e., ironic) music (by Georges Delerue). It was Ken Russell in his satirical TV commercial mode, which he employed in films like *The Music Lovers* and *Tommy*. Again, I'm sure that some viewers (and movie critics) took that scene literally, rather than ironically, as was clearly intended (look at the sequence again – there's no way that it is meant to be taken straight; it's two lovers walking towards each other in slow motion! Also, it's gorgeously done, and still very unusual – the camera on its side, the actors moving towards each other, the slow motion, the close framing, the backlighting, the angle having the effect of two lovers lying on top of each other).

The best moments of *Women In Love* were, as so often in a movie directed by Ken Russell, non-dialogue scenes: images plus music, such as the superb scene where Gudrun Brangwen gets up and starts to dance in amongst some trees and cattle, while Ursula sings 'I'm Forever Blowing Bubbles', one of the most popular songs of 1920 (the music was also employed over the opening credits, and is one of the signature music cues in the 1969 movie). The handheld shots of Gudrun facing off the cattle came after this.

The familiar Ken Russellian counterpoint approach is used with the music sometimes – for instance, the song 'I'm Forever Blowing Bubbles' is about wishing or dreaming, and the characters in *Women In Love*, as in movies such as *The Music Lovers* and *Savage Messiah*, have dreams or desires which are unreal and cannot be fulfilled. Russell argued that although the music doesn't appear in the novel, the two young women would've been aware of the popular music of the time. And of course the music places the scene in the 1920s period.

The setting – the trees by the lake – is a brilliant use of locations (and magic hour photography). The move from long shots in silhouette to handheld close-ups is a classic Ken Russell cinematic technique, as is the use of near-silence as Gudrun Brangwen dances with the music coming in later, to accentuate the change in the mood and purpose of the scene – from Gudrun to an illustration of her eccentric and even perverse delight in startling the cattle (it wasn't meant to be 'real', Russell commented in *An Appalling Talent*, not 'real' for him, as the director, but 'real' for Gudrun, to embody her character and the novel [Bax, 175]). And dramatically the scene's impressive, in the way it brings Gerald Crich into the scene, and puts Gudrun and Gerald together romantically (notice, too, the unusual dissolves in the midst of the exchange of dialogue, as Gudrun lies on the grass below Gerald, a marvellous way of suggesting the strangeness in the developing relationship between the two. Indeed, the erotic relationship of Gudrun and Gerald has strangeness heightened at many moments – the way that Gudrun seems coolly indifferent to Gerald's advances when she's with him, but how fascinated she is when she watches him from a distance. As if he disappoints her at close quarters, and she'd prefer him to remain a fantasy, seen from afar).

THE NUDE WRESTLING SCENE.

The famous nude wrestling match in *Women In Love* had originally been conceived by Ken Russell & co. as taking place outdoors, at night, when Gerald Crich comes upon Rupert Birkin bathing nude in the lake. They lark about, and get to fighting. Russell told the story, many times, how Oliver Reed stormed into his house when he found out about the nude scene (from his wife – he apparently hadn't read the novel), and showed him how it should really be played (how Reed was in an unstoppable mood (i.e., drunk). Another time, Reed used swords in his demonstration, which ended with Russell cutting Reed on the chest). Russell also often related how the shoot went, how the actors had a few drinks to set themselves up, how Reed compared his genitals with Alan Bates in the restroom the night b4 when they went out for a drink, and how Reed nipped into a corner to masturbate to enlarge his penis during filming (all rubbish, but now part of the legend).[50]

Still daring today, *Women In Love*'s nude wrestling scene is Ken Russell's cinema at its finest (and it's also a tribute to

---

50 Alan Bates dislocated his shoulder after shooting for 3 days, and Oliver Reed had bruises. The filmmakers had put rubber under the carpet, but that didn't look good, because they bounced on it. 'We took it out and they just landed crash bang wallop on the floor, time after time', Ken Russell recalled (Bax, 180).

Russell's standing as a director that he could get two major actors to do this scene. And still today there are plenty of stars who would *not* do that scene. Ever. For *any* money). Needless to say, nobody was looking forward to filming it – tough for the actors and for the crew.

In the chapter "Gladiatorial", the scene is described by Lorenzo thus:

> So the two men entwined and wrestled with each other, working nearer and nearer. Both were white and clear, but Gerald flushed smart red where he was touched, and Birkin remained white and tense. He seemed to penetrate into Gerald's more solid, more diffuse bulk, to interfuse his body through the body of the other, as if to bring it subtly into subjection, always seizing with some rapid necromantic foreknowledge every motion of the other flesh, converting and counteracting it, playing upon the limbs and trunk of Gerald like some hard wind. It was as if Birkin's whole physical intelligence inter-penetrated into Gerald's body, as if his fine, sublimated energy entered into the flesh of the fuller man, like some potency, casting a fine net, a prison, through the muscles into the very depths of Gerald's physical being. (348-9)

Plenty of *penetration*, then.

In the 1969 version of *Women In Love*, the nude wrestling scene begins with some dialogue, once again about the familiar Lawrencean themes of love and relationships, in particular male brotherhood and closeness. Importantly, it is a scene between equals – this is not Gerald seducing Birkin or vice versa: it's Gerald who suddenly stands up and asks Birkin to demonstrate, and it's Birkin who suggests that they should strip.[51]

That it's a gay sex scene the United Artists movie is in no doubt: this is two men at night in a room on their own, drinking by firelight, even before they get naked – i.e., it's already a very romantic setting (and the lighting – and intimate conversation – emphasizes that). But when the men strip off and begin wrestling, the scene becomes the longest love scene in the movie (and in much of Ken Russell's cinema).

The rapid cutting disguises long views of nudity, as per the censorship laws,[52] but it can't hide the fact that this is two men fully naked who're grappling each other (and men that we know

---

[51] Note the cutaway to the large, white bear skin – more animalistic, Lawrencean flesh and spirit.
[52] In the early Seventies, films such as *Zabriskie Point*, *M\*A\*S\*H*, *Fellini Satyricon* and *Women In Love* escaped the 'X' rating, which was death at the box office, when the MPAA under Jack Valenti raised the 'R' rating from 16 to 17.

are very friendly with each other). It might have been called 'Men In Love', as Ken Russell admitted. Only when the men have wrestled for some time do editor Mike Bradsell and director Russell bring in the music (and take down the local sound of pants and slaps). The scene climaxes – literally – with the two men face to face, very close together, with the kiss apparently inevitable. And when they slowly collapse to the floor, with Gerald on top of Birkin, the poses again suggest lovemaking.[53]

For feminists such as Luce Irigaray and Andrea Dworkin, women become commodities traded between men. In Irigaray's view of the narcissistic, phallocentric economy, women are not the endpoint of desire, but the means or carriers of male desire. As it's between men, this sexual economy is homosexual, governed by and for men. This is certainly at work in *Women In Love*: the book and the film may be about 'women in love', but it's men who have the final say, and the women for some feminists are commodities. And D.H. Lawrence's 1920 novel also makes clear the homoerotic relationship between Birkin and Crich – so clear, in fact, that there's a nude wrestling scene between the two guys! Lawrence doesn't depict gay sex, but has the nude wrestling scene stand in for it (with all the motifs pointing towards sex – the nudity, the sweat, the closeness, and even the fireside, nighttime setting). All of that is brought out in the 1969 movie.

*Women In Love* is unusual among mainstream commercial cinema in depicting not one but two gay relationships. That Herr Loerke and his companion are gay nobody can be in any doubt (or that Loerke swings both ways, having his eye on Gudrun from the get-go. But he is also the kind of personality that would try to seduce Gudrun Brangwen simply to cause trouble).

Some critics have chosen to see the central relationship in *Women In Love* between Rupert and Gerald as brotherhood or a Platonic ideal or companionship or whatever the current euphemism is for gay relationships. But no, this is a homosexual relationship. It might be unreciprocated fully from Gerald's point-of-view (he appears reluctant to go the whole hog), but Birkin certainly wants it. It's Birkin, of course, that's talking about

---

53 Ken Russell commented that when the censors in Argentina cut out much of the scene, but included the opening section, where Gerald and Birkin shake hands, and the final shots, where they are lying on the carpet together, it suggested the scene was even more erotic ('it became known as the great buggering scene and filled cinemas for months', according to the maestro).

wanting more than companionship and love with a woman. There must be something more, for Birkin – and the movie keeps coming back to that (to the point where it closes the picture).

So *Women In Love* portrays the courtship and intercourse of two heterosexual couples, but also the courtship and near-sexual relationship of two men. But one could argue, because of all of the devices and tropes employed, that the nude wrestling scene is a sex scene between two men in all but name. And once you combine those dramatic, romantic elements with some terrific performances, a great cast, and innovative and beautiful film-making, you can see why *Women In Love* is many folks' favourite Ken Russell movie.

SWITZERLAND.

The Swiss scenes in *Women In Love* were impressive – the endless reaches of snow contrasting dramatically with the soft undulations of the English countryside (they were filmed below the Matterhorn in Switzerland, including the Riffelberg Inn in Zermatt). Character actor Vladik Sheybal, another Ken Russell regular, as Loerke, added to the atmosphere of decadence, stifled sexuality, boredom, and impending doom.

Herr Loerke is a cliché of the decadent, purist artist, right down to his bisexuality – the first time he's introduced, in the German dance sequence, he's already got his eye on Gudrun Brangwen, but his blond lover (Richard Heffer) gets to dance with her first. Loerke also embodies the darker, sensual side of life that Gudrun hankers after (and all that's lacking in her relationship with Gerald Crich) – in the 1969 movie, Gudrun's depicted as someone who's simultaneously attracted and repulsed by violence and eroticism (or violent eroticism, or erotic violence). For instance, in the famous scene (superbly staged) where Gerald rides his white horse right at a passing train,[54] Ursula freaks out but Gudrun is fascinated.[55]

In the movie version of *Women In Love*, it's partly Gerald Crich's powerful physicality and drive that attracts Gudrun Brangwen (not, for example, his economic wealth or powerful job

---

54 And it does seem to be Oliver Reed riding the horse at a gallop beside the train – though the stunt in front of the train is likely a stuntman.
55 For Linda Ruth Williams, the scene in the book has a cinematic quality, with D.H. Lawrence shifting points-of-view from the third person to Gudrun's p.o.v., and the shot-counter-shot pattern of the text helps to render the movie version successful (*Sex In the Head*, Harvester Wheatsheaf, 1993, 66).

as mine manager). But after they've got together, Gudrun finds out that Gerald is not what she expected, and maybe he can't love her (and maybe she would've been better off admiring Gerald from afar). The scenes between them in the Swiss chalet are beautifully performed (and written) – Gudrun systematically (and quietly) demolishes Gerald and his idea of love and relationships. And in the lengthy master two-shot, Oliver Reed plays his moodiness at Moody Three, and simmers brilliantly. You know that Reed's Gerald is not going to sit back and take all this dressing down, even if it is the truth (Gudrun's right about Gerald's brutal form of loving – because in the next scene he fucks Gudrun like he's murdering her – and it's the first appearance of the characteristic, handheld, up-and-down, Ken Russell camera movement, which simulates sex).

The Swiss episode in *Women In Love* has a genuinely apocalyptic feel to it, a relentless surge towards self-destruction that seems unstoppable – like an ocean liner that can't stop and crashes into a harbour. The urge towards self-absorption which leads to self-immolation, the United Artists movie suggests, is a fatal flaw in the Crich family: the mother is insane, the daughter (Laura) killed herself *and* her new husband Tibby, and the son, that the family now relies upon, stalks off into the mountains to die.

And Ken Russell, Larry Kramer and the team find the perfect embodiment of the insanity of Gerald's act, as well as the desperation and sadness of it, by showing Oliver Reed trudging through the pristine snow. And, rightly, editor Mike Bradsell holds and holds on that shot. And this is just one of many, many memorable images in *Women In Love*. It might be for Russell one of his least-liked movies, but it contains numerous vivid images.

In conventional drama characters are usually changed at the end of a play or a novel. In *Women In Love* (the novel) there is no great change. Ursula Brangwen seems no different: instead, the characters are wearier, more cynical and more bitter. The war between love and solitude is not resolved, partly because D.H. Lawrence always sees things in terms of opposition, rather than two, complementary sides. Eugene Goodheart writes in *The Utopian Vision of D.H. Lawrence*:

Lawrence opposes an ecstatic, onanistic aloneness (don't be deceived by his insistence that he is not alone) in which the self absorbs and is enhanced by the cosmos to the romantic cult of passion, the dissolution of the identities of lovers into a death-like unity. Lawrence discovers the terror at the heart of sexual passion.[56]

The 1969 United Artists film does reflect that sense of circularity,[57] and characters getting nowhere. There is a tragic ending to *Women In Love*, with Gerald walking off into the mountains to expire, but Ursula and Birkin, it seems, haven't advanced spiritually or psychologically at all. As Joseph Gomez remarked, Ken Russell and Larry Kramer were much more sceptical and satirical about Ursula than D.H. Lawrence was, and it doesn't seem that Ursula has altered much at all (whereas she most definitely has in the 1920 novel). *Women In Love* ends with the lovers disagreeing.

MARKETING AND RECEPTION.

*Women In Love* was marketed cleverly in North America by United Artists, according to Ken Russell: they went down the academic/ literary/ college route, and showed the movie to psychologists, students, and intellectuals (Bax, 182). The tactic has been used many times with prestige or literary movies, to build strong word-of-mouth.

Though not his favourite movie, or his most typical movie, Joseph Lanza is right to point out that *Women In Love* contains many of Ken Russell's key themes, and was:

> perfect for summarizing Russell's courtships and inevitable conflicts between the sexes; his conflicted sympathies with homosexual relationships; his so-called love of nature and his phobias about its slimier side; his desire to tell a serious story while simultaneously slipping into farce; his love of art and his penchant for destroying art's mystique; his battle between visceral, irrational sensations and the more intellectual approach to life that Lawrence once derided as "sex in the head"; and spells of anger, pessimism and even nihilism that belie his frustrated love of life. (2)

---

56 E. Goodheart. *The Utopian Vision of D.H. Lawrence*, University of Chicago Press, 1963, 78.
57 There are repetitions and rhymes throughout the picture. For example, there's a visual rhyme where Gudrun takes Gerald to the same place under a bridge where she saw a miner and his girl embracing (which expresses her fascination and fear of sex and love).

## D.H. LAWRENCE AT THE CINEMA

> The film is only pictures, like pictures in the *Daily Mirror*. And pictures don't have any feelings apart from their own feelings. I mean the feelings of the people who watch them. Pictures don't have any feelings except in the people who watch them. And that's why they like them. Because they make them feel that they are everything.
>
> D.H. Lawrence, *The Lost Girl* (p. 144)

Ken Russell has contributed more than most to the D.H. Lawrence film and television industry, taking on three of Lawrence's biggest works. Films of Lawrence's work, up to the period of *Women In Love*, include: *The Rocking Horse Winner* (Anthony Pelissier, 1949, GB), with Valerie Hobson and John Mills, a real British curio; the superb *Sons and Lovers* (1960, Jack Cardiff, GB), with Dean Stockwell, Trevor Howard and Wendy Hiller; and *Lady Chatterley's Lover* (Marc Allégret, 1955), a French version, starring Danielle Darrieux; a North American version of *The Fox* (Mark Rydell, 1968), with Keir Dullea and Sandy Dennis; and *The Virgin and the Gipsy* (Christopher Miles, 1970, GB), with Franco Nero and Joanna Shimkus.

The 1960s was a decade of significant D.H. Lawrence movies and influence: there was the *Lady Chatterley* trial in 1960 (a version of *Lady Chatterley's Lover* had appeared in 1955); *Sons and Lovers* in 1960; then, in the late 1960s, when Lawrence was associated with counter-culture, the Summer of Love, free expression, hippy ideals and so on, there were three pictures: *The Fox, Women In Love* and *The Virgin and the Gipsy* (the 1970 *Virgin and the Gipsy* might not have been commissioned by producers inspired by the success of United Artists' film, but it was definitely of a similar type, and may have been influenced by it).

1960's *Sons and Lovers* was a terrific, if drastically curtailed, version of the 1913 D.H. Lawrence novel, and one of the first, major movies of a Lorenzo book. It enhanced the picture enormously by filming in many of the locations that inspired Lawrence for his novel (that doesn't automatically work, of course – because movies are pure illusion, but here it paid off).

Being directed by one of the great British cinematographers, Jack Cardiff (most famous for his collaborations with Mickey Powell), *Sons and Lovers* was always going to look great, and of course it did, with pin-sharp, contrasty, black-and-white photography (the DP was Freddie Francis). And although it missed out reams of Lawrencean prose and incidents, it did capture some of the erotic and psychological tensions in the relationships surrounding Paul Morel.

Dean Stockwell, an American Method actor who's made 100s of appearances in TV and movies, delivered an intense and convincing Paul Morel, as if James Dean had grown up in 1910s Nottinghamshire. Stockwell's Morel avoided the pitfalls of the role (such as not coming over as a smug, self-satisfied know-it-all, or someone wallowing in depression and narcissism, which's how some of Lorenzo's characters can appear. Because, let's face it, Morel can seem like a stuck-up prig in *Sons and Lovers*).

Since the Sixties the number of D.H. Lawrence adaptions has grown: there have been BBC TV versions of *Sons and Lovers* (1981, adapted by Trevor Griffiths); *The Captain's Doll* (BBC, 1982); *The Trespasser* (Colin Gregg, 1981, GB); *The Boy in the Bush* (Rob Stewart, 1984, Channel Four); *The Rainbow* (Stuart Burge, 1989, BBC), with Imogen Stubbs; an Australian *Kangaroo* (Tim Burstall, 1986), with Colin Friels and Judy Davis; *Priest of Love,* about Lawrence's life (Christopher Miles, 1981, GB), with Ian McKellen, Ava Gardner, Janet Suzman and John Gielgud; soft porn versions of *Lady Chatterley's Lover* (Just Jaecklin, 1981, GB/ Fr) with Sylvia Kristel and Nicholas Clay, a Czech TV version (1998), *The Young Lady Chatterley* (1977), and a sequel (1985).[58] Britain's ITV channel produced a version of *Sons and Lovers* in 2003 (it was scripted by Simon Burke and was truly awful).

It's a testament to the power of *Women In Love* that film and TV companies held off remaking it for such a long time. Finally, the BBC (inevitably) took up *Women In Love* for a TV rehash in 2011 (the year that Ken Russell died), combining it with *The Rainbow* (for a mini-series of two episodes). The crew included William Ivory (script), Miranda Bowen (direction), and 9 producers; the cast included Rory Kinnear, Rachael Stirling, Rosamund Pike and Joseph Mawle.

It was horseshit: I got thru 20 minutes before giving up. I loathed the writing (characters standing about pontificating in boring reams of dialogue), I hated the zero energy in the drama, I

---

58 Movies using the *Lady Chatterley's Lover* monkier or source material have been either prestige/ literary productions or softcore porn flicks.

detested the horrible, shaky, quasi-documentary camerawork, the hopeless, 'impressionistic' approach to staging scenes, the inept direction (which treated D.H. Lawrence like a crummy soap opera), and the useless, embarrassed, snippy interaction between the characters (why do so many Brit TV shows have this same crappy, downcast, apologetic, sarky style of performance?).

A dire version of *Lady Chatterley's Lover* and *John Thomas and Lady Jane* was produced by Pascale Ferran in 2006. A French production, it completely missed the essence of Lorenzo's famous novel of sex and liberation. What was interesting about *Lady Chatterley's Lover*, looking at it from the viewpoint of British cinema and English literature, was to see how a French film production took on a 'British' subject. Oh, *Lady Chatterley's Lover* looked fine (most movies do), because the French locations easily stood in for the English Midlands. But it was fascinating to see the French film industry trying to reproduce the idiosyncrasies of the English way of life, how people talk to each other, how they move. In other words, although the subject and setting was English, *Lady Chatterley* couldn't help but be thoroughly *French*.

What's striking about the list of films made from D.H. Lawrence's work is that nearly all of them, apart from the Australian *Kangaroo* and the 1968 version of *The Fox*, and the 1993 *Lady Chatterley*, are British adaptions (well, 'British' in the sense of being made in Britain with mainly British casts; the money for some of those films was of course American, including for Ken Russell's 1969 and 1988 movies). Hollywood has steered clear of adapting Lawrence; and most of the adaptions of Thomas Hardy have also been British. William Shakespeare has had many more big budget Hollywood adaptions, as have Charles Dickens (and, to a lesser degree, Jane Austen, the Brontës and E.M. Forster).

Perhaps Thomas Hardy and D.H. Lawrence are too regional, too 'British'. Emily Brontë and Charles Dickens, like James Joyce, Graham Greene and Joseph Conrad, seem to travel outside Britain. There have been 'international' versions of Lawrence's contemporary E.M. Forster; these films (*A Room With a View, Howard's End, A Passage to India*), and the spate of Jane Austen adaptions, are part of British 'heritage' cinema, the sort of pictures made by the Merchant-Ivory team, and favouring Forster and Henry James.

And most adaptions of D.H. Lawrence have been for

television, where they are typically put into the 'classic' or 'prestige' bracket. Lawrence's short stories have been turned into one-off TV films (resembling the TV play for the day), and the novels have sometimes become mini-series (like *Lady Chatterley* directed by Ken Russell in 1993).

It's also striking that many of the adaptions of D.H. Lawrence have been influenced by the 1969 *Women In Love*. And the biopic of Lawrence, *Priest of Love*, is very much a Ken Russell-style movie.

D.H. Lawrence's novels have not so far been part of the heritage film industry. It's no surprise that many of the adaptions of Lawrence's novels have been on television (it's the same with Austen, Dickens, Hardy and Brontë), like Ken Russell's last Lawrence adaption, in 1993.

In amongst all of these D.H. Lawrence film and TV series (there are others),[59] the United Artists *Women In Love* has been one of the most significant. It may not be Ken Russell's favourite among his films, but it's certainly had a lasting impact on how Lawrence's fiction has been adapted for the big and small screen. It's simply one of those movies anyone has to take into account if they're adapting D.H. Lawrence, and you can bet that anybody who has adapted Lawrence for the screen has seen *Women In Love*, and you can bet that if someone's seen a Lawrence adaption, it will be *Women In Love*. In short, *Women In Love* is probably *the* premier adaption of a Lawrence text.

---

Probably the single most challenging aspect of a D.H. Lawrence adaption is the script. Get that right, and you have *so much* of your work already done (but *no* adaption has cracked the screenplay, in my opinion).

Closely followed by the *casting*. Not the casting of the grotesques and the eccentrics in a D.H. Lawrence adaption, nor the children, nor the old coots and crones (much easier to cast). I'm talking about the lead characters; that is, the Lawrencean men

---

[59] *You Touched Me* (1949 and 2014, short), *Samson and Delilah* (1959 and 1985, short), *The Stocking* (1955), *The Widowing of Mrs. Holroyd* (1961, 1974, 1976 and 1995), *The Stories of D.H. Lawrence* (1966-67, ITV Playhouse, 12 stories), *The Princess* (1968), *The Daughter-in-Law* (1969, 1971 and 1974), *A Collier's Friday Night* (1976), *The Rocking Horse Winner* (1977 and 1983), *The Horse Dealer's Daughter* (1983, short), *The Story of Lady Chatterley* (1989), *Earthly Disturbance* (1993), *La fidèle infidèle* (1995), *Milenec lady Chatterleyové* (1998), *The Rocking Horse Winner* (1998, short), *Odour of Chrysanthemums* (2006, short), *The Blind Man* (2011, short), *Inside the Mind of Mr D.H. Lawrence* (2013), and *The White Stocking* (2014, short).

and the Lawrencean women – Ursula, Gudrun, Birkin and Gerald in *Women In Love,* Ursula and Skrebensky in *The Rainbow*, Mellors and Lady C in *Lady Chatterley's Lover,* Paul Morel, Clara and Miriam in *Sons and Lovers,* Kate and Cipriano in *The Plumed Serpent*, Aaron in *Aaron's Rod*, and so on. You can take your pick from the talent from the whole history of cinema, but I bet you won't find too many actors and actresses who can really pull off those lead roles and embody Lawrence's characters.

Why? Because they're practically unplayable.

And that's why I reckon *Women In Love* was among the more successful of adaptions of Lorenzo, because the casting (aside from Jennie Linden as Ursula), was spot-on, among well-known British actors of the time. And it's also one reason why *Lady Chatterley* and *The Rainbow* are so much less satisfying. (Casting *Women In Love* wasn't easy, though: Ken Russell said he and Larry Kramer saw dozens of women for the roles of Ursula and Gudrun [Bax, 171f]).

✻

I had a go at adapting D.H. Lawrence for the stage in 2006 – a version of his short story *The Horse-Dealer's Daughter*, which we put on at a theatre in London (as well as preparing it for a film adaption). Lawrence is supremely inspiring to adapt – partly because it's such an immense challenge – to reach those psychological, emotional and spiritual zones that Lawrence himself is striving for.

So I can appreciate the difficulties in adapting D.H. Lawrence's fiction for drama. For a start, you've got to have great actors who can deliver rock-solid performances, and the actors have got to be able to deliver lines which, although they're not as intricate as William Shakespeare, do need special care.

And then you try to use all the means at your disposal to explore the feelings and themes in D.H. Lawrence's text – so we had music, lighting, props, movement, etc. And the elements you'd expect in a Lawrence piece: the pre-World War One setting, the symbolism, the elevated dialogue, and of course some nudity. (I added some characters and scenes to the short story *The Horse-Dealer's Daughter*, partly because it wasn't long enough for a play). It's a challenge because you're dramatizing and visualizing feelings, philosophies, metaphysical ideas, and social and religious concepts, rather than 'characters' in 'real' situations.

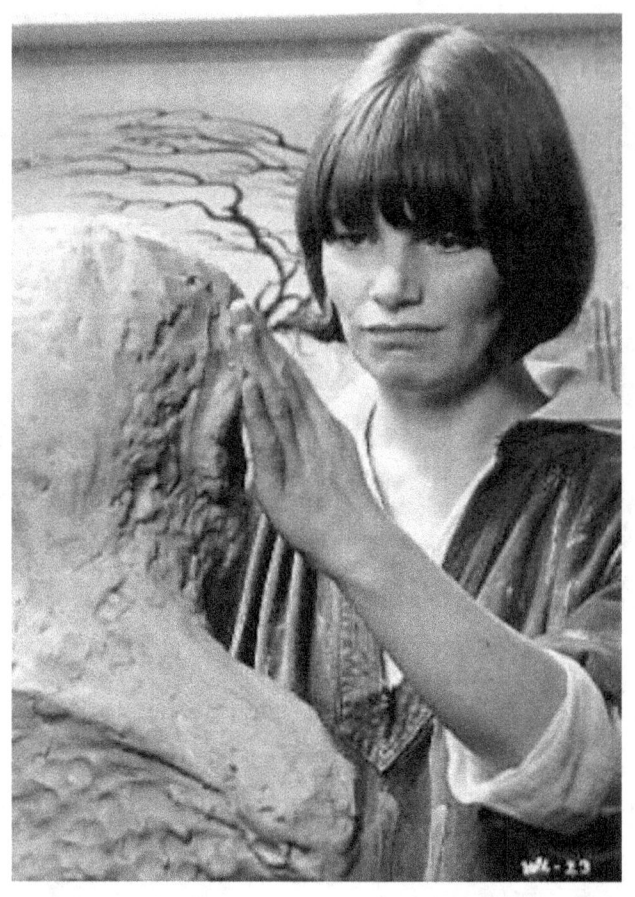

The stunning match cut in Women In Love
from the dead lovers at the bottom of the lake
to Birkin and Ursula after sex.
It's a good illustration of an invisible but
vital ingredient in Ken Russell's cinema: editing.

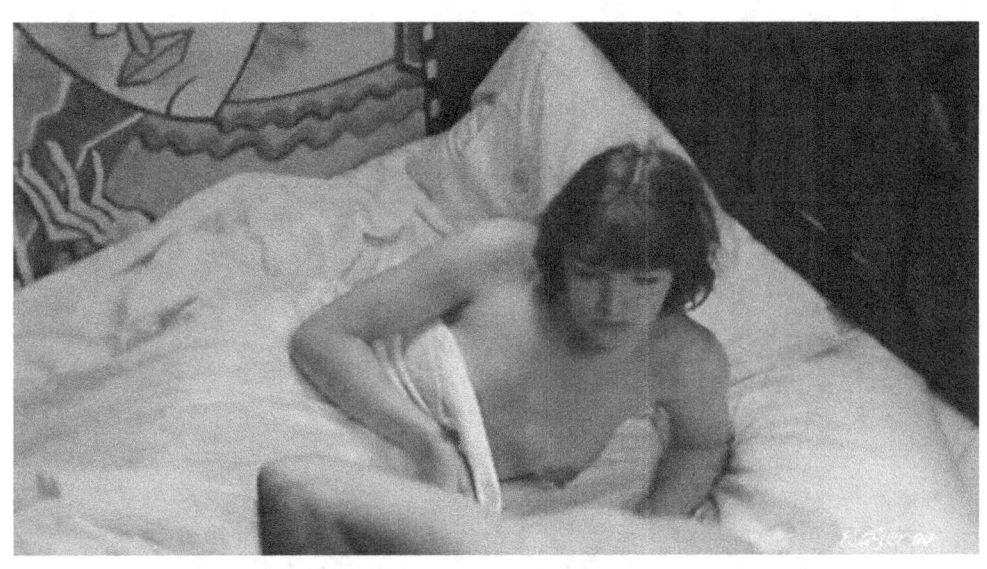

# 8
♪
## THE MUSIC LOVERS

> People call me self-indulgent, but [Peter Tchaikovsky] was the most self-indulgent man who ever lived, insofar as all his problems and hang-ups are stated in his music… His music, to me, has more pain in it than any music I know: self-inflicted pain, despair, suffering, precious little joy, and a kind of hysterical striving for love, a love so intense it could never exist.
>
> Ken Russell (*An Appalling Talent*, 183)

*The Music Lovers* (1970) is one of Ken Russell's favourites, among his own films. In 2010, Russell remarked:

> The film I'm most proud of is *The Music Lovers*, which featured the music of Tchaikovsky, because it was a masterpiece. It was the best film I ever made and I wouldn't change it in any way. I made a number of films on the great composers. My composers are my heroes because one never tires of them.

Without doubt, *The Music Lovers* is the first masterpiece among Ken Russell's feature films, though by this time he had already produced masterworks on television: *The Dance of the Seven Veils*, *Delius: Song of Summer*, *The Debussy Film*, *Isadora Duncan* and *Dante's Inferno* (the ambition and scope of those five TV docu-dramas, their flair and imagination, their narrative complexity and historical daring, even today beggar belief). *The Music Lovers* was his fourth theatrical feature.

Ken Russell spoke of a passionate love for Peter Tchaikovsky's music (*Piano Concerto No. 1 In B-flat Minor*),[1] when he heard it on the radio as a youth and was entranced by it.

> I became conscious of an incredible kind of beauty, the existence of which I had never dreamed. Even the bees stopped to listen and became as entranced as I.

It was akin to St Paul's conversion on the road to Damascus (of course a lapsed Catholic would make a comparison like that! But music really *was* that valuable to Ken Russell). Peter Tchaikovsky's music was fundamental in turning Russell on to classical music, a passion which would form such an important part of his professional life. For Russell, Tchaikovsky's music told the listener a good deal about his life and his psychology.

> A lot of his music is about frustrated love or the frustrated artist. Russell said that when he listened to Tchaikovsky's music, he heard all these mixed-up emotions, before I knew any details about his life I knew this man was a *mess*. (Bax, 183)

*The Music Lovers* was made when Ken Russell was at the height of his powers: organizing energetic crowd scenes, using locations and budgets imaginatively, indulging his penchant for visual and aural excess, and extracting strong performances from his lead actors (Glenda Jackson was outstanding as ever, turning in a remarkable performance, worthy of another Oscar, while Richard Chamberlain as Peter Tchaikovsky was never better. The casting of Tchaikovsky was of course vital to the success of the picture, and Chamberlain was absolutely superb, giving it his all.[2] He really throws himself wholeheartedly into this leading role, as you have to in a Russellini movie. No point in only going halfway!).[3]

On the basis of these two central performances alone, *The Music Lovers* is a major achievement, But there is more, so much more!

*The Music Lovers* was – and still is – a very significant movie for Ken Russell – it may be his most important production, at least

---

[1] And very soon afterwards, Russell went out to buy the music from a store, performed by Solomon Cutner and the Hallé Orchestra (PF, 22).
[2] That Richard Chamberlain was himself gay may have contributed towards the way he played the role.
[3] However, Alan Bates had been offered the role first, but had declined. Russell thought it might have been because Bates didn't want to play two sexually dubious parts in succession.

in terms of a film career. Why? For a number of reasons:

(1) Because it was a project he originated himself – on his previous three feature films, he had been a director-for-hire. But *The Music Lovers* was a project that Ken Russell was passionate about. *Women In Love* and *Billion Dollar Brain* are important ultimately because they enabled Ken Russell to make *The Music Lovers*.

(2) Further, it was the first time Ken Russell brought the approach of his television documentaries onto the big screen: at last he was able to stage a film about a classical music composer on a bigger scale (though still on a much lower budget than many a Hollywood flick).[4] Thus, *The Music Lovers* is the feature film version of the series of brilliant biopics of artists that Russell had developed over ten years in the 1960s: it's got everything that you find in *The Debussy Film, Isadora Duncan, Delius: Song of Summer, Dante's Inferno* and *The Dance of the Seven Veils* – the bohemian *milieu*, the late 19th century/ early 20th century setting, the explorations of art, the uneasy relations with patrons, the struggle to survive economically, and of course the messy, complicated sexual and familial relationships (it's a bonus that Tchaikovsky's gay and his wife's a nymphomaniac, but *The Music Lovers* doesn't need those elements, and without them it'd still be a masterpiece).

(3) And *The Music Lovers* brings to culmination all of the artist figures that Ken Russell had explored in his television work: the intensity, the self-absoprtion, the waywardness, the insecurity and vulnerability, the stubbornness, the pig-headness, the wilfulness, the promiscuity, and the craziness. And of course the Faustian bargain of being an artist, and the costs, and the effects on the people around the artist. (But now Russell and co. were able to mount the production in colour, and in widescreen).

(4) And *The Music Lovers* was the first time that Ken Russell was able to foreground in a feature film the utterly sublime human invention that is music. *The Music Lovers* is about the miracle of music, the beauty of music, the hypnotism of music, the terror of music. *The Music Lovers* is about 'the most incredible event in human history', as Russell so rightly called music.

---

4 The movie was 'deliberately done in a lush style,' Russell remarked. 'Though it cost only $1.6 million, UA said it looked like a $3 million film' (Bax, 187). Which today means a $150/ 200 million movie.

The title cards for *The Music Lovers* reflected that,[5] announcing that this was definitely a 'Ken Russell Movie':

> KEN RUSSELL'S FILM
> ON TCHAIKOVSKY
> AND
> THE MUSIC LOVERS

*The Music Lovers* was brilliantly shot by veteran Douglas Slocombe, one of the star cinematographers of all British cinema;[6] the screenplay was by Melvyn Bragg, based on *Beloved Friend* by Catherine Drinker Bowen and Barbara von Meck.[7] Roy Baird was the producer. André Previn[8] conducted Peter Tchaikovsky's music (with the London Symphony Orchestra), Rachel Orozco played the piano, and April Cantello was the soprano vocalist. Natasha Kroll designed the picture.[9] Other collaborators were Russell regulars, such as choreographer Terry Gilbert,[10] editor Michael Bradsell, set decorator Ian Whittaker, sound editor Terry Rawlings, production manager Neville Thompson, Russell's wife Shirley as costume designer, and actors[11] such as Ken Colley, Christopher Gable, Maureen Pryor, Iza Teller, Max Adrian,

---

5 Early titles for *The Music Lovers* included *Opus 74* and *The Lonely Heart* (*Opus 74* because that was the *Pathétique Symphony*).
6 Douglas Slocombe shot the three *Indiana Jones* movies; he lit some classic Ealing comedies (*The Lavender Hill Mob, The Man in the White Suit,* and *Kind Hearts and Coronets*), classic British films (*Dead of Night, Hue and Cry, The L-Shaped Room, The Young Ones, The Servant* and *The Italian Job*), also *The Lion in Winter, The Vampire Killers, The Great Gatsby, Rollerball, The Lady Vanishes, Nijinsky, Never Say Never Again* and *Lady Jane*. Slocombe had worked with Roman Polanski, Joseph Losey, Irving Kershner, Charles Crichton, Robert Hamer and Fred Zinnemann (on *Julia*).
7 Joseph Gomez has identified at least 5 other books which Ken Russell and Melvyn Bragg probably draw on – biographies by John Briggs, Edwin Evans, Rosa Newmarch, Modeste Tchaikovsky and Herbert Weinstock.
8 André Previn (b. 1929) was undoubtedly an important collaborator in *The Music Lovers:* the music director is such a vital talent in producing a musical movie. Previn was a movie veteran, with work going back to *Kiss Me Kate*, and including *Porgy and Bess, Gigi, Paint Your Wagon, My Fair Lady, Elmer Gantry, Rollerball* and *Jesus Christ Superstar*.
9 It's still rare for women to hold head of department jobs like production designer, but Russell liked to work with women – prior to *The Music Lovers*, such as Luciana Arrighi.
10 Terry Gilbert, Russell's regular choreographer, worked with Russell on the ballet tours of Russell's youth.
11 As with other Ken Russell productions, I reckon that certain roles should've been cast with more well-known actors (even tho' Iza Teller, Christopher Gable, Ken Colley and Sabine Maydelle are wonderful as Madame von Meck, Modeste, Anton Chiluvsky and Sasha).

Glenda Jackson, Ben Aris, Andrew Faulks, Imogen Claire, etc.[12]

Pretty much everyone is working at the top of their game on *The Music Lovers* – and, once again, one of the most important contributors to this extraordinary movie was the editor, Mike Bradsell.[13] *The Music Lovers* hurtles along at a rapid pace, never out-staying its welcome, never milking scenes beyond breaking point, but nevertheless allowing for all sorts of interludes and quieter moments. Bradsell and his assistants achieved a hypnotic momentum to the scenes, and how the scenes linked together. Within some scenes, however – especially the musical numbers – the editing was allowed to go wild.

And the other vital contributor, among many to note, was the screenwriter, Melvyn Bragg. Although *The Music Lovers* is perceived – rightly, I think – as 'a Ken Russell film' – it's Bragg who has the screenwriting credit. Of course, Russell's input to the script would have been considerable. And, although I haven't seen *The Music Lovers* script, I bet there would be moments in the screenplay where it would say 'THEY DANCE', but it was up to Russell and choreographer Terry Gilbert and the actors to work out how to shoot such a scene (the *Swan Lake* ballet scene, for instance). As well as *Swan Lake*, *The Music Lovers* contains numerous instances of dance, such as the dance of the fireflies, the many dance styles in the opening scene, characters moving like dancers (in the idyllic flashbacks, or in the scenes in Peter Tchaikovsky's living room), and in the *1812* satire.

Peter Illyich Tchaikovsky (born May 7, 1840, in Kamsko Votkinsk, died in St Petersburg, November 6, 1893), was one of Russia's most celebrated and well-known classical music composers. His works included three ballets (*The Nutcracker, Sleeping Beauty* and *Swan Lake*), seven symphonies (including *No. 6, the Pathétique*), the *Romeo and Juliet, Hamlet* and *The Year 1812* overtures, operas (*Eugene Onegin, Maid of Orleans, The Sorceress*), plus concertos, string quartets, etc.

---

12 Playing Peter Tchaikovsky's young assistant in *The Music Lovers* was a terrific British director, Bruce Robinson (b. 1946). He appeared in a number of movies (including *Romeo and Juliet* and *The Story of Adele H*), and went on to write and direct classics such as *Withnail and I* (one of the most perfect and perfectly fabulous scripts of recent times), and write movies such as *The Killing Fields, Fat Man and Little Boy, Return To Paradise* and *In Dreams*.
13 Michael Bradsell cut many of Ken Russell's TV films and the early features, and later movies like *Gothic, Hot Pants* and *Aria*.

Nadezhda von Meck (February 10, 1831 - January 31, 1894)[14] was Peter Tchaikovsky's benefactor, never meeting him, from 1876 to the disagreement which ended the arrangement in 1890. They corresponded by letter, and this aspect of Tchaikovsky's life takes up some of the most memorable scenes in *The Music Lovers*.[15]

Peter Tchaikovsky denied that he was homosexual, with several lovers (his brother Modeste was also gay),[16] and, according to Catherine Drinker Bowen and Barbara von Meck's biography, Tchaikovsky had a dubious, perhaps incestuous relationship with his sister, was highly excitable, very neurotic, was devoted to his mother Alexandra Andreyevna, and did try to harm himself (such as drinking the water, and trying to give himself pneumonia).

But for critic Jack Fisher, *The Music Lovers* is all about sex: sex sex sex!

Oh yes, SEX! Give us more sex, baby!

> That the film is about sex is beyond argument... There are several varieties of homosexuality, at least two varieties of inverted heterosexuality, incest, sadomasochism, voyeurism and even a suggestion of displaced necrophilia. There is so much sex in the film that if it were all removed, what would remain would be a fifteen minute entertainment starring Max Adrian. (49)

Part of the Ken Russell Legend is sex and nudity, which his movies of this period feed: *Women In Love*, *The Devils* and *The Music Lovers*: had he been Italian or French, maybe it wouldn't be such a big deal for some viewers and critics. But it's true that Russell employs nudity and sex far more than most British film directors. Among his contemporaries, nude scenes in the films of, say, David Lean or Ridley Scott, are thin on the ground.

For Ken Russell, Peter Tchaikovsky was a tormented soul, which was hidden beneath the respectable, calm exterior. Consequently, Tchaikovsky's music was 'absolutely hysterical' because he was hiding everything, including his homosexuality.

*The Music Lovers* is about delusion, particularly conscious,

---

14 The wife of Madame von Meck's grandson co-wrote the source book for the movie on Tchaikovsky.
15 The format of letters was employed by the primary sourcebook for *The Music Lovers*, the biography by Bowen and von Meck.
16 Notice that naught is made of Modeste's sexuality – however, he is seen with neither a man or a woman.

willing self-delusion – the lengths to which people will delude themselves with their dreams and wishes and fantasies. 'The core of the film is the destructive force of dreams, particularly on reality,' Russell insisted.[17] It's a movie about how damaging self-delusion is, and that's why so much of *The Music Lovers* is shot in a heightened, unreal style, and why many scenes are filmed like a television commercial. 'it was meant to be a huge send-up,' Russell said.

And *The Music Lovers* wasn't just about Peter Tchaikovsky and his music, it was 'a black comedy about the decadence of romanticism' (ibid.). And of course, Ken Russell and his movies are also ambivalent about Romanticism, because he is very much a Romantic artist, and is completely in love with Romantic art and artists.[18]

But Ken Russell also acknowledges in his movies that there are many destructive aspects to Romanticism – the death wish, for instance, or the need to go to extremes.

♪

That Peter Tchaikovsky was gay is one of those aspects of a famous and respected personality that even today is problematic for some audiences and fans. And of course Ken Russell and Melvyn Bragg seized upon Tchaikovsky's closet homosexuality and brought it into focus.

And then there was Peter Tchaikovsky's disastrous relationship with and marriage to Antonina Milyukova (July 7, 1848-March 1, 1917), which hastened on Tchaikovsky's mental collapse. Mix in conducting tours, retreats to the countryside to compose (after 1888), visits to London and America, and an early death by cholera (or maybe he took poison to avert a scandal involving a homosexual affair with an aristocrat's nephew, as some have suggested), and you have some of the key elements for a sensational movie.

Oh, and some fantastic music!: it's the music, after all, which draws so much of Ken Russell's interest, and he makes sure that *The Music Lovers*, the first of his feature films about composers,

---

17 Quoted in G. Flatley, 1972. '*The Music Lovers* wasn't so much about a person as an idea: about the destructive power of fantasy on people's lives', Ken Russell remarked in 1973 (Bax, 191).

18 One thing Ken Russell wished he'd got right was the look of Tchaikovsky: his hair was too curly, too glamorous (Bax, 186). That did play into the over-romanticism of Tchaikovsky and his music, however. And Christopher Gable sports wildly effeminate, bleached blond locks.

contains plenty of Tchaikovsky's music.

*The Music Lovers* was definitely crude, excessive and flamboyant, Ken Russell agreed, because that was what attracted him to the subject of Peter Tchaikovsky in the first place: 'the excessive romanticism. I was intrigued by the contrast between this destroyer, this monster, and the accepted picture of the unhappy, homosexual lovely man, that most people have'.[19]

Joseph Gomez has pointed that Peter Tchaikovsky and Antonina Milyukova are not meant to be 'real' characters, in the conventional filmic sense (G, 99), because Ken Russell, Melvyn Bragg and the team are exploring themes like the decadence of Romanticism done in a black comedy genre.

*The Music Lovers* looked a lot more expensive than its $1.6 million budget. Had *The Music Lovers* been produced in Hollywood, it would have cost at least five times that, and possibly more. $1.6m is an absolute bargain – the budget included the recreation of a whole Moscow street, and many extras, props, sets, costumes and set-pieces. (Look at what Ken Russell and his film crews put on screen for budgets of $1-2 million, compared to other movies of this period like *Paint Your Wagon* (1969, 26 million bucks), *Catch 22* (1970, $24m), *Fiddler On the Roof* (1970, $40.5m), *Dr Doolittle* (1967, $20m), and *Star!* (1968, $14m).)

*The Music Lovers* was based out of Bray Studios: on the backlot Peter Tchaikovsky's town house, streets, apartment blocks, the Kremlin, the fairground and part of a Russian church were constructed. Location shooting included Milford-on-Sea in Hampshire, Salisbury and Southampton (for Moscow's public gardens, the Davidov house, and the forests and fields) in the *First Piano Concerto* scenes); Wilton House in Wiltshire, a popular film location (*The Bounty, Barry Lyndon, The Madness of King George*), was Madame von Meck's house at Brailov (exteriors were shot at West Wycombe House,[20] with its Classical gardens, including the lake, the Classical temple, the lawn); a Greek orthodox church on Moscow Road in Bayswater, London, stood in for St Sofia's Cathedral; the Grand Union Canal in Camden, North London, was where Tchaikovsky tries to commit suicide; the Royal Artillery Barracks in Woolwich, South-East London, stood in for the asylum at the end. Nearby Greenwich was used for

---
19 In L. Langley, "The Right To Be Outrageous", *The Observer*, Aug 18, 1971.
20 18th century West Wycombe Park belonged to Sir Francis Dashwood, of the Hell-Fire Club.

downtown St Petersburg (Greenwich is one of cinema's favourite spots in all of Britain, employed in numerous pictures).[21] Many of those locations were used in other films of the time (and since), such as *Pirates of the Caribbean 4, Barry Lyndon, The Golden Compass* and *GoldenEye*).

*The Music Lovers* is an American movie made in Britain with a (mainly) British cast and crew – but it's wholly about Russians. And it's set entirely in Russia. With Russian music, and Russian culture. As Ken Russell oft told the story, he sold *The Music Lovers* to the United Artists brass as 'a story about a homosexual who fell in love with a nymphomaniac' (BP, 56). Russell wanted Alan Bates to play the lead,[22] but Bates pulled out close to shooting (after agreeing for a long time to do it).

One of the reasons Richard Chamberlain[23] got the part[24] was because he could play the piano (well, that's what United Artists told Ken Russell when they suggested Chamberlain); Russell didn't want an actor who couldn't look convincing on screen at the piano, and he didn't want to hide the actor's hands (only later Russell found out that, no, Chamberlain could not play the piano – he discovered the actor in his dressing room practising with a dummy piano and headphones.[25] It paid off, though: Chamberlain is convincing as a great pianist, and terrific as the doomed composer.[26] It helped too that the *Concerto* was the very last sequence filmed for *The Music Lovers*, so Chamberlain had ample time to practise. As Russell put it, 'I defy anyone to say he wasn't actually performing that concerto. He did it brilliantly' [Bax] 186).

Richard Chamberlain came away depressed and exhausted

---

21 A scene shot at a favourite Ken Russell location, Tollard Royal, standing in for a St Petersburg park, was cut.
22 One wonders if Oliver Reed was considered. His roles in *The Debussy Film* and *Dante's Inferno* made him perfect for playing tortured souls. Maybe he couldn't play the piano, either. We know he couldn't sing!
23 There is a good website at richardchamberlain.net, which contains many images from *The Music Lovers*.
24 Ken Russell wasn't convinced in casting Richard Chamberlain at first, associating him with Doctor Kildare (an image that Chamberlain was keen to move away from). But when Russell saw the actor in *Portrait of a Lady* (Henry James), he 'seemed sympathetic, romantic, intelligent and had no American accent' (Bax, 184). And Russell liked Chamberlain: 'I liked Richard very much, thought he was good for the part, and the fact that he said he could play the piano a little was the best bonus of all' (ib., 186).
25 Alan Bates also couldn't play the piano – and this was absolutely essential for Russell.
26 The Walt Disney Company also produced a life of Peter Tchaikovsky (*The Peter Tchaikovsky Story*, Charles Barton, 1959) – but theirs was a Hollywoodized docudrama involving live-action and paintings, made to help market their 1959 animated film *Sleeping Beauty*, which used music from Tchaikovsky's ballet.

by making *The Music Lovers,* and considered giving up acting. Chamberlain said he would do anything for Ken Russell, but Russell was also

> so serious and demanding that he made Glenda Jackson and me do those scenes over and over, sometimes twenty times, until we couldn't move. It was no fun. That picture nearly put me in a loony bin. But I loved the film. (PF, 101-2)

*The Music Lovers* was drawn first of all, Ken Russell said, from Peter Tchaikovsky's music, as with *Mahler.* Many of the scenes were based in historical fact, although Russell and Melvyn Bragg tended to give them their own twist. The scene where Nikolai Rubenstein (Max Adrian) berates Tchaikovsky about his *Piano Concerto* happened, and Tchaikovsky did write to Madame von Meck: 'Nadezhda Filaretonva, every note which comes from my pen in future is dedicated to you! To you I owe this reawakening love of work...'.[27]

It is a movie of the *inner life* of an artist, not the *external* aspects of his life. If you don't understand that, *The Music Lovers* is going to come across as confusing, to say the least. As Ken Russell put it in 1973, *The Music Lovers* shows some of the factual, external trappings of Tchaikovsky's life (such as him teaching at the Conservatoire), but Russell wasn't interested in that at all (Bax, 183). The problem is that audiences *and* critics often take scenes *literally*, even when the visual language is cueing them differently.

♪

As Huw Wheldon recognized, music was incredibly important for Ken Russell: 'music is tremendously important to him. All sorts of things suggest music to him. He has a first-rate musical memory. He is musically very well-read' (Bax, 122).

One of the aspects of Ken Russell's cinema that attracts me is music. Of course there are a bunch of film directors who are praised by critics for their use of music – Martin Scorsese, Stanley Kubrick, Peter Greenaway, Quentin Tarantino, etc. But Ken Russell goes way, way beyond any recent filmmaker in foregrounding music (except for Jean-Luc Godard). His movies are not only filled with music, they are often *about* music – to the point where some of Russell's major works are about musicians and

---

27 P. Tchaikovsky, in *The Musician's World,* ed. H. Gal, 363.

composers.

One wonders if Ken Russell would have preferred to work on the field of classical music more than any other (with dance and ballet as a possible second choice). Certainly he has confessed that if he could compose music, that's what he would do.

I wonder if Ken Russell might have had a career as a radio presenter – he could've presented classical music shows, for instance. But Russell loves images, and it's that combination – music plus images – that drives so much of his cinema. Clearly, Russell is a filmmaker who thinks in images, so that even if the music comes first, the images soon follow on. One thing's for certain, the films of Russell will have inspired some viewers to listen to Peter Tchaikovsky or Gustav Mahler again, or to look at the sculpture of Henri Gaudier-Brzeska, or maybe to read some of D.H. Lawrence's books.

Like Stanley Kubrick and Francis Coppola, Ken Russell often played music on set to get his actors in the mood. Famously, he played *The Fiery Angel* by Sergei Prokofiev during the nun's hysteria scene in *The Devils*, and a loop of 'the most barbaric fifteen-second section of Dimitri Shostakovitch's *The Execution of Stepan Razin* while shooting the famous train ride in *The Music Lovers*.

♪

THE OPENING SEQUENCE.

*The Music Lovers* opened with two lengthy music and image sequences, the kind that Ken Russell loves to shoot, his ideal mode of operation in cinema. The first, to Peter Tchaikovsky's 'The Dance of the Clowns' (from *The Nutcracker*), depicted a vivacious festival on the snowy streets of Moscow: images of people sledging on a wooden slope, cavorting in the snow, throwing snowballs, getting drunk (lots of drinking scenes), acrobats and gypsy dancers on a stage, Russian dancers with a band in an inn, marching soldiers, and visual introductions to some of the main characters: Peter Tchaikovsky, his male lover, Count Anton Chiluvsky[28] (Christopher Gable), Nina Milyukova (Jackson), who lusts after an officer (Ben Aris) in the cavalry, the composer's sister Sasha (Sabina Maydelle), his brother, Modeste (Ken Colley) and Sasha's family (including Davidov (Andrew Faulds), and

---

[28] Chiluvsky is a combination or representation of a number of Tchaikovsky's lovers, a typical filmic device. They might have included Vladimir Shilovsky, a companion, lover and pupil (G, 113).

daughter Tatiana, played by Victoria Russell – there are many scenes involving Russell's children, with some of them, such as Victoria, prominently featured in numerous scenes).

Ken Russell, Melvyn Bragg and the production team front-loaded the 1970 picture with that opening sequence, spending a large proportion of the budget on it (it showed off the production values of the film early on – the big Moscow set, covered in fake snow, many extras in costumes, and many of the key players). Followed by a segue into nighttime, with snow falling.

It was also shot in Ken Russell's familiar, loose, handheld style,[29] to convey the excitement and derangement of the scene. And, this being A Ken Russell Movie, it included plenty of dancing – Russian Cossack dances, gypsy dancers, and acrobats. Peter Tchaikovsky's music was pounding all the way through it, and Russell and co. ended the sequence by showing Tchaikovsky and Anton lurching into their home and collapsing in bed. The movie thus addresses the gay issue head-on: Tchaikovsky liked men. (The film could've continued by depicting a love scene between Tchaikovsky and Chiluvsky, but it didn't need to, because the scene set the following morning in the house was clear that these guys sleep together – Tchaikovsky is in bed asleep, when Modeste comes to call, and Chiluvsky is teasing and half-dressed).

The opening of *The Music Lovers* is thus another of Ken Russell's moves to grab an audience by the throat, and never let go. Or, put it like this: how many movies of this kind (a big, historical studio production) put the main character together with a guy in the first scene, showing them having a crazy day, b4 falling into bed together? No, not many, outside of gay cinema.

THE *FIRST PIANO CONCERTO* SEQUENCE.

The second music and image sequence in *The Music Lovers* has Ken Russell in his element, and lets Peter Tchaikovsky's music speak for itself. It was a lengthy rendition of Tchaikovsky playing his *First Piano Concerto* in front of a small audience at the Conservatoire (this event took place in 1874).

The sequence is amongst the finest in Ken Russell's cinema, a truly remarkable choreography of narrative, visual rhymes, meanings, looks, exposition, and photographic techniques. The

---

29 With the camera often operated by Ken Russell himself.

*First Piano Concerto* episode demonstrates Russell's total mastery of the giant train set of move-making. And, once again, the flamboyance and rapidity of the imagery deflects attention from just how skilful the storytelling and drama is.

It is perhaps the single most important sequence in the whole of Ken Russell's *œuvre*. It contains everything that's important to Russell's form of cinema:

♪ the overwhelming pre-dominance of *music*,

♪ the *performance* of music, live (and by the composer),

♪ the use of music with images and the visual storytelling,

♪ the pæans to the natural world,

♪ the 19th century setting,

♪ filming in England, with a British cast and crew (including many regulars, and including Russell's own children),

♪ the use of myriad cinematic techniques, including an approach that's simultaneously straight (i.e., conventional drama) and satirical (slo-mo from commercials, for example), subtle but also over-the-top,

♪ it contains the critic's viewpoint, at the end, and the artist's self-assertion,

♪ and finally the vital relation between music and life (or art and life).

Critics often lambasted Ken Russell's movies for their OTT scenes – I'm reminded of a reply that Orson Welles made to people who complained to him that his camera movements and angles were baroque or operatic or self-conscious. Are they? Welles would say: doesn't everyone film like that, or think like that? To Welles, it was simply natural to place the camera way up there, or to move the camera in highly unusual and idiosyncratic ways. It's the same with Ken Russell: he's not showing off or being 'arty' or self-conscious – it's just natural to him to do scenes like that.

The *First Piano Concerto* sequence in *The Music Lovers* was another big scene: many extras in costumes, many of the leading players were present, and a whole orchestra. The sequence opens with a lengthy and complicated master shot, tracking thru corridors, following Nina into the concert hall, and trucking up to the composer at the piano, as he begins his first notes on the piano.

This is Richard Chamberlain's Big Scene in *The Music Lovers* –

not only is the pressure high to convince the audience that he is a virtuoso pianist, and to really sell the high emotion of the music and the performance, he also has the film director operating the handheld camera himself, inches from his nose.

The concert was intercut with scenes from Peter Tchaikovsky's life, and the fantasies of some of the other characters (shot, Ken Russell explained, in a deliberately 'false and ultra-romantic' fashion, like TV commercials.[30] That's an important point: I'm sure some viewers take these scenes straight, but they are definitely meant to be ironic, as in films such as *Lisztomania*, *Tommy* and *Women In Love*).

Peter Tchaikovsky's sister Sasha, for example, dreams while Tchaikovsky plays of a Summer idyll with Tchaikovsky and her children rowing on a boating lake, blowing bubbles, gathering daisies (shot in glowing, backlit slow motion, all of the characters dressed in white,[31] like a commercial for soap powder or perfume. By contrast, the scenes from reality were lit quite hard, often from the front, with no backlighting or softeners). Ken Russell explained:

> We were after lyrical summery images to accompany the highly romantic second movement of the composer's great B-minor piano concerto. And capture them we did, with the happy couple running through silver birch woods, wandering through acres of golden fields of wheat, and rowing in slow-mo across their private lake at sunset. (DF, 56)

In another scene, Sasha and Peter Tchaikovsky are walking in a silver birch wood, smiling and talking, in slo-mo (one of those classic, Russian birch groves; a good example occurs in Andrei Tarkovsky's 1962 film *Ivan's Childhood*; Tarkovsky scouted 40 suitable woods before near Moscow finding the one he wanted. The art department in *The Music Lovers* had to paint the birches silver, however).

The strong hints at an incestuous relationship between Peter Tchaikovsky and his sister Sasha are much more than hints – they are extremely affectionate with one another, physically as well as emotionally (later, they discuss Tchaikovsky finding a wife, and

---

30 Using television advertizing techniques like slow motion, soft focus, backlight and reflected light (Bax, 187).
31 The white costumes for every scene is one of the stylistic hints that this is not a dream but a fantasy, or a heightened fantasy of a memory – or a memory purged of all darkness and difficulty.

Sasha looks on jealously when an opera singer (Olga Bredska, played by Joanne Brown) sings while Tchaikovsky plays the piano. Tchaikovsky mentions he wishes that Sasha could be on stage with the music, because it's all about her: to emphasize this, the camera moves over to Sasha lying back on a couch, in one Ken Russell's numerous handheld shots in *The Music Lovers* (probably operated by Russell), to a close-up).[32]

> No, I could not endure it
> I could not love another man.
> My fate is yours to leave or share it.

Thus run the lyrics to the song.

The relation between brother and sister is reciprocated, and the United Artists movie suggests, as strongly as it can, without showing any sex, the incestuous relationship. Brother and sister are depicted in numerous ways as lovers, with looks, smiles, shining eyes, holding hands, and many embraces (and they look at each other longingly during the concert). In fact, the Peter-Sasha relationship is the core of the first part of *The Music Lovers*, which's why she is so missed in the second part, when Madame von Meck moves into the limelight.

There's also a scene of Peter Tchaikovsky, Sasha, her husband Davidov and the children play-acting and dancing in front of a lake (with swans artfully arranged behind them, evoking *Swan Lake*), a scene of Tchaikovsky reaping the harvest in a wheatfield with a group of peasants (looking like a Soviet propaganda film),[33] and a scene in a Russian *dacha* (country house) in the woods (probably the New Forest), where Sasha plays the cello and her brother's at the Bechstein grand piano again. All of these scenes were lit with sunlight (often against the sun, to bring out the flattering backlight), emphasizing the idyllic nature of the previous Summer.

In these and other scenes in *The Music Lovers*, dear, old England makes a really good stand-in for the Russian country-side, and the Moscow back-lot set is terrific, too. Of course, a film with a $1.6 million budget can't do giant Moscow or St Petersburg city scenes (it's not as big as MGM's *Doctor Zhivago* of a few years

---

32 As Ken Russell pointed out, in Peter Tchaikovsky's *Manfred*, 'the poet's in love with his sister' (Bax, 183).
33 His sister Sasha brings him some water, which he drinks, foreshadowing his suicide attempt later.

earlier, for example, recreated near Madrid), or have quite the same look as Soviet epics such as *War and Peace* (1967).³⁴

Another sequence in *The Music Lovers* shows the love triangle between Peter Tchaikovsky, Sasha and Anton Chiluvsky, his lover, in a darkened pine wood (where the filmmakers stage the erotic conflicts between the three people in shorthand, silent cinema style). Each character's clad in white (so simple, but so effective – and Russell and Shirley Kingdon employed this costume design many times); Sasha and Tchaikovsky are in a kind of ecstatic state (there's lots of smiling looks up at the sky in all of the fantasy flashbacks); but after embracing (though not going as far as a kiss on the mouth), Anton is shown standing nearby, watching them, somewhat aloof. As Sasha runs off, and Anton saunters away, Tchaikovsky is left alone, in between two of the people he loves the most, looking anxious and downcast.

*Variety* commented (bitchily) that Richard Chamberlain plays Peter Tchaikovsky teary-eyed much of the time, which's true; he's always on the point of welling into tears. Before every take it seems as if Chamberlain was sprayed with water and had gunk applied to his eyes. The sweaty appearance of Chamberlain enhanced Tchaikovsky's impassioned, sensitive nature (Tchaikovsky's sweaty in almost every scene), and also looked forward to his death by cholera. But it also made Chamberlain sometimes look as if he's acting in a different movie – *The Jungle Book* or *The African Queen* perhaps, a jungle adventure movie).³⁵ Chamberlain plays Tchaikovsky at the height of a neurotic, fevered intensity.

But what's striking about these sequences of idealized memories of the previous Summer in *The Music Lovers* is not only the imagery itself, but how Ken Russell and editor Mike Bradsell have structured them within a network of close-ups and point-of-view shots of the people in the audience at the piano concert. There's a cut, for instance, from that scene in the dark, pine wood to Peter Tchaikovsky, then a Tchaikovsky point-of-view zoom shot of Anton Chiluvsky, his dandyish lover, who stands at the back of the hall looking at him meaningfully and listening to the music, while Tchaikovsky sits at the piano (as if both Sasha and

---

34 But then, *War and Peace* is possibly the biggest movie ever made – *Cleopatra*, *Titanic* and even *Intolerance* included. The battle scenes alone are beyond belief in scale and cost.
35 Richard Chamberlain did go on to make the Alain Quartermain movies in the Eighties.

Chiluvsky know the specific moments last Summer that Tchaikovsky is writing about in his music – and they're not the same moments!).

Finally, Nina Milyukova, sitting alone in the audience, behind the Hussar (Ben Aris), imagines she's getting married to the officer of her dreams in an idealized vision of a church ceremony and a wild ride in the countryside in a white carriage pulled by white horses, drinking champagne and eating chocolates. At the end of the ride, Nina and the Hussar step into some woods, over bridges and embrace. A wedding ceremony in a church concludes this OTT fantasy. When Nina emerges from her reverie, the Hussar has departed, and Glenda Jackson's acting neatly suggests: *damn,* back to humdrum reality.

At the concert, Peter Tchaikovsky's future rich patron, Madame von Meck (Izabella Telezynska, a.k.a. Iza Teller),[36] a widow (of a wealthy engineer) in black, enters the concert hall (late) and sits alone in the balcony.[37] Doug Slocombe's camera places them all in relation to Tchaikovsky at his piano by cutting rapidly from C.U.s of each, and also by crash zooms from Tchaikovsky in the foreground towards each figure (these are the 'music lovers' of the title).

Within 15 or so minutes, then, Ken Russell and Melvyn Bragg have established the major characters in Peter Tchaikovsky's life: his lover, Anton, his sister, Sasha, her husband, Davidov, his brother Modeste, his teacher Nikolai Rubenstein, and his future patron, Madame von Meck.

There's also a deaf and dumb protégé of Modeste's, Koyola (played by one of Ken Russell's children, Xavier – all of his children are in *The Music Lovers*, often in prominent roles – Victoria is one of Sasha's children, and is part of many scenes. By this time (1970), I guess the kids were used to appearing in their dad's movies). The boy (his deafness and dumbness looks forward to Tommy) is included in many scenes, including the one where Modeste visits Tchaikovsky the morning after the festival (which's odd – because Modeste tries to protect the boy from seeing the soldiers getting the gypsy woman drunk the day before, but he's

---

[36] Iza Teller was a Ken Russell regular, from TV shows such as *Dante's Inferno* and *Always On Sunday*. An unusual casting choice, perhaps, as Teller was a character actress, and not a name like Jackson or Chamberlain.

[37] This occurred historically at a different time – the 1970 film combined or telescoped a number of events and characters, which's standard practice in all Hollywood literary adaptions, and many biographical movies.

OK about the boy seeing Tchaikovsky and his lover in the morning. Modeste was also gay, so maybe it was no big deal for him).[38]

Peter Tchaikovsky's mother Alexandra Andreyevna (Consuela Chapman) is seen in another flashback, as Tchaikovsky tries to compose at the piano during a noisy party. It's in two parts: Tchaikovsky as a boy (played by Alex Bewer), all sweetness and rosy cheeks, playing for his mother in a drawing room, then some time later (weeks? months? years?), witnessing his mother undergoing harsh treatment for cholera in a steaming bathroom.

What the first two reels (the first 20 minutes) of *The Music Lovers* also do, apart from foregrounding Peter Tchaikovsky's music (which is absolutely vital), is to depict how people at concerts drift away into their private worlds, then come back to the music. And each person has their own interpretation of the music, and of their own past. These are not conventional flashbacks: they are the idealized past, memories as people would like them to be. That's the point of using a heightened, glossy, TV commercial style for the flashbacks – to show that these are not true memories, they are the desired versions of reality. The scenes also show how Tchaikovsky is affecting the people around him, and how the people in his life are connected to him partly by music (investing their own emotions and memories in his music).

That's unusual in cinema – to have music playing more than simply a decorative or even narrative role. The music in *The Music Lovers* is part of the psychological fabric of the 1970 movie. And if you don't understand that aspect of Ken Russell's cinema, you miss so much of what he and the production teams are trying to do.

In a conventional musical, music or songs or dances typically narrate or illustrate some of the story or something about characterization (like their emotional state). But in *The Music Lovers*, without using lyrics to point out people's feelings in neon, psychological connections are made which not only depict the interiority of each person, they also show some of their hopes and

---

38 In that scene, the boy is waving peacock feathers (and also in the *First Piano Concerto* scene). Why peacocks? Apart from looking good, maybe it's because peacock feathers're associated with Decadent and Romantic culture, and with paintings of love (Eros holds peacock feathers, for instance, in images of the Goddess Venus). In symbolism, peacocks're linked to the sun, one of Russell's prime symbols. But they're also suggestive of immortality, longevity, love, and more recently, vanity, pride and worldliness.

fears – and, above all, their *desires*.

In a conventional movie musical, a song might illustrate a simple emotion: 'I'm in love', 'I'm sad', 'I'm sexy', 'I'm tough', etc. In Ken Russell's musical cinema, music is used to try to depict some of the deepest experiences people can have – experiences which are beyond words, because they can only be put into music.

Ken Russell's films are *crazy* about music, and part of the time Russell just wants the viewer to *listen to the music*. So, in a way, all of that visual flashback montage during the *First Piano Concerto* is actually *secondary* to the music. In short: *Russell wants you to listen to Tchaikovsky*. (One must mention again the performers here: André Previn conducted the music, the London Symphony Orchestra performed it, and Rachel Orozco played the piano. The music advisers should be noted, too: Michael Moore and Elizabeth Corden, plus music editor Matthew Hutchinson and John Mordler, music recording producer).

And part of the reason that Ken Russell employs so many visual devices in his films, so many montages, or crash zooms, or jump cuts, or strange props, is that he is trying to find visual equivalents for music. He wants to illustrate the abstract, or to capture abstract music in film. He wants to share his enthusiasm for Peter Tchaikovsky's music with the movie audience.

In a way, it's a similar challenge that the religious artist faces: to depict the holy, to depict someone or something that's divine, or spiritual, or mystical. Renaissance art came up with devices such as haloes, or using lots of gold, or having characters surrounding someone (Jesus or Mary, say) looking up at them in awe. Ken Russell and his teams of filmmakers are searching for a similar sort of language – a vocabulary that can portray or find equivalents for the sublime, abstract and intensely enjoyable aspects of music.

But Ken Russell also employed much more conventional devices in *The Music Lovers*. One of these was the voiceover. There wasn't a great deal, but there was enough to offer either exposition or commentary. And some of that voiceover came from letters (and occasionally people read out letters aloud).

There's also a key scene at the end of the performance of the *First Piano Concerto,* in which Nikolai Rubenstien (1835-81), marvellously played by Max Adrian, lambasts Peter Tchaikovsky in terms instantly familiar to anyone who knows anything about Ken Russell, whose cinema has often been criticized like that – but it's also a typical attack on any artist: vulgar, sentimental, and just plain bad! as Rubenstein puts it.

After that ecstatic performance, Nikolai Rubenstein's criticism seems not only tactless and ill-timed – Peter Tchaikovsky is elated from his performance – but also insensitive and grudging. Tchaikovsky's vehement response is also essential to Ken Russell's cinema: it's the best thing he's ever written, he insists, snatching the manuscript out of Rubenstein's hands, and he won't change a note! Rubenstein is taken aback by the violence of Tchaikovsky's response, but that is Tchaikovsky's manner of course (and he's in that after-show high, too), but although it's exaggerated for dramatic impact, he still says what he really wants to say: it's the best thing I've done, and I ain't changing a note!

The scene is so important, because it illustrates what I've been saying about Ken Russell, and what Russell has demonstrated in his movies time after time: the critics were WRONG. They were wrong about J.M.W. Turner, they were wrong about Orson Welles, they were wrong about Peter Tchaikovsky, and they were wrong about Ken Russell.

One of the reasons for having the *First Piano Concerto* sequence be so long in *The Music Lovers*, and contain so much music, is that the filmmakers want the audience not only to listen to the music, but also to realize, as Ken Russell did, that the guy who wrote this music is not your usual movie hero. As Russell put it: 'before I knew any details about his life I knew this man was a *mess*'.

It's also necessary to show that this 1970 biopic is not going to be your usual Hollywood biopic. And it won't end well: you can see that from this sequence. The *First Piano Concerto* episode is clear that the rest of the movie will explore ambiguous and uneasy relationships and situations. And the portrayal of Peter Tchaikovsky (including the performance by Richard Chamberlain) also indicates that he is a haunted figure: he draws upon his life in his music, but there are clearly gaps between what his life is really like and the life he conjures up in his music. Those images of Summer and larking about in boats are meant to be self-consciously heightened and romanticized (*and* satirical): in short, you have not only the power of memory, which has exaggerated certain parts and ignored others (memory as cinema itself, editing and selecting real life), but also the deeply romantic approach to life and art. In sum, a romanticization of memories through art which are highly subjective experiences in the first place.

After the Conservatoire concert, Sasha comes up to her brother Peter and embraces him and cries that it seemed as if he had included all of last Summer in the *First Piano Concerto*. Yes, but it was *her* Summer (her memory of the Summer), as she saw it. Not his – because we know that for Tchaikovsky part of that Summer was a lie, because the opening sequence depicts Tchaikovsky with his lover Anton Chiluvsky: although he might've spent dreamy afternoons with his sister's family, he also had a secret relationship.

♪

COUNTER-POINTS AND CONTRASTS.

Counter-point or oppositions are a recurring device in Ken Russell's cinema, often introduced via editing montages. What better (easier, quicker) way to slam two conflicting attitudes/ moods/ styles/ modes together than with the editor's razor?

Editing is the magician's sleight-of-hand of cinema that even now very few people outside the industry really understand or appreciate. Even those critics and fans who understand the principles of editing in theory have no real idea what can be done with it (until they try it for themselves).

I wish they would: I wish folk would get some simple editing software and have a go at editing. Because if you're going to watch 4 hours of television and cinema per day for the rest of your life (the average in the U.S.A.), if you're going to spend years and years of your life watching movies and TV, a deep knowledge of editing enriches the experience enormously.

*The Music Lovers* contains some of the strongest contrasts using cutting in Ken Russell's work: when Madame von Meck and the sleeping Peter Tchaikovsky lie side by side chastely and platonically in von Meck's country house, the movie cuts to Nina fucking one of her clients (this one's called 'Rimsky-Korsakov', played by Alexei Jawdokimov, who was the mad poet in *Isadora Duncan*); when Tchaikovsky and his brother Modeste eat a refined dinner, with wine and butlers, and Tchaikovsky comments that Nina's mother Madame Milyukova assures him she's well cared-for, the picture cuts to grim images of Nina in the lunatic asylum.[39]

It's also very typical of Ken Russell's cinema to demonstrate that when things are going really well for some characters, others are having a really bad time: in *The Music Lovers*, when Peter Tchaikovsky, Modeste and Alexei and the young children of the neighbourhood are cavorting on the lawn at a party thrown by Madame von Meck for the composer, when everything seems laughingly, dancingly good for Tchaikovsky, Anton Chiluvsky has turned up and, spurned by Tchaikovsky, proceeds to inform Madame von Meck about Tchaikovsky's former life. It's the act of a jilted lover, cruel and jealous (we have seen Anton like this before, in the scene with Tchaikovsky at Nikolai Rubenstien's party, where he bitches about Alexei) – but Anton doesn't realize quite how far von Meck will go, to the point of locking Tchaikovsky out of her house and cutting off all contact with him.

And if Ken Russell and his team don't switch from one group of characters or situations to another, to provide the counter-point, they often do it by illustrating the music in an ironic, distanced manner. Russell knows that conflict is one of the essences of good drama, and his cinema is full of it. Yet one shouldn't forget that there are numerous moments of straight ecstasy in Russell's cinema, bliss without counter-point or contradictions.

♪

It's ironic that Peter Tchaikovsky, in the first half-an-hour of *The Music Lovers*, is a homosexual who's surrounded by women who dote on him, such as his sister, patron and future wife. Yet the woman that has most effect on him, that wracks him with guilt and remorse, is his dead mother, Alexandra Andreyevna.

In the first 30 minutes of *The Music Lovers*, Antonina Milyukova's parallel story has her daydreaming about romance and writing love letters full of lies to people she fancies but hardly knows (including Peter Tchaikovsky and the Hussar officer). Eventually, the army officer comes to visit her, drunk; she's shown after the act, lying ravished on her bed, legs open, her mouth bloody, her arms tied to the headboard, the room a mess. Within 30 minutes of *The Music Lovers*, the filmmakers have shown or suggested brother-sister incest, drunken rape (and SM),

---

[39] The filmic approach emphasized Nina's degenerating state with hard lighting, as in the break-up between Tchaikovsky and Nina, where cinematographer Doug Slocombe employed 'flat, cruel lighting' (Bax, 187).

homosexuality, sexual repression, mother fixation and love from afar.

*The Music Lovers* tries to show that most impossible thing – an artist at work, the creative impulse in action. Biopics of artists usually contain a sequence where the artist is shown at work. With a writer, it's about the most boring thing to portray, so films usually do something else. With painters there's often a montage of the painter painting (as in *Lust For Life* or *The Agony and the Ecstasy*).

And *The Music Lovers* is no different: it has scenes of Peter Tchaikovsky at the piano, composing, tinkling around and noting down the music. *The Music Lovers* also depicts artists trying to work in difficult surroundings – like one of Nikolai Rubenstein's parties. It's during this scene, after Anton Chiluvsky has tried to persuade Tchaikovsky to join the party, that the film introduces Tchaikovsky's mother. Again, it's done as the past intruding upon the present, with Tchaikovsky hearing his mother singing like a siren's call (it's *Porgi Amor* by Wolfgang Amadeus Mozart), and following the sound into a bathroom. There's some disturbing imagery of Tchaikovsky's mother dying of cholera, and having the boiling water treatment. Ken Russell and Mike Bradsell intercut this in a montage with Tchaikovsky dragging a woman out of a bath, in a hysterical effort to prevent his mother from dying. It's another classic Russell scene, covered in loose handheld shots. So in *The Music Lovers*, it's always ultimately about the mother.[40]

Incest: two forms of incest are presented in *The Music Lovers* – between Peter Tchaikovsky and his mother Alexandra Andreyevna, and the composer and his sister Sasha. Indeed, the movie suggests that for Tchaikovsky his sister Sasha was the closest connection he could have with his lost mother. Leave your copy of *The Portable Freud Reader* at the door, you won't need it: because *The Music Lovers* spells it all out clearly and vividly. (You will have noticed the total absence of Tchaikovsky's father from the proceedings).

The flashback becomes literal for Peter Tchaikovsky, when above the ruckus of the party he thinks he hears his momma singing, and stumbles into the bathroom where a woman's having a bath: the link is between the music of the present with the music of the past (Wolfgang Amadeus Mozart): for a

---

[40] As Joseph Gomez puts it, Tchaikovsky's relationship with his mother 'was not the ordinary love of a son for his mother' (1976, 103).

composer, music is the thread that binds past and present together. In a fit of remorse, Tchaikovsky drags the woman out of the bath, just as he did as a child, trying to save his mother from the cholera treatment. Throughout, the movie is cutting back and forth from the flashback to the present.

Why? The image needed to be extreme, Ken Russell explained in 1973, because Peter Tchaikovsky had confessed that the image of his mother Alexandra Andreyevna dying had haunted him. The image in the movie was exaggerated in order to penetrate the protective barriers people put up around death:

> So simply saying it isn't enough. If this was a central point in this man's life and triggered off things in his music – and even if it wasn't he *said* it was, which is also important – then it's worth showing, and showing in the most shattering way possible. (Bax, 201)

It's also extreme because it foreshadows Peter Tchaikovsky's own death at the end of the piece: in the 1970 movie, the composer expires after the hot bath treatment, which the viewer is already prepared for with the scene with the mother. (Similarly, the way that the two treatments are filmed, with the camera emphasizing the bare feet being dragged along the floor, link them together. Poor Nina Milyukova is treated in a similar fashion, when she's hauled from the exercise yard in the mental institution and put into a strait jacket. Strapped down to the bed, her pose echoes that of Tchaikovsky in the bath and on the floor, dead).

### THE MIDDLE ACTS.

The rest of *The Music Lovers* depicts the narratives strands mapped out in the first half-an-hour: first up is Nina Milyukova's seduction of Peter Tchaikovsky, and their marriage (much to the distress of Sasha, Madame von Meck and Anton Chiluvsky); Tchaikovsky's marriage (in 1877) to Nina falls apart, he moves out (he left after less than a month), is offered the use of a country home by von Meck (Nikolai Rubenstein's visits von Meck to broker the deal for the country retreat); there he returns to composing, seeing his friends and relatives intermittently.

The movie elides many other parts of Peter Tchaikovsky's life, such as his time in Switzerland and Italy after his marriage, or the period in the U.S.A. in 1892 and London in 1893.

Nina Milyukova goes into decline; her mother Madame Milyukova (Maureen Pryor) acts as her pimp, procuring men, while Nina deludes herself that Peter Tchaikovsky still loves her and will return one day (he never does). Towards the end of the 1970 picture, Anton Chiluvsky shows up during Tchaikovsky's birthday celebrations and, spurned by Tchaikovsky, goes to Madame von Meck and tells her the truth about the composer's sexuality (the only reason given in the film for von Meck to withdraw her patronage of Tchaikovsky is the revelation from Anton about Tchaikovsky's former life; it's enough, though, to burst the bubble, and the dream is over (this was 1890). At first, von Meck listens seriously, but then laughs – as if she doesn't believe it; she clearly does, though, in time, maybe putting two and two together. But note that what Anton tells von Meck isn't included in the dialogue (so it might be about Tchaikovky's homosexuality, but it might be other things), and neither is von Meck's last letter to Tchaikovsky, which Tchaikovsky finds when he visits Brailov for the last time).[41]

During this time, Peter Tchaikovsky has shared a love from afar relationship with Madame von Meck, delivering her his compositions as soon as they're complete, though they promise never to meet (in a memorable sequence, Madame von Meck enters her house while the composer's asleep, and lies next to him on the bed, fingers touching).

After Madame von Meck has withdrawn the use of the country retreat, and also his allowance, Peter Tchaikovsky's brother Modeste persuades him to turn to conducting. This works for a while, until Tchaikovsky, stricken with remorse over the wife he's let down, who's now in an asylum, also goes into a decline, deliberately drinking water that could give him cholera. *The Music Lovers* ends with Tchaikovsky dying (on his deathbed he's still muttering about how he should have done more for Nina, and when he says he loved her, as Joseph Lanza pointed out, he could be talking about Nina or von Meck or Sasha or 'most likely his mother' [PF, 101]). The 'her' can be any of those people, but it can also be life itself, or music (the Muse), or death.

The reluctance of Madame von Meck and Peter Tchaikovsky

---

[41] Indeed, biographers differ as to the reasons for von Meck's withdrawing her patronage. Maybe she began to feel guilty about it, partly because her son Vladimir was ill (recalling her to her late husband). Or maybe it really was when she discovered Tchaikovsky's homosexuality.

to meet was on both sides: Tchaikovsky was shy and ultra-sensitive, and von Meck didn't want to spoil their relationship by meeting. That comes out strongly in Tchaikovsky's letters. He found the proximity of von Meck troubling, when he was staying on her estate, even though he knew she wouldn't force herself upon him.

> I know my seclusion will not be disturbed. I am so accustomed to regard her as a kind of remote and invisible fairy that the consciousness of her mortal presence in my neighbourhood is rather disconcerting.

Thus he wrote to his brother Modeste in 1879.[42]

One of the key narrative elements in *The Music Lovers* was the link between music and life, between the music that Peter Tchaikovsky was composing and his life and the people around him. *The Music Lovers* established that connection early on, with the *First Piano Concerto* sequence. And the device was continued: thus, when Tchaikovsky is seen composing *Romeo and Juliet*, while his sister Sasha looks on, the film offers a bitterly ironic contrast in mood and meaning, when it cuts from the beauty of the music and the tranquil scene with Tchaikovsky and his sister to the shot of Nina beaten and bloody on her bed after being raped (or at least violently fucked) by the Hussar soldier. No need to show the rape itself – the aftermath, and Glenda Jackson's Nina spread across the bed (with her hands tied) says it all.

Another commentary on the narrative occurred with *Eugene Onegin*: the novel, and Peter Tchaikovsky's music inspired by it, were employed as counterpoints to the narrative of *The Music Lovers* in the middle of the movie. For *Eugene Onegin*, for instance, the filmmakers mounted a fantasy sequence (from Nina Milyukova's point-of-view) of Tchaikovsky duelling with the Hussar (and winning, of course), drawn from 'The Letter Song' in *Eugene Onegin*. It was about Nina's (doomed) search for love (and was couched in a consciously melodramatic style, like her first fantasy at the piano concert – complete with images of Nina staring out of her window while it rained outside – Nina does a lot of staring, and Glenda Jackson is brilliant at this kind of silent cinema acting).

What's striking about *The Music Lovers* is just how much Ken

---

[42] In H. Gal, 371.

Russell and his team played *against* the music, how much irony and satire there was. So Peter Tchaikovsky's music for the most celebrated love story in world literature – *Romeo and Juliet* – was employed in a viciously ironic manner when it comes to an abrupt end on the image of Nina raped on the bed (the gulf between Nina's fantasies and the harsh reality was enormous, and one of the primary themes of *The Music Lovers* is precisely the gulfs between desire and reality that people create for themselves. It's one of Russell's recurring themes).

Similarly, *Eugene Onegin* took up the themes and images of the novel by Alexander Pushkin, but played against them, with its jokey images of Peter Tchaikovsky duelling with the drunken Hussar, whom he shoots casually in the head.

And notice that when Peter Tchaikovsky invites Nina Milyukova to his house, the fantasy continues, with now Tchaikovsky not Nina continuing the fantasizing: when she enters the darkened house, he sees her still in the white dress from the *Eugene Onegin* fantasy. The scene dissolves to Nina in her usual clothes (when she's dressed up to the nines). To emphasize the sexual hypocrisy of the moment, just b4 Nina arrives, Anton Chiluvsky does (rather improbably, but this is a movie!): forget the dialogue, Anton's mere presence is enough to remind Tchaikovsky that he's gay, and that marrying is probably not the best idea for him.

Peter Tchaikovsky decides he needs a drink to get him thru this, and there's a shift into an alcoholic haze that lasts some time before Nina arrives.

PETER TCHAIKOVSKY AND NINA MILYUKOVA.

The central section of *The Music Lovers* dealt with the marriage of Nina Milyukova and Peter Tchaikovsky. Inevitably, Melvyn Bragg, Ken Russell and the team made sex one of the sticking points between the two: Nina wants sex, and Tchaikovsky can't bring himself to do it. All very familiar stuff in the movies. Occasionally, Anton Chiluvsky pops up to remind Tchaikovsky of his homosexual past and gay longings. Chiluvsky maintains that Tchaikovsky is really gay, but is trying to suppress it (even today, such a narrative is still controversial, and Hollywood, in pursuit of moolah, avoids it like the plague).

To illustrate the sexual tensions between Peter Tchaikovsky and Antonina Milyukova, Ken Russell created the most famous scene in *The Music Lovers,* the equivalent to the nude wrestling scene in *Women In Love*: the train carriage scene, where Glenda Jackson rolls around the floor nude while Richard Chamberlain looks on in horror, unable to escape (prior to the train scene, Russell and co. filmed Chamberlain and Jackson in Greenwich, which was standing in for St Petersburg).

Sex and music and trains – it's classic Ken Russell! Russell had the carriage built full-size, with grips rocking it to and fro, while he played Dimitri Shostakovitch's violent *Execution of Stepan Razin* loud (in a 15-second loop), to help the actors to create the crazed mood.[43] Cinematographer Doug Slocombe lit the unreal scene from a single lamp. And of course the scene is shot in the familiar Ken Russell Wild Crazy Handheld Camera Style, with very tight close-ups, with the camera inches from the actors' faces, accompanied by loud music (from the *6th Symphony*) and rapid cuts (and the tempo of the scene accelerates, akin to rising action in drama, and also to sex).

According to Ken Russell, Peter Tchaikovsky

> found himself locked in a sleeping compartment with Nina on a train hurtling through the snow at sixty miles an hour, rocking violently. It's like hell. Almost like *Huis Clos*. It's a little box six feet square. And he gets her drunk in it… We show her taking off her things, and suddenly he's with a piece of meat… She's a naked drunk. She passes out cold. And she just rocks about on the floor, and he is trapped with this… piece of meat. (Bax, 31)

The scene is there to depict the fear, the revulsion but also the desire in Peter Tchaikovsky. Sexual desire, the 1970 movie says, can't be ignored, even if it's desire for someone you can't bear (it's also of course a homosexual fear of heterosexuality, of a gay man confronted with a horny, straight woman). Nina of course wears a *red* dress before disrobing, and there's a shot of the wire frame of a skirt bustle which disturbs Tchaikovsky with its impression of women's devouring genitals, the *vagina denta*.[44] It's the reduction of a human being to a 'piece of meat', as Ken Russell intended.

In bed with Antonina Milyukova, Peter Tchaikovsky says maybe they could be like brother and sister (a telling comparison,

---

[43] Glenda Jackson told Russell not to turn off the music: 'Christ, if you stopped the music I couldn't do it' (Bax, 188).
[44] And champagne bottles are employed phallically in this nightmarish scene, as often in Ken Russell's cinema.

on the night of their honeymoon, when Tchaikovsky has not done his duty); Melvyn Bragg's dialogue consciously evokes Tchaikovsky's relationship with his sister Sasha, of course (the camera tilts down from an image of a classical nude, a Venus image, down to the newly-weds in the bed, to emphasize the irony).

Ken Russell called Nina Milyukova a nymphomaniac, but the movie doesn't really depict her like that. Rather, it shows her becoming a prostitute, reverting to her old ways. But prostitution isn't nymphomania. And enjoying a good fuck isn't nymphomania either. Nina is more a doomed lover, in the 19th century Romantic style, someone, like the characters in Thomas Hardy's novels, who puts all of their hearts and souls into love and relationships, which, when they backfire (as they always do!), end up destroying them.

To put it at its most simplistic: Nina Milyukova just wants to give love and be loved. Unfortunately, her choices of lovers lead to disasters. It's not all the man's fault, however: the movie depicts Nina as a *dreamer* from the beginning, when she admires the Hussar officer from afar (and the sexual politics are as ruthless as in Thomas Hardy's stories: when women throw themselves at men, the results are never good).

Antonina Milyukova is a lost soul, at odds with her social environment, and imprisoned by her gender, her social status, her relationships. As in a Jane Austen novel, it's all about men and marriage for Nina, and the 1970 movie depicts the savagery of patriarchal society, where women are second class citizens. For Nina, a good marriage is one way out of her life, while Peter Tchaikovsky has his music, his followers, and benefactors such as Madame von Meck (Tchaikovsky has *choices*, options, possibilities, while Nina seems to have none).

Nina Milyukova has only her mother, Mrs Milyukova, and her mother is ruthless in selling out her daughter to the highest bidder. It's one of the most vivid depictions of a completely twisted, cynical and exploitative relationship in Ken Russell's cinema – and in English language cinema – the way that Nina's mom pimps her child (even today, that relationship comes across as remarkably cynical – Russell is especially good at depicting exploitation).

For Glenda Jackson, Nina Milyukova was a self-destructive and rather pitiful personality. 'I felt sad about Nina. Nina was so much a victim of her lack of intelligence, her inability to control her own emotions. But she unlikable, too, because she was a continual fantasist and – like all fantasists – dangerous and destructive'. But where Peter Tchaikovsky had an outlet for his fantasy in his music, Nina didn't.

Ken Russell acknowledged that he hadn't really achieved enough in the characterization of Nina Milyukova:

> If the film has any failure I think it's that I didn't show Nina's background enough, what she'd sprung from, what she was escaping from; I think I got what she aspired to, but there wasn't enough of the fact that this was a desperate attempt to find a place, and that Tchaikovsky destroyed her with his self-indulgence.[45]

In *The Music Lovers*, everyone is either not what they seem, or not what they want to be, or not living with the one they want. They are people existing in a world of unreality and dreams (like Nina Milyukova), or denying their true selves (like Peter Tchaikovsky), or fantasizing about art and artists (like Madame von Meck), or hankering after someone they can never have (like Sasha), or someone they once had but who has spurned them (like Anton Chiluvsky), or putting on a pretence (like Nina's mother).

And nobody is anything near happy.[46]

But Peter Tchaikovsky is also prostituting himself: the United Artists movie is clear about that, and his brother Modeste acts as his pimp. Notice how Tchaikovsky resists Modeste's pleas for conducting tours (in 1888), because he knows it's a kind of whoring.

The gap between fantasy and reality is one of the 1970 movie's primary themes – between one's inner life and the real, outer life, between what people are striving for and what they actually get. The heightened, heavily romantic style of *The Music Lovers* enhances the gulfs. And the movie works on a number of levels, and I'm sure that some viewers respond to the romantic, emotional levels, which are so exaggerated, and ignore some of the other layers, where the movie is satirizing not only its characters, and their dreams and desires, but also the form of the movie itself. That is, although *The Music Lovers* isn't an obvious

---

45 Ken Russell, from an early draft of John Baxter's book, quoted in G, 99.
46 The word 'happy' does not describe Ken Russell's characters in the movies of this golden period: rather, they zoom up way past happiness into euphoria and bliss. And when they crash, they collapse far below simple unhappiness into grief, despair and suffering.

comedy like a Marx Brothers or Mel Brooks movie, with easy-to-see comedic moments, lines, gags, and pratfalls, it is certainly sending up the historical movie, the artist bio-pic movie, and the romantic drama movie.

♪

SWAN LAKE.

*Swan Lake* was another set-piece designed to show off Peter Tchaikovsky's work, include some of the ballet, but also to comment upon the relationships and tensions among the characters (particularly the sexual tensions between Tchaikovsky and Nina Milyukova, and Tchaikovsky and Anton Chiluvsky), a dramatic device of ironic commentary which Ken Russell had employed in *The Debussy Film* (when the Film Director takes the Actors to see a play about Claude Debussy's life), and in *Dante's Inferno* (in the scene of painting the murals in Oxford). The *Swan Lake* episode was filmed at West Wycombe House, in South-East England, by the lake near the North front, and included lengthy highlights from the ballet (ballet and dance being one of Russell's passions). Alan Dubreuil and Maggie Maxwell were the principal dancers.

Anton Chiluvsky provides a commentary upon the action (when he finds that Nina Milyukova really doesn't know the story of *Swan Lake*), delineating the people in Peter Tchaikovsky's life, including his 'true love', Sasha (Anton's attending the concert with a male companion, but sidles over to Nina and Tchaikovsky when he sees them entering the audience). Ken Russell and Melvyn Bragg fuse reality and fantasy here (and also employ the footage later), with Sasha appearing in the ballet. But when Anton talks about the 'true love' of the hero, he probably means himself (throughout the film, Anton seems to regard himself as Tchaikovsky's true soul-mate, and there's a cut to emphasize this to the 'true love' ballet dancer. But from Tchaikovsky's point-of-view, the 'true love' in *Swan Lake* is his sister Sasha: the importance of that image is suggested when it's included in the rapid montage of the people that Tchaikovsky loved as he's dying).

Yet another commentary on the non-sex life of Antonina Milyukova and Peter Tchaikovsky occurs in the *camera obscura* scene (possibly a reference to *A Matter of Life and Death* (a.k.a. *Stairway To Heaven*, 1946), but Ken Russell isn't the only film-maker to be fascinated by early forms of cameras and optical systems). Inevitably (well, this *is* a Ken Russell movie), as the optical device pans around the park, it alights on a couple making out. It's a tried and tested dramatic device – of course Nina is fascinated and giggles as the couple kiss and grope each other, and of course Tchaikovsky become more uncomfortable, and is relieved when the woman in the park pushes the man away (offscreen comments are included from the crowd watching the *camera obscura* which heighten the sexual tension – such as, I hope they don't go too far, voicing what Tchaikovsky is feeling).

When the marriage of Antonia Milyukova and Peter Tchaikovsky reaches its breaking-point, the filmmakers stage a terrific bust-up scene (Ken Russell is great at these, and Glenda Jackson and Richard Chamberlain play them brilliantly – these are two wonderful actors who can really let rip: this is why you cast a movie with actors who can really do their thing. It must've been such a delight for Russell as a director: to sit back and see what the actors would do. When actors are this good, they make everyone look better. And it's scenes like this which remind us that the performers are often the true *auteurs* in a movie – not the directors, producers, DPs, designers, costumiers, hairdressers, writers, or anyone else).

It's a full-on spat, with Nina Milyukova hurling stuff around (she scratches the carpet manically,[47] then Peter Tchaikovsky's cheek), and the couple grappling each other on the floor. Nina tries to seduce the composer again, tearing at his clothes and rolling on top of him. It doesn't work: as Nina wonders in previous scenes, 'how can I keep him?' In this fiercely patriarchal world, a woman such as Nina, the 1970 movie suggests, has only one weapon at her disposal – sex – and when that doesn't work, she's lost. (And in this part of the film, Tchaikovsky, returning from his suicide bid, tries to strangle Nina, who's still on the floor in the foetal position, but is pulled away by Alexei).

All in all, this domestic meltdown in *The Music Lovers* is the finest in Ken Russell's cinema: partly, I think, because the script is solid, partly because the characters are so intense and damaged, partly because the situation is so heightened, and partly because the actors are marvellous. Peter Tchaikovsky and Nina Milyukova are two lost souls, two people who are ill-suited and corrosive, yet

---

[47] I haven't seen an actor do that, but it fits perfectly. It's the kind of action that likely came out of rehearsals, on the set. Glenda Jackson is *incredibly* good, the kind of actor that makes other actors look decidedly tame and unadventurous.

are somehow thrown together (but the movie is careful to show not only Nina seducing Tchaikovsky, with that initial letter, but also Tchaikovsky's delighted response, and his determination that he's going to meet her – though, Modeste, in his role as the Jiminy Cricket conscience and voice of reason, isn't so sure. That is, they move towards each other – it's not simply Nina seducing Tchaikovsky and him going along with it).

THE BRAILOV COUNTRY HOUSE IDYLL.

When Peter Tchaikovsky leaves Antonina Milyukova, the United Artists film becomes far less stressful – the two volatile elements are separate and no longer combustible. Indeed, the picture shifts into a lyrical, dream-like idyll when it depicts Tchaikovsky in Brailov, at Madame von Meck's country estate (in the Zhmerinka district of Ukraine). Ken Russell indulges his (and Melvyn Bragg's) Romantic love of nature to the full; it's a soft, pleasant respite from the agony Tchaikovsky has undergone. It's also a new seduction, but this time carried out by letter, read in voiceover by both Richard Chamberlain and Iza Telezynska (narration being one of the classic ways of illustrating letters in cinema, especially in historical dramas). It's an idealized vision of the artist and his patron (if only filmmakers had patrons like this! If only Russell had someone who gave him free food and rent, full film resources, and healthy budgets!).

And it's also couched as a fairy tale: Peter Tchaikovsky visits Madame von Meck's main house at dusk and delivers his latest composition (the scene contains beautiful, magic hour cinematography from Doug Slocombe). Then he walks over to a window and spies on von Meck opening his manuscript.[48]

Peter Tchaikovsky wandering around the country manor in *The Music Lovers* while Madame von Meck is away recalls a prince or princess in an enchanted castle – like the princess in *Bluebeard* or like Belle in *Beauty and the Beast* (Jean Cocteau's 1946 film, which is a big influence on Ken Russell's cinema, is evoked here). Like fairy tales, everything is provided as if by magic for Tchaikovsky, from unseen servants. In one sequence, Tchaikovsky is shown dining alone, drinking and smoking and enjoying himself immensely. It's a dream of plenitude and fulfilment.

The sequence, which is completely without dialogue (but with

---

[48] Peter Tchaikovsky really did visit Brailov when von Meck was away.

plenty of Peter Tchaikovsky's music, of course – it never stops – here it's from *Romeo and Juliet*), continues when Tchaikovsky falls asleep (possibly on Madame von Meck's own bed), and she returns to find him there. The 1970 production sensualizes the already idealized relationship between von Meck and Tchaikovsky, by having von Meck caress the chair where Tchaikovsky sat, lick the peach he's half-eaten (classic Ken Russell!), and tenderly touch his fingers as he's asleep on the bed (caught in an overhead shot).[49] The scene climaxes with von Meck lying awake beside Tchaikovsky (with flash cuts of Nina and a punter making love). It's Platonic love and carnal love embodied, *eros* and *agape*, as Christian mediæval theologians would put it (and the movie is clear that, ironically, von Meck's idealized love-from-afar for Tchaikovsky could be as damaging in the long run as Nina's dreaming and sex with strangers).

Madame von Meck idealizes Peter Tchaikovsky's music passionately. She wrote:

> In your music, I hear myself: my notes that echo my feelings, my thoughts, my grief… Come to my house while I'm away and by the spirit of your presence envelop me. The love that is in your music is already in veins; it has become part of my flesh and blood, part of my being. Your music is mysterious, inexplicable, marvellous, intoxicating. One would like to die experiencing it. How I love you!

Nadezhda von Meck would no doubt have preferred to find Peter Tchaikovsky heterosexual and crazy about her. Well, he *is* crazy – but not about her, or about anybody (except perhaps his mother). Ultimately, he is a supreme narcissist, self-absorbed, wallowing in his own self. The portrayal of von Meck is of someone seeking affection and contact, but knowing that it cannot be with this particular person. There's an enormous welling-up of erotic longing in this part of the 1970 movie: look at the way that von Meck reacts when her twin sons come to carry the sleeping Tchaikovsky away from her bed (and, for some odd reason, depositing him, in a deeply out-of-focus image, outside, against a tree!). The twins, by the way – John and Dennis Myers – are delightfully conceived secondary characters, clad like boho artistes, and very protective of their mother.

---

[49] Joseph Gomez says the couple look like 'Gothic *gisant* sculptures' (1976, 109). Bird's-eye-view shots of bodies are a recurring motif in *The Music Lovers*: Nina's nude body in the train, Tchaikovsky and his mother in the bath, Nina tupping her 'composer' clients, Nina and Tchaikovsky in bed on their honeymoon, etc.

The gap between fantasy and reality is also emphasized in *The Music Lovers* in the use of close-ups of paintings in this part of the United Artists movie, and match cuts from paintings of Madame von Meck's Brailov estate to the exterior views (presumably these would've been 18th century workss from West Wycombe House).

THE BIRTHDAY PARTY SEQUENCE.

In the second half of the 1970 picture, Ken Russell and his production team mount two spectacular set-pieces. The first is at Peter Tchaikovsky's birthday celebrations: children with sparklers and other fireworks running around the woods and the country house garden (an interpretation of the dance of the fireflies); the main characters are shot dancing against waterfalls of shimmering light; a firework display, in the shape of Tchaikovsky's face, burning away into darkness, intercut with a M.S. of Count Chiluvsky (looking grim – he's just told von Meck about Tchaikovsky's murky past). There is some beautiful magic hour and nighttime photography in this sequence (and often lovely dusk cinematography is enough on its own; you don't need a story or characters or themes in any movie when there are enchanting twilight scenes to contemplate).

It's a truly magical sequence (but it's not too hard to do something good with fireworks, which, like thunder storms and lightning, or chases, are tailor-made for movies). However the worm[50] is in the apple: when Anton Chiluvsky has been rejected for the last time (let's forget the implausilibity of Anton turning up at Tchaikovsky's birthday party in the country), he goes to Madame von Meck to do his worst (the scene, staged on a balcony, reprises the first appearance of von Meck at the concert, while Tchaikovsky cavorts on the lawn with his friends below).

The aftermath of the birthday party sequence has Peter Tchaikovsky returning to his country home to find it locked, and, in one of Ken Russell's most memorable images, the fields in front of the building on fire (shot at West Wycombe House in Buckinghamshire). The fields on fire is a superb image of an idealized, Platonic love affair ending in disaster. It's another of numerous examples where Russell and his team find just the right visual emblem to suggest what's going on emotionally and

---

50 I mean *snake* – this is Ken Russell!

psychologically. (The rift between von Meck and Tchaikovsky occurred in reality in 1890).

The chain across the door, for instance, says enough, and would be sufficient for many filmmakers. But Ken Russell and his team go much further: they have whole pastures on fire. It's the kind of filmmaking that makes critics complain that Russell is OTT. Yes, he is, but what great imagery! You can't forget the end of a love affair being dramatized with fields on fire.

Not only that, Peter Tchaikovsky hurtles away into the flames, crying that it shouldn't end like this (meaning the break-up with Nadezhda von Meck), before Alexei and Modeste can pull him back. A stunning tracking shot captures the men walking behind a wall of fire. This is great cinema.

THE *1812 OVERTURE* SEQUENCE.

As they drive away, and Peter Tchaikovsky's brother Modeste persuades the composer to take up conducting for a living (using fire as an analogy), the second extravagant set-piece begins, based on Tchaikovsky's *1812 Overture*. And it's all about an artist selling out (and Modeste always has his eye on rouble$).

As with the *Piano Concerto No. 1* at the beginning of *The Music Lovers*, Ken Russell and Melvyn Bragg turn this into a dramatization of the key people and relationships in Peter Tchaikovsky's life, but with the emphasis on comedy and slapstick humour, more *Monty Python* or Buster Keaton than Pier Paolo Pasolini or Joseph Losey (as with the kitsch Wagnerian sequence in *Mahler*, or the TV commercials scene in *Tommy*).[51] Here are phallic canons firing, the heads of Tchaikovsky's sister Sasha, wife Nina Milyukova, lover Count Chiluvsky, copyist Alexei and patron Madame von Meck at a concert being shot off, leaving bloody stumps; Tchaikovsky conducting wildly on top of the Russian church with its golden towers; Modeste gleefully raking in money;[52] Tchaikovsky's family and friends pursuing the composer on foot and then horseback, and in a carriage, clawing at him (they all want a piece of him); Tchaikovsky running the gauntlet of their grasping hands in the street; and scenes of Tchaikovsky triumphant as a conductor, in a street procession,

---
[51] The surrealism of the sequence jettisons the Romanticism and Impressionism of previous scenes, for Surrealism, for Jack Fisher, and suggests Joan Miro, Pavel Tchelitchew and Marc Chagall (54).
[52] These scenes are paralleled by Nina's mother counting out dough while Nina entertains another man in the bedroom in the background.

carried bodily, and strewn with ribbons and flowers. The scene closes with a match cut from Tchaikovsky on a plinth conducting to a statue of the composer in snow, bringing the movie back to conventional narration. The *1812 Overture* sequence offers some of Russell's most exuberant and over-the-top imagery and ideas (and the sequence is cut by Mike Bradsell entirely to the music). And it exploits the backlot set to the max.

♪

One of the larger narrative holes in *The Music Lovers* was the disappearance of Sasha. The 1970 picture had built her up as a hugely important figure in Peter Tchaikovsky's life – to the point where she is Nina's rival for Tchaikovsky's love (along with Anton Chiluvsky). Yet her death is only mentioned in dialogue by Modeste and Tchaikovsky later in the film (in the scene at the coast). Maybe there was a scene deleted here (it needs to be shown in the foreground of the story), but Sasha's death, according to this particular portrait of Tchaikovsky, would surely have greatly disturbed him (particularly as the relationship had strong, sensual elements, and was, according to this movie, incestuous). There is a brief indication of Sasha's situation in the extreme close-up where she's weeping at the end of the later *dacha* scene – it's her final appearance in *The Music Lovers*.

THE FINAL ACT.

*The Music Lovers* ends with some gruesome scenes. The cost of creating his music has been high for Peter Tchaikovsky, as it is for most of Ken Russell's outsider artist figures: he dies after undergoing the hot water, bathing treatment that killed his mother (as the film tells it). Tchaikovsky's act of drinking the contaminated water is depicted as a kind of suicide (the circumstances surrounding Tchaikovsky's death are unclear.[53] But Tchaikovsky has a glass of wine and a glass of water beside him in the movie, and his hand shifts deliberately from one to the other, despite Modeste's protests. Water or wine, life or death – it's a classic piece of drama to present a fatal choice in such a simple manner. Death at the height of success).

Then comes the most disturbing image in *The Music Lovers*,

---

[53] None of Peter Tchaikovsky's biographers have suggested that the composer was in a suicidal mood when he drank the contaminated water, but he did drink the water when there was a cholera epidemic in St Petersburg. Also, the suicide bid by walking into the Moscow River really happened.

and certainly one of the most outrageous Ken Russell has ever shot: Glenda Jackson as the now-insane Nina Milyukova, with shorn hair, in a brutal mental asylum[54] (filmed in Woolwich, South-East London), crying to her visiting mother[55] that now she has lots of lovers: she straddles a grating on the ground below a wall, legs apart, giggling to herself, while the inmates' hands reach up from below and grope her.

Nina Milyukova's lolling eyes and gaping mouth, the hands all over her body, between her legs, is a gross, unforgettable image of social and psychological decay. It's scenes such as this which gives Ken Russell the label of *enfant terrible*. He doesn't stop there, either, but shows Nina in the chaotic refectory, surrounded by rows of cackling, mentally disabled people, reduced to an animal; and the final image of *The Music Lovers*: Nina in the exercise yard, reciting over and over that Peter Tchaikovsky loved her, then, when she realizes he didn't, and hated her, she starts to lose it, running at the walls; the warders rush to grapple her and put on a strait jacket, and strap her into a bed in a cell. Glenda Jackson is absolutely sensational in these scenes.

The final image of *The Music Lovers* is of Antonina Milyukova staring out through the bars of her prison,[56] condemned to a hellish life: for Ken Russell this's an unambiguous image of someone damaged by coming too close to a fiercely independent creative spirit (or maybe it's about sacrifice, another perennial Russell theme, Nina sacrificing herself for Peter Tchaikovsky):

> Sacrifice is the central pivot of the Catholic faith and one of the best things about it. It comes into a lot of my films, especially *The Devils*.

remarked Ken Russell (Bax, 136). But Nina Milyukova's fate also seems like punishment for her dissolute life – for being a prostitute and selling herself to men. In which case, it's very severe.

While some filmmakers return to hospital scenes, or scenes set in bars, or restaurants, the sheer number of scenes set in lunatic

---

[54] Nina Milyukova spent the last 20 years of her life in an asylum.
[55] And now her mother seems to pity her child, after all the exploiting of Nina she's done.
[56] The geometry of the asylum 'suggests Mondrian out of Edvard Munch' for Jack Fisher, and that close-up on Nina's eye 'fixed in the rigidity of the rectangular lines is one of the greatest single shots I have ever seen in a film' (55).

asylums is striking in Ken Russell's *œuvre*. They appear in, among others, *The Devils, The Music Lovers, Mahler* – and the gaol in *Valentino* is fairly crazy. (And although filmmakers such as Terry Gilliam and Tim Burton have depicted asylums, those in Russell's cinema are far, far more gruesome).

You really did *not* want to be in an asylum before the 20th century. For instance, the German Romantic poet Friedrich Hölderlin (a Russellian artist) became mentally unstable around 1802, and in 1806 he was taken by force to the Autenrieth mental clinic in Tübingen. Here the regime included immersion in cold water in a cage, strait jackets, drugs (belladonna, digitalis), and the Autenrieth mask, put on to stop patients screaming. The depictions of mental institutions in Russell's cinema are just a tiny glimpse of how horrific they would really have been.

SUMMARY.

Ken Russell's whole approach in *The Music Lovers*, as in his other films, is exaggeration in all things. Ultimately, you either go along for the ride or you don't. In a couple of respects I reckon Russell maybe went too far: Nina Milyukova's fate is simply way too grotesque: the asylum scenes can seem like vicious caricatures, and unnecessarily horrible. Because the 1970 picture has already shown how Nina is slipping into mental instability, how she sits around at home flicking through Peter Tchaikovsky's pages of music and murmuring how he loved her. And the scenes of her mother[57] inviting men to sleep with her daughter[58] (tastelessly pretending that they are famous composers such as Nikolai Rimsky-Korsakov or Alexander Borodin),[59] while she sits in the other room counting the money and toasting Tchaikovsky, though over-the-top, are very effective in portraying self-delusion and exploitation. So the images of Nina being groped and abused in the asylum seem out of proportion for her life and 'crimes', and also serve too severe a punishment.

Having watched *The Music Lovers* yet again, the asylum scenes still seem incredibly harsh, and few movies have depicted insanity in which such a gruesome fashion (the direction of the

---

[57] Maureen Pryor is OTT as the sly, materialistic momma, but she certainly gets across the baseness of the set-up. The broad acting recalls Fagin out of *Oliver Twist*.
[58] Her characterization was invented by Ken Russell, according to Joseph Gomez (1976, 107). Nina's mother wasn't like this.
[59] Nina has already tried to write real love letters to Rimsky-Korsakov and Borodin, as she had done with Tchaikovsky, but that didn't work.

extras – Jonathan Benson was first A.D. – is stunning). But they do ram home the costs to Nina Milyukova; it's also important Nina's mom appears and finally seems to have some pity for seeing her child reduced to such horrors. That Mrs Milyukova is preposterously over-dressed – she's taking the allowance that Peter Tchaikovsky sends to Nina and spending it wholly on herself – adds to the bitterness and hypocrisy of this scene.

The Milyukova mother-daughter relationship is probably the nastiest in Russell's cinema – one of his specialities is to depict intimate relationships that become sadomasochistic and exploitative. Russell is particularly strong on portraying how incredibly brutal people can be with each other, and it's usually people who are romantically linked, or family. The dramatizations that Russell and co. put on screen are extreme, of course, but they wouldn't have any dramatic value if they weren't based in real relationships and situations that audiences can recognize. That is, such extreme dramatizations work (the plays of William Shakespeare are full of them), because the audience recognize people they know, and even themselves, in such characters.

Peter Tchaikovsky's fate, meanwhile, was a kind of suicide: his remorse for Antonina Milyukova, as well as other disappointments (like Madame von Meck and his mother's early death) has him drinking water knowing there's a cholera epidemic in St Petersburg. *The Music Lovers* had already depicted Tchaikovsky trying to commit suicide by stepping into a canal (shot in Camden in London).[60] That in itself was another curious sequence, played entirely without dialogue (to the strains of Tchaikovsky's *String Quartet No. 3*): a finely-dressed woman in white with a dog (Ken Russell regular Imogen Claire) approaches Tchaikovsky as he stands in water only two feet deep. Her enigmatic and mocking (and permanent) smile as he climbs out emphasizes his predicament: this's not the grand act of self-immolation that the artist probably envisaged. She's a kind of figure of death.

*The Music Lovers* is a movie where the two main characters wind up either dead or insane. This is no walk in the park, no sugary movie with a happy ending. Peter Tchaikovsky is going to die, that is presaged very early on, in the sequence where Tchaikovsky thinks he hears his mother singing in the bathroom, and is confronted by the horrors of the past. The nervous tension

---

[60] In real life, Tchaikovsky had waded into the Moscow River in Autumn, 1877. Somehow, a canal in Camden isn't quite the same as the Moscow River!

and hysteria in which Tchaikovsky lives his life (and how Richard Chamberlain plays him) is bound to lead to disaster – in *movie* terms, that is.

In which case, *The Music Lovers* certainly has tragic overtones (or, as Modeste corrects his brother in the dinner scene – not *tragic* so much as *pathetic*). It's also true that Tchaikovsky is his own worst enemy, and many of his demons are self-created (a running theme in Ken Russell's cinema, especially with artists).[61]

*The Music Lovers* is a film about an artist, let's not forget – a very talented artist, to be sure, but also one beset by so many demons and neuroses. This Peter Tchaikovsky would be quite at home with the New York characters of Woody Allen, or the angst-ridden Swedes in the films of Ingmar Bergman (and Bergman was at the height of his popularity in film circles at this time, and Ken Russell draws a good deal on Bergman's movies).

So *The Music Lovers* is partly about an artist trying to find their place in the world – a way of living, a means of working. The rural idyll, for instance, cannot possibly last – and Ken Russell and Melvyn Bragg depict the dream coming to an end during an ecstatic dance of the fairies, complete with fireworks and children running in the trees. Disaster occurring at the height of bliss (like death at the moment of orgasm) is classic dramaturgy; Russell explores such heavy irony many times.

And in the *1812* sequence, the 1970 movie depicts another of Ken Russell's recurring concerns about artists: *selling out*. The style is OTT – canons firing, money fluttering through the air, Tchaikovsky's enemies being vanquished – but the message is clear: money corrupts, success corrupts. And right at the height of his success, Tchaikovsky contracts cholera.

♪

*The Music Lovers*, like most of Ken Russell's other work, deals in clichés and stereotypes when it comes to character psychology and emotion. Peter Tchaikovsky's depicted as guilt-ridden, intense, difficult, and mercurial, a brilliant artist but cowardly homosexual who won't admit to his sexual identity and over-compensates with Nina Milyukova. In fact, Tchaikovsky is the typical Russellian figure: an artist, misunderstood, possessed/

---

[61] As Joseph Gomez remarked, the ending of *The Music Lovers* only appears excessive if you don't understand that the movie is 'a radical critique of romantic self-indulgence and romantic evasions' (G, 111). It's a critique of precisely the things that film critics accuse Ken Russell's cinema of being.

obsessive, volatile, moody, complex, rebellious, combative, and highly individual. A mass of emotions, all of them extreme.

But slow-paced Bergmanesque explorations of character and psychology are not Ken Russell's and Melvyn Bragg's goal here (nor in most of Russell's cinema). Rather, their intention is to illustrate aspects of or events in the composer's life through his music, the emotion, atmosphere, meaning and allusions of the music, as with his other musical biopics.

> Most of my films on composers evolve through a stream of consciousness in which the man and the myth, the music and its meaning, time, place, dream and fact all flow and blend into the mainstream of the film itself [Russell remarked]. (K. Russell, 1971)

Ken Russell's musical biopics suggest a fan listening to the music and daydreaming, conjuring up sequences from immersion in the sounds. It's as if Russell hid himself away in the Lake District with a pile of records, put on the best bits from Peter Tchaikovsky's *œuvre* and wrote down his imaginings as the music plays. Then he called his chum Melvyn Bragg and asked him to shape the material into a script.

Such an approach is bound to be a little hit and miss, because it's an intuitive, emotional response to the music, not a dispassionate, controlled evaluation of the life. If they amount to nothing more than a series of vignettes from Tchaikovsky's life in *The Music Lovers*, as detractors suggest, that's fine, because these 'scenes in the life' are filmed with such energy, such breakneck speed, such a sheer love of music, dance, imagery and style, and such a love of making films.

It's wrong to demand a certain kind of awed, slavish kind of biographical portrait from a film which plainly doesn't want to be taken like that (why should all movies be the same, or conform to the same patterns or genres or forms?). From the very first image, of someone on a sledge hurtling down a slope in the middle of a crowd of noise, movement and people, Ken Russell, Melvyn Bragg, Roy Baird and the team announce that this isn't going to be staid documentary made for arts television with a solemn voiceover (courtesy of a snooty, BBC radio presenter) reading extracts from the diaries and letters over black-and-white photographs. It doesn't matter too much if this biopic is not factually accurate (one can get the facts on Peter Tchaikovsky from many a scrupulously-researched and stodgily-written biography), or has slips into self-indulgent Russellania (Anton Chiluvksy stroking a bottle suggestively, for example, while staring lasciviously at Tchaikovsky as the composer tries to work), because the filmmakers want to celebrate the music as much as anything, and the agony and the ecstasy that contributed towards the creation of the music.

Indeed, with some of Ken Russell's films, like *The Music Lovers* or *Savage Messiah* or *Mahler*, there's a sense that Russell was in such a rush to get it all on film he didn't bother with tripods or tracks, and shot the actors on the hoof, on the wing, with a handheld camera lurching about. The signature shot of *The Music Lovers* is of some 19th century, Russian interior lit with lamps and candles while Richard Chamberlain, Glenda Jackson, Christopher Gable and Ken Colley hurtle around, or dance, or sing, or stare hungrily. (Tchaikovsky's house is a red womb, richly furnished, with red walls, recalling *Cries and Whispers*, the celebrated Ingmar Bergman chamber piece of 1972. Did Russell influence Bergman?!).

♪

I'm going to indulge in a little theorizing here, just as a Ken Russell movie will be just a little self-indulgent. The work of French feminist Julia Kristeva is useful in discussing art and artists, particularly in relation to Peter Tchaikovsky and the other artists that Russell depicts (such as Dante Gabriel Rossetti or Gustav Mahler or Franz Liszt). Psychoanalyzing the artist, Kristeva reckons that art is born out of the pain of loss. She asserts in "A Question of Subjectivity: an interview":

> the creative act is released by an experience of depression without which we could not call into question the stability of meaning or the banality of expression. A writer must at one time or another have been in a situation of loss – of ties, of meaning – in order to write. (1992, 133).

In this intriguing reading of the artistic act, Julia Kristeva presents the artist not as a 'technician of ecstasy', as Mircea Eliade called the archaic shaman (there is a strong link between Ken Russell's artist figures and the shaman – and not only the Romantic artists), but as a technician of melancholia. The people on the edge – hysterics, obsessionals, lovers, artists – are often sufferers of depression. Underlying many of the complaints of our time, Kristeva said in 1986, is depression (1992, 133). Writing may be one way in which the writer writes her/ his way out of depression.

Julia Kristeva puts forward writers such as Fyodor Dostoievsky, Gérard de Nerval and Marguerite Duras to see this counter-depression at work, and we could add so many of Ken Russell's artist and composer figures. The angst-ridden artist may be a cliché of our times (Vincent van Gogh, Mark Rothko, Ludwig van Beethoven, Thomas Hardy), but it also fits the facts, it certainly fits personalities such as Peter Tchaikovsky or Gustav Mahler.

In *Soleil Noir* (*Black Sun*), Julia Kristeva developed her psychoanalysis of melancholy. For Kristeva, the melancholic is reduced to one, basic meaning – despair and pain (*douleur*), rather than a search for meaning. The melancholic fails to develop a sense of the imaginary and symbolic (this is certainly Peter Tchaikovsky's state). The inability to mobilize the imaginary and symbolic in the melancholic person makes melancholia a kind of living death. Kristevan melancholia is not neurosis, for melancholia does not eroticize the death drive, which results in hatred, and melancholia prevents an eroticization of the separation from the mother. The mother is not the lost object – instead, the subject dies in her place. The artist, though, is able to deal with states such as melancholia because s/he can control signs. The artwork, Kristeva suggests, can be the mark of a 'vanquished depression'.[62] For Tchaikovsky, though, the consolations of art and the psycho-dynamics of art just aren't enough.

♪

Pauline Kael, Judith Crist, William Wolf, Alexander Walker, Gary Arnold, Roger Ebert, Vincent Canby and many other film critics derided *The Music Lovers*. Crist dubbed it 'shockingly bad because it reduces the art of biography to a semi-porno film in Victorian-meller terms'. Yeah, maybe, but that's one of the things that's great about it! (And, besides, Victorian melodrama is the model for 99.99% of cinema that tells stories).

Poor Alexander Walker, one of Ken Russell's chief adversaries among crrrritics, felt that Peter Tchaikovsky'd been raped: 'I don't really like to see a composer raped for the delectation of a

---

62 J. Kristeva, *Black Sun*, 76.

director's sense of what is theatrical,' Walker griped on the BBC in 1971. Other critics (such as Roger Ebert) also felt that the movie had assaulted Tchaikovsky.

Raymond Murray raved in *Images In the Dark: An Encyclopedia of Gay and Lesbian Film and Video*:

> wonderfully overacted and filled with wildly overstated imagery... Chamberlain creates a fascinating picture of the Russian legend, and Glenda Jackson matches him all the way with a helterskelter portrait of his nymphomaniac wife. Though this is admittedly not all tastes, and is overpowering in its energy and emotion, the film is ultimately rewarding for the adventurous. (116, 175)

Ken Russell defended *The Music Lovers* against critics by saying that he loved Peter Tchaikovsky (which certainly comes across in the 1970 movie), but his love wasn't blind, and saw the blemishes as well as the greatness. His film wasn't all highs and lows, but had moments of tranquillity, he said; he used the facts of Tchaikovsky's life, but was making his own interpretation of the Tchaikovsky myth (BP, 56-57).

This page and over: images from an important production in Ken Russell's career: The Music Lovers

The two stars of
The Music Lovers:
Richard Chamberlain
and Glenda Jackson

The final shot of The Music Lovers
– the costs of getting too close to an artist.

Images of
Peter Tchaikovsky

# 9

✝

# *THE DEVILS*

The whole film was conceived as a black comedy, but the fact that people don't laugh isn't very surprising... What the film is saying is that this would be a terrible joke if it weren't all so horrible and hadn't actually happened. I find it extraordinary that Grandier was convicted and burnt on the strength of ludicrous statements which even a young child would find implausible these days in a fairy story.

Ken Russell (Bax, 202f)

Any film that sacrilegiously features frenzied nuns sexually attacking a giant crucifix is pure enjoyment in my cinematic book.

Raymond Murray, *Images In the Dark: An Encyclopedia of Gay and Lesbian Film and Video*

Ken Russell's most notorious hour was undoubtedly *The Devils* (1971),[1] based on the Loudun demonology trials in the 17th century, scripted by Russell from Aldous Huxley's *The Devils of Loudun* (1952) and the 1961 play by John Whiting (1918-63).[2] The project did not originate with Russell, however: it was set up by United Artists, who owned the property, and they approached Russell to direct it.[3] Russell, though, wanted to do the Peter Tchaikovsky movie first, and reluctantly UA agreed (Bax, 183).

---

[1] But Russell's had a few notorious moments, hasn't he? – more than many filmmakers!
[2] A Polish version of the events in Aldous Huxley's book, *Mother Joan of the Angels* (dir. Jerzy Kawalerowicz, b. 1926) had appeared in 1961, but Russell said he saw it after making *The Devils*.
[3] J. Gomez, 1976, 21.

However, the project passed to Warners.

A *tour-de-force* of direction (and organization and production), the most significant contribution to *The Devils* may well be the screenplay – and Ken Russell has the screen credit for the script. Which makes *The Devils* all the more remarkable. (As if writing the script and directing the movie wasn't enough, Russell also co-produced it.) Not enough credit is given to Russell as a screenwriter;[4] he also sometimes downplayed his contributions to scripts, and he also happily admitted that he re-used the ingredients of scripts in other movies (like large chunks of the unproduced *Angels* script in *Tommy*). Go watch *The Devils* and consider it in terms of screenwriting, and you'll appreciate even more what a masterpiece it is.

Aldous Huxley's 1952 book allowed the filmmakers,[5] Ken Russell explained, to go a little nuts (and *The Devils* certainly went just a little nuts!).[6] Huxley's treatment was a 'mind-blowing account of those fantastic events', and was

> just about the trippiest version of a historical event it has ever been my good fortune to happen upon. It was also largely responsible for the original look of the film. (DF, 41)

Although Ken Russell drew on both Aldous Huxley's book and John Whiting's play, the resulting screenplay – and movie – is very much his own interpretation. Russell reckoned he had employed Huxley's books for the atmosphere, but although he'd been knocked out by the play when he'd seen it in 1961,[7] he later found Whiting was too soft-centred in the end, and the play 'evaded the central issue'.

Aldous Huxley (1894-1963) was one of Britain's finest writers

---

4 Joseph Gomez commented: 'This film, more than any other, also best reveals Russell's genius as a creator-adaptor. He remains faithful to all of the major events in Huxley's book, captures the tone of the original, and, most importantly, delineates the major themes of the prose account in methods appropriate to the film medium. He also forcefully presents his own attitudes and responses, but in a way which never violates Huxley's vision' (1976, 161-2).

5 There have been fewer adaptions of Aldous Huxley's fiction than one might expect – fewer than contemporaries such as D.H. Lawrence or Graham Greene, for instance. Most adaptions have been on TV, rather than feature films. A BBC adaption of *Point Counterpoint*, and a couple of versions of *Brave New World,* have been made.

6 In his superb study of Ken Russell's cinema, Joseph Gomez described *The Devils of Loudun* as 'an apocalyptic statement which fuses biography, fiction, and essay to warn about present trends that can lead to world destruction, and to instruct people in the quest for the alternative "divine peace" which comes from upward self-transcendence.' (G, 125)

7 It had starred Dorothy Tutin, whom Russell would cast in *Savage Messiah*.

in the modern era, best known for novels such as *Brave New World, Eyeless In Gaza, Chrome Yellow,* and *Point Counterpoint*. He also wrote books of essays and non-fiction, including the influential *The Doors of Perception* and *The Perennial Philosophy*, with their explorations of mysticism, religion and drugs, which were taken up by the counter-culture in the Sixties. *The Doors of Perception* has links with *Altered States*, and Huxley was part of the literary circle that included D.H. Lawrence (indeed, Huxley parodied Lawrence himself in his novel *Point Counterpoint*).

Aldous Huxley had considered a dramatic version of his book back in the early 1950s, and a movie adaption was being talked of in the early 1960s. Commissioned by the Royal Shakespeare Company, John Whiting's play opened in February, 1961, at the Aldwych Theatre in Londinium.

Aldous Huxley also went to Hollywood (in 1938), working on *Jane Eyre* and *Pride and Prejudice*, and a biography of Madame Curie. There's an excellent Huxley website at somaweb.org.

Urbain Grandier (1590-1634) was burnt at the stake in public in Loudun in 1634 after being charged with inciting the Mother Superior, Jeanne des Anges,[8] and other Ursuline nuns, to demonic possession. As well as combining characters (characters such as D'Armagnac were dropped completely), Ken Russell's script also grants Grandier the powers of governor (departing from the book), when the current governor, Saint-Marthe, dies (it's Saint-Marthe's funeral at the beginning).

Ken Russell commented in the *Toronto Star* on Dec 4, 1971:

> The church has always been appalling. I'm an ordinary run-of-the-mill sinner who only pays lip service to the church, but I was trying to tell the truth about how it uses totally illiterate people to seduce everyone through terror.

It's clear from the first few minutes of *The Devils* that Ken Russell was on fire as a filmmaker[9] when he made this picture[10] (he was certainly on fire at the period in his film career – not only *The Devils* but also *The Music Lovers* and *The Boy Friend* were

---
[8] Jeanne des Anges became Prioress of the Ursuline Convent of Loudun at 25.
[9] Joe Gomez speaks of 'Russell's richly ornate images, his craving for the theatrical, his ambivalent attitudes towards his heroes, and his bizarre sense of humour' in *The Devils* (1976, 70).
[10] As Jack Fisher noted, 'it seems impossible that anyone can watch *The Devils* and not be aware of Russell's brilliance as a visual artist. The film is so totally visual that one has the feeling of watching a series of single frame paintings being displayed' (55).

playing at the same time in central London theatres. Incredible – I can't think of another British movie-maker with three big (and very different) movies in release at the same time).

It was a highly productive period for the maestro: not long after *The Devils* and *The Boy Friend* in 1971, Russell and his team were making *Savage Messiah* for MGM-EMI. (Also in 1971, Russell received awards for best director from the National Board of Review). 'He was fantastically proud of *The Devils*, and was willing to defend it to the death,' remarked Mark Kermode (2013, 43).

You can only make a movie as good as *The Devils* if you're feeling very confident and have immense organizational skills. And you can only really do this kind of movie with the backing and resources of a major film studio. Yeah, and plenty of imagination and skill and 95% hard work.[11]

And Ken Russell was happy with what he'd achieved in *The Devils*: '*The Devils* is the most successful film I've done, insofar as what I expected is there. The effects I aimed at seemed to work' (G, 162).[12] In *The Devils*, Russell was working on a giant canvas, and you can tell from the first few minutes that the director is in complete control of the form, and of this movie. With *The Devils* and *The Music Lovers,* Russell rises far above being merely an accomplished director, and joins the greats.

In fact, in this movie set in 17th century France, with French characters, filmed in England with a mainly British cast and crew (and drawing on two British writers), but paid for by a North American studio, everyone is a star, producing their finest work.

*The Devils* was a big movie, and Ken Russell's production team should always be mentioned when discussing the movie: David Watkin, DP, camera operator Ronnie Taylor, editor Mike Bradsell, costume designer Shirley Kingdon, production designer Derek Jarman, art director Robert Cartwright, set dresser Ian Whittaker, production manager Neville C. Thompson, make-up Charles Parker, hairdresser Ramon Gow, A.D. Ted Morley, unit manager Graham Ford, choreographer Terry Gilbert, composer Peter Maxwell Davies, special effects by John Richardson, and sound by Gordon McCallum, Terry Rawlings and Brian Simmons.

---

11 Elements of *The Devils* were arduous for cast and crew: as Ken Russell put it, '*The Devils* left many of us weak, miserable and shattered' (Bax, 211).
12 The Jesuit reverend Gene Phillips was a keen supporter of *The Devils,* and included it in the course he taught at Loyola University in Chicago.

Let's not forget that Russell also produced the film, along with Robert H. Solo, and his regular producer, Roy Baird.

*The Devils* was filmed on 35mm in Panavision widescreen (ratio: 1:2.35). Technicolor produced the prints. Running time was 111 minutes, 117 minutes (restored). Released: July, 1971 (G.B.), and July 16, 1971 (U.S.A.).

Ken Russell's extravagant, over-the-top take on the Loudun martyrs starred Oliver Reed, Vanessa Redgrave, Gemma Jones, and British character actors (such as Dudley Sutton, Murray Melvin, Michael Gothard, Georgina Hale, Kenneth Colley, Andrew Faulds, Judith Paris, and Max Adrian). Many of the actors were Russell regulars – the whole repertory of Russellians is here. Sutton and Gothard played the State emissaries sent in to break Loudun; Redgrave was the chief sister, Jeanne, deformed, and tormented by 'sinful thoughts';[13] Hale and Jones were Grandier's lovers (Hale would later star in *Mahler*).

*The Devils* may be Ken Russell's masterpiece (tho' for him his favourite movie was *The Music Lovers* – not least because it's a pæan to that most miraculous event in human history: music).[14] You can tell when filmmakers are really engaged with their material and when they are really reaching for something and extending themselves. And Russell and his team were certainly going for it big time in *The Devils*. Look at the staging and the way the camera is used, for instance: *The Devils* contains muscular, confident blocking and filming of scenes – from the big, crowd scenes to the small, intimate scenes. The subject matter and the themes are fully in tune with Russell's own sensibilities, and his form of cinema. With *The Devils*, as with *The Music Lovers*, Russell really found a way of exploiting his talents on a very grand scale.

The control of *mise-en-scène* in *The Devils*, as Joseph Gomez has demonstrated in his excellent close analysis of the movie (in his 1976 study of Ken Russell), is superb. Russell and DP David Watkin compose shots, for instance, which subtly underscore the drama, as well as images which express the key themes of the piece in an OTT manner. The blocking of actors within shots, for instance, illustrates many of the tensions inside the drama, such as

---

13 Giving Vanessa Redgrave the OTT movie hump of Igor in *Frankenstein* fits perfectly in this savage satire.
14 '*The Devils* stands as Ken Russell's major achievement, in part, because the flamboyance of his style is so perfectly suited to the film's subject matter,' remarked Joseph Gomez (G, 161).

having the people opposed to Urbain Grandier on the issue of the walls being demolished on one side of the frame (Mignon and Trincant), and two that support him (Rangier and Legrand) on the other side of the frame.

☦

In terms of production, *The Devils* displayed a slightly larger budget than the usual Ken Russell film: there was an impressive French, 17th century town square set, all in white, contrasting with the predominantly black costumes (the sets[15] were designed by Derek Jarman, with set dressing and art direction by Robert Cartwright and Ian Whittaker; Jarman would later make films such as *The Tempest, Caravaggio* and *The Last of England*, clearly influenced by Russell).[16] It's a stylization of Loudun, of a 17th century, French town (Russell wasn't interested in the real place, for the purposes of this movie). The first scenes in Loudun show off the big sets[17] (which took up a large portion of the backlot at Pinewood Studios), the many extras, and the costumes.

Derek Jarman is often praised and singled out by critics in relation to the look of *The Devils*,[18] but it's the way the design fuses with the other elements that really makes it work. In *The Devils*, everyone is working at their best.[19]

As accomplished and visionary as the sets are, for example, one could cite the dazzlingly brilliant, widescreen cinematography as being more important, or the editing, or the music – no one can forget Peter Davies' score for *The Devils*, by turns parping, florid, irreverent, stark, mawkish and nihilistic (there isn't a score quite like this one anywhere!).

When we're talking about such a stunningly visual movie

---

15 But the film studio – Warners – asked the filmmakers to cut back on some of the sets: the royal palace, for instance, and a court and garden for King Louis (PF, 107).
16 Derek Jarman had met Ken Russell through Janet Deuters (PF, 103). Russell found Jarman full of ideas and enthusiasm for the movie. 'We talked for days and days on end'.
17 Urbain Grandier's apartments comprise a circular room at the top of an Italian-style tower, containing a circular staircase. The luxury of such rooms emphasizing the vanity of Grandier, of course, and how he appears to be above everyone else.
18 Ken Russell and Derek Jarman drew on a Russell favourite movie, *Metropolis* (Bax, 207), a hugely influential picture of course; Jarman looked at Giovanni Piranesi (his *Imaginary Prisons*, 1760s), Étienne-Louis Boulée, and Claude-Nicolas Ledoux (PF, 107).
19 Including the camera department, headed by David Watkin, with Ronnie Taylor as camera operator; the costume department, headed up by Shirley Kingdon; the editing team led by Mike Bradsell (with Stuart Baird as assistant editor); the music by Peter Maxwell Davies and David Munrow; the hair by Ramon Gow; the make-up by Charles Parker; the set dressing and art direction by Robert Cartwright and Ian Whittaker; the choreography by Terry Gilbert; and the special effects by John Richardson.

like *The Devils,* the DP is incredibly important. David Watkin turns in a performance as lighting cameraman the equal of the superstar DPs of the period, like Vittorio Storaro, Geoffrey Unsworth, Gordon Willis, Vilmos Zsigmond or Sven Nykvist. In terms of the cinematography, *The Devils* is sensational. Illuminating the black Cathedral, for example, required an inventive approach to lighting (Russell recalled that Watkin employed a giant searchlight from WW2 and blasted it thru the stained glass, to throw colours onto the performers. It was very effective). The cinematography in *The Devils* is crisp, stylized yet also naturalistic.

The hair and make-up is particularly fine in *The Devils,* with Ramon Gow, Charles Parker and their teams delivering fabulous results, as well as gruesome visualizations of the plague, hunchbacks and torture.[20] Hairdresser Gow gives Vanessa Redgrave a deliberately over-the-top, long wig for Sister Jeanne's fantasies.

Masks (and masquerades) are favourite props in a Ken Russell movie, and *The Devils* has masks aplenty, as if everyone is wearing a disguise and no one is quite what they seem. It was a stroke of genius, for instance, to have Georgina Hale's Philippe Trincant sporting a face done in pale make-up.[21] And the king appears first in a high camp costume as the Goddess Venus.

There were crowd scenes, with many (maybe two hundred) extras in costume (for sequences such as the funeral procession; Urbain Grandier expelling the government from Loudun with the aid of soldiers bearing crossbows; and the climactic burning of Grandier). There were horses, animals, and numerous props (some were very large, like the wooden, wheeled engines).

And *The Devils* is a very grand, special effects movie – there are numerous special make-up jobs (for the plague victims, for instance, or Urbain Grandier as he's tortured), and a huge amount of practical effects (courtesy of special effects supervisor John Richardson and his team), ranging from fire and smoke to water and explosions (pretty much all of the exterior shots include smoke and many have fire). Richardson, a veteran of almost every movie made in Britain from the 1960s to today, commented in the *Times:* 'I was horrified sometimes at what we were doing.

---

20 And of course the special effects make-up for Urbain Grandier's last moments on Earth.

21 The green lipstick and white face make-up was historically accurate, according to Ken Russell: it was a fashion of the period. 'I thought: yes, it makes her look corpse-like and it does go with her jealousy, her wish to kill Grandier' (Bax, 223).

But seeing the picture I wasn't at all offended by it, it all had a rightful place in the film'.[22] Yes: *The Devils* is one of those movies that if people visited the set (such as studio executives or journalists, probably the people most resented on set by film directors), and observed some of the action, they might've come away with a negative impression (especially if they don't really know how movies are made – many journos don't): but put it all together, and it makes sense.

The fundamental design principle of *The Devils* was a scheme of black and white throughout the costumes, sets, props, and lighting. It's a film of opposites in everything: life and death, Protestantism and Catholicism, good and evil, God and the Devil, belief and non-belief, State and citizen, King and subject, Paris and Loudun.[23] Black and white, but with the red of blood, hate and fire superimposed over it, and running thru it (red's used in *The Devils* for Cardinal Richelieu's costume, the crosses on the costumes, and of course the blood – *The Devils* is Russell's bloodiest movie).

Ken Russell said he hated historical films, where everything is crumbling or in ruins.

> I really despise period films. Anything before the eighteenth century is automatically in crumbling ruins, all grey blocks of stone. It looks like a pageant with everyone in fancy dress. We wanted to do away with the cobwebs and grey stone and get a contemporary feeling. The people of Loudun who were so crazy about their city and trying to save it certainly didn't see it as an old museum relic. For them it was something new and modern. So we had to make if modern for people today. (Bax, 206).

So Ken Russell and his team went for a contemporary look. The simple, household brick was chosen as the basic building block for all of the architecture in the Loudun set (using Pinewood Studios' standard brick mould); everything was painted white (actually beige, so it photographed white), giving the set the look of a hospital, a clinic, an asylum, a prison, and a slaughterhouse. The chapel is extremely odd, with even the altar being built from white bricks. And the Catholic archive in Paris is constructed in the same way, looking like a prison that's been turned into an

---

[22] *The Times*, December 7, 1971.
[23] I wonder if the filmmakers were also linking the struggle between Catholics and Protestants in *The Devils* to the Irish Troubles: at the time of production, the acts of I.R.A. (including bomb attacks) were very much in the news.

archive and library[24] – not only implying the continuity between the convent and a prison, but also between Paris and Loudun, and the whole of France (but France has seldom appeared like this on screen!).

Ken Russell and his team took a line in Aldous Huxley's *The Devils of Loudun* as their starting-point: 'Barré had treated [Jeanne] to an experience that was the equivalent, more or less, of a rape in a public lavatory' (1970, 1924). The design æsthetic took that concept – 'a rape in a public lavatory' (a phrase guaranteed to get Russell's attention!) – and applied it on a grandiose scale. (Huxley is referring to gruesome tortures such as the 'miraculous enema'). The anachronistic sets of Loudun were analogous to Huxley's references to the present day – Huxley and Russell are sending out warnings about the present by using the past (like any decent production of a classic play, from say William Shakespeare or Sophocles, *The Devils* updates the material and makes it contemporary).

The score, by Peter Maxwell Davies, announces itself forcefully in the opening scenes of *The Devils,* too. It's a distinctive, modernist score which plays with dissonance. And in the later, hysterical scenes, the music comes close to cacophony, with instrumentation that emulates the mediæval street parade (horns, drums, flutes). Davies's music is vital to *The Devils,* partly because Mike Bradsell had edited some scenes to the music.

Peter Davies recalled that the musical language for *The Devils* was easy to find: it drew on the 1960s, and was meant to get louder and more disturbing as the narrative progressed: 'it becomes louder than it is because it's echoing back at you, and it begins to have a resonance which you want to get out of. There's a slight feeling that you don't want to stay there too long' (PF, 113).

It's not all rasps and hoots and drum-banging, however: many scenes are played alongside slow drones of strings; however, these are not the usual, soft strings of Hollywood movies, which gently enhance the mood. Rather, they are deliberately unsettling sounds, consciously melancholy and disturbing, underlining the fact that *The Devils* is *never* at rest: the entire film is in a state of flux and riot. Even the intimate scenes of Urbain

---

[24] The Catholic Church must've had enormous vaults holding information on everybody, Russell reckoned: hence the OTT archive set, complete with piles of books stored in prison cells and giant swing doors with a cross on them.

Grandier with his two lovers, for instance, are not really respites from the hothouse atmosphere, because the audience is always aware that the whole town is on the edge of erupting into chaos or violence. (There are also versions of *Dies Irae* (*Day of Wrath*), deliberately cheesy, melodramatic music, and of course the 1920s popular song 'Bye Bye Blackbird' – included perhaps to further piss off purists! Warners likely hated the score as well as everything about *The Devils*).

☥

*The Devils* was Ken Russell's first of two productions for the Warner Brothers studio (the second being *Altered States*). At the time, in the early 1970s, Warners was presided over by Ted Ashley. Russell was not the only filmmaker to run afoul of Ashley's regime: for instance, George Lucas and Francis Coppola[25] fell out with Warners over *THX 1138*, and would not do business with them for years afterwards. Lucas loathed the way Warners treated his film. When four minutes were cut from *THX 1138* by Warners' editor Rudy Fehr, on Ted Ashley's orders, Lucas said it was 'like watching someone cutting the fingers off of his child'.[26]

Needless to say, it's unlikely that Warners would've developed and produced *Altered States* had Ken Russell been the initial director: Warners took up *Altered States* after Columbia Pictures had dropped it. In a familiar story, Russell insisted that Warners had approved the script of *The Devils* (but may be they hadn't scrutinized it too closely), and he had shot what had been agreed in the screenplay (it's the famous scene in *Contempt*, Jean-Luc Godard's masterful 1963 satire on the film industry, when the producer (Jack Palance) berates the director (Fritz Lang) for not shooting the script as written and agreed; then, when he checks the script, he sees the rushes *are* as agreed. But he's still not

---

[25] Francis Coppola's relationship with Warners was rocky, to say the least: they backed his first three features (*You're a Big Boy Now*, *Finian's Rainbow* and *The Rain People*), all of which flopped; they invested in Zeotrope but backed out; they backed *Hammett* and *The Escape Artist*, but these failed; later, there were lawsuits brought by Coppola against Warners over *Pinocchio* and *Contact*.

[26] George Lucas hated the way Warners executive Fred Weintraub had spoken about it. Weintraub had liked the dwarfs, whom he called freaks, who appeared towards the end of *THX 1138*. Weintraub told Lucas that he ought to grab the audience's attention early on in the film: 'put the freaks up front', as Weintraub put it. Lucas later referred to the phrase to embody what he hated about the studio system, where the 'freaks' were the executives. 'Put the freaks up front' summed up for Lucas (and his contemporaries) the typical, dumb, Hollywood studio executive's mentality when it came to movies.

satisfied).27

✞

*The Devils*, performance-wise, was monopolized by Ken Russell regular Ollie Reed (not easy in a film of many eccentric acting turns),28 and Vanessa Redgrave's Sister Jeanne. Reed, with his substantial bulk, bulldog face, shaggy, black hair, moustache, and haunted look, was a formidable presence in *The Devils* (especially in the agonizing torture scenes, shaven-headed (and without eyebrows),29 broken, surrounded by Sutton, Adrian, Gothard and Melvin hissing 'confess!' at him, and maintaining his dignity to the end). But all of the way through *The Devils*, Reed is at his best; it's a remarkable performance, undoubtedly the biggest challenge of Reed's acting career. But it also needs a great supporting cast, which *The Devils* has in spades.

Urbain Grandier was certainly a challenging role,30 and one many an actor would jump at the chance to do31 – these sorts of roles simply do not come along that often.32 Oliver Reed's performance was certainly Oscar-worthy, and may be the best performance of his career – although *The Devils* was probably just a tad too Out There for the Academy in L.A.

Altho' Oliver Reed recognized that Urban Grandier was his greatest role, he also thought that his performance had been swamped somewhat by the extravagance of the filmmaking: 'there was so much going on that it was difficult to make a

---

27 That's also partly a joke about Jean-Luc Godard – he *never* shot what was in the script! And there wasn't a conventional script in the first place, anyway!
The amusing incident may derive from something that happened to Fritz Lang when he was directing *Fury* (1936) for producer Joe Mankiewicz: according to Lang: 'When *Fury* was finished, the producer came out of a preview and called me to his office and accused me of changing the script. I said, "How could I change the script when I can't even speak English!" So they went and got a copy of the script and he read it and he said, "Damn you, you're right, but it *sounds* different on the screen." Perhaps it did – to him.' (In *Films & Filming*, 1962).
28 Oliver Reed found the dialogue difficult, and sometimes read from pieces of dialogue written on the set.
29 Russell said that Reed's eyebrows had been insured by Lloyd's of London (if they didn't grow back). Reed had been reluctant.
30 Oliver Reed sometimes wasn't confident about his dialogue and his voice (he had the Latin quotations in *The Devils* reduced, for instance, and the lines hidden off-camera. Critics have wondered if Reed might've done some William Shakespeare – an aged King Lear, perhaps, or Macbeth (in the 1971 adaption which starred Jon Finch).
31 Filming *The Devils* had been intense, Oliver Reed admitted – he likened working with Ken Russell on this challenging production to sitting on a firecracker.
32 John Whiting's play added a character called the Sewerman, so that Urbain Grandier could have someone to talk to, rather than playing scenes alone (or using monologues). Among his symbolic functions was to act as a court jester or commentator, and to embody the notion of the world as a sewer (G, 126).

performance live. The performances got lost in the tirade of masturbation, flagellation and kissing God's feet', Reed complained when the movie was released. But when you consider Ollie's performance now, it seems magnificent.

Vanessa Redgrave (b. 1937) had not been Ken Russell's first choice to play Sister Jeanne: that was, as one might expect, Glenda Jackson. When she refused (not fancying the role),[33] Russell was furious – 'it produced the most bilious fury from him', as Jackson put it – it had seemed the perfect pairing, Reed and Jackson, and had proved so successful in *Women In Love*.

Glenda Jackson had liked the ending of *The Devils* in one (earlier) script version – when, after her death, Sister Jeanne's head was put on display in a casket and her followers approached it on their knees. In this version of the screenplay, the movie would've continued after Urban Grandier's demise to show Sister Jeanne becoming something of a saintly celebrity, cosying up to Cardinal Richelieu and the King. But the movie would've been long. Jackson wanted that ending, and didn't like the revised ending: in the movie, the ending for Jeanne is rather downbeat and unresolved.

But if you can't sign up Glenda Jackson, Vanessa Redgrave will do! – Redgrave is absolutely spell-binding as the tormented soul in a hunchback's body – again it may be the performance of her career (at least in cinema – Redgrave has worked extensively on stage, and her cinema performances have been a little patchy). Redgrave thought very highly of *The Devils*, calling it the chief work of genius of the postwar period, along with *The Charge of the Light Brigade* (which had been directed by her husband Tony Richardson in 1968, in which she appeared). Russell was full of praise for Redgrave, how she would throw herself into the role, without worrying about how badly she looked.[34]

Prior to *The Devils*, Vanessa Redgrave had appeared in *Isadora, Morgan, The Charge of the Light Brigade, Blow-Up, A Man For All Seasons, Camelot,* and *Oh, What a Lovely War!* Redgrave became known for her outspoken left-wing political opinions.[35] As well as *Isadora*, a 1968 movie version of the dancer who'd been the subject of Russell's incredible, 1966 TV biography, another connection

---

[33] 'I was worried about playing another neurotic, sex-starved lady, albeit a nun,' Jackson remarked in the *New York Times* in 1971.
[34] And it must have been difficult for Redgrave playing every scene with her head tilted to her left side.
[35] She apparently sold copies of the *Communist Manifesto* outside the commissary.

with Russell was Redgrave's daughters (by Tony Richardson) – Joely and Natasha – who appeared in *Lady Chatterley* and *Gothic*.

The supporting players are also outstanding in *The Devils*. Many were Ken Russell regulars, and actors such as Dudley Sutton, Michael Gothard, Christopher Logue, Max Adrian, Georgina Hale and Murray Melvin excelled themselves. Although *The Devils* was by most reports at times a difficult shoot, that never detracted from the performances. In every respect, *The Devils* is filmmaking at its very, very finest. (The roles played by Dudley Sutton, Michael Gothard and Christopher Logue – the chief heavies – perhaps called for more well-known actors – Jack Palance, say, or Trevor Howard. Logue, for instance, was a poet, not an actor, although he had been impressive as Algernon Swinburne in *Dante's Inferno*. Someone with more menace and weight on screen might've been more suitable casting. But Sutton and Gothard were terrific, and perhaps Logue playing the Cardinal as a scheming tho' clearly weak person enhances the picture).

✟

*The Devils* is Ken Russell's *hommage* to the silent movie classic *The Passion of Joan of Arc* (Carl-Theodor Dreyer, 1928). There are numerous affinities between the two: such as stylistic motifs like big close-ups, or setting actors against white and grey buildings (which comprise stylized, abstract versions of mediæval architecture). And of course *Joan of Arc* shares many themes with *The Devils* (including a French setting), such as the satirical representations of the Church and Catholicism, hypocrisy, religion, prayer, worship, religion vs. politics, etc. And both movies conclude with a martyrdom at the stake (the finale of *Joan of Arc* is evoked in many ways by *The Devils* – such as the use of street performers (jugglers, acrobats) mocking the event, the cuts back to big close-ups of the victim, the shaved head, the skull in the dirt, and even the descent into violence, as the soldiers set upon the onlookers).

✟

In a classic Russellian fantasy sequence (not in the Aldous Huxley book or the John Whiting play, needless to say!), Oliver Reed's Urbain Grandier appeared as Christ, walking on water (in a lake), towards Vanessa Redgrave's Sister Jeanne, now clad in a white dress with long, ginger hair – a Mary Magdalene who prostrates herself before Reed's Jesus. She wipes his feet with her hair, like the Magdalene does in the Christian story. The fantasy, which occurred early in the 1971 picture (as Jeanne watches the funeral procession), served to illustrate Jeanne's suppressed erotic desires for Grandier, which she couches in religions terms (the fantasies 'are projected by a very sick lady in heat', as Jack Fisher put it [1976, 64]).

Typically for a Russellian fantasy sequence, it all goes horribly wrong, when a righteous hurricane rises, coming straight from God or the moral majority (or maybe the mob), and blows Sister Jeanne's dress up, revealing her ugly hump. By the end of the fantasy, Jeanne is rolling around on the stones in agony, as the nuns laugh at her. 'I'm beautiful!' she insists. Urbain Grandier looks down at her pityingly. Poor Sister Jeanne – even her sexual fantasies don't come out right. Even in a sexual fantasy, the one place you can get everything just right (you just close your eyes!), *jouissance* is disrupted.

The fantasy then cuts to Sister Jeanne in the little alcove[36] where she's been spying on the procession,[37] caught in a contorted posture, crouched on the floor. She's a twisted, deformed body in cramped, claustrophobic spaces.[38]

This's one instance of many in the 1971 film of highly physical acting: although he's never described as an 'actor's director', Ken Russell certainly knew how to extract extraordinary and visceral performances out of his ensemble in *The Devils* (or he knew how to create an environment in which they could feel safe enough to experiment). It's something that critics tend to overlook – maybe because the visuals and behaviour in a Ken Russell movie are so compelling. But he is a master at drawing out from his actors really kinetic movements and gestures.[39]

And *The Devils* is full of them: actors lunge at other actors, gripping them tightly during the exorcism scenes; they fall to the

---

[36] The alcove is put there just for this scene: it's an example of production design describing a personality: it demonstrates how Sister Jeanne has her own ways of circumventing convention, how she has her own little spying places, while the nuns have to fight over getting the top place at the window.
[37] Narratively, the procession is there partly to offer an ensemble scene in which to introduce many of the main characters (G, 141). Such scenes also of course show off the production values of a movie. Ironically, Urbain Grandier will undertake the same journey in his own Calvary, at the end of the movie.
[38] As Jack Fisher pointed out, those confined spaces and deformities embody the turmoil of Jeanne's sexual and religious repressions (58).
[39] Which's also partly why some of the later works are disappointing, because that feeling for physical acting and gesture, and the *sheer energy* that infuses the high-water mark works, from the late 1960s thru the 1970s, is lacking in some of the later pieces.

floor; they loll about from the plague; and in the torture scenes and the frenzy in the church, all manner of contortions are on show (Vanessa Redgrave performs the 'hysteric's arc', for instance, and croaks in a demon's voice (at Grandier: 'devil!'), anticipating *The Exorcist* by a couple of years).[40] The actors throw themselves into these roles – they know that parts this juicy don't come along that often. How many times do you get asked to whip yourself up into (sexual/ religious) hysteria in a major, historical movie?!

In a later erotic fantasy of Sister Jeanne's, the real Christ on the Cross transforms into Urbain Grandier crucified. The *mise-en-scène* comprises smoke, extras in Biblical costumes, and a rocky cliffscape (it looks like the Lake District again, or maybe a quarry near Pinewood).[41] It's a full-on, Golgotha sequence, in gnarly black-and-white,[42] with three people being crucified against a rock face (drawing on Renaissance art, of course – a *Crucifixion* out of Rogier van der Weyden or Hans Memling, perhaps).

Vanessa Redgrave's Sister Jeanne[43] overacts in a silent movie manner (as if she's Lillian Gish in a D.W. Griffith melodrama), again clad in white with long hair – a Mary Magdalene figure or bride of Christ (the nun here as a literal 'bride of Christ'). Jeanne approaches Urbain Grandier, who steps down from the Cross (Oliver Reed doing 'Moody 3', of course, complete with a crown of thorns and blood on his face). Grandier/ Jesus embraces the hysterical nun; they kiss while the crowd jeer, and she licks her dream lover's wounds. Finally, they roll on the ground in an

---

40 *The Devils* would make a great double-bill with *The Exorcist* – two Warners movies which explore very similar, hysterical, Catholic territory, by filmmakers at the height of their powers. The shoot of *The Exorcist* was by most accounts more difficult than *The Devils*, however.

41 *The Devils* was shot mainly at Pinewood Studios. Bamburgh Castle was also used for the approach road to Loudun (it was seen in *Macbeth* (directed by Roman Polanski) the same year). Locations near Pinewood Studios included Black Park for the forest scene, and a small lake, for the scene where Urbain Grandier walks on the water in Sister Jeanne's dream.

42 Joseph Gomez suggested that Ken Russell and the team employed b/w here because the scene is 'meant to parody such motion pictures as C.B. DeMille's *King of Kings* (1927)' (G, 162). In *An Appalling Talent*, Russell wished he'd filmed both dream visions in black-and-white, to maintain consistency (Bax, 209). The final image of *The Devils* is an optically printed shot which bleaches out to black-and-white.

43 Another echo of the *Gospels* has Sister Jeanne hanging herself on a tree in a rainstorm.

erotic embrace, with the Grandier on top of Jeanne.[44]

And while Jesus/ Grandier is fucking Sister Jeanne, the movie cuts back again and again to Jeanne conducting a religious service on her knees, in close-up, surrounded by her nuns, all holding their rosaries. The music is working frantically to enhance the atmosphere of intense eroticism and intense religious repression. At the climax, Jeanne digs a crucifix into her palm, creating a bloody hole that recalls stigmata. Wow! (The cross as phallus, the hole as vagina, plus menstrual blood). She hides, embarrassed (Jeanne is always being overtaken by her erotic desires).

The evocations of classical Hollywood cinema in Sister Jeanne's sexual fantasies (and in particular Cecil B. DeMille) is intentional, of course: DeMille famously sexed-up Biblical stories, happily conflating sex and religion (ancient world epics were a legitimate way of getting a lot of naked flesh on screen, for instance, in Production Code-era Hollywood: the Hays Office and the Legion of Decency might complain about lines of suggestive dialogue, or keeping one foot on the floor in a bedroom scene, but Salomé or Delilah or Cleopatra could justifiably be clad in skimpy costumes). And the *form* of a sword-and-sandal Biblical epic from the 1930s-60s also shows how corny and clichéd Jeanne's fantasies are, how she sees herself in camp, OTT settings. Because by 1971, when *The Devils* was produced, those sorts of toga sagas were very old hat.

Certainly the erotic fantasy aspects of *The Devils* have been noted by viewers. In one of American author Nancy Friday's books of women's sexual fantasies, for instance, we find this entry from 'Rose Ann', a 23 year-old college grad:

> When the movie *The Devils* came out, a whole new fantasy world opened to me. I don't know if you're familiar with it. The "nun-possessed-by-sexual-demons-that-must-be-exorcised-through-sexual-means" type of thing. Vanessa Redgrave, the nun in question, had to go through the most delicious tortures (having her breasts bound with barbed wire, etc). It turned me on so I had to leave in the middle to go home and masturbate.[45]

---

[44] Igniting several taboos, principally those surrounding religion and religious imagery, *The Devils* was adding nothing new to well-known works on the margins of mainstream art. For instance, British artist Eric Gill (another passionate, Catholic Romantic, like Ken Russell, who exalted a particular brand of British/ English tradition), had portrayed a nude, long-haired Mary Magdalene embracing Christ on the Cross. (Gill had produced other images which combined sex and religion, such as his illustrations to the most erotic book in the *Bible*, the *Song of Songs*, in which couples fuck while blessed by the hand of God).

[45] N. Friday, *Forbidden Flowers*, Arrow, London, 1994, 279.

Filmmakers, like any artists, love it when people react powerfully to their work, so if they're leaving halfway thru a movie to get themselves off at home, wow! (Even the exhibitors're happy, 'cos they've already paid to see the movie!).

Yeah – take that crrritics Pauline Kael, Vincent Canby, Judith Crist and Alexander Walker: here's a happy customer!:

> It turned me on so I had to leave in the middle to go home and masturbate.[46]

Yes, the erotic fantasy scene in *The Devils* is the cliché of all nun movie genre clichés – taking the 'bride of Christ' fantasy to an erotic conclusion, and depicting Sister Jeanne and Jesus getting it on. Nuns and candles, nuns and lesbianism, nuns and Jesus – you can't expect Ken Russell *not* to include those clichés! So, yes, there're scenes of nuns jerking candles, nuns a-kissin' and a-frolickin' naked, and nuns getting intimate with Christ.[47]

Immediately after the gruesome death of the plague victim (played by one of the Russell regulars, Maggie Maxwell), which ironically brings together Urbain Grandier and Madelyn de Brou (the victim's daughter), and the eternal themes of love and death (they pray over the dead body),[48] the 1971 Warners film shifts into a humorous moment.[49] The outraged father of Philippe, Magistrate Trincant (John Woodvine), accosts Grandier (and he's egged on by Adam and Ibert, the town fools and quacks, who love any social disruption). A little bit of *The Three Musketers*-style swordplay crops up here, when Trincant draws his sword on Grandier, and the priest employs a stuffed crocodile to defend himself (Adam and Ibert having been using crocodiles, among other crazy cures, to treat the plague victim).[50]

Ken Russell gleefully *refuses* to put a serious sword fight on screen in any of his movies – they are always sent up (in *Lisztomania* or *Dante's Inferno*, for instance). He just *won't* do it! He won't

---

46 That should be put on the ads and posters: 'this movie got me off five times!'
47 Even so, a movie such as *Behind Convent Walls* (1977, a.k.a. *Interieur d'un Convent, Sex Life in a Convent* or *Within a Cloister*), directed by Euro-art-'n'-erotica maestro Walerian Borowczyk, was more sexually explicit: the picture (set in a convent) depicted nuns carving dildos from wood and masturbating with them. But the filmmakers of *The Devils* probably knew that being so graphic wouldn't get past the studio or the censors in an American, studio-financed picture in 1971.
48 As they pray, Urbain Grandier has discovered a new potential lover.
49 Some of the in-jokes include the word 'RUSSEL' daubed on a building (but you'll miss it on panned-and-scanned versions).
50 Russell said he came up with the idea of wasps in glass jars as a cure (wasps?! How would that work?!).

he won't he won't! Imagine Russell directing one of those Hollywood blockbuster, action movies, like *Lord of the Rings* or *King Arthur Decapitates the Pirates of the Caribbean In Troy*, which call for thirty-minute-long sword fights. After three seconds the swords would become stuffed crocodiles and ten foot bananas, everyone's costume would fall off to reveal silver bikinis, and on come the chorus girls dressed as nuns and Nazis!

Just writing these little skits on Hollywood movies, where a Hollywood Action Movie Sword Fight becomes an Over-The-Top Ken Russell Dance Number, reminds me just how ridiculous those Hollywood blockbuster movies are, with their incessant and insane insistence on, and its glorificatino of, endless violence. They are far, far dumber, and far more perverse, twisted and sick, than anything Russell produced.[51] And just how much *fun* Russell's approach to movies can be. Oh, once again, I wish that a Hollywood studio had been ballsy enough to give Russell $150 million to see what he could deliver!

Detractors who dislike Ken Russell's movies could criticize the sword-'n'-crocodile fight scene in *The Devils* for being foolish and pointless, but it's not: first, it demonstrates that the townspeople can't touch Urbain Grandier, and he knows it; it shows that Grandier thinks he can get away with being a bad boy (like horsing around with Important People's Daughters), and not suffer any consequences; it shows that Philippe Trincant is not going to take being thrown over by Grandier for a younger model (Madelyn de Brou) lightly (she has already appealed to her father, but he's ineffectual); and it lightens the movie with some humour after the horrors of the death of the ill woman. (Thus, the movie skilfully uses humour to get across some key points. And that, folks, is clever screenwriting. Not every bit of exposition or information in a movie needs to be delivered in a solemn, sit-down-and-shut-up-and-listen manner).

The instant rejection of poor Philippe Trincant when she tells Urbain Grandier that she's pregnant (in their post-coital scene), demonstrates his cold-hearted side ('so it ends', he mutters). And once he's made his decision, none of her frustrated protestations have any effect on him: to emphasize his indifference (and also

---

51 The *Lord of the Rings* flicks, for instance, are *extremely violent*, at least in terms of what they are trying to portray – a world war in a fantasy land called Middle-earth. The body counts of *The Return of the King* (836) and *The Two Towers* (468) far excel those in *Saving Private Ryan, Hard-Boiled, Braveheart* or *We Were Soldiers* (according to www.moviebodycounts.com).

his vanity), the movie has Grandier looking in a mirror and combing his hair, in C.U., while the nude Philippe frets and rages out of focus in the background. (Her father, Trincant, presents her – naked – to the Baron in attempt to obtain some justice. But that slur against Grandier doesn't stick). However, Grandier's cavalier-Casanova attitude to the town's women works against him in the end, persuading Trincant to become involved in the conspiracy to oust Grandier.

You could say that while all around him there is twisted sexuality – repressed sexuality, too-intense desire, sexuality that erupts via the suppressions of Christianity into something tormented and self-loathing – Urbain Grandier's sexuality is actually straightforward and simply heterosexual. The guy just likes a good fuck. He's a Henry Miller character or Giacomo Casanova who unfortunately finds himself in the middle of a lunatic asylum putting on a play of Dante's *Inferno* at a time of plague.

Yes, Urbain Grandier moves on from one mistress to the next, and sometimes has to hear them confess in church, but his sex life is familiar, heterosexual, traditional. It's what men have always been like (yeah, men're shits, but what're you gonna do? Kill them all? 3 billion men?!). In fact, it is through Grandier that one sees much of the insanity of *The Devils*. Meanwhile, the other main viewpoint of the narrative, Sister Jeanne's, comes from someone who is literally twisted in her body as well as her mind (but the most twisted mind in *The Devils*, according to the filmmakers is the power behind the throne, Cardinal Richelieu. Twisted minds who have access to political power are the worst of all).

Thus the scene where Urbain Grandier and Philippe Trincant are seen making love is an important scene (rather than being merely titillating), because it offers a familiar and conventional, central, emotional/ psychological axis for the narrative: b4 the rest of the crazy story splatters across the screen, the audience has seen 'honest lovemaking between two loving people', as Jack Fisher put it (58). Similarly, there is a scene where Grandier and Madelyn de Brou share a meal and talk. Just that. A simple, non-dramatic and harmonious scene (but not a scene that critics who dislike Russellania, and this movie in particular, ever comment upon. What movie reviewer would discuss a modest scene like that? – but there are quite a few in *The Devils* (and loads in

Russell's whole output), including a very lengthy two-shot of Madelyn and Grandier later on where they do naught but talk quietly).

✞

Who are the 'devils' in this movie? The nuns when they go nuts at the end? The State's bullies who persecute them and the townspeople of Loudun? Is it Urbain Grandier and Sister Jeanne? Is it Christianity, or Catholicism, or French society, or themes like sin and guilt and retribution?

No. Joseph Gomez is right when he states in his illuminating book on Ken Russell that the real devils in *The Devils* are Cardinal Richelieu and the King of France: because the movie opens not with Loudun, but with the pageant involving the King and Richelieu (presumably in gay Paree), and when the main title comes up, it is over close-ups of Richelieu and the King (that is, the movie *shows you* who the devils are, by placing the title right over their faces).

Church and State, religion and politics: when Cardinal Richelieu talks to the King in the prologue, he says, 'I pray that I may assist you in the birth of a new France in which Church and State are one'. He also adds that he wishes to rid France of Protestants. At that point, dispensing with the usual opening credits (of who-did-what), the film cuts straight to a close-up of a maggot-filled skull, attached to the skeleton of a dead Protestant on a wheel on a post in the countryside.

The shock cut does a lot of narrative work: it's all about contrasts, for a start: life and death. It's about the hypocrisy and corruption of the ruling powers. It's about the relationship between mere talk at court and what that talk leads to in reality – death for people who follow the wrong religion. Words and acts.

And that close-up of the skeleton slowly rotating on a wheel functions as vivid *mise-en-scène* for the rest of the 1971 picture, evoking the setting of grim, political times, a world where death is a hair's-breadth away. It also defines the two primary settings: city and town, Paris and Loudun, and the ideological and social contrasts between them. The shock cut also defines where we're going in *The Devils* (and in our own lives): to d-e-a-t-h.

✞

The religious atmosphere in *The Devils* is at fever pitch. It's a hothouse – and the more the religious fervour emerges, the more the religious repression asserts itself – as well as the State oppression (the irony being, of course, that the more political pressure the State exerts on their hothouse, the crazier it gets, which in turn demands more policing and suppression).

Everyone's highly sensitive or already mad, like the Mother Superior. They're all praying, or confessing. (Once again, I insist on the elegance of the script written by Ken Russell, how it builds and builds, so that when the full force of the hysteria erupts, some of the key influences on it have been carefully established. The hysteria[52] doesn't explode out of nowhere: it has a number of dramatic motivations, and is given a historical-religious context. Of course, the structure was already in place in the play by John Whiting and the book by Aldous Huxley, but it was Russell who adapted that structure to make it work in a movie. Sounds easy? It's not: thousands of movies fail at exactly this. Scripts of this kind don't just write themselves: you can't just switch on a camera and point it at the actors in their costumes and tell 'em to recite the lines from Whiting's play or Huxley's novel).

✝

Perhaps the most infamous scene in *The Devils* was Oliver Reed's priest Urbain Grandier being tortured at length (having his tongue stretched and pierced, his limbs smashed with a hammer, his head shaved, pulled along the ground behind a donkey, crawling along the scaffold with his legs smashed), culminating in being burned at the stake. Some of the tortures that were historically enacted (i.e., people really did this stuff! those torture devices really did exist!) wouldn't pass any film censor,[53] but what's on screen is already tough enough to endure (it's how the victim is portrayed that really makes such scenes work, and Reed is marvellous in the torture sequence. Boy, he *really* sells it!).

Urbain Grandier is surrounded in these scenes by the venomous, scheming, manipulative Baron de Laubardemont, the

---

[52] *Häxan* (Benjamin Christensen, 1922), also known as *Witchcraft Through the Ages*, is a truly remarkable, Scandinavian silent movie, which includes many scenes which prefigure *The Devils* (nuns in hysteria in a church, mediaeval torture devices, and trials where victims're accused of witchcraft). Produced by Svenska, photographed by Johan Ankerstjerne, *Häxan* starred Maren Pedersen, Clara Pontoppidan, Elith Pio, Oscar Stribolt and Tora Teje. The Danish director – Benjamin Christensen (1879-1959) – appears as the Devil (of course!).

[53] Shots had to be curtailed, such as the close-ups of Grandier's mutilated legs (on screen for a brief flash only). The stake scenes took 3 weeks to film, according to Murray Melvin.

hysterical, vain Father Barré, and the oily, sanctimonious Father Mignon (plus the two comic sidekicks, the chemist and the physician, Ibert and Adam,[54] who are always on hand with their collection of grotesque instruments and their crazy schemes and theories).

For Joseph Gomez, the anachronistic costume and look of Father Barré was a misfire, even in Ken Russell's definition of using anachronisms to make a point. He sports hippy hair, wire-rim specs like John Lennon's in the late 1960s, and black and white garden gloves (G, 149f). I'm not convinced the present day trappings of Barré's costume work either (the hippy trappings form the wrong associations).

And sometimes it does seem as if Ken Russell allows Michael Gothard's portrayal of Father Barré to go too far, to be too silly and OTT. Yes it is a caricature performance, a send-up of the mediaeval exorcist and witch-finder (as played so solemnly and seriously by Vincent Price in *The Witchfinder General* (a.k.a. *The Conqueror Worm*, 1968), and by Max von Sydow in *The Exorcist* (1973). But it does threaten to drag *The Devils* too far into farce.

It's a vital element of the overall impact of *The Devils* that Urbain Grandier is being tested and tortured by a gaggle of men who are either insane and sadomasochistic, or who *play* at being insane and vicious (but the result, for Grandier, is just the same!). Father Barré is as out-size in his hysteria as Sister Jeanne. It's wonderful the way that Barré doesn't hesitate for a second to launch himself at Jeanne or the nuns or Grandier; he only requires the slightest provocation, and he leaps into the fray. It's apt too that Ken Russell has Mike Gothard play Barré at fever pitch in many scenes, so that the persecutors turn out to be just as mad as the nuns or Jeanne. But during the scene where Barré enters the pit holding the quaking, weeping nuns, there's a look exchanged between Barré and the Baron: he's enjoying it.[55]

That scene is crucial to the narrative of *The Devils* too: the nuns don't get hysterical without a very good reason: Baron de Laubardemont has them corralled in a pit in the woods, and threatens them with death. If he sets them free, they are commanded to make merry hell. Which they do. (Just like a film

---

54 Adam and Ibert are inspired additions to the Huxley book, deriving from the Whiting play. Wherever there is the potential for mischief to be made, they slyly appear. In later eras, they would be journalists and film critics!
55 In the book, Aldous Huxley described the nuns as 'cabaret performers and circus freaks', while Grandier 'behaves exactly like the proprietor of a sideshow at a fair'.

director cajoling his actors to go nuts).

Spike Milligan had appeared in the scene where soldiers smash Urbain Grandier's home to bits. But although Milligan played it straight (without the comic flourishes he often seemed unable to resist inserting into every performance, even if they were great), it was decided it didn't quite fit, so it was reshot with Dudley Sutton. It is a very effective scene, with obvious ideological symbolism (the thugs destroying Grandier's collection of classical nude statuary), which works (why be subtle when you're portraying the violence of the State?).

One of Hollywood cinema's curious traits is to combine contemporary and period fashion and appearance. Thus, although a film is supposed to be taking place in mediæval times, like *The Devils,* the film's stars will either retain a modern haircut or will have an approximation of a mediæval hairstyle but in modern terms. Costumes are rarely 'authentic' versions of period costume, down to the tiniest detail. Blatant and camp misrepresentations of costume occur in films such as *One Million Years BC* (1966), when Raquel Welch wore a 'prehistoric', Sixties-style bikini. In a film such as *In the Name of the Rose* (1986), Sean Connery went barefoot in mediæval garb, which seemed 'authentic' – but the film's dialogue was in a 20th century, 1980s idiom. Even if, as in BBC TV costume dramas, every detail is 'authentic' and of the period, the speech, language and interactions of the people will be distinctly 20th or 21st century. Movies can never be 'about' earlier times, it seems, but only about the era when the film was made. *The Devils* is no different: but it is also one of those movies which transcends its time.

Aldous Huxley wondered if the events he related in his book *The Devils of Loudun* would prove too much for some audiences. He wrote to playwright John Whiting about Whiting's early draft of the play:

> I wonder if some of the scenes in the last two acts may not prove almost too powerful. The possession, exorcism and torture episodes were hair-raising enough in the narrative (incidentally, I exaggerated nothing; everything in the book is drawn from original sources). Dramatized and well-directed and acted, they may be almost more than many people can take. In any case, it will be very interesting to see how an audience reacts to the horror and strangeness of the story.[56]

---

[56] *Letters of Aldous Huxley*, Chatto & Windus, London, 1969, 896.

And in the end, Ken Russell and his team did tone down some of the wilder events described in Aldous Huxley's book (G, 137).[57]

The Baron de Laubardemont, Cardinal Richelieu's instrument in Loudun, is a wily and brutal politico, wonderfully performed by Dudley Sutton, an ever-dependable character actor (and it's a great role for an actor, too). The Baron is a wholly believable character, who is rightly kept this side of credibility by the filmmakers. It might have been tempting to let the Baron be played over-the-top. But there's no need to do that when you've got Father Barré doing all the crazy eye-rolling, Latin-spouting and larking about with the nuns. Instead, the Baron's cool, menacing quality and calm, cold efficiency as a military man renders the mania of the final scenes all the more unnerving. The Baron just wants to get the job done: he's a professional, a soldier, a tactician (yet he remains a commander all the way thru – you don't see the Baron getting his own hands dirty, such as physically attacking any of the townspeople himself, which makes the violence of what he and his underlings are doing in Loudun all the greater).

Again, if you consider the characterization of Baron de Laubardemont in the movie, and the way he's played by Dudley Sutton, you can once again appreciate just how good Ken Russell is as a film director, and as a film writer. If this were Sam Peckinpah or Howard Hawks, *cinéastes* would be marvelling at how brilliantly Russell creates a military leader, brutish and canny, worthy of standing alongside William Holden's Pike Bishop in *The Wild Bunch* or John Wayne's Ethan in *The Searchers*.

The Baron has a striking introduction in *The Devils*, too: the camera picks up a skull filled with maggots, then pulls back to reveal the skeleton chained to a wheel, and lastly to the Baron on horseback looking up at the victim (the first shot after the amazing prologue). The subsequent scene depicts the Baron ushering a convoy towards Loudun along a road lined with skeletons on wheels. There's a large wagon pulled by many people carrying something bulky but mysterious – it's foreshadowing: all will be revealed at the start of the second act, when the Baron's overseeing the destruction of the walls of the town.

---

[57] Russell said that *The Devils* had to be harsh, because the topic was harsh. But the facts, from the book, were 'far more horrible than anything in the film' (PF, 105).

The last third of *The Devils* has a marvellous, mesmeric and cruelly logical momentum. It begins when Cardinal Richelieu decides to do something about Loudun, in the archive scene set in Paris, where he confers with the Baron in a slow tracking shot. Once that decision has been made, the events accelerate in their unreality and horror.

For a start, it's not only Urbain Grandier who is tortured: Sister Jeanne is subjected to a horrific bout of punishment, culminating in stomach-churning enemas. It's staged with immense flair in the white-brick convent, with the spectators wearing black eye-masks, and Jeanne being man-handled by Father Barré, Ibert and Adam onto the altar. The camera is now handheld, and right next to Jeanne's legs as they're forced apart. The low angle shots of the large clyster used for the enema enhance the chaos and madness of the scene.

Yes, *The Devils* is a movie where someone's given an enema on an altar. It's not something you see everyday! (And if film censorship allowed it, Ken Russell and his team would surely have gone further, and been more explicit with the enema scene. Although they went way too far for many viewers and critics, and certainly too far for Warner Brothers).

So *The Devils* isn't one long bout of craziness from start to finish: there is a logic, cruel as it is, to the events, as the powers that be (headed up by Cardinal Richelieu and Baron de Laubardemont) try one thing after another. When the torture of Sister Jeanne doesn't turn up the required results, the State tries different tactics, such as intimidating the nuns into hysteria. (That scene is also staged anachronistically – the reference here being a firing squad in a forest,[58] in particular the kind of scenes in WW2 movies where dissidents or Jews have been rounded up and then shot).

*The Devils* is one of those movies that's *meant* to be exhausting and an assault on the senses and mind. It's like *The Texas Chainsaw Massacre* or *The Exorcist* or *Straw Dogs* or *A Clockwork Orange*,[59] to mention films of the same era (the latter two were released the same year as *The Devils*). It's *supposed* to be grim and overwhelming. Yet it is also, like *The Exorcist* or *Texas Chainsaw Massacre* and *Straw Dogs* and *A Clockwork Orange*, flamboyant and

---
58 Filmed in Blackwood Park, near Pinewood Studios, used in zillions of movies.
59 At one time Ken Russell had been interested in making *A Clockwork Orange*.

supremely confident filmmaking, from filmmakers who were pushing at the confines of acceptability and taste. It's not meant to be a walk in the park followed by a cup of tea and a snooze in front of the fire.

✝

The torture of Urbain Grandier is truly relentless; if it's meant to be camp and comic, then this's very black humour (but Ken Russell conceived the movie as black comedy).[60] Maybe certain areas of *The Devils* have to be so intense (and serious), in order to exaggerate the black humour of the other parts. Only rarely is this level of suffering inflicted on an individual depicted in mainstream cinema, outside of horror movies. It recalls the end of *Braveheart* (1995), and films of the time like Pier Paolo Pasolini's infamous *Salò* (1975).

(There's a link between Ken Russell and Pier Paolo Pasolini: in the early 1970s Russell was offered *Gargantua and Pantaguel* (1532-52) by François Rabelais, a film which apparently Pasolini was going to do but pulled out. But when Russell saw Pasolini's version of *The Canterbury Tales*,[61] he was horrified. The director of the excesses of *The Devils* found *The Canterbury Tales* 'the most disgusting film I've ever since in my *life!*' [Bax, 229]). (It's a recurring sentiment of Ken Russell's – that he can be very put off by seeing the violence and excesses of some movies, yet he can portray that kind of thing in his pictures. It's the difference between seeing someone else do it, and doing it yourself, perhaps. I'm also reminded of Steven Spielberg finding the violence in *The Gangs of New York* (2001) off-putting, and telling director Martin Scorsese that he found it difficult to watch such material, even though he did it in his own films (such as *Saving Private Ryan*).)

✝

YOU ARE WATCHING A KEN RUSSELL MOVIE!

The king, Louis XIII (Graham Armitage), who reigned from

---

[60] Similarly, some viewers can't believe that Alfred Hitchcock saw movies such as *Psycho* as black comedies. But then, Hitch had a very macabre sense of humour!
[61] One of the odd things about *The Canterbury Tales* (for a British audience) was that much of it was shot in locations in England (such as Canterbury, Rye and Wells). It was curious seeing a cool, European *auteur* like Pasolini, whose films are full of images of sun-kissed, Southern Italy, or the cultured corridors of power in Rome, or the Middle East, winding up on little, English streets under overcast, English skies. The English locations, plus the appearances of British TV and film actors (such as Tom Baker, Hugh Griffith and Robin Askwith), plus the bawdy humour, linked *The Canterbury Tales* to films such as the *Carry On* or *Confessions of...* series – camp, British, sex comedies.

1610 to 1643, is introduced in *The Devils* as a buffoon from the off: the 1971 film opens with King Louis appearing as the Goddess Venus in an ultra-camp dance number at a theatrical masque (no Ken Russell film is complete without a dance number).[62] He wears a silver codpiece and bra, a silver cape and high crown, while the (male) dancers're in similarly silvery and thoroughly anachronistic costumes[63] (dressed as women). The choreography (by Terry Gilbert) is deliberately camp.

It's hard to think of another serious historical movie, not a comedy, which introduces a king like this (yeah, and even comedies have to go some way to be sillier).

But it's based in fact, according to Ken Russell, who said that King Louis was

> an extravagant homosexual, a great shot, hater of Protestants, lover of shooting blackbirds and dressing as a woman and choreographing his own numbers; all are used in the film. (Bax, 206).

As Jack Zipes noted in 2012's *The Irresistible Fairy Tale*:

> In all the court entertainments in Italy and France during the baroque period, the spectacle was of utmost importance, consisting of magnificent displays based on myths and fairy tales that celebrated the glory as well as the power of the court, which was likened to some kind of enchanted fairy realm. Those ballets, masquerades and operas were taken seriously in various European courts; they often were made up of ten to fifteen tableaux of scenes: the stories were danced and sung by gifted actors and acrobats, machines and traps were invented and used to create illusions; and characters such as fairies, witches, wizards, gnomes, gods, ghosts, devils, and noble protagonists were involved in plots that demanded the intervention of some good higher power, either a fairy, god, or goddess. (26)

A filmmaker devoted to the magic of theatre like Ken Russell is not going to pass up an opportunity like this, especially when backed up by the historical evidence for such spectacles, festivals and extravagance (one imagines that Russell would be quite happy organizing royal festivities in the French court of the 1600s!).

The opening of *The Devils* demonstrates the total confidence of

---

[62] The costumes are outrageously anachronistic, employing plenty of shiny silver – very early 1970s, very glam rock. Another anachronism has *Dies Irae* by Hector Berlioz being played during the funeral procession.
[63] Shirley Kingdon once again drew on pop culture – glam rock – for the anachronisms.

Ken Russell and his team, to be bold enough to open a historical drama like this: there is no slow, ponderous scene-setting, no long shots of castles or towns, no reams of captions to wade thru, no expositional dialogue, no ponderous Charlton Heston or Orson Welles voiceover... Instead, the King of France appears as the Goddess Venus wearing nothing but a bra and silver shell codpiece... and indulging in some *outré* choreography!

The scene's a 'fuck you' to the historical movie genre, but not to the audience. The scene also announces to the viewer: 'YOU ARE WATCHING A KEN RUSSELL MOVIE!' (as if they didn't know: in 1971, Russell had no less than *three movies* playing in first-run theatres in London – and three *big* movies, not shot-in-two-weekends indie flicks).

The portrayal of the king and the cardinal in *The Devils* are very different from their usual portraits in movies – think of any *Three Musketeers* movie, for instance (two *Musketeer* flicks were made not long after *The Devils* in Britain and Spain, helmed by Dick Lester, and starring, incidentally, Ollie Reed and Richard Chamberlain).

Cardinal Richelieu (1585-1642, played by Christopher Logue), humours and indulges the king like a child, but is the real power in France (Richelieu took over the government of France in 1624: 'his main aim was the establishment of absolute royal power in France, and also of French supremacy in Europe').[64] Richelieu dismisses the King's performance with a single reference to Venus – as if Venus (i.e., mythology, or love) is completely off the point: for Richelieu, life is about politics and power, and dressing up and pretending to be the Goddess of Love is a frightful bore (Richelieu's shown yawning at the King's performance, which marks Richelieu out as superior and dismissive; it may also be a taunt to the audience: in this show, the movie says, you won't yawn, you won't be bored! Yes, but some of those real, French, 17th century *masques, ballet comiques* and operas went on for five hours!). Notice that it's the king who kisses Richelieu's hand at the end of the scene (emphasizing the power relationship). The title credits run over Richelieu and the King in close-up.

It's the power-behind-the-throne scenario, but *The Devils* exaggerates that cliché by making Louis XIII an over-dressed (and cross-dressed) superficial dilettante, a dabbler and fashion plate

---

64 I. Robertson, *Blue Guide: France*, A & C Black, 1997, 37.

who's only really interested, it seems, in having a good time.⁶⁵ While Cardinal Richelieu puts forward the case for breaking down the fortifications of France's towns, for example, in the blackbird scene, the king is more concerned with firing at the Protestants in bird costumes.⁶⁶ (That's the single scene in *The Devils* which doesn't work so well for me: the satire or comedy or whatever it's meant to be jars with the rest of the movie. And it seems to come from a different picture. But Russell liked to include satire like that from time to time, and it does make its ideological and thematic point well).

☥

There are some impressive montages in *The Devils* – such as the one when Urbain Grandier is giving his speech to the townspeople, which's intercut with King Louis and Cardinal Richelieu talking in a garden (it's the scene where the king shoots at Protestants dressed as blackbirds, among the silliest scenes in Ken Russell's cinema).⁶⁷ Another montage follows Sister Jeanne's story and cuts between the Mother Superior masturbating in her cell – and whipping herself afterwards (she has lots of gruesome, steel, flagellation devices, sex toys for the extreme S/M of Catholicism) – and Grandier and Madelyn de Brou having their secret, night-time, marriage ceremony (a 'blasphemous nuptial mass') in the church. (In terms of the controversy of these scenes, and *The Devils* as a whole, there isn't that much that's shown – much of it is implied but offscreen. For instance, when the film depicts Jeanne masturbating, it occurs in a long shot with the camera soon dollying back and panning, to reveal one of the nuns – Sister Agnes – watching (and loving it); and the flagellation with the whip is done offscreen, on a C.U. of Sister Jeanne's hand clutching yet another crucifix, with sound effects.⁶⁸ Compare that to thirty

---

65 Yet Richelieu is also crossdressing, in the Catholic manner of clergy in red dresses; the characterization of Richelieu being pushed about by two nuns also emphasizes his oddness. Not quite a cripple, Richelieu's characterization is the familiar cinematic one of the disabled bad guy who has the most power in the movie.
66 However, the king isn't wholly a fool who can be manipulated by Richelieu; he has the measure of the hysteria erupting in Loudun, when he visits the town and exposes the trickery (in Aldous Huxley's book it's a nobleman who performs this act; the king also combines the character from the novel of the debauched royal prince Henri de Condé).
67 The cross-cutting pattern was already established in the script, Russell and Bradsell said, not discovered during post-production.
68 It's a standard tactic in cinema – to show the effect of something nasty or explicit, you use someone else's reaction to it, and let the audience imagine the real thing for themselves. It gets around the censor, but it also provides a commentary on the act (and also emphasizes the act of looking).

years later and the endless flagellation on-screen in 2004's *The Passion of the Christ*).

Again, much of the criticism surrounding Ken Russell's work draws attention to his visuals, but often it's the editing that really brings out the impact of those visuals. The montages are one example in *The Devils,* as well as some of the shock cuts (the opening cut from the King and Richelieu to the C.U. of maggot-ridden corpse is one shock cut – another is the cut from the chaotic Cathedral scene, where Urbain Grandier is arrested, to the close-up of his tongue being pierced which begins the torture sequence). Much of the credit must go to Russell's regular editor Mike Bradsell, whose editing and pacing adds so much to *The Devils* (Bradsell recalled that editing *The Devils* had been relatively easy, and shots had fallen into place organically and naturally; it wasn't a picture where the editors had to struggle to complete the movie. However, preparing re-edited versions for the censors and the studio wasn't so easy).

The plague scenes in *The Devils* were also highly exaggerated: Urbain Grandier walks through a devastated Loudun, with fires burning and plague victims gasping, staring wide-eyed, being winched down from houses above, and expiring. Cue close-ups of extras with revolting, decaying faces.

In one scene, Urbain Grandier enters the home of a dying woman who's being administered quack cures by the two doctors (Ibert and Adam) who become instrumental in Grandier's torture. The woman's naked body's covered with glass jars containing leeches and a wasp. Fire flickers in the background from an oven (the lighting, by cinematographer David Watkin and his team, is stunning in this sequence).

There's also a large plague pit full of bodies, which Urbain Grandier visits the following morning. And corpses being piled onto a cart and a guy yelling, 'bring out your dead!' The *Monty Python* team were probably thinking of *The Devils* when they sent up plague scenes in *Monty Python and the Holy Grail* (they had satirized Russellania in their TV show, in a piece called 'Ken Russell's Gardening Club, 1958'). The plague doesn't feature in either Aldous Huxley's book or John Whiting's play, according to Russell: the fact was discovered by a French scholar (Bax, 223). So the 1971 movie used it: why? because it enhanced the already crazy goings-on, and played into the themes of the corruption and decay underneath the surface of the life of the community.[69] (Depicting big plague scenes was also Russell's chance for scenery like that in *The Seventh Seal,* or the popular Biblical epics of the 1950s and 1960s, where scenes involving lepers were mandatory. But in those sword 'n' sandal epics, Jesus was on hand to cure the lepers. In the helhole that is Loudun in *The Devils,* there's nobody around with such a miraculous touch).

But the most controversial scene in *The Devils* was cut out of the film, a decision made by Warner Brothers and the censor. It featured the so-called 'rape of Christ', the climax of the convent possession sequence, where the naked nuns cavort crazily around and on top of a wooden Cross and a figure of Christ in the Cathedral (meanwhile, Father Mignon watches from above and masturbates, as any self-respecting Catholic priest would!).[70]

It was an over-the-top scene, as Ken Russell and his team intended, combining nudity and religion, sexuality and Christianity,[71] but it was, for Russell, the central scene of *The Devils*. Russell intended the 'rape of Christ' to be intercut with a scene of Urbain Grandier alone in the mountains, a very quiet, reverential scene:

> The naked nuns tear down a wooden figure of Christ and throw themselves on it, having it in every possible way… Both Warner Brothers and the censors thought it was too strong so I took it out… But it was really central to the whole thing, intercut as it was with Grandier finding himself and God in the solitary simplicity of Nature. Over-ripe, perverted religion going as bad and wrong as it can possibly become, with the eternal truth of the bread and the wine and the brotherhood of man and God in the universe. (Bax, 210)

Some of the 'rape of Christ' images survived in *The Devils*: nuns stroked phallic candles; women masturbated, and writhed

---

[69] Russell certainly does have a fascination 'with the decayed, the used, the soiled, the defective, and eventually with the grotesque', as Jack Fisher remarked (42).
[70] Ken Russell played *The Fiery Angel* by Sergei Prokofiev and *The Rite of Spring* during the 'rape of Christ' scenes, to help his actors get in the mood. As Aldous Huxley put it in *Along the Road*, 'since Mozart's day composers have learned the art of making music throatily and palpitatingly sexual'.
[71] Again, in Aldous Huxley's book it was based on eye witness accounts: in a letter to Walter Montague, Thomas Killigrew related how he was invited to hold the limbs of the nuns in order feel how the Devil was possessing them. Other Britishers visited Loudun and described what they saw, including Lady Purbeck and Sir George Courthop. For Huxley, the scene became like a grotesque fairground sideshow, with onlookers invited to step right up and touch the nuns: 'these spouses of Christ have been turned into cabaret performers and circus freaks' (1970, 157).

around on the floor, eyes rolling and tongues lolling out;[72] they whipped themselves, fell on top of each other, danced, shook and shrieked. The scene involves many elements – not only naked nuns, for instance, but also the townspeople who've come into the Cathedral to watch, gape and laugh. The background action is brilliantly chaotic and animated, and the scene also includes Barré and Sister Jeanne in prominent roles (Jeanne performs the hysteric's arc, for example, in a disturbing moment). And into it all comes King Louis XIII and his entourage.[73] You can appreciate that it was a nightmare to shoot – definitely one of the most challenging scenes in Russell's whole career.

For the actors playing the nuns, the rape of Christ scenes required not only nudity but plenty of physical acting. Not easy. On top of that, the actresses were required to have their heads shaved. To persuade some of the more reluctant actors (plenty of actresses would refuse), the production offered them 150 quid ($225). But it certainly enhances the scene that not only are the nuns nude, and hysterical, they are also shaved, like prisoners or concentration camp inmates.

But even without all of the 'rape of Christ', *The Devils* is still *immensely* powerful. And it still does cut from the mayhem in the Cathedral to Urbain Grandier conducting his mass beside the lake.

Rarely have movies – well, British movies at least – depicted such chaotic, intensely hysterical scenes with so much nudity (albeit female nudity – priest Barré strips off his top). And Ken Russell was probably the only British director who could have done it, at the time (and very few filmmakers since then would dare do it; and many producers would no doubt try to persuade the director to drop it from the script).

But it's the end of the 'rape of Christ' scene that's vital: when Urbain Grandier turns up, framed in the doorway. The staging and camerawork is brilliant here, with David Watkin and his camera team producing elaborate tracking shots worthy of Orson Welles as they follow Urbain Grandier into the church, thru the chaos, past the smoking, swinging censer, and all the way up to Sister Jeanne.[74] It's the moment when Grandier and Jeanne meet

---

[72] Apparently, some of the rape of Christ takes got out of hand, Russell recalled, and Equity (the actors' union) got involved (PF, 116-7).
[73] When the king arrives in the Cathedral, celeb couple Twiggy and Nigel Davies (a.k.a. Justin de Villeneuve) can be glimpsed in the background as fops.
[74] A grand shot that probably took hours to rehearse, set up, light and shoot.

face to face, and right after that momentous encounter, Grandier is arrested (when the Baron exploits the feverish atmosphere and orders Grandier's arrest).[75]

The 'rape of Christ' sequence is carefully constructed dramatically: as screenwriter (rather than as director), Ken Russell doesn't simply cut straight to the mayhem inside the Cathedral, which's such sensational material. No: the entire sequence has a narrative logic, building up from the orgy to major dramatic beats, such as Sister Jeanne being urged to confess, and finally to the two big reveals: the arrival of the King and his entourage, and the finale, Urbain Grandier appearing in the doorway.

Ignoring the out-there nature of the sequence – sex-plus-nudity-plus-violence-plus-religion – you can see how meticulously the episode has been planned and scripted. For critics who complain that Ken Russell's cinema emphasizes shocks and vulgarities and over-the-topness, the 'rape of Christ' episode is solid proof that those shocks and brazen images can only work if the foundations have been laid correctly, if the context has been set properly, and if the hysteria builds in a convincing and dramatically logical manner.

And it does: Ken Russell and his team know so well how to construct a scene: that is, to literally *construct* a scene, piling it up piece by piece, shot by shot. Take away some of the beats and the shots, some of the looks and lines of dialogue, and it won't work. In short, *The Devils* is so powerful largely because it is so brilliantly staged and delivered. Yes, the material is incredibly strong on its own, but it's the way that the movie is presented to the audience with such assurance, such flair, such wit and such imagination, that makes it a true classic. (And a true one-off: there is nothing like this in all of British cinema).

✞

It is also the *complexity* of the portrayal of the characters and the issues that is so impressive in *The Devils*. Urbain Grandier is a conflicted personality; he's a hero with flaws (the movie makes sure the audience understands some of those flaws early on). His penchant for women might be understandable or forgivable to a modern cinema audience (it was OK for James Bond and Our Man Flint in the 1960s, for instance), and not count as a fault; but the film clearly outlines the levels of sexual repression and sin that

---

[75] Grandier entering the church consciously alludes to Christ in the temple with the money-changers, and his arrest parallels Christ in Gethsemane.

run through this community of Loudun. Vanity, the love of power and authority, arrogance and insensitivity are further flaws in Grandier's character, yet he acts at times as one of the most sensible people in the town.

*The Devils* is specially good at delineating the *motives* of each of the major characters. Everyone has their reasons and their goals. It's true that in some films directed by Ken Russell, narrative or dramatic elements such as motives aren't so fully developed. In *Tommy*, for example, Russell persuaded Pete Townsend to insert some backstory for Tommy's father, and *The Music Lovers* develops a marvellous use of flashbacks, but in other films he prefers to dispense with backstories.

✝

As a respite from the political and religious machinations of the plot, and the downbeat nature of much of the material in *The Devils*, there is a romance, between Urbain Grandier and Madelyn de Brou (Gemma Jones[76] – another terrific performance. Jones is perfectly cast). Madelyn might be the most 'normal' character in the piece, and Grandier is probably at his most humane in the scenes he shares with her.

And although most viewers probably think of *The Devils* as being dominated by Urbain Grandier and Sister Jeanne – which it is – it's actually Madelyn de Brou who is in some ways the central figure. Introduced early on – when she begs Grandier who's passing by to look at her mother, a plague victim who's being treated with bonkers medicine by the comic pairing of Adam and Ibert – Madelyn soon develops a desire for Grandier.

It's Madelyn de Brou who further links Sister Jeanne and Urbain Grandier, when she goes to Sister Jeanne asking to join the convent (Jeanne pours scorn and bile on Madelyn from the outset of their unusual interview (conducted through the bars of the convent's window), deprecating her appearance (the downcast eyes),[77] her pretty rosary, and her sin of pride). Jeanne despises Madelyn for possessing the quiet spirituality she pines for but can't manufacture (Madelyn is how Jeanne might've started out when she was younger and idealistic); but Jeanne is also right that Madelyn is a somewhat stuck-up, goody-two-shoes. In her negative aspects, Madelyn represents the pious religiosity

---

[76] In recent years, Gemma Jones has appeared in Jackie Chan movies, *Harry Potter* movies and Woody Allen.
[77] As if Madelyn de Brou is a caricature of a painting of a Catholic saint.

that Catholicism aspires to but which too often is misdirected, or is corrupted; and Madelyn is also too 'pure' and 'innocent' to be wholly convincing (could you remain 'pure' and 'innocent' growing up in a town with crazy people like Adam and Ibert around?!).

And it's Madelyn de Brou who's the last person to be seen in the 1971 Warners production, when she walks away from the town. Yet the romance does not slow the movie down, or deflate some of its power, but enhances it (and when Ibert and Adam witness the marriage in the church at night, it becomes part of the accusations hurled at Urbain Grandier).

It's no 'walk into the sunset' image, though: at the end of this bleak, unrelenting movie, there can be no happy ending, and nothing approaching a happy ending. Because what's happening in Loudun is happening across France. (Joseph Gomez compared the marvellous final shot to *The Triumph of Death* by painter Pieter Brueghel [G, 161]).

✞

The theme of the nuns spying on each other and on the world outside the convent recurs numerous times in *The Devils*. That's partly to do with dramatic necessity, to connect the worlds inside and outside the nunnery, but the evocation of paranoia is fundamental to stories of political corruption, whether it's in the White House in 2014 or London in 1592. It begins with the nuns watching the funeral procession at the beginning of the film (and fighting like kids over who gets to watch from the top of the ladder). Sister Jeanne spies on her sisters, then dismisses them – only to sneak into a basement alcove where she can ogle Urbain Grandier for herself and swoon into an erotic reverie (she also overhears the townspeople remarking of Grandier – 'he can have me any time!', and: 'there's a man worth going to Hell for!').

Later, Sister Agnes spies on Sister Jeanne masturbating then whipping herself. Sister Jeanne watches the nuns goofing around with a re-enactment of the nighttime nuptials of Urbain Grandier and Madelyn de Brou. And the nuns themselves are watched avidly by the crowd at the public trial, and during the 'rape of Christ' scene.

✞

Torture scenes run throughout *The Devils*. In the middle of the 1971 film, for instance, the denizens of Loudun are put inside giant, wooden wheels which drive ropes to pull down the fortifications. (Torture wheels on poles are one of the signature images of *The Devils* – famously in the opening sequence, lining the road to Loudun (filmed at Bamburgh Castle), and in the final shot.)

Full of Ken Russell's over-the-top imagery, with not a few comic moments ('it's not everyday baby sees daddy being burned at the stake', Max Adrian quips to Urbain Grandier's bastard child while Philippe Trincant stands beside him, joyously drinking as Grandier is burnt at the stake), *The Devils* is Russell's sustained attack on hypocrisy, obsession, religious bigotry, the manipulations of the State and politics, and mob mentality (it was his only political film, Russell sometimes remarked; but, actually, Russell has tackled politics head-on many times). It wasn't so much that Russell wanted to 'shock' (almost impossible to achieve anyway, especially today, and a dumb, limiting ambition for an artist), his project was rather to expose intolerance (religious and political).

It was mainly the manner in which Ken Russell and the team tried to achieve those aims that created the negative response to the movie: by using extravagant performances, outlandish imagery, and the irreverent treatment of religion. For some people even today, images, even if they're a fantasy, of a Christ figure sexually embracing a Mary Magdalene character, can be disturbing. *The Last Temptation of Christ* created a similar (much more widespread) controversy in 1988: in that Universal movie, a clearly signposted fantasy sequence showed Jesus and the Magdalene having sex and bearing children, the point being to show what Christ's life might have been like had he not died on the Cross. As expected, religious fundamentalists took the dream sequence at the end of *The Last Temptation of Christ* literally.[78]

Besides, Ken Russell wasn't interested in so-called 'realistic' violence or shock. He was being intentionally fantastical and exaggerated:

> People are used to watching television and seeing the Korean War or the Vietnam War or Ireland. I think even that, in the end, becomes associated with fantasy. It becomes a fantasy of reality, of handheld cameras running down the street. That's why I would never do a modern film like that. People have come to expect that sort of violence. They don't stop eating while it's going on. I do want to shock people into a sense of awareness. (1973)

Ken Russell stressed that the material in the book by Aldous Huxley was far more horrible than anything put in the film. *The Devils* had to be harsh, because the subject was harsh (Bax, 202). The gross humour was part of Russell's project of exploring religious hypocrisy: 'designed to point out the nonsensical irony of these horrors being committed in the name of God' (ibid.). It's not supposed to be taken literally or totally seriously. Here, Russell's penchant for over-the-top drama serves the themes and material very well. It's not the sombre seriousness of Arthur Miller's *The Crucible*, or the solemn horror of *Salem's Lot*. It's deliberately camp, silly, and out-size.

At the same time, there is a real power of rage running throughout *The Devils,* which erupts most passionately in the portrayal of Urbain Grandier. Everyone in *The Devils* seems to be off-kilter or plain crazy. And the once sane folk only require a slight nudge to send them into hysterics. The sanest character is definitely the Grandier, and also his wife Madelyn de Brou. If there is a mouthpiece of Ken Russell and the team in *The Devils,* it's definitely the Grandier.

---

[78] The evangelical groups claimed they had over 3 million signatures on their petitions against the film. Bill Bright, of the Campus Crusade for Christ, offered Universal $10 million for the destruction of the picture. Between 7,500 and 25,000 people protested outside MCA/ Universal Studios' 'Black Tower' in the week before the film's opening on August 12, 1988. The protesters included the Eastern Orthodox Church of America, the National Catholic Conference, the Southern Baptist Convention, the Archbishops of Canterbury and Paris, and people from the American House of Representatives.
There were scenes of protest against *The Last Temptation of Christ* in New York, Washington, San Francisco, Chicago, Seattle, Toronto and L.A. Around a thousand people protested at cinemas in New York and Salt Lake City. Screens were slashed by protesters; a print was taken. In Paris, at the UGC Odéon cinema, when the film opened in September, there was a riot, with Molotov cocktails being hurled. Similar protests occurred in Marseilles, Avignon and Besançon. There was a fire at the Cinéma St Michel on October 22, 1988.

Ken Russell saw Urbain Grandier as 'the fall guy in a political conflict', whose greatness took him by surprise, who was out of step with his times but managed to effect great changes (Bax, 205). He loses the battle (his life), but wins the war. After this, no one could be burnt as a witch in France, Russell insisted, and the people must've realized that Grandier couldn't have been guilty of the 'crimes' he was charged with.

In Ken Russell's conception, Urbain Grandier doesn't take *everything* in Catholicism seriously. He acknowledges that religions are made up of human beings with all their frailties and desires. And you can't expect even a priest to be the perfect Catholic 24 hours a day. Sometimes they will be reciting the sacred words parrot fashion (as in the plague pit scene).

But it *was* important for Ken Russell to show that Urbain Grandier did take the central ritual of the Catholic religion seriously, the Eucharist, which's one reason why the filmmakers placed Grandier away from Loudun, in the mountains, to perform the Mass on his own (and with Madelyn de Brou).

The rise of Urbain Grandier to greatness is depicted in a face-off with Baron de Laubardemont and his cronies, who are pulling down the walls of Loudun (with the aid of some enormous wooden wheels and ropes).[79] In that instance, Grandier wins – he arrives in the town square with a group of soldiers who train guns and arrows at de Laubardemont.

☦

*The Devils* alters the historical time-scale of the events in Loudun and Paris – for instance, there were more appeals, the King changed his mind about the walls, Barré left for Chinon (and was recalled), and there were much more legal wrangling (G, 163). The events in Loudun stretched on for years, but *The Devils* compresses it into maybe months or even weeks (but movies typically compress time, combine characters and events, and leave out masses of material).

But when Ken Russell was attacked for altering history, he insisted that what was depicted in *The Devils* was historically accurate. A caption opens the movie to state this: 'this film is based on historic fact. The principal characters lived and the major events depicted in the film actually took place'. Of course, there is artistic licence being employed all over the place – but that occurs

---
[79] The destruction of the town walls had to be filmed twice, when the cues to time the explosions went wrong. The scene was re-set ten days later.

with any historical movie, or play, or novel, or painting, or whatever.

*The Devils* is not a documentary, it's history portrayed within the context and modes (and limits) of a feature movie. And Ken Russell and his team were concerned with getting the central issues right.

☦

The final scenes of *The Devils* are a *tour-de-force* of staging, performance and wielding the whole, technical arsenal of cinema. The equal, I would say, of anything in British – or world – cinema. Really? Oh yes. Go back and have a look at the last 10 or 15 minutes of *The Devils*. It's astonishing.

*The Devils* is one of those movies where the hero dies. A martyr. A victim. A scapegoat. A hero. A sacrifice. (Take your pick).

No Hollywood Last Minute Rescue here. It's Death all the way. The grand trajectory of the drama – that Urbain Grandier has to make his way to the stake, be tied to it and burnt alive – is all-encompassing. But along the way the filmmakers include all manner of incidents and details, such as: the use of black and white costumes, and the black masks; the sideshow of capering players on a stage in front of an enormous Mouth of Hell (who send up the story);[80] the gallery of rogues up on the balcony (Magistrate Trincant and his daughter Philippe, gleeful that justice is being done and Grandier is going to die, accompanied by the equally joyful Adam and Ibert); Grandier being hauled along behind a mule then thrown off; Grandier bound on the ground; the condemnation of Sister Jeanne and her sisters; Father Mignon's confused, ambivalent response (a look of anger then horror); the compassionate, hooded hangman, who offers to strangle the priest before the fires are started; the astonishing images of Grandier crawling in a low angle close-up while the circus cavorts behind him; Father Barré kicking Grandier's feet and Grandier's screams…

Still the State emissaries and bully boys hiss and bellow for a confession, but of course Urbain Grandier does not give anyone the pleasure. The kiss – of compassion which becomes a kiss of

---

[80] And also demonstrate that it all amounts to nothing but fuel for a story and an entertainment, in the end. The ultimate in exploitation and cynicism. The troupe of players would become, in the 20th century, a film crew, cannibalizing history and suffering to provide entertainment.

betrayal – is a marvellous and grotesque touch, bringing together the crowd (the idea that they sway in unison is terrific (like a rock concert audience) – and the assistant directors (Ted Morley and Nicolas Hippisley-Coxe) in a big, challenging scene like this did their work beautifully).

It's truly remarkable filmmaking, so many stages to the sequences, so many details, though of course a hero going to the stake is fantastic dramatic material to climax a story. But even if you've seen it before (in *Joan of Arc* movies, for instance), this interpretation is still riveting and heart-rending (not least for Oliver Reed's outstanding performance).

And, no, Ken Russell and his team are not going to stop at the beginning of the fire, and step away with a long shot and a fade to black... they are going to depict Urbain Grandier in different states of flamey decay. Wow – it's truly gruesome, but even in the midst of excruciating agony, Grandier still manages to appeal to and sermonize the crowd (that might be unconvincing at the level of realism, but it works dramatically superbly).

But Oliver Reed in gory, fire-scarred make-up is not only what makes this scene so startling: it's the *point-of-view images* seen *through* the flames (achieved one imagines with optical super-impositions and mirror shots as well as practical effects), of every character in the movie. And also cuts to the mummers and their skeleton costumes dancing manically. (You can see why *The Devils* might play well in Italy – or in Mexico – where it comes across as a Mexican Day of the Dead carnival). The flames make the simple but important point too that the town has become Hell on Earth.

A triumph of montage editing by Michael Bradsell and the sound editors, this is Ken Russell and his team at their wildest and most incisive (certainly Russell didn't top this sequence in the rest of his career): because the point-of-view images of each character seen though the flickering flames condemns all of them, yes, but also begs them, implores them, denounces them, but doesn't expiate them.

What is being burnt here, sacrificed here, torn to shreds here, apart from poor Urbain Grandier? It's the society's faults, their obsessions, their intolerance – their sins, to use the Catholic term.[81]

---

[81] One of Grandier's final cries is to implore the people to look to themselves, to their town, to their *country*. He might have finished with saying to their *world*. The implication is the modern world, too.

But also some better part of themselves. The film condemns actions and ideas which make humans less than human, when humans lose something of their humanity.

When Urbain Grandier undergoes his lengthy Cavalry – a crawl to Golgotha along the wooden scaffold – one person is conspicuously absent from the vast crowd gathered to witness the event. Everyone else is present, the complete cast of crazy characters in this Christian circus – except for Madelyn de Brou. During the whole torture and court trial sequence, Madelyn is kept off the screen. Though it might have been tempting to cut to her shocked expression as she watched the idiocy of the trial or the utter horror of seeing her husband being burned alive at the stake, *The Devils* doesn't need it. The imagery is already so sensational (and Madelyn is being saved for the final scene).

☦

The *dénouement* of *The Devils* involving Sister Jeanne and Baron de Laubardemont, which follows the stake scene, is brilliantly modest and small-scale, which only heightens the total cynicism of the Baron (and by implication the government of France). At the start of the scene, Sister Jeanne has her back to the camera and seems about to plunge a hot poker into her vulva, to drive out those sexy demons (Christianity has some of the most bizarre self-harming practices in history). By now, we've seen so much craziness, this scene doesn't startle.[82]

But when the Baron appears, all of Sister Jeanne's craziness disappears, and she seems quite normal and lucid. The matter-of-fact tone of the Baron's appraisal of events, and what will happen next, enhances the attitude of the State: all of this madness has simply been an excuse for exercising power. That's all it was: a way of the State gaining control of the provinces. And now that Sister Jeanne[83] has ceased to be useful, she can, as far as the government is concerned, fade away into oblivion.

☦

So the final shot of *The Devils*, which ironically employs the classic crane shot of the Hollywood ending, is not much of a way out or a sop or a means of finding something positive to express in

---

[82] There was more to this scene, with Sister Jeanne using the bone that the Baron gives her (part of Grandier's remains) as a dildo (of course the bone looks like a cock and balls – the dick's gotta be the bit of Grandier that Jeanne receives after his death!).

[83] When Sister Jeanne tells the Baron that she has wronged an innocent man, it is not what the Baron or the State want to hear.

amongst all of the madness of the preceding two hours. It's a symbolic ending, however: Madelyn de Brou, one of the only sane people left in Loudun (or one of the only people who don't go along with the lunacy that grips the denizens of the town), decides she's had enough and flees the town, scrambling over the broken walls.[84]

At least someone gets out alive, you might say. But what sort of life will Madelyn de Brou have now (assuming she's not traumatized by what she's witnessed)? The cut from the chaos of the apocalyptic execution scene to the utter banality and nothingness of the man shovelling black ashes and bones says it all: all of this terror and horror has amounted to… a heap of ashes.[85] To nothing. And the cut from the ashes below the stake to Madelyn's reaction also speaks volumes: she is beyond tears, beyond feeling anything. She just knows she's got to get out of there.

☦

Was *The Devils* worth making? Ken Russell wondered. 'To me, yes, *The Devils* was a political statement worth making' (BP, 193). And it has resonances that were very much of the present moment – and Aldous Huxley had inevitably made comparisons with France in the 17th century and the contemporary era in *The Devils of Loudun*:

> Though frequently Manichaean in practice, Christianity was never Manichaean in dogmas. In this respect it differs from our modern idolatries of communism and nationalism, which are Manichaean not only in action, but also in creed and theory. Today it is everywhere self-evident that *we* are on the side of Light, *they* on the side of Darkness, they deserve to be punished and must be liquidated (since *our* divinity justifies everything) by the most fiendish means at our disposal. (1970, 192)

Ken Russell resolutely stood by his film, throughout the period when it was attacked as blasphemous and flopped in North America (though it was 'an all-time hit in Italy where the Doge of Venice was burnt in effigy when he tried to ban it', Russell

---

[84] Of course, Madelyn de Brou would have stayed for Grandier's burial and funeral service, and in reality would also have taken some other belongings, food and maybe a friend or relative or two (this is not the time to be wandering around France unaccompanied).

[85] 'In terms of pictorial qualities alone the ending is triumphant cinema' (Jack Fisher, 59).

claimed [BP, 193-4]).[86] 'They said *The Devils* was blasphemous,' Russell told *SFX Magazine* in August, 1999, 'whereas I see it as being about abuses within the Church. It's a very moral tale.'

*The Devils* is a movie of now, of course (or 1970-71, when it made, but also of now (like all classics), because it still resonates big time). As Joe Gomez put it, *The Devils* is 'not merely a supercharged historical recreation of the last years of Urbain Grandier; it is also an æsthetically exciting, visionary film about our own time' (1976, 70). Of course, *all* movies are *at least* about the time when they made (because they are always that, no matter what else they might be). But some historical movies pretend to ignore the present day, as if you can have a 'pure' re-enactment of the past, as if you can re-create history from scratch, in a 'pure' form. You can't. *The Devils* in fact is very conscious of the contemporary period of the late 1960s and the early 1970s.

☦

I've not bothered with extensive theoretical explorations in my study of the cinema of Ken Russell (because I want to focus on the movies as much as possible, without veering off the subject), but it's worth noting that there is a huge amount of theoretical writing about the links between insanity, hysteria and altered states of consciousness and the relation to religion. Contemporary feminism, for instance, has studied mediæval religious hysteria, which relates directly to *The Devils*.

Instead of using the usual approach of Sigmund Freud, the writings of French feminism are useful in thinking about the depiction of the nuns and the religious communities in *The Devils*. The French feminist Luce Irigaray, for instance, has been concerned with the notion of women as 'outsiders', of the otherness and outsideness of women in a patriarchal regime. Irigaray is interested in those women who have been 'outsiders' in history – the hysteric, the witch, the mediæval mystic, those people who 'stand outside' culture, using the techniques of ecstasy ('ex-stase', Irigaray spells it, 'ecstasy' meaning, from the Greek, 'stand outside'). Both Irigaray and Julia Kristeva spoke of the special, creative positionality of the mediæval women mystics, who occupied the maternal, liminal place of the mother, where

---

[86] Apparently, the Vatican criticized *The Devils* as 'the perverted marriage of sex, violence and blasphemy'. It was banned but then shown in Italy (and *Women In Love* was allowed to be released, too). According to Robert Sellers, reaction to *The Devils* helped to change the out-dated censorship laws in Italy.

the object of devotion became less fixed, more open, less dogmatic, more 'feminine'.

For Julia Kristeva, Christianity offers a limited number of ways in which women can participate in the 'symbolic Christian order': for women who are not virgins or nuns, who have orgasms and give birth

> her only means of gaining access to the symbolic paternal order is by engaging in an endless struggle between the orgasmic maternal body and the symbolic prohibition – a struggle that will take the form of guilt and mortification, and culminate in masochistic *jouissance*. For a woman who has not easily repressed her relationship with her mother, participation in the symbolic paternal order as Christianity defines it can only be masochistic. (*Tales of Love*, 147)

Two of the classic ways in which women have been allowed to participate in Christianity is the *'ecstatic* and the *melancholy'* (ib.). According to Elizabeth Grosz in "Lesbian Fetishism?" (1991), women can disavow their own castration (*contra* Sigmund Freud) through hysteria – women phallicizing part of their bodies; the 'masculine complex' – women taking the phallus as their love object; and narcissism – women turning their bodies into the phallus.

Even at the most simplistic and childish level, *The Devils* activates some of these concerns – with phallic imagery, a favourite with Ken Russell, with the eruption of sexual and religious repression in the 'rape of Christ' orgy, and with the twisted sadomasochism of Catholicism. And it's not only the community of the convent and the nuns, it's also the community of Urbain Grandier, the priests and their Church which's explored for its repression, extremity, S/M, hypocrisy and hysteria. (You could also link the evocations of witchcraft in *The Devils* with the rise in popularity of occultism, paganism and wicca in the late 1960s/early 1970s, figures such as Aleister Crowley (a perfect subject for a Ken Russell movie!), books like *The Occult* by Colin Wilson, and popularized in the dabbling with satanic themes in rock bands like Led Zeppelin, Black Sabbath and the Rolling Stones).

✝

Video and DVD versions of *The Devils* have been the focus of much contention, with critics and fans hoping for a full, uncut version, and the distributor (Warners) reluctant to deliver (the 117 minute restored version remains unavailable on home entertainment formats – the longest cuts are 108/ 11 minutes). *The Devils* has been screened in restored versions (including with the director presented for Q & A afterwards – in Southampton in 2007 and in Montréal, Toronto and L.A. in 2010, and in London in 2011, for instance).

Inevitably, *The Devils* was a problematic film for the censors (ironic, too, because it was partly about State censorship). In Britain, that meant John Trevelyan (out-going censor), new censor Stephen Murphy, Lord Harlech and the British Board of Film Censorship; in the U.S. of A., the film was given an 'X' rating[87] by the M.P.A.A.[88] *The Devils* was banned in Ken Russell's hometown of Southampton, and 16 other local councils. In the Land of the Free, 2 minutes were cut out of *The Devils*, including some of the shorter, more graphic images (G, 163). According to Mark Kermode, the movie was trimmed of the 3-4 minute 'rape of Christ' scene before being submitted to the censors in Feb, 1971 (on the advice of Trevelyan).

The Festival of Light (led by Peter Thompson) protested against *The Devils* outside theatres (however, compared to some movies, such as *The Last Temptation of Christ, Hail Mary*[89] or *The Passion of the Christ*, the protests against *The Devils* were much milder).

Censor John Trevelyan had drawn the line at allowing the word *cunt*, however: the script had included a line where Sister Agnes says cunt, but as Trevelyan told Russell, 'I'm afraid we can't have Vanessa saying 'cunt'. It's taken me ten years of fighting just to get 'fuck' accepted. I'm afraid the British public isn't ready yet for 'cunt'' (Bax, 211). And for the next forty years

---

[87] No studio wanted to receive an 'X' rating from the MPAA, because distrib-utors and exhibitors didn't want to show 'Xs'; they wanted 'Rs'.

[88] Warners re-cut the movie to gain an 'R' rating in 1973, when they saw their own movie *The Exorcist* doing incredibly well, and released *The Devils* to cash in.

[89] From the outset, even before the cameras had rolled, *Je Vous Salue, Marie* (Jean-Luc Godard, 1985) was a controversial film. A range of institutions, organ-izations and individuals protested against the film (as usual, many of these hadn't seen it, or had misunderstood it). The controversy surrounding *Hail Mary* resulted in the film being banned, or withdrawn, and theatres being picketed; in North America some 5,000 people demonstrated against the film at its premiere at the New York Film Festival, at the Lincoln Center. (Thirty years later, I'm sure many people still haven't seen the film).

*Hail Mary* created controversy when it depicted the Blessed Virgin as a gas station attendant. There were bomb threats, 5,000 protesters reciting the rosary to cinema queues, and the 'film bears the distinction of being the first ever con-demned by a pope (Pope John Paul II), and being the first instance in 400 years that a pope directly intervened in the suppression of a work of art' (Steven Dubin, 93).

or more, it was still rare for movies to include the word cunt. (Other language was also trimmed. Russell remarked that Trevelyan had been more helpful on *Women In Love* than *The Devils*).

In Blighty, local administrations can prevent the screening of a movie if they wish, even if the BBFC has passed it. And local councils have done so – with pictures such as *Monty Python's Life of Brian*,[90] *9 1/2 Weeks, Salò, or 120 Days of Sodom* and *The Last Temptation of Christ*. There have been films that the BBFC has banned but which have been shown (such as *The Texas Chainsaw Massacre*, which the Greater London Council gave an 'X', so it could only be seen in London).

*The Devils* proved a difficult movie to re-cut to suit the censors and Warners, because the requested cuts damaged the movie dramatically. Both Ken Russell and editor Mike Bradsell have recounted how satisfying the censors (and Warner Brothers) drove them nuts. Warners, for instance, wanted to cut back on the nudity – on the pubic hair ('pubic hairs get you an automatic X', a sales rep at Warners told Russell [PF, 122]). Nudity was pruned, as was Sister Jeanne masturbating, the enema/ exorcism scene, Grandier's torture, and the 'rape of Christ'. But even after the censors had wielded their scissors, *The Devils* was 'still without doubt the most savage film ever released in Britain', noted Robert Sellers in *Oliver Reed* (203).

In one of Ken Russell's many run-ins with the press, he bopped newspaper critic Alexander Walker over the head on BBC TV with a copy of the newspaper (the London *Evening Standard*) in which *The Devils* had been denounced ('the masturbatory fantasies of a Catholic boyhood').[91] That has become one of the infamous Russell events: it's surely something that many film-

---

[90] In the case of *Monty Python's Life of Brian*, despite being rated 'AA' (14 and over), 11 local councils banned it, 62 enforced the classification, and 28 reclassified the film 'X'.

[91] It was also the use of the Dread Word *fuck* that viewers objected to. In those quaint days of the Sixties an' Seventies, a mere word could drive audiences nuts. Like the moment when theatre critic Kenneth Tynan said 'fudge' on television in the Sixties, and 20 million people rioted (and it took Britain 15 years to recover), or when the Sex Pistols were interviewed by Bill Grundy on British TV in 1976. The following day, the *Daily Mirror* yelped 'a pop group shocked million of viewers last night with the filthiest language heard on British television'. The newspaper headlines became famous: 'THE FILTH AND THE FURY', 'ROCK CULT FILTH' and 'PUNK? CALL IT FILTHY LUCRE'.
A truck driver, James Holmes, had apparently kicked in his TV set, outraged that his 8 year-old son had heard the bad language. 'It blew up and I was knocked backwards. But I was so angry and disgusted with this filth that I took a swing with my boot' (*Daily Mirror*).

makers would love to do – bash a film critic over the head (preferrably with a loaded Magnum that accidentally fires into the schlub's skull).

At the time, Alexander Walker was one of the premier film critics in Blighty – and Ken Russell was by then a major name not only in the British cinema, but internationally. Many other critics came out against *The Devils*. George Melly, the camp jazz dandy, dubbed it 'vulgar, camp and hysterical' and 'a hideous pantomime'. Judith Crist admitted in *New York*: 'we can't recall in our relatively broad experience (400 movies a year for perhaps too many years) a fouler film'.[92] For the *Christian Science Monitor* it was 'an offensive mockery of Christianity'. Vincent Canby called Russell 'a hobbyist determined to reproduce *The Last Supper* in bottle tops'. *Variety* reckoned that Russell had 'gone berserk'. For Paul D. Zimmermann, 'Russell has gone beyond extravagance to insanity'. And in the *L.A. Times*, Charles Champlin said *The Devils* was 'a degenerate and despicable piece of art' (G, 114-5).

They were all wrong.

The critics were all *wrong*.

*The Devils* is a masterpiece.

✝ ✝ ✝

---

92 Oliver Reed challenged Judith Crist to a showdown on a chat show on TV. Of course she declined!

This page and over: images from The Devils,
Ken Russell's 1971 masterpiece.

Above: Ken Russell on the set of The Devils with the two stars,
Oliver Reed and Vanessa Redgrave.

# Video ★ WatchdoG®

the Perfectionist's Guide to Fantastic Video

No. 35
$6.50

## THE DEVILS
### A Plea for Restoration

**Ken Russell**    **Donald Cammell**
*On Film Censorship*    *Final Performance*

ANIME   **SOUNDTRACKS**   BOOKS   RETITLINGS

Urbain Grandier

# 10

# THE BOY FRIEND

*The Boy Friend* (1971), made for MGM-EMI and produced by Ken Russell and Harry Behn, was based on Sandy Wilson's 1953 play, set in the 1920s.[1] There's no doubt who is the star of this particular show: Ken Russell: he not only produced the movie, and directed the movie, he also wrote the screenplay (adapting a musical play for the screen is not simply a cast of taking the play onto the set and shooting it as it is). Direction alone of a big movie like this is impressive, direction plus production is rarer, but to write as well as produce and direct is very unusual (and exhausting).

*The Boy Friend* starred Twiggy and many Ken Russell regulars: Christopher Gable, Max Adrian, Vladek Sheybal, Bryan Pringle, Antonia Ellis, Georgina Hale, Graham Armitage, Murray Melvin, Sally Bryant, Glenda Jackson, Catherine Wilmer and Brian Murphy. Also appearing were Barbara Windsor, Ann Jameson, Caryl Little and Moyra Fraser. Similarly, among the crew were regular collaborators, such as David Watkin (DP), Graham Ford (AD), Michael Bradsell (editor), Peter Maxwell Davies (music), Tony Walton (production designer), and Shirley Kingdon (costumes). Also in the crew were Barbara Ritchie (hairdresser), Freddie Williams (make-up), Simon Holland (art director), Brian Simmons (sound), and Neville Thompson

---

[1] According to Ken Russell in *An Appalling Talent*, he came to direct *The Boy Friend* via Twiggy, when a journalist discovered the model and the director having a drink and asked them if they were going to work together. Somehow he wound up making a musical (Bax, 213f). But it was inevitable that Russell would make a musical like *The Boy Friend* at some point.

(production manager). The choreographers were Christopher Gable, Terry Gilbert, Gillian Gregory, and members of the cast. Many of the cast and crew had completed *The Devils* not long before making *The Boy Friend*. (So it was '*The Devils* Take a Holiday – but it wasn't a happy shoot).

Shooting took place at Elstree Studios (then owned by MGM-EMI), and at the Theatre Royal in Portsmouth. Unfortunately, *The Boy Friend* was cut by the studio, MGM-EMI, so some prints run longer (the U.S. version was trimmed by 25 minutes).[2]

Twiggy (a.k.a. Lesley Hornby, born 1949) was absolutely one of the faces of the period – a famous supermodel.[3] Twiggy, who played the lead, Polly Browne, is a terrific find for the 1971 movie: she can sing, she can dance, and she can act![4] Finding all three in any performer is a rarity. Finding all three so accomplished is even rarer. Finding someone who also looks right for the role adds to the challenge (and it doesn't hurt that she looks fabulous, too, romancing the camera like the greatest Hollywood star).

Twiggy, in short, has to carry so much of *The Boy Friend*: it is Polly Browne's story, first and foremost. And this is Twiggy's movie. However, the supporting cast is sensational. By the time of *The Boy Friend*, Ken Russell and his team had worked with an ensemble of actors for some years, and they are all here in *The Boy Friend* (the production is a good illustration of just how valuable it can be to develop working relationships with a bunch of collaborations, in front of and behind the camera. And a musical movie tests everybody to the limit).

The camera absolutely loves Twiggy's appealing, open features, especially those colossal eyes, as big and wide as a Japanese *anime* star (and always meticulously made up with mixed colours of eye shadow).[5] One of the enduring images of *The Boy Friend* is Twiggy's face in close-up, with those baby blues eating up the screen. Twiggy's is one of those actors who have to do nothing but just *be there*, in front of the camera. You can't take

---

[2] At the behest of James Aubrey, head of MGM. Some scenes were dropped from the final cut, including an ancient Greek fantasy, and a lesbian relationship between two women in the cast. And the wheel-chair ballet was cut by MGM for the U.S.A. release.
[3] Other celebrities of the time would include Mary Quant, Vidal Sassoon, Ossie Clark, John Lennon, Jean Shrimpton, Dusty Springfield, Mick Jagger, Kenneth Tynan and Joe Orton.
[4] Twiggy won Golden Globes for best actress and newcomer.
[5] By Freddie Williams.

your eyes off her.

One wonders if some of the executives at MGM were not sure about casting Christopher Gable: they had an established star of the era with Twiggy, and Gable was probably not enough of a name for some of the suits. True, a star name of the time (such as Malcolm McDowell or Terence Stamp), might've enhanced the marquee value of *The Boy Friend*. But could they sing and dance as well as act? When you factor in singing and dancing, as well as being right for the role (and looking 1920s), your choices dwindle down rapidly.

Christopher Gable, one of the unsung stars in the Ken Russell Repertory Company, who had the role of a lifetime in *Dance of the Seven Veils* the year before, is terrific in *The Boy Friend* as the millionaire's son Tony Brockhurst going undercover as a bell-hop and messenger boy. As the blond prince in this fluffy, backstage fairy tale, Gable's Tony convinces. Gable also works really well with Twiggy: their scenes together are very fine (you can believe that Twiggy is nuts over Tony, and that Tony is fending off advances from a no. of women).

Because, whaddya know?, *The Boy Friend* is an out-and-out romantic comedy: it is a love story in which Polly Browne's love for bell-hop Tony Brockhurst finally bears fruit (well, romantic stories are the primary narrative motifs in all musicals). *The Boy Friend* really does end with the lovers dancing off into the sunset. They are a golden-haired couple, with the bright, toothy smiles of the young innocents of moviedom, the kind of characters that only exist in winsome movies and Victorian fairy tales. (Critics complain that Ken Russell can't do straight drama or romance (or anything straight), but he can – when he wants to, that is!).

The whole movie opens with a shot-counter-shot set-up that depicts Polly Browne looking longingly at a photograph of Tony Brockhurst; and that simple, reverse angle sequence also introduces the two stars, and the two main characters, at the outset, which's standard practice. And, in her Assistant Stage Manager role, Polly Browne is hurrying about delivering the cast their tipples and nibbles. She saves an apple for Tony – no need to note that a woman is symbolically giving a man an apple (at least it's not a banana!). And it's in keeping with Tony's characterization that he says he's already had one (Tony's adultery is the friction that comes between Polly and Tony: the film has Tony getting friendly with one of the young women in the cast, which upsets our Pol).

It's surprising perhaps that Ken Russell didn't direct more movie musicals – there are two, really: *The Boy Friend* and *Tommy*, altho' *The Music Lovers*, *Lisztomania* and *Mahler* can also be classed as musicals (among the theatrical releases). But when you add up the number of dances and songs that Russell manage to sneak into most of his TV and film works, you have a director who's put more musical and dance performance on screen than pretty much anyone else.

★

Britain isn't known for its movie musicals (the mainstream, movie musical is essentially an American form), but it has produced many – traditional ones (like *Oliver!*, *Half a Sixpence*, *Scrooge*, *The Red Shoes*, *Absolute Beginners* and *Bugsy Malone*), plenty of pop musicals (*A Hard Day's Night*, *Help!*, *Summer Holiday*, *Espresso Bongo*, *Flame*, *That'll Be the Day*, *Stardust*, *Catch Us If You Can*, *Quadrophenia*, *Spice World*, *Rude Boy*), and musical biopics like *Sid and Nancy* and *Backbeat*. In amongst British musicals, Ken Russell's entries – *Tommy*, *Lisztomania*, *The Music Lovers*, *Mahler* and *The Boy Friend* – are superbly crafted and wildly over-the-top. And Russell has carved out his own niche in British musicals – none of which are as insane as *Lisztomania* or *Tommy*.

Despite all the familiar faces surrounding Ken Russell, though, *The Boy Friend* was a troubled production, with fall-outs between Russell and the cast and crew, technical problems which stretched the production's resources and skills, and the budget allocated by Metro-Goldwyn-Mayer ($1.7 million) wasn't large enough for a musical of this scope (G, 166). The budget is clearly a big problem for staging a major musical movie like *The Boy Friend* – there have been musical movies with far smaller budgets, but the kind of effects that Russell and his team were going for, $1.7m wasn't enough, by a long way (it wouldn't have been sufficient even in the 1950s).

For Shirley Kingdon, *The Boy Friend* was a miserable experience for all involved:

> There was something strange in the atmosphere. We had nervous breakdowns and near suicides among the company. Over one weekend, one girl nearly tore another's eyes out, somebody else kicked

another person's door down, and one of the guys, a very nice person, was coming back to the location from London by train, and when the train halted at a siding, he just got out of it and wandered away into the middle of a field, and we had to go and fetch him. It had a peculiar effect on everyone, that film. (PF, 135)

There was an atmosphere of bitchiness and bitterness amongst the cast and crew, Ken Russell recalled. And jealousy – over who was getting more lines, or being on camera more. 'The film should have been called *The Devils Take a Holiday*' (Bax, 218).

Among the challenges of making *The Boy Friend* were that British studios weren't high enough or large enough for what Ken Russell and the team were trying to achieve (a 70mm camera was hired from the U.S.A. to get the effects). Sets were late in construction or didn't work. The crew wasn't used to filming big musicals. Obtaining a really shiny floor was a nightmare, Russell explained, because no matter how often they were cleaned, the studios were so dusty they would be covered with dust again. 'A lot of the time I wasn't directing dance numbers; I was down on my hands and knees trying to get the floor polished' (Bax, 212). (Actually, the British film industry *had* filmed some big musicals by this time – *Oliver*, for instance, was an enormous production that constructed giant sets at Shepperton Studios, by John Box).

Musical movies such as *The Boy Friend* are pre-production movies: that is, most of the important stuff has already been done by the time the cameras roll on a soundstage (true on any movie, but vital with a musical). The music has been chosen (and cleared for permissions), and arranged, orchestrated and re-recorded; the dancers have been rehearsed; the actors have been pre-recorded singing. Even so, with all that preparation, the 1971 movie was challenging to shoot.

MGM were putting pressure on the production which they thought was going over-budget (this occurred far less with Ken Russell than the critics might lead you to think. And films going out of control are more fun to write about. But when Russell went over-budget, as with Orson Welles, it was *tiny* compared to the truly abysmal movies that have gone over-budget – like *Raise the Titanic* or *Honky Tonk Freeway* or *Spider-man 3*).

★

The framing story in *The Boy Friend* is a theatrical company in a provincial theatre putting on *The Boy Friend*; the movie plays the usual Russellian game of the framing story commenting upon (or altering) the fictional story, and vice versa. There are further narrative layers, however: one is the fantasies and daydreams of the main characters: Polly Browne, while she's in the midst of singing or dancing a number, drifts off into fantasies (usually about her and Tony Brockhurst. One of the best is pure Isadora Duncan, as Polly and Tony dance together in front of a lake). Impresario Mr Max also has daydreams – about how his theatrical career might be if he were conducting a show with a full orchestra (and a full house) for visiting royalty. And the film director Mr De Thrill also has fantasies: he imagines Tony and Polly dancing on a giant gramophone (the viewpoint of De Thrill, throughout the movie, adds another layer to the proceedings. Indeed, many scenes are filmed from his perspective, especially in the second half of the picture. Too many, I think: once De Thrill's presence (and influence) have been established, with the cast playing up to him shamelessly, it spoils some of the numbers by the over-use of the high angle, stage right angle simulating De Thrill's viewpoint).

Thus, altho' Ken Russell is often thought of as a crude, rude and vulgar director, there is a narrative complexity to *The Boy Friend*: it might be at first glance a simple love story (a romantic comedy), and a simple let's-put-on-a-show story (a theatrical, backstage comedy), but there is much more to it than that.

★

*The Boy Friend* (1953) was conceived by Sandy Wilson as an *hommage* (as well as a mild send-up) to the 1920s and its music. It became a huge hit, running for over 2,000 performances.[6] Julie Andrews played Polly Browne in the first Broadway production (one of her first roles. Andrews was also going to appear in the 1971 movie, as the injured star Rita Monroe, which was played by Glenda Jackson).

The setting of the story-within-a-story is the French Riviera, and a finishing school for young women. The setting of the theatre company putting on a show in a suburban theatre in Portsmouth, England, adds a further layer (jokes're made at the expense of dreary, provincial England – Tommy, for ex, goes from Broadway to Portsmouth, and a big shot, Hollywood producer ends up in Portsmouth. Those two dream factories –

---

6 So a movie version was probably in the works somewhere.

Hollywood and Broadway – seem far away from li'l old Portsmouth on the South Coast of li'l old England. But in the hands of a master magician like Ken Russell, and aided by the magic of movies themselves, *anywhere* can be Hollywood, *anywhere* can be Broadway).

Sandy Wilson had been concerned by the alterations that Ken Russell and co. were making to his beloved material (such as shifting the action into the 1930s). But if you want a 'faithful' version of a play or a musical (impossible for numerous reasons), don't hire Ken Russell! Russell naturally complicates any material he takes on – his natural tendency is to make things richer, deeper, more exaggerated and more colourful (and in the early 1970s, he was at the height of his all-out colourfulness and wildness).

★

*The Boy Friend* is another design piece from Ken Russell and his team, with each department excelling itself: Tony Walton, production designer, Simon Holland, art director, Shirley Kingdon, wardrobe, Barbara Ritchie, hair, Freddie Williamson, make-up, George Ball, props master,[7] and David Watkins (cinematography). It's drenched in saturated colours, a comicbook version of a Metro Hollywood musical of the heyday in the 1940s and 1950s (MGM-EMI were the financers of *The Boy Friend*).[8]

It was a dream project for a production designer: it's the kinda movie where designers're encouraged to go nuts. And they know, it being a Ken Russell movie, it's going to look amazing. 'I was like a child let loose in a candy store,' recalled Tony Walton; 'I never dreamed I would have the opportunity to create such things as an *Arabian Nights* extravaganza, an airplane with dancers on the wings, a giant, revolving gramophone turntable for another number, and even a complete Pixieland'.

*The Boy Friend* is self-consciously artificial, a show-within-a-show, and contains many allusions to famous Hollywood musicals, such as *The Bandwagon, The Wizard of Oz, 42nd Street, Flying Down To Rio, Sunset Boulevard*, Federico Fellini, Busby Berkeley, humour from *Monty Python* and the *Carry On* movies, and perhaps the best loved musical of them all, *Singin' In the Rain*.

*The Boy Friend* is Ken Russell's *History of the Movie Musical*: in

---

7 There are some inventive props in *The Boy Friend* constructed by the prop department.
8 MGM had acquired the rights in 1957.

it Russell and co. get to stage a host of favourite scenes, motifs, effects, routines and dances (Gerald Mast and Bruce Kawin call *The Boy Friend* 'as pure a style piece as has ever been made, a self-contained history of the musical film').[9] It is also a compendium of theatrical effects and stereotypes – it's a *History of Theatre*. It's Russell's *History of Popular Songs* (the movie is wall-to-wall songs from the 1920s and 1930s). And it's also Russell's *History of Modern Dance*, with the choreographers (Gable, Gilbert, Gregory) delivering a very large amount of dance in a single movie (there's no scene that goes on for long without someone dancing in it).

If you love musical movies and theatrical musicals (and who doesn't?), you will love *The Boy Friend*. The affection it lavishes on musicals is irresistible; you can't help but be won over by *The Boy Friend*'s passion for its subject.

*The Boy Friend* is delightfully fluffy, indulgently romantic, unashamedly nostalgic, and vividly self-conscious. Like the great musical movies which it emulates and pays homage to, there isn't an ounce of reality in *The Boy Friend*. *The Boy Friend* is like watching the music of the Bonzo Dog Doo-Dah Band (one of the great British bands of the late Sixties era) visualized on celluloid (right down to the 'voh-doh-de-oh' chorus in the 'Charleston' number).

*The Boy Friend* is Ken Russell's backstage musical: it's his *42nd Street*, his *All About Eve,* his *Singin' In the Rain*, his *Sunset Boulevard* (Russell's knowledge of Hollywood movies is of the order of film obsessives such as Jean-Luc Godard, Martin Scorsese and Steven Spielberg). *The Boy Friend* contains numerous ingredients of the backstage genre, from the Innocent Understudy who gets to take over the Injured Star's role, to the Pompous Serious Actor always threatening to walk out, to the Ambitious, Scheming Actress, to the dictatorial Stage Director. The bitchiness, the ruthless ambition, the competition, the boredom, the stupidity, the razzle-dazzle (and the blandness behind the glitz), it's all in *The Boy Friend*. Some backstage stories make all of that nastier, but *The Boy Friend* plays it more sweetly, and for comedy.

The camp factor[10] in *The Boy Friend* is built-in, so hardly needs to be pointed out: *The Boy Friend* doesn't need the Ken Russell

---

9 Gerald Mast, 1992, 396.
10 The restored version of *The B. F.* was advertized in San Francisco (at the Castro Theater) thus: 'Ken Russell's Uncut Boyfriend!'

camp approach which emphasizes vulgarity and crudity. It's already in there (but how could it *not* be in there?). *The Boy Friend* also doesn't need (or want) the wicked sense of humour that Russell brings to many projects: in the end, *The Boy Friend* is a much sweeter product than later Russell musicals, such as *Lisztomania* or *Tommy*. The cynicism inherent in those musical movies would be out of place here: not because *The Boy Friend* is so thoroughly romantic and romanticized (which it is), but the cynicism of the showbiz folk and the show business *milieu* is enough.

It's worth remembering that the 1953 musical play was of its time: *The Boy Friend* was the 1950s looking back fondly on the 1920s: the 1971 MGM-EMI movie is the 1970s looking back on the 1920s, thru the filter of the 1950s play. It is altogether more knowing, more ironic, and of course the sensibility of filmmakers such as Ken Russell, Harry Behn, Christopher Gable *et al* is very different from Sandy Wilson and co. in the 1950s. Wilson in 1953 conceived a sweet nostalgiafest which evoked his youth: Russell and co. in 1971 didn't want to do that.

★

If a theatrical effect exists, *The Boy Friend* makes sure it's included. One of the pleasures of the theatre is its artifice, its contract of suspending disbelief btn the audience and the performers (and the play). In some movies, such self-conscious effects can be irritating and intrusive. In *The Boy Friend* they added to the appeal of the piece.

Ken Russell and cinematographer David Watkin were right to retain the proscenium arch for many of the routines in *The Boy Friend* – to keep the actors in full body shots, so you can see their feet as well as their heads. I agree with Woody Allen, Fred Astaire and John Badham (*Saturday Night Fever*) that for dance movies, full-body shots are preferrable (though of course *The Boy Friend* punctuated scenes with close-ups – there are numerous shots of feet, for instance – and not only in the dance numbers. The injured star Rita (Glenda Jackson), for example, is introduced with a tracking shot on her legs).

Ken Russell and editor Mike Bradsell were also right to keep showy editing to a minimum in *The Boy Friend*: it worked for previous material such as *The Devils* and *The Music Lovers*, but shock cuts were inappropriate for this material. Also, I for one am glad that rapid cutting was not employed during the dance numbers. It drives me nuts in movies such as *Moulin Rouge* (2001), *Dreamgirls* (2006) and *Chicago* (2002), which're edited like MTV pop promos, and literally cut bodies to bits. As if multiple images of the same thing is somehow more exciting. It can be, but not often with dance. The template for how to edit bodies moving in space in live-action is without doubt Hong Kong action cinema. (However, some of the numbers in *The Boy Friend* are rapidly cut – the 'Charleston' number, for example. And the editing is actually complex at times – especially when it is intercutting the fantasies of the characters with their performances in the theatre, plus cutaways and inserts of the audience, and the cast and crew watching from the wings. That is of course one of the reasons that filmmakers enjoy the theatrical setting for movies, because it means there can be a continuous commentary on the artifice of putting on a show).

*The Boy Friend* is a style piece, like many musicals: it's not about the story, the romantic comedy elements, or even the characters, it's about the style, the look, the music, the dancing, the costumes, the whole experience (yet even professional critics, who should know better, keep going on about the story or the characters of a musical movie). It's also a movie about movies, and about watching movies (as many of Ken Russell's films are). And it's definitely a trip down memory lane for Russell (he was born in the 1920s – in 1927).

The sound of feet pounding the stage is emphasized in *The Boy Friend* – and clearly (and ironically) many of those sound effects are foley work (that is, added after the fact). The sound of feet at work enhances the sense of effort involved in dance, as well as the earthy, provincial aspect of the Portsmouth theatre. It was also over-done, I think: after it had been established, it wasn't necessary (though you will often hear clunky and too-obvious foley work in movies of the 1960s and 1970s. Fashions come and go in sound as in everything else in cinema – and in the 21st century it's simply not deemed desirable to have actors accompanied by thudding footsteps everywhere they go).[11] Similarly, the sound mixing and editing in *The Boy Friend* was a little self-consciously clunky and rough, as if we always needed to be reminded that this was a provincial theatre group putting on a

---

11 Footsteps were added in *Saturday Night Fever*, until the filmmakers were told by club-goers that you'd never hear the sound of feet under the disco music!

show (though in the fantasy sequences, the sound rightly altered, as did the music, shifting from piano and drums to a fuller, orchestral sound).

*

*The Boy Friend* boasts three choreographers: Christopher Gable, Terry Gilbert and Gillian Gregory, all of whom had worked with Ken Russell before (the cast are also credited). I guess three choreographers were needed because of the sheer amount of choreography that the production required (and also the large, ensemble cast – this wasn't *Dirty Dancing* or *Flashdance*, where one or two stars dance (or their stand-ins). And *The Boy Friend* is not a musical movie with, say, 6 or 7 numbers: it has many numbers, each requiring choreography (and Russell, as usual, often stages non-musical scenes like dance numbers).

Not everybody in the cast of *The Boy Friend* is a sensational dancer, but plenty of rehearsal (and enthusiasm) makes up for that, as well as some people who really *can* dance – such as Tommy Tune (as the token Yank), and Christopher Gable. Tune delivers his scenes in constant motion: he doesn't talk so much as he dances his way thru the movie (Tune's Tommy offers *hommages* to the great hoofers of cinema, such as Fred Astaire and Gene Kelly). Tune, an accomplished tap-dancer, is great to watch. And he seems even taller and skinnier than Fred Astaire – his legs seem to go on and on.

And plenty of the cast in *The Boy Friend* throw themselves into the *melée* – apart from the stand-outs, Twiggy and Christopher Gable, Max Adrian is marvellous as the passionate diva of a theatrical impresario, the fussy, anxious stand-in for the director himself, trying to stave off chaos. A strong actor in this sort of role helps a story like this immensely. As usual, Adrian threw himself wholeheartedly into the role (even though he was ill at the time, and played his dance with Georgina Hale in a wheelchair).[12] Antonia Ellis is incredible as Maisie, Polly Browne's rival in the troupe, a wild bundle of dancer's energy and lascivious close-ups (she gives Ken Russell exactly what he wants from a leading lady – the sexier and sluttier the better for our Ken!). The rest of the supporting performers are superb, providing solid ensemble playing, with a real feeling for a theatrical company struggling

---

[12] A filmmaker such as Ken Russell, after hearing from an actor or assistant director that they were too weak to perform the number as rehearsed, would get over his disappointment and relish the challenge.

against the odds (every actor has been there!): the women (including Caryl Little, Sally Bryant, Georgina Hale and Barbara Windsor), and the guys (Murray Melvin, Brian Murphy and Graham Armitage).

★

Ken Russell thinks you can put *everything* into a movie like *The Boy Friend*. So he does. He's right: the form of the musical comedy, in movies or musical theatre, is broad enough to take in slapstick comedy, romantic comedy, all-out musical extravaganzas, as well as lyrical, fantasy sequences and even some social or political commentary. If you've been to a musical show in London or New York City, or seen musical theatre at the level of amateur drama or a college drama group, nothing in *The Boy Friend* will surprise you: it all fits. If you've seen any of the classics of musical cinema – *The Bandwagon, 42nd Street,* Busby Berkeley, *Singin' In the Rain, An American In Paris,* or more recent movies, such as *Everyone Says I Love You, The Nightmare Before Christmas Beauty and the Beast* or *Rock Star* – *The Boy Friend* will be comfortingly familiar. The *love* that the 1971 movie has for musical movies pours out of every frame.

The amount of dancing is very impressive, and the number of dance styles runs from freeform, modernist ballet *à la* Ken Russell's beloved Vaslav Nijinsky and Isadora Duncan, to popular dances such as the Charleston. Along the way, *The Boy Friend* takes in Hollywood tap-dancing in the manner of Fred Astaire and James Cagney, vaudeville and British musical hall (there's even an 'Any Old Iron' sketch), and the graceful, romantic style of mid-20th century, Hollywood musicals *à la* Gene Kelly, Vincente Minnelli and Stanley Donen.

★

The group of four dancers/ actresses surrounding Polly Browne were especially wonderful: Antonia Ellis (Maisie), Caryl Little (Dulcie), Georgina Hale (Fay) and Sally Bryant (Nancy).[13] They took the simpering, cooing, ooohing and aaahing of ditzy, young women to new heights – coupled with marvellous, over-the-top postures (legs and torso bent to one side, knees together, hands clasped in merriment, giant eyes sparkling, with Cheshire Cat grins).

The cut lesbian subplot (between Maisie and Fay) would've

---

13 And they outshone the guys – who included Murray Melvin, Graham Armitage, Brian Murphy and Tommy Tune.

diverted too much attention into unnecessary areas. *The Boy Friend* needs only the primary plot (of putting on a show) and the secondary plot of the romance between Polly and Tony. There are other sub-plots (such as the Mr De Thrill plot), but romances btn the cast are way down the list. (However, some remnants of the lesbian relationship emerge in the movie, where Maisie and Fay are often depicted together (in the final scene, fr'instance, when Maisie is gutted to find that De Thrill has shot off into the sunset with his long-lost son Tommy, she looks up to exchange a Meaningful Glance with Fay.

★

As usual, *The Boy Friend* divided critics – Gene Siskel and John Coleman liked it, but Pauline Kael and Judith Crist (no surprise) didn't. Sandy Wilson, needless to say, wasn't crazy about it. For him, the only redeeming feature, the single glow in the walpurgisnacht, was Twiggy. As usual, some critics didn't know quite what to make of *The Boy Friend*: they tended to be far too literal in their perception of this movie, and other Ken Russell movies, still not grasping the fundamental confluence of art and vulgarity which Russell's cinema is founded on. Most critics don't 'get it', and they just can't move past that initial block. (But why send critics known to dislike Russell's work as a director to review *The Boy Friend* in the first place?!).

Anyhoo, film critics often don't react well to musical movies (or comedies), unless they have some social or political comment to make (like *Cabaret* or *Jesus Christ Superstar*, which came out a coupla years later), or, like the Walt Disney Studios' cartoons, are so obviously fluffy and superficial.

For me, there's very little *not* to enjoy in *The Boy Friend*. It's pure entertainment: you can see what it's trying to do from the opening scene; it's not hiding anything; and, like a professional Broadway company, it sure knows how to deliver a good night out. None of the out-size Russellania bothers me at all. The camper the better! But I'm a fan: only occasionally does Ken Russell and the team miss the mark here, I reckon. The only negative thing to say about *The Boy Friend* is I wish that Russell had made more movies like this! And particularly in the 1990s and the 2000s.

✯

But the story in *The Boy Friend*, as well as the framing story, and the levels of daydream and fantasy, are only for producer-writer-director Ken Russell a springboard for all of the stuff he *really* wants to do:

✻ stage Busby Berkeley God's-eye-view shots of dancers on a giant, rotating gramophone;

✻ put exotically-dressed dancers on the wings of a biplane in swirling clouds;[14]

✻ create a colourful pixieland of enormous toadstools and jolly, dancing elves;

✻ set Twiggy atop a Rolls Royce as a living statue of the 'Spirit of Ecstasy';

✻ stage dancers as playing cards on ladders with huge, shiny headdresses of clubs, diamonds, spades and hearts;

✻ put dancers in the sea in swimwear (with, of course, painted waves rolling to and fro);

✻ recreate a French *fin-de-siècle* musical extravaganza with sad Pierrots and sparkly moons;[15]

✻ and stage plenty of Isadora Duncan and Vaslav Nijinsky-inspired routines.

When you consider all of the inventive situations and routines that Ken Russell and the production team have delivered in *The Boy Friend*, it's pretty remarkable. As a musical film director, Russell has no equal in all of British cinema. Russell makes it all look so easy, so simple – yet we know from the accounts of making *The Boy Friend* that it was challenging (any dance number in any movie means days and often weeks of rehearsal).

*The Boy Friend* is very much a Let's Dress Up movie for Ken Russell and the team, a Let's Lark About, Let's Dance, Let's Sing, Let's Put On a Show kind of movie. In *The Boy Friend*, it's all about the costumes. It's all about the hair and make-up. It's all about the sets. It's all about the lighting. It's all about the moving camera, the framing, the juxtapositions of editing.

*The Boy Friend* is a *musical*: music is pounding throughout the movie: there is never more than a minute or so of non-musicality. As well as Sandy Wilson's songs, there is music from Peter

---

[14] Taken from *Flying Down To Rio* (1933), a Russell fave.
[15] Lindsay Kemp, who appeared in *Savage Messiah*, had performed as Pierrot in a revue show with David Bowie in 1967-68 (as well as being Bowie's lover for a while, until the inevitable acrimonious fall-out).

Maxwell-Davies, and also a coupla numbers from *Singin' In the Rain* ('You Are My Lucky Star'[16] and 'All I Do Is Dream of You'). And much of the music comes from an upright piano, accompanied by drums. (The music supervisors, producers and editors on any musical movie contribute a huge amount: on *The Boy Friend* it was two Peters, Maxwell-Davies and Greenwell (Greenwell also played the pianist, thumping the joanna throughout the movie in the orchestra pit and grinning up idiotically at Mr De Thrill).)

★

*'You're going out there as a youngster; you've got to come back a star!'*

You wanna be a ★, right? Sure, *everyone* in the backstage theatrical genre is on the make: the genre is a perfect analogue for Western capitalism. To make it, to be a star, it powers along the backstage genre just like it does in the contemporary capitalist world – even more so decades later, in the postmodern era of celebrity culture and instant stardom (Ken Russell had a taste of that with his *Big Brother* TV appearance – where 'ordinary' people could become stars in a postmodern, surface-is-everything television show).

There is an over-the-top recreation of a Hollywood film studio of the 1920s in one of the fantasy sequences towards the end of *The Boy Friend* (which features Mr De Thrill in his Cecil B. DeMille/ D.W. Griffith/ Rex Ingram mode. It's the Film Director as a master of chaos, revelling in the madness of a big production with special effects (snow, smoke, dry ice) and pretty women dancing.) Ken Russell would revisit this territory a no. of times (most memorably in *Valentino*).

---

[16] Sung by Twiggy alone in the dressing room as she moons over Tony yet again.

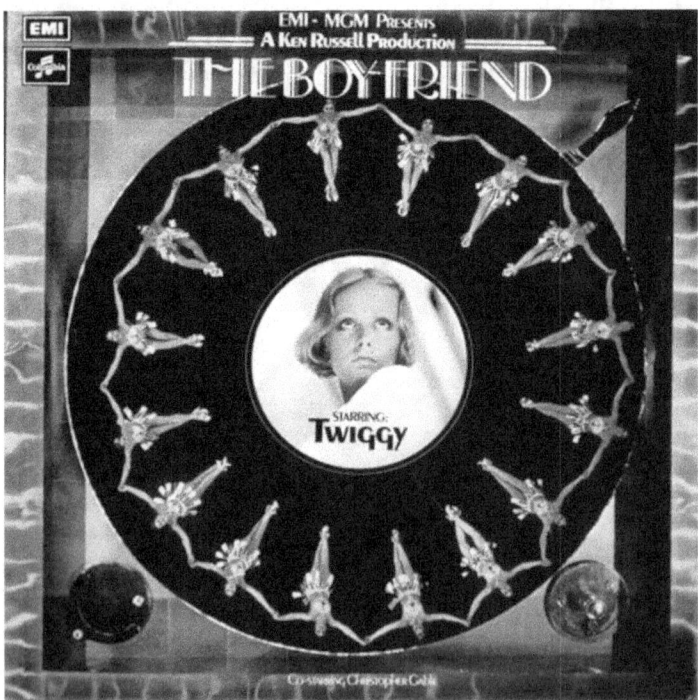

The Boy Friend (this page and over).

# 11

# *SAVAGE MESSIAH*

Everything that I saw became something to be made, and it had to be exactly as it was, with nothing added. It was a new freedom: there was no longer the need to compose. The subject was there already made, and I could take from everything. It all belonged to me: a glass roof of a factory, with its broken and patched panels, lines on a road map, a corner of a Braques painting, paper fragments in the street. It was all the same: anything goes.

Ellsworth Kelly

*Savage Messiah* (1972), directed by Ken Russell for MGM-British and Russ-Arts, his follow-up to *The Boy Friend*, was another of his many biopics about artists. It starred Scott Anthony as Henri Gaudier-Brzeska (October 4, 1891 - June 5, 1915), the French, modernist sculptor who lived in Paris and London, and who was associated with the Vorticist group. It was based on the 1931 book by Jim Ede,[1] and scripted by Christopher Logue. The budget (around $750,000) came from John and Benny Lee, and Russell's second mortgage and savings; MGM picked up the film for $750,000.[2] The schedule was 10 weeks. Russell and Harry Benn produced.

---
[1] H.S. Ede, *Savage Messiah*, 1971. Other books about Henri Gaudier-Brzeska include *Gaudier-Brzeska: A Memoir* by Ezra Pound (1916), and *Henri Gaudier-Brzeska* by Horace Brodzky.
[2] As Ken Russell recounted in his autobiography, 'the Lee boys' (John and Benny Lee) were 'a couple of Cockney sparks who put up some money and let me use their studio, a derelict biscuit factory on the banks of a putrid canal in North London' (BP, 81).

Henri Gaudier-Brzeska was influenced by Auguste Rodin, Jacob Epstein and Michelangelo Buonarroti, among others. His art has affinities with Constantin Brancusi, Jean Arp, Pablo Picasso and Rodin, as well as the Cubists and Vorticists. He was born near Orélans in France and worked in Bristol, Nuremberg, Munich and Paris, ending up with Sophie Brzeska in Londinium from 1910 onwards.

Henri Gaudier-Brzeska contributed towards the Vorticists' manifestos and publications, such as *BLAST*, and showed work at the 1915 Vorticist show. The Vorticists included Wyndham Lewis, Ezra Pound, Christopher Nevinson, and Edward Wadsworth. Associated with the Futurists in Italy, the Vorticist movement was self-consciously radical and aggressive.

After the trials of producing *The Boy Friend*, Ken Russell said he wanted to get back to something much smaller in scale – i.e., a production much easier for him to control: 'I wanted this film to be totally different, away from the big companies and back into the small studio; back to the BBC sort of style with a small unit. I mean it's as small as can be' (in P. Buckley).

The production was based at Lee International Studios in West London, like many of Ken Russell's films of the time.[3] Location work included parts of North London (instantly recognizable, as Paris), the countryside around Bath, Somerset, which stood in for France (the centre of Bath, next to the Abbey, a well-known tourist spot, stood in for Paris, and the scene set in the Musée de Louvre was shot in a church, which is probably Bath Abbey). Other locations included Portland in Dorset (for the stone quarry).

As well as a much lower budget than Ken Russell's previous few films, *Savage Messiah* had something like a family atmosphere, and was one of Russell's most enjoyable shoots. Many of the crew acted in the film, as did most of Russell's family, and the 65-strong crew felt like a family. Even the weather was great (in England in March!). According to Russell, the only time shooting stopped for weather was when the sun came out in the middle of a rain shot, when it's usually the other way around (Bax, 225).

Christopher Logue wrote the screenplay for *Savage Messiah*, drawing a good deal on the biographies, and H.S. Ede's book in particular. Much of the dialogue, for instance, comes from the biographies (a standard Ken Russell tactic). However, Russell

---

[3] For much of this period Ken Russell's film operation was based out of Lee International Studios.

added all sorts of elements to Logue's first draft, which he hadn't been wholly happy with.[4] The anti-war demonstrations were added by Russell, and 'Gosh' Smith-Boyle being pro-war too (an intriguing twist on Smith-Boyle's initially left-leaning politics). Major Smith-Boyle was another addition that Russell made to Logue's script (making 'Gosh' Smith-Boyle a daddy's girl).

Ken Russell had discovered H.S. Ede's book about Henri Gaudier in his early 20s, and the story of the sculptor who died young impressed him. Gaudier, Russell recognized, was convinced that 'somehow or other there was a spark in the core of him that was personal to him, which was worth turning into something that could be appreciated by others. I wanted to find that spark in myself and exploit it for that reason', Russell said in 1977.

A significant addition to Christopher Logue's screenplay was to alter the ending: Ken Russell put the exhibition of Henri Gaudier-Brzeska's work *after* his death in the Great War, not before. That's Russell's cinematic instinct at work, and it's absolutely right. Instead of Gaudier-Brzeska being there, reacting to the visitors looking at his work and commenting upon it, the scene gains enormously in emotion.[5]

Like pretty much every historical movie, *Savage Messiah* telescopes events and time, so that events that took place in Henri Gaudier's life over years occur within maybe weeks of each other in the film. For instance, in London it seems as if Gaudier and Sophie Brzeska lived in the Putney Arch studio for most of the period, but they were there only for the last part of Gaudier's life (G, 172).

Ken Russell and the team used the low budget wisely. If Hollywood had made *Savage Messiah* in 1972 (unlikely, but possible in the experimental heyday of the 'New Hollywood'), it would have cost perhaps 4-5 million dollars. There were a lot of speaking parts, many locations and sets, and plenty of extras. And the film being historical would have bumped up the budget further. However, Russell and the team used some of the settings to their advantage: *Savage Messiah* was set not only in early years of the 20th century, but in an artistic bohemia, which was poor (there are scenes of Henri Gaudier and Sophie Brzeska stealing

---

4 M. Dempsey, *Film Heritage*, 9, Winter, 1973.
5 The tactic has been employed in other movies – *Andrei Rublev* (1971) is a good example, with the added bonus of shifting from black-and-white to colour.

vegetables from market stalls, and begging for money, with Brzeska using a doll to stand in for a baby, until a cop uncovers the ruse). Many of the sets, then, didn't need to be pristine, aristocratic worlds,[6] but dusty, grimy streets and grubby lodgings. It was not the Edwardian or pre-war England of *Brideshead Revisited* or *Howard's End* (the E.M. Forster and Evelyn Waugh 'heritage' adaptions of the Eighties), but the world of struggling, starving artists (the scenes in post-Victorian London, with whores lining the streets at night, were the gritty, Dickensian flipside to the glossy, TV commercial visuals of your usual costume drama). There were scenes in upper-class settings, though, such as the Smith-Boyle country house, and the West End art gallery.

Henri Gaudier and Sophie Brzeska spent much of the 1972 picture in a dingy room below pavement level near a railway station, and underneath a railway bridge (all arches, dust, bricks and iron railings; a metal frame bed, stripey pillows without pillow cases; a stove; hardly any furniture). The set, built at Lee International Studios, was meant to be the Putney Arch studio, which Gaudier used at the end of his life (G, 172). And there's a view to the sidewalk above, where *tableaux* are staged, behind the action: a protest march against the war, weaponry (canons) going to war, or soldiers marching accompanied by a brass band[7] – heading for war, or triumphantly returning.

But there were bigger scenes in *Savage Messiah* too, where Henri Gaudier and Sophie Brzeska walk through the streets of Paris or London, or meet on a railroad platform in Dorset, scenes which require extras in costumes, horses and carriages, trains and other vehicles. These scenes helped *Savage Messiah* look ten times its budget of under $750,000. The production was also aided by some hugely talented professionals, such as DP Dick Bush, costume designer Shirley Kingdon, designers George Lack and Derek Jarman, and editors Michael Bradsell and Stuart Baird.

The music was by Michael Garrett, plus selections from Claude Debussy and Alexander Scriabin (from Scriabin's *Divine Poem*, used in the sequence where Sophie Brzeska and Henri Gaudier are sketching and writing together in the park). There was brass band music, embodying the establishment and the

---

6 However, dirty, boho sets can be as costly as shiny, upper-class ones.
7 The martial music of brass and drums expressed the forces of tradition and establishment in the world of *Savage Messiah,* the society against which Henri Gaudier was rebelling.

military machine (as they usually do in a Ken Russell movie).

The more I look at *Savage Messiah*, the more I think it is one of Ken Russell's most accomplished feature films: the casting is spot on (from the two leads through the gallery of grotesques, to supporting players like Helen Mirren, John Justin and Lindsay Kemp, down to the bit parts and extras), as are the performances • the script is superbly put together (tender and poetic when it needs to be, but also literate and historical, and ironic and bitter too) • the look and design is very impressive and wholly convincing and lived-in • the title is great • and the filmmaking is completely confident (flamboyant where necessary, but also restrained and simple too).

Ken Russell acknowledged that *Savage Messiah* was a similar sort of biopic about an artist to his previous ones: it was the artist against society, etc. But Henri Gaudier-Brzeska was quite a different personality from other artists he'd filmed: 'much younger, more revolutionary, more anti-establishment and everything'.[8]

Ken Russell said that *Savage Messiah* was about

> passion and sweat, it was about a poverty-stricken artist who stole a tombstone from a cemetery, sculpted it into a nude and, when the dealer who had commissioned it refused to pay, threw it through the window of his Bond Street gallery. It was about revolution and fuck the art dealers of Bond Street and Madison Avenue and fuck Pinewood and Hollywood, who have never made a proper film on an artist yet! (BP, 81)[9]

Ken Russell's Henri Gaudier-Brzeska was, as one would expect from Russell, the artist-as-outsider, misunderstood, passionate, courted by the *avant garde*, living in Bohemian circles. Henri Gaudier is portrayed as mercurial, intense, tender, physical, driven, and exhausting. And during the film he becomes wilder (a tiring person to be around, one imagines, but also never a dull moment!). Russell enjoyed piling on shock effects and absurd behaviour – his hallmark. For Russell, art is 'simply exploiting to the full one's natural gifts', but it is also 'really bloody hard work, misery, momentary defeat and taking a lot of bloody stick – and giving it' (BP, 220).

As Joseph Gomez pointed out in his study of Ken Russell,

---

[8] In P. Buckley, 1972. When he leaps onto the fountain, he declaims: 'art is dirt. Art is sex, and art is revolution!'
[9] Russell had worked in an art gallery in Bond Street as a youth, so that scene must've been satisfying to shoot.

*Savage Messiah* seemed to be a more personal account of the artist for Russell, a movie in which he poured many of his concerns about art and artists, and turns out to be 'an accurate portrait of both Henri Gaudier-Brzeska and Ken Russell' (G, 167).

There are some terrific scenes in *Savage Messiah*: Ken Russell was at the top of his game: the visit to the stone quarry at Portland, with Sophie and Henri excitedly planning Henri's first exhibition of 1914 (Sophie thrilling at the thought of what she's going to do in the catalogue); Gaudier drawing the tiger in London Zoo; Gaudier sketching a naked 'Gosh' Smith-Boyle in a vast, 18th century country house; the Vorticist dinner; Smith-Boyle's suffragette song and dance at the Vorticist club, Vortex; Gaudier sculpting Major Boyle while the old man rides about on a white horse in his house in full uniform (a caricature of an officer); and the centrepiece, the carving of the marble, female torso overnight.

*Savage Messiah* was a modest movie – not because of the small budget, but the scope of the film, and Uncle Ken's intentions. It was not meant to be a big, sprawling, historical epic about a famous artist like Michelangelo Buonarroti[10] (such as *The Agony and the Ecstasy*, Carol Reed, 1965), or a study in solitude, suffering, alienation and a descent into creative madness, like the many films about Vincent van Gogh.

Dying at age 23 meant that Henri Gaudier-Brzeska never reached artistic maturity; though the filmmakers portrayed him as a volcanic talent, bursting with energy, he still had a long way to go, a long way to develop. Yet, although the ending of the 1972 film was inevitable, with its poignant montage of Gaudier-Brzeska's sculptures and drawings linked to his death in the trenches of World War One, the filmmakers did not play the film as a tragic story of a young man and a young artist who died before his time. There might have been a temptation, as in other artists' biographies, to freight the narrative with portents of the artist's doom. Ken Russell steers clear of hectoring the viewer about the senselessness of war, or piling on the tragedy and melodrama for Sophie and Gaudier's friends, or making political points. Instead, Russell keeps the artist's work centre stage.

---

10 A running gag in *Savage Messiah* has Henri Gaudier expressing his dislike for Michelangelo Buonarroti, but growing to like him. Art critics have found definite influences from Michelangelo in Gaudier-Brzeska's art. Indeed, Michelangelo is the towering presence in all of modern sculpture.

The core of *Savage Messiah*, as Ken Russell saw it, was the scene where Henri Gaudier-Brzeska carves a sculpture all night (after promising to show Lionel Shaw his sculpture). Russell wanted to portray the creative act as an intense but also very physical thing, something that takes great physical effort. It's one of the key scenes in all of Russell's cinema – and more effective, too, than the scenes in *The Music Lovers* of Peter Tchaikovsky at work. Russell has never been better at depicting the artist at work.

> …writing a symphony *is* hard work but you can't convey that by showing the composer writing down a few notes – but if you really want to show the hard work behind a work of art, then a sculpture is your very best subject. I was very conscious of this in the sequence where Gaudier sculpts a statue all through the night. It's the heart, the core of the film, the most important scene to me. (Bax, 221)

Ken Russell was going to have Henri Gaudier-Brzeska carving the female torso to the strains of Ludwig von Beethoven's *Fifth Symphony*, but Christopher Logue, who wrote the script, and Russell's wife Shirley, talked him out of it (Bax, 222). Instead, Gaudier rattles off his philosophy of art as he chips incessantly and restlessly at the block of marble, with the Neo-Classical, female nude appearing gradually. Sophie Brzeska and Angus Corky sleepily listen, fading in and out of sleep as the film cuts back to them. Gaudier works all night, in a whirlwind of creative activity.[11]

Art is mysterious, yes, Henri Gaudier admits, but it's as much a mystery to the artist as to the viewer. And art has to please the artist first, because if it doesn't how can it talk to the observer? Gaudier continues:

> Why anybody else wants to look at the work someone like me does and give good money for it – amazing. Why don't they just do their own? I'm not interested in somebody else's work, unless I can steal from it – unless it gives me something I can use.

The scene is beautifully staged and blocked, with the camera tracking or craning slowly around the block of marble, while dust

---

[11] The scene may have some basis in fact: according to his friend Horace Brodzky, one time Henri Gaudier stayed up all night and talked to him while chipping away at a stone (H. Brodzky, 50f). And Frank Harris recalled that Gaudier worked all day and night after Jacob Epstein had promised to visit Gaudier to see his work (E. Pound, 76).

and pieces of stone fly off (presumably the camera crew wore goggles – there's a later scene where you can see actor Scott Anthony dodging the pieces of flying stone as he chisels away). Ken Russell said in 1972 that he attracted to Henri Gaudier because

> one recognizes in him what one hopes one might aspire to oneself. He had marvellous things to say about art, very simple, straightforward things, and he knew he was good.[12]

Scott Anthony plays Henri Gaudier-Brzeska with a winning enthusiasm that often erupts in wild, physical activity. His is an artist who seldom keeps still for long, whose youthful exuberance continually threatens to disrupt whatever situation he finds himself in. Anthony turns in some very physical acting – leaping onto tables, rushing up and down stairs, getting thrown out of museums, jumping over beds, and so on.

The out-size and unstoppable physicality is introduced in the early scene where Henri Gaudier leaps onto the fountains and statues outside the Parisian library (St Genevieve Library) where he meets Sophie (20 years his senior).[13] The last thing Anthony's, Logue's and Russell's Gaudier is is staid and restrained. Russell turns the artist into something like a dancer or a circus performer, someone who won't walk across a room if he can run or jump. It's a little over-the-top, if the viewer mistakenly slips into reading *Savage Messiah* as 'realistic' or literal. It isn't. Russell's films aren't. *Savage Messiah* is Russell's *Singin' In the Rain*, in a way, with Anthony reminding me of Gene Kelly.[14]

Dorothy Tutin played the frustrated, neurotic writer Sophie Brzeska (1873-1925), the older woman with whom Henri Gaudier became involved (their relationship in the 1972 picture is portrayed as affectionate, tempestuous at times, but non-sexual. They live together as brother and sister).[15] She wants to be a writer, but faces reality and takes jobs as a nanny[16] (the film is more sympathetic than many movies about artists-as-lovers, where the woman's artistic pursuits are regarded as secondary to the man's –

---

12 Quoted in P. Buckley, 13.
13 Sophie Brzeska was writing a book, *Truth: A Novel of the Spirit.*
14 In H.S. Ede's study of Henri Gaudier, the artist is much feebler, skinny, neurotic, depressed, weepy and often ill.
15 According to biographer H.S. Ede, Brzeska and Gaudier may have had sex once or twice, but in the main co-habited.
16 In Dodford, Frowlesworth and Felixstowe.

the situation would crop up again in *Mahler* and *Gothic*). Tutin makes Brzeska a totally believable person who wants to write and have people read her books, but who faces up to the reality that she has to work and provide money and food. The two artists encourage each other, but it's Gaudier who finds success first.[17]

Dorothy Tutin (1930-2001), more known as a stage actress,[18] was not Ken Russell's first choice: he wanted Jeanne Moreau, darling of the European New Wave (that could've been amazing – Moreau would've added the glam, the enigma, the star quality. It might have been more difficult for the audience to believe that the Gaudier—Brzeska relationship *wasn't* sexual, though, had Moreau played Sophie Brzeska. It would be assumed from the get-go that Moreau's Brzeska was automatically bedding Gaudier).

But Dorothy Tutin is terrific. A very different actor from Jeanne Moreau,[19] her relationship with Scott Anthony's Henri Gaudier is touching. Similarly, Anthony was not Ken Russell's preferred choice for Gaudier: he was after John McEnery (but McEnery looked too old – Gaudier died at 23, killed in action on June 5, 1915, in an attack at Neuville St Vast).

Dorothy Tutin and Scott Anthony make for one of cinema's odd couples, and they work well together. She calls him 'boy'; he calls her 'Mamalushka'. It's certainly one of the tenderer, more emotional couples in Ken Russell's cinema.[20] Even if they weren't the first choices, Tutin and Anthony make the roles their own, completely, and it's impossible to imagine *Savage Messiah* with other actors.

They embody, as the script wants them to, youth and middle-age, idealism and realism, art and life, sex and restraint. The movie exalts Henri Gaudier's art but not always Gaudier himself – it draws attentions to his flaws as well as his talent and idealism and creativity and sense of fun. For instance, Gaudier is portrayed as somewhat selfish and insensitive, and also so energetic and idealistic it wears out the people around him. Some are upset by

---

17 And it's true that Sophie Brzeska's writing does take second place to Henri Gaudier's sculpture.

18 There's a previous link with Ken Russell – Dorothy Tutin had appeared in *The Devils* as Sister Jeanne in a 1961 production in Stratford. In *An Appalling Talent*, Tutin said: 'when I saw the Delius and Isadora Duncan films I *longed* to work for him' (Bax, 194).

19 In one scene, Sophie eats monkey nuts non-stop, which you can't imagine Jeanne Moreau doing!

20 *Savage Messiah* was for Russell, 'the story of two people in a room'. Which is of course the basic unit of all drama, and all movies, really.

his crudity in social situations (like the art snobs and avant gardists), and some find him simply exhausting (as Brzeska and Corky do many times).

As a character in love with life, though, Henri Gaudier as portrayed by Scott Anthony is wholly convincing. The sheer energy of his performance is among the best in all of Russell's cinema. And as a portrayal of an artist as a life-force, *Savage Messiah* is stunning.

There are typical Ken Russellian scenes in *Savage Messiah* of artists at work, depicted in short montages: Henri Gaudier's sketching ducks in a park, while Sophie writes (and later scenes when she watches him as he works). The early montages fuse art with love, as the couple move closer, hands entwined, and kissing.[21] Another art-making montage occurs in a zoo, with Gaudier sketching the animals, accompanied by a choral cue (animals were popular subjects in the art of the time, and there's a famous poem by Rainer Maria Rilke about a panther in a cage, padding around the cell in the Jardine des Plantes in gay Paree:

> Sein Blick ist vom Vorübergehn der Stäbe
> so mid geworden, daß er nichts mehr hält.
> Ihm ist, als ob es tausend Stäbe gäbe
> und hinter tausend Stäben keine Welt.[22]

Henri Gaudier-Brzeska possibly produced fakes, when he was in Munich, of paintings by Rembrandt van Rijn (in the movie Sophie Brzeska spies Gaudier faking a Jean Honoré Fragonard work at the Lartique Gallery).

The Vorticist dinner in *Savage Mesiah* is brilliantly done, delivering a series of eccentric performances which stay just this side of outrageous. The scene looks as if the actors were encouraged to add any silly, eccentric business they fancied (Ken Russell has always been indulgent towards extravagant acting, but it pays off well in his scene of the modernist *avant garde*). Instead of depicting real people from the time – the Ezra Pounds, John Middleton Murrys, Katherine Mansfields and Wyndham Lewises

---

[21] Close-ups of hands are one of the visual motifs in *Savage Messiah,* as Joseph Gomez remarked: hands chiselling at stone, hands sketching or writing, chopping vegetables, fluttering in a new dance, holding hands, Shaw squeezing grapes, and a drawing by Henri Gaudier of a hand over the opening titles (G, 179).

[22] 'His gaze, going past those bars, has got so misted with tiredness, it can take in nothing more. He feels as though a thousand bars existed, and no more world beyond them than before' (R.M. Rilke, *New Poems*, Hogarth Press, 1963).

– *Savage Messiah* opts for broad caricatures of poseurs and dilettantes (all of them are depicted as impotent and uncreative, compared to the full-of-life Gaudier-Brzeskas).[23]

As well as the Vorticists, Henri Gaudier-Brzeska also met Katherine Mansfield and John Middleton Murry (two of D.H. Lawrence's best friends), Lovat Fraser, and Enid Bagnold. However, the friendship between Gaudier-Brzeska and Murry and Mansfield ended badly; Mansfield found Sophie repulsive (G, 169). Gaudier-Brzeska also met well-known figures on the literary and intellectual scene such as Roger Fry, Ezra Pound, Jacob Epstein, Frank Harris, Horace Brodzky and Wyndham Lewis.

The positive atmosphere the production enjoyed as it was made (one of Ken Russell's happiest) rubs off on screen: you can see Scott Anthony really throwing himself into his first leading role, and trying anything the director asks him to do; and set designers and dressers George Lack, Ian Whittaker, Christopher Hobbs and Derek Jarman looked like they had a good time building settings like the consciously anachronistic Vorticist club, and recreating the moments when Henri Gaudier's art was produced. You can't always tell if a film was made in good or difficult circumstances, but with some movies the good feelings seep through the celluloid, as in *Savage Messiah*.

In the background of *Savage Messiah*, which is essentially about Henri Gaudier and the writer Sophie Brzeska, are some fine British character actors: Peter Vaughan as a Louvre museum attendant, Michael Gogh as Gaudier's sombre, distanced father, John Justin as the pompous, pretentious, foppish gallery owner Lionel Shaw,[24] Robert Lang as the stuffy, very old school, military man Major Boyle, Judith Paris, catty and sleek in a Pre-Raphaelite wig, and ultra-camp Lindsay Kemp as art dealer Angus Corky.[25] Helen Mirren was luscious as a young suffragette 'Gosh' Smith-Boyle.[26]

---

[23] As Joseph Gomez notes, Mavis Coldstream might be Enid Bagnold, Thomas Buff might be Middleton Murry, and Kate might be Katherine Mansfield (G, 173).
[24] John Justin, one of Ken Russell's regular actors, was the lead in a movie revered by numerous contemporary filmmakers, including Francis Coppola and Steven Spielberg: *The Thief of Baghdad* (1940). Shaw was based on Roger Fry, one of the key figures in the art scene of the period.
[25] Corky was, according to Joseph Gomez, a character mixing elements of Horace Brodzky and Haldane Mcfall (G, 173).
[26] Mirren played one scene, as Gaudier's model, while he sketches her, nude except for a necklace and Vorticist slippers – Mirren had suggested it would be sexier to be nude but wearing stockings. But they were left out: the effect was sexy, but the camera crew voted the other way.

The introduction of 'Gosh' Smith-Boyle was another comic set-piece: she chucks a petrol bomb at a mail box and cries 'votes for women!' to the crowd that's gathered (inevitably, Henri Gaudier joins in – he can't resist any moment to create a bit of noise).[27] Smith-Boyle's sent up, as Joseph Gomez rightly points out, not because she's a feminist, but because she's a 'shallow, spoiled fool with silly illusions of grandeur' (G, 176).

Helen Mirren offers some delectable nudity in the scene shot in another country house, where Henri Gaudier has arrived to sculpt 'Gosh' Smith-Boyle's father, the Major[28] (in the film, Gaudier's relationship with Smith-Boyle is that of artist and model, at least at first, but doesn't depict their lovemaking – except in the unusual and bitter scene where Smith-Boyle is horsing about with Gaudier on a bed, lying on top of him, while Sophie Brzeska scrubs the steps and sings. It's over-the-top: emotionally true but dramatically greatly exaggerated. But Sophie, after this scene, wants to leave).

'Gosh' Smith-Boyle was based on a woman that Henri Gaudier knew (she modelled for him). According to Jim Ede, she went to Paris and returned with crazy tales of dancing naked:

> greatly to the delight of the artists; how Isadora Duncan had wanted to meet her, and how several theatres had offered to engage her. Also Modigliani had wanted to sleep with her, but she had refused because he drank and had no money. (150)

I wonder if the scene in the Musée de Louvre, where Henri Gaudier, in his Gene Kelly, physical, visionary mode, climbs atop an Easter Island statue, was a nod to the scene in *Bande à Part*, where Anna Karina and co. run through the Louvre (which's also inspired other movies, such as *Pulp Fiction* and *The Dreamers*).

The people around Henri Gaudier treat him like a precocious child at times, and indulge him. On the Easter Island head, Gaudier declaims: 'art is alive. Enjoy it. Laugh at it. Love it or hate it, but don't worship it. You're not in church'.

In his letters, Henri Gaudier-Brzeska expressed his love of a beautiful man that he saw, a Hindu in Kew Gardens, which correlates to the dialogue in the movie that sometimes he thinks

---

[27] The narrative structure of *Savage Messiah* was a little false at the point where Sophie handily exits the film for Dorset so that Henri Gaudier can encounter 'Gosh' Smith-Boyle.

[28] There is some blether about art and war, and Gaudier humours the old coot.

men are more beautiful than women:

> He walked like a tiger, proud and haughty, with eyes that flashed like steel. I think he was the most lovely man I have ever seen, the sight of him made me wild with pleasure; and would you believe it, the English, with their hideous mugs, laughed like idiots as he went by. In this country, it's a kind of crime to be beautiful. (In H. Ede, 61)

Ken Russell would definitely go along with that view, especially the notion that in Britain being beautiful is seen as a crime. And I'm sure that anyone who likes beautiful bodies and forms can see that it doesn't make any difference about the gender of the seer or the seen.[29]

The set-piece in Vortex, the Vorticist club,[30] is typical Ken Russell – as stylized as it comes. It's art history as performance art. Helen Mirren's 'Gosh' Smith-Boyle appears on stage to cut up a framed copy of Francisco de Goya's *Reclining Maya* (1801), the *naked* version, *of course* (based on a real incident in the National Gallery, London, when a feminist attacked the painting). Smith-Boyle then sings about getting women the vote (one assumes that Mirren is acting singing badly, and can really sing). And Henri Gaudier has a song, too, of course (a crude one, naturally – Russell likes folk songs and street songs, and includes them in quite a few pictures). Smith-Boyle and Gaudier indulge in some silly stage antics, and Gaudier persuades Smith-Boyle to start undressing. So they are thrown out of the club (and Gaudier's exit line – 'damn, I've thought of a better one' – is great).

The Portland, Dorset sequence veers from the contrived (the landladies at the lodging houses turning away Sophie and Henri, presumably because 'they be foreign', as the locals might say in Darrset), to the wild: Henri Gaudier is Fred Astaire, barefoot, leaping from stone to stone and climbing up a crane while declaiming about the exhibition he's going to have (including the customary Russellian worship of the sun). The scene shifts from the stones to using the sea as a background (when Sophie Brzeska realizes how beautiful it is there). DP Dick Bush covers part of the scene with a lengthy take.

The lovemaking in the workman's hut comes to nothing in the second part of the Portland sequence, as Sophie turns away

---

[29] I remember seeing a gorgeous, young, Latino guy walking along Broadway with the grace of a dancer recently who was breathtakingly fabulous to look at.
[30] Partly based on gatherings at the Cafe Royal.

from Henri. The 1972 movie employs the classic device of indicating the emotional separation of the couple when Gaudier moves into the distance, walking away from Sophie by the hut. (That scene was rustled up at the last minute, and was shot as the light was failing. Ken Russell asked writer Christopher Logue for some dialogue on the spur of the moment; Logue was taken aback, and couldn't come up with something, according to Russell).

Sex is another battleground in *Savage Messiah* in the tense, troubled relationship between Henri Gaudier and Sophie Brzeska (it's one of those relationships where they split up and get back together a few times).[31] The film has Gaudier eager for sex, and Brzeska repulsing him (i.e., it's age-old story of men and women). When desire becomes too much for Brzeska, they quarrel, and Gaudier visits a prostitute (played by Maggie Maxwell, who reprised a similar role in *Valentino*), whom he also sketches in the nude (in the 1972 movie, the fact that Gaudier draws the whore is much more significant than having sex with her). Like Gaudier's erotic dalliance with 'Gosh' Smith-Boyle, Brzeska is deeply upset by Gaudier's other relationships.[32]

As in a Thomas Hardy novel, the lovers promise to marry, but never get round to it (Sophie Brzeska is more reluctant than Henri Gaudier). *Savage Messiah* closes the sexual relationship between Gaudier and Brzeska in a classic melodramatic manner, with Gaudier calling up to Brzeska outside her bedroom (she has moved out nearby), but walking away before she can talk to him. It's the last contact they have in the film (apart from letters).

*

*Savage Messiah* is a tightly-plotted, impressively-structured screenplay:[33] it doesn't simply whisk Henri Gaudier off to the First World War, for instance. Although it is only 100 minutes long, there is time in this British movie for Gaudier to express his anti-war sentiments, and his reluctance to join up (he makes fun of 'Gosh' Smith-Boyle when she turns up and shows him the bag

---

[31] For Joseph Lanza, Brzeska and Gaudier are 'so highly strung, insecure, angry and obnoxious that all the drama at least stays fevered, even if the two characters end up being not all that sympathetic' (PF, 136). Maybe I know too many people like this, but Gaudier and Brzeska don't strike me as too neurotic or angry, but they are certainly irritating at times.

[32] Yet Brzeska and Gaudier are presented as soul-mates: as Joseph Gomez pointed out, they are filmed in the same shot so often Gaudier comes to be associated with the right side of the frame and Brzeska with the left (G, 177).

[33] Among the scenes dropped from *Savage Messiah* was a fierce argument between the couple, and a cameo by Russell.

she's made to go with her uniform – war is that superficial to her at that point. Again, it's a theatrical presentation, with a procession of soldiers and guns under the bridge right next to the actors).

Henri Gaudier is the liberal, revolutionary artist who would rather stay at home and contribute to the war and to society in his own way. His art is important, he says, as he chips away at the giant, stone sculpture he never finishes. Those scenes where Gaudier is resisting the call to war and refusing to be swept along with everyone else with the excitement of going to war make his eventual decision to sign up even more moving.

One of the great montages in Ken Russell's cinema occurs in the build-up to and revelation of Henri Gaudier's death. It takes place in the Vorticist club, with a show in progress involving dancers (naturally), including Susanna East (as Pippa) in silver make-up, and a conversation at a table between Angus Corky, Lionel Shaw and Thomas Buff. Corky is reading aloud some of Gaudier's letters from the Front.

The montage orchestrates the dialogue, the music (with cuts on the piano glissandos), the dancers (and Pippa in close-up), and photographs of Henri Gaudier surrounded by soldiers. It's one of Ken Russell's familiar, ironic montages, combining the frivolous and the tragic. At this point, it might have been tempting to include much more of Gaudier's letters, or even scenes in the trenches, which Russell has done before, but there is just enough to give an impression of the artist in a war zone, and how he has fashioned a sculpture from the butt of a rifle. Shaw and Buff pour scorn on Gaudier's sentiments, and Shaw cynically notes that his sculpture would be 'a saleable item' (an obscene remark in the light of Gaudier being in the war, under fire, but fully in tune with Russell's contempt for commercialism).

*Savage Messiah*'s montage, aided by the music and increasingly rapid cutting, reaches a climax as Angus Corky informs Lionel Shaw and Thomas Buff that Henri Gaudier has died. At that point, there's a smash cut to a close-up of a stricken, tearful Sophie Brzeska, and a sudden switch in the music to something highly emotional, fitting the drama.

And this montage, folks, is one of many reasons why Ken Russell is an absolutely stupendous filmmaker.

*Savage Messiah* closed with a montage of Henri Gaudier-Brzeska's works, shot at the Vorticist exhibition (in 1915), intercut with close-ups of Sophie Brzeska reacting to the news of Gaudier's death, black-and-white photographs of Gaudier in the trenches, and accompanied by classical music.

*Savage Messiah*'s ending was typical of Ken Russell's cinema: a montage not with dialogue (everything has already been said), but with music, of BBC *Monitor*-style documentary footage of close-ups of the artist's works and photographs of the artist combined with the melodrama of his death and the reaction of his lover. It's the cinematic form that Russell loves best: when he's done the narrative work of exposition, and building characters and situations, and is now free to take the basic elements – the faces and images of the film up to that point – and edit them into a montage to music.

(After Henri Gaudier-Brzeska's death, Sophie Brzeska fell into melancholy for a time, and sometimes blamed herself for Gaudier-Brzeska's passing – she thought her last letter to him, in which she again refused his offer of marriage, 'had perhaps driven him into danger' (H. Ede, 160). Brzeska lived in London for seven years, until she was taken to Gloucestershire Asylum, so much like a Ken Russell character, dying 3 years later in 1925. Yet Russell doesn't refer to Brzeska's fate after Gaudier's death at all. That close-up of her weeping is enough.)

§

Let's compare *Savage Messiah* with another biopic of a modern, European sculptor: *Camille Claudel* (Bruno Nuytten, 1988), about Camille Claudel and Auguste Rodin. It's the same era, the same European, modernist *milieu*, the same sorts of examinations of art and creativity and the role of the artist in contemporary society (Henri Gaudier-Brzeska lived in Paris for a time, and was influenced by Rodin).

But *Savage Messiah* is a far superior movie: yes, *Camille Claudel* does feature two of the biggest French stars of recent times – Gérard Depardieu and Isabelle Adjani (Adjani is impossibly gorgeous to look at),[34] and it has a budget twenty zillion francs bigger than *Savage Messiah*, but it is soooo long, soooo obvious, soooo superficial, and is utterly ruined by completely inappropriate orchestral music.

Worst of all, *Camille Claudel* takes itself so fucking seriously! You yearn for some *humour*, some *irreverence*, some light-hearted-

---

[34] She was also nominated for an Oscar – it's a classic 'gimme the Oscar' performance. Adjani's always watchable, but even her talents couldn't save this movie.

ness to alleviate the string-music-smothered gloom. As Ken Russell has shown, repeatedly, you don't have to be po-faced and serious all the time. Now, I love French historical movies – I think they make 'em better than just about anybody apart from the Chinese film industry. And *Camille Claudel* has a luscious, lived-in *mise-en-scène*. But what a waste of 300,000,000,000 francs.

For Joseph Lanza, Ken Russell took a too pious, too reverential approach to Henri Gaudier and his art (which apparently Derek Jarman found uncomfortable [PF, 136, 138f). I don't agree. It's true that *Savage Messiah* enhances Gaudier's naïve, idealistic youth – but you also have to remember that this is about a young man who's in his late teens at the start of the 1972 movie, and Sophie Brzeska I think contributes plenty of cynicism and bitterness and irony to counter-balance Gaudier's irrepressible energy and revolutionary ideals.

Pauline Kael griped about *Savage Messiah* that it contained no truth at all, and its exaggerations were of nothing the viewer could recognize:

> we no longer know what world we're in. That's why, at a certain point in a Ken Russell movie, I always says to myself, "The man is mad." But it's why those who adore his movies say, "He's a genius." (1972)

Ken Russell was being far too tough on himself I think when he remarked that *Savage Messiah* was 'although worthy, wasn't cinematic enough. I leant too heavily on the script; it could have been a radio play' (PF, 141). Ah, if only all radio plays were as cinematic as this!

# 12

# *MAHLER*

> When one is trying to compose music, one mustn't try to paint, write poetry, or present descriptions. But *what* one puts into music, all the same, is the entire (feeling, thinking, breathing, suffering) human being. There can be no particular objection to a 'programme' (even if it is not exactly the highest rung of the ladder) – but it is a *composer* who has to express himself in it, not a writer, philosophy or painter – all of whom are included in the composer.
>
> Gustav Mahler, letter to Bruno Walter (1906)[35]

*Mahler* (1974) was a biopic about Gustav Mahler (July 7, 1860 - May 18, 1911), which Ken Russell had been planning since 1970.[36] Mahler moved from growing up in a small, provincial town (Olmitz) to the centres of the classical music world (Kassel, Leipzig, Budapest, Munich, Hamburg and Prague). He worked for many years as a conductor (where the real money was), and headed the Vienna State Opera between 1897 and 1907. He also spent time in New York City (from 1908), as principal conductor at the Met (which the film only alluded to in the dialogue, but didn't use as a setting).[37]

*Mahler* starred Robert Powell and Georgina Hale – and these

---
[35] G. Mahler, in H. Gal, 380.
[36] Joseph Gomez has pointed out some of the affinities between Russell and Gustav Mahler, such as converting to Roman Catholicism, or an outsider status, on the cultural map, assimilating influences from many sources (184), which Kurt Blaukopf called 'synthesis' (K. Blaukopf, *Gustav Mahler*, Praeger, New York, 1973, 104.)
[37] Gotham can be simulated in England, of course, but it's cheaper to refer to it in dialogue rather than recreate it, or go there.

were star roles for both of them, not only for Powell: Alma Mahler-Werfel was far more than the dutiful wife and mother of the composer's children. Both Powell and Hale are outstanding: *Mahler* simply wouldn't work with the wrong actors in these parts. Both Powell and Hale throw themselves into the drama, which's the best way to perform in a Ken Russell movie. No good holding back, no good being too technical or analytical: the instinctive, intuitive approach is best.[38] Acting in A Ken Russell Movie is a physical and visceral experience.

*Mahler* looks amazing, considering its tiny budget (Ken Russell said it cost some £168,000 ($268,000) [BP, 144]). $268,000! How does Russell do it?! And for a historical movie! It's remarkable. (The average movie budget in the West in the mid-1970s was $4 million).

*Mahler* was originally set up with German backers,[39] who abandoned the show at the last minute; David Puttnam was instrumental, Russell recalled, in keeping the movie afloat, and transferring the production from Bavaria to England (BP, 144).[40]

*Mahler* was shot in 9 weeks. However, the lack of production value showed at times: in the train journey, for example: the landscape outside the windows and the cosy, little stations the train passes through do not look very Middle European; and there is the low budget film's dearth of big city shots, streets, and crowd scenes. *Mahler* was filmed in the Lake District (Lake Derwentwater, Borrowdale, Keswick), in Kent and Sussex, and Black Park Country Park near Pinewood Studios (yet again).

It was unusual for so much a film to take place on a real train – many productions would opt to stay in the studio for much of that, with second unit or selective scenes shot on a real train. Maybe it was due to the budget.

---

38 Like many an artist, Ken Russell didn't always like to analyze himself too closely, or his films, or his motives or choices. he preferred to keep all that stuff unexamined (Bax, 198). 'I just make them' (RC, 250). Of course, they have to do a number of things: they had to be cinematic, they had to flow, and they had to communicate (ibid.).
39 There was a longer gap between *Savage Messiah* and *Mahler*, partly because of projects which failed to get off the ground, and scripts that were abandoned (according to Joseph Gomez).
40 The production required the 'yes' from Gustav Mahler's daughter, Anna Glucki Mahler, which she had declined at first. (One can imagine that sons and daughters of famous artists are going to be a little wary of Ken Russell taking a run at their parents – because his movies tend to be sensational, and warts 'n' all!).

Yet again in Ken Russell movie, this was a British train[41] done up to look Middle European: the quaint railway stations, for instance, with their white-painted roofs and metal railings and Victorian windows, are instantly recognizable to Brits.[42]

In *Mahler*, Ken Russell and his team may only have $268,000 to play around with, but it doesn't matter a jot, really, because the filmmakers are really enjoying themselves (or the director is, at least – it's often that way). Russell was clearly inspired making *Mahler*, and if even that small budget had been cut in half he would still have delivered something inspirational. (Credit is due to producer Roy Baird, DP Dick Bush, production designer John Comfort, art director Ian Whittaker, costume designer Shirley Kingdon, choreographer Gillian Gregory, and editor Michael Bradsell, among others, for making *Mahler* such a great film).

Ken Russell again indulged his love of classical music, *mittel* Europe of the late 19th century, flamboyant acting styles, 'bad taste', and excess in imagery, spectacle, and rhetoric.[43] *Mahler* is a little gem in Russell's cinema – not nearly as well-known as the controversial films like *The Devils* or the D.H. Lawrence adaptions, but it deserves to be. It's not as frantic or hysterical as *The Music Lovers*, doesn't have the starrier casts of his bigger pictures, but it manages to foreground Gustav Mahler's music in a very impressive way (the music was played by the Concertgebouw Orchestra of Amsterdam, and conducted by Bernard Haitink; Russell regular John Forsythe was music co-ordinator). Once again, Russell and his production team have found methods of re-presenting familiar pieces of music and rejuvenating them. No doubt some of *Mahler* is too over-the-top and too in-your-face for some classical music lovers. And 'The Convert' fantasy sequence, with its camp send-up of the symbolism of Catholicism and Judaism, is bound to offend some viewers.

For me, *Mahler* is not only very enjoyable and entertaining, it's one of Ken Russell's more modest films which achieves its goals, which makes it more successful, in its own small-scale way, than some of the bigger films. One of the great Gustav Mahler conductors, Klaus Tinstead, told Ken Russell that his movie was

---

[41] The railway employed was the Bluebell Railway in Kent and Sussex, which you can still visit – a classic piece of olde worlde Englande. (Russell used it at other times).
[42] Ollie Reed has a cameo as a railway conductor.
[43] Joseph Gomez points out that *Mahler* is not meant to be a literal portrayal of the composer's life. And it shouldn't be judged on those grounds (185).

the best he'd seen about a composer (RC, 246). In the picture, Mahler tells the news reporter Krenek: 'I conduct to live, I live to compose'.

❉

Once again, a Ken Russell picture foregrounds *music*, and the amount of music played during *Mahler* is one of the most impressive aspects about it. And the quality of it: *Mahler* reminds the viewer once again of the beauty and power of classical music, and Gustav Mahler's music. If nothing else, *Mahler* is a compendium of great music, and on that level it is very successful. Once again, Russell tells his audience, OK folks, we're going to listen to some terrific music. And sometimes the visuals, affecting though they are, are very much secondary to the music. For Russell, the film was shaped by Mahler's music.

*Mahler* continued Ken Russell's aim of illustrating aspects of a composer's music by using their life (not necessarily a biopic in the traditional sense). Thus, moments from Gustav Mahler's childhood, young adulthood, his marriage, his family, and so on, were set to his music.

When he took up the *Mahler* project, just about his favourite composer (with Edward Elgar), Ken Russell said he 'searched for the soul of the man in his music' (BP, 141). That tells us everything you need to know in viewing this movie. Russell wrote that he found in Gustav Mahler's music 'the sound and fury of a tormented artist', and

> music that was brutal, vulgar, grotesque, macabre – and [I] was inevitably pilloried for reflecting these elements in the film. I found joy, poetry and magic too and included them as well. (BP, 141)

In Ken Russell's conception, Gustav Mahler is no straightforward personality. The 1974 British film portrays him as creative but also selfish, mercurial and moody, tender but also downright difficult. Russell and his adaptors have never held back from pointing out the flaws in the artists they present in their films and TV documentaries. They never whitewash them, never sit back and coo and gawp at the artists' genius.

Thus, *Mahler* draws out the excess in the maestro's music, how he would include 'low-brow' or 'populist' elements, such as folk songs, as well as self-consciously 'high art' elements.

The structure of the narrative was seemingly simple: on a

train journey in the film's present tense (near the end of Gustav Mahler's life), the composer remembers aspects of his life. Ken Russell explained that *Mahler* was structured as a flashback film;, and compared the format of *Mahler* to a *rondo* musical form: A-B-A-C-A-D: original theme-new material-original theme-new material (DF, 98). Love was the recurring theme, the 'A' theme, Russell explained: 'the love of Mahler for his wife'. Meanwhile, the variations, B, C, D, etc, were variations on death (such as the death of innocence or the death of trust). The most significant variation was the death of love, embodied in the funeral and crematorium sequence.[44]

As well as flashbacks, there were fantasy sequences, and dream sequences, constituting the film's project of manifesting an individual's inner life. It was a more thematic or emotional structure, however, not a chronological one. Although the lengthy section concerning Gustav Mahler's troubled youth was placed in the first third of the movie, the other flashbacks moved around the composer's life (thus, it isn't a 'simple' narrative structure at all!).

The working screenplay was also more conventional structurally and less metaphorical. The earlier versions of the *Mahler* script had Alma's lover Max based only on Walter Gropius, not a soldier. The character of the princess was altered: in the early script, she was a 'somewhat foolish bohemian blue-stocking' (G, 189).

Ken Russell also intensified the allegorical and political aspects of *Mahler* from his earlier script – for instance, he changed the pall-bearers in the funeral sequence from being Alma Mahler-Werfel's future lovers, who were also Austrian soldiers, to being members of the S.S.[45]

❃

*Mahler* opens in classic Ken Russell style: a wooden summerhouse beside a lake bursts into flame. Doesn't matter what it *means*, or how it plays into the rest of the film, it's simply a strong opening image. And right after that, there's a brief montage of later moments from the movie (and the main title), followed by a lithe, young, human form clambering and clawing its way out of a white cocoon, then crawling over to a stone bust of Gustav

---

44 K. Russell, "Mahler the Man", 1974.
45 Nationalism and the military is an important ingredient of each version of *Mahler*.

Mahler and caressing it (only a little later is it revealed that the naked cocoon-woman was Alma Mahler-Werfel: it's Alma's rebirth into life following Mahler's death. The movement of Georgina Hale is choreographed to the music in the style of Isadora Duncan; that is, consciously stylized in a modernist, theatrical manner, which Russell has employed many times).

Among the vignettes that *Mahler* delivered about the Viennese composer's childhood were evocations of a rather anxious, tricky childhood: his father Bernhard (Lee Montague) is a well-worn, tired-out, old stereotype: a lazy, drunken, aggressive and violent man who tups the family servant Bertha (upsetting poor, sensitive, young Gustav, who bursts into tears, framed in a shot which superimposes a phallic spike in focus over Mahler's face). It's the primal scene, of course, which also disturbs the young Tommy in *Tommy*.

Gustav Mahler's family is also rather stereotypically rendered (it's not one of the great portrayals of Jewish working-class life in cinema, and it does trot out plenty of clichés concerning a Jewish meal time,[46] which could be viewed as vaguely anti-semitic, like some of Ken Russell's other depictions of Jews and Jewish culture). There's the strained, caring mother, Marie (Rosalie Crutchley), the easily impressed and ditzy Aunt Rosa (Miriam Karlin), the all-wise, pontificating grandfather (Arnold Yarrow), and so on. Meanwhile, Mahler senior is interested only in paying to train his son to become a concert pianist, so they'll be rich (even if he's half as good as Franz Liszt, he opines, they'll make lots of dough). It's Wolfgang Amadeus Mozart[47] and his father all over again (and it's bound to end in tears – which it does).

The vignette of the piano lessons depicts a teacher, Professor Sladky (Otto Diamant), who prods Gustav Mahler with a violin bow and demands that he learn scales instead of trying out his own compositions (which he derides, like Nicholas Rubenstein with Peter Tchaikovsky in *The Music Lovers*). The bullying music teacher is yet another cliché – the scenes are necessary, dramatically, but a bit of a bore to watch.

Turns out that this is another movie where a gifted, young artist is a skinny outsider figure who's bullied by authority

---

46 At times the *Mahler* childhood scenes come across as a dour *Fiddler On the Roof*, but without larger-than-life Topol singing gutsily through them.
47 Gustav Mahler's dad tells him there's no money in composing – playing piano at concerts is where the lucre is.

figures, such as a father and a teacher. We've been here countless times before, and this isn't the most revealing portrayal of such a scenario. It's also true that Ken Russell the image-maker can't quite find really good images to illustrate the drama.

Until, that is, the young, rather hapless, rather weedy, rather neurotic Gustav Mahler finds solace in the natural world (a recurring theme in Ken Russell's cinema), and encounters a wandering musician, Old Nick (Ronald Pickup) who's more of a shamanic inspirer figure than a real person (he plays a concertina, for instance, in a self-consciously sentimenalized fashion – the songs are 'Ach, du Lieber Augustin' and 'Frère Jacques').

The encounter with Old Nick is set by the lakes yet again (Ken Russell told the story of how his young actor, Gary Rich, had insisted that he could swim, but when it came to do the scene where Gustav Mahler tries to swim out to a boat, Rich couldn't manage it. But they did get some good drowning footage). Later, Old Nick teaches Mahler to swim.

After that scene, which depicts young Gustav Mahler as an outsider teased by the neighbourhood kids, there is a classic Ken Russell scene of the wandering musician pointing out the wonders of nature to Mahler (telling him he can't be a great composer unless he knows about nature, framed in a magic hour, two-shot tracking shot near the lake). Is there any British filmmaker who has infused their work so diligently and enthusiastically with pantheism, with a love of nature? Michael Powell, maybe, but very few others, and no one like Ken Russell.[48]

The nature poetry scenes continue with Gustav Mahler once again in the woods, covered with slow, lateral tracking shots through silver birches and pines. The shot of Mahler throwing stones into the water is particularly beautiful – classic magic hour photography (by Dick Bush), with the camera filming through the trees with a long lens, and the figure silhouetted against the blue and silver water (a reprise of a similar image in *Women In Love*).

There are inserts of stock footage of foxes, owls, hedgehogs, birds and the like. And images of clouds, lakes and forests. It's not meant to be realistic at all, but a distillation of the feeling of childhood, as the adult Gustav Mahler remembers back to his younger days. Looking at it yet again, it isn't wholly convincing, and that's partly due to the child actor, who simply can't convey

---

[48] The creepy aspects of a man horsing around with near-naked young boys is not addressed.

the complexity of emotion necessary, or even simply the wonder of being in the natural world.[49] I guess you either buy this kind of Disneyesque stuff or you don't.

A little of the spirit of D.H. Lawrence rears its head here, in the form of a large, white horse.[50] It startles the pint-size Gustav Mahler at first, but soon he's riding off on it ('the little bugger couldn't ride a horse either', Ken Russell commented of Gary Rich, 'so we tied him to the saddle and whipped the stallion into a gallop – only kidding! HONEST!' [DF, 64]).[51]

Many of the elements of Gustav Mahler's childhood were taken directly from *The Awakening* by Isaac Babel, such as the dinner table scene, Mahler hiding in the toilet, Mahler meeting Sladky, and Old Nick. Meanwhile, the conflict between Mahler and his father over the music scholarship comes from Babel's short story *The Story of My Dovecot*.

Ken Russell justified using the Isaac Babel material because Babel's childhood was 'a lot closer to Gustav Mahler than anything I could have dreamed up – they seem uncannily similar' (G, 193). It came about partly because Russell likes to use elements from his films that don't get made – thus, he re-used aspects of his scripts of *The Angels* and *Music, Music, Music* in *Tommy*, and in *Mahler* he employed the Babel stories because he was going to adapt Babel for the Beeb in the period before making *Mahler*.[52]

One of the outstanding montage sequences – one of the finest in Ken Russell's cinema – occurred at the beginning of *Mahler*, a brilliant illustration of the artist in his garret and the companion or wife or lover who tries to make everything right so the maestro can get to work (the garret here was one of the signature images in Ken Russell's cinema, the small, wooden summerhouse on the lake, shot at Derwentwater and Keswick, favourite Russell locations (standing in for Mahler's summerhouse at Maiernigg, and used in *Dante's Inferno*). Cumbria looked amazing. How

---

[49] Finding really good child actors is incredibly difficult, even more so when they have to look a little like the adult actor. But Gary Rich is allowed to over-act, and it unbalances the movie.
[50] A nod back to *Women In Love*, in the scene with Gerald Crich and the train, and also to Russell's famous *Elgar* documentary. The origin is *Die Niebelungen*.
[51] Actually, it was a stunt rider, who, as often with stunt riders, doesn't look much like the actor at all.
[52] For Joseph Gomez, Russell used too much of the Isaac Babel material in *Mahler*, and it didn't belong in the movie (G, 190).

could Mahler compose in that little house, with that incredible view out of the window? Russell should be receiving payments from the Lake District or Cumbrian tourist boards).

There was an appealing sweetness and tenderness to the vignettes of Georgina Hale's Alma Schindler (clad in a white dress)[53] running around the entire neighbourhood in order to silence all of the distractions that her husband was complaining about.[54] Cow bells (taken from the necks of a bunch of cattle), church bells, stealing a shepherd's flute with a kiss, comforting her baby, and encouraging a local folk band to halt a while with some big mugs of beer.

The climax of this *First Symphony* montage had Alma Mahler-Werfel standing on a table conducting the dancers silently and comically, intercut with Gustav Mahler back at the summerhouse, striding around in a circle, miming conducting the music in his head, with the camera in the centre of the room (meanwhile, the real music of Mahler's *First Symphony* (1883-88) is playing on the soundtrack. It's a *tour-de-force* montage[55] (and a triumph for the sound editors), and the film doesn't top it – until, perhaps, the OTT 'The Convert' sequence, and the funeral episode).[56]

*Mahler's First Symphony* sequence is like a Ken Russell movie in a single episode: it's got so many Russellian elements. Such as: new love, romantic love, married life, children, horsing around, swimming, the Lake District, water, sunlight, mountains, animals, dancing (and drinking), live music (the band), creating art, the artist and his/ her lover, and of course classical music.

And, most of all, the *First Symphony* sequence – for all its dazzling visuals, its lovely, humorous touches, its tenderness, its high romanticism – is a *tour-de-force* of *editing*.

Images + music = cinema.

And the magic ingredient is: cutting.

The real star of *Mahler* among the crew is editor Mike Bradsell: *Mahler* is a beautifully orchestrated piece of cutting. Every editor loves to cut footage to music (and without being tied down

---

[53] The costume neatly evokes early marriage, when the relationship was still romantic.
[54] Gustav Mahler moans about the noise on the train – this guy doesn't like any distractions when he's working.
[55] The sequence includes some bought footage – helicopter shots among snowy mountains, for instance, and an image of planet Earth.
[56] It has some basis in fact, when Mahler was working on the *Third Symphony* in 1896. But it's really about the lengths that an artist's loved ones or friends will go in order to ensure they can work.

by dialogue or a voiceover), and *Mahler* is gift times a million. The montage sequences in particular are breathtaking – the rapidity of the cutting is a decisive factor in keeping *Mahler* alive after decades.

❖

What Ken Russell was really interested in were not so much the connections between the composer's life and his music, but finding ways of illustrating Gustav Mahler's music with the composer's life. The music seemed to come first: it certainly dominated the film, to the extent that the movie was cut to the music, and scenes were orchestrated to the music (down to details like pans and zooms). Russell clearly knew Mahler's music backwards, and was a huge fan. What's also remarkable about *Mahler* is how the film revitalizes the music, and makes you realize, again, how wonderful Mahler's music was.

The central tension in *Mahler* was between Gustav Mahler, his music, and his wife Alma, herself a composer (with adultery added to the mix, between his wife and a young soldier, Max (Richard Morant), who was a composite figure of several lovers, and between Mahler and an opera singer, Anna von Mildenburg (Dana Gillespie)).[57]

The scene where Gustav Mahler finally plays one of Alma Mahler-Werfel's compositions, and the opera singer Anna von Mildenburg sings it, is bitter: the viewpoint is not with Mahler, this time, but with Alma, as she listens to Anna and her husband perform one of her songs. The subtext of sexual betrayal and artistic superiority is barely concealed (the blocking of the scene, for instance, says it all: Alma sits surrounded by empty space some way off, while her husband and Anna sit on the piano stool together, looking at each other and smiling as they perform. And Anna's in dark clothes, while Alma wears white again). The way that Mahler dismisses his wife's musical abilities is pretty harsh, and all the more vindictive for being so casual. Leave the real music-making to professionals, he tells her.

Alma Mahler-Werfel (1879-1964) was a striking figure herself, with three marriages (including Franz Werfel and Walter Gropius), and a colourful life, of which her marriage to Mahler (in

---

[57] Dana Gillespie (b. 1949) was a singer/ actress/ pin-up who recorded many albums, and also appeared in movies (such as *The People That Time Forgot* as a cute cave girl). She was Mary Magdalene in one of the early runs of *Jesus Christ Superstar*. Gillespie famously went out with David Bowie (and dated his manager, Tony DeFries, too).

1902, aged 23) was only part. Antony Beaumont, in his introduction to her diaries, commented that Alma's idols remained sacrosanct during her life: 'Wagner, her musical god, Schindler, the deceased father, and Nietzsche, her household philosophy'.[58]

There are moments where *Mahler* explains what the audience has seen, as Joseph Gomez noted. Perhaps so the audience will understand what's going on. Gustav Mahler's wife said she felt like a shadow, for instance, and the film both depicts that (in a scene where fans crowd around the composer, ignoring Alma Mahler-Werfel, clad in black, with a black veil over her face), and explains it.

*Mahler* also cites musical predecessors and contemporaries, sometimes in the dialogue, and sometimes visually. Thus there are references to Ludwig van Beethoven, of course, and Richard Wagner, of course, and Peter Tchaikovsky, Franz Liszt, and Sergei Rachmaninov (there are busts and paintings of the composers placed prominently in the *mise-en-scene*). Ken Russell knows this world of classical music so well, he can slip in the references in the script seamlessly. So that the allusions to classical composers never seem pretentious or self-conscious, because they are so deeply interwoven with Russell's films.

*Mahler* acknowledges author Thomas Mann, too, in this vignette, putting together Gustav Mahler, Gustav von Aschenbach in Mann's story, and the film *Death In Venice*. It's thus a commentary upon a commentary.

One can discern the influence of (or affinities with) Luchino Visconti on other aspects of Ken Russell's cinema: the operatic style (Russell also directed operas, like Visconti), the penchant for emphasizing the decadent, the narcissistic and the erotic, adaptions of classic literature, the use of high culture (such as classical music), the love of (mainly European) historical subjects, and exploring history through extraordinary individuals (such as Gustav Mahler in *Death in Venice* or the king in *Ludwig*; Russell had planned to make a biography of Ludwig).

Luchino Visconti's treatment of Nazism in *The Damned*, for instance, may have influenced Ken Russell (Visconti staged scenes of debauchery and decadence – nude figures in opulent rooms – which recalled Russell's approach at the time).[59] Like Visconti and

---

[58] A. Mahler-Werfel: *Diaries 1898-1902*, ed. A. Beaumont, Cornell University Press, Ithaca, New York, 1999, xvi.
[59] Or maybe it was Mel Brooks! In *The Producers*.

other European contemporaries, Russell tended to make films about European history, shot in Europe, films which were basically art cinema, but with some cross-over appeal into the mainstream (give me *Mahler* any day over *The Damned*, which drags on interminably – what was Visconti's editor doing?).

*Mahler* was another of Ken Russell's explorations of the artist; creative energy; the relation between art and life; the artist and those around him; how the artist relates to society, to authority, to institutions; the artist and his past; the artist and religion, and so on. *Mahler* developed Russell's sense of the artist at the centre of life, a heroic, angst-ridden, Existential figure, suffering for his art, trying to make something extraordinary in amongst poverty, pain and mediocrity.

To illustrate Gustav Mahler's religious music the movie resorted to a montage of images from the art of Gustave Doré.[60] That's one way of saving money: having several minutes of film comprising rostrum camera work of 19th century illustrations. It's a technique more often used in television documentaries than movies.

Gustave Doré (1832-83) is a favourite with other filmmakers (such as Walt Disney, Cecil B. DeMille, Terry Gilliam, and Carl-Theodore Dreyer – and he also inspired Vincent van Gogh). *Mahler* employs images from Doré's illustrations to Dante Alighieri's *Divine Comedy*, in particular the images depicting the last book, *Paradiso*, when Dante and his poet guide Virgil enter heaven, and see visions of angels dancing in circles of light. (But hell is also included, of course – and Doré can certainly deliver incredible imagery of angels and demons and everything in-between).

According to Joseph Lanza, the scene with Gustav Mahler and his brothers Otto (Peter Eyre) and Alois (Michael Southgate) was a skit on the Marx Brothers: Alois in a blond, curly wig as Harpo, Otto, at the piano, is Chico, and Mahler with his cigar is Groucho (PF, 161). There are Marx Brothers flourishes, such as Mahler wielding his cigar like Groucho, or Otto playing a glissando on the piano *à la* Chico, with one finger. Ken Russell would reprise

---

[60] The dramatic device of having Gustav Mahler's two daughters carry around the Dante-Doré book and ask their pa questions about theology, like 'is God everywhere?', was a little laboured and contrived. But, once again, it's the quality of the music that elevates the sequence.

that cinematic spoof approach in *Lisztomania*, where Franz Liszt and Comtesse Marie's married life is done over as a Charlie Chaplin silent comedy.

*Mahler* also had more than its fair share of dream and fantasy sequences, one of Ken Russell's specialities. Outstanding among these was 'The Convert' sequence set in a Wagnerian Valhalla (filmed, yet again, in the slatey, rocky *purlieus* of Russell's beloved Cumbria), an encounter with Cosima Wagner (Antonia Ellis) as a valkyrie, a goddess dressed as a sexy, Nazi storm-trooper, in boots, whip, short, black skirt and German helmet (another fab Shirley Kingdon costume), the muse as an operatic, Hitlerian diva, standing in front of a giant sword like a Cross, or wriggling lasciviously before of a boxy, red cross (like a cross made from coffins).

For Ken Russell, Gustav Mahler betrayed himself when he converted to Cosima Wagner's form of Catholicism (in 1897). The betrayal was even worse because it was to Cosima Wagner's religion, for Russell a misguided religion which also included anti-semitism, leading towards Nazism.

In this self-consciously 'bad taste' scene, Ken Russell and his team made hackneyed but hilarious links between Richard Wagner and Nazism (Gustav Mahler's Jewish background and anti-semitism had also been running themes in *Mahler*. In the scene where Mahler visits his brother Hugo (David Collings) in an asylum, Hugo orders Mahler to drop his pants so he can check if Mahler is circumcised).

'The Convert' sequence also allowed Ken Russell and his colleagues to make a version of *Die Niebelungen*,[61] one of Russell's favourite movies, fashioning his own take on the famous German Expressionist 1924 epic directed by Fitz Lang[62] (Russell had screened *Die Niebelungen* as a youth, on his own film projector[63] – he had probably wanted to recreate the Gothic splendour of the

---

[61] *Die Niebelungen*, written by Fritz Lang and Thea von Harbou, produced by Erich Pommer and directed by Lang, is a prime slice of German silent cinema fantasy. Indulgently old-fashioned and conventional (and 'simple'), as far as storytelling goes, *Die Niebelungen* is a giant production which shows off the technical resources of the big German studios of the era. This is lavish filmmaking which delights in the mechanics and the spectacle of what cinema is and what it can do when you really push at the boundaries.
[62] The tasks that Brunhilde/ Cosima has Mahler perform are partly inspired by the scene in *Die Niebelungen* between Brunhilde and Siegfried (PF, 162).
[63] In his autobiography, Ken Russell said he preferred to watch movies at home rather than at the cinema (BP, 231). Russell was fond of sitting on the couch! (He has related attending some disastrous screenings, which seem to be a part of every professional filmmaker's career).

mythological film for years. Unfortunately, the low budget of *Mahler* prevented Russell filming anything as spectacular as the famous, giant, mechanical dragon in the German opus, which took 17 people to operate. *Mahler*'s dragon is two spotlights and a flamethrower in a cave,[64] but it's still fun – it works because 'The Convert' episode is a comedy).

The point of the fantasy was Gustav Mahler's conversion to Catholicism in order to please the powers that be, embodied by Cosima Wagner (one which Ken Russell himself had undertaken). Woody Allen also filmed sequences involving a conversion from Judaism to Catholicism for comic effect (in 1986's *Hannah and Her Sisters*, for instance; Allem loves to spoof religions and cults). In *Mahler*'s 'The Convert' (mounted as a silent movie, complete with captions),[65] the symbols of Judaism and Catholicism are playfully exploited: crosses made from swords, a giant sword as a cross, Mahler eating a pig's head, swastikas, S/M gear (boots, a whip),[66] and Mahler leaping through black hoops of fire.[67] (Veteran fx man John Richardson headed up the special effects team: and this sequence demanded a large array of effects and gags, with fire used throughout).

It was all very camp, jokey, very silly, very Ken Russell, climaxing with a song ('then came the talkies!') set to Richard Wagner's 'Ride of the Valkyries'. (Why does Gustav Mahler's conversion to Catholic religion, so he can marry, have to be staged in such a crazed fashion? Because it's a Ken Russell film? Maybe. Or because such social manœuvring is inherently ridiculous).

Ken Russell said in 2005 that some of that comedy was in Gustav Mahler's music: a movement in the *Ninth Symphony* (1908-09) is called 'Burlesque', which was the piece Russell chose to accompany 'The Convert'.

Other dream sequences in *Mahler* included another Ken Russell favourite, the burial and cemetery scene, and Gustav

---

[64] The cave was also employed in *Dance of the Seven Veils*, for Zarathustra's lair.
[65] 'The Convert' starts as a silent movie, but following the caption 'Along Came the Talkies', Brunhilde/ Cosima sings.
[66] Some of the clothes at the World's End shop of Malcolm McLaren and Vivienne Westwood – the swastikas, stockings, S/M gear – were used by Ken Russell in this fantasy sequence.
[67] On set photos show Ken Russell himself wielding the whip – of course! He's the director!

Mahler imagining what would happen after his death.[68] This extended sequence began with a funeral scene in what seemed to be a real cemetery, with Alma leading the coffin, in which Mahler was trapped, still alive, looking at his own funeral through a glass panel, screaming to get out, unheard by his wife (it seems that Russell and the team were inspired by Carl-Theodor Dreyer's extraordinary 1932 film *Vampyr*, which features a dream sequence where the lead character Allan Gray is carried in a coffin with a glass opening in it. *Vampyr* includes unbelievable point-of-view images from inside the coffin as it is taken to a burial site past a church. Gray is frozen inside, dead but still alive, a lost soul unable to stop the nightmare). And of course Alma dances on the coffin, right on top of Mahler, while it's being lugged by her lovers (and of course there's a point-of-view shot looking up her legs through the glass of the coffin).

Following the cemetery scene was a fantasy sequence in a crematorium, all stark, stylized black and dark purple, with the sexual tensions of the film writ large: Alma Mahler-Werfel and lover Max happily embracing and dancing, while Gustav Mahler looks on, sweating, red in the face, impotently locked up in his coffin (which's soon burnt – apocalyptic fires being one of the themes of the film – the opening shot of the picture is Mahler's wonderful wooden hut beside the lake exploding into flames, with the camera zooming in).

Alma Mahler-Werfel's other lovers appear in this musical and dance scene, carrying the coffin (with S.S. goose-steps), then becoming Alma's chorus line. It's Georgina Hale's set-piece: she is the centre of attention,[69] cavorting around the crematorium, and gradually stripping off her widow's weeds to reveal sexy underwear, until she's topless (another stunning piece of costume design by Shirley Kingdon).

It's a grotesque[70] send-up of a rejoicing widow: the funeral/crematorium scenes blend into a posthumous exhibition about the

---

68 When the black woman on the train mentions the word D-E-A-T-H, it is clearly a taboo term for Gustav Mahler: the sound dips out, and perhaps the primary theme of *Mahler* is highlighted. It recalls William Randolph Hearst, who forbade references to death (or illness).
69 Georgina Hale was nervous shooting this scene – she's the star, she's nearly nude, and she has to dance. But it works so well, helped by Gillian Gregory's choreography.
70 There are comic touches, such as Gustav Mahler's ashes in a box emerging from the crematorium with two eyeballs.

composer,[71] within the same space, with images of Alma Mahler-Werfel now semi-nude and clad in stockings writhing over Gustav Mahler's death mask and a gramophone (with a huge phallic horn, of course!). Classic Russellania.

A macabre fantasy interpretation of *Kindertotenlieder* (1901-04) features Gustav Mahler's children in a storm (by the lake again), and a child's coffin (placed on a grand piano). Mothers and children – and *dead* mothers and *dead* babies – is a theme that Viennese artist Egon Schiele took up (there are echoes too of *Isadora Duncan*).[72] Naturally, Alma's incensed when she discovers the musical manuscript of the *Kindertotenlieder*; Gustav Mahler's answer is classic Romanticism: he can't dictate what his music is, it comes to him from outside. (The death of Mahler's child is linked to his first heart attack, and foregrounds the theme of death yet again).

A visit to a mental asylum is played as a tease for the audience: it seems as if Gustav Mahler and his sister are really visiting the emperor – the scene was filmed at one of Britain's grand country houses and gardens. But it turns out that the emperor is actually Mahler's brother Hugo. Nevertheless, the sequence is another Ken Russell dance scene,[73] with Mahler and his sister waltzing around the lavish gardens and fountains (this place must have the most luxurious gardens of any asylum in Europa).

What is the visit to the asylum scene doing in *Mahler*? It's there to depict the alternative paths that Gustav Mahler's life might have taken… He might've ended up like his brother Hugo, mad and naked in a dark cell, but still writing reams of music and songs. It shows a tenderer side to Mahler, too, in caring for his brother.

The asylum is part of a sequence which depicts Gustav

---

[71] There are reproductions of Oskar Kokoschka's paintings of Mahler (and also in the Egon Schiele style) – Alma Mahler-Werfel and Kokoschka had a passionate affair (which was celebrated in the painting *The Tempest*, 1914).

[72] *Death and the Maiden* (1915), *Cardinal and Nun* (1912,), *Holy Family* (1913), *Pregnant Woman and Death* (1911) and *Dead Mother* (1910) – these are Egon Schiele's strangest images, bringing together the themes of the family, loss, death, desire and religion. Cardinals or monks embrace women, or the figure of Death embraces women, or mothers hold dead babies, or living babies are swathed in cloth by dead mothers, or pregnant woman sleep beside monks.

[73] In *Mahler* Ken Russell manages to cram many dance sequences: the revellers at the inn, waltzing at the asylum, Alma Mahler-Werfel and Max in the crematorium, etc. The funeral musical number is a major dance routine.

Mahler's youth: see what happens to another brother of Mahler, Otto: he shoots himself at home. The revelation comes at the end of the scene where Mahler has converted to Catholicism, and is happily hurrying home with his sister and a bottle of champagne. And there's Otto: a gun, blood and more music manuscript (in the Marx Brothers scene, Otto's depicted as another struggling composer). It's grim stuff – it's striking just how much Ken Russell's cinema explores the sadder parts of life.

*Mahler* also answered *Death in Venice* (Luchino Visconti, 1971), which had been released three years previously (so audience in 1974 would've been familiar with it): an early scene in *Mahler* replayed the Visconti scenario: a middle-aged man in a white suit (with more than a passing resemblance to Dirk Bogarde) looking at a wistful youth who swans around a railway station platform, spinning around the columns which hold up the roof, while the *Adagio* from Gustav Mahler's *5th Symphony* (1901-02) is played (the *Adagio* was the music that was runs throughout *Death In Venice*). *Mahler* was a critique of *Death In Venice* – Russell had been irked at the way that the Mahleresque composer had been portrayed in the 1971 picture.

❦

Like biopics such as *The Music Lovers* and *Savage Messiah*, *Mahler* has a narrative momentum which moves inexorably towards Gustav Mahler's demise. *Mahler*, for example, concludes on a note of simultaneous bliss and death, Hollywood sappiness and European pragmatism, when one doctor (Andrew Faulds) tells Mahler he's going to be fine, and another (Dr Roth, played by George Coulouris) knows he won't last long at all. 'The ending of the film out-Hollywoods Hollywood', Russell commented.

The death of the main character gives Ken Russell's films a shape that accords to tragedy, but few of Russell's pictures have a tragic form or approach, in the literary sense or the philosophical sense (tho' *The Devils* could be defined as a tragedy, as could *Women In Love* and *Dante's Inferno*). And the movies remain ambiguous – they refrain from stating that the characters 'deserved' death, or that their lifestyles led them to ruin. They are not stories with black-and-white characters, with heroes and villains, with join-the-dots morality and ethics. Part of the point of using an artist as a central character is to show that people are both: they have the angel and the devil inside them, they are both good and evil, light and dark, beautiful and ugly.[74]

Ken Russell's pictures don't need villains to drive the plot along, because all of the seeds of destruction and alienation and sorrow are already inside the characters. (They are placed within the genres of dramas, melodramas, romances and relationship movies (occasionally thrillers), rather than genres such as action or adventure or fantasy, genres which need quests, goals, threats and chases).

*Mahler* closes with a classic ending that fuses love and death – and it's a classic Viennese finale, too (think Sigmund Freud, Egon Schiele, Gustav Klimt, etc). First, Gustav Mahler's escape from death, when he's examined by a doctor (Andrew Faulds) and declared fine for now (despite earlier ill-health: throughout the railway trip Robert Powell sports subtle, pale make-up).

Second, a lengthy take which is Gustav Mahler's final love letter to his wife Alma Mahler-Werfel: caught in a two-shot close-up, the composer explains that all of his music was about her, *was* her.[75] At this point, the dramatic device of whether Alma is going to leave at the next station with her lover Max or stay with her husband is foregrounded. In the event, Alma opts to stay with her husband.

So much for love: because at the train station another doctor appears: it's Doctor Roth, played by none other than George Coulouris, who appeared in the movie that for many is still the greatest picture ever made: *Citizen Kane* (Coulouris played Thatcher, Kane's long-suffering, parental surrogate and financial adviser). In the brief cameo in a telephone booth, Roth explains that Gustav Mahler hasn't got long to live.

But the music lives on: as Gustav Mahler told his wife Alma Mahler-Werfel moments b4, as long as his music lives, their love will live. Hence too the longevity of cinema, of all art. Cinema is filming death at work, as Jean-Luc Godard asserted, but cinema also transcends death. *Mahler* lives on.

---

74 And if you burn bright, as an artist, your fire will affect those around you – this's one of Russell's key views.
75 Earlier, Gustav Mahler had insisted that his most important piece of music was not 'what nature tells me', but 'what love tells me'.

This page and over: scenes from Savage Messiah (1972), starring Scott Anthony (above), Dorothy Tutin and Lindsay Kemp.

Helen Mirren in Savage Messiah

Gaudier in the Louvre in Savage Messiah

Henri Gaudier-Brzeska

Henri Gaudier-Brzeska

Scenes from Mahler (1974), this page and over.

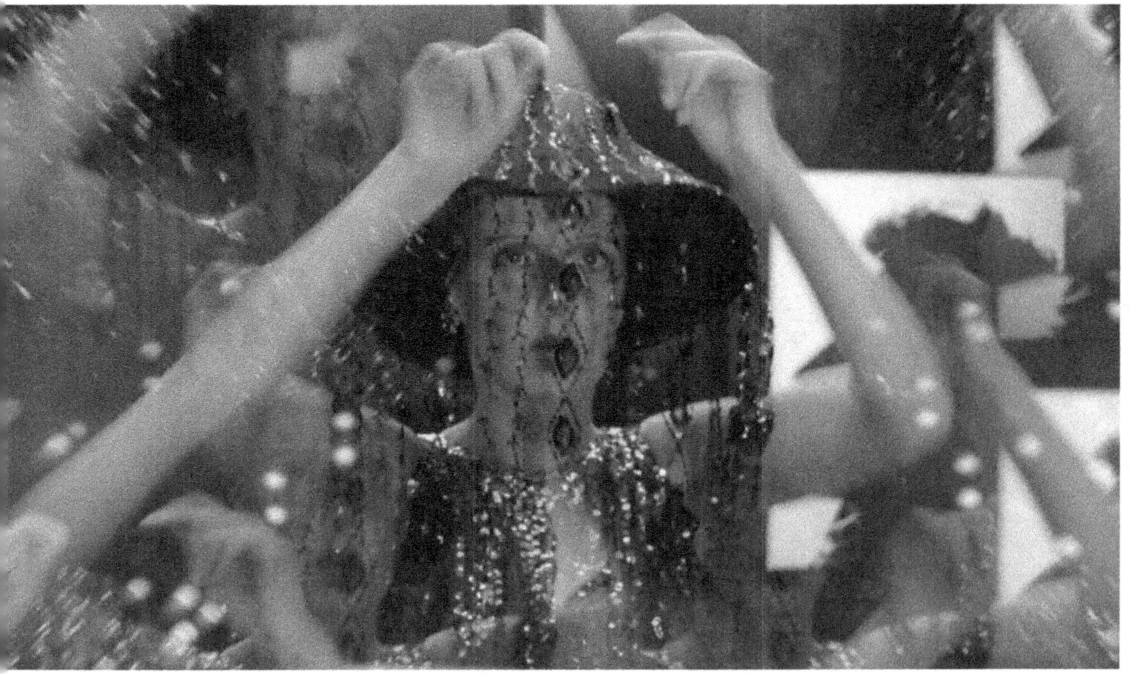

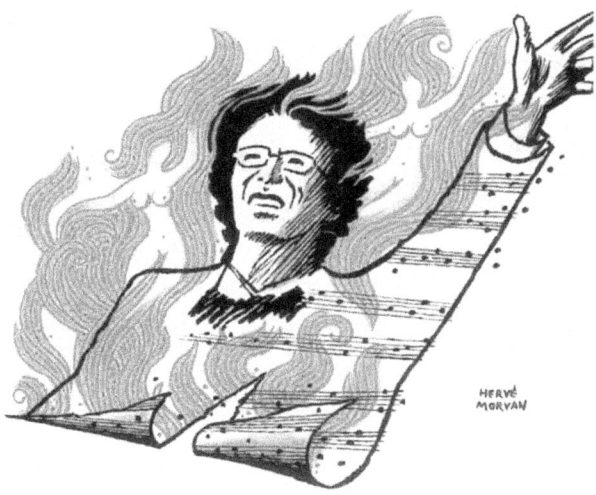

GAUMONT DISTRIBUTION
PRÉSENTE
A GOODTIMES ENTERPRISES PRODUCTION
UN FILM DE KEN RUSSELL
HERVÉ MORVAN
MAHLER
AVEC
ROBERT POWELL
GEORGINA HALE
PRODUIT PAR
DAVID PUTTNAM
SANDY LIEBERSON
PRODUCTEUR DÉLÉGUÉ
ROY BAIRD
ÉCRIT ET RÉALISÉ PAR KEN RUSSELL
LES SYMPHONIES DE MAHLER PAR LE CONCERTGEBOUW ORCHESTRA, AMSTERDAM,
SOUS LA DIRECTION DE BERNARD HAITINK

Ken Russell in full-blown OTT satire mode:
"The Convert" sequence from Mahler

# 13

## *TOMMY*

That's one of the things I like about film, it's sort of an odyssey, you get a lot of people on a ship, and you go off on a Grecian adventure, meet the cyclops and the sirens and the hydra with the head full of snakes and cross the Styx and some people die along the way.

Ken Russell[1]

INTRO.

*Tommy* (1975) would have to rank in the top three of anyone's Ken Russell films. It's one of those movies where every element comes together beautifully, and where everyone in the production seems to be working at their best. *Tommy*'s not perfect, but you wouldn't want to change anything.[2] (But *Tommy* is also a movie which divides viewers, music fans, and film critics: as with all of Ken Russell's movies, many hate it, and many love it. And the ones who don't get it can't be persuaded to like it!).

*Tommy* is shamelessly over-the-top,[3] silly, wild, dynamic, primitive, glitzy and violent. *Tommy* ain't subtle: it presents pop psychology (of Ken Russell's usual Freudian kind) which's crude as a sledgehammer, symbolism which's heavy-handed like a pinball machine hurled out of a hotel onto Sunset Strip, it's decked out in Pop Art colours and costumes by way of glam rock,

---
1 K. Carroll, 1975.
2 Except maybe Oliver Reed's singing!
3 When Ken Russell worried that some of the performances in *Tommy* were going to be too over-the-top, Oliver Reed retorted, 'me over the top? Have you ever seen any of your films?'

it's proudly and bizarrely *English* and parochial and provincial, it's perverse and kinky, it's shrill and hysterical, and it contains some of the finest music every included in a musical movie. If Richard Wagner was making movies out of his music in the 1970s, this is what it would look like.

Ken Russell said *Tommy* was one of his happiest shoots, and one of his favourites among his own films (the two are related, of course: a movie that was an absolute bastard to shoot and edit and release might not be your favourite picture – Russell wasn't so fond of *Billion Dollar Brain* partly for that reason, and films like *The Boy Friend* had been difficult. But Russell also confessed afterwards that *Tommy* 'really was very tough and upsetting').[4]

Pete Townshend noted in his autobiography *Who I Am*:

> I found Ken Russell bombastic, energetic, funny, tireless and inspiring. He had an obsessive eye for detail and planning that I now realise every great film director needs, together with the ability to adapt to fluctuating circumstances. (264)

*Tommy* is an ideal project for Ken Russell – it has an existing musical score which Russell can exploit, including some showstoppers; it is filmed in Russell's favourite style – images cut to music; it has a strong narrative line but also allows for numerous embellishments; it has powerful religious (and Christian) aspects; it is a coming-of-age story; it has many youngsters in the cast; it is a high energy piece; and it has a British setting in the 20th century.

In other words, there were enough elements to give the 1975 project a strong, clearly-defined structure (such as the story of Tommy itself, from semi-catatonic child to reborn messiah), but also plenty of leeway so that Ken Russell could bring his own vision to the piece. And he did, he so did!

It was *balance* of the elements that encouraged everyone involved to such heights in *Tommy*. If Ken Russell and his team had been handed the project, for instance, and been told that they could do *anything* with it, including completely altering the characters and story, it might not have been so compelling, because the story and characters give the film a very strong foundation. On this project, the limits of the script (and of the budget) were perfectly in tune with Russell's sensibilities and

---

[4] Quoted in K. Carroll, 1975.

talents as a filmmaker. An unlimited budget and endless freedom creatively simply might not have worked (besides, no filmmaker has been given unlimited freedom recently, not on big, commercial productions. And Russell has of course made many films on relatively low budgets – but the low budget has of course granted more creative latitude and less interferrence).

It's important on *Tommy*, for instance, that Ken Russell and his team were in the main left alone by the financial backers (and producer Robert Stigwood). Had Ken Russell & co. been battling with the front office, with hatchet line producers, with power-mad writers, with vain stars, with studio executives visiting the set, as has happened on many a movie, it would certainly have been a different piece. Some of that made *Altered States* such a tense, draining project for Russell.

No doubt about it, Ken Russell was simply ON FIRE when he directed *Tommy*. Utterly on fire. The energy that blasts off the screen in this hyper-active musical movie is just astounding. You can see that the filmmakers, headed up by Russell, were having a ball making this picture. The inventiveness of the filmmaking can be found in every single frame and every single scene.

For instance, look at the way that the camera is deployed in *Tommy* – Ken Russell and his DP (Dick Bush) are using every trick in the book, extreme close-ups, crash zooms, rapid cranes or tracking shots. Particularly striking is the number of tilted camera shots and upside-down shots (presumably Russell operated the camera for some of those moves, as often on his movies, so many of those spontaneous camera movements come from him).

The staging of the scenes is second-to-none among musicals of this type – indeed, I would put *Tommy* on the same level as the great musical movies of cinema – that is, the MGM musicals of the 1940s and 1950s. Is *Tommy* really *that* good? As good as *An American In Paris, Meet Me In St Louis, Easter Parade* or the top-flight musical of them all, *Singin' In the Rain*?

Yes, I think it is. Because within its field of operation, within its themes, within its popular culture *milieu*, within its peculiarly British sensibility, *Tommy* really does fulfil on all its promises, in all areas. It really is that good.

TOMMY – THE 1969 ALBUM.

*Tommy* was a pop opera which Pete Townshend had begun to develop in 1967 (the first song he wrote for *Tommy* was 'The Amazing Journey',[5] which acted as a kind of summary for the rock opera's story, and works as a suitable sub-title). Early titles for *Tommy* included *Deaf, Dumb and Blind Boy, Omnibus, The Brain Opera, Journey Into Space* and *Amazing Journey*.

(The first opera that Pete Townshend created was *Rael*,[6] about geo-politics between Israel and Communism (it grew out of the political events of the late 1960s, when Israel and Egypt were at loggerheads (again), and had Red China invading Israel).[7])

Concept albums (as they were called) were fashionable in the late 1960s/ early 1970s for pop acts with intellectual, spiritual or artistic aspirations. They included *Days of Future* by the Moody Blues, *Ogden's Nut Gone Flake* by the Small Faces, *S.F. Sorrow* by the Pretty Things, Keith West's *Excerpt From a Teenage Opera*, and *The Village Green Preservation Society* by the Kinks (altho' 'what we were doing owed more to British music hall than to grand opera', Pete Townshend recalled [164]).

The one that tops them all, and is still regarded as the greatest pop album ever, was *Sgt Pepper's* by the Beatles. It was *Sgt Pepper's* that challenged the Who, like everybody else, in the late 1960s. If there's a single 'concept album' that influenced everyone at the time (and since then), it was *Sgt Pepper* (or it was *Pet Sounds* by the Beach Boys).[8] 'The shockwave it caused challenged all comers,' said Pete Townshend, and *Sgt Pepper* and *Pet Sounds* 'redefined music in the twentieth century: atmosphere, essence, shadow and romance were combined in ways that could be discovered again and again' (123). *Tommy* (and other Who operas) can be seen as post-Beatles and post-Beach Boys works.

In his autobiography *Who I Am*, Pete Townshend dispelled some of the legends that'd grown up around *Tommy*. It wasn't put together in the studio with lengthy discussions about the songs (tho' occasionally they would talk about the story. Townshend

---

5 An early concept for *The Amazing Journey* was to have events seen twice – from reality, and from illusion. That idea was dropped, but it does emerge in a small way in the album and the movie – often, we are inside Tommy's head or mindscreen, when incidents take on a fantastical quality.
6 The forerunner of Tommy was Damon, the hero of the earlier project, *Rael*.
7 Pete Townshend wrote a more recent opera, called *Floss*, which would include theatricality and technical challenges – '*The Wall* meets Cirque du Soleil' (499).
8 Moony was a passionate fan of the Beach Boys (his previous band was called the Beachcombers).

recalled that his fellow band members often found it difficult to understand what he was attempting).

Not all of the songs for *Tommy* were written specially for the concept: Pete Townshend adapted existing songs. So 'It's a girl' (from 'Glow Girl') was changed to 'It's a boy'. Songs like 'We're Not Gonna Take It' and 'Sensation' had lyrics altered to fit the story. 'We're Not Gonna Take It' didn't have the 'listening to you' chorus originally, and had been about something else, Townshend explained in 1974:

> When I decided to put *Tommy* together as an 'opera', I simply amassed all the songs I had, and remarkably about 80% of them fit somewhere. I seem to have been unconsciously writing on a theme for almost a year without realizing it.[9]

The story on the 1969 album is sketchy and ambiguous, as Who critics have pointed out: 'one should be wary of considering the *Tommy* album to have one sole and clear narrative meaning', as Steve Grantley and Alan Parker put it in their excellent study, *The Who By Numbers* (63). Indeed, the story was developed further *after* the album was released, by the different productions, by Pete Townshend, and of course by the Columbia movie of 1975.

The name Tommy is meant to evoke an everyman character, like Joe Bloggs: until the trauma, Tommy is just a regular kid, like anyone. 'Tommy' also evokes the regular soldiers in the British Army (Pete Townshend liked the links to war and heroism in the name). Townshend also found word games inside the name: it meant 'to me', for him, and it also contained the Hindu mantra OM in the middle (also, it begins with the same letter as his surname – authors often choose names like that).

♫

A few aspects strike you when you listen to the original 1969 album of *Tommy* now: one is the lack of the celebrity singers, and most especially the diva performance of Ann-Margret. The second thing is the lack of synthesizer noodlings and additions, which do water down the original recordings somewhat (these were added for the movie soundtrack). And the third thing is the songs themselves, how some of the arrangements and the performances are quite different from the soundtrack album of the movie.[10] I

---

[9] Quoted in C. Heylin, 61.
[10] 'Now I'm a Farmer' was an early song dropped from *Tommy*.

guess purists'd prefer the 1969 *Tommy* album (but maybe not the newly-mixed or releases of later years), but the movie soundtrack album is a very fine piece of work too. And if you saw the film first, this'll be the one you're used to. (However, the soundtrack album differs again from the music used in the actual movie, as is often the case. You can find lists of the differences between the studio and soundtrack albums and the movie's score online).

The first recording sessions for *Tommy* took place on September 19, 1968,[11] at I.B.C. Studios in dear, old London (next to the British Broadcasting Corporation in Portland Place).[12] A good deal of money and effort and time was expended on putting the album together: it was due out at Christmas, 1968, but was over-schedule, and was released in May, 1969 (May 17 in the U.S.A., May 23 in Blighty), at the same time as *The Village Green Preservation Society* (the Kinks), *S.F. Sorrow* (the Pretty Things) and *Ogden's Nut Gone Flake* (the Small Faces).[13] The recording sessions were a happy time, Pete Townshend recalled, with the band working well together, and hanging out in the pub afterwards.

The *Tommy* album cost $60,000 to make, a huge sum for the time, and took 8 weeks to record (of course, bands since then have taken a *lot* longer, and spent a *lot* more money! And with *far* less spectacular results!). Kit Lambert mixed the album (Pete Townshend wasn't happy with the mix, which put the vocals way in front of the band). Mike McInnerney designed the famous album cover, and inner sleeve paintings (it was McInnerney who introduced Townshend to Meher Baba; McInnerney was a key influence on Townshend in the *Tommy* period).

Track listing for the May, 1969 album of *Tommy* runs thus:

Overture - It's a Boy - 1921 - Amazing Journey - Sparks - Eyesight To the Blind (The Hawker) - Christmas - Cousin Kevin - The Acid Queen - Underture - Do You Think It's All Right? - Fiddle About - Pinball Wizard - There's a Doctor - Go To the Mirror! - Tommy Can You Hear Me? - Smash the Mirror - Sensation - Miracle Cure - Sally Simpson - I'm Free - Welcome - Tommy's Holiday Camp - We're Not Gonna Take It

---

11 The recording sessions for *Tommy* at I.B.C. included February 3-7, 17-21, 24-28 and March 3-7, 1969. At the time, the Who were touring throughout Britain.

12 Other studios used included Ramport Studios and Apple Studios (the Beatles' studio). Ken Russell had visited Pete Townshend's Ramport Studios and saw what could be done with synthesizers (Russell was after an orchestral as well as rock music score). (Ramport had been built for the *Quadrophenia* project in Battersea, with Ronnie Lane's mobile studio being hired for the sessions).

13 In 1969, the Who operation was in debt to the tune of $2 million (N. Cawthorne, 9). So they needed a successful project.

For *Tommy*, brass was added (by John Entwistle), French horn and trumpet, and keyboards (by Pete Townshend), principally organ and piano. Plus gongs, timpani, and tambourines (but not the orchestration that Kit Lambert pushed for). There were also more backing vocals than in previous Who outings, requiring both Townshend and Entwistle to sing. Musically, *Tommy* is more complex and layered than previous Who records.

The orchestrating of *Tommy* was something that Kit Lambert wanted, but Pete Townshend resisted: Townshend aimed for an album that the Who could play on stage as a four piece act (which they did, many times). Townshend preferred something 'operatic', but not necessarily with a full orchestra. (It was Lambert who nudged Townshend towards opera, however: Townshend said he argued with Lambert, but Lambert insisted, 'No, no, no! This is fucking OPERA!'[14]).

Among the tracks recorded but not included in the final running order of the *Tommy* album were 'Young Man Blues' by Mose Allison, 'Cousin Kevin Model Child' by Pete Townshend (tho' credited to John Entwistle), and 'One Room Country Shack' by Mercy Dee (which was abandoned).

Pete Townshend was very proud of the *Tommy* album: 'Keith's playing has never been better, John's playing has never been better, Roger's singing has never been better'.[15] The Who knew they had a hit on their hands as they were making it, and *Tommy* became hugely important for the band. It went on to sell over two million copies.[16] *Tommy* became a live favourite, and possibly the Who's most famous album and song cycle. It made the Who a lot of money, and after it they were elevated to the front rank of rock acts. *Rolling Stone* enthused: 'the most important milestone in pop since Beatlemania'.

The most famous performance of *Tommy* was at Woodstock, where 'See Me, Feel Me – Listening To You' was played at dawn. The Who presented *Tommy* live throughout 1969 and 1970. The Who enjoyed performing the album, and they came to prefer their live interpretations to the one on the album. Live, the

---

14 Quoted in C. Heylin, 2012, 58.
15 *Tommy* wasn't finished when the album was done, for Pete Townshend: he saw all the flaws. Townshend would spend a good deal of time tinkering with *Tommy* over the decades.
16 The *Tommy* double album was split into two in some territories, so punters could buy one or the other. It was also released as a series of singles, and by Jun, 1970 had apparently accumulated sales of $5 million. *Tommy* made the Who rich.

presentation of *Tommy* ran to 50-55 minutes (shorter than the album). The live recordings from the Leeds, the Isle of Wight and Hull shows of 1970, clock in at 54 minutes.

Nik Cohn's review of *Tommy* (in the *New York Times*) ran:

> *Tommy* is rock's first formal masterpiece. *Live At Leeds* is the definite hard-rock holocaust. It is the best live rock album ever made... Townshend is intelligent, creative, highly complex, and much given to mystic ponderings, but the things that he values most in rock are its basic explosions, its noise and flash and image.

Meanwhile, *Rolling Stone*'s Al Aronowitz dismissed the album. The story meant nothing to Aronowitz, and 'the whole thing may as well be sung in Italian'.

*Tommy* was a double album. In the rock and pop world, there were precedents for this prior to *Tommy's* release, the most significant probably being the Beatles' *White Album*. Other pop acts who released doubles included Jimi Hendrix, Frank Zappa, Chicago, Cream, and Bob Dylan.

Although *Tommy* has Ken Russell's fingerprints all over it, it is very much 'a Pete Townshend film': Townshend's music dominates the movie, pounding away all through it (with Townshend's guitar very prominent, as well as Townshend's experiments with early synthesizers and sequencers). Townshend wrote most of the music, and most of the lyrics. The concept, story and themes are by Townshend (although Russell had the screenplay credit). He also produced the recordings for the movie. Not only that, Townshend also appears in the movie. And he has the all-important musical director role, so vital on a musical. So it's very much Townshend's baby.

TOMMY AS ROCK OPERA.

*Tommy* was conceived by Ken Russell as an opera, a 'long-haired opera', with duets, arias, quartets and choruses, and '*leitmotivs à la* Wagner' (1993, 130f).[17] Russell admitted that he didn't know much about rock music, his love being classical music, of course. This needs to be emphasized: that Russell's love and knowledge was wholly in the world of classical music (and

---

17 'Rock opera' – some dub these albums and movies, and Ken Russell and his team approach the piece as an opera, with arias, choruses, recurring motifs, and so on. Richard Barnes, Who biographer, has described *Tommy* as a rock cantata or rock song cycle (rather than an opera) with a Christ-like pinball player at its centre.

also folk, music hall, theatrical and movie musicals, and popular songs), and he only came to pop and rock music much later (Russell was 29 when North American rock 'n' roll hit Britain in 1956).

Ken Russell had seen a performance of the orchestral version by Lou Reizner; according to Pete Townshend, it was seeing the classical interpretation that helped Russell to consider the possibilities of doing *Tommy*.[18] (Reizner (d. 1977 aged 43) was a producer and vocalist who produced Rick Wakeman and Van der Graaf Generator). Townshend recalled meeting Russell in his Ladbroke Grove home where the maestro had encouraged him to use an orchestra as well as pop music. Townshend had enjoyed Russell's movies about art and musicians, in particular *Savage Messiah, Elgar* and the piece that many musicians can relate to, *Delius: Song of Summer*.

1975 marks the highpoint of the British rock musical movie in many ways – two of the finest were released that year: *Tommy* and *The Rocky Horror Picture Show*. Both had fantastic soundtracks, outstanding performances, eye-popping visuals, a brilliant reworking of pop icons and pop music and pop culture, and an irreverent take on what a musical movie is or could be. Both were based on musicals which were centred in British culture (though *The Rocky Horror Picture Show* was a much more fully developed theatrical show). Both also celebrated American pop culture (such as movies and music) Both were U.S.-financed. And both *Tommy* and *The Rocky Horror Picture Show* are fabulously enjoyable movies – they're audience movies, movies which the *audience*, not the critics or the establishment, owns.

*Tommy* is very much part of the pop and rock operas of the period, which included *Godspell, Hair, The Rocky Horror Show, Stardust, Jesus Christ Superstar, Evita* and *Joseph and His Technicolor Dreamcoat*. On film, *Tommy* was about the finest of these rock operas – although *The Rocky Horror Show* is in a class of its own, as one of the great, great feel-good movies (and *The Rocky Horror Show* certainly tunes in to the same send-up and celebration of

---

[18] However, Russell said he preferred Reizner's orchestral *Tommy* to the Who's version. In time, he came to like the original (N. Cawthorne, 16).
Ken Russell said he had seen a version of *Tommy* performed by the Who and an orchestra in London in December, 1972 (with the London Symphony Orchestra and the English Chamber Choir). It had been partially staged at the Rainbow Theatre: Roger Daltrey was Tommy; Keith Moon was Uncle Ernie; Peter Sellers was the Doctor; and Rod Stewart was the Pinball Wizard.

popular culture and movie genres that is Ken Russell's speciality).[19]

MUSICALS.

*Tommy* was a part of the 1970s cycle of rock and pop musicals, on stage and screen (many of these musicals started out on stage): *Grease, Jesus Christ Superstar,*[20] *Joseph and the Amazing Technicolour Dreamcoat, Godspell, The Wiz, Pippin, Evita, War of the Worlds* and *Hair* and the one which was released the same year which became more successful (and enduring in some quarters) than *Tommy*: *The Rocky Horror Picture Show*. But *Tommy* was not the film version of the stage show (like many of those musicals noted above), altho' there had been many stage versions prior to filming, but it did partake of the musical theatre tradition as well as the film musical, and the rock music world.

The 1972 album was recorded over 8 months (at a cost of $100,000), with the Who helping to oversee the sessions. The album contains a cast of guest musicians: Maggie Bell played Tommy's mom (and sang 'Love, Reign O'er Me');[21] Ringo Starr was Uncle Ernie; Traffic's Steve Winwood was Tommy's dad; Richard Harris was the Doctor; Sandy Denny (of Fairport Convention) was the Nurse; Merry Clayton[22] was the Acid Queen; Richie Havens was the Hawker; and John Entwistle was Cousin Kevin. This all-star *Tommy* sold very well (over a million copies in 4 months).

But that show and 1972 album wasn't used as a basis for the 1975 film. There was also an orchestral album recorded by Lou Reizner of this production, entitled *Lou Reizner's Tommy* (1972). (The Who would revive guest star versions of *Tommy* from time to time, and also record them on video).[23] However, Ken Russell did say that he saw 'immense possibilities in it. I wasn't into rock as such, but I recognized this was something very special' (PF, 168).

Casting pop stars in dramatic roles in movies aimed at the youth market was a common practice in the 1970s: David Essex, Adam Faith and Ringo Starr in *That'll Be the Day* and *Stardust*, for

---

19 Meanwhile, Nell Campbell from *Rocky* was Olga in *Lisztomania*.
20 Incidentally, Ted Neeley had appeared in the musical *Tommy* b4 being cast in the lead in 1973's *Jesus Christ Superstar*.
21 'Love, Reign O'er Me', was written for Bell; it appeared on *Quadrophenia*.
22 Clayton is one of the key singers on the soundtrack of cult movie *Performance*.
23 For instance, a show featuring David Essex, Roy Wood, Marsha Hunt, Viv Stanshall and Steve Marriott (Small Faces), in the U.K. in 1973, and in Australia a TV broadcast of the show.

example, or David Bowie in a film released the same year as *Tommy*, *The Man Who Fell To Earth*.

## BACKGROUND, SCRIPT, PRE-PRODUCTION.

*Tommy* was co-produced by David Puttnam and Sandy Lieberson – that enhanced the influence of the rock music world, according to Ken Russell (Lieberson had produced *Performance*, for example, while Puttnam was known for his work on films such as *Stardust*,[24] *That'll Be the Day* and *The Final Programme*,[25] and later *Bugsy Malone*, *The Mission* and *The Killing Fields*).[26]

*Tommy* was released on March 19, 1975 in North America and on March 26, 1975 in Blighty. 108 minutes.

The script for *Tommy* was 66 pages long (short for a feature movie, which's usually 110 or so pages). One of the reasons that *Tommy* is so good is that it had a long lead-in time, when the script, ideas, casting, props, costumes, make-up, hair, special effects, designs and all the rest were developed at length.

Had it been rushed into production, *Tommy* wouldn't have been nearly so accomplished. Movies like this, especially musicals, require a huge amount of preparation. The music, for instance, had to be re-recorded, using the new cast members. And that took 6 months.

Ken Russell told Pete Townshend that the music had to be locked before any of the movie was shot.[27] That's one of the essential prerequisites of making a movie musical (and for a somewhat undisciplined musician like Townshend, that would've

---

[24] *Stardust*, the 1974 follow-up to 1972's superb *That'll Be the Day*, is another movie that links with *Tommy*: it takes in a rock star, a rise and fall structure, pop music and popular culture, and also includes a messianic trip (the stage show). *Stardust* also shared personnel with *Tommy*: it featured Keith Moon, and was produced by Sandy Lieberson and David Puttnam (one of the reasons that Moony didn't drum on much of the music in the movie of *Tommy* was because he was appearing in *Stardust*). Another link: *Stardust* was edited by Mike Bradsell, Russell's regular editor.
[25] *The Final Programme* (1973) was based on Michael Moorcock's *Jerry Cornelius* books (it was co-produced by Sandy Lieberson and Goodtimes Enterprises). Unfortunately, *The Final Programme* is dreadful. Moorcock bemoaned how bad it was in a letter to me, and sadly there have been no other movies of Moorcock's work (as there have been of his contemporary, J.G. Ballard, who's had movies made from *Empire of the Sun* and *Crash*).
[26] Since the early 1980s, and his Oscar-winning success with *Chariots of Fire*, David Puttnam had been in the forefront of the British film industry. As well as a producer, he was a contributor in Goldcrest; a governor of the National Film and Television School; and a member of Harold Wilson's Interim Action Committee on the Film Industry. Jake Eberts said Puttnam was one of the very few people able to spot talent even in a poor film, was brilliant at selling ideas for films and promoting them; James Lee said Puttnam was amazing with negotiations over money and talent (J. Eberts, 30, 103).
[27] The soundtrack began recording in January, 1974.

created immense pressure, as Townshend acknowledged). Musicals demand rock-solid, accurate and hard-working music producers, music editors, orchestraters, arrangers and engineers. Indeed, musicals produced today have whole teams of producers, composers, arrangers and ancillary staff. (Hollywood movies are stuffed to the gills with music nowadays, pushing the costs of music production way up, and demanding more and more of musicians).

Pete Townshend hadn't really known what was involved in producing a movie soundtrack. It meant *a lot* more work than simply recording or re-recording a bunch of songs. By the end of it, he was exhausted. (He didn't do it all on his own – Nicky Hopkins and Martyn Ford are credited as arrangers).

During pre-production, Pete Townshend, aided by Ken Russell, added six new songs to the rock opera (including 'Prologue 1945', 'T.V. Studio', 'Champagne', 'Mother and Son' and 'Bernie's Holiday Camp'). Also, the order of the songs was altered, and some of the lyrics were changed. The movie also required incidental music to link scenes, adjusted timings for songs, and other re-organizing (thus, the movie's *actual* soundtrack isn't the same as the soundtrack album).

*Tommy* was very much the Who's baby, and very much a Peter Townshend concept and production. However, when Ken Russell and his team came on board, the concept was developed. For instance, one of the key additions that Russell made was to provide a much more detailed back-story for Tommy. 'Bernie's Holiday Camp' and 'Prologue 1945' were added by Russell: now Tommy's father is Group-Captain Walker (Robert Powell), a RAF pilot who dies (or seems to die) in the Second World War, shot down in his plane. There's a lyrical interlude featuring Walker and Nora, Tommy's parents (with conscious references to the Garden of Eden, with Tommy's folks as Adam and Eve), which is where Tommy is conceived (and, this being a Ken Russell movie, where else are they going to go for a picnic, but Russell's beloved Lake District?).[28] A spiritual guide for Tommy – a stranger in a silver robe – was dropped for the film (the figure appeared in a vision in the song 'Amazing Journey').[29]

The reason for Tommy's deafness, dumbness and blindness has to be something traumatic – and the Freudian primal scene is

---
28 It's Borrowdale.
29 The glowing, white sphere performs the guide function.

chosen: Tommy sees his father being killed after Captain Walker's come home to find Nora and Frank in bed. It's the primal scene *plus* the father's murder. (But it is also filmed in a stylized manner, close to a nightmare). The deaf, dumb and blindness was symbolic[30] for Pete Townshend: 'the hero had to be deaf, dumb and blind, so that, seen from our already limited point of view, his limitations would be symbolic of our own'. Ken Russell needed to include the motives and reasons: 'you never knew exactly who the father was, why the father was killed or why the boy went blind, deaf and dumb'.

Pete Townshend also acts as the narrator of *Tommy* (he's credited as 'the Narrator') – he sings songs which explain parts of the plot (such as 'Captain Walker' and 'Amazing Journey', including self-contained episodes such as the 'Sally Simpson' sequence). In fact, Townshend's is the one major singing voice which's featured in the movie but doesn't belong to one of the characters on screen.

One of the chief people in the Who camp, Kit Lambert, had produced the *Tommy* album (Lambert had written his own film version of *Tommy* (entitled *Tommy, 1914-1984*),[31] and was very keen to produce it, but the project languished).[32] Pete Townshend became disenchanted with the idea of *Tommy* becoming a movie,[33] and it was his disagreements with Lambert over it that poisoned their relationship: 'it was *Tommy* that destroyed the relationship', Townshend said (S. Grantley, 103).[34] Filmmakers such as Joseph Strick had expressed an interest in scripting *Tommy*, with Hollywood legend Ray Stark producing at Universal (who owned Decca).[35]

Kit Lambert didn't guide the story of *Tommy*, according to Pete Townshend (156), but he did type up the story after the album had been completed (partly for a film treatment, and

---

30 For Pete Townshend, the deaf, dumb and blindness of Tommy was 'a symbol of our own everyday spiritual isolation' (147).
31 Kit Lambert had an idea for an Ages of Man story for the stage show, which Pete Townshend said he combined with his story of a deaf, dumb and blind boy.
32 Two months after the 1969 album was released, Pete Townshend was considering a film version.
33 The first movie idea for *Tommy* was along the lines of *The Magical Mystery Tour* which the Beatles had filmed for TV (this was announced by the Who in January, 1969).
34 Also, Lambert had been criticizing Townshend's pet project, *Life House*, behind his back, which further pissed off Townshend, as *Life House* meant a good deal to him (S. Grantley, 85).
35 Joseph Strick (b. 1923, director of *Ulysses*, *The Savage Eye*, *The Balcony* and *Tropic of Cancer*), had visited Pete Townshend a few times in London (222).

partly to protect the copyright). Later, Lambert (and Track Records) were engaged in legal wrangles with the Who over the movie (Lambert complained that he hadn't received a credit or any money).

Ken Russell said he and Pete Townshend had worked for 6 months prior to production on the script. They didn't always get along or agree – both were independent-minded, highly creative, strong-willed and potentially volatile personalities. They never defined exactly what *Tommy* was about, Russell recalled.

Pete Townshend recalled that Ken Russell had helped him to recognize that *Tommy* was about his own story, but also about a whole generation. It was a way of holding up a mirror, a way of encapsulating what was happening to postwar youth. For Townshend, speaking in 2004 on the *Tommy* DVD, Russell was perfect as the director of *Tommy*: he had that kind of pop video approach – 'he just seemed to be perfect'.

I doubt that any of Kit Lambert's script was used in the 1975 film of *Tommy:* it's likely that Ken Russell, when he was hired, would've jettisoned as much of the previous drafts or ideas as possible (in fact, probably all of 'em): film directors like to exert their influence (and power and ego) over a project as soon as they sign on, and rejecting *all* previous versions of a script and ordering rewrites of the script with a writer of *their* choice is a common practice. Lambert was influential on the production of the *Tommy* album, and had suggested doing an overture (which was much further expanded by Russell in the movie), as well as coming up with the title *Tommy*. The movie deal for *Tommy* was initially brokered by Chris Stamp, Pete Townshend said.[36]

MUSIC.

The music for *Tommy* was recorded before any filming took place, over three months (some said 6 months).[37] Pete Townshend supervised the recording sessions (Ken Russell said he attended all of them, and that Townshend drove the musicians and singers pretty hard). Townshend wrote new material for the film,

---

[36] The first offer to produce *Tommy* as a movie came from the famous Hammer studio, in a deal planned by Chris Stamp. Producer Michael Carreras at Hammer Films suggested Ken Russell as director (he had been approached by the Who in 1970). Apparently, George Lucas had also been considered – presumably on the basis of *American Graffiti*.
[37] During a period of power cuts and the three-day week, when Britain experienced an energy crisis. Ann-Margret recorded her role in one 11-hour session.

including music to bridge scenes, and provided new arrangements. Every song from the 1969 *Tommy* album was re-recorded.

Among the many musicians who contributed to the *Tommy* recordings were Nicky Hopkins (piano), Mick Ralphs (guitar, from Bad Company), Caleb Quaye (guitar), singers Alison Dowling, Margo Newman, Liza Strike and Vicki Brown,[38] Simon Townshend (vocals), Gerald Shaw (theatre organ), Fuzzy Samuels (bass), Eric Clapton (guitar and vocals), Graham Deakin (drums, from Ox), Alan Ross (guitar, from Entwistle's band Ro Ro), Paul Gurtvitz, Mylon LeFevre, Phil Chen (bass, from the Streetwalkers), Tony Stevens (bass), Dave Wintour (bass), Ron Wood (guitar, from the Faces), Chris Stainton (organ/ guitar, from Joe Cocker's band), Elton John's band (Davey Johnstone, Dee Murray, Ray Thomas, drummer Nigel Olsson), and drummers: Kenny Jones, Mike Kelly, Tony Newman, and Richard Bailey. And more musicians: Howard Casey, Dave Clinton, Geoff Daley, Bob Efford, Ronnie Ross, . Among the backing singers were Billy Nicholls and Jess Roden (on 'Listening To You'). So it wasn't the Who on every song, and it wasn't members of the Who providing bass, drums or even guitar on every track.[39] (Some of those musicians were session musicians, and most were veterans that you'll have heard on numerous recordings).

The soundtrack for *Tommy* has a density beyond many musical movies. Look at the enlightenment scene, when Tommy wakes up on the beach, discovered by his mother. The sound mixers add synthesized wave sounds to coincide with the heavy waves crashing on the rocks behind the actors. (That is, the sound team add other layers of further sounds to the musical recordings made for the movie).

According to Billy Nicholls, a singer and songwriter, Ken Russell became more excited by the possibilities of the music as the recording sessions drew to a close:

> he would be walking around the studio with a stick in his hand, beating out rhythms, getting more excited, suggesting more ideas, maybe getting a bit more pissed than he would have done earlier on. You could see he was beginning to feel things happening, beginning to see what he'd be doing with the music. (In N. Cawthorne, 171)

---

[38] Newman and Brown sang the nurses in 'It's a Boy'.
[39] However, on some songs, Pete Townshend played everything – on 'Captain Walker/ It's a Boy', he plays the guitars, keyboards and drums.

Russell helped out with some of the recordings. For 'We're Not Gonna Take It', Russell encouraged the singers to become an angry mob (clearly he had already envisaged the scene where Tommy's followers turn on him, and wanted a suitably irate crowd in the background).

Pete Townshend had prepared the soundtrack for the movie of *Tommy* in his home studio, where a lot of the Who's music started out (Townshend produced demos[40] as a matter of course, like many acts, bringing them to the studio for the rest of the band to hear). The Who were also performing during the recording period.[41]

The movie required further time in the recording studio for Pete Townshend (about 4 weeks) when the film was in post-production. As the picture was edited, it needed adjustments to the soundtrack for timing (Townshend was responding to editor Terry Rawlings as well as Ken Russell's changes).

Who critics Steve Grantley and Alan Parker dub the soundtrack album for the movie

> a well-meaning but sprawling mess, drenched in keyboards and soaring choirs. The Who's songs and performance are submerged beneath a welter of inappropriate star turns, non-singing vocalists and a surfeit of synthesizers. Jack Nicholson's and Oliver Reed's voices are particularly tuneless and embarrassing. (134)

THE PRODUCTION OF *TOMMY*.

Ken Russell regulars on *Tommy* included actors Robert Powell, Oliver Reed, Imogen Claire, and Ben Aris, DP Dick Bush, costume designer Shirley Kingdon, sound man Ian Bruce, set dresser Ian Whittaker, associate producer Harry Benn, and editor Stuart Baird. John Clark was art director, Tim Hutchinson was another set designer, hair was by Joyce James, make-up by George Blackler and Peter Robb-King, choreography by Gillian Gregory, and visual fx by John Richardson.

Design-wise, *Tommy* has its own special look, a colourful, Pop Art, pop culture, comicbook approach. Set designer Paul Dufficey made significant contributions (Russell pointed to the wallpaper, which was another element among many that were commenting

---

40 In his home studio at the time of writing *Tommy*, Pete Townshend had two Revox tape machines, a mixer, a limiter, an electric piano, two organs, bongos, echo and reverb machines, and of course guitars.

41 A concert in South London was filmed by the BBC (for $1200): it was originally going to be shot for the movie, to add to the movie's finale.

upon the narrative).

The budget for *Tommy* was over $3 million ($3.5m according to some reports, and $5 million in others – it would be $140m in 2010. But that's a bargain compared to bloated, high budget musical movies of the era like *Annie* or *The Blues Brothers*). Columbia backed the movie, and released it in the U.S.A. (the involvement of Columbia led to the casting of Americans). Robert Stigwood Organization and Hemdale produced. Rank Film Laboratories processed the film. It was filmed in 35mm, using the regular ratio of 1: 1.85. *Tommy* was released on March 19, 1975 in North America and on March 26, 1975 in Blighty. Running time was 108 minutes (some sources say 111 minutes).

The schedule was short: according to some reports, the initial schedule was twelve weeks,[42] using $1.5 million. The actual shoot ran to 22 weeks, and $3-5 million. Making a musical movie that cheaply and that fast would only have been possible with amazing organization, a really dedicated, professional crew, and a ton of preparation (it was pre-production, as usual, that was the key: all of the important work on *Tommy* had already been done before the cameras rolled).

Cinematographer Dick Bush left halfway through the production – often that's a disastrous turn for a film production (partly because no one else wants to take up the job). The cameraman who assumed the post – Ronnie Taylor – was the camera operator, so, Ken Russell explained, it wasn't too difficult a change-over. In fact, Taylor was a veteran by then of films such as *Barry Lyndon, Oh! What a Lovely War!, Saturday Night and Sunday Morning* and *Room At the Top*. And Russell's own *Savage Messiah* and *The Devils*.[43]

*Tommy* was produced at Lee International Studios in West London (owned by the Lee brothers), which was Ken Russell's production base also for *Mahler* and *Savage Messiah*, and Shepperton Studios. Principal photography ran from late April[44] to August, 1974. The crew worked six-day weeks (not five), and usually until 7 p.m. (not 5.30 p.m., as is usual in the British film

---

42 Some said the schedule was 8 weeks.
43 After *Tommy*, Taylor was camera operator on *Star Wars*. As DP, Taylor shot *Gandhi, A Chorus Line, Cry Freedom, Sea of Love, The Phantom of the Opera* and many other flicks.
44 Weymouth was one of the first locations.

industry).[45] Pete Townshend was struck by how hard everybody in the crew worked (the disciplined and unionized world is a different regime from making a rock album, where musicians roll in at noon or later and work into the night).

THE RELEASE.

*Tommy* premiered in New York City on March 18, 1975, at the Ziegfeld Theater. Celebrity premieres followed in L.A.[46] (at Grauman's, of course), and London (in Leicester Square, of course). Many of the cast and crew attended; the film was also shown at Cannes, closing the film festival. In Gotham the audience had applauded Tina Turner's star turn as the Acid Queen, as Pete Townshend related, 'every song after that received applause, even the linking sections' (270). The movie was doing well and money was coming in from the Stigwood organization, according to Townshend, very soon after the film's release (277).

*Tommy* was prepared for release in quintaphonic sound – the first film, apparently, to do so. The quintaphonic mix was a complex technical challenge (it was one of the forerunners of domestic 5.1 surround sound,[47] developed by John Mosely,[48] and used the DBX noise reduction system (left and right front, centre screen, and left and right back). It turned out to be the only quintaphonic release ever, being supplanted by Dolby). John Mosely, Terry Rawlings and others worked on the mix (which ran until mid-December, 1974). The sound editors and mixers recalled that the room set up to mix *Tommy* had speakers on scaffolding, like a rock concert, and was so loud they had to communicate with flashlights. Rawlings[49] said it was the loudest thing he'd ever heard (the Who's concerts, like other rock acts of the time, were known for their ear-bursting volume. Joan Baez told Pete Townshend that the Who were 'very loud'. The Who even got into *The Guinness Book of Records* for being 'the World's Loudest

---

45 Knocking off at 5.30 instead of 7.00 drives North American directors visiting Britain nuts.
46 Among the people attending the L.A. premiere were the McCartneys, Ryan and Tatum O'Neal, Tommy Smothers and Dean Martin.
47 Pete Townshend said that *Tommy* was the 'first and only matrix-encoded five-channel surround film', apart from *Fantasia* (272).
48 Using a QS matrix system from Sansui.
49 Ken Russell said that Terry Rawlings had been a great help on *Tommy*.

Pop Group').[50] Actually, it's common for sound mixers on movies these days to wear earplugs because the sound mixing sessions, to emulate theatres, are so loud.

There were disagreements over the sound mixes for *Tommy*, inevitably. Everyone had their opinions, but ultimately it was Pete Townshend who had the final say.[51] (Ken Russell had final cut in the UK for the movie). As well as the quintaphonic mix, there were regular stereo, double stereo and mono mixes done. The quintaphonic mix meant that only a few cinemas could show it, which's one reason for the limited release of *Tommy*.

The sound of *Tommy* – either the 1969 album, the stage musical or the 1975 Columbia film – was very much Pete Townshend's (the sound *musically*, that is). Although the Who's sound relied hugely on Keith Moon's crazily idiosyncratic drumming, John Entwistle's intricate bass lines, and Roger Daltrey's gutsy vocals, it was Townshend who was the driving force.

*Tommy* played in cinemas for over a year – for 14 weeks it was the number one movie at the box office in Britain, following its release in March, 1975. At the Leicester Square theatre it broke records (taking $40,500 in its first week). The biggest movie in 1975 was of course *Jaws*; others included *The Rocky Horror Picture Show*, *Dog Day Afternoon*, *Rollerball* and *One Flew Over the Cuckoo's Nest*.

## THE INFLUENCE AND RECEPTION OF *TOMMY*.

The influence of *Tommy* was considerable. You can find instances in many places, not only the obvious ones like MTV and music promos. It's certainly apparent in *Pink Floyd: The Wall*: the 1982 movie (directed by Alan Parker,[52] very much made in the Ken Russell mold), was virtually a remake or a sequel to *Tommy*. Every single aspect of *The Wall* had already been covered by *Tommy*.

> As mythic, absurd and exaggerated as the film may have been in some ways, the denouement remained true to the album and centred on the spiritual benefits of growing up in troubled circumstances

---

50 120 decibels was recorded from a distance of 55 yards from the stage at a concert the Who gave at the Valley soccer ground in the mid-1970s.
51 Townshend also thought the sound quality was terrible. He was never happy with the sound of *Tommy*.
52 *The Commitments* (1991), also directed by Alan Parker, is also very Russellian. But not nearly as much fun!

Pete Townshend remarked of Ken Russell's take on his concept in his autobiography (261).

Film director Alan Rudolph (*The Moderns, Choose Me, Mortal Thoughts*) had some reservations about *Tommy* (a lot of commentators voice their reservations first, before going to praise aspects of the 1975 movie, as if it's too embarrassing or dumb to offer outright adulation), but he did admit that altho' 'Ken Russell threw in kitsch and the kitchen sink', there were 'things in it that make you go, 'Oh man! How did they know that?''[53]

For Mark Sinker, *Tommy* was to blame for 'most of the worst of 70s rock's pretensions to seriousness'.[54] Rubbish! But Sinker insisted that *Tommy* made the limitations of the album and the stage show by the Who even more obvious; the movie was too slavishly tied to the album, Sinker reckoned, it became a ragbag of cameos, an episodic and too literal interpretation of the LP (ibid.).

THE CASTING OF *TOMMY*.

Pete Townshend influenced the casting of *Tommy*: Elton John, Tina Turner and Eric Clapton were stars in the music world, and (at the time) not part of the film world (Ken Russell would later direct some of John's pop promos). John had declined the first time he was offered the role (but Robert Stigwood waited until John agreed).

Pete Townshend wasn't sure that Roger Daltrey (b. March 1, 1944) should play Tommy (at 30 during filming, he was perhaps too old),[55] but the advantages were obvious: Daltrey knew the part inside out, and had performed it many times already. It was a role that Daltrey had made his own (performing the character of Tommy live was 'an absolute dream' for Daltrey. He loved it).[56] For Ken Russell, this was a great blessing: there were no fights with his star: it was simply a case of Daltrey showing Russell what he could do. Russell called Daltrey 'faultless' as Tommy (and, crucially, Daltrey trusted and greatly admired the director). And it's certainly hard now to think of other actors in the role. In

---

53 In J. Romney, 1995, 123.
54 In ib., 108.
55 It's true that Roger Daltrey is a little old to play the young teenager in some scenes – many movies opt to have a number of younger actors play a child character (at different stages). Thankfully, *Tommy* only used one (Barry Winch).
56 Following *Tommy*, Roger Daltrey appeared in *Lisztomania*, and a pet project, *McVicar* (1980). Daltrey was in many TV shows and movies, including: *The Beggar's Opera, Mack the Knife, Tales From the Crypt, Sliders, Highlander* and *Rude Awakening*.

short, Daltrey is simply fantastic in *Tommy* – he not only looks the part, he can act every part of it. And boy can he sing!

Ann-Margret (b. Ann-Margret Olsson, 1941) was outstanding in the lead role of Tommy's mother (and rightly nominated for an Oscar;[57] she won a Golden Globe). Really, it's one of the great musical performances in any movie. Margret is on fire in *Tommy*. With Roger Daltrey, Ann-Margret brought a great energy and sexy presence[58] to *Tommy* – in some ways, she is even more the centre of *Tommy* than Tommy/ Daltrey himself. Together, Daltrey and Margret make a terrific team, forming a solid, emotional centre which carries the 1975 Columbia picture along. Even if everyone else had been terrible, the film would've still been immensely watchable.[59] As well as singing like a diva, Ann-Margret also undertakes plenty of physical acting (as many actors are required to do in a Ken Russell picture; you've got to be pretty healthy and fit to keep doing some of this stuff again and again). 'Ken pushed his actors very hard indeed and wore a few people down', Pete Townshend recalled (265).

Prior to *Tommy*, Ann-Margret had appeared in numerous North American movies, such as *Carnal Knowledge, State Fair, Viva Las Vegas, The Cincinnati Kid, Made In Paris, The Swinger, The Train Robbers*. Afterwards, she was in *Joseph Andrews, Magic, Return of the Soldier, Twice In a Lifetime, Pick-Up, A New Life, Grumpy Old Men, I Ought To Be In Pictures*, and many TV shows.

Ken Russell regular Ollie Reed[60] was wonderfully lecherous, slick, rugged, devilish and humorous as the redcoat (or rather, greencoat) at Bernie's holiday camp who seduces Tommy's mother (however, Reed's singing was awful! I love Reed, but sometimes his singing in *Tommy* is soooo bad! Pete Townshend's reaction when he sat down at a piano in the recording studio to hear Reed sing was typical: 'are you fucking joking?' But Russell was adamant that Reed's performance as Uncle Frank more than made up for his lacklustre vocals. And it's true: Reed is fabulous

---

[57] Pete Townshend was nominated for an Oscar for his music on *Tommy*.
[58] As well as Ken Russell (whose fondness for Ann-Margret is clear to see), some of the other members of the show found the Hollywood star attractive (such as Eric Clapton and Keith Moon, who called her 'a lovely girl with big tits').
[59] Garry Mulholland, who complains about many rock movies in his book *Popcorn*, grudgingly acknowledges that *Tommy* is 'imaginative, memorble, funny, offensive, bizarre, risky, vivid, technically impressive… and entertaining' (166).
[60] Apparently casting Oliver Reed in *Tommy* was needed to ensure some of the financial backing. (Moony apparently coveted the role – but that was never gonna happen!).

in *Tommy*, and it's doesn't matter a jot that he can't sing at all).[61]

Apparently, Lou Reed had been thought of for the Acid Queen (!) and Tiny Tim (Pete Townshend's preference) for the Pinball Wizard. Mick Jagger had also been considered, but the Who had stolen the Stones' thunder in *The Rolling Stones Rock 'n' Roll Circus*, so that might've nixed that idea. Besides, Jagger was well-known for getting cold feet about numerous film roles at the last minute. He just wouldn't commit. A pity – altho' Tina Turner is magnificent as the Acid Queen, it would've been amazing to see Jagger adding to his memorable film role in *Performance* (indeed, Turner (who dated Jagger) is doing a bit of a Jagger as the Acid Queen).

Robert Stigwood was another high power personality involved in the *Tommy* film, with his own ideas about casting (according to Ken Russell, the casting was decided mainly by Stigwood[62] and Pete Townshend.[63] Stigwood had left the production pretty much alone, Russell said: he just let them get on with it). It's important to remember that Russell did *not* cast the major players in *Tommy*, and one doesn't need to emphasize the significance of the principal cast in a specialized cinematic form like a musical. But he was happy with many of the casting decisions; and of course, he brought in many of his regular actors in the minor roles, including his daughter Victoria to play Sally Simpson.

Known as a music manager and promoter, by the mid-1960s the Australian Robert Stigwood (b. April 4, 1934) had become one of the most important people in the entertainment business (he had moved to Britain in 1954). Stigwood was involved with promoting (among many others) artists such as: Mick Jagger, Cream, the Who (they were signed to Stigwood's Reaction label, as was Paul Nicholas),[64] the Bee Gees, Rod Stewart and David Bowie (Stigwood's links to the music industry made him a more suitable producer than others for the movie).

---

61 Not only could Oliver Reed not sing, by any standards, he couldn't remember lyrics. Recording Reed's vocals was a nightmare, and had to be done line by line.
62 Robert Stigwood had forged links with the Who and Eric Clapton, for example, in the 1960s.
63 Pete Townshend wasn't sure about Ann-Margret, whom he thought was too glamorous, too Broadway, too musical theatre, and Reed couldn't sing. Townshend came round to liking Margret's approach, tho', with her 'drawling theatrical' way of singing (263).
64 Robert Stigwood's Reaction label was linked to Polydor. In 1966, the Who signed a deal with Polydor for £50,000 ($75,000). In the U.S.A. they were with Decca.

Among Robert Stigwood's theatrical shows were *Evita*, *Hair*, *Oh! Calcutta!*, *Jesus Christ Superstar* and *Sweeney Todd*, and movies such as *Jesus Christ Superstar* (which has affinities with *Tommy*), *Bugsy Malone*, *Staying Alive*, *Gallipoli*, and two of the biggest (and best) musical movies of the Seventies: *Saturday Night Fever* and *Grease* (which included very successful albums and merchandizing).

*Saturday Night Fever*, for example, produced by Robert Stigwood for Paramount, boasted an incredibly successful soundtrack: six number one singles, and 35 million copies of the soundtrack album were sold. *Saturday Night Fever* cost $3.2 million and made $159.8 million in the U.S.A. alone. *Grease*, also produced by Stigwood (and also for Paramount), was another massive hit: *Grease* cost $6 million to make and grossed $207.3 million in North America (the 2005 equivalent of $520.5m). Not only enormous hits, then, but with a cost-to-profit ratio which make film studio executives go ga-ga.

Christopher Lee had been put forward (by Ken Russell) for the psychiatrist (Lee has a fine singing voice, and has recorded albums, but he was filming *James Bond* in Thailand). It was Robert Stigwood who brought in Jack Nicholson (and when Pete Townshend asked if Nicholson could sing, and Stigwood told him no, he retorted: 'I'm not having another fucker in this film who can't sing. Oliver Reed is giving me nightmares as it is' (Townshend has a point – to have *two* stars playing prominent roles in a musical who can't sing and won't be dubbed is taking the piss).)

There are four rock music stars in *Tommy* – Elton John, Tina Turner, Eric Clapton and the Who; but presumably Robert Stigwood could've used his connections in show business to include many more (it was Stigwood who insisted that Turner appear as the Acid Queen). John Lennon as Uncle Ernie, say, or David Essex as Cousin Kevin. Indeed, with such a large cast, *Tommy* could've had one of those all-star cameo casts, like *The Blues Brothers* or *It's a Mad, Mad, Mad, Mad World*. The trouble with that approach is that the star power can deflect attention from the story and the characters, and the movie can become a variety show (still enjoyable, but a different kinda movie: with *Tommy*, the filmmakers were aiming for something with a bit of substance).

The casting was too old, as so often in movies of any era: Ann-

Margret was only three years older than Roger Daltrey; Daltrey was too old (at 30) to play a teenager, as was Paul Nicholas (at 30).

*TOMMY* AS A KEN RUSSELL MOVIE.

While *Tommy* is very much Peter Townshend's and the Who's baby, and while Ken Russell had little to do with the casting of some of the main roles, Russell's influence is all over this picture. It's true that the characters, the music, the story and the themes were all present in the piece before anyone else came on board, and it's true, as Russell states, that he didn't have that big a say in the casting of some of the major players.

But when Ken Russell arrived, *Tommy* became heavily influenced by the director. Russell, for instance, has the screenwriting credit. Russell and his team added hundreds and hundreds of elements to *Tommy*. Because while the songs might have described scenes in the lyrics, and gotten over the gist of what was supposed to be happening, it was Russell and the team who had to show exactly what those songs were about. They brought literally thousands of ingredients to the album that the Who had released a few years previously.

For instance, listen to one of the stand-out songs in *Tommy*, 'Eyesight To the Blind'. Eric Clapton sings: 'you talk about your woman, | I wish you could see mine', and so on. Great song, great guitar solo, but nobody could've guessed that it would be filmed the way that Ken Russell and his crew staged it – with Marilyn Monroe taking the place of the Virgin Mary (as a statue!), and a host of real, disabled extras lining up to be healed (today that scene would be even more controversial).

And when we say that 100s of elements were added by the film production, that needs to be emphasized. On the album, as with a radio drama, the listener can imagine whatever they like. But the filmmaker has to visualize everything in front of the camera. If the album sings 'Tommy can you hear me?', the audience can imagine that any way they want, but filmmakers and actors have to make all sorts of decisions about how to deliver that line, in what context, with what props, costumes, lightning, sets and all the rest.

In short, Ken Russell brings his Russellania to the show, the whole, extravagant Ken Russell Circus. I'm sure that many another film director could've produced summat entertaining and fascinating from this material (imagine Bob Fosse coming to li'l ol' England after making *Cabaret* and giving *Tommy* the hat-and-cane Fosse treatment – wow!). All sorts of filmmakers might've made an interesting *Tommy* at this time – Robert Altman, John Schlesinger, Herbie Ross, Norman Jewison, Mike Nichols, etc.

But *nobody* could've brought *Tommy* to life the way that Ken Russell did – just on the level of celebrating and sending up British popular culture, for example, Russell can't be beat. And to bring the elements of English Romanticism and the poetic English spirit to *Tommy* – to open and close the whole enterprise in the glorious mountains and lakes of Northern England – was a genius move. Putting *Tommy* into the Lake District, and filming the sequences with the emphasis on beauty and landscape, pushes *Tommy* into the 19th century, Romantic tradition of visionary poetry. How many rock musical movies evoke the tradition of English Romantic poetry and painting? It's peculiarly *English*, yet it works, and it fuses with the spirit of British rock music.

FILMING *TOMMY*.

The production of *Tommy* was based at Shepperton Studios and Lee International Studios, and shot on location mainly in Southern England, including Portsmouth, Southsea and Hayling Island. The blitz war scenes were shot in Fratton, Portsmouth (Cumberland Road) • Wesley Hall in Fratton Road was used for the Sally Simpson sequence • Sally Simpson got married in All Saints Church in Commercial Road • Hilsea Lido and Southsea stood in for Bernie's holiday camp (it wasn't a proper holiday camp like Pontin's or Butlin's – more a row of beachside chalets, shot at Eastney Esplanade, but it was enhanced by the Lido, and looked fine)[65] • Portsdown Hill was used for some scenes • the tunnel of Southsea Castle was filmed for the scene where Tommy goes to the fun fair with his mom and Uncle Frank Hobbs • the ballroom was in South Parade Pier, Southsea (the pier burnt down during shooting, with the film production working nearby – the circumstances were mysterious)[66] • the King's Theatre in Southsea

---

[65] Apparently, Ollie Reed had flashed his schlong (which he was apt to do from time to time), and the resort's owner had told the production to leave (PF, 177). It's probably not a good idea for your star to flash their dick to the owners of your location – particularly if they're British, the most sexually-repressed nation on Earth. But the story's probably not true.
[66] The film includes a shot of the burning pier, which had been started by the production's lights overheating.

was the location for the pinball duel[67] • the Church of Marilyn Monroe was filmed at St Andrew's Church,[68] Henderson Road, Eastney • Warblington Church near Havant was another location • Harefield in Hertfordshire was the scene of Tommy's birth. The sheer number of locations in *Tommy* is striking, but Shepperton Studios was employed a good deal too.

*Tommy* ended with Roger Daltrey joyously running, swimming and climbing towards a mountain-top, greeting the rising sun with raised arms (the sun was added later, optically); the image was placed on Ken Russell's coffin (tho' enlarged to appear Russell-like, along with pretty pictures of the Lake District).[69] It was meant to be a mythic finale of rebirth and fulfilment (accompanied by the Who's 'Listening to you I hear the music'). Certainly it's one of the most ecstatic endings in the Ken Russell canon, Tommy apparently having overcome all of the traumas and abuses he's undergone (for Russell, the sun was a pagan symbol, and sun-worship crops up in his cinema often, as in the fiction of D.H. Lawrence). The image is of totality and a re-immersion in the natural world: Tommy literally goes back to nature, racing along the beach, climbing the mountains, swimming in the pools, and running through the fields of the Great British Isles. (Tommy is also going back to his roots – to the place where he was conceived, and where his parents were happiest, in the opening scenes).

Ken Russell saw *Tommy* as a hymn to pop culture, to Marilyn Monroe, pinball machines and rock 'n' roll. *Tommy* used deliberately striking (and often simple) set-ups and bold colours. It had a series of camp celebrity cameos: Elton John on stilt-size platform shoes ('bovver' boots) for 'Pinball Wizard', Jack Nicholson as a psychiatrist (called the Specialist, or the Doctor in some versions of *Tommy*),[70] Eric Clapton as a Fender Strat-wielding evangelist and, most memorably, Tina Turner as the exuberantly soulful, but also scary and untameable Acid Queen.

---

67 And the set had to be dismantled at the end of each day's filming and re-built the next morning, because an amateur production was using the theatre at the same time.
68 The vicar complained about the filming (altho' the church was deconsecrated). Stories appeared about the bad boy director filming naughty scenes in a church.
69 A man standing against the giant sun had been used a few years earlier, at the end of *THX-1138* (1971).
70 Jack Nicholson came in for a day to record his part, and to shoot it, while he was on his way from the U.S.A. to somewhere else. A hot actor at the time (and even hotter since), Nicholson had already appeared with Ann-Margret (in 1971's *Carnal Knowledge*).

Tina Turner's own life was given the biopic treatment in the superb but gruelling *What's Love Got To Do With It?* (Brian Gibson, 1993). It was based on Turner's book *I, Tina* (with Kurt Loder). Turner's stint on *Tommy* and the sound recording was only 6 days (and her scenes were filmed in few takes, usually less than four). At the time, Turner was touring, and only had a few days to spare in her schedule.

Other stand-out scenes in perhaps Ken Russell's most over-the-top movie included Keith Moon leading a procession at the seaside holiday camp playing a mobile organ (reminiscent of *Monty Python*),[71] and Ann-Margret rolling around in a sea of baked beans, detergent and chocolate, which poured out of a television. (The Who had explored the territory of consumer capitalism in their concept album *The Who Sell Out*, with its Pop Art collage of radio jingles and commercials.[72] Indeed, there is even a spoof jingle about Heinz Baked Beans on *The Who Sell Out*. The concept of selling out and commercialism chimes perfectly with one of Russell's pet hates).[73]

*Tommy* depicted a psychedelic landscape kitted out with iron canisters, glitter spectacles, and skeletons crawling with reptiles. *Tommy* delighted in idiocy and excess, and didn't hold back for an instant: it reflected the glam rock and heavy metal culture of the mid-Seventies, as well as being part of the Who's mod culture (there were Teddy Boys in there, too, and a chapter of Hell's Angels from Newcastle).

Yet, despite the movement towards North American culture (in the use of American stars and American icons such as Marilyn Monroe), pinball machines, a comicbook style and Pop Art sensibility, *Tommy* was indubitably British. It evoked the much disliked (but fondly remembered) British holiday camps like Butlin's and Pontin's (called Bernie's),[74] creepy, raincoated old men like Uncle Ernie, and saucy, seaside, postcard humour (Uncle Ernie and Frank Hobbs preside over a revue). And the locations that the filmmakers discovered and exploited give *Tommy* an instantly recognizable British – and *English* – flavour. It

---
71 Keith Moon had the idea for making the holiday camp the venue for the Tommy cult (Townshend gave him a co-writing credit, altho' Moon didn't write the song).
72 Parts of the music in *The Who Sell Out* album was used in *Tommy*.
73 *The Who Sell Out* had employed the sound of Radio London, one of the pirate radio stations of the late 1960s that broadcast from a ship off the coast.
74 The 1963 musical and 1969 movie *Oh! What a Lovely War* explored similar seaside territory (with heavy irony).

was typical for Russell to make a film among so many locations he knew so well – Portsmouth, Hampshire and the Lakes.

For these reasons, although *Tommy*, like the Who's music, and rock 'n' roll, and popular culture, is steeped in North American culture (rock 'n' roll, despite what some music critics claim, is an *American* form), *Tommy* may be one of Ken Russell's most *British* and *English* of movies (Russell remarked that the production of *Tommy* went very well, and was one of his most enjoyable shoots.[75] It was also his favourite among his musicals, with *The Boy Friend*).

STYLE, MOTIFS, EDITING.

*Tommy* allowed Ken Russell and the team to indulge in every cinematic trick in the book: crash zooms, jump cuts, surprise reveals, optical burn-ins, multiple images, over-size props, different film speeds, rapid montages, and animation. *Tommy* is another visual effects movie – there are numerous optical and post-production trick effects (Colin Chilvers was special effects supervisor, aided by Nobby Clark, with optical effects by Malcolm Bubb and Sheldon Elbourne). And there are many scenes involving the practical effects of water, smoke and fire (John Richardson was the practical vfx man on the show). There's a surprising amount of animation in *Tommy*: it's not something you associate with Russell, yet animation is suited to Russell's comicbook approach to cinema. In *Tommy*, the animation is relatively technically simple, but it's bold and graphic, and does the job.[76]

While the set designers, costume designers, cameramen, hairdressers, make-up artists, assistant directors, sound editors and special effects people, and all the rest, deserve every credit for this extraordinary movie, it is Stuart Baird and the editing team that contribute so much: *Tommy* is a film edited to within a frame. It's pin-sharp editing, and not only *within* scenes (the music helps enormously when editing a film like this), but also the *relationship* of the scenes, and how the scenes flow to form the whole piece.

In short, one of the main technical reasons that *Tommy* is so effective is the cutting. Stuart Baird and his team were clearly

---

[75] Pete Townshend said that he and Ken Russell had been driven to the 'brink of alcoholism' by the production: 'Ken and I would be up till two in the morning talking about the next day's shooting, and he used to get up at five!'
[76] Sheldon Elbourne and Les Pace did some of the animation and rostrum work.

inspired by the material – *Tommy* is a film that bounces out of the cutting room with excess energy. (The influence of *Tommy* crops up in all sorts of places: for instance, editor Baird, who became a well-known film director (in particular of action movies), included an *hommage* to the Acid Queen scene in *Star Trek: Nemesis* (2002), the best of the *Star Trek* movies, when Patrick Stewart is captured by the bad guys in a device reminiscent of the iron maiden in *Tommy*).

Theatricality was enthusiastically foregrounded in endless ways in *Tommy*. For instance: the camera tracked past sets built next to each other illustrating different times and places (Tommy's birth, for instance, occurs in a hospital while outside the window there are homecoming celebrations for soldiers at the end of the war – that situates Tommy in a memorable historical moment – V.E. Day).

COSTUMES.

Roger Daltrey looks amazing – and his costume for much of the latter part of the movie comprises nothing more than a pair of flared, blue jeans. But that is perfect – not just for the mid-1970s, in which long hair and blue jeans (usually flared) was a classic look – but for youth rebellion everywhere in the Western world. In the era of James Dean and Marlon Brando, it might have been jeans, a white Tee shirt and a leather jacket (plus sunglasses for Brando in *The Wild One*). By the time of the hippy era in the late 1960s, jeans alone sufficed – and topless, too – the epoch of the musical *Hair*, the Summer of Love and Haight Ashbury (although Tommy sports a white Tee shirt in many scenes, and one of the chief items in the range of merchandizing is white Tees,[77] with his high-key, Jesus-like face on them).

And jeans plus a toned, tanned torso hasn't gone out of style – it's a look that remains as luscious and sexy now as it was then. In terms of costume design, *Tommy* isn't out of date at all and still looks marvellous (unlike some other youth-oriented or pop music-led movies). This's largely due, of course, to Shirley Kingdon, and her assistants, combined with the hair (Joyce James) and make-up dept (George Blackler and Peter Robb-King). On a production like *Tommy*, which so emphasizes the look of the performers, the hair and make-up people are *so important* (Pete Townshend might sing

---

[77] Other merchandize includes albums, posters, and the curious shades-ear-plug-and-cork combo

about Tommy on the 1969 album, but the filmmakers had to decide exactly what Tommy looked like).

Yet costume-wise, although the looks in *Tommy* comprise classic teen motifs, such as blue jeans, or the subcultural elements, such as the Teddy Boy gear or the bikers and Hell's Angels, there are plenty of really extraordinary costumes, and many of them are one-off, special creations by Shirley Kingdon and her department. For instance, the bovver boy/ skinhead outfit which's brilliantly combined with glam rock for the Pinball Wizard (the glittery hat that Elton John wears, for instance, or those fabulous, out-size bovver boots).[78] Or the stage togs for the backing band, consisting of money motifs (Pete Townshend wasn't keen on wearing these costumes, until Ken Russell pointed out that he wasn't being the Who in this part of the movie, he was working as the Elton John/ Pinball Wizard backing band. Elsewhere, though, the Who did wear their regular stage gear).

One of the most memorable looks was the truly creepy use of Marilyn Monroe masks (I bet that was Shirley Kingdon's idea), which was combined with a loose fitting dress that simultaneously had religious aspects (resembling a monastic outfit, like something out of *The Devils*), but also something contemporary.

Shirley Kingdon has a lot of fun with the changing appearance of Tommy's folks, as the era shifts from the late 1950s to the early 1960s. This's an era that Kingdon (and Ken Russell) knew inside-out, and *Tommy* relishes the prospect of delivering a send-up and celebration of the postwar era in Britain. Russell said that many of the costumes were off-the-peg, culled from used clothes stores.

One of the running gags in *Tommy* is the vanity of Tommy's folks – not only his mother Nora, but also his step-father Frank Hobbs. Tommy's step-dad is often shown admiring himself in the mirror or combing his hair, just as his lady applies her lipstick or does her hair (and also while singing – another repeated joke has mom slurring her words while she sings – in the 'do you think it's all right?' sequence).

Simply for her invaluable contribution to Ken Russell's movies, Shirley Kingdon is one of Britain's great costume designers (and even more remarkable when you consider that so many of Russell's movies were relatively low budget, compared

---

78 Elton John apparently wanted to keep the Dr Martens boots as part of the conditions for accepting the role.

to Hollywood movies of the same era, and also that so many were period movies, always more expensive to pull off).

COLOURS.

The colour red is all-over this 1975 movie, and it is one of the key devices of the Russellian *mise-en-scène*. As Ken Russell explained, he and his wife Shirley Kingdon were 'costume fanatics', and they loaded the wardrobe in *Tommy* with red: the Acid Queen, the Christmas party, the red light over the revue bar, the fire in the airplane, the pinball machines (later, white, an antiseptic, paralyzing white of money and success, was employed – for the costumes and decor in Nora Hobbs' luxurious bedroom, for instance).

The significance of the colour green in the set dressing, the props, drinks, and the costumes of Tommy's messiahdom is uncertain: is it the green of Spring, birth and growth? The green of money? Or envy? Or is it the green of things rotting? It's certainly an unusual colour to pick for the costumes of Tommy's acolytes (they sport overalls which recall workman's clothes, as well as something military). In the first two-thirds of the 1975 picture, the colour red was predominant, so green is clearly employed as an opposite, but it's not a healthy green of growth, but something more utilitarian, or military, or sickly. The military hints of the costumes suggest the negative aspects of the new Tommy cult – the regimentation and lack of individuality (everyone dressing the same), and the social oppression.

MIRRORS.

A terrific sequence had Tommy following his alter ego through a mirror (*à la Alice's Adventures in Wonderland*), and into a junk yard, where the youth discovers the pinball machine in amongst the abandoned cars, TV sets and washing machines (and is found by the police, the following morning). Here the motif of the shining, white globe (introduced by a vision of Tommy's father in the Lake District hillside where he and Tommy's mother had their picnic and conceived Tommy) is the angelic guide to Tommy's future.[79]

Some of the symbolism and pop psychology in *Tommy* was

---

[79] But it's still not all plain sailing for poor Tommy – because his alter ego abandons him, and he's left alone in the junk yard at night. Then it becomes a matter for the police, and his parents to come and rescue him.

deliberately crass, obvious, simplistic, in-your-face. That comes as much from Pete Townshend and the Who as from Ken Russell and the team. For Russell, the starkly obvious approach was chosen over the subtle, refined approach, if both worked well. That tended to lead *Tommy* into areas of the grotesque, the exaggerated, the silly, and the obscene.

The visual staging in much of *Tommy* is symmetrical and central, and also theatrical: that is, the chief character, usually Tommy, is placed in the centre of the frame, with other characters on either side of him. The staging also emphasizes the theatricality of the scenes – actors are blocked often as if they are part of a *tableau*, or on stage. And the movements within the frame often also recall how staging is employed in the theatre – when Tommy appears riding the hangglider, supported by the disabled acolytes dressed in green, they all walk towards the camera, arranged symmetrically, while the camera zooms back slowly. It's exactly the sort of staging that's employed in musicals, as the cast walks down stage (the staging also echoes the mirroring theme).

SCHIZOPHRENIA AND MAGIC.

One aspect of the 1975 Columbia movie that was dramatically vital was showing just *how* Tommy gains his præternatural ability with pinball. It isn't really in the 1969 recording or the lyrics. Undoubtedly, this was one area where Ken Russell brought a good deal to the piece: just *how* do you show on screen a youth suddenly becoming hugely talented at something? (Many movies have to tackle this problem: if you go too fast, the audience won't believe it; if you dawdle, viewers'll get restless).

The solution in *Tommy* was primarily visual, and I would guess it came from Ken Russell: Tommy's interior life is evoked with mirror psychology (mirrors being one of cinema's favourite motifs).[80] The 1975 movie depicts Tommy standing in front of a mirror (circular, of course), which's an intriguing situation for a blind person. *Tommy* employs that paradox to suggest the boy's mental landscape – you don't need to know about the symbolism

---

80 Tommy spends a lot of his youth staring into mirrors, even though he's blind. *Tommy* employs some heavy-handed symbolism by splitting Tommy's reflection into (different-coloured) alter egos, which are meant to represent the three traumas that Tommy undergoes. And when they are united, Tommy overcomes his traumas and becomes whole, and finds his calling in life – depicted in the scene where the three coloured spectres merge to form a full-colour reflection of Tommy, who then turns and leaves, leading Tommy into the car junk yard, where he finds the pinball machines.

of mirrors and circles and souls.

Splitting Tommy's image of himself into other selves is another device that the movie deploys – again, you don't need to know anything about Carl Jung or Sigmund Freud or Jacques Lacan to see that something very odd is happening to Tommy here. It's enough to suggest schizophrenia, with different-coloured reflections of Tommy's selves in the circular mirror (also using movement, showing the selves sliding apart from Tommy in the middle).

And the schizophrenia starts early – after the traumatic scene when Tommy sees Frank Hobbs kills his father. There's also a curious image of the young Tommy on a sunny beach, next to the water, with a box on his head, spinning, like a blind man's buff game (but there are no kids playing with him). Even if it isn't wholly coherent, (somewhat sadistic) images like this hint at Tommy's psychological separation from the world.

The moment when Tommy discovers his magical ability is one of the extended musical sequences in *Tommy* – no lyrics here, no narrators or characters describing what's happening. It's all Ken Russell and his band of talented filmmakers: they put Tommy in front of the mirror, re-unite the youth's split selves, and have his inner self walking off in the reflection. Tommy duly follows, ending up at a car junk yard at night. The circular motif appears – now it's the magical, white sphere, which can represent anything you like (Tommy's spirit guide, soul, his future, his inner self, his God, his enlightenment, whatever).

That might be enough for some filmmakers, but *Tommy* continues to develop this vital scene – the moment, for instance, where Tommy's enlightened inner self disappears and leaves Tommy alone is important. Tommy is abandoned once again, and distressed, but now has the inner resources to heal himself – by finding the pinball machine, and playing it.

Again, the dramatic contrasts in *Tommy* are crucial: between the ecstasy of the nighttime experience of playing the pinball machine, with the coloured disco lights flashing inside the cars around him, and the aftermath of the morning after, with its bleak daylight and the arrival of the distraught parents (and the police). It's an unusual depiction of teenage rebellion, to say the least.[81]

---

[81] You can bet that Pete Townshend and the Who hadn't imagined the scene playing out like this back in 1969!

And Ken Russell's intuitive narrative choices work well, too: why, for example, is it a junk yard? That pinball machine could appear anywhere (and knowing Russell's sensibility, it might materialize on a windy mountainside in Cumberland). But the junked cars provide a great setting – is it that Tommy finds something miraculous even amongst the trash of society? Even buried in the stuff that everybody throws away and thinks is worthless? Is it that summat as superficial and apparently worthless in popular culture can provide the means of transcendence?

The used car pound corresponds to the desert in a Biblical epic movie – the prophet or messiah goes out into the desert to commune with God (coming back enlightened after his trials). The whole sequence is certainly freighted with religious motifs.

CIRCLES.

One of the recurring motifs in *Tommy* is the circle, as in the rest of Ken Russell's cinema: the giant sun from the opening and closing images; the big, circular mirrors in Tommy's mother's bedroom; the circular mirror that reflects Tommy's alter egos; the little sphere atop the Tommy crosses; the baubles in the Christmas party scene; and the big close-ups of eyes. And that glowing, white globe which is Tommy's inspiration, guide, future.

Linked with the circular motifs is the sun: many times Ken Russell and DP Dick Bush point the camera at the sun, or have Tommy standing in front of the sun. Also aligned with circles and suns are mirrors. *Tommy* contains a huge number of mirror shots – often they're employed as indications of identity.

Water is another very prominent device in *Tommy*: Tommy falling into a swimming pool; Tommy's disciples swimming around him; the holiday camp by the sea; Tommy's mother in the pool at the camp; Tommy in the bath; Kevin hosing Tommy down in the garden; Tommy speaking with his mother on the rocks by the sea; Tommy baptizing his mother in the sea; Tommy standing under the waterfall (if you do a Ken Russell picture, you will be getting cold and wet!); Tommy climbing rocks alongside and through a stream; Tommy's mom and Captain Walker swimming under the waterfall (the couple are later seen near a lake); the Hell's Angels fighting beside (and in) a quarry pool (and later dancing next to a lake); and Tommy running in front of process footage of ocean waves.

Many times the filmmakers blend the simple but striking symbols together. For instance, when Tommy is finally woken up, three symbols – circles, water and the sun – are deployed. His mom Nora wakes Tommy up when she pushes him through a circular mirror in her bedroom; he falls backwards into water, lit in sunlight.

Ken Russell would often employ symbolism with the lack of finesse of an tenth grade art student trying to do a Salvador Dali, but it works. Russell wields his cinematic motifs with a sledge-hammer, and makes sure the viewer *really* gets it. Thus, in *Tommy*, water = life and rebirth, baptism, plenitude, the maternal realm and spirituality. Sun = awakening, wholeness, fulfilment (and rebirth). Circles = the self, the soul, as well as the search for wholeness or what Jungians call 'self-realization'.

THE PRIMAL SCENE.

It was Ken Russell who switched the emphasis of the primal scene that the young Tommy stumbled upon: on the Who's original album, it was the father who killed Tommy's mother's lover. There was a trade-off in doing that, of course. However, it's also possibly a fantasy or dream sequence: because Group-Captain Walker appears to be already dead by that time.

The primal scene scene in *Tommy* doesn't make sense in some respects: in it, Tommy's dad appears to the boy when he wakes in bed (in both guises – in his uniform, disfigured moments before death, and as he was before the fatal mission. He's meant to be an amnesia victim). Tommy's dad appears in his wife's bedroom, and sees her with Uncle Frank. Tommy goes to his mom's room, and witnesses the traumatic moment when Frank kills Captain Walker.

In Ken Russell's script, the scene's described thus:

TOMMY gets out of bed, opens his door and creeps along the deserted corridor. His MOTHER's bedroom door is partially open. Through the crack he sees a flurry of bodies, sheets, naked flesh – a bedside table lamp raised and the base brought down in a crushing blow onto his father's head. At the moment of contact the image freezes for a moment. CAPTAIN WALKER's agonised face is illuminated with an intense light which burning everything out before it explodes with a shatter of glass and plunges the room into darkness.

However, though this scene makes dramatic sense (but not

entirely), and it fits into the flow of the movie beautifully, it isn't logical. For a start, Tommy has never met his father; so much of this is what he is imagining, presumably (who must've been at war soon after Tommy's conception, and isn't there at the birth or afterwards).

It is the usurping of the father's place by Frank Hobbs, of course, with the mother at the centre. Yes, all of the (Freudian) psychosexual dynamics are in place. But there are further eccentricities about this scene: for one thing, Tommy appears to be about six here (it's meant to be 1951 – it's also 6 years after WWII), while the œdipal scene typically occurs much earlier (Sigmund Freud and Jacques Lacan and countless others have written of the primal scene and the œdipal tensions between mothers and sons).

For instance, let's indulge in some theorizing here: French feminist Julia Kristeva has drawn on both Sigmund Freud and Jacques Lacan to develop her own version of early, psychosexual growth: in the first stages of differentiation, identity is still shaky, and the individual confuses her/ himself with the maternal image (as in *The Music Lovers*, the mother dominates the protagonist in *Tommy*). The way out of this confusion, in the classic scenario, is via the age-old (Freudian) œdipal triangle (which *Tommy* illustrates). But Kristeva introduces her notion of abjection: the (male) child must split up his mother in order to take up his masculine gender: she is split into the abject and the sublime, Kristeva says in her book *Powers of Horror*.[82] Abjecting the mother enables the child to separate himself from the mother. To counter the mother becoming a phobic object, if she is only abjected, the phobic substitutes a sign for the absent object (ib., 45). Abjection thus operates in an in-between zone, as Kristeva calls it, 'of phobia, obsessions, and perversion' (ibid.). A loving 'imaginary' father is necessary for this journey through the stages of Kristevan abjection: the imaginary constructs encourage the separation from the mother. Only when the child identifies with the space opened up by the archaic or imaginary father, the paternal space, 'the father of individual prehistory',[83] can narcissism occur. Love always involves separation in Kristeva's psychology of the individual.

Let's get back to the young artist (or individual): that is, to those primal and primary zones of the womb, fluids, the

---

[82] J. Kristeva, *Powers of Horror*, 157.
[83] J. Kristeva, *Tales of Love*, 26.

maternal, the first few months of existence outside of the mother. For Julia Kristeva, the artist activates the tensions between the realms of the symbolic and the semiotic, between expression and repression, between the maternal and the individual.

And the whole thing may be in Tommy's dream, or imagination. It doesn't help that the scene isn't wholly convincing from a staging or action point-of-view; the act of Frank Hobbs whacking Captain Walker with a lamp doesn't quite have the violent impact it should possess. It's as if Ken Russell and the team pulled back here slightly from depicting something more explicitly violent (however, there is more violence later, particularly in the last act, when Tommy's followers rebel against his religious cult). No, it's not the violence, it's the decisiveness and the dramatic significance of the act.[84]

But if it isn't in Tommy's dream or imagination, the scene still possesses some odd elements – such as Captain Walker returning very late at night, at the bedroom door – no scenes downstairs, for example, of his return. And he looks exactly the same as the day he left for his mission in 1944 or 1945 (what was he doing for the intervening six years?). But what counts is the effect on *Tommy*, which the filmmakers emphasize by placing the camera behind Tommy at a low angle, while his mom and Frank yell at him on either side, very close to his face, that he didn't see anything or hear anything.

The relationship between Tommy and his mom Nora is sometimes clearly eroticized, with hints of incest. And it comes from both of them, not just, as is often in cinema (and literature), from one person. But the resolution to the sexual relation doesn't occur.[85]

CHRONOLOGY.

As to the time scale within the *Tommy* movie, the filmmakers pinpoint it very precisely when they have Tommy being born on VE Day (Victory in Europe Day), which was May 8, 1945 (Pete Townshend was born on May 19, 1945, so the birth date also ties Tommy to Townshend). That makes Tommy 6 in 1951, when his father Captain Walker returns and is murdered. So the opening scenes, in Cumbria, depicting the romance of Tommy's parents,

---

[84] None of the legal consequences Walker's murder are explored. No disposal of the body, etc, *à la* Alfred Hitchcock. No time for that!
[85] See J. Smith, 2010, 140.

would be nine months earlier – in August, 1944 (because the scenes in the waterfall and pool are (presumably) meant to depict the time of Tommy's conception). The attempts at healing Tommy in the church, for instance, and Tommy's awful experiences with Uncle Ernie and Cousin Kevin, would take place about 10 years later, when Tommy's 16 (in 1961).

Thus, when Tommy's revelation occurs and he wakes to form a new spiritual cult, he would be about 25 (or 1970), or maybe 30 (in 1975, when the film was released).

While much of *Tommy* is accurate historically, it also happily mixes time periods. Although the early part of the movie's set in WW2 and the 1950s, it employs all sorts of props and costumes and paraphernalia from later epochs, such as the 1960s and 1970s. For instance, there are scenes in fairgrounds where Frank and the young Tommy are playing an arcade game, shooting down bombers. This is the 1950s, and there were no video games then.[86]

All of that video game imagery in *Tommy*, including the animation that it segues into, with the bombers fusing into memorial crosses, comes out of the early-to-mid Seventies. But it works, because the film works emotionally and dramatically, and such oddities of mixing up the historical periods is only noticed after repeated viewings. And one of the pleasures of *Tommy* is that it is so well worked out and so heavily detailed, it bears up to repeated screenings (if you're clocking such details, you have of course missed the point!). The audience goes along with such inconsistencies because the narrative and dramatic line is so strong.

THE ACID QUEEN.

As Ken Russell conceived the 1975 musical movie, *Tommy* was about the journey of a person in a 'pilgrim's progress', towards self-discovery. The film begins and ends, for instance, with a man exultant on top of the mountain – his father at the beginning, and Tommy, going back to where he was conceived by his parents at the start of the movie.

As well as a coming-of-age story for the main character, *Tommy* was also a series of extravagant set-pieces in the Grand Ken Russell Style. Tina Turner's wild turn as the Acid Queen, high priestess of getting high, laid and loaded, was one of the

---

[86] There is also the added niggle that it would be unusual for a *British* arcade game to involve shooting down *British* aircraft – Germans, yes, Russians, yes, but not Brits.

best sequences. 'The Acid Queen' was a fantasy of hallucinatory drug abuse (which Russell mined later on in *Altered States*) and debauchery. Although it was a great song (sung by Pete Townshend on the album), Turner made it completely her own.

The centrepiece of 'The Acid Queen' sequence was the outrageous prop of the shiny, metallic iron maiden in which Tommy is entombed, festooned with hypodermic needles (and set in an attic with a sloping roof, again looking like a church).[87] The iron maiden (designed by Shirley Kingdon) opens to reveal, at different times, Tommy's father Group-Captain Walker in RAF uniform, half his face burnt; his father, smiling (as he'd like to remember him); Tommy, in white loincloth, recalling Jesus or a Catholic saint, trembling (in agony or ecstasy), adorned with poppies; and a skeleton garnished with live snakes (a Ken Russell favourite motif).[88]

> I'm the gypsy, the acid queen,
> Pay me before I start.
> I'm the gypsy, I'm guaranteed
> To break your little heart.
>
> ...I'm the gypsy, I'm guaranteed
> To tear his soul apart.

Tina Turner, eye-popping, lip-trembling, in diaphanous red, dominated the scene of Tommy's drug initiation by strutting about like a tornado in giant, wide angle close-ups or rapid handheld shots.[89] (Ken Russell said he wasn't a drug-taker himself, and had tried a magic mushroom in L.A. once but it had been a very bad experience. So the Acid Queen sequence was his interpretation of what a bad trip might be. Of course, the rock fraternity associated with the film – Eric Clapton, Pete Town-

---

[87] The setting was the 'Sin City Revue Bar', a clichéd, seedy, sleazy nightspot where Frank Hobbs and Uncle Ernie lurk shiftily.

[88] Although they crop up regularly in his cinema (they are all over *The Lair of the White Worm*, for instance), Ken Russell is scared of snakes, but operated the camera for that scene, when the camera operator chickened out. 'I shot it up a ladder with cycle clips on my trousers in case I was invaded; but I got away scot free', Russell recalled on the DVD commentary. (A scene where Daltrey was going to be covered with snakes was dropped).

[89] Visiting the set, Joe Gomez reported that Ken Russell operated the camera himself for these scenes, moving 'with the music as he followed the action, and soon the director and the actors were part of a riveting ballet. There was no awkwardness or sudden jerking of the camera – but instead a single, sustaining flowing motion with Russell lunging forward, tilting the camera, sliding back, bending up, and finally capturing that last close-up of Uncle Frank's sinister smile' (1976, 93).

shend, Keith Moon *et al* – could've offered plenty of advice on substance abuse).

Who is the Acid Queen? She is death, she is life – she is the wild experience, the uncontrollable urge. Pure id, pure desire. She's dressed in the bright, shiny red of blood and life and wounds and pain. There's no holding back – the Acid Queen scene's about breaking through boundaries and transgressions. And after this bout of drug-taking and being bad, Tommy will not be the same again; the casualties of drug habits have been a staple of rock 'n' roll movies, as well as underground cinema (even Frank Sinatra played a drug addict, in *The Man With the Golden Arm*, 1955). And the real-life casualties, of drugs such as LSD and heroin, are well-known (in the rock music world, Syd Barrett, Sid Vicious and Nancy Spungen).

It's not only sex. Yes, sex is part of it, but because sex is part of the Uncle Ernie scenes, in the Acid Queen sequence it's also drugs (note that Tommy's a real loner – he has no brothers or sisters, and no friends of his own age – or any friends at all. And he certainly doesn't have a lover, even when he's awakened, and can see, hear and speak).

For Pete Townshend, 'The Acid Queen' song was 'not just about acid. It's the whole drug thing, the drink thing, the sex thing, wrapped into one big ball' (in S. Grantely, 65). In his autobiography, Townshend calls the Acid Queen 'a prostitute, drug-pusher and gypsy' (158).

DRUGS.

Viewers who don't understand what an artist does – they make stuff up – often wonder if the creator is on drugs, especially if the artist delivers crazy images, like Ken Russell. Nope, Russell's drug, as he says, is music, and, like all artists, it's the creative work itself (though of course he loves a drink – particularly champagne).[90]

*Music*.

But I bet Ken Russell's been asked loads of times: *are you on drugs?* Or: *do you get all these crazy ideas from drugs?* It's as if when you snort some coke or shoot some heroin, you instantly become Leonardo da Vinci. If only!

Nah, Ken Russell is an artist, and that's what artists do: they

---

[90] People often asked the comedy filmmakers Zucker-Abrahams-Zucker (*Airplane!*, *The Naked Gun*, *Hot Shots!*, etc) if they were took drugs. Uhh, no.

make stuff up. Writers do it. Sculptors do it. Dancers do it. Painters do it. Musicians do it. And sometimes they come up with some crazy shit (which's often not crazy to the artist). Any good artist can access all of that mad stuff whenever they like – because it's part of their job. (In Russell's case, music was his drug, it was his way of coming up with the visions of his movies. A sip or two or champagne helped, of course!).

However, drugs do crop up in Ken Russell's movies and TV shows: Claude Debussy in *The Debussy Film* gets hooked on chloral, for insomnia. Dante Gabriel Rossetti's wife Lizzie Siddal in *Dante's Inferno* is addicted to laudanum (and Rossetti also to chloral – and booze). And of course the Romantic poets (in *Gothic*) partook.

And we should also note that Ken Russell's highest budget movie of all – *Altered States* – was very much about drugs and a very hi-falutin' use of drugs, too: this wasn't a character descending into pathetic self-pity and self-immolation, like a depressed poet or out-of-work rock star, it was a scientist using drugs to explore the secrets of the universe.

Because that's usually what drugs – and drink – are used for in movies: they're a theatrical device to suggest weakness, vulnerability, self-absorption, selfishness, insecurity, addiction, whatever (and in rock movies – also: excess! Wow! Wild parties! Wow!). That's all, just like the dramatic convention of having one actor wait until another actor has finished speaking their line before they say their line – when in real life everybody talks over everyone else all the time. Do you wait patiently until someone else has stopped talking then say your bit? No! Yet this is one of the commonest conventions in all drama, but one that nobody notices.

Because unless a ton of other stuff is going on in a druggy movie, it sucks. Which's why *Trainspotting* is a piece of crap and *Performance* is a masterpiece (to choose two British movies).

ABUSE.

Tommy is systematically abused as a youth. And there are *two* people tormenting Tommy: bullying and persecution from Cousin Kevin, and sexual abuse from Uncle Ernie (clearly one wasn't enough for the Who!). Paul Nicholas played the psychotic school bully from hell, Cousin Kevin (a sensational turn from

Nicholas),[91] who tortures Tommy every which way he can (cigarette burns, dunking him in the bath, spraying him with a hose,[92] and ironing him on an ironing board). Even in its camp, comicbook form, those scenes are still sinister and nasty – this is comic slapstick with the darker aspects of violence easily visible.

> I'm the school bully!
> The classroom cheat,
> The nastiest playfriend
> You ever could meet.

In 'Fiddle About', Keith Moon hammed it up as a cackling, lecherous pædophile, Uncle Ernie (in cloth cap, raincoat and gap-toothed grin), who brings along a suitcase of sex toys (!) when he babysits Tommy. (Ken Russell said that Moon was doing an impersonation of Robert Newton in *Tommy* – Newton is amongst the most over-cooked of British actors – have a look at *Treasure Island* (1950)[93] for one of the hammiest performances in the history of cinema).

> Down with your bedclothes,
> Up with your nightshirt!
> Fiddle about, fiddle about, fiddle about!

And when they leave Tommy with these dubious relatives, Nora and Frank Hobbs sing to each other:

> Do you think it's all right,
> To leave the boy with Uncle Ernie?

And Frank always answers: 'Yes, I think it's all right' (and the audience yells, 'No it isn't!'). The reprise of the same lyrics and the same situations outline Tommy's neglect and abuse over many years, but also lay out his childhood (and even though Roger Daltrey is meant to be playing a boy around 12 years old or teenager in these scenes, it doesn't matter – the movie gets away with it (just), instead of employing a teenage actor, as many

---

[91] Paul Nicholas (b. 1945) would scorch up the screen in the follow-up to *Tommy*, *Lisztomania*, as Richard Wagner. The Who had known Nicholas from the 1960s – Pete Townshend had given Nicholas (then called 'Oscar') the song 'Join My Gang', originally written for the *Quick One While He's Away* mini-opera.
[92] These were the first scenes filmed, according to Roger Daltrey.
[93] When Ken Russell took on *Treasure Island* (1995) for British TV, it wasn't your usual pirate show: he made Long John Silver a woman (played by his wife Hetty Baynes).

other films do).

Looking back at it, Pete Townshend said the one aspect that seemed harder to take in *Tommy* were those of abuse and bullying.[94] Child abuse, neglect, bullying and related issues had a different impact in the 2000s than they did at the time. Or it was the 1975 movie that was a little too jokey, a little too throwaway about issues and experiences that were too painful. (Townshend recalled that some of that sinister stuff came from staying with his grandmother as a child: 'I can't remember particularly clearly, but I know it was very, very unpleasant. I got involved with weird shit which involved some erotic and sexual stuff; that's all I know' [PF, 169]).[95]

Certainly, the scenes where Uncle Ernie and Cousin Kevin torment poor Tommy are difficult to take as comedy. They are aspects of *Tommy* that would probably be altered if it were produced today (Ken Russell remarked in the DVD audio commentary that it was be impossible to make *Tommy* today; it would cost too much, for a start). In one early draft of the album, the boy's father would've beaten his child, frustrated that the kid was deaf, dumb and blind.

However, both the 'Cousin Kevin' and 'Fiddle About' songs in *Tommy* were written by John Entwistle, not Pete Townshend: the latter said he wouldn't have been able to come up with such murky lyrics (finding the subject matter too traumatic in relation to his own childhood). Entwistle later said that Cousin Kevin was partly based on a bully he knew at school.

PSYCHOLOGY.

*Tommy*, although it appears to be dealing with superficial, Pop Art and popular culture elements, also contains all sorts of narrative developments. Frank Hobbs, for instance, doesn't remain the same character throughout the film: he shifts from being a greencoat and wide-boy character to a would-be aristocrat (appearing in one scene in hunting gear, for instance). That

---

[94] Pete Townshend had asked the Ox to write these two songs, because he found the subjects too disturbing. 'Fiddle About' was 'disturbing, relentless and powerful, although I was sad that it also seemed to turn into a dark joke about something I myself had found so disturbing as a child', Townshend remarked (159).
[95] And Pete Townshend was subject to a police investigation in 2003 when he had accessed a website about child abuse, when he was doing research for his autobiography (S. Grantley, 66). In 1996, Townshend said that his grandmother had boyfriends (all called 'Uncle'), and that some of them visited him in his bedroom. Townshend had tried finding out what happened thru therapy.

certainly echoes supergroups like the Who, the Beatles and the Rolling Stones, who bought fish farms (as Roger Daltrey did),[96] country houses, and ranches, and played at being upper-class toffs (which also reflects the capitalist aspirations of the British working class). Frank's – and Nora's – conspicuous consumption also mirrors the times of the 1960s and 1970s (the 1980s, 'greed is good' super-capitalism, were not far away). Later, Frank appears in the dark, green uniform of the Tommy follower, as one of the kingpins in the Tommy empire (Frank, of course, is also a spiv character, eager to exploit any situation for moolah. It's Frank who sings the song about running the Tommy cult's merchandizing operation. And in the movie of *Tommy*, it's Frank who's taking the money from the kids for the Tommy tie-in merchandize. The movie itself had its own merchandize, including Tees, badges, mirrors, stickers and a'course the soundtrack album).

Tommy's mother Nora Hobbs undergoes striking character developments, as does Tommy himself. This is why *Tommy* is no simple rock musical which strings together a collection of rock songs with a join-the-dots narrative. It has a genuine narrative and dramatic development, and depicts its main characters evolving over the course of the film. In other words, although *Tommy* didn't have a conventional script, it contained all of the character development, the rising action, the conflicts and pay-offs of a traditional narrative.

There's a lot more dramatic development and characterization in *Tommy*, for instance, than there is in many another musical (think about your favourite musicals, and how the characters change over the course of the movie. Often they don't, much). *Tommy* really does tell a story and explore characters, even though it's not your average musical show of a *Boy Meets Girl* story or a *Let's Put On a Show* story. *Tommy* is certainly a very strange story with a very strange central character (the prime story in musicals is romance). It's simultaneously a modern messiah story and a depiction of post-World War Two Britain (and the Western world emerging from WWII); it is at once a disaffected youth story and a dissection of popular youth culture in Britain (and the West). Few other musicals, and even rock musicals, could boast of exploring of so many themes – of teenage angst and alienation (in Tommy), of middle-aged anxiety and

---

96 Roger Daltrey bought a mansion in Burwash, Sussex; he became one of rock's land-owner gentry types, with two farms and a trout pond.

depression (in Tommy's parents), of youth culture and religion and modern messiahdom (in Tommy's followers).

So the frequent criticism launched at Ken Russell – that his movies are visually extraordinary but are lacking in terms of scripts and narrative – can be thrown out of the window here (like a TV set hurled from a Tinseltown hotel where Keith Moon and Led Zeppelin stayed in the 1970s). Because if you follow *Tommy* scene by scene and sequence by sequence, there are all of the narrative developments and story points and characterizations you might require.

Yet, let's not forget, *Tommy* is a *musical*, and musicals have a narrative form quite different from a melodrama or a Western or a screwball comedy. And many musical films get by with a very thin narrative (usually about love). Which doesn't matter at all. It doesn't matter that *An American In Paris* might have a flimsy narrative, because it is one of the most sublimely wonderful movies ever made. Ditto with *Grease*. Or *Summer Stock*.

A musical movie is a *genre* piece, too, with particular expectations, and motifs, and narrative demands. *Tommy* is exceptional in delivering not only narrative progression and character development (even if it is a weird story, and, on many levels, unbelievable), but also tackling really big themes, such as religion, religious cults and followers, and the exploitation of fans and followers. And there are also themes such as child abuse, the neglect of children, dysfunctional families, teenage alienation and depression, the consumer society, the commodification of popular culture, and the undercurrent of violence in everyday relationships.

### GREAT BRITISH LIFE.

*Tommy* was also a portrait of British society and history, as well as a rock opera about a 'deaf, dumb and blind' kid who becomes a kind of rock messiah. *Tommy* took a vignette and *tableau* approach to the portrayal of large chunks of pre-war and postwar British history. *Tommy* included depictions of the Second World War,[97] the Blitz, RAF planes on a mission over Germany, daddy lost in combat, a boy's bedroom with model planes, the bombed-out suburbs, a memorial service attended by widows in

---

[97] The 1969 *Tommy* album had focussed on the First World War, which Ken Russell changed to WW2, partly, he said, because he knew more about it, and had lived through the Blitz (and it would also resonate better with a modern audience).

black at a village monument,[98] V.E. Day celebrations (intercut with Tommy's birth, in 'It's a Boy'), the British seaside holiday camp, a 'lovely legs' competition, a dance, a strip club, a pinball competition, a British Christmas[99] (in 'Christmas'), and youth cultures such as teenyboppers, pop concerts and Hell's Angels.

One of the key images of *Tommy*'s overture is the complex tracking shot across the blitzed suburbs, involving many extras, props, smoke and fire, and classic Ken Russell details, such as the chorus girls from a local theatre in sexy costumes, wearing gas masks. It's one of the signature shots in all of Russell's cinema, and crystallizes the evocation of British life (in war-time).

The story of *Tommy* was in part the exploration by a British rock star of his roots, going back to pre-war Britain, the life-defining experience of WW2, the rebuilding of Britain in the Fifties, the emergence of rock 'n' roll and youth culture, the British family, the British vacation, the British Christmas, the increasing commodification in the 1960s, television, advertizing, and so on. 'Everything I write will always have the post-war thing running through it, because that's my period,' Pete Townshend explained. Similarly, World War Two had an enormous impact on Ken Russell's life: it, too, crops up in many of the movies he directed (he was 12 in 1939). But it was Russell & co. who widened out the 1969 *Tommy* album to include so much of British culture and history.

The time scale of *Tommy* is roughly twenty-five years – from before World War Two to Tommy as a young man. While Roger Daltrey (then 30) isn't aged up much, Oliver Reed and Ann-Margret have to be as the Hobbses (the costume changes and hairstyles help too – such as Tommy's mother's beehive hair, and that inspired leopardskin, which Ken Russell rightly called 'absolutely phenomenal').

The relentless commodification of society was embodied in the scene everyone remembers from *Tommy*: Ann-Margret in her plush, all-white den with its circular windows and mirrors and

---

98 Featuring a shamelessly phallic bomb as the centrepiece.
99 One of the more disturbing images in *Tommy* is where Frank sports a Santa Claus mask, holding it right next to the young, catatonic Tommy at the Christmas party, and singing at full throttle ('Tommy, can you hear me?'). Ann-Margret recalled that when Oliver Reed sang like that, it was a 'husky growl that comes right up from his stomach'.

bed, clad in a sexy, white cat-suit,[100] writhing around on the floor as detergent, bean and chocolate[101] gush from the TV set (in 'Champagne'). Tommy's mother's room is an image of 1960s wealth and achievement: the circular bed, the silk sheets, the enormous fur, the shiny chrome and plastic furniture. What Nora sees on TV is consumer culture run rife: TV adverts for chocolates, soap powder and baked beans.[102] (Parody television ads are something many filmmakers seem to enjoy making and putting into their films,[103] partly, one suspects, because many of them – including Ken Russell – have made ads themselves. Russell commented that he had shot all of those sorts of commercials, including the baked bean ad. Some of the material attacking the world of commercials derived from Russell's scripts *Music, Music, Music*[104] and *The Angels*).

The scene in *Tommy* is also about maternal guilt: the mother tries to change channels from the image of her boy staring at the viewer and singing 'feel me, see me, touch me, heal me', but the TV set reverts to Tommy every time Nora tries to escape her motherly duties (also a commentary on the sameness of television – whatever channel you switch to, it's always the same stuff).

> But what's it all worth, what's it all worth,
> When my son is blind?
> He can't hear the music
> Nor enjoy what I'm buying.
> His life is worthless, affecting mine.
> I'd pay any price
> To drive his plight from my mind.

LOVE.

Something is left out of *Tommy*. The 1975 picture is unusual in Ken Russell's cinema in leaving out one of his recurring themes

---

[100] Certainly Ken Russell wasn't the only one in the production who found Ann-Margret a sexy star; Roger Daltrey recalled that he had to remind himself that she was playing his mother, when she was slinking about in tight or revealing costumes.
[101] Ann-Margret's husband had objected to her doing this scene.
[102] The parody ad for Rex Baked Beans used costumes from *The Three Musketeers* (1973), which had starred actors such as Olly Reed, Roy Kinnear, Spike Milligan and Richard Chamberlain, who'd appeared in Russell's films.
[103] Joke commercials occur in the cinema of Jean-Luc Godard, Zucker-Abrahams-Zucker, and Stanley Kubrick, among others.
[104] In *Music, Music, Music*, an unmade Ken Russell script, the composer John Fairfax has to compromise: he has to write music for TV commercials in order to survive. Art is 95% hard work and 5% inspiration or talent in Russell's cinema. Witness Henri Gaudier working away at the sculpture all night in *Savage Messiah*. Even in a cartoon, satirical movie, like *Lisztomania*, the composer is shown at work composing.

and motifs: love. I mean, love between lovers, men and women, men and men, women and women, whatever. Tommy is alone: there is no young woman, no man, no girlfriend, no boyfriend, in his life. His major relationship is with his parents, and in particular with his mother.

So this is not your usual Ken Russell movie in that respect, because pretty much every Russell movie is stuffed with erotic entanglements, to the point where the romantic relationships take up large chunks of the running time. (It's also not a typical Pete Townshend story: romance is just about the key theme of the Who's music, as it is of all pop music).

For instance, it would've been easy to go the route of rock music groupies (who were at the height of their wildness in the mid-Seventies, if you believe the rock biographies), and have some of the women following Tommy in his messiah mode seduce him.

But the groupie or fan scene that the 1975 movie included was decidedly non-sexual and innocent: the Sally Simpson episode, where Sally is nuts about Tommy. (Even so, that sequence did evoke prepubescent adulation, which includes sexual desire, and the accoutrements of adulthood within pre-teens, such as make-up and clothes for older teenagers).[105]

As for Tommy, there is the Acid Queen scene, and the Uncle Ernie scene, which both include sex. Perverse as they were, those scenes did not suggest a longterm relationship for Tommy (how could the 'Acid Queen' and Tommy become an item?! or maybe they could – an addict and his dealer!). So, no Mary Magdalene, no long-suffering wife, no groupie, no teenage sweetheart for our Tommy.

Instead, by far the strongest erotic relationship in *Tommy* is between a mother and son. D.H. Lawrence and Sigmund Freud would've loved it!

'EYESIGHT TO THE BLIND'.

Undoubtedly one of the stand-out sequences in *Tommy* was the religious meeting in a church, presided over by Eric Clapton and the Who in long robes wielding guitars.[106] (Arthur Brown, best known as 'the god of hell-fire', fronting 1960s rock act the

---
[105] The Who have other songs about fans.
[106] Eric Clapton had been reluctant to be in the film, but had been intrigued by it, and was eventually persuaded to appear.

Crazy World of Arthur Brown, also appears, as the Priest holding communion with the kneeling faithful).[107] The song 'Eyesight To the Blind'[108] is by Sonny Boy Williamson:[109]

> You talk about your woman,
> I wish you could see mine.
> You talk about your woman,
> I wish you could see mine.
> Every time she starts to love,
> She brings eyesight to the blind.

The movie's interpretation of 'Eyesight To the Blind' turns the familiar emphasis on love and sex and the healing power of lovemaking that's everywhere in pop music into something spiritual. Now it's about healing in a specifically religious and institutionally religious manner. Instead of love and sex between two people, it's about a mass ritual of worshipping idols.

It was a religious service in which the congregation was led by British rock stars. As in his other films of the era (such as *Mahler*, *The Devils* and *The Music Lovers*), Ken Russell deployed his love of parodying Catholic imagery to mischievous, blasphemous effect. The sacrament, for instance, became hard spirits instead of wine (the petitioners glug from a whiskey bottle), and drugs not wafers representing the Body of Christ. The amazing extras in the scene were playing blind and disabled people,[110] some in wheelchairs.[111] They attended the service presumably to be healed.

Most extraordinarily, Marilyn Monroe replaced the Virgin Mary as the object of supplication, devotion and healing (in her famous incarnation in *The Seven Year Itch*).[112] A statue of the Fifties sex icon was the centrepiece of a procession through the nave of

---

107 Arthur Brown's 1968 album *The Crazy World of Arthur Brown* had been co-produced by Pete Townshend, and Brown was known for including much religious imagery and themes in his rock shows. (In fact, Townshend had intended to write a 25-song opera for Brown). The opera *Rael* grew out of the Arthur Brown opera. One of the songs written for *Rael* was 'The Motherland Feeling', part of which was used in *Tommy*.
108 Pete Townshend had first heard 'Eyesight To the Blind' performed by one of his favourites, Mose Allison (it was reworked by Townshend and dubbed 'The Hawker'). Townshend was also considering 'Country Shack'.
109 But Pete Townshend adapted it somewhat, and changed the lyrics.
110 Today, that scene would create even more of a fuss.
111 There's a cameo from Ken Russell in a wheelchair later on. Russell liked to put wheelchairs in his movies, and like Stanley Kubrick and other filmmakers, used a wheelchair for camera movements.
112 Ken Russell explained this as an organic progression – churches, he said, were filled with images of pretty women.

the church (a Pop Art version of the holy virgin/ holy whore duality of Western religion). There are Monroe pictures all along the nave. A creepy touch had women wearing Monroe masks and wigs, waving censers and dancing. There's a refracting filter on the camera lens, spotlights, coloured lights, candles, and smoke, all enhancing the theatricality of religion.

In the outrageous climax of the religious service the suppliants filed past the Marilyn Monroe statue, and touched the hem of her white skirt (Ken Russell included point-of-view shots up Monroe's skirt towards her crotch, and shots reflected in the round mirror at the base of the statue). But the religious ritual does not help Tommy – he's been brought there by his mom to heal him, as with all of the other followers. But the statue smashes into pieces on the floor[113] – another false idol and false religion.

There was so much the conservative, Republican, right-wing and Christian fundamentalist organizations could be offended by in this sequence: the combination of sex and religion, religion and popular culture, religion and movie icons was brilliant. And not least annoying to authorities and watchdogs was the depiction of disability, and the linking of disability to this heady mixture of eroticism, Pop Art, rock music and Christianity (the extras, invited from local hospitals and clinics and homes, knew what they signing up for and were happy to be in the film). The healing sequence ended with a sustained, trippy montage, a series of rapid images which were self-consciously silly but also bitter parody.

The 'Eyesight To the Blind' sequence also drew upon the trend in late 1960s/ early 1970s popular culture for blending rock music with (generally Christian) religion (as in rock musicals on stage and film like *Jesus Christ Superstar, Godspell, Stardust* and *Joseph and the Amazing Technicolour Dreamcoat*. Those musicals are regularly revived).

The notion of a 'rock messiah' was not too far-fetched, either: Jim Morrison, Elvis Presley, Bob Marley, Stevie Wonder, Tupac Shakur and John Lennon would all be regarded as messianic and guru figures in time (and some, like Elvis, Morrison and Lennon had – and have – their own shrines, maintained by acolytes). There are still people who make pilgrimages to, for instance, the

---

[113] The statue was made of plaster for this gag, and needed to be built twice, because the first take hadn't worked (it's filmed with a camera running at high speed). The other statue is fibre-glass (and it's larger).

Père-Lachaise cemetery in Paris, to see the Lizard King's grave, or visit Graceland, or Strawberry Fields in Central Park.

As Pete Townshend noted in *Time Out* in 1971, *Tommy* 'has a mystical thread flowing through it, and it's about the spiritual revolution of a man rather than about the sub-teenage frustrations I used to write about before'.

The spiritual journey in *Tommy* (the 'amazing journey' of the title) is towards spiritual perfection, or realization, or enlightenment, or union, whatever you wanna call it (the terms become interchangeable – especially in the 'perennial philosophy' of the late 1960s!). Reincarnation (*à la* Hermann Hesse) was an important element (Hesse (and *Steppenwholf* and *Siddharta*) being a favourites of the period: the hero would be reborn seven times on the quest to mystical union (so there are seven stages that the hero passes thru).)

The master/ disciple relationship was another important ingredient in the 'amazing journey' of *Tommy*, stemming from Pete Townshend's interest in Meher Baba (Baba was the master, his followers were the disciples, in the usual relationship in spiritual culture; but in *Tommy*, Tommy's father is the focus of the spiritual quest: he's the guru; but, in the end, Tommy himself becomes the guru).

'PINBALL WIZARD'.

Elton John[114] was given the biggest song from *Tommy* – 'Pinball Wizard' – shot in a traditional theatre in Southsea with 1,500 arm-waving, banner-holding extras[115] culled from local colleges.[116] Stevie Wonder had been considered for the part (which didn't make sense to Pete Townshend – a blind guy who's meant to be a pinball wizard, playing against a blind, dumb and deaf boy). Rod Stewart had played the role in the 1972 production by Lou Reizner of *Tommy*, and wanted the part in the movie.

'Pinball Wizard' is one of the Who's finest songs, and the version by Elton John and his band is marvellous (it reached no.

---

114 Elton John had supported the Who at the Roundhouse in London in 1970. The Who had included a tribute to Elton John in their 1991 version of 'Saturday Night's Alright For Fighting' (they included part of John's 'Take Me To the Pilot' at the end of the song).
115 The Who played a concert at the Guildhall in Portsmouth for the extras at the end of filming, as a 'thank you'.
116 The screams were aparently taken from *A Hard Day's Night*.

7[117] in the pop charts in Britain in 1976),[118] with a superb use of the piano replacing Pete Townshend's chiming guitars[119] (in the movie, though, it's the Who who serve as John's backing band, but on the soundtrack it was John's regular band who recorded the song – and they did it in less than four hours, including backing vox and solos).

> Ever since I was a young boy,
> I've played the silver ball.
> From Soho down to Brighton,
> I must have played them all.
> But I ain't seen nothin' like him
> In any amusement hall,
> That deaf, dumb and blind kid
> Sure plays a mean pinball!
>
> He stands like a statue,
> Becomes part of the machine,
> Feeling all the bumpers,
> Always playing clean.
> He plays by intuition,
> The digit counters fall,
> That deaf, dumb and blind kid
> Sure plays a mean pinball!
>
> He's a pinball wizard,
> There has to a twist,
> A pinball wizard,
> 'S got such a supple wrist.

For the 1969 *Tommy* album, the track had been recorded at London's Morgan Studios in February, 1969. In the U.S.A. the single reached no. 19, and no. 4 in Britain.[120] Pete Townshend recalled that the song had been written 'to try and get my friend Nik Cohn to accept rock opera':[121] Townshend included pinball because he knew that Cohn was into pinball[122] (and his girlfriend was a pinball champ): if the song was a little too obvious and on

---

[117] The single had originally reached no. 4 in Britain and no. 19 in the U.S.A.
[118] Nigel Olsson, Dee Murray, Ray Thomas and Davey Johnstone, and produced by John's regular producer, the wonderful Gus Dudgeon.
[119] 'Pinball Wizard' was an experiment, Townshend recalled, to see how many chords he could make using a running B. Townshend jammed (for some 15 minutes on the demo) around 30 or 40 chords using B.
[120] The pop singles from *Tommy* were there, Townshend said, 'to reflect and release, prefigure and inspire, entertain and engage' (164).
[121] Nik Cohn had heard the *Tommy* album and found the story 'a bit po-faced and humourless', according to Townshend (161).
[122] Cohn, also a friend of Kit Lambert's, was writing a book at the time called *Arfur: Teenage Pinball Queen*.

the nose, 'in the end it worked', said Townshend.[123] (Nik Cohn also worked on a film project (with Chris Stamp) which would star the Who, entitled *Rock Is Dead (Rock Lives)*. It was linked to an idea for a double album in which each member of the Who would take a side each (other bands had tried similar concepts, such as Led Zep and ELP). The four-cornered idea would later develop into *Quadrophenia,* as *Tommy* developed Cohn's story of the four Who members (the character was called Tommy in *Rock Is Dead*) into Jimmy in *Quadrophenia* (241).)

Why pinball? Well, it could be anything that Tommy turns out to be genius at, but pinball is a suitably odd pursuit, not a sport, but leisure, and also popular, and keyed into popular culture (there are pinball machines decorated with every pop fad. Still today, at least in Britain, pinball machines can be found in every seaside town and amusement arcade.) It was true, Pete Townshend admitted, that it didn't make sense that Tommy should be playing pinball when he was deaf, dumb and blind. It was 'daft, flawed and muddled,' Townshend confessed, 'but also insolent, liberated and adventurous' (ib., 162).

But in movies, forget the Who and 'Pinball Wizard' and *Tommy,* it's *Jean-Luc Godard* who's *the* Pinball Wizard. No filmmaker has ever included more pinball machines in their movies than the French genius – extras bang away at pinball machines in every café scene in a Godard movie (and not only those of the Sixties).

The idea of 'Pinball Wizard' in *Tommy* was to allow the hero to have an epiphany, to

> have some sort of colourful event and excitement. Suddenly things are happening... 'Pinball Wizard' is about life's game, playing the machine – the boy and his machine, the disciples with theirs, the scores, results, colours, vibration and action. (In S. Grantley, 67)

The 'Pinball Wizard' scene in *Tommy* is another of the out-size concerts that Ken Russell has staged throughout his movie career.[124] Russell is undoubtedly one of the great film directors of

---

[123] The title 'pinball wizard' (and 'mean pinball') also came from Nik Cohn (ib., 162). According to *Time Out* (1973), the machines to look out for were Gottlieb, Williams and Bally. The Pinball Wizard plays Gottlieb's *Buckaroo*, and Tommy plays Gottlieb's *Kings & Queens*.

[124] 'The entire 'Pinball Wizard sequence, with Elton John on stilts as the ultimate glitter-hooligan, at the front of an extraordinary shot stretching back to encompas a theatre full of screaming teens,' as Garry Mullholand put it (167).

live musical performances. He is one of the few filmmakers to *genuinely*, properly and fully capture the excitement and power of a rock show or a classical concert. It's not simply a case of covering the show from a variety of angles, or of rapid cutting, as so often in your average musical number or rock concert recording. It's about really understanding the multi-layered links between music and images; it's about knowing when to cut and when to hold on an image; and it's about rhythm and timing.[125]

Ken Russell has those abilities times a million. And in British cinema, there hasn't been anyone quite like him. *Tommy* is a classic, and one of the great musical movies in British cinema, partly because of the sheer power of the musical numbers.

THE SPECIALIST.

Ken Russell and the team of filmmakers added enormously to the Specialist (Doctor) sequence – the lyrics and the music deliver plenty of dramatic action, but the Columbia movie enhances it hugely. In the recording, the Specialist sings about the tests he performed ('he seems to be completely unreceptive, | The tests I gave him showed no sense at all'), but the movie shows them in detail, and adds numerous elements, from unusual props (the Specialist's machines, the odd equipment on Tommy's head), to the twin nurses (Jennifer Baker and Susan Baker),[126] to the obvious flirting between the Specialist and Nora Hobbs (while Frank's present).[127]

The Specialist scene is a little bitta realism in the story of *Tommy*, as some medical cause or solution to Tommy's predicament is searched for: here Tommy's parents actually act like caring parents (instead of leaving Tommy with Uncle Ernie or Cousin Kevin!). That the weirdness of the visit is enhanced (such as the examination of Tommy, or the appearance of the twin nurses), undermines the attempts at naturalism or regular drama. It's notable, for instance, that the Hobbses only take Tommy to see

---

[125] *So many* television tapings of pop shows, for instance, simply cut-cut-cut, too rapidly, too haphazardly, via video vision mixing, and misunderstand what music is, what a show is, and how best to portray a show on TV.

[126] As well as twin nurses in the Specialist scene, there are also twins employed as the Acid Queen's assistants: Juliet King and Gilliam King (Lefkowitz). Why twins? Presumably to play into the theme of split personality. And cinema likes twins, of course, because they look weird and play into perennial themes of doubles/ *doppelgängers*, etc.

[127] The flirtation once again undercuts Nora's character, so that instead of being the caring mom, she's still a kid, selfishly pursuing her own goals.

a doctor when they have enough dough to afford seeing a private doctor (that is, in Britain, at least, with its National Health Service, established after WW2, there would've been more help for Tommy). It's significant, for instance, that in *Tommy* the parents are depicted as somewhat clueless, and also shallow. As long as they've got enough money for some champagne and nice clothes, they don't bother too much with anything else. They sure have no idea what to do with Tommy when he becomes deaf, dumb and blind.

'SALLY SIMPSON'.

Another crazy sequence in *Tommy* concerns one of Tommy's fans, the young girl Sally Simpson (played by Victoria Russell, who appeared in many of her dad's films, right back to when she was a baby).[128] Sally becomes Tommy's number one fan: the walls and ceiling of her room are decorated with Tommy's pin-up image, wall to wall, a great touch – not *one* poster, but loads (the poster is a superbly conceived, high-key image of Tommy as a messiah, exactly the sorta pic that might've been included free with girls' magazines). (Her father (played by Russell regular Ben Aris) is – naturally – a vicar, who spends his time narcissistically polishing his black Rolls-Royce. Of course, Reverend Simpson doesn't approve of his daughter's infatuation with the rock god messiah, and neither does his wife, played by Mary Holland).

Sally Simpson is wounded at one of Tommy's concerts (inspired by an incident at a Doors gig), when she gets too close to the stage and Ollie Reed's Frank steps on her hands.

> The crowd went crazy
> As Tommy hit the stage!
> Little Sally was lost for the price of a touch
> And a gash across her face!
> Her pretty face!

Pete Townshend had seen a girl running onto the stage when they were supporting the Doors in the U.S.A. (to get close to Jim Morrison), and being hurled away by some bouncers. Townshend was among those who comforted her (148). The concert was at the Singer Bowl in Flushing Meadow, New York, on Aug 2, 1968.

The 'Sally Simpson' sequence is the story of a prepubescent

---

[128] Victoria Russell became a costume designer in her own right, like her mom, mainly in her dad's movies.

groupie, as seen from a rock star's perspective on the stage. It's fitting that it's Pete Townshend who sings the song about Sally in the movie. She gets to marry an American rock star. Her beau is a teen dressed as an adult (with a Frankenstein's monster make-up),[129] who wears a guitar around his neck at the altar (he was played by Gary Rich, who had been the young Gustav Mahler in *Mahler* the previous year).

*Tommy*'s 'Sally Simpson' episode is a self-contained sequence of its own, with a beginning, middle and end, all staged in Ken Russell's favourite approach of music plus images. But it's very important, narratively, because it's all about how fans worship their idols. The idols become interchangeable – they could be rock stars or they could be religious messiahs.

Sally Simpson's injured at the rock concert because this little morality tale is about the *costs* of fandom. The costs to the fan, not to the performer. It's exaggerated dramatically (well, that's what drama is/ does), and it also shows that even your kid sister can become a victim (that it's a young girl of course ties in to teeny-bopper culture, and it enhances the drama when a young, innocent girl is hurt (rather than a burly, hairy Hell's Angel!), but the morality tale applies to any fan).[130]

THE MESSIAH.

The satires on gurus and followers in *Tommy* are vicious too – or are they simply realistic? – because gurus (and their millions of followers) are everywhere today, as they were in the 1970s when the film was made, and the 1960s when the rock opera was composed. In *Tommy*, there's a scene where Tommy sits atop a building, with the sun creating a halo behind him, making hand gestures to a group of disabled people below who try to emulate him. The soundtrack emphasizes the guru–acolyte scenario with birdsong and quasi-Indian, New Agey music.

The Tommy cult is for everybody – the folk drawn to Tommy's home, church meetings and later the holiday camp include soldiers, teachers, bakers, hunting types (in red jackets), businessmen, children, grannies, etc.

As well as fishermen on the beach, there are numerous other

---

[129] The Frankenstein's monster motif was taken up in Ken Russell's next film, *Lisztomania,* and of course in *Gothic*.
[130] In fact, a girl was injured during the filming: Pete Townshend threw his guitar in the air and it landed on her (it's also a slice of traditional Who behaviour, when Tommy's backing band performs like the Who).

Christian references in *Tommy*, including Tommy baptizing his mother, the church meeting that begins with gospel hour and ends with a Tommy sermon (in the 'Sally Simpson' sequence), followed by a wedding, Tommy singing, 'I am the light', Tommy drawing the hurt and needy to him, a Last Supper (with green wine!), and the 'T' turned into a cross (used everywhere in the Tommy cult – the microphone, the lights on the stage, etc). And the 'Eyesight To the Blind' of course satirizes countless Christian rituals and symbols – that scene is going to remain offensive to many Christians for years to come.

The Tommy merchandize includes Tee shirts, stickers, glasses, crosses, mirrors, and records. The oddest aspect is the caustic satire on fandom and the lengths that fans and groupies will go in following their idols: Tommy eye-shades, earplugs and corks, so the fans can emulate Tommy's pre-enlightened state of being deaf, dumb and blind.

The ending of *Tommy* is broad satire, an attack, as in *The Devils*, on organized religion and the concept of worship. Thus, it can appear a little confused, because the narrative flow doesn't always make sense. The new messiah's followers turn up at the holiday camp (now called 'Tommy's Holiday Camp'), buy merchandizing, surround Tommy's house and generally worship him. At an outdoor park dominated by giant, silver spheres, the disciples play at pinball machines (a tall order for the art department to source so many machines;[131] the silver pinballs were actually buoys at Pound's ship-breakers in Portsmouth,[132] which had been redressed as Tommy's holiday camp). But they rebel, singing 'we're not gonna take it' (one of the better *Tommy* songs), smashing up the machines, setting fire to them, and killing Tommy's parents.[133] In the final scene the movie goes psychedelic again, with Tommy's grinning, running figure at the centre of a torrent of images.

Pete Townshend acknowledged that the endings of both *Tommy* and *Quadrophenia* were disappointing – because he was advancing intuitively, and hadn't conceived the whole story from the outset. However, the ending of the 1975 movie's convincing

---

[131] But Ken Russell said they found plenty in the Portsmouth area.
[132] The buoys needed to be repainted several times, as anyone stepping on them wore off the paint.
[133] This is one of the big practical effects and special effects sequences, with a 300 foot long row of pinball machines being rigged for fire. Roger Daltrey was burnt on the third take.

and satisfying (and at least a protagonist in a Ken Russell doesn't die at the end! Death provides the sometimes too easy, too pat ending of a Russell flick. Instead, there is a powerful and unequivocal affirmation of *life*).

One of the more bizarre scenes in *Tommy* is a battle between two Hell's Angels gangs in a quarry.[134] The fight's covered with rough and ready stunts and cutting – not quite *West Side Story*, but a lot of fun. And very silly, too. But when Tommy appears in a hang-gilder above them, they seem to learn the error of their ways (now reformed, the grisly bikers are seen doing the Status Quo boogie dance at a lakeside).

It's all about the power of Tommy's messianic influence: he can even tame bunches of no-goods like Hell's Angels, and bring them into the fold, as well as a satire on movies about Jesus. (Sequences dropped from *Tommy* included a scene where office workers and soldiers would drop what they were doing when they heard Tommy's evangelical callings on a P.A. (In the movie, other characters, such as the Hell's Angels gang, hear Tommy's message).)

The final quarter of *Tommy*, where the 'deaf, dumb and blind' becomes a messiah, is truly dotty, with Pete Townshend and Ken Russell giving free rein to their imaginations. Tommy appears to his followers, for instance, singing from a hang-glider (this must be the only movie where the hero sings from a hang-glider, and a hero who's a messiah!).

> You'll feel me coming,
> A new vibration
> From afar you'll see me.
> I'm a sensation!
> I'm a sensation!

The lyrics – 'I'm a sensation!' – work on a number of levels: it's about awakening, of course, spiritually but also physiologically, because Tommy has been deaf, dumb and blind for years. As Pete Townshend put it, the experience in 'Sensation' is 'that of divinity. Tommy is worshipping himself, knowing what he is and speaking the truth'. Tommy becomes the sensation itself.[135]

---

[134] The Black Angels were led by Dick Allan.
[135] But 'Sensation' had originally been inspired by a woman Pete Townshend met on tour in Australia called Rosie.

In another scene, Tommy addresses his congregation from the top of a church tower (with the hang-glider above him). In another scene, his acolytes (including the disabled folk) carry him along suspended from his hang-glider in a religious procession. And another scene has Tommy singing to his converts from a diving board above a swimming pool (they jump into the pool behind him). Truly bonkers. (The compositions of some of these scenes consciously evoke the Biblical spectaculars of the Fifties and Sixties, the blockbuster flicks that're still shown every Easter and Christmas).

Then there's the scene in *Tommy* where a crowd of the disabled extras worship Tommy. (Incredibly Roger Daltrey performed most of the stunts himself, though not the jump in a hang-glider off the church tower.[136] In many scenes in the last quarter, Daltrey is perched atop roofs or walls or diving boards, striking messianic poses as he addresses his followers.[137] Ken Russell said they didn't really think about it, they just asked Daltrey to do the hang-glider and other stunts, and he agreed (without cables and safety devices).[138] You can see Daltrey throwing himself into the role wholeheartedly – as well as the precarious moments on walls and roofs, he's often climbing around piles of disused cars or rocks. At the end of *Tommy*, Daltrey's wading and clambering through freezing, rushing streams.[139] There are many performers who wouldn't do that. One scene Daltrey balked at – climbing the rocks of the final hill in the Lake District – Russell told him he'd do it to show him it was OK. So Russell did, and after that of course Daltrey had to do it).

Roger Daltrey admired Ken Russell, and thought he was probably the only director who could've done it: 'we need a guy who we can relate to, feed information in to him, and get something back. Ken's the first bloke that's done that since our manager Kit Lambert dropped out of the scene'.

---

[136] Daltrey did some of the hang-glider stunts: it took guts, he said, 'but I would do anything for Ken'.
[137] Altho' he is known as a perfectionist who sometimes pushes his performers to multiple takes, Ken Russell also filmed scenes in one or two takes. For *Tommy*, there were times when multiple takes were required: Russell asked Roger Daltrey to run thru a field of mustard 32 times b4 he was satisfied.
[138] In the commando scenes, Daltrey was knocked unconscious for an hour.
[139] 'This is the first and last film I make,' Daltrey asserted at the time.

RELIGION.

Part of *Tommy* was about the followers of a false religion. The Tommy cult starts out well-meaning but becomes corrupted. Part of that narrative element derived from Ken Russell and his abandoned script *The Angels*, which was to have followed up *The Devils*. *The Angels* was about corrupt religion, and Russell duly adapted elements from *The Angels* for *Tommy*. (Russell had developed *The Angels* during the production of *Savage Messiah*, aided by Derek Jarman. It was dubbed his *48 1/2* (*pace* Federico Fellini, and how old Russell was). One of the characters in *The Angels* was a film director, Michael Mann (this was b4 the American director Michael Mann became well-known, of course), who undertakes an 'amazing journey' to a film festival in some Eastern European country. When the star of Mann's movie, Poppy Day, the 'Pantella pin-up', apparently dies, a shrine is developed, which includes a lifesize statue. That notion found its way into *Tommy* in the form of the Marilyn Monroe statue and the acolytes in the church.)

Ken Russell also incorporated elements from another original script idea in *Tommy*, with the very Russellian title *Music, Music, Music*. This was about a recurring Russell theme – selling out, and in particular selling out to advertizing and capitalism. *Music, Music, Music* concerned a composer called John Fairfax who sells out to the commercial world instead of pursuing his rock opera *Jesus On Venus*.[140] As Russell explained, *Music, Music, Music*

> will be about the things you have to do for money, from writing music for mad dukes to writing commercials for canned lamb. The artist has always been at the mercy of the commercial, or of somebody who will butcher his work.

The Catholic imagery is laid on thick in the final reels in *Tommy*, where Tommy becomes a messiah: the 'T' for Tommy is shaped like a cross (a *tau* cross),[141] and has the steel pinball atop it (Tommy also sports a microphone with this motif; in a similar manner, Prince had a prop mic shaped like a gun); Tommy's face on the posters (and the wallpaper in Sally's bedroom) is lit with a glowing light, recalling Catholic posters of Christ (*Tommy* sends

---

[140] The baked beans scene came from both *Music Music Music* and *The Angels*, Ken Russell admitted. And the shrine sequence was in both *The Angels* and *Gargantua*, the abandoned François Rabelais adaption.
[141] As well as a *tau* cross, it also recalls the ancient Egyptian *ankh*.

up cheapo, cheesy religious art); Tommy runs on the beach past some fishermen and a boat; Tommy 'baptizes' his mother in the sea (and is re-baptized in the waterfall); and in Tommy's house, Tommy, his parents and some others sit at a table suggesting the Last Supper.

THE ENDING.

Set free from his parents in the closing scene, Tommy disappears into the world, running and cartwheeling along a sandy beach, past rows of people sitting in cars on a South Coast promenade,[142] and running against process screen shots of lava and waves and undersea fish. Roger Daltrey's Tommy is certainly a memorable sight at this point in the film: topless, in blue jeans, he grins and stares into camera (Daltrey plays much of the final part of the film topless – it helps that he has a great body).

Tommy stands under a waterfall, and sings. It's the triumphant sounds of the Who's 'Listening To You', a terrific song, with lyrics which match the ebullience of the music, delivered by Roger Daltrey at full throttle:

> Listening to you, I get the music,
> Gazing at you, I get the heat.
> Following you, I climb the mountain,
> I get excitement at your feet!

And Ken Russell took that lyric about climbing the mountain literally, because now Tommy's in Russell's beloved Lake District, climbing the rocks beside white water and finally scaling one of Cumbria's peaks. The 1975 musical culminates with an image of Tommy saluting the rising sun, his small figure silhouetted against the enormous, yellow orb, raising his arms to greet it (this was how the movie opened, with Tommy's father). The image is meant to evoke wholeness, one supposes, and fulfilment. Tommy's finally come to life, finally grown up, and finally free of all of the shackles and disturbing events which held him back throughout the film.

It's significant that at the end of the Columbia picture Tommy is seen on his own, in the midst of the natural world, far away from civilization – and other people. Significant, too, that Tommy's journey ends in one of Ken Russell's favourite places, on

---

[142] Which they do all over Britain, all the time, staring out at the ocean.

a Cumbrian peak. Up there, in the sun, on a hill, in the wilderness, is one of the prime Ken Russell places – and soul states. It's the end of the 'amazing journey'.[143]

---

[143] If you're going to end up anywhere in Britain at the end of your 'amazing journey', on the peaks of Cumbria will do just fine.

On this page and the following pages:
images from a truly remarkable movie, Tommy (1975)

There is more satire and irony in Ken Russell's cinema
than many critics realize: the illusions and false promises
of commercials and capitalism are one of Russell's key targets,
seen here in this stupendously OTT scene in Tommy.

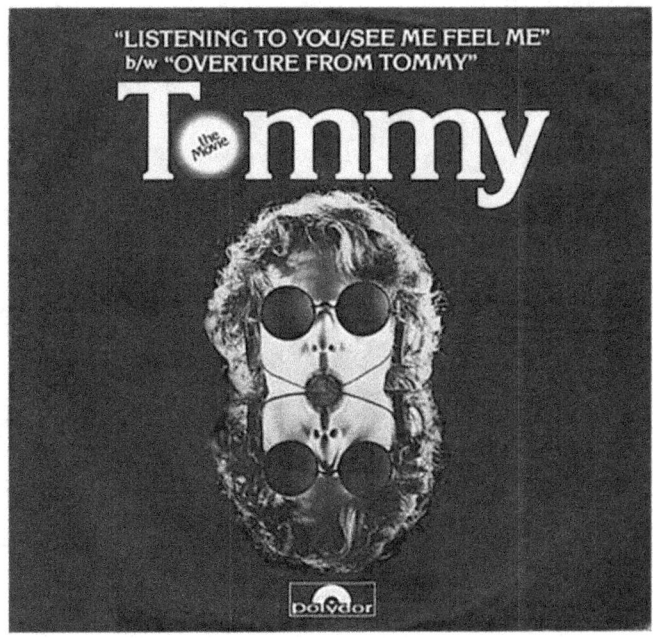

The Tommy film poster (above).
The Tommy album cover (below).

The Who on stage. Hamburg, 1972 (left). 1975 (below).

# 14

♪

# *LISZTOMANIA*

Courage is the mainspring of our best qualities: where it is lacking they wither, and without courage one is not even sufficiently prudent. One must, of course, consider, reflect, calculate, weigh the pros and cons. But after that one must make up one's mind and act, without paying undue attention to the direction of the wind or to any passing clouds.

Franz von Liszt, 1868[1]

I came to *Lisztomania* quite late, having seen most of Ken Russell's movies many times over the years. I'd wanted to see *Lisztomania* for ages. What a treat *Lisztomania* is! *Lisztomania* is a real gem of a movie, though probably one of the lesser-known items in the Russell œuvre (it only appeared on DVD, for instance, in 2009.[2] I wish I'd caught// it on a giant screen in 1975).[3] If you haven't seen it, you must! *Lisztomania* is vintage Ken Russell – and that means *a lot*.

There is something very beautiful and hypnotic about *Lisztomania*: it seems to have magically produced (along with *The Music Lovers*, its obvious forerunner) just about the most successful mix in Ken Russell's cinema of classical music, a biopic of an artist/composer, historical research, extravagant visuals and designs, extreme stylizations, staging, editing, over-the-top camp and lurid

---
[1] F. Liszt, letter to Richard Pohl, Nov 7, 1868, in H. Gals, 218.
[2] There is a wonderful audio commentary from Ken Russell on the DVD.
[3] So many great movies haven't been released on video or DVD yet – for countless reasons, of course, many to do with copyright, ownership, money and rights.

kitsch, comedy, romance, sex, and beauty.

I also find it one of the more emotional and moving of Ken Russell's movies: it's something about the struggle of the artist and the relation between art and life, and between an artist and their relationships – and it's about the beauty of music, and how *Lisztomania* puts ♪ centre stage. Again and again, it's about Russell's remark: 'the most incredible event in human history' is music ♪.

*Lisztomania* (1975) is a satire, as Ken Russell explained. That is, it is *a comedy*. That simple fact explains everything, and applies to many other Ken Russell movies. So all those criticisms that film reviewers have about Russell's works, that the film establishment has about him, that the media have about Russell, all of the attacks on Russell can be set aside if one considers the form, the genre, the approach of his movies in the right fashion.

It can be summed up as a series of questions and answers:

Q: Why is a Ken Russell film so over-the-top?
A: It is a comedy.
Q: Why is it all so silly, so theatrical, so bonkers?
A: It is a comedy.
Q: Why are Russell's movies so crude sometimes, so vulgar?
A: It is a comedy.
Q: Why do Russell's pictures rush around at a frantic pace, without pausing to make 'serious' or intellectual statements?
A: It is a comedy.
Q: Why doesn't a Russell film situate itself properly in a historical time and place?
A: It is a comedy.
Q: Why does a Russell movie hurtle from broad farce one moment to political satire the next to a moment of loss and nostalgia the next?
A: It is a comedy.
Q: Why can't Ken Russell be more restrained in his movies?
A: It is a comedy.[4]

LISZT AND WAGNER.

Franz von Liszt (October 22, 1811, Doborján, Hungary - July 31, 1887, Bayreuth, Germany) was one of the superstars of the

---
[4] You could also add: If it's a comedy, why isn't it funny? And the answer is simply: it is a comedy!

classical music world of the 19th century,[5] and, according to Hans Gal, perhaps the greatest pianist 'the world has ever known' (212). Born in Hungary, he was brought up in France, and was probably most at home in Paris. He knew most of the celebrated names in the music world of the time – Robert Schumann, Hector Berlioz, Frédéric Chopin and of course Richard Wagner, whose music he adored.

Among Franz Liszt's works were symphonies (*Dante, Faust*), numerous piano pieces (*Hungarian Rhapsodies, Liebsträume, St Francis*), symphonic poems, oratorios and masses, and *Tasso, Orpheus, Prometheus, Hamlet*, etc.

The ambiguous relationship between Franz von Liszt and Richard Wagner (May 22, 1813, Leipzig - February 13, 83, Venice), shifting from warmth through paranoia and doubt to open hostility, formed much of the backbone of Ken Russell's 1975 movie.[6] (Similarly, with *Delius: Song of Summer*, Russell remarked that he'd written a script about Frederick Delius years before he made his movie, but it was finding out about the odd relationship between Eric Fenby and the composer that really enhanced the prospect of doing a film about Delius).

> Without any regular income, prevented from doing anything for the promotion of his works in Germany, [Wagner] found in Franz Liszt a generous friend who supported him financially to the limits of his resources [wrote Hans Gal], and an inspired prophet who incessantly worked for him both as a performer and a propagandist.

According to Hans Gal in *The Musician's World*, Richard Wagner was

> fantastically argumentative. As a musician, dramatist, politician, philosopher and philanthropist, he held his own strong views and was indefatigable in formulating and communicating them. He won his battles as much by the drumfire that came from his pen as by his artistic achievements. One may often find his methods demagogic, his reasons spurious, his propaganda crude, but one cannot help admiring a man of such burning conviction and tremendous vitality. (279)

*Lisztomania* happily rewrites history and turns Richard Wagner into a really nasty villain – a key influence on Nazism,

---
[5] Movies had been made about Liszt before – such as *Song Without End* (1960) starring Dirk Bogarde.
[6] 'What really intrigued me was [Liszt's] strange relationship with Richard Wagner' (BP, 143).

no less. And Wagner is transmogrified into a Frankensteinian monster, a combination of Wagner and Adolf Hitler and the Teutonic Superman.

Ken Russell assassinated Richard Wagner in *Mahler* and *Lisztomania*. While for some music fans and critics, Wagner is a god (best known for his *Der Ring des Niebelungen*, 1869-82), for others his music is decadent, bombastic, crude and ideologically dubious (as Woody Allen quips in 1993's *Manhattan Murder Mystery*, 'when I hear too much Wagner it makes me want to invade Poland'). Russell is also particularly critical of Cosima Wagner's role in distorting Wagner's music with anti-semitism and right-wing politics.

Cosima Wagner (1837-1930) had appeared in a Ken Russell movie before: in *Mahler* (when she was played by Antonia Ellis in the guise of Brunhilde the Valkyrie). The affair between Richard Wagner and Cosima created a scandal; by 1866, Cosima had left her hubby Hans von Bülow and joined Wagner in exile in Lucerne in Switzerland. She and von Bülow were divorced in 1870, and she married Wagner.

CAST AND CREW.

*Lisztomania* is a kind of companion piece to *Tommy* – at least in terms of the production, which used many of the same cast and crew. Roger Daltrey, for instance, was the lead in both movies, and the following actors were in both pictures: Olly Reed as Princess Carolyn's (Franz Liszt's lover) assistant, Imogen Claire as George Sand, and Paul Nicholas as Richard Wagner. Russell regulars also appeared in *Lisztomania:* Ken Colley as Frédéric Chopin, Georgina Hale as an actress, Murray Melvin as Hector Berlioz, Andrew Faulds as Lévi-Strauss, Andrew Reilly as Hans von Bülow,[7] Cosima's hapless husband, Otto Diamant as Felix Mendelssohn, etc.[8] Fiona Lewis was Countess Marie and Sara Kestelman was Princess Carolyn.

Philip Harrison was production designer, Shirley Kingdon and Richard Pointing did the costumes, Wally Scheiderman

---

[7] Hans von Bülow had been Richard Wagner's conductor during the composer's time at the court of Ludwig II of Bavaria, in Munch.
[8] Many of Franz Liszt's fellow composers appeared in the backstage scene at the concert: Frédéric Chopin, for instance, clinging in tears to George Sand's thigh, while she embraces Lola Montes (Anulka Dziubinska). As well as Berlioz and Lévi-Strauss, Gioachino Rossini (Ken Parry) appears, and Johannes Brahms and Felix Mendelssohn (Otto Diamant).

applied the make-up, hair was by Colin Jameson, John Allenby was props manager, the art direction was by Tim Hutchinson and Ian Whittaker, Stuart Baird cut the film, Peter Suschitzky was DP, Peter Rice was production manager, Jonathan Benson was AD, sound was by Ian Bruce, Colin Chilvers did the visual effects, John Forsyth and Rick Wakeman arranged and co-ordinated the music.[9] Roy Baird and David Puttnam were the producers.[10]

And only one person in the world (now as then) could've written this movie, or written like this – or even wanted to! – and that was of course Uncle Ken. Nobody else would've included a Giant Penis Scene next to intellectual discussions about classical music and creativity, or featured cultural and musical references that only professors of music would understand, or filmed the extermination of the Jews in 1930s Germany by an Adolf Hitler-Richard Wagner-Frankenstein's monster wielding a guitar-shaped machine gun (backed up by acolytes dressed as Superman), or cast a Beatle (Ringo Starr) as the Pope, or staged a battle of wills between two classical music composers as a pitched battle with spinning, flame-throwing pianos!

Oh, don't you wish that Ken Russell could be making movies from now until the heat death of the universe in 15 billion years' time!?

*Lisztomania* was produced for Goodtimes Enterprises (and Warners), the company run by David Puttnam and Sandy Lieberson (Ken Russell had made *Mahler* for Goodtimes too.[11] Among Goodtimes' other films were *Performance, Stardust, That'll Be the Day, Bugsy Malone, The Final Programme* and *Glastonbury Fayre*).

As Ken Russell recounts in *A British Picture*, he had offered two movies to David Puttnam, and the producer went for Franz Liszt rather than *The Gershwin Dream*. According to Russell, Puttnam wanted a script that was more pop music than classically-oriented, and Russell rewrote his concept to suit that (BP, 143).

Casting was another area in which David Puttnam had a

---

[9] Wakeman didn't compose and arrange the music for *Lisztomania* on his own: John Forsyth and a group of orchestrators also contributed.

[10] The Dolby, stereo-encoded, optical soundtrack was first used with *Lisztomania* (it used left, right and centre encoding). *A Star Is Born* followed by adding surround to left, right and centre encoding.

[11] In *A British Picture*, Ken Russell spoke waspishly about David Puttnam and his producing work on *Mahler* and *Lisztomania*; Puttnam had brought in keyboard wizard Rick Wakeman, altered Russell's conception, turning it into a 'Panavision pop video' (BP, 143).

'heavy input', recalled Ken Russell (BP, 143). And those two items alone – script and casting – contribute *an enormous amount* to any movie. Indeed, if the script and casting are right, a movie is much easier to make, and will turn out well, according to many film-makers. It was Puttnam of course, who brought in people like Rick Wakeman.

Ken Russell wasn't so sure about some of David Puttnam's suggestions – as to casting, as to the script, on Rick Wakeman re-orchestrating Franz Liszt's music, and decisions like going widescreen, all of which drove up the budget (which became £1.2 million/ $1.8 million).

According to Rick Wakeman, there was 'an almighty row with financiers and production people', and Ken Russell had been obliged to rework the movie (very likely to reluctantly omit expensive sequences). It wasn't the first or last time that Russell had to cut back his vision.

Paul Nicholas in *Lisztomania* gives an ultra-high energy, Oscar-worthy supporting actor performance as Richard Wagner. First appearing in a white sailor's outfit (with 'NIETZSCHE' on his cap!), an allusion to the film *Battleship Potemkin* (Wagner as a Communist revolutionary!),[12] by the second half of the movie, Nicholas' Wagner is dominating the narrative, to the point of dressing up as Superman and commanding his Hitler Youth, and finally appearing as Adolf Hitler in the form of Frankenstein's monster, wielding a guitar shaped like a machine gun, and killing Jews.[13]

Fiona Lewis should also be praised for her performance as Countess Marie (Franz Liszt began romancing the Comtesse d'Agoult in 1833,[14] when he was 22); the gorgeous Lewis gamely cavorts in the nude in the lengthy opening scene, and seems up for whatever Ken Russell wants to do (not all actors are like that, particularly with nude scenes). Notice, though, that Roger Daltrey has enough time before the sword duel in that scene begins to wrap a torn sheet around his hips – *he's* not going to do the duel nude! (The double standards yet again of movie-making – where actresses are expected to disrobe, but not actors so much).[15]

---

[12] Sergei Eisenstein was one of Ken Russell's early favourites.
[13] The film plays Richard Wagner younger at this point – in real life, Wagner was in his 50s when he met and romanced Cosima Liszt.
[14] They split in 1844.
[15] The 1975 film includes shots of both Marie and the Count gawping at Liszt's penis, but the film doesn't cut to a shot of it.

However, Daltrey does, as in *Tommy*, play some scenes near-nude. (But the duel *should* be fully nude, and would be funnier if it was).

Although the role of Countess Marie is rather under-written (most the roles in *Lisztomania* are a little under-developed compared to the central duo of Franz Liszt and Richard Wagner), Fiona Lewis skilfully embellishes it with all sorts of gestures, expressions and performances. She is especially good in the Chaplin skit of her married life with Franz Liszt.

Both Sara Kestelman (as Princess Carolyn, the Muse and patron from Hell),[16] and Veronica Quilligan (as Cosima Wagner, moving from dutiful daughter to fascist aide), seem to be having a good time. Kestelman is unusual casting – but Ken Russell and his team have often moved away from obvious choices – for instance, Dorothy Tutin in *Savage Messiah* (this is where a Euro starlet like Jeanne Moreau, considered for *Savage Messiah*, might've been more effectve).

And Veronica Quilligan,[17] only 18 at the time of filming, is very impressive in playing both young and middle-aged, as well as evoking a truly evil daughter to Franz Liszt. Ken Russell remembered that Quilligan knew what she was doing, and needed very little direction. Liszt also had two other children (Blandine, b. 1835, and Daniel, b. 1839), but they only appear in minor roles (played by Russell's children, inevitably).

This is Roger Daltrey's movie, though, in terms of roles – although Paul Nicholas threatens to steal each scene he's in. Daltrey has the advantage of looking somewhat like Franz Liszt, and was of course a rock star – and the conception of Liszt in this movie is of the composer and pianist as an early form of rock star ('the first pop star of them all', as Ken Russell called him [BP, 143]). As he showed in *Tommy*, Daltrey is an appealing actor – completely unpretentious, down-to-earth, enthusiastic, athletic, and easy on the eye. And the boy can sing!

Franz Liszt was touring from an early age: visits to Vienna, Paris, England (where he played in front of Queen Victoria),

---

16 Princess Caroline Sayn-Wittgenstein was the wife of a rich Russian land-owner. Franz von Liszt met her in 1847 in Kiev and they fell madly in love. They went to live in Weimar in 1848, where Liszt produced operas (including Berlioz' *Béatrice et Bénédict* and Wagner's *Lohengrin*).

17 Veronica Quilligan (b. 1956) was in *Robin and Marian*, *St Trinian's*, *Angel* and *Anchoress* after *Lisztomania*, but has appeared mainly in British television.

Germany, Turkey, Denmark, Russia, etc.[18] And audiences really did go hysterical over his performances, to the point where they snatched his belongings and tore them to shreds. 'Lisztomania' was a real phenomenon.

PRODUCTION DESIGN.

Critics have drawn attention to Derek Jarman's sets for *The Devils*, and rightly so, but pretty much every major Ken Russell film contains truly outstanding set design. Clearly, Russell encourages his production designers to go nuts – John Clark and Ian Whittaker on *Tommy*,[19] Ian Whittaker and Roger Christian on *Mahler*, Luciana Arrighi on *Women In Love* and the TV films, Syd Cain and Bert Davey on *Billion Dollar Brain*, Natasha Kroll, Ian Whittaker and Michael Knight on *The Music Lovers*, and Philip Harrison on *Lisztomania*.

Simply in terms of production design, then, Ken Russell's features are extraordinary. And when you combine that with co-ordinated hair and make-up and wardrobe, plus of course the free-standing props, not to mention the lighting, and camera movement, plus the practical effects like fire, water and smoke, you have some of the most startling *mise-en-scène* in British cinema.

Simply at the level of *imagination*, this is incredible work.[20] Oh yes, costume dramas on TV are praised for accuracy or beauty of their costumes, but that isn't too difficult to achieve: if you're doing a Jane Austen or Charles Dickens adaption, and you've got some dough, you're automatically going to have lovely frocks and grungey suits. But a Ken Russell movie is in *another realm* from the average historical drama.

For *Lisztomania*, Ken Russell encouraged Philip Harrison to ever greater heights, and Harrison and his team delivered some fabulously luxuriant and excessively stylized sets (the budget of $1.9 million was larger than Russell's usual movies up to that point – but, as Russell pointed out, *Lisztomania* still looked better than a movie like *The Mission*, which cost $17 million and was also produced by David Puttnam).

Superior even to *The Devils*, and the finest design work in a

---
18 Over 1,000 appearances in 8 years, in the 1830s and 1840s.
19 Ian Whittaker went on to work on *Alien, Dragonslayer, Highlander, The Remains of the Day, Sense and Sensibility, Anna and the King*, etc.
20 For Joseph Lanza, *Lisztomania* is 'one of Russell's most visually dynamic, comically raucous, and intellectually charged efforts' (PF, 191).

Ken Russell production, every single set in *Lisztomania* is a masterpiece of radical stylization, emphasizing blacks and whites and reds. When Franz von Liszt is at home composing, for instance, he has a giant, white room with an enormous, circular window, the far wall stacked with suitcases (and a white, grand piano, of course). Even minor sets, such as the corridor outside Liszt's monastic room, towards the end of the movie, is a triumph of European Art Nouveau in black and white. Pattern in particular is employed to striking effect (down to the checkerboard appearance of the floors, or the black-and-white, piano keys around the raised platform in Liszt's home with the Countess).

Perhaps the most extravagant set is Princess Carolyn's palace – a vast, dusky chamber of a Goddess-spider's lair in blacks and reds and golds, with a platform at the end where Carolyn holds court, flanked by three, orange phallic columns (with Art Nouveau waves). Simultaneously it's a church, a palace throne room, an S/M dungeon, and the setting for a Busby Berkeley dance number. Forget the dialogue, or the story, just look at the visuals! These are sets which do all of the talking – and this particular one is employed to the full, as it becomes the setting for the jumbo, phallic dance number (and the lengthy tracking shot through the room, plus the big music cue, allows the audience to look at the set in detail).[21]

Peter Suschitzky's widescreen cinematography is beautiful and remarkable in *Lisztomania,* and one of the many delights of this amazing movie.[22] *Lisztomania* is one of the great British movies in terms of its look and lightning. And the widescreen enhances it, too; although Ken Russell might have been reluctant to add to the expense of the piece with scope photography, it does help *Lisztomania* to look truly gorgeous. And Suschitzky masterfully lights the increasingly dark-hued sets, especially the ones in Franz Liszt's black bedroom, or the Wagnerian Nazi rally set-piece.[23]

---

21 Prior to this scene, Franz Liszt has been led into an ante-chamber by Oliver Reed which has white asses fixed to the wall which let loose noxious gases. Liszt is fumigated and near-naked by the time he reaches the grand throne room – after trying to stop the gas by stuffing his clothes into the assholes.
22 It was David Puttnam's suggestion to shoot in anamorphic – most of Ken Russell's movies up to that point were in regular 35mm formats.
23 Peter Suschitzky had previously shot *That'll Be the Day,* which Puttnam had produced, *Leo the Last,* and *The Rocky Horror Picture Show.* Suschitzky was later cinematographer on *Valentino, The Empire Strikes Back, Krull, Naked Lunch, Mars Attacks!* and *The Man In the Iron Mask.* He became David Cronenberg's regular DP, and shot all of Cronenberg's movies from *Dead Ringers* onwards.

The gleaming, contrasty appearance of the celluloid in *Lisztomania* – it would be great in black-and-white – fuses brilliantly with the comicbook colours that Phillip Harrison, Ian Whittaker and Tim Hutchinson employ.

Like many other Ken Russell films, *Lisztomania* is full of paintings and references to paintings: there are Russian ikons (including pop stars like Elton John, Bill Haley, Elvis Presley, and Pete Townshend done in a kind of Andy Warhol-style, ikon fashion), Art Nouveau in the style of Aubrey Beardsley, religious paintings, and so on.

PIANOS.

The prop that I guess everyone remembers from *Lisztomania* is the giant phallus (which, Ken Russell recalled, mysteriously went missing one day after shooting – that sometimes happens to favourite props). But actually the key prop and motif in *Lisztomania* is undoubtedly the piano and the keyboard: there are pianos everywhere in this movie (and you'd have to go a long way to find a movie which employs more pianos and more keyboard motifs than *Lisztomania*): (1) the old upright piano in the Charlie Chaplin sequence; (2) the elegant grand piano that Franz Liszt and his wife the Countess sit on top of at home, using it like a couch; (3) the shiny, show piano at the concert; (4) the piano that Liszt and Marie tup next to in the opening scene (and are later imprisoned inside; this piano also explodes when a railroad train hits it); (5) the white grand piano that Liszt later composes on; and, most incredibly, (6) the spinning piano that fires canonballs and flames.

As well as pianos, *Lisztomania* is stuffed with deliriously, deliciously anachronistic costumes and sets adorned with black-and-white keyboard motifs. The comicbook approach to classical music is more extravagant in *Lisztomania*, in terms of design and look, than in any other Ken Russell movie (partly because the budget allowed for it).[24]

The costumes in *Lisztomania* in particular (by Richard Pointing and Shirley Kingdon) are full of delightful, historically inaccurate

---

[24] The comicbook approach is reminiscent of Walt Disney cartoons, such as *Musicland* (1935), a stupendously imaginative *Silly Symphony* about the rivalry in love and war between two islands – one of classical music and one of jazz. Every character is a musical instrument, music predominates as a motif across all of the design; there's no dialogue, but the music does all of the talking. Which's how Ken Russell likes to make movies.

elements (bodyguards wearing jeans, or the Pope with a movie-star robe, or Richard Wagner in a fab, leopard-skin beret and jacket combo). Russell remarked in his commentary on *Lisztomania* that it was pæan to costume design, and it certainly is.

THE MUSIC.

For *Lisztomania*, Ken Russell, Roger Daltrey, Jonathan Benson and Rick Wakeman wrote some lyrics for the music of Franz von Liszt (including 'Love's Dream' ('Liebstraum'),[25] 'Peace At Last', 'Funerailles' and 'Orpheus Song'), and Wakeman also composed some new songs, inspired by the music of Liszt and Richard Wagner. Finally, Wakeman performed some of the music in the film (the synthesized versions of Liszt's music, for instance). Wakeman was thus a key influence on *Lisztomania* (John Forsyth was musical co-ordinator – he also worked on *Mahler*).[26] The performers of the music in *Lisztomania* included Jack Bruce (bass), Dave Mattacks (drums), William Davies, David Wilde, Linda Lewis, Paul Nicholas, and of course Daltrey and Wakeman.

You have to admit that Rick Wakeman and John Forsyth do a brilliant job in *Lisztomania*: not only do they orchestrate and edit a lot of Franz Liszt's music and Richard Wagner's music (which is a big task in itself), they also incorporate many pastiches, some in a classical music manner, some in a rock music manner, and some in a jokey manner. The soundtrack for *Lisztomania* is very sophisticated, culturally as well as musically.

*Lisztomania*'s June, 1975 soundtrack (released by A & M) includes the following tracks:

> Rienzi (Chopsticks Fantasia) - Love's Dream - Dante Period - Orpheus Song - Hibernation - Excelsior Song - Master Race - Rape, Pillage and Clap - Funerailles - Free Song (Hungarian Rhapsody) - Peace at Last

Rick Wakeman released *The Real Lisztomania* in 2002 (on the Voiceprint label), which includes the following tracks:

---

[25] 'Liebstraum' (1853) is one of Liszt's loveliest piano pieces, composed in a florid, High Romantic style.
[26] It was producer David Puttnam's idea, not Ken Russell's, to have Rick Wakeman rearrange Franz Liszt's music. Wakeman accepted, knowing that Russell had a reputation for being a hard taskmaster, and for being fierce at times. Wakeman did have a team helping him, of course. If you don't know about scoring for movies, and you see that single credit 'music by', you might think that Hans Zimmer or Jerry Goldsmith did it all. But no, movie scores require teams of arrangers, producers and technicians.

The Scene - The Metronome - The Country Sword Dances - Free Song - The Freudian Dream - Dante Period - Orpheus Song - For the Chop - Hell - Wagner's Dream - The Dream of Hell - The Inferno Ride - Master Race - The Ride of Thor - Excelsior Song - The Guardian Virgins - Rape, Pillage and Clap - Love's Dream

There are rock versions of the music of Franz von Liszt and Richard Wagner, composed by Rick Wakeman, which further modernize the classical music of the 19th century. The approach is quite different, musically, from some of Ken Russell's earlier bio-pics about classical composers, in which the music was largely the original works (though played by modern orchestras. No doubt Russell carefully considers which recording and orchestra of each piece to use).

There's *a lot* of Franz Liszt's music and Richard Wagner's music in *Lisztomania*. Some of it is played straight (though by a modern orchestra), some of it is updated with electronic instrumentation, some of it uses Liszt's music as a starting point but departs from it, and some of it is spoofed.

Musically, *Lisztomania* is a very accomplished movie, with some clever re-interpretations of Franz Liszt's and Richard Wagner's music. This is not a traditional rendition of the music of the period or of Liszt's music. There are scenes where Liszt's music is played straight – such as the scene where Liszt plays the piano alone in his rooms, but much of the time the music is artfully re-arranged. For instance, following that scene, Liszt sings in a musical movie manner, with lyrics added to Liszt's original music (from 'Funerailles', 1849). And watches his wife and children being blown up on the street below.

And in some sequences, such as the climactic duel between Franz Liszt and Richard Wagner, Rick Wakeman and John Forsyth are delivering a mini rock opera based on Liszt's music and Wagner's music. They provide rapid shifts in musical styles and moods to accompany the velocity of the imagery and drama.

THEMES.

*Lisztomania* is partly about the perversion of art, about art being used for evil purposes, and about the artist selling out, all recurring themes in Ken Russell's work. Franz Liszt discussed the topic of the artist in society in his letters, such as this one of 1857:

> The artist, in our sense, should be neither the servant of the audience nor its master. He is and remains the representative of *beauty*, in all the inexhaustible multiplicity of which man's thought and feeling are capable – and his unfaltering conviction of this is sufficient warrant for him…[27]

One can imagine that Ken Russell agreed with such a view of the artist.

*Lisztomania* covers very familiar themes and territory for Ken Russell, and for the biopic in general. And you can see the filmmakers becoming impatient with it from the beginning: the erotic triangle, for instance, between Comtesse Marie, the Count d'Agoult and the piano teacher Franz Liszt is dealt with in an over-the-top manner, instead of the straight melodrama of many another movie. The subsequent scenes of the early romantic life and then married life and young family life of Marie and Liszt are rendered in a rapid montage form that apes Charlie Chaplin's cinema. The scenes of Liszt playing piano at a concert – well, Russell and his teams had already done plenty of before, including in *The Music Lovers* and *Tommy*.

Thus, *Lisztomania* takes on very familiar themes and relationships and situations, but from the outset is already bored with them. Instead, *Lisztomania* approaches the subject and situations in a very stylized, incredibly heightened manner. This is no longer a movie about an artist struggling to become well-known and successful, or about his relationships, his children, his wives and lovers, his rivals, his hopes and dreams, his failures and highpoints. Instead, *Lisztomania* is a movie *about* movies about those subjects: it's a comicbook movie *about* a comicbook biopic.

But even at that level, of a film-about-a-film-about-a-life, *Lisztomania* is bored with it. Ken Russell knows he can do all of that:

*Level One*: the Straight Biopic. Ken Russell has been there, done that.

*Level Two*: the Movie-About-Biopics, or the Movie-About-Movies. Ken Russell has been there, done that too (in *The Music Lovers*, for instance). *Lisztomania* posits a new level:

*Level Three*: A Comicbook-Movie-About-a-Movie-About-a-Biopic, or the A-Movie-Within-a-Movie-About-a-Movie.

*Lisztomania* is so rich partly because of this multi-layered

---

[27] F. Liszt, Feb 11, 1857, letter to Dionys Pruckner, quoted in H. Gal, 217.

approach. There are many things happening at once in *Lisztomania*: it's the multi-layered cake approach to cinema of Orson Welles. As Welles might say, why not have all these layers? As such, *Lisztomania* is a movie that certainly plays to music critics even more than film critics (and not only for its references to classical music, some of which are pretty obscure, and which probably only people who know quite a bit about classical music will understand).

At this level, *Lisztomania* is fabulously, indulgently obscure – or arcane, or intellectual. Certainly, *Lisztomania* is never going to play to a broad audience like, say, *Tommy* or *Women In Love*.

And *Lisztomania* is not conventional melodrama. The movie gets bored with routine relationships and situations, which Ken Russell and his teams have explored many times before. Instead, two major elements are introduced which take the narrative of *Lisztomania* into unusual areas: one is of course Princess Carolyn Sayn-Wittgenstein, the lover-as-muse *par excellence*, the embodiment of the Faustian bargain with money, creativity and fame. But the Princess Carolyn scenes are very extravagant and bizarre, especially in the early stages of the relationship, and take *Lisztomania* far, far away from your typical biopic (or your typical movie).

The second grand move the narrative makes in *Lisztomania* is Richard Wagner. The all-out assassination on Wagner is truly remarkable – these are some of Ken Russell's angriest and also most inspired pieces of celluloid. Here the OTT approach of *The Dance of the Seven Veils* and *Mahler*, about selling your soul to the Devil – i.e., Nazism – reaches a visceral highpoint.

Those two narrative strands alone are plenty for most movies – but *Lisztomania* adds a third: Franz Liszt's evil daughter Cosima Wagner. A fourth strand is Liszt's hankering for mysticism: his religiosity is actually portrayed in a modest manner, at times, but is tempered by his continued womanizing.

In the wedding scene, for instance, *Lisztomania* employs a simple but clear dramatic opposition: while Princess Carolyn is bustling about in the nave of the church, organizing the ceremony, Franz Liszt is someplace else, playing serene, melancholy music on a gigantic church organ. The scene dramatizes the conflicts between love and domesticity with music and mysticism.

The narrative twists and turns that the 1975 movie takes are very striking, particularly the way that they are *mixed together*. *Lisztomania* doesn't take one narrative strand and pursue it to a conclusion then move on to another one. Further, the heightened and heavily stylized approach makes *Lisztomania* like a dream of a life, a dream of history, a dream of music.

And in *Lisztomania,* the stylization becomes the content of the movie: but *not*, I think, in the way that film critics (such as Pauline Kael) often mean when they dismiss a filmmaker as producing empty images or flashy scenes which don't have any value or meaning or worth.

If you don't understand that the spiritual and emotional content of a Ken Russell movie is in the visuals, you miss so much. In fact, the same accusations of flashy images and showy scenes can be made at Ingmar Bergman and Carl-Theodor Dreyer, for example, filmmakers who delighted in the gorgeous machinery of making movies, who loved to pull off intricate shots. But their movies are regularly described as being the height of spiritual, weighty, 'meaningful' cinema.

♪

One of the confusions about the reception of the movies directed by Ken Russell is their ambiguity. The movies tend to be multi-layered: one layer of storytelling is deep into the melodrama, evoking the interactions of the characters and their often tempestuous relationships. But another layer will be ironic, cynical, ambivalent, commenting upon the emotional/ psychological melodrama. So one part of the movie will be trying *desperately* to create feelings in the audience in tune with the characters, while another part will be pushing them away with Brechtian distancing devices, ironic asides, satirical music, or vulgarity.

Well, which is it? Does the movie want us to cry along with these suffering people, or to laugh at these pathetic people? In *Gone With the Wind,* the most successful movie financially ever made, there's no doubt that the filmmakers hope that the audience is rooting for Scarlett O'Hara all the way.

By contrast, in many movies directed by Uncle Ken, one mode of viewing modifies the other (and maybe cancels the other out). And this is a key reason why Russell's movies are not always *emotionally* moving (there's no question about their cinematic brilliance). And that, I would suggest, is partly why they haven't been as successful as other films. Because audiences *want* to be moved: they *want* to be weep with joy at the end of *The Searchers*, when John Wayne lifts up Natalie Wood, holding up against the bright sun, and says, 'let's go home'.

ROCK MUSIC.

*Lisztomania* was very much of its time – the mid-1970s. Pop music and pop culture influences, such as glam rock, screaming pop fans, groupies, glitter rock fashion, and rock concert staging, were prominent (this was also partly due to *Tommy*, which mined similar territory, and the producers wishing to exploit a similar rock musical vein).

And *Lisztomania* was conceived by Ken Russell and his team as a film about a classical composer and performer who was the first rock star. Other precursors of rock stars from the 19th century have been evoked over the years: Lord Byron, Arthur Rimbaud, and Percy Shelley.

And rock musicians such as Jim Morrison, Led Zeppelin, Genesis and the Enid have drawn on 19th century literature and Romanticism. The spinning piano, a piano that can blast out fire – these are part of the paraphernalia of rock concerts of the Seventies, particularly those of the supergroups such as Emerson, Lake and Palmer,[28] Pink Floyd and Led Zeppelin. The Rolling Stones had famously used an inflatable penis on stage on the tour of the Americas in 1975 (they dubbed it 'Tired Grandfather', because it didn't perform too well).

There are many scenes where Franz Liszt is playing the piano, but also many scenes where Liszt is singing in the rock musical manner, in the postures of a performer in a musical.

RICK WAKEMAN.

Rock music keyboard wizard Rick Wakeman (b. May 18, 1949) composed the soundtracks for two of Ken Russell's pictures, *Lisztomania* and *Crimes of Passion*.[29] Wakeman was one of the

---

[28] At the California Jam in the 1970s, Keith Emerson performed the famous stunt of playing a piano on a rig that spun the piano and player round and round.
Emerson's stage act was famous – playing the Hammond organ from behind, using knives to sustain notes (he had started out using wooden pegs, but knives seemed showier), throwing knives at the organ and speakers. These theatrical antics were part of the same excess that was included in the Who's stage act.
[29] It was David Puttnam, a big fan of prog rock, who had proposed that Wakeman provide the soundtrack for *Lisztomania* – and also to arrange Liszt in a pop music mode.

superstars of the British rock music scene in the 1970s:[30] he played up the Merlin/ wizard circus act to the full, with his long, bleached blond locks, conical caps and a silver cape. Surrounded by pianos, mellotrons, Moogs, synths and Hammond organs (he had 36 keyboards on stage on four tiers), Wakeman became the focal point of his bands the Strawbs and Yes

Prior to Yes, Rick Wakeman had played keyboards with David Bowie (contributing the memorable piano on 'Life On Mars' and other marvellous *Hunky Dory* album tracks,[31] and mellotron on 'Space Oddity' – which he'd never played b4 the session);[32] he also played with Cat Stevens, Brotherhood of Man, Edison Lighthouse, and Kenny Lynch.

Rick Wakeman's performances were marked by incredible runs up and down the keyboards, and, octopus-like, playing many keyboards at once.[33] On the sleeve of the album *White Rock*, Wakeman said he played harpsichords, Hohner Clavinets, Steinway grands, mellotrons, Mander pipe organs, Moog synths, Fender Rhodes pianos, Hammond C3 organs, RMI Computer Pianos, and St Paul's Cathedral organ. You can hear quite a few of those keyboards on the soundtrack of *Lisztomania*.

It took years for Rick Wakeman to shake off the Progressive Rock Tendency: throughout the Seventies, Wakeman created concept albums, each weightier and more pompous than the last, each produced with an orchestra, choir and retinue of choice session musicians. There was Jules Verne's *Journey to the Centre of the Earth* (1974), complete with ponderous narration (*à la* Jeff Wayne's version of H.G. Wells' *War of the Worlds)*; there was King Henry and his six wives (each wife had her own five-minute piece on the LP *The Six Wives of Henry VIII*, 1973); there was Arthurian romance in *The Myths and Legends of King Arthur and the Knights of*

---

30 Producers of 'symphonic' prog rock of this era included Camel, ELP, the Enid, Yes and Genesis. Some of the prog rockers were classically-trained, or had classical pretensions: for instance, keyboard players such as Wakeman, Keith Emerson, and the Enid's Robert Godfrey.
31 You can hear Rick Wakeman making his instantly recognizable presence felt throughout *Hunky Dory* (playing the Bechstein piano used for 'Hey Jude', which the Beatles had recorded at Trident Studios); it's Wakeman that adds so much to the anthemic, timeless 'Life On Mars', blending perfectly with Mick Ronson's string arrangement. Wakeman provides a solid, rhythmic gounding for many songs on *Hunky Dory*.
32 This was the first time that Wakeman had seen or played a mellotron (but it would become a favourite instrument on Wakeman's subsequent recordings and concerts).
33 He liked to close his eyes when he played, he said, in order to see and feel the music.

*the Round Table*, 1975 (Wakeman turned his *King Arthur* show into a rock musical on ice, at Wembley's Empire Pool, complete with inflatable castles and mediæval knights with cardboard swords. It was one of the most fun shows Wakeman'd been involved in, he said. It wasn't meant to be taken seriously, as with some of Ken Russell's films).[34]

Rick Wakeman also produced film soundtracks: apart from the Ken Russell movies *Lisztomania* and *Crimes of Passion*, there was *White Rock* (1977), *The Burning* (Tony Maylam, 1980), and *G'Olé* (Tom Clegg, 1982).

Rick Wakeman was one of more prominent of the prog rock era stars, happy to appear on TV in documentaries (*Rock Family Trees, Grumpy Old Men*) or quiz shows (*Never Mind the Buzzcocks*), and many times on radio. He also wrote jokey memoirs of his rock star days (2008's *Grumpy Old Rock Star*). Indeed, Wakeman had an alternative career as a media pundit and minor celebrity, coming across as a cheerful, personable Londoner, who was great at interviews and the kind of light-hearted banter that television thrived on.

One can see why Rick Wakeman might have got on well with Ken Russell: both were passionate about music, and classical music in particular; both were serious about their work, but didn't take themselves too seriously; both loved English/ British culture, such as 19th century literature; both have a deep, spiritual strain in their art; and both are definitely on the more eccentric side of British popular culture. (And both liked a drink!).[35]

And Rick Wakeman was a prolific composer – he wasn't only a musician in a band (in several bands), performing other people's music, he wrote a huge amount of his own music. And his music for movies such as *Lisztomania* was impressive, ranging from individual songs (such as 'Excelsior Song', 'Peace At Last' and 'Master Race'), to complex cues to accompany the climactic battle between Richard Wagner and Franz Liszt.

Rick Wakeman recalled:

---

34 Other Rick Wakeman outings included his music for the 1976 Winter Olympics (*White Rock*), *No Earthly Connection* (1976), *Criminal Record* (1977), *1984* (1981, a musical collaboration of George Orwell's book with Tim Rice), the New Age-ish *Country Airs* (1986), *Rhapsodies* (1979), *Rock 'n' Roll Prophets* (1982), *Live at Hammersmith* (1985), *Silent Night* (1985), *The Family Album* (1987), *The Cost of Living* (1987), *Suite of God* (1988), *Time Machine* (1988), *Zodiaque* (1988), *Sea Airs* (1990), and *Beyond the Planets*. It was inevitable that Wakeman would turn to the *Bible*, producing *The Gospels* in 1987.

35 Wakeman struggled with alcoholism.

Ken was such an entertaining man to be around. His reputation for being quite fiery did reveal itself on occasion though, but it was always with the best intentions of making the finest film.

THE FIRST ACT.

From the beginning, *Lisztomania* announces itself as a comedy, with a joke about the speed that Franz Liszt used to play piano at, plus his womanizing. The camera tracks from a metronome (music) to Liszt and his lover Marie (sex). Music and sex (and women) are two of the major themes of the 1975 film, and of all of Ken Russell's films. But it's done in a deliberately stylized manner, so that nobody will be fooled into thinking that this is a serious movie, or a movie that is intended to be taken seriously.[36] The scene begins with Liszt kissing Marie's breasts, going from one nipple to the other, faster and faster as the metronome is speeded-up (by the woman, of course). If you don't get that this is a comedy, you've completely missed the point.

The appearance of Countess Marie's husband, Count d'Agoult (played by John Justin), introduces the cuckolded husband scene followed by the sword fight. There is much capering, jumping, Errol Flynn or Douglas Fairbanks swinging from the chandeliers, *Carry On*-style sex gags (such as water squirting from a sword-pierced statue), and other nonsense.[37] The scene's as much a movie spoof as anything – a send-up of sex comedies, of costume dramas, and of swashbuckling movies (though apparently Liszt did undertake duels for similar reasons).

The scene also gets the fact that Franz Liszt was a womanizer out of the way – by introducing nudity and sex so early on, the audience is told that this is not going to be a film about love and sex.[38] Because if it was, the topic wouldn't be portrayed like this, as well as sent up, in the first few minutes. That is, sex is only part of the equation in *Lisztomania,* and sex is used more for its power-gaming or relationship aspects, than as pure erotic *jouissance*. (There's plenty of nudity in *Lisztomania,* tho' – from Marie d'Agoult, Olga Janina, Lola Montes, the Rhinemaidens, etc – and Liszt.)

And, in particular, it's how *sex* and *love* relate to *art*: because

---

[36] However, Peter Suschitzky does a brilliant job of lighting the elegant set by Philip Harrison with a cool, blue moonlight.

[37] Ken Russell never liked the American Square Dance music that he said that David Puttnam had put on the scene without consulting him (BP, 144).

[38] Let's face it, a Ken Russell movie opening with a sex scene is nothing except-9999999ional.

what happens at the end of this comic prologue? A piano appears, and the old, sex triangle comedy of the husband, the wife and the piano teacher[39] is trotted out (yep, folks, the piano teacher is commissioned by the husband to teach his wife, and of course he ends up tupping her – one of the reasons is the Count's inability to satisfy his wife – pantomimed by the Countess with a drooping candle. Ken Russell can never resist the urge to include a phallic joke, so here there are bananas, which the Countess chomps on, and candles, which Franz Liszt holds up and the Count slices to pieces).[40] All harmless fun, and delivered with rapid cutting and out-size gestures. (The square dance, which includes American voices singing about Liszt's predicament, was not Russell's idea. For a director so meticulous about music, it must've rankled *a lot* to have David Puttnam and co. put in the American Country & Western song, with vocals narrating the events, a style that Russell has never used).

Count d'Agoult finally punishes the lovers extravagantly: first they're trapped inside the piano while he pounds on it (a funeral march from Frédéric Chopin, naturally), then in another silent movie spoof, he has the piano placed on a railway line. Cue another of Ken Russell's favourite motifs, a steam engine, which of course smashes into the piano.

THE CONCERT.

After that comes the title of the film – but all of the main credits are placed at the back of the film, a common practice now, but still unusual in 1975 (the movie cuts straight into the sex scene, without titles). And then, following the dressing room sequence (a vital scene), there's the extended concert sequence, staged as a modern-day rock show (modern elements include the glitter, the scurrying spotlights, the security guys standing in front of the stage, the screaming (and fainting) fans, the clapping, the chanting of 'Franz Liszt!', the stage invasion, and all the rest of it).

Most important, though, is the music itself. Yes, there are dramatic parts to the stage show, such as Franz von Liszt taking Richard Wagner's music and re-arranging it (much to Wagner's

---

[39] Liszt made a substantial living as a piano teacher – he taught many, many students over many years. Inevitably, some of them were women, and inevitably Liszt had affairs with some of 'em. This happened quite a few times with classical composers.
[40] Later on, Princess Carolyn smokes cigars, which she apparently really did.

consternation), or weaving in *Chopsticks,* inaugurating the rivalry between the two composers, but as this is a movie about a classical composer, it's important for the film to play some of his music. Ken Russell and the team did the same with *The Music Lovers* – in the first reel there is a lengthy performance of Peter Tchaikovsky's music (one has to admit, though, that Dick Chamberlain did a better job of miming Tchaikovsky than Roger Daltrey does of hammering out Liszt).

There is a conscious nod to the *Piano Concerto No. 1* scene in *The Music Lovers* when Iza Teller appears in the balcony (by the time of *Lisztomania,* Ken Russell had made enough movies to be able to quote himself if he fancied). This section of the Beethoven Memorial Fund concert (in 1840) is about Franz Liszt and his women: a woman appears on stage with a baby in a pram; Hans von Bülow scurries around the auditorium to find out about (procure) the women, communicating to Liszt on stage via cue cards: Teller plays a millionairess; Georgina Hale is an actress, and Sara Kestelman is a princess.

In *Lisztomania,* as in *The Music Lovers* and other films about composers, the filmmakers want viewers to sit back and listen to the music, as well as take in what is happening dramatically at the same time. Because in a feature movie, it's not enough to have an audience sit back and listen to music for ten minutes, though if Ken Russell and the team could get away with it, they would probably do that. But producers, film studios and distributors want a product that's fast-paced as well as one that contains the mix of elements deemed by film people and marketers to be essential to a successful flick: romance, jeopardy, action, comedy, thrills, sex, etc.

The Beethoven Memorial Fund concert is also portraying Franz Liszt's egotism, his smug sending up of the business of show business – the way he turns to grin inanely at the audience (and at Richard Wagner), and his sense of showmanship (the Liberace candelabra on the piano, the glittery background, the spangly jacket, the phallic joke with the glittery gloves, and the dance he does on it – the grin to the audience is also a Liberace gesture).[41] (Notice how the audience consists entirely of young women in yellow and green bonnets – which makes the hapless Wagner, in his white, sailor suit, stand out all the more –

---

[41] Joseph Lanza described Ken Russell's take on Franz Liszt as a 'combination rhinestone Elvis and cockney Liberace' (PF, 181).

especially when Liszt cruelly persuades him to take a bow before he plays his arrangement of Wagner's music).

After the concert sequence, including the important backstage meeting between Richard Wagner and Franz Liszt, Wagner disappears from the 1975 movie, not reappearing until around halfway through. From his entrance as a losing revolutionary onwards, Wagner's presence is enormous. The concert scene is important in the picture, whatever the historical reality was, because it establishes the animosity between Wagner and Liszt: it grounds the struggle between them in musical terms (that Liszt took Wagner's music and made fun of it, and that Wagner was publicly humiliated).[42]

THE DRESSING ROOM SCENE.

The dressing room sequence in *Lisztomania* is crucial, in situating Franz von Liszt in amongst his contemporaries, with whom he was friendly and appreciative (though not always in this movie): Hector Berlioz, Robert Schumann, Frédéric Chopin, Gioachino Rossini, Felix Mendelssohn, Lévi-Strauss, etc. These are satirical vignettes, not meant to be taken literally on any level (yet, as Ken Russell explained, all of the satirizing had foundations in truth).

The dressing room scene in *Lisztomania* also shows the adulation that Franz Liszt was surrounded by, the groupies wanting access, the fans, and the bodyguards hired to keep them at bay. His uptight manager (Aubrey Morris, the sleazy social worker in *A Clockwork Orange*) is desperate to get him on stage. The scene shows Liszt lapping it all up, and also fooling around with another lover (the infamous courtesan and dancer Lola Montes, played by Playboy Bunny and Playmate Anulka Dzuibinska), kissing her naked breasts (*Lisztomania* doesn't make too much of Montes, probably because she was the subject of Max Ophüls' 1950s, widescreen, colour masterpiece *Lola Montes*, the kind of extravagant and highly cinematic movie that Ken Russell

---

[42] It's likely that *Lisztomania* influenced *Amadeus*, a very Russellian movie – certainly other Russell movies did (*The Music Lovers* and *Mahler*, for instance).

loved).[43]

THIS IS NOT HISTORY.

Although *Lisztomania* follows some of the key points of the life of Franz Liszt, it doesn't set them out like a conventional documentary. There is no opening crawl introducing the world of the movie (it's straight into Liszt kissing Countess Marie's tits!), no voiceover explaining everything for the audience,[44] no long shots of cities or towns. Instead, it is completely fantastical and cartoon-like.

And that is a fault if the intended audience is a young viewership, for the people who enjoyed *Tommy*, who probably wouldn't know that much (or anything at all) about Franz Liszt, or Richard Wagner, or about 19th century classical music, as Joseph Gomez noted (1975, 200). How many teens in the 1970s – or today – have heard of Liszt?!

*Lisztomania* does not have much of a sense of place: it evokes a Middle European zone, but there are no establishing shots with captions saying 'PARIS' or 'ROME'. And no dates, either. In reality, Franz Liszt lived in Paris, Rome, Como, Geneva, Vienna, London, Kiev, Weimar, Budapest and other places.

*Lisztomania* works much better if you know something about the subject, and about 19th century culture. But Ken Russell's historical films have not been too keen on explaining everything, or getting across the historical context. As Joseph Lanza put it, *Lisztomania* needs 'more footnotes than most of today's art-house independents' (PF, 182), while *Film Quarterly* called it a 'brilliant, unique and intensely personal film in search of an audience which perhaps doesn't even exist'.[45] (So you could say that *Lisztomania* is a movie with an audience of one: Ken Russell! A kind of Howard Hughes or Charles Foster Kane idea – you create

---

43 Indeed, there are extended sequences involving Franz Liszt and Lola Montes in *Lola Montes*, including when they travel in a luxurious horse-drawn carriage which includes a piano and a stove. This sort of highly stylized, artificial movie-making might've influenced *Lisztomania* (Liszt tinkles on a piano as he talks to Lola, as he does in *Lisztomania*). There are numerous other links between *Lola Montes* and *Lisztomania*. For instance, the colourful, high energy opening sequence in the circus, where Lola's life is staged with dancers, jugglers, dwarfs, acrobats and animals. This shifts into the flashback *rondo* form (a film-within-a-film) that Russell employs many times. The levels of artifice, performance, stylization and narrative complexity are favoured devices in Russell's cinema.
44 But the Square Dance includes lyrics which explain a bit – and they stand out a mile, not being used like this anywhere else in the movie, and in any of Ken Russell's other works.
45 Ross Care, 1978.

a whole film studio just for yourself! And maybe the one (female) star you want to see in a movie!).

*Lisztomania* is not a movie with a voiceover explaining everything, as in your conventional television documentary about an artist. How tiresome that would in a movie like *Lisztomania*. Ken Russell and the team simply dispense with that: yes, there *is* some exposition in the dialogue, but probably not enough for many viewers. *Lisztomania*, in short, is not going to lay everything out for the audience all neatly described and labelled. If you want to follow *Lisztomania* on that level, you have to work it out for yourself. However, *Lisztomania* is not really a movie to viewed on that analytical, historical, documentary level.

Right away you'll notice that much of *Lisztomania* takes place inside, on sets, and so much of the companion film, *Tommy*, is shot out of doors, and on location. The studio-bound quality of *Lisztomania* gives the piece a particular flavour (as with *The Boy Friend*) – especially when combined with so many sets painted black. In short, *Lisztomania* foregrounds cinematic artifice and stylization, to the point where the outside world barely exists. This is not realism and it's not naturalism – but it might be, as Orson Welles would put it, *truthful* ('not *real* but *true*'). 'Realism' and 'reality', as we have seen, are just not very useful terms to describe Ken Russell's cinema – but also, I would say, not useful in defining *any* cinema.

LOVE AND SEX.

A subtitle of *Lisztomania* might be *Liszt and His Women*, although *Liszt and Wagner* might be just as accurate (the 'mania' of the title refers to the adulation Franz Liszt received, and that his concerts have been interpreted by Ken Russell and the team as akin to rock concerts).

Franz Liszt is, from the beginning, portrayed as a womanizer, with many female admirers. There is a woman in his life throughout the film, from the romp with the Countess Marie in the opening scene, where he's tupping someone else's wife, to his married life with the Countess, to Lola Montes (Anulka Dziubinska), to the meeting with a diabolical muse, Princess Carolyn, to his girlfriend Olga Janina in Rome, to the final scenes, where Liszt is playing the harp as an angel in heaven, surrounded by admiring women, including his daughter Cosima.

*Lisztomania* shows that although Franz Liszt's ideals might be high and mighty – he later becomes a Franciscan abbé – he is still a womanizer. The scene in Liszt's black-walled, monastic room, for instance, has no less a personage than the Pope bursting in upon Liszt and his latest lover (Olga Janina) in bed together (Olga was another of the many people that Liszt taught piano).

MOVIE SPOOFS.

*Lisztomania* is mounted in a comicbook style, or a style that incorporates comicbooks,[46] dance, vaudeville, silent movies, the musical, and genre jokes. It's a film, like *Tommy* or *Mahler*, done in the bright colours and bold designs of a comicbook (a couple of years later, *Star Wars* would inaugurate a whole sub-genre in Hollywood of comicbook movies, which continues today: at least a few of the Summer blockbusters are comicbook adaptions. Ah, but if only they could be as much fun as a Ken Russell comicbook movie! They are all so bloody *serious*, and take themselves so darn seriously).

*Lisztomania* mounts exuberant spoofs of movie genres – the silent comedy in the Charlie Chaplin scene and steam engine-and-piano Buster Keaton scene (as in Keaton's *The General*), the Hollywood backstage musical in the second scene, at the concert, and the horror film, in the *Dracula* and *Frankenstein* send-ups. There are also allusions to *Battleship Potemkin*, a favourite Ken Russell movie (the burning pram rolling along, for instance, and Richard Wagner's sailor suit), *The Exorcist*, *The Perils of Pauline* and *A Matter of Life and Death*.

The Charlie Chaplin sequence in the log cabin sends up *The Gold Rush* (1925), a film Ken Russell knows very well (though it's also spoofing other Chaplin flicks), with Fiona Lewis and Roger Daltrey both acting up a storm in this parody of young love (Lewis is excellent). It's another reminder of Russell's debt to silent cinema, but also cinema's debt to silent cinema. And it shows, again, that cinema can get by very nicely without the thing that film critics slaver over – dialogue (there aren't any captions in this sequence, either). The use of props is inspired, from the red, heart-shaped motifs in the blankets and food to the diapers hanging on a line indicating the arrival of each baby. Employing Chaplin is a treat, and works perfectly. It simul-

---

46 At one point, Franz Liszt refers to comics.

taneously updates the historical genre setting, but also portrays it as idealized nostalgia (using Chaplinesque humour is a way of getting across the joy of young love without it becoming too mawkish).

Especially fun in *Lisztomania* are the two spoofs of the horror genre: *Dracula* and *Frankenstein*. The send-ups begin with Franz Liszt being drugged by Richard Wagner, who turns into Dracula, with pointed fangs, which he sinks into Liszt's neck (after yanking off his crucifix) as he plays in a drugged state at the piano.[47] Outside, the moon slides across the sun (yet more circular imagery), in a suitably apocalyptic, astrological moment, and the lighting dims down to a close-up of Wagner's maw.[48]

Yes it's another of those ultra-obvious cinematic ideas that Ken Russell loves to portray – one artist sucking the art out of another artist, Richard Wagner as vampiric – but it works (partly because of the sheer flair of the filmmaking). Wagner spouts some megalomaniacal dialogue about firing up the German imagination with some rousing music.[49] Having Franz Liszt play the piano while Wagner sucks his blood, staged in a montage of close-ups, accentuates the artistic theft. *Lisztomania* suggests that Wagner is never good enough musically – Liszt either sends up his music (as at the Beethoven Memorial Fund concert), or doesn't take it seriously. The only way that Wagner's going to get anywhere in his music is by stealing other people's work.

The theme of the people surrounding an artist who feed off him/ her is a recurring one in Ken Russell's cinema (as well as the artist's ambivalent attitude towards them). In *Lisztomania*, Russell simply exaggerates the experience in comicbook form, using Dracula and vampirism. (Vampirism also works on much deeper levels, too: cultural critics have discussed vampires at length: it's not just theft or rape or sexual exploitation or phallic teeth sinking into voluptuous, female flesh, it's about blood and race and ethnicity and otherness, and corruption, and pollution. In fact, you can use vampirism to explore any issue you fancy).

When Franz Liszt approaches Richard Wagner's Castle (sent

---

[47] The reference is not to the 1931 Universal *Dracula* (though it is that too), but very much the famous Hammer *Count Dracula* movies with Christopher Lee.
[48] Taking down the lighting is a standard practice in the theatre, but is still rarely employed in cinema. Yet it's very effective.
[49] When Richard Wagner drops Communism and revolution and takes up right-wing nationalism, *Lisztomania* once again illustrates the Ken Russellian theme that what is idolized or worshipped can be interchangeable.

by the Pope to 'exorcise' Wagner),[50] Russell, Suschitzky, Harrison *et al* produce some marvellous send-ups of horror movies, in particular the famous Universal movies of *Frankenstein* (1931) and *Dracula* (1933). So there's plenty of lightning and thunder, wind, big, imposing doors, a courtyard, and scared citizens who scurry off at the mention of Wagner. Remember that at this time – the mid-1970s – the Hammer film studio was still churning out *Dracula, Frankenstein,* vampire and horror movies, so all of this was very familiar to movie-going audiences. (And, whaddya know?, contemporary cinema still releases plenty of horror movies each year, and Hammer-style horror movies, from filmmakers such as Tim Burton, Wes Craven and Gore Verbinski).

You're not supposed to take any of this seriously – but you weren't supposed to take the original *Dracula* and *Frankenstein* movies of the Thirties seriously, either (let alone the countless adaptions since). It's all a big yarn, an old wives' tale, it's 'dark and stormy night' stuff. A bit of fun. But, unusually, there's also a political point being made here.

The following scene of Richard Wagner addressing his Hitler Youth is one of the grand spectacles that Ken Russell delights in staging: everything is grotesquely exaggerated: the naked Rhine maidens worshipping the giant, stone phallus atop of which rests the glowing Rhinegold; the very young Hitler Youth (these are pre-teen Hitler Youth, which makes the satire all the creepier), all dressed in superhero outfits, blonde, holding candles and swaying gently to the music and grinning inanely; and Wagner himself clad as Superman, holding a black guitar (this was three years before Warners revived the *Superman* franchise yet again, in 1978, this time with Christopher Reeve in the red and blue suit).

The 1975 movie sends up Richard Wagner in the lyrics composed for the movie to Wagner's music: in the song 'Excelsior Song' (a witty, electronic rock version of a famous and lovely Franz Liszt piano piece), for instance, the lyrics run:

> The new messiah,
> His day has come.
> We'll drive the beast from our land.
> He will restore Teutonic godhead,
> The hour of the Aryan soon will come.

---

50 The Pope calls Richard Wagner the 'Anti-Christ' and the 'Prince of Darkness'.

At this point, *Lisztomania* is more like a conventional rock musical, as Richard Wagner sings and the children add the *oohs* and *aahs* of the chorus, and Cosima stands next to Wagner, smiling. There are rock dances and gestures, too. Well, it's conventional in some respects; in others, this is completely mad. (Quite crazy: it's a movie about the late 19th century, featuring classical composers Franz Liszt and Wagner, but it's staged as a Nazi rally in Germany in the 1930s, and it's mounted as rock musical of the 1970s. The mix of genres – classical musical biopic<>horror movie<>political satire<>rock musical – is brilliant).

The scene where the wild, semi-naked demon of Alberich appears (from the *Ring* cycle),[51] cackling and laughing, and carries off each of the Rhinemaidens to fuck them manically then discard them in a pile, is pure Ken Russell, right down to the very rapid cutting, the vigorousness of the sex, the laughing of the brute, and the use of a spinning camera (few filmmakers have enjoyed spinning the camera like Russell. Many filmmakers use tilted camera, of course – Orson Welles being the most celebrated advocate – but Russell likes to tilt it right over on its side, or to spin it).

This satire on Wagnerian music and Nazi theology is completely bonkers, at once marvellously childish, flamboyantly achieved, and very sinister. The moments where Richard Wagner makes the sign of the swastika in the air, copied by the Hitler Youth below him, and the way they march off to the strains of *Ride of the Valkyrie,* played in a deliberately tinny, silly manner (this was four years before *Apocalypse Now*), are pure Ken Russell.[52] There is something very disturbing about the corruption of children – it is the perversion of the whole human race. Putting those swaying, smiling children into this scene of megalomania and fascism is extremely creepy. (It sends up the way that people follow leaders blindly – which they still do. And worshipping a hero and a saviour – all of that idolization is still around today).

---

51 To the loud electronic re-working by Wakeman and Forsyth of 'Magic Fire Music' by Richard Wagner.
52 One wonders if Ken Russell's brilliant send-up of the dubious aspects of the Wagnerian cult in *Lisztomania* and *Mahler* inspired filmmakers such as Francis Coppola and Walter Murch to use Richard Wagner ironically in *Apocalypse Now*, or the portrayal of the dreaded Illinois Nazis and another outing for the *Ride of the Valkyries* in *The Blues Brothers* (1980).

It is extra disturbing that these children are not the usual depictions of the Hitler Youth – people in their late teens, who can join up and go to war, but younger children. That they are each dressed in Superman costumes is further satire – they have Wagner's 'W' on their chest instead of the Superman 'S' symbol, and the 'W' is a send-up of the Nazi eagle insignia.

Even if the scene is hackneyed or obvious or offensive, the way it's done is absolutely outstanding. There are very few filmmakers who can produce this kind of spectacle this well (and even fewer who would dare to). It might look as if anybody could stage this kind of musical scene, but no, they can't. Indeed, when was the last time you saw a Nazi rally staged in a rock musical theatre manner to the strains of Richard Wagner updated electronically and featuring everyone wearing Superman outfits?!

♪

Following the intense *Dracula* crossed with *Superman* crossed with *Triumph of the Will* crossed with *The Rocky Horror Show* send-up, *Lisztomania* moves into a full-on *Frankenstein* spoof, in particular the famous laboratory scene from the 1931 Universal film (Mel Brooks had parodied it the year before 1975's *Lisztomania,* in the genius comedy *Young Frankenstein*).

In Ken Russell's version, Richard Wagner is now put into the role of Viktor Frankenstein, the mad scientist creating a monster in the form of a god (Thor), a modern-day Siegfried who, armed with a sword, will rid Germany of the Jews. The monster (played by composer Rick Wakeman, in probably his oddest cameo in movies)[53] is dressed in the familiar garb of Siegfried from Wagner's *Ring* opera (though with silver make-up, a blond wig, and glam rock additions, like platform boots).

It's all very silly, and fun, expressing 'Russell's worst fears of what can happen when art is perverted by show business and political fanaticism', as Stephen Farber put it (1975). The scene allows for the horror genre to be sent up vigorously (and simultaneously celebrated), with the full arsenal of gadgets and machines that always surround Frankenstein and his monster in

---

[53] Rick Wakeman has related how he took his mom and elderly relatives to see the film and how they were embarrassed by the scene where Thor pisses on the fire. He also noted how the scene grew and grew, with Ken Russell adding more bits of business for Thor to do.

the scientist's laboratory[54] (there's a joke about 'stein', too: the 'steins' are the Jews that Richard Wagner is cackingly encouraging his monster Siegfried to slay with the sword he gives him – Steins, and maybe a couple of Cohens).[55]

Thunder growls and lightning flashes throughout the scene. Once again, Philip Harrison and his team provide a black-on-black set, masterfully lit by DP Peter Suschitzky (there's a terrific use of sickly green, for instance).[56] There is a genius touch, which is total Ken Russell, when Richard Wagner sets in motion multiple gramophones placed on either side of the monster on the table, playing skewed versions of Wagner's music.

The face-off between Franz Liszt and Richard Wagner continues, however, when Liszt decides to attack Wagner with his music: this's staged as a special effects battle, with Liszt playing a piano encased in a metal frame and mounted on a rotating podium which acts first as a cannon, then as a flame-thrower, hurling bolts of fire at Wagner.

All sorts of crazy stunts and gags ensue – Richard Wagner holding onto the spinning piano and being thrown off, Wagner hurtling around the room on a lamp, jets of fire issuing from the piano, sparks flying when Wagner crashes into the machinery, with the camera spinning too, or capturing the mayhem from a bird's-eye- views.

It's knockabout humour, deliberately schoolboyish and dumb – and it needs to be this big (and expensive), because it has to climax the rivalry between the two composers that has been festering throughout the narrative. And it's Ken Russell being delightfully, self-consciously literal – he has Franz Liszt destroying Richard Wagner using music![57] It's an OTT portrayal of how two music composers might duel in their wild fantasies.

Franz Liszt plays *Dance of Death* (of course), and Richard Wagner is crushed when his phallic, stone pillar is blown apart and collapses on him. Another great touch has Wagner being reduced to an ape-like wreck of his former self, croaking, with red

---

[54] The flashing lights of the machinery in the famous 1931 *Frankenstein* movie, the Van der Graaf generators, Tesla coils, and an assembly of weird machines, were created by designer Kenneth Strickfaden, who dubbed them 'bariton generator', 'nucleus analyser' and 'vacuum electrolyser'.
[55] When Richard Wagner grabs the sword later, it becomes a snake.
[56] Sickly green would become popular in movies of the 1990s and after, being employed in the *Matrix* and *Lord of the Rings* movies, for instance. But there the influence was Japanese *animé*.
[57] That's partly a skit on the real, musical duels that Liszt was involved with.

contact lenses, as he dies (looking forward to the extreme make-up and creatures in *Altered States*). Cosima appears to admonish her father, Liszt, and her ex-husband Hans von Bülow knocks him out. (Cosima's quip about Liszt's 'decadent religion' – Catholicism – is highly ironic, given Wagner's cult of Germanic music).

But Richard Wagner doesn't die, though, and *Lisztomania* hasn't given up its relentless attack on Nazism and the perversion of art. Because in the following scenes, Wagner is back from the dead, now in the figure of Adolf Hitler embodied in Frankenstein's monster, with his black guitar in the shape of a machine gun (he rises from his grave in a set out of a Leni Riefenstahl movie like Count Orklo in *Nosferatu*. And right away he begins mowing down his followers).

The 1975 film is now satirizing Nazi Germany in the 1930s, in particular the treatment of the Jews. So as Jews panic in a street of stores, struggling to take down their Stars of David, Wagner-Hitler-Frankenstein appears, with Cosima Wagner (still in her Superwoman outfit) at his side, backed by the Hitler Youth (also in their superhero costumes). And of course Wagner-Hitler-Frankenstein mows them all down (including Cosima's husband, Hans von Bülow).

Remember that Ken Russell spoke of films being like a mediæval play, simultaneously serious and silly, didactic and poetic, pedagogical and satirical? Well, this is how to take scenes such as Richard Wagner in the guise of Adolf Hitler as Frankenstein's monster gunning down Jews in a street. Nazism, music, performance, women, sex, marriage, the perversion of art – *Lisztomania* includes all of these themes, favourites of Ken Russell's, of course – but we have forgotten religion.

RELIGIOUS SATIRE.

*Lisztomania* contains plenty of satires on religion, and, what a surprise, it's Catholicism again.[58] Thus, there's a lengthy wedding ceremony in a church, presided over by Princess Carolyn, and some amusing scenes with Ringo Starr[59] in a cameo as the Pope.[60] The same sorts of comedy and satire techniques are employed from *Tommy*, *Mahler* and *The Music Lovers* – the Pope

---

[58] Franz Liszt had taken minor orders in 1865, and had retired to Rome in 1861.
[59] Ringo Starr as the Pope was, according to Rick Wakeman, part of the reworking of the movie.
[60] The battle between the Pope and Princess Carolyn had a historical basis, when the Pope declined to give her a dispensation.

appears in Franz von Liszt's bedroom, for instance, on a throne mounted on a trolley pushed by nuns and cardinals (accompanied by a fun fair siren). And of course he sports a fabulously over-the-top costume by Shirley Kingdon and Richard Pointing (which includes images of some of Ken Russell's favourite movie stars on the cloak). The Pope's all in white,[61] while Franz Liszt's room is decadently black – the bed's black and the sheets are black, forming a striking contrast with the lovely Olga Janina (played by the lovely Nell Campbell),[62] nude in bed (and blasé about the Pope entering the room while she's naked).[63]

*Lisztomania* is *absolutely stuffed* with religious imagery: there are statues of the Virgin Mary and Christ, crucifixes (around Franz Liszt's neck), paintings of monks and the Virgin, Russian ikons of saints (and pop stars as saints), the Pope, nuns, cardinals, incense, and a number of churches.

THE GIANT WIENER SCENE.

One of the famous scenes in *Lisztomania* is of course the Giant Penis Scene: again, there's nothing new here, because giant erections in art have been around for millennia, going back way beyond ancient Greek theatre into the mists of time. Phallic humour has been a staple in the Western literary tradition, too, whether it's in William Shakespeare's plays or Geoffrey Chaucer's poems, with their bawdy allusions, or the famous illustrations by Aubrey Beardsley for Aristophanes' *Lysistrata*. Around the time of the 1970s, big cocks had been used elsewhere – famously by the Rolling Stones, as well as in stage shows (such as nudie shows).

However, there aren't any giant cock scenes quite like this in cinema – not big pricks combined with a Busby Berkeley dance number which includes Maypole dancing and the Parisian can-can!

In *Lisztomania,* the out-size erection is used in a very particular manner: it is all about artistic creation, about art as an erection, about art and phallic energy. Wheeling in Ken Russell's favourite psychoanalyst, Sigmund Freud, here isn't necessary, because the theories are so familiar (and not only Freud, but also contemp-

---

[61] In the wedding scene, the Pope turns up in a hooded monk's garb – with a glittery eye-patch!
[62] Nell Campbell's best known as Little Nell in *The Rocky Horror Picture Show*.
[63] The snatch from *film noir*, when Olga pulls a gun on Liszt and demands that he never leave her, is great. This was based in fact, when the real Olga threatened to kill Liszt.

orary philosophers such as Julia Kristeva, who calls the art object the ultimate fetish).

Prior to the Giant Mr Happy Scene, Franz Liszt and Princess Carolyn get down to some 69, which's what inaugurates the fantasy sequence: Liszt stumbles between some huge, inflatable, stockinged legs, and back into the womb. The movie cuts to Liszt tumbling along a red tunnel, a crazy back-to-the-womb scene which makes explicit what all those scenes in numerous other movies are about when they have characters entering long, winding tunnels.

In the Phallic Energy Sequence in *Lisztomania*, Ken Russell and the team orchestrate a bunch of linked motifs – as soon as the weenie appears (with Franz Liszt now significantly crossdressing – Roger Daltrey wears a dress)[64] – so do the groupies materialize, who act now as harpies or mænads. They are the mænads or dancers of Dionysius or Bacchus, who in Greek mythology tore the god to shreds. Here, they are five of Liszt's women, the women he has betrayed (including Countess Marie, Lola Montes, Olga Janina, and George Sand), but now clad in sexed-up versions of their characters (sporting stockings and revealing outfits).

To help Franz Liszt placate the five women dancing around him and threatening to rip him to shreds, Princess Carolyn (who's been lounging about on a red couch in front of red lips), throws him a lyre.[65] Liszt proceeds to use the lyre like an electric guitar. It's wild. (A musician with a lyre evokes the famous god of poetry, Orpheus, an icon certainly in German (Romantic) culture, as well as many other sophisticated cultures of poetry and music in history. Look at the writings of Friedrich Nietzsche or the sublime poesie of Friedrich Hölderlin or Johann Wolfgang von Goethe, where Orpheus is a favourite deity). All of these high culture allusions are absolutely intentional in *Lisztomania*, even though the visuals and wild scenes of Roger Daltrey being attacked by luscious women threatens to obscure the hi-falutin' elements.

The version of the Dionysian orgy in *Lisztomania* follows the ancient Greek mythological model closely, drawing on the myths

---

[64] There is a practical reason for Liszt's dress, of course, and that's to hide the mechanisms for attaching the big prick to the actor's body.
[65] The lyre is appropriate – Franz Liszt composed an orchestral piece in 1854 entitled *Orpheus*.

of Orpheus (torn to shreds by mænads, until he was just a singing head floating down a river), and the Bacchic god of wine, Dionysis: it moves from celebrating phallic power and orgasmic pleasure (the women riding atop the cock, or lying underneath with their legs opening and closing), all staged in a Busby Berkeley style with the performers arranged in patterns for the camera, viewed from overhead or at floor-level, to the mænads and the Muse as castrating forces, tearing at Franz Liszt, and in the climax of the scene pushing him and his giant penis towards a guillotine (behind the guillotine Carolyn sits, her vulva a bull's-eye). She sings, now as a screaming banshee, from Liszt's *Dante Symphony* (1856), about taking Liszt's soul.[66]

There's also a hilarious scene where the groupies dance around the erect phallus like a Maypole – that came from an idea that Ken Russell had for his version of *Gargantua* by François Rabelais (Russell regularly employs ideas from abandoned projects).[67] It's a scene that occurs in no other movie in history.

Dancing and sex moves into dancing and death: Princess Carolyn shifts from being the gentle (but imperious) Muse figure for Franz Liszt to the Muse as devouring, castrating mother, the Muse as the Hindu Goddess Kali. She becomes a demon, with plastic wings, and a spider in a web, at once desirable and horrific.

It's about the costs of the artistic endeavour: that phallic, creative potential has a cost. And the scene's also about the relation between art and life, in particular art and personal relationships – here inevitably depicted as the relationships between the artist and the women in his life, a recurring Russellian theme (in other contexts it might be parental figures, or children).

But the giant penis scene in *Lisztomania* has numerous fun elements too, and can be enjoyed solely on the level of camp spectacle – from the fab, groovy costumes designed by Richard Pointing and Shirley Kingdon, to the incredible set design by Philip Harrison and the art department. And the music. And not forgetting the complex choreography of the camera and the performers, as Ken Russell and the team deliver a bunch of gags

---

66 Franz Liszt also produced, like so many composers of the era, a symphony drawing on *Faust* (1854-57), which's one of the key emblems of selling your soul, one of Ken Russell's primary themes.

67 But, yes, Maypoles and similar pagan and folk imagery and motifs have always had a strong phallic and erotic content. That's what Spring rituals are all about, after all – rebirth, energy, sex, growth.

and shots founded on the Hollywood musical, in particular the Thirties musicals of Busby Berkeley (the scene 'looks as if it had been staged by a berserk Busby Berkeley hard at work on a porno flick', as Joseph Gomez put it [201]. Yes, *precisely*). And as Ken Russell noted in his DVD audio commentary, it took quite a bit of work to make all of this look good, and you can believe it. These scenes are tough to do, requiring a lot of physical labour, rehearsals and retakes to pull them off.

THE ENDING.

The ending of *Lisztomania* is truly out-there. It has to be one of the wildest in the *Wild 'n' Wacky World of the Works of Ken Russell*. It features Franz Liszt now as an angel,[68] playing a harp, accompanied by five of his 'clever ladies', as Ken Russell called them on the DVD audio commentary (the women in his life – Marie, Cosima, Lola, Fifi and Carolyn). On a Greek-style dais (though still supported by phallic columns – now painted white – penises that're suitably demure for heaven!), with much dry ice below (for clouds), and a sky cyclorama behind, Liszt and his women beam at each other (the women are clad in diaphanous dresses and play cellos and violins). And, once again, the movie emphasizes the *music*: after the carnage of the Holocaust scenes, the 1975 film slips into pure music.

This might be the ending, but the movie decides it has to punish its villain – who's become a combination of Richard Wagner, Adolf Hitler, Frankenstein's monster and the nastier aspects of the German national psyche. So Franz Liszt takes a rocket down to Earth to attack Wagner-Hitler-Franksenstein's monster in Berlin in 1945.

But not in a conventional manner, oh no, that wouldn't be wacky enough for this extravagant movie: Franz Liszt's rocket ship is in the shape of a silver lyre, piloted by Liszt operating a colourful, organ keyboard, and powered by each of his Muses standing in huge, steel, organ pipes as the rocket exhausts. It's their love, their souls, their joy, their whatever you like that fuels the Liszt-ship. And it's music, yet again, that powers this vessel, and it's music that once again destroys Richard Wagner – Liszt represents 'pure' music, and Wagner 'debased' or 'corrupt' music,

---

[68] One can imagine what fun Ken Russell is having in heaven right now – with a cast of angels, God as the producer, all the classical composers ever lived and died, with final cut and an unlimited budget!

art perverted by political power.

The visual effects budget might be running out a little here (the models, matte paintings, and animation are a little scrappy by today's standards, though that doesn't matter in a comedy), but it gets the point across: Franz Liszt and his 'clever ladies' waste Hitler-Wagner-Frankenstein's monster in a war-torn Berlin, then ascend to the heavens and the stars, while Liszt reprises his song about love and peace.

Wow!

This is why we love Ken Russell!

(What would Ken Russell have done with a $100 million visual effects budget in a $200 million blockbuster movie? Something a lot more entertaining than the rancid shit churned out by Hollywood, I bet! Even a movie as vulgar/ offensive/ schlocky as Russell could make it would be more fun than unspeakable garbage like *Snow White and the Huntsman*, *Hannibal* or *Casino Royale*).

It's an unusual ending to a very unusual movie: *Lisztomania* has the hero being murdered by his daughter, in revenge for him killing her husband, and a lifetime of neglect. The scene is grotesque: Cosima Wagner not only imprisons her father (extreme enough, one might think), she systematically tortures him with her voodoo doll (this was set up in an earlier scene, when Franz Liszt was due to leave for a concert in Russia, and Cosima said, don't worry, dad, I've got this doll of you to play with).[69]

*Lisztomania* takes another element from the horror genre: it has Franz Liszt's daughter punishing her father by attacking a voodoo doll with a hat-pin. It's a pretty dark and desperate scene, too: Cosima stands outside a room and Liszt is locked inside. As she attacks his head, ears and neck, he howls in agony on the other side. And the scene goes on and on, to the point where, during the Jewish pogrom, she kills Liszt with a stab to his heart.

And finally, Cosima Wagner jabs a needle into the heart of the doll, and Franz Liszt dies inside the room. The camera catches Liszt in the reflection of a segmented mirror – he is now literally shattered to pieces. All of this is taking place at a heightened, symbolic level, of course, but it's still very unusual (and very Gothic). Ken Russell has a very low opinion of Cosima Wagner!

But the filmmakers, as so often, want to have it both ways

---

[69] What do Ken Russell's kids think of this, I wonder?! Ah, but I would imagine that they were used to dad's fantasies and excesses by then!

(well, do you know a filmmaker who doesn't?!). They are going to have a tragic and grotesque scene where a daughter kills her father because he murdered her husband[70] (even though she stands by while her monstrous, second husband kills her first husband). And the filmmakers are also going to have the hero enacting his revenge – from beyond the grave – launching an aerial attack from heaven, no less!

The scene in heaven in *Lisztomania* acts initially an epilogue or coda, in which some of the main characters gather to discuss the story and movie, and if it's a Hollywood movie, they might also talk about morality or lessons being learned. The music unfolds first – as Franz von Liszt leads his lady orchestra in a harp-and-strings arrangement of his own work, 'Peace At Last'. Then comes some conversation, in which all seems to be forgiven (feminists would no doubt find this appalling – the women in Liszt's life seem to forgive him everything).

But the Goodtimes Enterprises movie then shifts from a coda or epilogue back into conventional narrative, as Franz Liszt snaps into action to deal with Richard Wagner as the Frankensteinian monster terrorizing Europe, Adolf Hitler. Piloting his ship using music is an inspired idea, as is the notion that the power of art can defeat the power of politics (Princess Carolyn yells the same idea, that art is far more powerful than politics – clearly a concept close to Ken Russell's heart).[71]

So when Franz Liszt and his lovely ladies dive-bomb Wagner-Hitler-Frankenstein in a war-torn Berlin and zap him into oblivion, it's a return to the conventional ending of a traditional movie (i.e., on the North American model): bad guys must always be dealt with, and always by the hero. It's no different from James Bond or Indiana Jones wasting the chief villain. (And the movie has jumped from 1887, when Liszt died – Richard Wagner died four years earlier – to 1945).

Does it work? Hell, if you're complaining now, after all you've seen in *Lisztomania,* you've been wasting your time!!! *Lisztomania* is a movie where you go along for the ride, and watch a group of enormously talented filmmakers delivering some stupendous material. It may be bonkers, it may be twisted and sexist and violent and dumb, but it sure is entertaining! And it

---
[70] The scenario's reminiscent of *King Lear*.
[71] The visualization of music as different colours – the organ pipes and the beams of light that attack Wagner-Hitler, is also an ancient idea, links to synæsthesia.

does make a serious point: if you're an artist and you debase your art, you've sold your soul to the devil.

But *Lisztomania* doesn't stop there; there is a second 'happy ending' sequence, a positive, life-affirming ending, like at the end of *Tommy*: Franz Liszt pilots the lyre-shaped spaceship out amongst the stars, and sings, 'Peace At Last'.[72] This section of *Lisztomania*, beginning with the Nazi rally at Wagner's Castle, is mounted in a rock opera manner, with the characters singing:

> Now love, sweet love,
> Oh now that love has won,
> Oh now that love has won.
> Now love, our love,
> Our love has ended war;
> He'll torture man no more...

And it's smiles all round as the rock-slanted music kicks in and Franz Liszt and his women fly off into infinity (and beyond).

I don't know who suggested that ending (who would dare?! Only Ken Russell himself!), but it's typically Russellian – it's OTT, it employs the power of music, it shows fascism being defeated, it uses a ton of visual effects, and it's unexpected. One can imagine that ending being proposed at a production meeting: what if we see Franz Liszt in heaven with his lovely ladies, and he creates a rocket ship made of an organ and a lyre, and flies down to Earth and blows Wagner-Hitler to pieces? And the response might be: Err, OK, Ken. How much is it going to cost?

FLAWED BUT FUN.

It's true that there are flaws in *Lisztomania*, and many fans probably wouldn't put it in the same class as *Tommy* or *The Music Lovers* or *Delius: Song of Summer* as a piece of fully-realized and wholly-satisfying Ken Russell movie-making (and Russell-haters wouldn't even get past the first act). But the flaws in *Lisztomania* don't matter, they really don't. Because *Lisztomania* is *not* a conventional movie, it's *not* a melodrama, it's *not* a historical piece, it's *not* a dramatized documentary about a composer, it's *not* a traditional piece of fiction or biography in any accepted sense.

Rather, it's more like a fantasy of a few biographical elements of an artist's life, or it's more like a dream-laden Federico Fellini movie. *Lisztomania* is deliberately, exuberantly stylized and

---

[72] With lyrics by Roger Daltrey and the first A.D., Jonathan Benson.

artificial and heightened (look at Fellini's movies of the mid-1970s, such as *Amarcord* or *Roma* or *Casanova*, where Fellini and his teams go to town with studio-based fantasies. And in Fellini's later work, you just have to go along for the ride. If you resist, there's no point. For some critics and audiences, they won't or can't surrender, so they fight the movie, and that's a waste of time. Fellini – and Russell – don't want you to struggle against their movies, they want you to have some fun and go along for the trip).

Or, put it another way: *Lisztomania* is *hugely enjoyable*. At the level of entertainment and imagination and fantasy, *Lisztomania* is marvellous. 'The film *isn't* biography. It comes from things *I feel* when I listen to the music of Wagner and Liszt, and when *I think* about their lives', Ken Russell remarked at the time (PF, 182; my italics).[73]

It's what Ken Russell *feels* when he listen to the music of Richard Wagner and Franz Liszt. What he *feels*. This needs emphasizing. And the film's what he *thinks* about their lives. Not their lives in a documentary fashion, but what he *thinks* about their lives. It's a world of difference.

THE CRITICS.

*Lisztomania* was the movie 'that many feel took Russell over the top; resulting in an outlandish, phallic-symboled biographical assault on the life of Franz Liszt', according to Raymond Murray in *Images In the Dark: An Encyclopedia of Gay and Lesbian Film and Video* (117). Russell, of course, had been going over-the-top for years before *Lisztomania*!

*Halliwell's Film and Video Guide* called *Lisztomania* 'the most excessive and obscene of all this director's controversial works' (2000, 489); Tony Rayns called it 'Russell's first completely unmitigated catastrophe in several years'; and *Sight and Sound* magazine dubbed it a 'camp compendium of camp, second-hand Freud and third-rate pastiche'.

There's no need to quote any more critics on *Lisztomania* you can guess that most critics at the time found something to dislike in *Lisztomania*. Because it confirms all of the things they don't like about Ken Russell's movies in the first place.

I find *Lisztomania* among the most emotionally moving of Ken

---

[73] 'He does genuinely feel what's in his films', Glenda Jackson said (1972).

Russell's works – the feelings stream from a combination of the passion of the movie for art and artists, for being alive, for the things that bring joy as well as heartache, and, above all, for *music*, my own religion.

This page and over: images from 1975's Lisztomania,
a hugely enjoyable comicbook approach to a composer biography movie

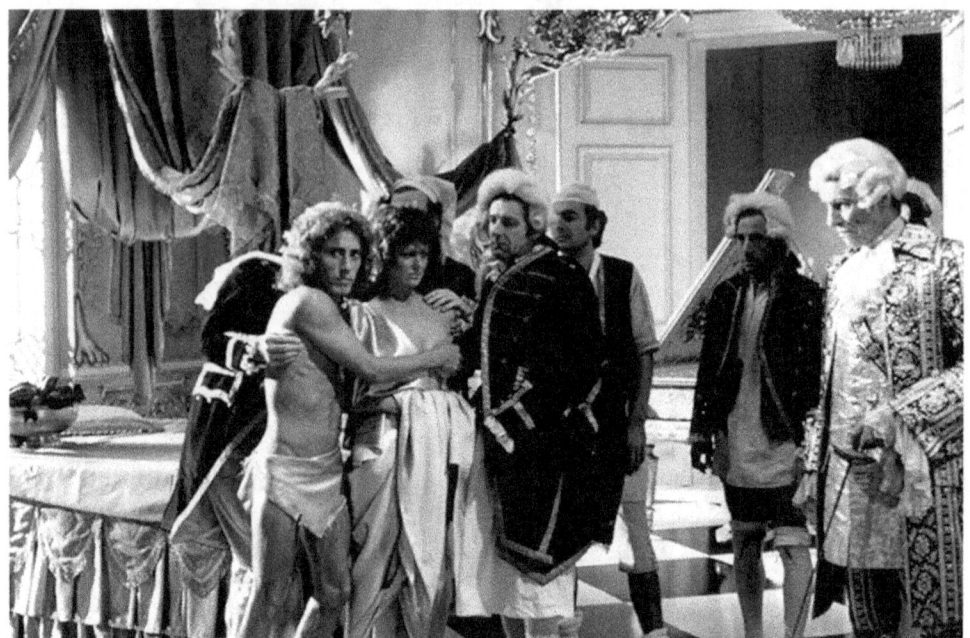

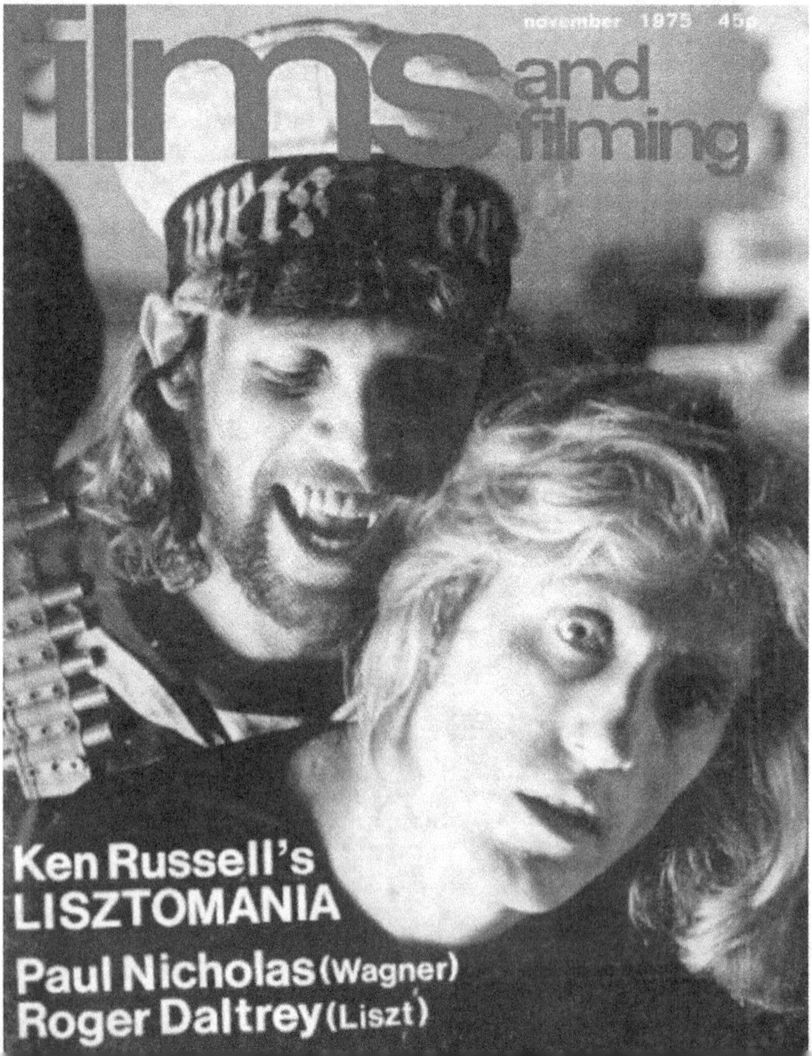
november 1975 45p
films and filming
Ken Russell's
LISZTOMANIA
Paul Nicholas (Wagner)
Roger Daltrey (Liszt)

# 15

# VALENTINO

Why doesn't *Valentino* (1977), Ken Russell's film of Rudolph Valentino's life starring Rudolf Nureyev, work? Err... It's partly the script, which doesn't get inside the character of Rudolph Valentino much, and partly that he turns out to be rather dull (he's a fantastic dancer, though, and the film exploited Nureyev's dancing talent to the hilt).[1] Maybe it's because Valentino and his lover Natasha Rambova are somewhat under-written, or not that appealing.

Also part of the problem with *Valentino* is that we have seen this kind of movie *many* times before.[2] Audiences are so familiar with the rags-to-riches narratives of movie stars or famous artists – or music composers. So the filmmakers must add something new, or demonstrate to the audience just why they want to tell *this* particular tale. And the script and the concept for *Valentino* doesn't quite do that.

And it's also that *Valentino* doesn't gel as a whole: it has marvellous scenes, and many entertaining moments, and some wild ideas, but all of the elements don't quite add up. It is a film that works in sections or in individual scenes, but not as a flow of narrative. And this, it has to be said, is a fault found in some other Ken Russell movies.

---

1 Well, *of course*: you wouldn't cast a world-class ballet dancer and *not* have him dance – especially in a Ken Russell movie! (Russell had trained a ballet dancer and did some theatrical tours).
2 Valentino had been the subject of a previous movie, *Valentino* (Lewis Allen, 1951), and a TV movie, *The Legend of Valentino*, starring Franco Nero.

And the casting isn't quite right, either: not only Rudolf Nureyev (but who else would you cast at that time?), but also Natasha Rambova (Michelle Phillips), Valentino's 2nd wife, and June Mathis (Felicity Kendal), the Metro executive, and Seymour Cassel (George Ullman). Kendall and Ullman really need replacing.

Yes, Rudolph Valentino *is* fascinating, yes the scenes of his funeral (100,000 fans thronging the streets of Gotham) were spectacular, and yes the silent movie era (and Hollywood history and legend) is *enormously* compelling. But the movie *Valentino* doesn't get to grips with that fascination – not in its portrayal of Valentino as a rags-to-riches celebrity, or the movie world of the 1920s, or the nature of fame, or entertainment.

Ken Russell in his autobiography agreed that if *Valentino* were seen as a mirror held up to a movie marriage, it 'reflected all of the pain and none of the fun' (BP, 129); Russell's marriage to Shirley Kingdon was also in trouble.

Rodolfo Alfonso Raffaello Piero Filiberto Guglielmi di Valentina d'Antonguolla, 1895-1926, was born in Castellaneta, Italy. Valentino was the desert sheik lover, the tango dancer, the Latin Lover. Valentino's movies included: *The Four Horsemen of the Apocalypse* (Rex Ingram, 1921), *Uncharted Seas* (Wesley Ruggles, 1921), *Camille* (Ray Smallwood, 1921), *The Sheik* (George Melford, 1921), *Blood and Sand* (Fred Niblo, 1922), *Monsieur Beaucaire* (Stanley Olcott, 1924), *Cobra* (Joseph Hendabery, 1925), *The Eagle* (Clarence Brown, 1925) and *The Son of the Sheik* (George Fitzmaurice, 1925).

*Valentino* was released by United Artists and produced by Robert Chartoff, Irwin Winkler[3] and Harry Benn. The script was adapted by Mardik Martin and Ken Russell from a book by Brad Steiger and Chaw Mank (*Valentino: An Intimate Exposé of the Sheik*).[4] Philip Harrison and Peter Suschitzky, who had done such brilliant jobs on *Lisztomania,* were back as production designer and cameraman, as was Shirley Kingdon designing the costumes, Stuart Baird editing, and Gillian Gregory as choreographer. Steve

---

3 Among Chartoff and Winkler's productions was the controversial movie *The Last Temptation of Christ*, which they had set up with Paramount in the early 1980s. They made a *ton* of money from United Artists' *Rocky* series (the first *Rocky* movie cost $1.5 million and took $55.9 million in North American rentals alone).
4 *Valentino* by Irving Shulman was also used. It was Schulman, for instance, who drew attention to the mourners at the funeral parlor (PF, 198).

Cooper was set designer, and Stanley Black composed the music.[5]

*Valentino* had one of the biggest premieres for a Ken Russell movie: Andy Warhol and Diana Vreeland came to the opening in Gotham (at the Iranian Embassy), and Princess Margaret attended the London premiere.

❊

Structurally, *Valentino* was *Citizen Kane*: a bunch of people gather after the death of the central character and the film flashes back to each of their stories. It was the rondo form again, that Ken Russell and his team had employed in *Mahler:* A-B-A-C-A-D-A-E.

*Valentino* is partly an exploration of stardom itself – it could be about anyone famous. The film is fascinated by the charisma and glamour that makes up a star, that a star projects. Ken Russell's films have often been curious about fans as much as stars, about the people who worship artists and stars, about the artists and stars themselves (and the nature of adulation). Films such as *Delius, Savage Messiah, Lisztomania* and *The Music Lovers* are about the people who surround the artists, the entourages, as about the artists themselves. *Valentino* asks the question 'what is a star?', and has fun exploring it, even if it doesn't come up with any answers beyond the obvious one of: people need stars, need something to worship. Worship and awe: for Russell, it might be awe of classical music, and mountains, and the Lake District, and for others it could be Valentino or another movie star.

Take *Tommy*, which was very much a study in modern religious feeling, a modern religious cult that develops around an individual – *Valentino,* like *Lisztomania,* is virtually a sequel to *Tommy*, with similar themes (and images). Consider, for instance, the scenes where the mourners on the street outside the funeral parlour burst in and storm the place. Or the powerfully staged sequence outside Valentino's mansion, where the fans are crowded in the gardens at night and are chanting, led by a young woman who yells 'YOU!' at the beginning of each phrase. There's something about the way the filmmakers have captured the woman screaming 'YOU!' that's unforgettable.[6] And *The Devils*

---

[5] Other music included 'The Sheik of Araby', sung by Chris Ellis, 'There's a New Star In Heaven Tonight', sung by Richard Day-Lewis, and Ferde Grofé's *Grand Canyon Suite*.

[6] The scene where the crowd of fans outside Valentino's mansion and scream 'YOU! are the spirit that moves the universe!' was masterfully intercut (by Stuart Baird) with Natasha and Valentino conducting a séance inside (the movie sends up Natasha's occult leanings towards divination, and includes a scene where she casts bones), and also a hysterical love scene on the table.

was of course all about the religious impulse to worship.

Although it was an American production, *Valentino* was shot mainly in Britain and Europe (based in Elstree Studios, Borehamwood), with many British actors and crew. Ken Russell regulars in the cast included Linden, Justin, Sutton, and Kemp.

There's a cast of British character actors (Alfred Marks, Felicity Kendall, Jennie Linden, Peter Vaughan, John Justin, etc) doing American accents in *Valentino*: everyone denounces Hollywood stars when they attempt British accents, but some of the British actors in *Valentino* aren't particularly wonderful at accents either.

And the star is a Russian inhabiting an Italian-American. Rudolf Nureyev (1938-1993) had done a little acting prior to *Valentino* (including *Don Quixote*, *Romeo and Juliet* and *The Nutcracker*), but no one would say he was wholly satisfying (being best known as a ballet dancer, which's a different kind of performer).

However, Rudolf Nureyev had been closely involved with the production of films such as *Swan Lake* (1966), and he had co-directed *Don Quixote* (1973) in Australia with Robert Helpmann. So he knew about movies on both sides of the camera, and had also been involved with important records of ballet performances.

Rudolf Nureyev studied with the Kirov Ballet, defected to the West in 1961,[7] appeared with the Royal Ballet (most famously with Margot Fonteyn), and ran the Paris Opera Ballet. He appeared in *Marguerite and Armand* (1963), directed by Frederick Ashton, from Alexander Dumas, *The Moor's Pavane* by José Limón, *Appalachian Spring* by Martha Graham, *Aureole* by Paul Taylor, *The Nutcracker* (Royal Swedish Ballet, 1967), and *Romeo and Juliet* (London Festival Ballet, 1977). Prior to *Valentino*, Nureyev had appeared in documents of ballet performances (such as *Romeo and Juliet*, 1966, with Margot Fonteyn and the Royal Ballet, choreographed by Sir Kenneth MacMillan, and *An Evening With the Royal Ballet*, 1963, two years before his defection to the West), documentaries (*I Am a Dancer*, 1973), and a film of his *Don Quixote* (1973), with Robert Helpmann, Ray Powell, Lucette Aldous, Francis Crose and the Australian Ballet (Nureyev played Basilio in Marius Petipas' ballet, with a score by Ludwig Minkus. It was photographed by Geoffrey Unsworth). Later films included *Giselle* (1979), *Fonteyn and Nureyev* (1985) and *Rudolf Nureyev* (1991).

---

[7] Mikhail Baryshhnikov, Natalia Makarova and Alexander Godunov followed Nureyev.

Certainly Rudolf Nureyev looked the part (but didn't look much like Rudolph Valentino), and moved like a dream, but he didn't quite have the acting chops to deliver on the rest of the role. And the chemistry with Valentino's lovers, including Natasha, was a little strained (sometimes that plays into the media image of Valentino as the cinema's Lothario, but it works against love scenes which're meant to be intimate and tender). The experience of shooting *Valentino* was not the happiest for Ken Russell – not least because his marriage to Shirley Kingdon was falling apart – and Vivian Jolly, Russell's second wife, was on set, which caused friction.[8] *Valentino* was the last film of Russell's that his wife did the wardrobe.

And there were problems with Rudolf Nureyev, who was something of a diva, and wanted to be the centre of attention in every scene. Michelle Phillips, too, didn't have the best time making *Valentino*: the former singer with the Mamas and the Papas called it 'the most miserable working experience of my life' (PF, 2060.

Certainly Rudolf Nureyev wasn't the easiest actor to get along with, and there are accounts in Ken Russell's autobiography of his prima donna antics, upstaging of scenes, and tantrums. Later, Nureyev told James Toback that he 'detested the director', and he regretted doing *Valentino*.

But you couldn't help looking at Rudolf Nureyev when he was on screen: if he didn't have the same acting skills or experience of a professional actor, he certainly had bagfuls of charisma and screen presence. Besides, although Nureyev's dialogue wasn't always delivered perfectly (and that accent wavered, too), Ken Russell's films have never been about the dialogue. So when it came to fitting in with the visuals, Nureyev moved beautifully.

It was a trade-off, similar to the one with Oliver Reed in *Tommy*: while Reed couldn't really sing, his acting presence made up for that. And if Nureyev couldn't act as well as Paul Scofield, he moved – and looked – like a star.

Casting *Valentino* was difficult – the producers Irwin Winkler and Robert Chartoff said they looked everywhere. It had to be, preferably, a star, and it had to be someone who could

---

8 Onlookers have said that Ken Russell and his wife would have arguments on set, in front of the crew (such as when Kingdon found Vivian Jolly sitting in Russell's director's chair), and the tense atmosphere may have contributed to the tougher approach that *Valentino* has (PF, 197).

convincingly play Rudolph Valentino. Nureyev was cast as Vaslav Nijinsky, in a bit part, but was eventually cast in the lead.[9] The appeal was obvious.

But one performer in *Valentino* was unequivocally wonderful, and that was Leslie Caron, as Alla Nazimova, Rudolph Valentino's ageing admirer.[10] She gets the best entrance in the 1977 film: swanning into Campbell's Funeral Parlor in NYC with a vast train flowing behind her. The white-and-black cloak patterned with camellias (an *hommage* to the illustrations that Aubrey Beardsley produced for *Salomé* by Oscar Wilde, which Ken Russell reprised in *Salomé's Last Dance*), is placed around Valentino's coffin).

Leslie Caron was right up to the mark for Ken Russell's swooning, hyped, camp form of acting, and all of the scenes featuring Alla Nazimova are some of the most satisfying in the picture. (Aspects of her character were mixed with Pola Negri, an actress who fainted at Valentino's funeral. And when some of the newspaper photographers miss the moment when Nazimova faints, the actress performs it again to make sure they all get it).

Leslie Caron, a true Hollywood legend, made one of the most stunning debuts in movies when she starred opposite Gene Kelly in just about my favourite Hollywood musical, *An American In Paris* (1951). What a truly, transcendentally beautiful experience that film is.

On a sidenote, Alla Nazimova (1879-1945) is worthy of a biopic herself: a Russian emigré (in 1905), Nazimova was the first actress trained by Konstantin Stanislavsky to appear in movies, Nazimova starred in *Camille* (1921) and *A Doll's House* (1922), collaborated on six movies with her lover Natasha Rambova (Rudolph Valentino's second wife), who was the art director, and directed a homosexual version of *Salomé* by Oscar Wilde, with, apparently, a cast and crew that was all gay. According to Raymond Murray, 'the story of Herod's vixen stepdaughter who danced for the head of John the Baptist is even more outrageous here than in Ken Russell's entertainingly over-the-top *Salomé's Last Dance*' (228).

Alla Nazimova was also one of the famous hostesses of

---

9 Apparently, because of Rudolf Nureyev's commitments, casting Nureyev meant delaying shooting for a year. According to Ken Russell, it was Shirley Kingdon's idea to cast Nureyev.

10 Nazimova appeared as Salomé in a 1923 movie.

Hollywood's lesbian community, and her Garden of Allah mansion on Sunset Boulevard was well-known for some wild Tinseltown parties. (Jeez, why didn't Ken Russell make a film about her instead of Valentino?!).

So we come to one of the central issues of *Valentino*: the star's sexuality. It's *The Music Lovers* all over again, with homosexuality and bisexuality set against heterosexuality. Except in *Valentino* it becomes one of the central battlegrounds of the drama, as the press and later the public pick up on the ambiguity of Valentino's sexual preferences, and Valentino's increasingly desperate measures to prove his heterosexuality and machismo.[11]

Certainly Rudolph Valentino is portrayed as gay or sexually ambiguous from the start: the first time he's seen alive (following the lying-in-state scene), he's dancing with his ballet dancer partner, teaching him the tango (this is no less than Vaslav Nijinsky, played by Anthony Dowell (b. 1943), a well-known British ballet dancer). As well as that fairly obvious indicator of the hero's sexual preferences, there are many allusions in the dialogue to Valentino's homosexuality (even though Valentino is surrounded by women from this moment onwards).

In *Valentino*, Ken Russell and the team recreated Vaslav Nijinsky's performance of *L'Après-midi d'un faune* of 1912, which had Valentino appearing in Nijsinky's role nude, in body make-up. It's another example of Uncle Ken finding ways of squeezing in more dance (and more Nijinsky) into a movie.

There's sex, and nudity, too, in *Valentino*, including scenes of Natasha and Valentino lovemaking in the sheik's tent, just prior to filming of one of Valentino's most famous pictures.

One of the intriguing elements of *Valentino* is that it explored a male pin-up, a man who was the object of a sexual gaze from both women *and* men. As David Thomson put it in *A Biographical Dictionary of Film*:

> it seemed likely that he was bewildered by his fame and the wealth of characters it opened up for him. His screen personality and his reputation are both inaccessible now because they depended upon the fashion of the moment. Men have always had an insecure hold on the camera, and male sex appeal vanished much quicker than the sway exerted by actresses. (1995, 767)

---

[11] Needless to say, some have linked the sexual ambiguity in *Valentino* to Nureyev's own sexuality.

*Valentino* thus reverses the usual gender make-up of celebrity biopics which focus on sex icons: *Valentino* also gives us an idea of what Ken Russell's *Nijinsky* project might've looked like, where men – and their bodies – are the focus (Russell's cinema has not been afraid of sexualizing men's bodies – indeed, the most famous scene in all of his work is exactly that, two nude men wrestling, and not a woman in sight).

Michelle Phillips (b. 1944), who plays Natasha, is a willing participant in the Ken Russell School of Filmmaking, but doesn't seem wholly comfortable, and not just in the nude scenes (where, like Eve in Biblical movies, she has very long hair to cover up her breasts).[12] Phillips said that Nureyev hated kissing her, and the sex scenes with him were very difficult for her. However, Phillips – and Nureyev – are delicious to look at. In this film of the glamour of stardom, the nudity and the sex isn't gratuitous – this is what it's *all* about.

And there's a scene where Rudolf Valentino and his starlet Lorna Sinclair (Penny Milford) get jiggy with it during the lunchhour at the studio, which Ken Russell and his team typically depicts as a film fantasy. And there's the madam Billie Streeter (Linda Thorson) who runs the dance hall, who's tupping Bianca's (June Bolton) mobster husband (Robin Brent Clarke) (before Valentino and his chums catch them *in flagrante*, on camera).

There was a scene where Valentino is tortured in a cage in a jail by several British characters actors (such as Dudley Sutton, playing a mad masturbator, called 'Willy the Wanker' in the credits). He's given summat nasty in his drink, but the bastard jailor won't let him out to use the bathroom.[13] It was typical over-the-top Ken Russell, but United Artists let Russell keep it in. The producers however, Robert Chartoff and Irwin Winkler, wanted to cut it.[14]

Of course the abuse scene had to go when *Valentino* was

---

12 To prepare for the part, Michelle Phillips said she tracked down Rudolph Valentino's sister, and also read Valentino's autobiography (G. Gholson: "Michelle Phillips", *Interview*, July, 1977).

13 Ken Russell wanted Rudolph Valentino to piss himself, and one of the many anecdotes about shooting *Valentino* was the debacle with Rudolf Nureyev and the hose-pipe that had to be inserted in the star's pants (cue gossip about Nureyev's weenie). The scary prison guard was one of the hillbillies in *Deliverance* – Billy McKinney.

14 'Not one of the backers could stomach the gaol scene. It was out of character with the rest of the film, too violent, too disturbing', Russell recalled (BP, 102). It is pretty OTT, and does seem to belong in another movie – and the bitter, vicious treatment of Valentino is already covered in other scenes.

shown on U.S. network television. Ken Russell saw it then and said it was 'a million times better without it' (1993, 67). He was right: the scene is vicious and nasty and crude, and too schoolboyish.

⁂

Theatricality, putting on a show, is foregrounded in *Valentino*, as in many Ken Russell movies (Russell never passes up the opportunity to put on a show). There are numerous scenes where a performance is taking place and an audience watches it – right from the second scene, where Valentino dances with Vaslav Nijinsky, to the German-themed bar, Baron Long's. And the many scenes of a film being screened for an audience, whether for an agent and a producer, or for an audience in a cinema.

One of the more memorable scenes in *Valentino* has a cinema packed entirely with women, all wearing hats and red lipstick, staring at the screen (reprising the concert sequence in *Lisztomania*). In the centre towards the front is June Mathis: after imagining herself in a fantasy from *The Sheik* where Rudy Valentino whisks her off on a horse in the desert and kisses her, Mathis exits in tears (and presumably every other woman in the cinema is having similar erotic fantasies. In its own, modest way, this is as a good a commentary on the nature of film itself, and fantasy, as anything by, say, Jean-Luc Godard or any postmodern filmmaker you care to consider).

The big scene in Baron Long's club in Los Angeles is another of Ken Russell's flamboyant portrayals of show business combined with personal relationships going to pot. It's wild and theatrical and cruel, delighting in the moment when Marjorie Tain (Leland Palmer) dances in a drunken stupor with Rudolph Valentino, or when Valentino takes Mr Fatty's girlfriend (Carol Kane) away from him. These are sequences of grand spectacle and emotional barbarity that Russell is particularly brilliant at portraying.

I agree with Joseph Lanza that *Valentino*'s 'tempo starts to skid a bit' when George Ullman appears (PF, 204). Part of the trouble is that Ullman is too much like one of those characters invented by producers and scriptwriters to cover holes in the narrative, or a character invented to combine other characters. Also, he's not a particularly interesting character.

*Valentino* filmed in many British locations, standing in mainly for U.S. locations, including Blackpool Tower and London's Hyde Park Hotel. The Russell-Cotes Art Gallery in Bournemouth, which I know well and like very much,[15] stood in for parts of Rudolph Valentino's mansion in the later scenes of the film. The production visited Spain for the scenes of Valentino's appearance in 1921's *The Four Horsemen of the Apocalypse*. This was Almeria in Spain standing in for California, which in turn, in the silent film *The Four Horsemen of the Apocalypse*, was standing in for World War One France. (*Valentino* also employed Spain for the desert scenes for the recreations of *The Sheik*).

*Four Horsemen of the Apocalypse*, adapted by June Mathis from Vicente Blasco Ibáñez's novel, was a Metro Pictures epic, with a budget rumoured to be $800,000 ($800,000 in 1921 is plenty expensive; the novel had been optioned for $20,000; during re-negotiations the deal went to $190,000). Director Rex Ingram, said *Variety*, had 14 assistants (and each had a cameraman), and a cast of 12,000. Shooting ran for 120 days (six months). 125,000 tons of building materials were employed (they shot a million feet of film). Sets were built for the village and the castle near Griffith Park, where Warner Brothers is now.

*Four Horsemen of the Apocalypse* brought in $5m in domestic box office (equivalent to $188m in 2005), and made Rudolf Valentino a star. Needless to say, the 1977 United Artists movie could not reproduce a silent movie epic on that scale (pity!), but the scenes are crowded and chaotic enough to give the impression of a historical epic being filmed.

*The Four Horsemen of the Apocalypse* put Rex Ingram into the A-list among directors. In his autobiography *A Life In the Movies*, Michael Powell described Ingram when he first met him in the 1920s:

> Rex was about twenty-nine and was one of the best-looking men I had ever seen. He had straight black hair and eyebrows, a perfect profile, and was about medium height. His eyes were remarkable, a dreamer's eyes. He wore a gold bracelet on his left wrist. He was dressed in khaki, long pants and bush shirt with short sleeves. Bare brown feet in sandals. Long slender fingers and toes… an artist, but

---

[15] When I was at film school in Bournemouth we used to visit the Russell-Coates Museum, which was on the cliffs, not far from the college. Today it still looks pretty much the same as it did when it was used as the film set for *Valentino*.

an amateur artist, a show-off; a bit of an actor, because of his good looks, but not a good actor; a showman, certainly, with a sure instinct for and appreciation of the theatrical. He was loyal to his likes and dislikes, and his friends were loyal to him. (1986, 124, 148)

❦

*Valentino* was in many ways another Ken Russell musical: although it was about a Hollywood star, it contained a large amount of dancing (more dancing than songs). It wasn't just that Rudolph Valentino was a dancer and gigolo before he became a movie star, it was because if there's an opportunity to present a scene as a dance, Russell will take it. And especially when his leading man is a famous and fantastic, Russian ballet dancer.

Natasha Rambova and Rudolph Valentino dance when promoting 'Mineralava' (set in a theatre/ ballroom, it's yet another of Ken Russell's scenes of performances and audiences). Valentino dances at the bierkeller. And a dance troupe dressed in pink with powder puffs send up the Sheik's sexuality in a restaur-ant (talk about bitchy and catty! Meoww!). *Valentino*'s reminiscent of the sordid, gossipy tales of Olde Hollywoode which Kenneth Anger mined for his book *Hollywood Babylon*.

*Valentino* enabled the filmmakers to have their digs at Hollywood, and also to recreate some moments from the history of cinema, including filming silent movies (and reproducing some silent comedy, one of Ken Russell's favourite genres). Russell clearly enjoyed recreating the shooting of Westerns and war movies in the desert (taking a cameo as the brash film director Rex Ingram). And there's a lavish recreation of a historical romance film (*Monsieur Beaucaire*, 1924) – the scene where Valentino has a pink powder puff thrown at him (the pink powder puff was part of the Valentino legend – in *U.S.A.* by John Dos Passos, Valentino wakes up from his operation for peritonitis and says, 'well, did I behave like a pink powder puff?').

In his autobiography, Ken Russell describes how the actor cast to play the film director Rex Ingram was too drunk to do the part, and Russell ended up doing it himself. Equity didn't like Russell taking over the actor's role for the cameo, but Russell found out that he had been an Equity member since 1950. Russell would have problems with Equity later on, during the pre-production of the abandoned *Moll Flanders*.

*Valentino* was full of real people, including movie moguls

such as Jesse Lasky (1880-1958), and actors such as Mr Fatty (clearly based on Fatty Arbuckle, 1881-1932). And some of them were sent up, which's inevitable in a Ken Russell movie. Lasky (Huntz Hall), for instance, was depicted in his office with a gorilla in a cage behind him. And the 1977 movie satirizes Hollywood's money-love by having three movie moguls literally arguing over Valentino's corpse (Richard Rowland from MGM, Joseph Schenck from United Artists and Lasky from Paramount).

A further satire on the fakery of Hollywood and entertainment was included in the script, but not in the movie: the Sheik's corpse would have been revealed to be a wax model by the funeral director Lindsay Kemp, with the real Valentino elsewhere, in a morgue.

It's in the recreation of particular movies that *Valentino* really comes alive. Because *Valentino* is Ken Russell's film about film-making, it's his *The Bad and the Beautiful*, his *Sunset Boulevard*, his *Singin' In the Rain,* his *8 1/2.* And in *Valentino*, Russell and the team deliver numerous in-jokes about movies and Hollywood, just as Russell did about the classical music world in *Lisztomania* and *The Music Lovers* and *Mahler*.

*Valentino* continued Ken Russell's penchant for covering scenes with single master shots, choreographing the actors with the camera. And for using extreme wide angle lenses.

Rather than use extracts from Rudolph Valentino's films themselves (which may have been considered, but rights issues have to be taken into account), Ken Russell and the production team recreated them – iconic scenes from *The Sheik*, for instance, or from *Monsieur Beaucaire*. A wise decision, because it makes the leap between the drama presented in the foreground by the people impersonating real people of the past so much smoother. Employing footage of the real Valentino, for instance, might draw attention to the differences between Nureyev and Valentino (thus, we don't really see the actual Valentino in this movie).

As well as recreating some silent classics, *Valentino* also depicted newsreels (as in the opening credits),[16] using the age-old strategy of degrading the film so it looked like old newsreels (after presenting newsreel footage of the Sheik's funeral and mob scenes outside the funeral parlour, the film then switches from black-and-white to colour).

---

16 Newsreels are a rapid and clear method of delivering slabs of exposition, of course, and *Valentino* is inspired by the best – *Citizen Kane*.

*The Sheik* (George Melford, 1921), perhaps Rudolph Valentino's most famous movie, is sent up in sepia tones, with Jennie Linden over-acting in silent movie style as the star Agnes Ayres encountering the Arabian prince in a tent. *Valentino* cleverly uses another classical Russellian montage as *The Sheik* merges with June Mathis's fantasies in the cinema, and is also re-worked again when Valentino and Natasha get freaky in the same tent used for *The Sheik*.

*Valentino* is very much Ken Russell's *hommage* to Olde Hollywoode, to the films he enjoyed as a youth. The silent era in Hollywood *did everything*, in terms of stories and types of movie. Absolutely everything. By the late 1920s, everything had been done, and all that follows afterwards is in many respects a repetition, a remake, a rehash. Maybe it was enough in *Valentino* that Russell & co. simply delivered a loving tribute to glory days of Hollywood.

Rudolph Valentino (1895-1926)

# 16

## *ALTERED STATES*

'Why don't you take your turkey sandwiches and your script and your Sanka and stuff it up your ass and get on the next fucking plane back to New York and let me get on with the fucking film.'

Ken Russell, *A British Picture* (181)

Ken Russell was brought in late to the *Altered States* (1980) project (it had already been through a number of directors – some 26, apparently. Eh? 26!).[1] The writer Paddy Chayefsky disagreed with Russell about the film and subsequently disowned it;[2] Chayefsky (doing well following the success of 1976's *Network*), had handpicked Arthur Penn to direct it; Penn was originally going to make the film, budgeted at $12.2 million (it came in finally at $14.9 million), for Warners. Penn walked when he and Chayefsky disagreed about the kind of film they wanted to do.[3] (Much of the information in this section comes from Ken Russell's books, but some is from Joseph Lanza's study, which Russell (in his *Times* newspaper column) found revelatory and upsetting.

---

[1] Including, according to Ken Russell, Steven Spielberg, Stanley Kubrick, Sydney Pollack, Robert Wise, Orson Welles, Martin Scorsese, Fred Zinnemann, Woody Allen, Ingmar Bergman, Brian de Palma, Bernardo Bertolucci, John Boorman, Andrei Tarkosvsky, Irwin Kershner, Francis Coppola, Roman Polanski, George Lucas, John Schlesinger, François Truffaut, Franco Zeffirelli, Bryan Forbes, Sidney Lumet, Nic Roeg, Richard Donner and Michael Winner (BP, 169).
[2] Even though Paddy Chayefsky took his name off the movie, and used his real name instead (Sidney Aaron), he was still paid.
[3] One sticking point was the basement – Penn wanted it to look hi-tech, but Chayefsky wanted a simple setting.

Lanza, Russell said, had illustrated his account of *Altered States* with opinions from all sides, but some of the material in his book was news to Russell).

Starring William Hurt as a scientist, Edward Jessup, who goes too far in his experiments, and Blair Brown[4] as his wife Emily who stays with him for the journey, *Altered States* presented cinema as a psychedelic trip, with some extraordinary imagery, even by Ken Russell's standards – colourful, kinetic, and over-the-top. As Jessup experimented with sensory deprivation tanks, hallucinogenic drugs such as peyote in Mexico, and so on, eventually regressing mentally and physically to a primal ape-like creature (nimbly and athletically played by Mexican Miguel Godrean),[5] and beyond, to a foetal, pre-human form, Russell and his team piled on the visual effects, the flashing lights, the make-up, the rotoscoping and the computer animation.

Howard Gottfried produced; Daniel Melnick was executive producer; Stuart Baird was associate producer; Jordan Cronenweth was DP; Eric Jenkins was editor; Richard MacDonald was production designer; Thomas Roysden was set decorator; Robert Blalack, Brian Ferren and James Shourt did the vfx; Ruth Meyers was costume designer; and John Corigliano composed the score.

*Altered States* was set in New York City, Harvard Medical School, Boston, San Francisco and Mexico. Location shooting included Columbia University for the opening scenes[6] (later used in *Ghostbusters*, *Spider-man* and Woody Allen's *Hannah and Her Sisters*); Harvard Medical School, Boston Logan Airport, and Beacon Hill in Boston; Mexico, for the unusual rock formations, and the peyote sequence; the Bronx Zoo (for the scenes where Jessup as a prehistoric man runs amok); and Los Angeles (at the Biltmore Hotel, for the scenes where Jessup transforms into a blob).[7]

Paddy Chayevsky (1923-81) made his name with a group of TV dramas in the 1950s, topped off by *Marty*. The 1955 movie version of *Marty* won the Oscars for Best Film, Actor, Script and

---

[4] Blair Brown underwent a few auditions before she got the part.
[5] That was another scene that Paddy Chayefsky – what a surprise – hated: 'the janitor hears something in the lab and creeps in to check. Then a ballet dancer suddenly jumps out of the tank doing a *grand jeté*. You're into *Planet of the Apes*!' (PF, 231).
[6] The movie introduces the hero (Edward Jessup), his buddy (Arthur) and the woman in his life (Emily) very quickly.
[7] No shooting in Frisco, though – it's clearly not San Fran, but looks like somewhere along the Hudson River, on a hill.

Director. The movies that Chayefsky wrote include: *The Catered Affair, The Bachelor Party, The Goddess, Middle of the Night, Paint Your Wagon, The Americanization of Emily, The Hospital,* and *Network*. There were plays on Broadway, too. *Altered States* was Chayefsky's last movie.

Paddy Chayefsky had written *Altered States* as a novel first, which he vowed never to do again, because by the time he'd rewritten the novel he was bored with the whole thing (he also preferred drama to novels, regarding them as *declassé*: drama, Chayefsky said, had been around since the Orphic rites).[8] When it came to writing the screenplay, 'all the holes came out', Chayefsky recalled, so he started over.

Ken Russell was an unusual choice as a director for hire: he wasn't the kind of filmmaker who could be pushed around, told what to do; he wasn't a young novice, eager for experience, which the studio could dictate to.[9] Further, he had his own way of seeing things, which would inevitably clash with Paddy Chayefsky's way. Chayefsky wanted things done his way: 'Paddy could never readily accept any idea that was not his own,' as Russell put it (BP, 172). Columbia dropped *Altered States*, and Warners took it up (Russell claimed that Warners' president Ted Ashley would only take over the production if the director was fired. Ashley was among the suits at Warners who profoundly disliked *The Devils*. Hiring yet another director so close to principal photography would have been very difficult – especially when so many big names had already turned it down).

But Ken Russell needed a gig, so he accepted: he knew going in that this was going to be tough: a noted director had walked out; he couldn't use his choice of cameraman; the show had switched studios; and there was a difficult, fussy, control freak writer to deal with. Paddy Chayefsky, for instance, insisted on attending the rehearsals, which must've been taxing, judging from Russell's account in his autobiography. Chayefsky was eager to have his input acknowledged and acted upon. Russell agreed,

---

[8] Quoted in J. Brady, 59.
[9] Producer Howard Gottfried remarked of Ken Russell that, 'in hindsight, if I knew he was going to be such a putz, such a miserable son of a bitch, I would never have recommended him' (PF, 226). Gottfried sided with Paddy Chayefsky, and both called Russell a monster, who was using any means possible to undermine Chayefsky's influence on the movie. It can't have helped the tensions on set when Chayefsky insisted on having headphones so he could monitor the dialogue. Russell was clear: 'I can't possibly direct this movie with all your incessant talk going on', Russell told Gottfried.

but told Chayefsky that 'when it came to shooting I would brook no interference from him' (BP, 175).

Ken Russell related some of the arguments between him and Paddy Chayefsky,[10] with his agent Bobby trying to act as an intermediary. After one memorably tense phone call –

> 'Why don't you take your turkey sandwiches and your script and your Sanka and stuff it up your ass and get on the next fucking plane back to New York and let me get on with the fucking film.' (BP, 181)

– Russell thought he'd be asked to leave. He wasn't, and although Paddy Chayefsky apparently had to relinquish some rights or input at Warners, he still had plenty of influence:

> All the rushes were flown to New York for his approval and we were forbidden to exchange a single word of dialogue, no matter how trivial, without his permission. So I shot the script just as it was – typos and all. But I shot it in such a way that the excess dialogue could be junked later if I should get lucky… (BP, 181)

It seems that Paddy Chayefsky had met his match with Ken Russell, but also that Russell had met his match with Chayefsky. Both could yell and fume, both were used to getting their own way (in the main), and both had strong ideas about what they wanted from a movie.[11]

Paddy Chayefsky was used to getting what he wanted: for *Marty*, he asked for sole credit as writer, casting vetos, stipulated that Delbert Mann would direct, and that he could co-direct if needed. Producer Harold Hecht acceded to these demands.

Needless to say, Paddy Chayefsky took a dim view of auteurism: 'all humbug, pure humbug, rubbish'. There were only four or five true *auteurs* for Chayefsky – Ingmar Bergman, Stanley Kubrick, Bob Fosse, Orson Welles, Robert Altman and Woody Allen.[12] Ken Russell and nearly all directors agree that the *auteur* theory doesn't reflect reality.

Apparently, Stanley Kubrick had wanted to film *Network* by

---

[10] Paddy Chayefsky could be morose, paranoid, tyrannical, difficult, and hyper, according to his biographer Shaun Considine (*Mad As Hell*, Randhom House, New York, 1994).
[11] There are further similarities between Russell and Chayefsky, such as being fans of Edgar Allan Poe, which Joseph Lanza outlines in his book (221). 'Chayefsky and Russell both liked to eat, gab, throw their weight, and fuel their work on anger, frustration and tortured love,' remarked Lanza.
[12] Quoted in J. Brady, 80.

Paddy Chayefsky. But Chayefsky was well-known for being totally bullish and protective when it came to his scripts, and according to Joe Eszterhas (in *The Devil's Guide To Hollywood*), he 'wouldn't work with him, and stopped the studio from hiring him' (2006, 230). It would've been two control freaks clashing head-on! The struggles between filmmakers and Chayefsky are infamous – and some of the toughest occurred during the making of *Altered States*.

In a script, Paddy Chayefsky said, you're attempting to do a number of things:

> one of those things is life. You're trying to produce and create a moment of life that people will believe. On top of that, you're trying to produce a certain theatricality. There are a lot of things you're trying to do.[13]

Paddy Chayefsky's friend Garson Kanin said that 'Paddy, more than most [writers], was a little bit cuckoo'. According to writer J.P. Miller, Chayefsky knew how to fight and how to manipulate people:

> Paddy was an extraordinarily good human manipulator. He knew his way around a scrap as very few writers do. Most writers, if they get into a fight or a bad situation on a movie, call their agents. But Paddy knew Hollywood and he wouldn't back down. He would go head to head with anybody – and at the same time he has this incredible writer's sensitivity.[14]

That Paddy Chayefsky could be a son-of-a-bitch was well-known, and he knew it too. He was described by a producer thus:

> When he was crossed, his entire body would tighten like steel. He'd scowl, clench his fists, glare, then the verbal avalanche would begin. He could level armies with that tongue of his if he didn't explode first, because his whole body would shake in a fit of apoplexy.[15]

The production of *Altered States* was full of problems, and the filming became one of the legendary shoots in Hollywood history (no wonder so many directors turned the project down, and as they heard about the ruckus, they were probably very glad they did!). Ken Russell has related some of Paddy Chayefsky's inter-

---

13 Quoted in J. Brady, 60.
14 Quoted in J. Eszterhas, 2006, 90.
15 Quoted in J. Eszterhas, 2006, 91.

ferring tactics in his autobiography *A British Picture*: Paddy Chayefsky comes across as a difficult, possessive writer who wanted things to be done *his* way. He was also one of the few writers in the film industry who had some power and influence. He wasn't someone that the studio could simply fire, and go out and hire twenty other writers (as they would do in every other instance). As Russell reminisced in *The Times* in 2008:

> We sparred from the start, over the high-falutin' sci-fi dialogue, the colour of the set, the luncheon script sessions, the meetings over Sanka (a brand of decaffeinated coffee) and pressed turkey sandwiches, camera angles, tracking shots and over Paddy taking the actors aside for private chats on how to play the scene.

The script, as Ken Russell explained, was the *Bible*, and you couldn't mess about with it:

> Every page, every paragraph, sentence, word and comma was as sacrosanct as the script engraved by Moses on Mount Sinai. Paddy's script was holy writ and Paddy's word was law... it was a no-win situation. (BP, 171)

Paddy Chayefsky said that Ken Russell ruined his book; Russell became the scapegoat for the failure of the film, artistically and financially.[16] But when a director is brought in late to a troubled production, there are plenty of other people to 'blame' (although if a film tanks, the director is often blamed first). Besides, if Chayevsky didn't put any credence in the *auteur* theory, how could he blame Russell alone? Ah, it works both ways!

Some critics said that Paddy Chayefsky's book would have been difficult to make a decent film out of anyway: 'if you don't like *Altered States*, blame Chayefsky. I find no director as infuriating as Ken Russell, but I admit some admiration for his work on *Altered States*', commented Danny Peary in *Omni's Screen Flights, Screen Fantasies* (3). And check out that script – it's not an easy script to shoot. *Tons* of scientific and philosophical dialogue to include, for a start. Yes, it's not only scientific and technical information that the characters spout at each other, there's also philosophical and religious ramblings.

There's no doubt that *Altered States* is a very impressive

---

[16] Ken Russell said that Chayefsky hated him, hated the rushes, hated everything to do with the film (BP, 185).

movie, on its own terms. It didn't do blockbuster business, like *Alien* or *Star Wars* (but neither did *Blade Runner* on its initial release). *Altered States* is a very good *movie* of the *script*, but the script and the whole concept is *Paddy Chayefsky's*, not Ken Russell's. Of course, when a movie's regarded as bad or a flop, the director usually gets attacked. But on this show, Russell was a hired hand, and the production was most definitely not his idea – it's not a concept or story that Russell would ever originate on his own (and many of the troubles the production ran into were nothing to do with Russell).

So it's not accurate or fair to blame Ken Russell for the deficiencies in *Altered States*. And anyway, it's a much better movie than the general perception of it. It's the same with movies like *Heaven's Gate* (from the same period): these movies, when you get to see them and forget about the hype or bad buzz, are often far better than other people's views suggest.

Ken Russell wasn't allowed to change a single word of dialogue, Danny Peary said, so he had the actors deliver their awkward, over-written monologues at speed, over-lapping each other, or eating food (the first exchange between Edward Jessup and his future wife Emily, at a party, has both William Hurt and Blair Brown speaking with their mouths full). In the scene in the Italian restaurant, the actors play drunk, while swigging from bottles, with the dialogue (including Jessup's ramblings) partly incoherent.[17]

For Ken Russell, the important thing about *Altered States* was the budget: for the first time he had a decent amount of money to play with, to mount his cinematic visions (the budget was about ten times what Russell had been used to; it would be the biggest budget that Russell used in his career).

All of his previous films (and especially the *Monitor* documentaries) had been produced with much less money than he would have liked. However, Ken Russell was one of those filmmakers who appreciated the necessity to be inventive, to make budgets stretch. Despite his creative use of low budgets, some of Russell's films do look like they were produced on close to a shoestring. One of the key effects of the low budgets in Russell's films was the lack of location shooting: many of Russell's

---

17 Paddy Chayefsky hated that: 'He keeps his actors moving all the time. You can't concentrate on what they're saying,' Chayefsky griped (PF, 227).

films were set in Britain, which was fine, because Russell was able to find locations that generally matched the fictional world of the films (*Women In Love, The Rainbow, Lady Chatterley, Tommy*, and so on). However, many of Russell's films (especially those about composers) were set in Europe, or further afield: *Mahler, Lisztomania, The Music Lovers, The Devils* and *Gothic*, among others; parts of Great Britain can look like Austria, Germany, Russia or Scandinavia, but (especially when it comes to cities and towns), there is no substitute for the real thing. When a railroad station, town square or a long shot of a city is required, stand-ins can look more like stand-ins.

With *Altered States*, Ken Russell was playing with a budget close to $15 million. A good deal of the budget was taken up with the visual effects – there were no stars in the show, for example, to soak up the money (it was William Hurt's first feature, while actors like Bob Balaban, Blair Brown and Charles Haid were known to some audiences, but certainly weren't stars commanding star fees).[18] Incidentally, Drew Barrymore appears in an early role as Margaret Jessup, one of the Jessup kids.

Much of *Altered States* was put together in post-production – true for many movies, of course, but especially true of visual effects movies, which require a huge amount of work on the backlot or in fx houses, putting together the optical and aural effects. As he noted in *A British Picture*, Ken Russell stayed on in L.A. working on *Altered States* for nearly a year, off and on:

> my days were mostly spent in talking to boffins at optical houses, supervising 'small shoots', devising and recording terrifying sounds, arguing with lab technicians and, between times, editing down hours of dreary dialogue. (BP, 186)

*Altered States* had previewed badly, Ken Russell remembered, but that might have been because Warners chose to show it in a San Diego in a shopping mall, and the audience (comprising 'mainly of overweight women in slacks with beehive hairdos') hated it. It's a very familiar story with the previewing process, of course (there are literally 1,000s of stories surrounding previews, most of 'em disaster tales). Russell said that executive producer Howard Gottfried had arranged another preview, near UCLA in

---

18 Bob Balaban may have been cast due to his similar role in *Close Encounters of the Third Kind*: he would reprise it in *2010* (1984).

Westwood, and it was college kids, Russell said, who would be the film's keenest audience.[19]

At the box office in the United States of America (in the years before the overseas box office became over half of a film's total revenue theatrically), *Altered States* performed modestly. 1980 was the year of *The Empire Strikes Back* (no. 1), *Superman 2* (no. 2), *Nine To Five* (no. 3), *Stir Crazy* (no. 4), *Coal Miner's Daughter* (no. 5) and *Any Which Way You Can* (no. 6). *Altered States* took 25 million dollars in domestic (US) gross (though it's rentals, roughly half of gross, that really count). It's the sort of movie, tho', to do well on video and DVD.

1980 was a year in which sci-fi, horror and fantasy were prominent: *The Empire Strikes Back, Superman 2, Flash Gordon, The Shining, The Fog* and *The Final Countdown*. Unfortunately, *Altered States* simply hasn't become one of those science fiction or fantasy flicks revered by fans, in the manner of *Blade Runner, Alien, Star Wars, Terminator* or *Jurassic Park*. Which's a pity, because it deserves a high reputation, and it looks amazing on DVD. (It does have a minor following, tho').

Jordan Cronenweth (1933-96) was offered to Ken Russell as DP: he was told, he later recalled, that he couldn't have his own selection (BP, 173). For Russell, as for many directors (Werner Herzog, Steven Spielberg, Orson Welles, etc), the on-set relationship with the cinematographer is crucial. Cronenweth was one of the superstar DPs of the era: his most famous film was the one he made after *Altered States*, another sci-fi flick with a British director produced in La-La Land: *Blade Runner*.[20]

*Altered States* has the Jordan Cronenweth look, with some very intricate lighting effects, and plenty of the back-lighting popular at the time (and still now). Even some of the simpler effects, such as the red glare from an electric fire, or the slanting sunlight of late afternoon, are classily achieved. And for the deprivation tank scenes, Cronenweth and his team constructed elaborate but convincing lighting schemes (such as the under-floor lights in the

---

19 Ken Russell recalled that youths would get stoned in the theatres, popping back in from the foyer to see the hallucinations (BP, 187). A similar thing had occurred with 1968's *2001: A Space Odyssey*.
20 Prior to *Altered States*, Jordan Cronenweth shot *Brewster McCloud, The Front Page, Handle With Care* and *Rolling Thunder*. After *Altered States*, Cronenweth filmed *State of Grace, Best Friends* and two Francis Coppola pictures: *Peggy Sue Got Married* and *Garden of Stone*.

opening sequence, through grids of bars, evoking a dungeon, a motif that Ken Russell and DP David Watkin had employed so effectively in *The Devils*). And in the corridors of the Harvard Medical School, the overhead slanting light, visible amongst smoke, is instantly recognizable as an American science fiction film classic look (appearing not only in *Blade Runner*, but also in *Alien*, *Close Encounters of the Third Kind*, *Jurassic Park* and *The Terminator*).

In the major, deprivation tank trip, towards the end of the 1980 picture, the scene shifts into the brilliant lights (and smoke) that DP Vilmos Zsigmond had developed on *Close Encounters of the Third Kind*. This would become *de rigeur* for any sci-fi flick: any scene where an experiment goes wrong or something weird is happening inside a building simply has to have waves of light blasting into the camera lens. (Jordan Cronenweth and his lighting crew pulled out all the stops in this part of the movie, and, coupled with the sound effects, the result is tremendous).

As well as falling out with Paddy Chayefsky, and the producer, Howard Gottfried, Ken Russell also differed with visual fx wiz John Dykstra, replacing him with the much less experienced Brian Ferren.[21] If Ferren and his team didn't have the high profile of Dykstra (who's one of the great visual effects supervisors in contemporary cinema), they still performed very well. *Altered States* contains some absolutely outstanding effects work, comparable with any of the other visual effects films of the time, such as *Star Wars*, *Star Trek* or *Alien*.[22]

Veteran Dick Smith, a Hollywood legend, contributed the wonderful special make-up effects (which included muscles rippling under Edward Jessup's arms and torso, a prehistoric man suit for actor Miguel Godreau, and a 'blob' look for Jessup when he regresses to a primitive life-form). *Altered States* got there before *An American Werewolf In London* and *The Thing* with the rippling-muscles-under-limbs make-up effect (it also included effects on Jessup's head and chest, and an extra toe). The scenes of Jessup waking up to find the skin on his arm bubbling are really

---

[21] Out went Joe Alves (the designer of *Jaws* and *Close Encounters of the Third Kind*), Arthur Penn's production designer, and Ken Russell hired Richard McDonald. That also meant the sets were scrapped – no incoming designer is going to use the old guy's sets.

[22] Trouble is, if the movie sucks, no one cares how good the vfx were – *Battlefield Earth*, for example, contains some outstanding vfx, but nobody noticed as they were fleeing theatres.

powerful.

The drug-taking sequences allowed for some wild imagery, which Ken Russell and the filmmakers put together using Russell's customary shock cuts and jump cuts, slamming back and forth between two or three different images (Eric Jenkins was editor). It was a technique that Russell loved, and was founded on tried and tested montage methods going back to Sergei Eisenstein and the silent era. As well as shock cuts, *Altered States* also employed very rapid editing, using just a few frames of celluloid, and sometimes coming back to show more of the same shot.

Pretty much every trick in the book was used in the hallucination sequences in *Altered States*, including macro and high speed photography of liquids, mattes and models, special make-up, and plenty of optical printing and superimpositions. The Columbia movie also included numerous practical effects, such as fire, smoke, wind, fireworks, special lighting, and explosions. And plenty of bought footage and second unit footage – of lava, oceans, galaxies, mountains, deserts, animals (sourcing and assembling all of that footage was a huge undertaking).[23] This was Ken Russell working on a big budget Hollywood movie – and it showed: compare *Altered States* with 'The Convert' sequence in *Mahler*, for instance (however, from *Billion Dollar Brain* onwards Russell has made some big movies with American backing, though usually shot in England. The climax of *Billion Dollar Brain*, for instance, is enormous).

*2001: A Space Odyssey* is the high watermark for the kind of visual effects sequences dealing with grand, cosmic themes: the 1968 film has influenced numerous science fiction and fantasy films, including *Star Wars, Alien, Blade Runner, Close Encounters* and *The Terminator*. *Altered States* is no exception: look at the hallucination sequences, which employ many of the techniques of the famous Stargate sequence in *2001: A Space Odyssey:* shifting, gooey liquids in close-up against black backgrounds, moving star fields, landscapes optically treated to produce psychedelic effects, etc. And also the sounds of the Stargate sequence in *2001: A Space Odyssey,* the low, bassy rumbles, the eerie noises, etc. (However, *Altered States* wasn't hampered by *2001*'s sticking to cosmic-style imagery, and included a host of other images).

One memorable sequence (the first vision/ trip) has a many-

---

[23] Where did the footage of mass crucifixions come from? Maybe some Biblical movie?

eyed goat-head appearing, like something out of Aleister Crowley's magickal ramblings. It's all very *New Testament* and the *Book of Revelations*: the goathead, Edward Jessup on a Cross (wearing the goat mask), the speeding clouds and Jessup fucking Emily. The religious imagery is set up in the previous scenes – Emily mentions that religion (Christianity) and sex are linked for Jessup (lovemaking as crucifixion – passion as the Passion). The 1980 movie takes up that, and also Jessup's mumbling about the death of his father (it's pure Freudian psychology again, which Ken Russell likes to employ – but the sex and Catholic motifs would have been there in Paddy Chayefsky's script).

Cancer – death – hospitals – daddy on his deathbed in pain (with wounds like stigmata) – sacrifice – knives – the 1980 movie weaves all of that (and plenty more) into the first hallucination. The colour red and the motif of fire will recur throughout the picture (as in the rest of Ken Russell's cinema).

The hallucination scene where Emily and Jessup sit at a table in front of a landscape of giant, orange flowers (California poppies in a big, fish eye image) is terrific, as is the way that editor Eric Jenkins cuts back to Jessup in the deprivation tank, watching his hallucinations (the dreamer and the dream).

In *Altered States'* peyote sequence (the second hallucination), all the stops are pulled out once more: the build-up is lengthy and intricate, and includes a climb up into the mountains of Mexico, the introduction to the locals (including their bulgy-eyed spokesman, culled from Weird-Looking Extras, Inc.), explanations about the drug, the preparation of the drug in a cauldron over an open fire in a cave, the circle of participants (sporting white face make-up), etc. The filmmakers slide in oddities and discontinuities in the editing – for instance, a reverse angle reveals *two* fires, with the locals grouped around the second fire, leaving the first one, with the bubbling cauldron, free for Jessup.[24]

And when Edward Jessup takes the peyote, the filmmakers employ simple, practical fx – fireworks – very impressively, cascading all around Jessup (the fireworks are a cheeky reprise of the cheapo effects Ken Russell used in his early TV shows). And there are many other effects (some complex), such as flashing lights and coloured lights, masks on the locals, flames, flash cuts, rapid cutting, painted symbols in the cave, special make-up, and

---

[24] This being a Ken Russell film, there had to be some dancing – and there was: in the peyote ceremony sequence (and the party).

animation. The effects of peyote have been well-documented,[25] and *Altered States* depicts some of the physical and sensory effects closely.

The second part of the peyote trip, which's all about Edward Jessup's wife Emily, features a powerful scene where a big lizard (a komodo dragon?) crawling near Jessup is transformed (via cuts) into Emily lying naked on the sand in a sphinx pose (there are paintings of this sort of image in 19th century Symbolist art, by Franz von Stuck).[26] It's an image of woman as erotic temptress, a Goddess figure, part-animal, part-deity, of women as sphinxes, as eternally mysterious, simultaneously loathed and lusted-after creatures.

The peyote trip closes with the wind machines blowing on full and a gradual transformation from the actors lying on the ground into sand sculptures, which blow away. And the 1980 movie holds on this gag for a *long* time, with the soundtrack losing the music and focussing on the sound of the high wind. (The baaaad trip ends with one of Ken Russell's favourite tricks: the abrupt shock cut – this time to the lizard with its entrails hanging out – later, Jessup's buddy tells him the locals said that he did it – a submerged rape fantasy).

One of the most effective hallucinations in *Altered States* occurs when Edward Jessup is sleeping with one of his students and wakes to find his skin bubbling like liquid. The film puts Hell right into the bedroom, with Jessup cowering at the door to the room while his bedroom opens up to reveal chasms of lava and fire. And before that, there's a creepy scene in the shower where bits of Jessup's body change.

A vital element in the impact of *Altered States* was the sound design and music (the film was rightly nominated for Best Sound and Best Original Score Oscars). John Corigliano's music enhanced the film immensely, evoking abstract, menacing atmospheres in many scenes, and not only in the visionary sequences. It's a very fine soundtrack (and possibly the finest of the scores composed specially for Ken Russell's movies).

Unusual instrumentation (such as Tibetan horns) aided in producing unreal worlds. The sound design added rumbles, wails,

---

[25] The classic text on the peyote cult and rituals among the Plains Indians is *The Peyote Cult* by Weston La Barre, which I have re-published.
[26] As in Franz von Stuck's *The Sphinx* (1904, Hessisches Landesmuseum, Darmstadt) and *The Kiss of the Sphinx* (c. 1895, Museum of Fine Arts, Budapest).

drones and bleeps which complimented the onslaught of visuals in the hallucination segments, with the sound editors keeping up with the flash cuts that editor Eric Jenkins was producing (supervising sound editor was Michael Colgan). (Unfortunately, for the sub-plot scenes, concerning Edward Jessup's personal life, much more conventional Hollywood music was employed (strings, woodwind). Maybe it was needed, to ground the film in some kind of recognizable reality, in between the more extreme scenes).

▼

*Altered States* boiled down dramatically to four characters: the hero who's exploring uncharted territory, the woman who loves him (despite everything), and the two guys who help him (the gruffer, sceptical one, Mason Parrish (Charles Haid), and the nerdy believer, Arthur Rosenberg (Bob Balaban)). It has to be said that, apart from his quest to find the Ultimate Truth of Human Life, Jessup was a bit dull. He's serious, and driven, but a little one-dimensional and unsympathetic. And also the single sub-plot – of Jessup's personal life, i.e., his relationship with Emily – was utterly predictable, down to the separation of the year in Africa with the kids, the re-uniting, and the final Big, Loving Hug.

It's a pity that the two buddies in the movie aren't given deeper characterizations – I mean Arthur Rosenberg (Bob Balaban) and Mason Parrish (Charles Haid). Yes, Parrish is the doubting one, who continually rejects Edward Jessup's crazy notions, while Rosenberg's curiosity overcomes his scepticism, and he aids Jessup in the quest to discover the Meaning of Everything. Two fine actors, Balaban and Haid,[27] but they're held back by the limitations of the script – and the genre. Even so, their characterizations are a lot more rounded than thousands of other movies in the sci-fi genre.

Similarly, the Columbia movie never wants to leave Edward Jessup and his quest for the Ultimate Truth – the movie's always about him, and he's in most every scene; so it doesn't follow Emily on her trips – for instance, her field trip to Africa, where she recorded the cries of baboons, which might've provided fascinating thematic material for the movie, as well as lightening the heaviness and sameness of always being around the perenn-

---

27 Charles Haid joined Ken Russell for some of the screenings of Russell's movies in the U.S.A. later in his career.

ially-serious Jessup.

Edward Jessup is more than a little tiresome, and morose, and just not much fun to be with (for a whole picture) – Blair Brown is much easier on the eye than Bill Hurt. Jessup's characterization is the big kid, the kid who won't grow up, a selfish, self-obsessed man that Emily should've dumped years ago.

One of the flaws of *Altered States* is that Edward Jessup isn't a particularly engaging or interesting character, even when he's the scientist obsessed with discovering the Secrets of the Universe. However, the central hook or concept of *Altered States* – that consciousness might have a material form, that the consciousness of people today might include remnants of prehistoric people's thought or physicality, and that drugs or deprivation tanks might bring that out – is intriguing.

The notion is definitely strong enough to sustain a movie (many sci-fi flicks have been produced on far less) – it's just that the characters involved in this exploration aren't the finest put on celluloid. However, Ken Russell's *direction* of this particular *script* is excellent – just for the spectacle of those hallucinations, *Altered States* is worth the price of a cinema ticket (and not including the production difficulties).

William Hurt's (b. March 20, 1950) a much-respected actor, but there is something a little too self-conscious about his acting in *Altered States* at times. However, as this was his first lead role in a movie, it's a pretty good job (Hurt's delivery of the dialogue was less than satisfactory, though – Hurt has a tendency to underplay and mumble his lines (which continues in his performances today); it didn't help either that much of the dialogue in *Altered States* is techno-speak). And the quirkiness of Hurt's acting style certainly enhances the character (it must have been tempting for Ken Russell to let Hurt go much further – Russell adores over-the-top acting – but the film's better because he doesn't).[28]

There was quite a bit of nudity in *Altered States*, but in this particular Ken Russell film it was largely required by the material. It meant that both Blair Brown and Bill Hurt had to play many scenes nude – and Hurt more than Brown. (And that would automatically have put off some actors contemplating auditions).

---

28 Ken Russell wrote in his autobiography that 'the trouble with Bill is he can't stop talking. In the end his eternal nattering, usually about himself, became so unbearable that Viv and I would only take him out to dinner if he remained silent throughout the meal. If he spoke he paid he bill. He never got further than the fish course before having to get out his cheque book' (BP, 184-5).

*Altered States* was one of a long line of movies about scientists going to extremes with scientific experiments – back to *Frankenstein* and *Metropolis*. Contemporary with *Altered States* were films like *The Fly* remake, and *Brainstorm* (and perhaps *Back To the Future*). The packaging of *Altered States* was also similar to those movies: the high production values, the quirky, 1950s B-movie storylines, the visual effects, and the casting of actors like Jeff Goldblum (*The Fly*) and Christopher Walken (*Brainstorm*).

*Altered States* gave the mad scientist movie a manic, visionary twist, with cosmic ruminations on voyaging back in time to the origin of all life. It took in some big themes, such as the origin of life, the nature of human consciousness, the relation between the mind and reality, as well as the familiar themes of the sci-fi and mad scientist genre: the quest for truth, and the obsessive need to probe the mysteries of the universe.

*Altered States* also used the formula of the scientist's relationship with a woman, again very familiar emotional territory, as the scientist Edward Jessup can't give up his quest to pursue the experiments to their ultimate, with the woman always pulling him back to reality, to family life, children, to being reasonable and sensible.

There was quite a bit of technical jargon to be delivered to the audience – and Ken Russell and his team weren't that interested in it. *Altered States* was basically *Frankenstein* all over again (Russell had already mounted laboratory scenes out of *Frankenstein* in *Lisztomania*, of course, and would return to the origins of Mary Shelley's story a few years later in 1987's *Gothic*). So the scientific elements – about genes and DNA and regression – were included but weren't the point of the movie.

One could link the quest or theme of *Altered States* also to Ken Russell's own concerns about art and the artist: one of the battlegrounds of the film is between the mind and reality, between thinking and doing, between thoughts and physical things. Which is what art is all about: so in *Altered States* the artist – Edward Jessup – is using himself as the canvas or marble slab to make something out of. And he finds that what's happening in his mind is coming true in the real world. As a question of æsthetics that's fascinating, and also as a metaphysical question.

*Altered States* was the second time Ken Russell was associated with Aldous Huxley, whose book *The Doors of Perception*, which explored drug-taking, had been taken up by 1960s counter-culture (providing the name, via William Blake, for one of the key rock acts of the era, the Doors; their music is heard in the film, at the 1960s college party).

There is some basis in *Altered States* of science – or psychology at least. Have a look at the book edited by Charles C. Tart in 1969, for instance, called *Altered States of Consciousness* (the movie is a kind of adaption of *Altered States of Consciousness*).[29] What Paddy Chayefsky has done is to take some of the research about drugs and deprivation tanks and exaggerated it, until the point is reached where the real world is altered by the changes in the mind.[30]

It is pure Hollywood hokum, though, that, for instance, there should be so much horror and terror involved. Why, for instance, is *terror* the primæval state, millions of years ago? When Edward Jessup has regressed to a blob with one arm, he tells Emily about the terror of being at the beginning of all life. Why should the origin of life be so terrible, though? Maybe the Big Bang was actually a lot of fun! And surely prehistoric forms of life, like amoebas and fish, had fun now and then! (Maybe dark matter was *so* bored and aching for the creation of the universe; at last, something's happening!).

And when Edward Jessup regresses to the state of a prehistoric man, why is there so much violence involved? The horror genre element of that scene is understandable: it's *Dr Jekyll and Mr Hyde*,[31] of course, when the thing that emerges from the deprivation tank ain't Jessup but a hairy beastie. And when the caretaker and the security guard go to investigate, the movie switches into classic horror film mode, complete with the setting of a basement filled with pipes and stuff for the critter to hide in.

But that the prehistoric man would instantly become wildly aggressive, attacking two guys, is pure Hollywood wackiness (although that whole episode, which's extended far longer than it

---

29 An excellent book, by the way.
30 For his research, Paddy Chayefsky spoke to anthropologists at the American Museum of Natural History, scientists at Harvard Medical School, Duke University, the Maimonides Medical Center, Brooklyn, City University of New York and doctors at Columbia University (PF, 223-4).
31 Paddy Chayefsky admitted that some of the Jekyll and Hyde aspects of the piece came from his own split personality.

needs to be,[32] is delivered with high energy by everyone involved. And it's more impressive than some of Ken Russell's action sequences: when he wants to, Russell can deliver some punchy action scenes).

※

Some critics reckoned *Altered States* was one of the great sci-fi movies (J. Brosnan, 347); for others, it was Ken Russell simply doing another Ken Russell. David A. Cook said that *Altered States* 'oscillated between the outrageously vulgar and the outrageously brilliant' (601). It's an impressive film in many respects, with perhaps only the ending seriously letting the movie down. The climax boils down to Jessup regressing to a pre-human, blob-like state, infecting his wife Emily when he touches her, and saving them both, when he first brings himself back to normal, after a struggle – involving much slamming of his arm against the wall and floor, then saving his wife. One might expect that this ending was included by powers other than Ken Russell (i.e., the producers or the studio or Paddy Chayefsky) – the final shots show Jessup and Emily hugging each other on the floor (both naked), with Jessup using the classic eight letters of the schmaltzy, Hollywood closer: *I love you*.[33] Of course, no way was *Altered States* going to end any other way – with Jessup dying, for instance. He has to come back to reality, to humanity. Yep, and it's a good woman who'll rescue you from the abyss every time.

But as cinema, as an experience of sound, music and images, *Altered States* is terrific, and lives up to the subject matter of a scientist exploring the outer reaches of consciousness. *Altered States* might not be regarded as one of the 'classic' sci-fi films of the period – *Alien, Star Wars, Blade Runner, The Empire Strikes Back, The Thing*, etc, but the story, the themes and the flamboyant treatment are just as impressive as those movies. The narrative of *Altered States* is more compelling than that in *Blade Runner*, for instance. And *Altered States* at least *is* science fiction – while *Alien* was a monster in a spook house tale (as director Ridley Scott acknowledged), and the *Star Wars* movies were really space operas, cowboy or swashbuckler movies set in outer space, but with few genuine, science fiction concepts in them.

---

32 There's the fight with the dogs, with a car, and the elephants, and a tiger, and all the rest – as if Ken Russell and the team are doing a mini version of *The Jungle Book* or *Tarzan* or a Ray Harryhausen movie in the middle of a sci-fi flick.
33 Early versions of the script had Jessup and Emily winding up hating each other.

John Brosnan in his history of sci-fi cinema, *The Primal Screen,* wrote:

> Ken Russell has made a stunning piece of cinema out of the original material. It would have been too easy to make it all seem infuriatingly pretentious or simply ludicrous, but Russell avoided all the pitfalls, even during the apeman sequence that could easily have drifted into absurdity. *Altered States* is a dazzling torrent of light and sound that succeeds in being intellectually stimulating and rather disturbing all at the same time… I never thought I'd live to see the day but I've got to admit that Ken Russell – *Ken Russell* – has made what will probably rank as one of the all-time great science fiction movies. (346-7)

Of course, *Altered States* did explore the sensational aspects of altering consciousness, with its scenes of Edward Jessup regressing to an athletic, prehistoric guy, but the relationship between consciousness and physiology (and evolution) was an intriguing one. There were serious themes in *Altered States* – such as the notion that altered states of consciousness have affected human evolution. The idea that taking drugs has played a part in human history – and evolution – is very Sixties, but also appealing.

The series of experiments that Edward Jessup conducts gives the 1980 picture its structure, as Jessup travels further back in time with each dive into the subconscious. Each experiment is treated slightly differently, and the filmmakers were aware of having to startle the audience in new ways each time.

*Altered States* departed from the conventional Hollywood formula in *not* having a villain: nobody embodied the bad guys or evil in this movie – Edward Jessup was his own worst enemy. It was Jekyll and Hyde, the good and bad sides of man incarnated in a single individual. (A more conventional script might've had a villain or corporation wanting to get hold of Jessup's scientific findings for nefarious ends).

# 17

# CRIMES OF PASSION

My sister Mandie and I went to see *Crimes of Passion* (1984) on its first run at the Odeon cinema in Haymarket, London, and we loved it. How can you not enjoy this energetic send-up of Middle America?

The openly-gay writer Barry Sandler was very much the force behind *Crimes of Passion*: he wrote the script, and was the producer. So the set-up, the characters, the situations, the plot and the themes all come from Sandler, not Ken Russell. Of course, Russell added so much to the piece, and I wouldn't take away from what Russell brought to the movie, but it's worth remembering, once again, that Russell did not originate many of the films he directed. (But once you bring Ken Russell onto a project, you don't have a director-for-hire who's going to run through the movie just for the money, you have a filmmaker who will bring plenty of themselves to the piece, as well as possibly reworking it. Russell has writing credits on many projects).

*Crimes of Passion* is an odd film: a black comedy about sex, sexual repression, marriage and (American) society, it pivots around Kathleen Turner's (b. 1954) professional fashion designer Joanna Crane who has a secret night life as the hooker China Blue in a seedy, downtown hotel in the red light district of an unspecified American city.

The movie records her encounters with several punters: (1) John Laughlin's straight, caring New Man Bobby Grady, a sexually frustrated husband and family man, with a marriage that's falling apart and a nearly non-existent sex life; (2) fat, anonymous men who like to play rough games (including masochistic cops); and (3) Anthony Perkins' (1932-92) neurotic, sex-obsessed, self-righteous priest, the Reverend Peter Shayne.

*Crimes of Passion* would be a little more conventional if it only concerned John Laughlin's husband's search for sexual satisfaction in the arms of a prostitute, and the prostitute's curious double life, but with Anthony Perkins' religious fanatic Shayne in the mix it enters bonkers territory.

The art film has of course explored the relations between sex and religion from the early Surrealist films of Luis Buñuel and Salvador Dali onwards, but this kind of sexual paranoia, degradation and perversion is much rarer in the mainstream, Hollywood film.

*Crimes of Passion* tackled a number of targets: sexual conventions, marriage, religion, morality and the American way of life (Ken Russell called *Crimes of Passion* 'an extremely anti-American film' [DF, 55]). Russell had explored these issues many times before *Crimes of Passion* (notably in films such as *The Devils* and *Lisztomania*), and wasn't adding to anything he hadn't already expressed previously.

*Crimes of Passion*'s trajectory was conventional: the hard-nosed, cynical, seen-it-all-before prostitute learns to love, and finds true love, while the alienated husband flees his ailing marriage and finds comfort in the hooker's arms.

As in previous Ken Russell movies, *Crimes of Passion* had a dogged intent about it; it was going to tackle its issues and nothing else, with no meandering. Consequently, it had a claustrophobic atmosphere, emphasized by staging much of the action in China Blue's hotel room at night.

A prostitute entertaining her clients in a hotel room offered Ken Russell and his team opportunities to indulge Russell's love of theatricality and dressing-up, of sleaze and sex, of sensational subject matter (these scenes were lit by Russell's regular DP Dick Bush in lurid reds and blues and flashing lights). Meanwhile, the down-to-earth, everyday scenes between Bobby Grady and his wife Amy were lit flatter and much more naturalistically.

*Crimes of Passion* depicted many sex scenes – between China Blue and Bobby Grady, China Blue and a policeman, China Blue and the priest, China Blue and an upscale couple in the back of a limo,[34] and China Blue and anonymous punters. Having an eye on the censors meant that the filmmakers couldn't go as far as they wanted in depicting sex (a scene, shot from above, where China Blue, straddling a cop manacled to the bed, sodomizes him with his night stick, was shortened when the BBFC requested cuts), but they did manage to squeeze in blowjobs (in the first few minutes), a *Kama Sutra*-like run through sexual positions (seen in *Rocky Horror Picture Show*-style silhouettes on a semi-transparent cloth), and dressing up in kinky air hostess, nun and stripper outfits.

*Crimes of Passion* was put before CARA (the Code and Ratings Administration)[35] five times before it gained the 'R' rating which the distributor, New World Pictures, required. Ken Russell and editor Brian Tagg cut 15 minutes: this was later restored in the 'X' rated video version (Barry Sandler recalled that Russell found it dispiriting to keep cutting the movie and still receiving the dreaded 'X'.[36] New World weren't prepared to go the whole hog and stand behind the picture, Sandler reckoned, partly because of the conservativism of the political period [PF, 257]). Eminent movie critic Andrew Sarris, who was 'unalterably opposed to all censorship', said he was 'grateful for the opportunity to see and judge for myself', but found the added scenes 'somewhat loathsome'.[37]

Ken Russell said *Crimes of Passion* had previewed badly in San Francisco, partly due to the ending (you'd think an audience in Frisco would go for it, if anywhere in the U.S. of A.).[38] The audience, Russell said, didn't like the ambiguity of the original ending. So a new one was shot, in which the hero says, 'I guess you're all wondering what happened to the hooker and me. Well, we decided to shack up together – then we went home and fucked our brains out' (DF, 106). Thus, *Crimes of Passion* was yet another movie, like *Altered States*, that was rejigged as a result of the preview process.

---

34 The couple prattle on – or the woman does – while the man gropes China Blue. But the hooker gets out of the car in frustration.
35 There were six categories for CARA examiners to consider when rating films: nudity, sex, drugs, violence, language and theme.
36 Russell complained that 'you can be as violent as you want in America but you talk about sex and everybody reaches for their chastity belt'.
37 Andrew Sarris: "To Cut or Not to Cut", *Village Voice*, 12 March, 1985.
38 Also, the scene where China Blue visits a guy sick with cancer was taken out (but then put back for the theatrical version).

*Crimes of Passion* was intended to be a comedy, and Barry Sandler's script full of wisecracks about sexual *mœurs*; but although it wasn't always funny, Ken Russell and Sandler did include some amusing gags: China Blue like a queen on a throne with a man's head between her legs, seen from end-on, as if he's licking her caboose (a cut to a side angle shows they're just talking); Bobby Grady's party piece as a penis, with basket balls tied round his ankles for balls, spouting a cloud of milk for the ejaculation; Grady giving a solemn speech to a quietly attentive psychotherapy group about his sexual problems and his marriage, ending up with the line 'and then we fucked each other's brains out' (the film's closing line); Anthony Perkins' turn as a nutty, lusty preacher provided a few laughs (such as when he's in his den, kneeling in front of a shrine of pornographic photos, religious icons and candles, stroking a large, silver vibrator, and watching China Blue fucking her clients through a hole in the wall (reprising Perkins' most famous role, as Norman Bates in *Psycho*),[39] or when he's muttering about what he's going to do to China Blue, crouching under some bushes, stroking a dildo,[40] wearing a crown of thorns).

The dialogue does have its amusing moments – particularly in the exchanges between China Blue and Peter Shayne:

> Shayne: 'do you recognize me child?'
> Blue: 'I never forget a face, especially when I've sat on it'.
> Shayne: 'you're the head of your class, or is it the class of your head?'
> Blue: 'Oh, a man of words. He makes up in diction what he lacks in dick'.

Shayne rants at one point:

> Behold this wicked woman; she falls, she mends, she crawls, she bends, she sucks it, fucks it, picks it up, and licks it; you can whip her, beat her, maul her, mistreat her; anything you want, as long as you don't touch her.

With dialogue like this and some dynamic two-hander scenes between China Blue and Peter Shayne, *Crimes of Passion* might make a cracking stage play.

---

[39] Apparently, Perkins designed Shayne's shrine himself (PF, 250).
[40] Originally the dildo was going to be a Superman figurine, but the idea was nixed because of potential legal problems with DC Comics and Warners (PF, 256).

When I first saw *Crimes of Passion,* I thought it was spoilt by Rick Wakeman's music; Wakeman, though a hugely talented progressive rocker – and I'm a huge fan of his – turned in a soundtrack of synthesizer squeals and *muzak*-style jazz which didn't fit the film; his music unbalanced the narrative; while it might have fitted the sensational underworld of prostitution and vice, it cheapened the picture. Russell's use of rock composers such as Wakeman and Thomas Dolby (on *Gothic*), known as keyboard wizards, might seem odd, coming from someone like Russell, who was so committed to, so in love with, classical music (the synth pop soundtracks also date badly).

On further viewings, Rick Wakeman's soundtrack seems much more in tune with the material. Especially fun are the hard rock segments, and the quirky variations on China Blue's signature tune.

From the viewpoint of mainstream Hollywood output, *Crimes of Passion* was another Ken Russell excursion into kinky, sleazy territory, amusingly eccentric but ultimately a small-scale film that wouldn't make much money because it was only for a narrow audience (the subject matter would probably put off large chunks of a non-metropolitan audience). Any film which climaxes with Anthony Perkins in female, hooker drag being stabbed with a vibrator by Kathleen Turner in priest's robes is bound to have a somewhat limited appeal.

The 1984 movie goes a little flabby during the scenes between Bobby Grady and his wife Amy (Annie Potts): clearly, as Barry Sandler noted, Ken Russell was more interested in the scenes featuring China Blue and Peter Shayne. You can see that immediately, in the performances as well as the direction.[41] And it's also true that scenes between a hooker and a crazy priest are going to be potentially more intriguing than those between a married couple who are moving apart from each other (at least to a filmmaker like Russell!).

The problem is that the issues and situations portrayed in the domestic scenes at the Grady house are soooo predictable, down to every line of dialogue and every dissatisfied sigh. Whereas you don't always know what a mad vicar and a tough prostitute are

---

[41] Barry Sandler commented that Russell wasn't particularly keen on the North American way of life in suburbia, and that there were scenes that were dropped that were sympathetic towards Amy (PF, 254).

going to do in their scenes.

Yet *Crimes of Passion* maybe needs those everyday scenes of unhappy domesticity – because without them, it would fly off too quickly into fantasy and mania. That is, from the commercial filmmaking point-of-view, those domestic scenes are necessary to ground the piece in some kind of everyday reality. Yet, as anyone who knows anything about Ken Russell's cinema recognizes, Russell is not much interested in everyday reality. Other filmmakers do that all very nicely, but it's not Russell's cinematic territory.

*Crimes of Passion* would be torn apart by feminist critics if they took it on. There are so many aspects of the movie that feminists could attack, it's not even worth bothering to point them out here. You know what they are!

Well, if you insist: to cite one, look at the portrayal of Amy Grady. Oh dear. Oh deary dear.

All three people in *Crimes of Passion* are neurotic and frustrated. Sex is the battleground – so *Crimes of Passion* can be viewed as a sex comedy, though with psycho-thriller aspects. There are nods to Anthony Perkins' former movie roles, including of course his most famous role, as Norman Bates in *Psycho*. For instance, in the showdown, Shayne is dressed in China Blue's costume, complete with the shiny, blonde wig, echoing the climax of *Psycho*. Meanwhile, Joanna (now wearing *his* costume), lunges for Shayne with the dildo held high, just like Bates on his murdering sprees in *Psycho*. (Two sequels to *Psycho* appeared around this time – in 1983 and 1986).

I guess all of those allusions to the Alfred Hitchcock classic movie of 1960 were just too tempting to pass up (and Ken Russell enjoys quoting from other movies just as much as anyone else). And, hell, *loads* of filmmakers have delivered *hommages* to (or spoofs of) *Psycho*.[42] And when *Crimes of Passion* was being filmed in the early 1980s, it was a time when the horror film, in the form of the 'stalk 'n' slash' flick, a cycle partly inaugurated by 1978's

---

[42] Brian de Palma, Mel Brooks, Wes Craven, Dario Argento, and Steven Spielberg, to name a few.

*Hallowe'en*, was enjoying a renascence.⁴³

*Crimes of Passion* received very mixed reviews: 'dismal, over-the-top... inanely written' according to Dennis Schwartz (*Ozu's World*); 'good performances and an interesting idea are metamorphosed into one of the silliest movies in a long time', complained Roger Ebert; it may have been 'over-done, overripe, and overloaded', as Jay Carr put it in his review in the *Boston Globe*, but 'it isn't boring. Russell makes the screem jump'.⁴⁴

---

43 The 'slasher' and 'video nasty' horror films of the late 1970s/ early 1980s, also called 'stalker' or 'slice 'n' dice', 'body count', and 'teenie-kill' movies, included: the *Friday the 13th* films (1980 onwards), the *Nightmare On Elm Street*/ Freddy Kruger series (1984 onwards), the *Hallowe'en* series (1978 onwards), the *Psycho* sequels, the *Amityville Horror* films (1979 onwards), *The Exorcist* sequels (1977 onwards), *Final Exam* (1981), *My Bloody Valentine* (1981), *Deadly Blessing* (1981), *New Year's Evil* (1981), *The Burning* (1981), *Happy Birthday To Me* (1981), *Night School* (1981), *The Slumber Party Massacre* (1982), *Visiting Hours* (1982), *Driller Killer* (1979), *The Toolbox Murders* (1979), *Terror Train* (1980), *Prom Night* (1980), *Hell Night* (1981), *Graduation Day* (1981), *The Evil Dead* (1983), the *Hellraiser* films (1985 onwards), the *Lawnmower Man* series (1992 onwards), the *Candyman* films (1992 onwards), and the seminal slasher, *The Texas Chainsaw Massacre* (1974).
44 *Boston Globe*, Nov 9, 1984.

Crucifixions, Christianity, death, illness, goat's heads, fire, blazing skies and agony.
Visionary scenes from Ken Russell's 15 million dollar visual effects head trip, Altered States.

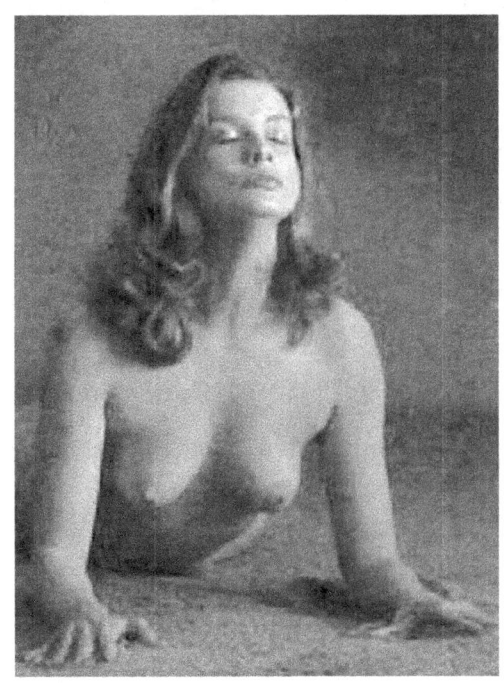

1984's Crimes of Passion

# 18

# GOTHIC

> I couldn't believe it: here was an Englishman asking me to make an English film on an English subject by an English writer for an English company in England! The age of miracles was not dead.
>
> Ken Russell, *A British Picture* (273)

*Gothic* (1987) was about the famous, fateful night in 1816 at Lord Byron's Swiss Villa Diodati at Lake Geneva when Mary Shelley's *Frankenstein*[1] and Dr John Polidori's *The Vampyre* were conjured up. Other films which concerned the creation of Shelley's landmark novel include *Haunted Summer* (Ivan Passer, 1988) and *Frankenstein Unbound* (Roger Corman, 1990). And one of the most famous horror films ever made, *The Bride of Frankenstein* (James Whale, 1935), had depicted Byron, Shelley and Mary Shelley

---

1 As well as *Frankenstein,* Mary Shelley (1797-1851) produced a novella, 5 novels, 2 travelogues, letters, essays, poems, reviews, and many short stories. Shelley's novels included *Valperga* (1823), *The Last Man* (1826), *The Fortunes of Perkin Warbeck* (1830), *Lodore* (1835), and *Falkner* (1937). Her novella, *Matilda*, which dealt with father-daughter incest, was not published until 1959.
Mary Shelley's great novel and the mythical monster have been the subject of many readings: as class struggle, industrialization's product, a symbol of the French Revolution, as technology, the danger of scientific experimentation, and a 'totalizing monster', in Franco Moretti's term, like Dracula, who can never be vanquished. Frankenstein's monster is a multiplitic chameleon, open to a multitude of interpretations.
*Frankenstein* has also been interpreted as being about the fear of the population explosion; a warning about colonialization (Viktor takes apart the old in order to make the new); about the French Revolution and the Terror; and a protest about about classism.

discussing ghost stories on the stormy night in Switzerland[2] that Russell, Volk, Corke, Southon, Hobbs *et al* explored in their picture (*Gothic* is thus a kind of remake of *The Bride of Frankenstein*, as well as countless other horror films).[3]

Ken Russell had employed aspects of *Frankenstein* before: *Lisztomania* contains not only an elaborate recreation of the famous laboratory scenes of reanimation in Universal's movies of the 1930s, it also depicts the resurrected Richard Wagner as Adolf Hitler in a Frankenstein's monster guise. Meanwhile, in *Tommy*, the Sally Simpson episode featured Gary Rich as a teen pop star Frankenstein's monster. And in *Dante's Inferno*, Ken Russell and co. had explored a poet and his coterie – and *Dante's Inferno* is far, far more successful than *Gothic*.

1987's *Gothic* is virtually a remake of 1967's BBC film *Dante's Inferno*. Same British-boho-Romantic-poetic-erotic *milieu*, same cast of kooky, Brit aristo-artists, same slide into fantasy and dream, same use of the horror film genre, and some of the same crew (such as editor Mike Bradsell). But *Dante's Inferno* is infinitely superior to *Gothic*.

Among the topics taken on in *Gothic* were vampirism, incest, murder, blasphemy, abortion, pregnancy, self-mutilation and homosexuality (PF, 261).

Or, business as usual for a Ken Russell movie!

*Gothic* starred Gabriel Byrne, Julian Sands,[4] Natasha Richardson, Miriam Cyr and Timothy Spall in a chaotic, stormy séance during a single night of revels, full of the usual Ken Russell obsessions. It was shot mainly at Wrotham Park in Hertfordshire (also where *Peter's Friends* and *Princess Caraboo* were filmed, and later Russell's own *Lady Chatterley*), and at a favourite Russell location, Gaddesden Place in Hemel Hempstead.[5] In *A British Picture*, Russell remarked that there was a 'monumental piece of miscasting' in *Gothic* (274). I wonder which actor this refers to:

2 Played by Elsa Lanchester, Douglas Walton and Gavin Gordon. The rest of the cast of *The Bride of Frankenstein* included Colin Clive, Vlarie Hobson, Ernest Theisger, and Una O'Connor.
3 Richard Corliss remarked that *Gothic* wants to be 'the last horror show. Byron is Count Dracula, feeding on his guests' dreams and demons. Shelley is every weak hero, Polidori every mad doctor, Clairmont every wench whose lust turns her into a succubus. And Godwin, racked by visions of her stillborn child, becomes the cursed mothers of *The Exorcist* and *Rosemary's Baby*' (*Time*, Apl 20, 1987).
4 Julian Sands compared the filmmaking approaches of James Ivory and Ken Russell: while Ivory watches his subjects from a distance through binoculars, Russell 'is a big-game hunter filming in the middle of a rhino charge' (PF, 268).
5 Gaddesden Place has appeared in numerous TV productions, and movies such as *A Kiss Before Dying, Hidden Agenda, Fanny Hill* and Russell's movies.

probably not Natasha Richardson, Tim Spall or Gabriel Byrne. It must be either Julian Sands or Miriam Cyr (I would think probably Cyr – she seems to be acting in a different film. But I also find Sands too self-conscious. But then, he always seems to be like that to me).[6]

*Gothic*'s crew included Penny Corke (producer), Mike Southon (photography), Stephen Volk (script), Mike Bradsell (editor), Thomas Dolby (music), Kay Gallway and Victoria Russell (costumes) and Christopher Hobbs (production design). As Ken Russell put it, 'it was great to be making a feature film in England again after nearly a decade' (BP, 273).[7]

FIRST VIEWING.

This is my first response to *Gothic*, which was largely disappointment, when I first saw it in the 1980s: it could be seen as truly appalling, considering it was made by one of the U.K.'s once-great talents; true, some of Ken Russell's penchant for startling image-making was in evidence, but the film lacked narrative pace, suspense, genuine terror or horror. *Gothic* was curiously uncinematic at times, filmed in many static, wide angle shots, betraying a vacuum of imagination, in a story that was supposedly all about the flash of inspiration, symbolized by the lightning striking and setting alight a tree. However, DP Mike Southon went to town on the lighting, all shadows, flickering light from log fires, enormous silhouettes on walls; the set design consisted of sparsely furnished rooms dominated by floating veils and curtains.[8]

*Gothic* consisted largely of actors Gabriel Byrne, Natasha Richardson, Timothy Spall, Julian Sands and Miriam Cyr dashing about a country house, swooning, flailing, screaming, abusing each other, acting scared, or pontificating *ad nauseam*. The performances lacked weight, subtlety, or authenticity. As the 'mad, bad and dangerous to know' Lord Byron, Byrne was lacklustre, while Spall overacted a ton as the homosexual, lech-

---

[6] One of the clues to the less than satisfactory aspect of Julian Sands' performance is that many of his scenes seem to be looped – in scenes where the other actors aren't looped.

[7] The script was ideal for a director, Al Clark of Virgin Vision remarked, and it was quite different from the usual sort of screenplay that's received by production companies in Britain (PF, 268).

[8] *Gothic* contains the whole retinue of horror film clichés, including skulls, skeletons, cobwebs, basements, rats, masks, lightning, rain, thunder, blood, fires, candles, horses, mist, shadows and snakes.

erous (literally leech-erous) Doctor Polidori.

All highly unbelievable, without resonance. Thomas Dolby's soundtrack, all parping synths and glissandos, was a camp mix of a Hammer horror soundtrack and pop classical. *Gothic*, too po-faced, didn't even have the camp charm of the Hammer horror films. This was great material and potential, ideally suited to Ken Russell's sensibilities – the Romantic poets Byron and Shelley,[9] the creation of *Frankenstein*, one of the key books (and myths) of the modern era – but the filmmakers wasted it all. It's as if the filmmakers had forgotten what cinema could do, and hadn't the energy or imagination to reinvent it.

This was true of some of Uncle Ken's films of the Eighties and after, from *Altered States,* and the Vestron films, *The Lair of the White Worm, Gothic, Salome's Last Dance,* and *The Rainbow*. Many of these 1980s and after movies were clearly made on a cut-back budget: the single, main location (Wrotham Park country house in *Gothic*), the inappropriate buildings of D.H. Lawrence's Nottinghamshire in *The Rainbow,* the use of Russell's beloved Lakes to stand in for Switzerland,[10] the lack of big name stars,[11] few crowd scenes, extras, special effects or set-pieces, and so on.

But no, it's not the budget or the production values – nearly every mainstream entertainment feature film is full of compromises (they couldn't get this actor, or the rights to that piece of music, or permission to film in the Taj Mahal, or whatever). A small budget doesn't equal a bad movie: the tiny budgets of the following films didn't stop them from being superb: *Breathless* (Jean-Luc Godard, 1959), *Eraserhead* (David Lynch, 1976), *Chimes At Midnight* (Orson Welles, 1965), *Effi Briest* (Rainer Werner Fassbinder, 1974), *The Blood of a Poet* (Jean Cocteau, 1930) and *Un Chien Andalou* (Luis Buñuel, 1928). François Truffaut's *The Four Hundred Blows* (1959) cost $65,000; Ingmar Bergman's *Prison* (*The Devil's Wanton* [*Føangelse*], 1949) cost $40,000, as did Akira Kurosawa's *Rashomon* (1950). *Mad Max* (George Miller, 1979) cost $350,000 (and looked it, with its postpunk post-apocalyptic chic), but it made $10 million worldwide.

Ken Russell seemed to have lost the knack of making his low

---

9 Prior to *Gothic*, Ken Russell made TV films about Romantic poets: *The Rime of the Ancient Mariner* and *William and Dorothy* (under the title *Clouds of Glory*, 1978), about William Wordsworth and Samuel Taylor Coleridge. Both poets were of course associated with Russell's beloved Lake District.
10 Shot during one of the worst Summers on record, said Ken Russell (BP, 273).
11 In *Crimes of Passion*, Perkins and Turner worked for less than their usual rate.

budget, post-1980s films look decent. *Mahler* had cost £168,00 ($250,000), but was a powerful film. The must-needs inventiveness which young filmmakers had to have was gone, only resurfacing at odd moments (such as on his late 1980s *South Bank Show* documentary on classical music, made in conjunction with his longtime LWT friend, Melvyn Bragg).

In *Gothic* Ken Russell and his team threw everything they could lay their hands on into the mix, particularly in the nightmarish visions: of a goat; Polidori's cut-off head on the floor; demons in a carriage; a Turkish, belly dancer marionette (Linda Coggin);[12] Claire Clairmont with eyes in her breasts; Polidori drinking a glass of leeches; Polidori banging his palm on a nail while Byron and Claire tup in a room nearby; Byron, nude, covered in leeches; Mary trapped in a maze of doors, as in a funhouse, with horrors or visions behind each door; images of a funeral of Mary's aborted baby;[13] Shelley, nude, clambering on the rootops at night during the storm and chanting; a vision of Shelley drowning and his body being burnt on an Italian shore.

Ken Russell said that the 'hysterical pace' he and Mike Bradsell had employed on *Gothic* was a mistake:

> I'd fallen into the trap which has been the undoing of many an unsuspecting pop-video director – punchy, roller-coaster cutting, short sequences and non-stop action. (BP, 274)

Lord Byron was seen in *Gothic* as a precursor of Count Dracula, seducing Claire, approaching her in bed in the classic Dracula manner, lying on top of her, his mouth covered in blood after licking her. Byron was at the centre of the film, rakish, cynical, promiscuous, bisexual.

---

12 The full-size female automata or marionettes which play the piano or dance seductively were fun nods to topics like re-animation, and giving life to the dead. All very E.T.A. Hoffmann and properly Gothic (Michael Powell had mined similar territory in *Tales of Hoffmann* (1951), and *The Thief of Baghdad* (1940) contains one of the most memorable automata scenes in British cinema). Russell had also been here before, in the Victorian nightclub scene in 1967's *Dante's Inferno*.

13 Plenty of critics have related the fictional world of *Frankenstein* to Mary Shelley's own life, to issues such as motherhood, childbirth, pregnancy, abortion, illness, etc. To her relationship with Percy Shelley, with Lord Byron, with her father William Godwin (who features prominently in Shelley's life), and so on. To early 19th century attitudes towards death, disease, sex, science and marriage. And to Romanticism.

Mary Shelley had four children, but only one survived beyond childhood: a daughter born prematurely in 1815 died after 11 days; William (born in 1816), died aged 3; born in 1817, Clara Everina died one year old; Percy Florence (born in 1819) survived.

*Gothic* played with the legends of the Romantics: Lord Byron as a sexual polymath, having erotic relationships or flirtations with everyone in the film; incest between Byron and his half-sister; Shelley as an idealistic, tormented poet; and Mary unable to recover from losing her first child.

Everyone in *Gothic* was seen as wrestling with their demons, such as Mary and her agony over her aborted child (portrayed as the seeds of the *Frankenstein* novel); Byron with his creative impasse; and everyone's addicted to something.

Drug-taking is foregrounded – in this case, laudanum. Percy Shelley especially is swigging tincture of opium every chance he can get. Medicine and disease is another theme touched on – narcolepsy for Shelley, Dr Polidori with his blood and leeches, madness for Claire, Mary Shelley and her concerns with pregnancy, birth and creating a monster.

The only really true moment of 'horror' in *Gothic* were the shadowy images of the 'monster' stalking the house, glimpsed through the windows; there were also horror clichés, such as the slime found where the monster had been (evoking the fluid in the womb), or the muffled groans of the monster in the distance, creepy, off-screen sound effects, and the play with shadows on the wall. In one memorable sequence, P.B. Shelley, unable to sleep, goes outside to investigate a barn, in true, horror film style, and has a vision of demons in the carriage. And poor Dr Polidori, in the act of hanging himself on the back of a horse, sees the monster, which drops from a beam onto the horse and gallops away.

The end of *Gothic* jumps to the morning after (most of the picture takes place at night), with the five main characters having a picnic (or breakfast) on the lawn outside the country house. Then it shifts to the present day, and has tourists in modern dress wandering around the grounds, while through a PA system a tour guide on a boat on Lake Geneva tells of what happened subsequently to the famous night (within 8 years they were all dead, for example).[14] The film ends on a tilt-down shot to the water, and a dissolve (then a freeze frame) to an image of a baby, Mary's aborted foetus, under the water (with a distinctly Frankensteinian monster shape to its head).

---

14 This was Ken Russell's preferred ending: writer Stephen Volk wanted the framing story to be Mary as an old woman looking back (how boring!). But both framing stories do the same sort of job.

The above musings were my first reactions, seeing *Gothic* in the 1980s. Watching *Gothic* again, it doesn't seem as bad my first response. But it does have a frenetic, throwaway pace which scuppers many of the effects it's trying for.[15] Much of the problem with *Gothic* is the fault of the script, however, not the director, producers, backers, actors or crew. To put it simply: the screenplay by Stephen Volk is too obvious, too join-the-dots, too predictable. There needs to be much more going on – we've covered this ground a zillion times before (or maybe it's because I know too much about the Romantic writers and their literature (so the exposition is redundant and tiresome for me), or I have seen too many movies – including Russell's own flicks – come on! Russell did all this twenty years previously, in the divine *Dante's Inferno*).

*Gothic* also suffers from making the literary references to Lord Byron, Dr ......Polidori and the two Shelleys too in-your-face. *Gothic* looks as if a screenwriter has picked up a *Student's Guide* or *Dummies* book to the Romantic poets and created a drama around their lives and works. Maybe if you didn't know *loads* about Byron, Shelley, Polidori and Mary Shelley, *Gothic* would work (and movies do have to work without an audience reading footnotes at the same time). But if you do, then like me you'll find it too much like a 17 year-old college student's view of Romanticism and the Romantic poets.

The script for *Gothic* seems to want to lecture the audience about Romantic culture, too: or maybe it feels it has to deliver *some* exposition on Romanticism, to put it in context for the audience.

No.

The audience will come along for the ride, I think, and if it gets the Romantic cultural aspects, all to the good. But you don't need to give the viewer a college-level *Introduction To English Romanticism* lecture.

The recreation of the famous painting of *The Nightmare* (1781, Detroit) by Henry Fuseli is an example of too-literate, too-clever filmmaking (it has been quoted many times – including, recently in the *Twilight* vampire saga). It's on the wall in the women's

---

15 For Vincent Canby, *Gothic* was 'as ghoulishly funny and frenzied as a carnival ride through 'The Marquis de Sade's Tunnel of Love'' (PF, 262). Maybe – but many viewers would go for that!

bedroom, and is recreated on the bed (when little Kiran Shah[16] squats on Natasha Richardson's torso as the incubus).

The low budget does hamper some of *Gothic*: the country house (Wrotham Park and Gaddesden Place) looks like all of the furniture has been carried out by the art directors and their team, so there's nothing left. Drapes seem to be used to cover up bits the owners of the houses or the filmmakers don't want the audience to see.

So the setting doesn't feel real or lived-in at all – but that's true of so many historical films that set up camp in country houses. They clear everything out until it appears exactly like that: empty, echoey rooms that look like the owners are moving house. A studio is so much better in some respects.

The music for *Gothic* by Thomas Dolby still sounds very odd at times: it can really punch along some of the scenes, and it's an interesting departure for the usual Ken Russell soundtrack (*Altered States* had of course gone further in this direction – and more successfully, I think. And Russell had of course had electronic soundtracks in films such as *Lisztomania*).

The *tone* doesn't seem to have been agreed upon by the filmmakers and the actors in *Gothic*: what kind of film are they making? Who is this movie *for*? How much should be played for laughs, or played straight? When it comes to the horror genre, Ken Russell does tend to want to send it up. He can't take people creeping around corridors with candles seriously. But when he does present this kind of genre straight – as in *Altered States* – it can really work. And then the *audience* can decide if wants to interpret it for camp or kitsch value, or to laugh, or to go along with the thrills and scares.

In other words, if *Gothic* had been played straight, with the camp hysteria toned down, and the winks at the camera dispensed with, it might have been more successful. Oh, it would still very likely have been interpreted as a camp spectacle by many viewers. But, like *The Devils*, it might also have had more impact.

As it is, *Gothic* comes across too much like a bunch of people playing dressing up as Romantic icons, rushing around, performing a séance, stumbling into exotic boudoirs, etc. It becomes a silly pantomime. But that is Ken Russell's habit, of course: his films

---

[16] Shah has appeared in numerous movies – he doubled for Frodo in the *Lord of the Rings* movies, for instance.

like to have it both ways, and be both camp and straight, both silly and serious, at the same time.

In the last third, Claire Clairmont thankfully is pushed to the sidelines – because she is an irritating character. She becomes the witchy trickster, cackling off-screen, and playing tricks on the others. Claire is an epileptic, and rapidly goes insane as the movie progresses. By the end of the crazy night of revels, she's reduced to gnawing on rats in the dark basement, covered in dirt. She's incomprehensible – and nude, of course.

⁂

But there are many sequences which work well in *Gothic*: the scene where the five-some read some ghost stories from a book (it's *Fantasmagoriana*, 1812),[17] and the film acts them out. At these moments, *Gothic* becomes cinematic, exploiting montage and voiceover to the full, as each character reads a story that relates to their desires or personal life. The tales then become the fantasy of each character. In these scenes, *Gothic* transcends its too-literary, too-writerly script, and cinema takes over.

*Gothic* is lit with red and blue lights – very reminiscent of the nighttime photography of the horror films of Italian maestro Dario Argento. It's an attractive, self-consciously artificial lighting scheme which suits the frenzied subject matter. (Imagine, however, if *Gothic* had been filmed in black-and-white, which would have also suited the subject matter perfectly; it would also have moved *Gothic* away from that garish, loud, frantic atmosphere).

There are nods in *Gothic* to the feminist interpretation of the horror genre – to menstruation, for instance (Lord Byron's face's bloody after going down on Claire). Peter Redgrove and Penelope Shuttle, in their book *The Wise Wound* (1978), have analyzed the relations between menstruation and horror movies (for them, Dracula is an incarnation of the menstrual animus). It would make perfect sense that Claire is menstruating, for instance, during this crazy night (here, everyone is menstruating). And feminism has long enshrined Mary Shelley as one of the icons of feminism – no need to draw attention to the huge amount of critical and feminist writing about *Frankenstein* (and also of course Mary Wollstone-

---

17 This had been translated from *Gespensterbuch* (1811-12) by Johann Apel and Friedrich Schulze (from German into French).

craft).[18]

*Gothic* is certainly informed by some of the more recent developments in feminist and critical theory on the horror film and *Frankenstein* and *Dracula*. But it's a movie, not a critical essay being published in *Diacritics* or *Yale French Studies*.

✽

The recurring theme in Ken Russell's cinema that the artist makes real what's in their mind or soul is again central to *Gothic*. The five people in Lord Byron's country retreat are all artists – and four of them are, significantly, *writers* (not composers, or painters, the usual subjects in a Ken Russell film about art and artists). What's significant, though, is that all five of them are creative people. If you ignore all the trappings of the séance, the challenge to compose a ghost story, the frantic to-ing and fro-ing and the yelling and the thunder storm and all the rest of it, you have a situation involving five creative people who create something. They each create their own hell as well as their own heaven. And what they create has a life outside of themselves.

As this is a horror or fantasy movie, what the artists create is a monster. But it might be anything. And this is a theme that Ken Russell returns to again and again: that the mind creates the world, that your mental state determines your reality. That what you think about becomes real. In *Altered States,* Edward Jessup uses his own body and mind as the vehicle or clay to mould; in *Gothic,* what's created becomes externalized in flesh and blood.

---

[18] There's also an enormous critical interest in horror movies, which draws on feminism and cultural theory, far too much to mention here (some good starting points are: *The Horror Reader*, edited by K. Gelder, *Planks of Reason: Essays on the Horror Film* and *The Dread of Difference: Gender and the Horror Film*, both edited by B.L. Grant, and Kim Newman's *Nightmare Movies*).

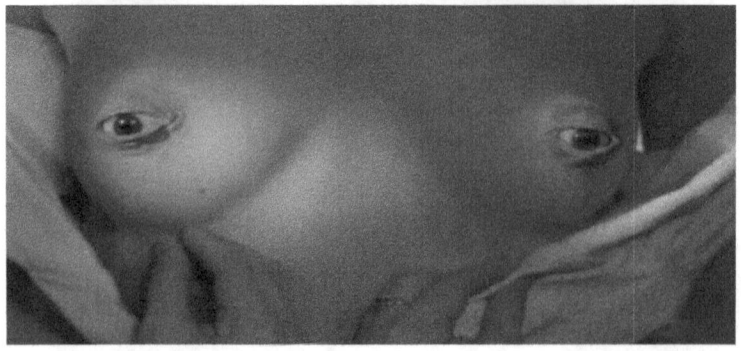

The Romantic stars of Gothic:
Lord Byron (below right).
Percy Shelley (below).
Mary Shelley (right).
John Polidori (below left).

# 19

# SALOMÉ'S LAST DANCE

I can resist everything except temptation.

Oscar Wilde, *Lady Windemere's Fan*

*Salomé's Last Dance* (1988) – Ken Russell meets Oscar Wilde – featured a terrific cast (which *really* delivers): it starred Nikolas Grace, Glenda Jackson, Stratford Johns, Douglas Hodge, and Imogen Millais-Scott,[1] with Penny Corke, Robert Littman, Dan Ireland, William Quigley and Ronaldo Vasconcellos producing, and Ken Russell writing the script from his American wife Vivian Jolly's translations of Oscar Wilde's play of 1893[2] (which had been written in French). The crew included: Harvey Harrison (DP), Timothy Gee (editor), Michael Buchanan (prod. des.), Christopher Hobbs (sets), Arlene Phillips (choreography), Michael Arrals (wardrobe), and Michael Jeffrey (jewellery and headdresses). *Salomé's Last Dance* was filmed at Elstree Studios.

---

1 This was Imogen Millais-Scott's last film, according to my research, and she'd only been in a couple of things b4 *Salomé's Last Dance*. Casting Millais-Scott was quite risky, in view of her lack of experience for such a challenging role (and she was too unwell to perform the all-important dance, so that was achieved with a double, played by Dougie Howes). However, for an actress with little experience, Millais-Scott does very well with some lengthy and intricate monologues (which're captured in some very long takes – a huge challenge for any actor). And of course she's surrounded by some great actors who *really* know their stuff.

2 Who knows what Oscar Wilde would've made of Ken Russell's interpretation of his play? At least he kept many of the lines verbatim! But Wilde and Russell are definitely a perfect match.

A French/ Italian version of Oscar Wilde's play appeared not long b4 *Salomé's Last Dance* (Claude d'Anna, 1985). Al Pacino produced one of his *Looking For Richard*-style documentaries on the play in *Wilde Salomé* (2011). Incidentally, Alla Nazimova, who appeared in *Valentino*, starred as Salomé in a 1923, all-gay movie version of Wilde's play which apparently out-Russells Russell).

Oscar Wilde (1854-1900) has been a favourite with theatre producers since forever (and critics, intellectuals and poseurs, from André Gide to Steven Morrissey of the Smiths): *The Importance of Being Earnest* (1895) has probably been playing somewhere on Earth every year since it was written. *Salomé* was Wilde's last play. Banned in England, it was performed in Paris in 1896 with Sarah Bernhardt (and first shown in England in 1905, at the Bijou Theatre, in a private performance). There's another link with Ken Russell: the play was used as the libretto for an opera by Richard Strauss (which Russell directed in Bonn in 1993).

Among the cinematic treatments of Oscar Wilde's work are *Lady Windermere's Fan* (1925), *The Picture of Dorian Gray* (1945, 1970, 1983), *The Importance of Being Earnest* (1952), *The Canterville Ghost* (1986), as well as biographies (1959, 1960, 1980, 1998).

Only much more recent Oscar Wilde film adaptions have drawn attention to the sexual and gender issues in his work: a movie of the late 1980s, whether it was directed by Ken Russell or not, was almost bound to address those issues. But, being directed (and co-written) by Russell, it was definitely going to do that! And *Salomé's Last Dance* did. This was a movie in which Russell's penchant for camp was fully justified – and fully explored!

♣

The first time I saw *Salomé's Last Dance* I found it a curiously lacklustre and unengaging film. Too static, too theatrical, too staid for a Ken Russell picture. No, that's not right – no Ken Russell movie is 'static', and no Ken Russell movie can be 'too theatrical'!

Further viewings, however, reveal the richness – and the fun! This is not a movie to take solemnly and seriously, like a Biblical epic flick from the 1950s and 1960s, when white light and twittering choirs heralded portentous and divine occurrences, and Hollywood stars in sandals and togas stood in the Californian or Utah deserts revisiting their Sunday school teachings.

This is a sit-back-and-pass-the-champers-darling kinda movie, a self-consciously silly slice of Russellian camp and vulgarity coupled with art historical allusions which only art historians will get, and yet also it's simultaneously a genuine attempt at putting on a late Victorian play by a highly-regarded playwright, and there is even a serious, theological under-pinning to the crazy proceedings.

And, in amongst the camp surface, the in-jokes and the OTT costumes, jewellery and make-up, *Salomé's Last Dance* packs a strong, dramatic punch. Altho' Ken Russell is often derided for being vulgar and showy, *Salomé's Last Dance* is actually a tightly-plotted and carefully-scripted movie (with a superb cast). And despite the plethora of effects, tricks and showiness, *Salomé's Last Dance* is *always* locked into the main story – the struggle between King Herod and Salomé, between Salomé and John the Baptist, between Herod and Herodias, and the framing story, of Oscar Wilde and his lover Bosie (Lord Douglas).

*Salomé's Last Dance* took place in a brothel (based on a real brothel) that Oscar Wilde had visited, set on the night before Wilde's arrest by the police for sodomy.[3] Glenda Jackson called it a 'visually extraordinary thing to do' (B. McFarlane, 318). The multiple narrative levels were another of Ken Russell's responses to a reduced budget (some said it was around $1 million,[4] others reckoned $800,000): that is, making a movie about a bunch of amateurs putting on a play in a private setting meant that the shabbiness of the enterprise could be part of the deal. Yet, of course, *Salomé's Last Dance*, like Russell's other 'low budget' pictures, is simultaneously crude and sophisticated, simultaneously self-conscious 'cheap' and 'low rent' yet also cinematically refined (the number of times that Russell's been promised a higher budget, only to have it slashed as shooting approaches, or during filming, is so many he must've got used to it pretty early on in his career). Besides, he started out making films for the British Broadcasting Corporation on budgets so small you would not believe the minuscule amounts. We are talking very, *very* small! Not what Hollywood calls 'low budget' – their idea of 'low budget' is $30 million! I mean, come on, how could *The Shining* cost $18 million at 1979-1980 prices?! Roger Corman could've made two hundred *Shinings* for that money! And how about turkeys like *Kingdom of Heaven, Prince Caspian, Lara Croft, Casino*

---
[3] But when Oscar Wilde is taken away by the police, he is utterly unruffled – and, in true Ken Russell style, is still holding his glass of champagne.
[4] That was what producer Robert Littman had told Vestron, apparently.

*Royale* and *Batman Begins*? (There are plenty more disasters from the 1990s and 2000s to choose from). Add up their budgets, each $100-plus million, and you could have financed *every single one* of Russell's many unmade, long-cherished projects![5] We'd all rather have 100 *Salomés* (at one million bucks each) than any one of those car wrecks of movies!

The 1988 *Salomé* film is set in 1892, on Bonfire Night, the anniversary of the famous incident when Guy Fawkes and co. attempted to blow up Parliament.[6] The establishing shot which opens the movie has people running around with fireworks in a London night, a scene that reprises moments in *The Music Lovers*.[7]

In this version, Oscar Wilde's play has been banned from performance by the Lord Chamberlain[8] (and that censorship organization remained in place in dear, old Blighty for many decades after the 1890s), so it is being performed by the people who work at (or visit) the London bordello, with Alfred Taylor (who runs the establishment) as the impresario (he also takes the lead role of King Herod).

Deep blues, rich reds, and burnished golds comprised the colour palette of *Salomé's Last Dance* – it might be the closest thing to a Gustave Moreau painting in the history of cinema (and, like Moreau's Salomé, Ken Russell's Salomé is both sexy and innocent, forthright yet eternally enigmatic – woman as cultural and spiritual force more than anything resembling a real person).

It's all about the costumes, the hair and the make-up: for *Salomé's Last Dance,* make-up artist Pay Hay devised a high camp, Venice Festival, Hallowe'en look, which included golden, green, blue and silver face make-up (even the slaves' boobs are gilded). As to costumes, the special headdresses and jewellery by Michael Jeffrey[9] enhanced Michael Arrals' wardrobe wonderfully (hair stylists were Liz Michie and Daphne Vollmer).

Combined with the sets (by Christopher Hobbs) and product-

---

[5] Russell would probably start with a crate of 1924 Dom Perignon to celebrate the movie being green-lit!

[6] Thus evoking political manœuvrings, as well as scapegoats and sacrifice, with Oscar Wilde as the ultimate fall guy.

[7] And filmed at the Royal College of Physicians in Regent's Park, London.

[8] Apparently because Biblical figures could not be depicted on stage. That reverential reticence continued with the early depictions of Jesus, of course – in *Intolerance*, the messiah is always shown in long shot, for instance (but that was also partly due to actor Howard Gaye's appearance). What would the Lord Chamberlain's office have made of *The Passion of the Christ,* the Mel Gibson-helmed whip-me-senseless movie?!

[9] Michael Jeffrey worked on many of Russell's 1980s productions.

ion design (by Michael Buchanan), the costumes, hair, jewellery and make-up delivered an operatic, Fellinesque look (reminiscent of Fellinian extravaganzas of the 1970s, such as *Satyricon*[10] and *Casanova*), which would be fine and dandy for a live opera (Ken Russell was directing opera around this time).

No electronica from Rick Wakeman or Thomas Dolby this time, but a soundtrack culled from public domain compositions: Erik Satie (*Gymnopédie No. 2*), Jacques Ibert (*Ports of Call*), Claude Debussy, Edvard Grieg (*Peer Gynt, In the Hall of the Mountain King*). The London Phil was conducted by Richard Cooke.

The out of copyright music in *Salomé's Last Dance* has been used by Ken Russell and the post-production teams have employed many times. Unfortunately, there are one or two scenes where Russell makes one of the biggest mistakes that Hollywood movies make: he allows the music to burble along underneath scenes for far too long. To the point where, as in so many recent Hollywood movies, it loses its dramatic impact and its function, and becomes mere muzak.

*Salomé's Last Dance* is a movie with obvious nods Derek Jarman; some in the team had worked with Jarman (such as Christopher Hobbs, set designer, and Michael Arrals, costumes). The late 1980s were the height of Jarman's influence on British cinema (following his biggest success, with *Caravaggio,* and the Super-8 oddity *The Angelic Conversation*) – which today has almost completely vanished (and Jarman's cinema seems wholly post-Russellian and Pasolinian now).

The actors in *Salomé's Last Dance* relished the roles offered them in *Salomé's Last Dance* – you can see them getting their teeth into the dialogue and the over-the-topness of it all: Stratford Johns, who steals the picture (despite fierce competition), as the weak-willed, superstitious, over-bearing (but curiously vulnerable), and unashamedly lascivious King Herod; Glenda Jackson as the

---

[10] *Satyricon* (a.k.a. *Fellini-Satyricon,* 1969) is a key intertext with *Salomé's Last Dance* (and with other Ken Russell outings). *Satyricon* was the maestro's interpretation of Petronius's (died AD 66) incomplete account of ancient Roman life during the reign of the Emperor Nero. With *Satyricon*, Federico Fellini and his team seemed to be aiming to make the most extravagant film possible, to out-do the Roman and Biblical epics of the 1950s and early 1960s, to counter Hollywood's version of ancient Rome with their own fantastical, overblown vision. In *Fellini-Satyricon,* Fellini and an army of phenomenally talented filmmakers created a world of grotesques, midgets, giants, prostitutes, pimps, soldiers, slobs, gluttons, actors, and so on. *Fellini-Satyricon* contains more weird characters, more outlandish sets, more strange make-up, more bizarre gestures, more unusual faces and actors, and more crazy costumes than most pictures. You have to go *a long way* find a movie as *genuinely* strange and over-the-top and lavish.

harrassed diva of a wife, Herodias; Douglas Hodge, terrific in a double-layered role as John the Baptist the firebrand prophet and Wilde's current lover Lord Douglas ('Bosie'); and Imogen Millais-Scott's highly quirky, kooky Salomé.

The play by Oscar Wilde is usually dominated by King Herod when it's performed, and that is the case in the 1988 Vestron picture; there's no doubt that Stratford Johns' formidable screen presence towers over the movie. Johns is *sensational* (and what a role for an actor!). Yet the filmmakers give a generous amount of screen time to Imogen Millais-Scott's Salomé.

*Salomé's Last Dance* allows Ken Russell and the team to indulge to the max their love of *fin-de-scièlce* culture: *Salomé's Last Dance* alludes to (or directly quotes from) Gustave Moreau (who produced without doubt the finest images of Salomé in the history of painting), Aubrey Beardsley,[11] the Pre-Raphaelites, J.K. Huysmans, and of course numerous quotations from Oscar Wilde himself (Russell and Jolly made sure they included some of Wilde's famous lines, including a'course the 'handbag' line – given in the movie, rightly, to Glenda Jackson).

Any number of Wildean quotes apply to Ken Russell's cinema:

> Art is never expressing anything but itself.
> All art is quite useless.
> In matters of grave importance, style, not sincerity, is the vital thing.
> I can resist everything except temptation.
> Other people are quite dreadful. The only possible society is oneself.
> Truth is rarely pure, and never simple.

It's a Biblical story, too, of course: Ken Russell revisits many of the themes and the characters of previous movies. Although he doesn't appear in the foreground, Jesus is discussed at length in the play (including the conundrum which crops up every time in any scene in cinema involving Herod and Herodias: what is a messiah? who is Jesus? why is he such a threat? Herod in particular is terrified of John the Baptist and the Jewish Jehovah. He refuses, again and again, to grant Salomé's wish of delivering the head of John the Baptist, in some of the movie's finest scenes).

The issue of (sexual) betrayal, of selling someone out, which occurs within the 1890s drama, also plays out in the framing story

---

[11] Russell adored Beardsley, and put the main titles of *Salomé's Last Dance* superimposed over a version of the *Yellow Book* which Oscar Wilde leafs through.

(principally between Oscar Wilde and Lord Douglas, with the golden page boy of Herodias (Russell Lee Nash) as the pretty boy coming btn them). *Salomé's Last Dance* portrays characters indulging in sex – Wilde takes a shine to the page boy, and spends quite a bitta time on the couch caressing him (then slinking around the corner). The sexual tension between Wilde and Bosie is another aspect of the framing story (Wilde blames the police arriving on Bosie, for instance).[12] Meanwhile, Herodias (or it is Lady Alice?) climbs into a wooden chest (of all places!) to fool around with two of the King's bodyguards. There is yet another element added to the framing story, when King Herod orders Salomé to be executed, and she's killed with a thrown spear[13] (as the maid is carried out, apparently murdered, there's a suggestion that the execution really took place, yet another crossing-over of the twin layers of reality in *Salomé's Last Dance*).[14]

*Salomé's Last Dance* is also a comedy of erotic dalliance, where everybody is as mad as the moon on this eternal night of topsy-turviness: Herod lusts after Salomé, and Salomé after the Baptist; the hapless and lovelorn Young Syrian (Warren Saire) moons over Salomé (and kills himself when spurned); meanwhile, Wilde dallies with Herodias's page boy, but the Baptist is played by his lover (who also has his own assignations). Meanwhile, there are topless guards (with gold breasts) in many shots.

The three slaves, introduced early on, are played by buxom, topless actresses in black leather fetish gear (Linzi Drew, Tina Shaw and Caron Anne Kelly),[15] offering the customary tits and ass quotient in a Ken Russell movie (*Salomé's Last Dance* stages the torture of John the Baptist as it has never occurred in any Biblical epic: the dominatrices playfully whip and stab the Baptist in a small cage, and clamber over it, in a stripshow routine (to the sounds of *Peer Gynt*). Russell just loves sending up the sword 'n' sandal flicks he saw as a kid.

'Here reenacted full of pulsating sexual innuendo, Russell eagerly sinks his teeth into Wilde's poetry and renders the play,

---

12 As the climbs into the police wagon, Oscar Wilde remarks to Alfred Taylor that maybe Bosie shoulda been Salomé, with himself as the Baptist.
13 Did it really happen? Oscar Wilde congratulates Taylor on the verisimilitude of the event – a little bitta Grand Guingol.
14 Even tho' the cowardly, superstitious Herod would *not* kill the daughter of his wife!
15 Arlene Phillips, the choreographer, was known for her troupe of sexy dancers *Hot Gossip* who appeared on British TV's *Kenny Everett Show*. Phillips was also the choreographer on *Annie, Legend, The Meaning of Life* and *Escape To Athena*.

in its entirety, at a frenetic pace' (Raymond Murray in *Images In the Dark*, 118).

'Who else can I offend?' Kenneth Russell might've asked himself. Well, Jews for one: the three Jews included in *Salomé's Last Dance* are played as grotesque, arguing caricatures by dwarfs (Mike Edmonds, Willie Coppen, and Anthony Georgiou).[16] Later, one of the Jews tups one of the topless slaves, cartoon-style, and then all three are at it. Queen Herodias gets freaky with the two bodyguards towards the end, in a wooden chest.

Some of the finest effects in *Salomé's Last Dance* are very simple: the stand-out sequence is where Salomé visits John the Baptist in his cell and taunts him, teases him, praising him then berating him: for most of this sequence, Ken Russell and his DP Harvey Harrison use a simple, over-the-shoulder shot, and editor Timothy Gee holds back on the reaction shots, so that the Salomé is held on screen in close-up. Imogen Millais-Scott over-acts plenty, but the filmmaking forces the audience to contemplate the dialogue, which's taken from Oscar Wilde's play. (In fact, a good deal of *Salomé's Last Dance* is filmed in long takes, which focusses the attention on the acting and the writing.[17] See the appendix for an extract from the play).

And straight away you notice that the language of the play is a send-up of overly ornate, poetic verbiage: it's Oscar Wilde sending up the kind of praise of a beloved that appears in the poetry of Sir Philip Sidney or William Shakespeare (Salomé offers pæans to the Baptist's black hair, white skin, red lips, repeating lines such as: 'I will kiss you on the mouth, John the Baptist'). Yet it also functions as a scary scene in which a *femme fatale* (one of the great *femme fatales* of late 19th century culture), taunts and teases a chained-up guy. Salomé embodies the linking of power and sex, religion and brutality, the ancient world and the modern world, which so many artists in the late 19th century adored. This is Salomé as the 'evil woman', the satanic spirit, the 'fallen woman' of the late Victorian era.

Thus, in spite of the OTT campness of the piece, and the wilfully perverse performance of Imogen Millais-Scott (you never *like* this Salomé, on any level, and certainly not at the level of

---

16 With Russell voicing one of them.
17 This is how Paddy Chayefsky wished Ken Russell had filmed his dialogue in *Altered Statesi!*

attraction and romance – she ain't Rita Hayworth!),[18] the 1988 Vestron movie does, I think, capture some of the authentic atmosphere of *fin-de-siècle* culture.

Ken Russell cast himself as the photographer Alfred Russell (a name he uses when he's operating the camera on his own films): the bushy, white beard look evoked *Dr Caligari* (a favourite movie) as well as Santa Claus (and, Russell said, hammy actor Donald Wolfit). His turn in *Salomé's Last Dance* included more lines than the occasional cameo (though if there're any characters that a director might identify with, it's Wilde and Herod. You can certainly see some of Russell the film director in Alfred Taylor's role as the play's director – especially his waspish comments!).

*Salomé's Last Dance* has to be extreme and excessive, partly because the story, the characters and the themes have already been seen a zillion times in the history of cinema. Like sword fights or a romantic kissing scene, Ken Russell can never play this cod spiritual/ Biblical stuff straight. He can't, he won't, won't, won't! He *has* to send it up.

So he has a Roman-style feast with farting guests (courtesy of a visiting Roman ambassador Tigellenus, played by Denis Lill, who's also the butler), a sweaty, pudgy patriarch lusting over his Lolita step-daughter, a middle-aged man fondling a pretty youth, and on the floor a midget humps one of the semi-naked lovelies (including the inevitable pun on the word 'come'). It's Ken Russell! You gotta love this guy!

Yet, *Salomé's Last Dance* also does capture the hothouse atmosphere of the 1893 play, and recreates an ancient world setting and characters, even as it sends them up. There is a real drama being explored here. The movie wouldn't work if there wasn't at least some psychological investment by the performers in the characters, and by the audience in the situations and the characters.

But it *is* very stagey – that's part of Oscar Wilde's play, of course. It's one of those British plays which're *stuffed* with dialogue, where characters don't say one word, as in William Shakespeare, where 557 will do. Where characters pontificate at length. There is plenty of actorly emoting and actorly business in *Salomé's Last Dance*. The actors in 1988 are pretending to be people of 1892 who are in turn being amateur actors for one night,

---

18 Rita Hayworth starred as Salomé in one of the famous Hollywood interpretations, *Salomé* (William Dieterle, 1953).

pretending to be famous figures from history of the AD 30s. That the author of play is watching them enhances the multi-layered aspects of *Salomé's Last Dance*.

There are some serious theological questions being raised by Oscar Wilde's play and the wacky adaption delivered by Ken Russell and his ensemble. One is the notion of a Saviour. What is a Saviour? asks King Herod at one point. Someone who saves the world – by *dying*? Someone who dies for your 'sins'? Indeed: the idea of a messiah in the Christian model was a blasphemy to Hebraic religion (as were many other elements in Christianity, like God having a Son, and a man also being divine. Christianity, we recall, was a syncretic religion composed of at least 13 different strands of beliefs, cults and religions).

# 20

# *THE LAIR OF THE WHITE WORM*

*The Lair of the White Worm* (1988) was based on Bram Stoker's last novel *The Lair of the White Worm* (a.k.a. *The Garden of Evil*, 1911), with Amanda Donohue donning the fangs as a reptilian *femme fatale*, Lady Sylvia Marsh, in a camp amalgam of *Carry On* humour and Hammer horror.[19] *The Lair of the White Worm* also starred Peter Capaldi, Hugh Grant, Catherine Oxenberg, Stratford Johns and my friend Sammi Davis.

Ken Russell, who wrote the script, updated Bram Stoker to the present day,[20] setting the film in a Northern, rural landscape (it was shot in the Peak District National Park, and in Derbyshire, at Gaddesden Place, a favourite Russell location, and Knebworth House, scene of many shoots, including *Batman*, *Jane Eyre* and *Eyes Wide Shut*). The show was based at Elstree.

*The Lair of the White Worm* involved many Ken Russell regulars, such as Dick Bush as DP, producers Ronaldo Vasconcellos and Dan Ireland, editor Peter Davies, and actors Christopher Gable and Imogen Claire.

The music for *The Lair of the White Worm* was by Stanislas Syrewicz: it was another electronic score, typical of the mid-1980s,

---

[19] 'Russell's flair isn't lost as this slimy tale of rampant vampirism oozes with an abundance of camp humor, serpentine symbolism, phallic symbols and just about every daft snake joke in the book', noted Raymond Murray in *Images In the Dark: An Encyclopedia of Gay and Lesbian Film and Video* (118).
[20] Bram Stoker's novel included a slave who uses voodoo that was dropped.

which Ken Russell also explored in films such as *Gothic* and *Crimes of Passion*. Syrewicz delivered one of the better soundtracks of this period, suitably moody and ominous. And for James D'Ampton's dream sequence, he composed a mini symphony.

*The Lair of the White Worm* is also Ken Russell's vampire movie – remember that Russell had wanted to produce a version of *Dracula* in 1979. So much of the movie in fact resembles Bram Stoker's famous 1897 novel, and the numerous interpretations of the vampire theme: you've got the fangs, the bites, the hypnotism of victims, the spread of the disease via blood and biting, the Christian vs. paganism conflict, the villain being spooked by the Cross, and Sylvia as a Dracula figure, aristocratic, debauched, seductive, and living in grand style in a mansion.

The novel wasn't as good as *Dracula*, Ken Russell said, but it did have potential (RC, 249). In updating the novel, Russell was also drawing attention to the fact that nothing much has changed in 500 years, since the time of the lords of the manor and simple country girls.

*The Lair of the White Worm* was the kind of film that British cinema hadn't made for at least a decade: a low budget horror film, in the tradition of the Hammer horror films. *The Lair of the White Worm* wasn't a conventional horror flick, though (what Ken Russell picture is 'conventional'?). Instead, the filmmakers delighted in sending up the horror genre and horror tropes, exaggerating the camp sexuality of the set-up (Russell will do music and biopics straight, but not horror or action!).

The plot, such as it was, concerned the revival, by Amanda Donohue's Lady Sylvia Marsh, the rich lady of the manor, of a long-dead, Roman cult of worshipping Dion, a worm-god. Sylvia was clad in improbably luxurious outfits and high heels, driving an E-type Jaguar, and luring unsuspecting youths back to her country house. *The Lair of the White Worm* came alive when Donohue's Sylvia was on screen: Ken Russell clearly likes powerful women a lot, preferably wearing some S/M gear, and preferably into domination and bondage.

Despite a reasonably adept cast, *The Lair of the White Worm* is very much Amanda Donohue's movie, and Ken Russell has clearly encouraged her to go all out. And she does. Donohue hits exactly the right key for A Ken Russell Movie, halfway between sexy seductress and camp vamp. If only everything else in the movie were up to the same standard, it might be a terrific piece.

In one scene Lady Sylvia entices a spotty, teenage rambler, Kevin (Chris Pitt) to her mansion (picking him up during a rain storm), plays snakes and ladders with him in front of the fire, bathes him, and bites off his dick. This's also the scene where the villain goes all megalomaniacal, and declaims loudly – to no one in particular – about the worship of the snake.

One of the more amusing scenes in *The Lair of the White Worm* has Sylvia Marsh appearing as the serpent coiled in the tree above Eve in Paradise – here, clad in red hues, she hypnotizes Eve to come back to her lair, so she can have her wicked way with her.

The young people in a nearby bed and breakfast place – sisters Eve Trent (Catherine Oxenburg) and Mary (Sammi Davis), who lost their parents mysteriously a year ago, and student archæologist Angus Flint (Peter Capaldi) – gradually uncover the pagan serpent cult with the aid of upper-class toff Lord James D'Ampton (Hugh Grant, playing his usual screen persona, which he would milk for decades – charming, stuttering, wimpy and dim).[21] *The Lair of the White Worm* starts with Angus unearthing a giant, serpent skull in the same place as a Roman villa, on the same site as a mediæval nunnery.

All jolly hokum, shot in the trademark style of Ken Russell's late work (low budget location shooting, few crowd scenes or expensive sets or costumes, and the occasional wild dream sequence). Russell complained that British critics insisted on taking it seriously:

> How on earth can you take seriously the vision of Catherine Oxenberg, dressed in Marks & Spencer's underwear, being sacrificed to a fake, phallic worm two hundred feet long? (1993, 145)[22]

It's only in the dream sequences did the old Ken Russell of craziness rear its head unfettered, with a grotesque rape 'n' pillage scene (recalling the familiar, over-the-top Russell of *The Devils* or *The Music Lovers*). In Eve's dream (when she touches the crucifix that Sylvia has vomited venom over), Roman centurions rape terrified nuns in a luridly coloured set, while a white serpent screeches and curls around Christ on the Cross.

---

21 And aided by a terrific OTT cameo from Stratford Johns.
22 Catherine Oxenberg wouldn't do nude scenes, and retained her underwear. Somehow the white bra and panties make the scene look even sillier.

In James D'Ampton's nightmare, the phallic connotations of the snake are further exploited by Ken Russell and his team: on a Concorde jet Grant imagines Sylvia, Mary and Eve as air hostesses having a cat fight, struggling on the floor in a lesbian embrace, while Grant's sexual arousal is indicated by his red felt-tip pen erecting. The dream sequence runs on and on, and includes numerous bits of business, some of it dopey, some of it dumb, and some of it inspired. Stanislas Syrewicz knits it all together with an impressive music cue. (The dream was added by Russell, needless to say: and in it he presented an explanation for all of the mysterious goings-on: 'it tells the whole of what happened. It tells who everyone is and what they're up to. It's a mystery, but it's solvable' [RC, 253]).

As well as the two chief dream sequences in *White Worm*, there are shorter ones, such as the one that Mary Trent has, and includes a clever superimposition over Sylvia's giant, blue face that makes it seem as if her mouth is full of crazy, snake people. These images are flashed on the screen in the manner of the hallucinations in *Altered States* – so fast you don't quite know what you've seen. And some of the images are really out-there. For instance, the images of nuns being raped, and stabbed by crucifixes.

But parts of the 1988 movie are curiously chaste. When you'd think Ken Russell and his team would include some nudity and sexuality in *The Lair of the White Worm*, the opportunities are oddly passed up. For instance, in the classic scene in horror movies where a young, romantic couple first glimpse the villain in a forest at night, there's typically some erotic fumblings at least before the bad guy appears. But no, nowt more here than a chaste kiss between Mary and Angus.

And this is Ken Russell! Similarly, when Lord James D'Ampton visits Lady Sylvia, the movie presents an eroticized encounter between the two, but once again, it's only a kiss. And in the previous scene, where the snake woman seduces the hapless youth who just wants to get dry and reach his youth hostel in one piece, there is plenty of saucy *Carry On*-style dialogue and gesturing, but no sex.

The restraint in depicting sexuality maybe is intended to play into the horror and campness of the piece. *The Lair of the White Worm* is all tease and no seduction, all titillation but no arousal.

Despite all of the snakes and phallic emblems on display, the movie just can't get it up.

However, later on, Sylvia appears nude, and wields a giant dildo,[23] employing it to test Eve's virginity. In fact, Amanda Donohue is nude in many scenes, and towards the end is clad in a fetching make-up job of blue body paint.

*The Lair of the White Worm* is disarming in its narrative strategies: it is an ensemble piece, and shifts around a bunch of characters, none of whom are especially appealing or interesting, apart from Lady Sylvia. When Sylvia's on screen, the film visibly brightens. But when she's elsewhere, the film dips.

In other words, because Sylvia is the most alive character in the piece, the one who seems to be having the best time, you end up identifying with her, and rooting for her. Why shouldn't she revitalize the ancient snake cult, and polish off all these boring, white Brits? Would you rather live in a world of Lady Sylvias, or dreary folk like James D'Ampton and his nouveau riche fiancée Eve Trent?

The roles in *The Lair of the White Worm* are under-written, perhaps deliberately so: they are also stereotypes, and speak in banalities (even the odd pearl of British humour doesn't add much dimension). As such, *The Lair of the White Worm* is a slow-burning piece, which lacks the high tension and threat and jeopardy of a really good horror movie. But if it's all a skit, it doesn't wholly work either. There *are* good genre send-ups which simultaneously spoof the genre but also act as decent comedies or dramas or suspense thrillers (and some, like the *Scary Movie* series, are *very* funny, too!).

It's not the easiest balance to effect, and while *The Lair of the White Worm* gets the tone right, and has the visuals and settings to match, the pacing is too slow,[24] the situations and characters are too uninvolving, and the humour is too flat, and not punched across enough.

One of the more macabre parts of *The Lair of the White Worm* is genuinely creepy – Eve and Mary's mom Dorothy (Imogen Claire) is one of Lady Sylvia's zombie-like victims. In one scene she watches television in a trance, in an empty room (staring at

---

[23] According to Ken Russell, the prop is a replica of the dildoes used by Malaysian pygmies to enhance their manhood (PF, 283).
[24] But when the cutting is rapid, as in *Gothic*, that doesn't solve the problems either, because the *pacing*, not the *editing*, is off.

footage of a snake charmer). *The Lair of the White Worm* enters some bizarre territory when it has James D'Ampton playing snake charmer music from North Africa (which his father picked up on his travels) on loud speakers set up on the roof![25] And, lo and behold, some snake people are duly attracted by the warbling pipes like the Pied Piper (later, Angus Flint uses bagpipes to lure crazed snake man PC Erny (Paul Brooke) away from his girlfriend, Mary. Very silly). Mary's mom Dorothy enters the D'Ampton home and is sliced in two by D'Ampton (though, like a worm, she's still wriggling).

Snake motifs[26] were packed into the 1988 film: the white worm curled around Christ on the Cross, and on a ring; a sundial; a Roman mosaic; a serpent's skull; a snakes and ladders board game; a painting of James D'Ampton slaying the worm; a watch's hand that goes snakey; a vacuum cleaner pipe, and so on. This being Uncle Ken, most of the snake symbols were seen as phallic.

There are numerous quotes in *The Lair of the White Worm*: the quotes include paintings and sculptures, a reference to one of Ken Russell's favourite films, *Citizen Kane* ('Rosebud'), *The Importance of Being Earnest*, and two scenes where characters watch television.[27]

And the ending of *The Lair of the White Worm* was over-the-top,[28] as it should be: it involved the must-have, underground cave set, with eerie lighting and tunnels, *de rigeur* on any horror movie. In the villain's set-piece, Amanda Donohue's Sylvia presides over the sacrifice of a virgin (Catherine Oxenburg tied up over a deep tunnel). Sporting the huge dildo for deflowering Eve, and covered in blue body paint, Sylvia is one of the more arresting of Russell's villains. (The scene was also another re-run of one of the movies that so influenced Ken Russell – *Die Niebelungen*, the silent German epic. Only Russell and his team had a fraction of the budget that director Fritz Lang and author

---

[25] Here technology is employed to battle the snakes: music and loud speakers. Does it convince? Not really. But it music being used as weapon, which Russell has explored before.

[26] It can't be a coincidence that Ken Russell is scared of snakes and worms, and filled the movie (and other films) with some of his phobias.

[27] The sisters' mom Dorothy watches a snake charmer, and D'Ampton contemplates an old movie on TV which looks like one of Georges Méliès' fantastical extravaganzas.

[28] The ending of *The Lair of the White Worm* featured the common twist coda, in which after the demise of the villain and her monster snake, the possibility of further mayhem is suggested.

Thea von Harbou commanded at Berlin's Universum Film Aktiebgesellschaft in 1924 for *Die Niebelungen*. But the giant snake practical effects and the visual effects ain't too bad).

In *The Lair of the White Worm*, the filmmaker seem to be piling parody upon parody, but the result doesn't always gell together, the performances are not convincing and too often dull, and the parody or pastiche isn't always fun. *The Lair of the White Worm* exhibits mistakes in conception as well as execution, and is further scuppered by the relentless pursuit of the oddball in any situation, giving rise to an eccentricity that isn't endearing, but tiresome. The camp irony just isn't always pleasurable in Russell's late films, compared to pictures made at the same time, such as Tim Burton's *Beetlejuice* (1988) or John Waters' *Hairspray* (1988), both far superior movies.

But there is something intriguing about *The Lair of the White Worm*, even if the movie can't quite decide whether to be an out-and-out spoof or a *hommage*,[29] even if the action is sometimes fudged, even if the characters seem greyed-out and unengaging, and even if the atmosphere is beautifully evoked one minute and flat the next.

And *The Lair of the White Worm* does benefit from Ken Russell's kooky way of looking at the world, particularly when he brings together elements that are disturbing or camp or just plain bonkers. It's no surprise that *The Lair of the White Worm* has a cult following (according to Joseph Lanza, it has been shown on the Sci-Fi Channel a few times).

Part of the lack of success of *The Lair of the White Worm*, and why it's still not well-known among Ken Russell's works, is I'm sure because viewers don't know quite what to make of it. It's the kind of movie that confuses audiences. It's too gruesome and strange to be a straight comedy or a send-up, like *The Rocky Horror Picture Show* or *Little Shop of Horrors*, but it's also so camp and silly it can't be taken seriously.

For me, *The Lair of the White Worm* would have benefitted from a stronger opening scene: after the slow-burn of the l-o-n-g and s-l-o-w zoom into the cave of Thor's Cave in Staffordshire the movie cuts to Angus digging up the snake skull, and the subsequent exposition dialogue with Mary Trent around the excavation site.

---

29 *The Lair of the White Worm* wasn't a spoof of the novel, but it was definitely a send-up of the horror film genre (RC, 249).

In other words, it was a scene of two people talking – just too lifeless and routine for a Ken Russell movie. At this point, it would've been relatively easy to cut some rapid images of the ancient snake cult, the crazy kind included in the dreams or fantasies of other characters when they encounter the snake cult. Or the opening needs Sylvia cornering a victim, with some gore or action, to quicken the blood in the viewer. Russell is a master of the hook, jarring the audience into watching, but not here.

There are also many scenes in *The Lair of the White Worm*, especially towards the end, which would have benefitted from night shoots, scenes that cry out for the Gothic look of smoke and darkness. Instead, the daylight tends to diffuse any atmosphere (night shoots are more costly).

Salome's Last Dance

The Lair of the White Worm on this page and over.

Below: Amanda Donohe's scene-stealing turn as a Bram Stoker femme fatale

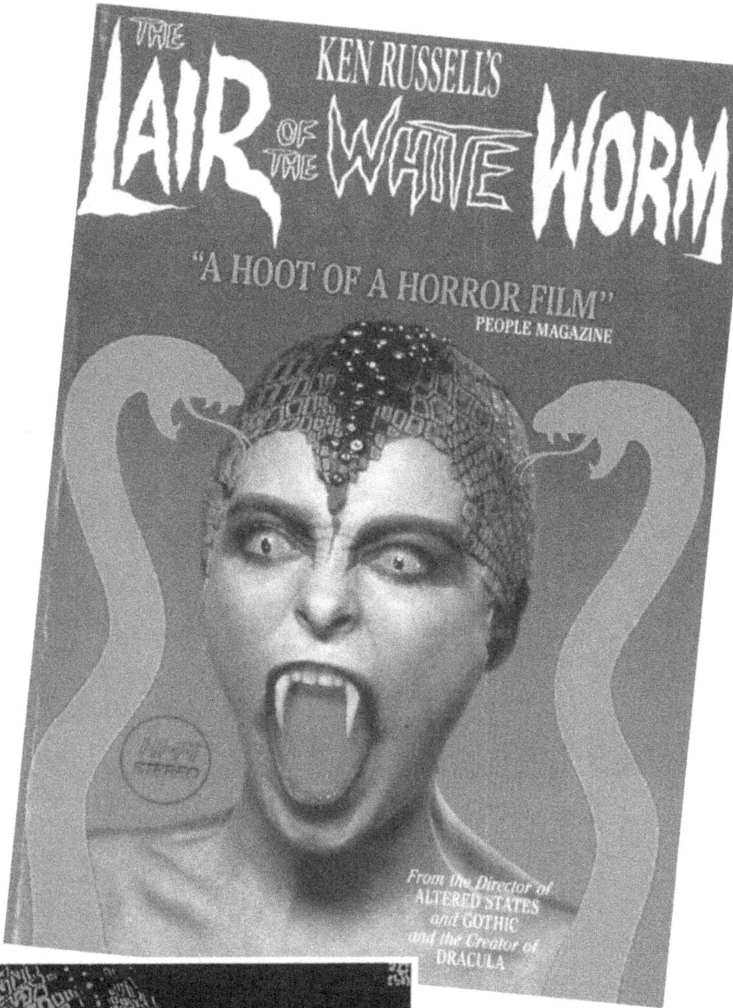
THE
KEN RUSSELL'S
LAIR OF THE WHITE WORM
"A HOOT OF A HORROR FILM"
PEOPLE MAGAZINE
From the Director of
ALTERED STATES
and GOTHIC
and the Creator of
DRACULA

A
KEN RUSSELL
FILM
ケン・ラッセルの
白蛇伝説
The Lair of The White Worm
ケン・ラッセル監督作品
ヒュー・グラント主演

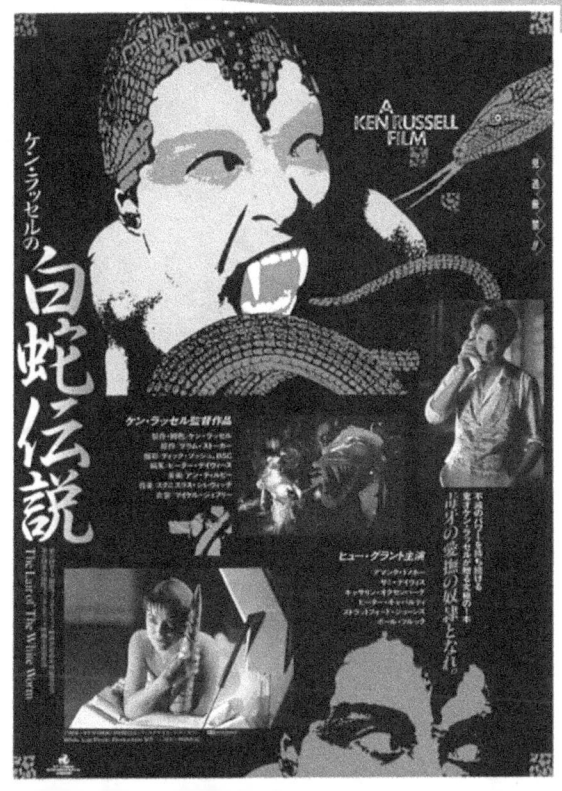

# 21

# THE RAINBOW

I find *The Rainbow* (1989) difficult to write about, partly because it's my favourite D.H. Lawrence novel and a book I know very well (and have written about in other studies). So I'm precious about it, partly because I know the star, Sammi Davis, really well, partly because I know that D.H. Lawrence's fiction is bloody difficult to adapt, and partly because I love Ken Russell's work, and know that it's a film he's proud of,[1] but I think it is really not very good at all.

Many in the cast and crew on *The Rainbow* were Ken Russell regulars: Judith Paris, Imogen Claire, Glenda Jackson, Dan Ireland, Ronaldo Vasconcellos, Billy Williams, Peter Davies, Luciana Arrighi,[2] Christopher Gable, Dudley Sutton, Ken Colley, etc. (Many had also worked on *Women In Love*).

*The Rainbow*'s script,[3] by Ken and Viv Russell, was shopped around the studios, according to Russell: EMI, Paramount, Fox, Metro, and Goldcrest, and they all declined (BP, 141). It eventually found a home at Vestron.[4]

The initial budget estimate – £2.5 million ($4m) – was too much for Vestron, and the company wanted half a million to be cut (BP, 275). The production trimmed some of the bigger scenes (including a village crowd scene, a dream sequence, and two

---
[1] *The Rainbow* was 'a British Picture I could really be proud of' (BP, 274).
[2] Luciana Arrighi designed *Women In Love* and the TV films of the Sixties.
[3] The novel was published on Sept 30, 1915.
[4] Ken Russell said he waited 8 years before he was able to make *The Rainbow* (RC, 247).

night shoots out of doors were combined into one interior scene (the scene where Ursula Brangwen and Skrebensky make love by moonlight). The production was shifted to near London (at Pinewood Studios) instead of the Lake District (though some of it was filmed in Cumbria).[5] The shooting schedule was 51 days (the schedule, and the budget, were much more than many of Russell's earlier works, but that still didn't make it a better movie than, say, *Dante's Inferno* or *Delius*).

THE CAST.

For Vestron, one of the problems of *The Rainbow* was the lack of star names. David Hemmings played the uncle (after Elton John dropped out, and others such as Alan Bates and Ollie Reed had been tried but said no). By then Hemmings was more an ageing character actor than the famous star of *Blow-Up* and *Alfred the Great*. Christopher Gable was cast as the father (after Jeremy Irons and Charles Dance had declined). Amanda Donohue played Winifred Inger (Theresa Russell, Kelly McGillis and Mariel Hemingway turned the part down because it was too small), but Donohue wasn't then known internationally (*LA Law* was some years off; Donohue had been the amazing villain in *The Lair of the White Worm*).[6] Glenda Jackson was a name, but only had a small part, as the mother (Vestron were happy with Jackson; Julie Christie was considered). Paul McGann as Anton Skrebensky was known for his TV roles, such as *The Monocled Mutineer*, and the cult film *Withnail and I*.

As to the casting, well, there are certainly problems there. *The Rainbow* is nowhere near cast on-the-nail, like some of Ken Russell's other movies. No one could dispute that Christopher Gable, Judith Paris, Ken Colley and the rest of the team in *Delius: Song of Summer* weren't fabulous, or that Roger Daltrey, Fiona Lewis and Paul Nicholas weren't spot-on in *Lisztomania*.

However, as I keep harping on and on, casting a D.H. Lawrence film or TV adaption is *very* tricky. Because Lawrence's texts require a talent for delivering arch, heightened dialogue, fit into a historical setting, bags of charisma, enormous acting skills, a lot of physical acting, and nudity. In a way, the *look* of an actor is the least of considerations in a Lawrence piece (though in much of

---

5 The novel of *The Rainbow* was set mainly in Cossall in the Midlands, which Lawrence called Cossethay.
6 Vestron wanted more of a name.

movie casting, it's the *primary* consideration).

Or, to put it another way: you could meet and audition a hundred actors over the course of a few days (as I have done), and find only one or maybe two people who could be one of your leads. And that would be lucky.

SAMMI DAVIS.

The biggest part, and the most problematic to cast, was Ursula Brangwen. When Sammi Davis (b. June 21, 1964) was chosen, she had appeared in a few British movies (such as *Hope and Glory* and *Mona Lisa*) and TV literary adaptions (such as the Thomas Hardy story *A Day At the Fair*), but certainly wasn't a 'star name' (but there were few actresses who were right for the part).

Sammi Davis and I dated for a while. In fact, we came from the same town (Kidderminster in the English Midlands), and I'd cast her in her first film – and *my* first film. It was a romantic drama called *Soosie and Lune* which we made in 1981-82.

When we were living in London, we'd meet up a lot and talk about movies – Sam (I always call her Sam) was just starting to get some good roles, in films like *A Prayer For the Dying* and *Hope and Glory*. We'd sit in the Godfather café on Tottenham Court Road (and many other places), drinking endless cups of coffee and smoking endless cigarettes, and always talk talk talking.

I remember Sam saying how she went to see a fringe theatre production of *The Rainbow* with Ken Russell. We bitched about a rival production of *The Rainbow* (starring Imogen Stubbs, it was a BBC TV series), which couldn't possibly be a patch on Ken's film. I also recall Sam saying how tough the nude scenes had been – not the love scenes, but running around the hills of Northumberland naked.

Ken Russell was full of praise for actress Sammi Davis in his autobiography *A British Picture*, enduring many wounds:

> Despite her wounds and battle fatigue, she continued to soldier on and was a wonderful example to the men. She braved rapids, swam rivers, survived a stampede of wild horses and ran naked to a dangerous mountain peak; she destroyed a field of lettuce single-handed, was sexually assaulted by a soldier, chased by a miner, endured torrential rain and being screwed against a tree in the spray of a raging waterfall... (1989, 291)

Ken Russell described the scene where Anton Skrebensky

fucks Ursula Brangwen against a tree beside the deafening waterfall thus:

> All thoughts of directorial subtleties are drowned out but Sammi, with the camera playing on her face, which is visible over Anton's shoulder, wants to know how to grade her orgasm. So I tell her to go for it in four stages and we turn over with someone holding the loud hailer to my lips:
> "One" – she grinds away. I'm operating the camera and she's acting really turned on. "Two" – her face begins to glow. "Three" – she's beginning to smile… "Four" – ecstasy. Perfection in each of the seven takes. If only it were always that easy, I thought, especially against a tree with 25 people looking on. (ibid.)

Sammi Davis told me that the most challenging aspects of *The Rainbow* was the nudity:

> The most difficult scenes to deal with during my time on a Ken Russell set, were the numerous nude scenes in *The Rainbow*, I was young and being naked in a movie is a huge step to take when you are new to the business. I had to run naked up hills, stand on a platform to have my portrait painted and my bum slashed with red paint, jump naked into a freezing lake, and be tied (for safety reasons) to a tree for a sex scene. Ken made no big deal about any of it, never made me feel on show or out of context in any way. I had to portray having an orgasm up against the tree. I asked Ken how to do that; he said he'd count out loud to ten as I built up intensity, ten was the moment, and in that way it was easy (and has been ever since!).[7]

THEMES.

Ken Russell and Vivian Jolly weren't much interested in D.H. Lawrence's politics or religious arguments in *The Rainbow*, and cut out most of his metaphysical discourses. Similarly, the 1988 Vestron movie did not address issues of class, gender and labour (the recurrent Lawrencean discussion of work was only covered in the school sequence). It also meant that whole slews of chapters and dialogue were dropped, because *The Rainbow* is very much a *spiritual* and *philosophical* book, in which Lawrence is exploring what it means to be alive, to be human, to connect with other people.

Maybe it's partly because in *The Rainbow* that irony or satire which goes along simultaneously with straight drama in Ken Russell's cinema was somewhat lacking. A Ken Russell Movie will typically send up the characters and situations and the drama

---
[7] S. Davis, letter to the author, 2007.

even as it presents them as 'real' or straight. There is always at least two levels to the experience. Russell's films like to have it both ways: they like to present stories and dramas, but also to send them up, or add camp or theatrical layers, or whatever.

THE OPENING SCENE.

But from the beginning of *The Rainbow*, which depicts the five year-old Ursula Brangwen running happily through the fields near her home in pursuit of a rainbow in the sky ('I want that,' she tells her father), the approach the movie takes seems uncharacteristically straight. Worse, it appears really schmaltzy, in the treacly, Hollywood manner (I love treacle and schmaltz, but in this case, it's not good treacle or good schmaltz). The sunshine, the smiling child, the summery setting and the clearly fake rainbow – we might be in *Wizard of Oz* or *Alice's Adventures In Wonderland* territory. But we ain't, because this is not a send-up, this is *straight*.

It really *is* meant to be *poetic*, it's meant to be a cinematic representation or equivalent for D.H. Lawrence's prose. And it *doesn't work*. It doesn't work *from the opening scene*, which is *not good* for a movie. But the beginnings of, say, *Mahler* or *Lisztomania* are spot-on, because they announce the kind of movie that's coming up – and not only the subject of the film, but the *approach* the film will take. And if we're meant to take the opening of this adaption of *The Rainbow* literally… oh dear, oh dear, oh dear.

Because that opening is misjudged, and awkward, and all wrong. Your heart sinks. This is *The Rainbow* we're talking about! One of the great, great novels in English literature. It's <u>THE RAINBOW</u>. I repeat: it's *The Rainbow*!!

You just can't start an adaption of *The Rainbow* with that silly scene of little moppet Ursula running through the sunny fields trying to catch a rainbow!!!

OK, let's forget about the novel and D.H. Lawrence. Let's look at that scene just as a *movie* scene. Folks, it *still* doesn't work or convince or send out encouraging signals for the rest of the movie!

If it was a Disney movie about a family from Philadelphia who're going on vacation somewhere pretty and outdoorsy like the Pacific North-West, fine. But not for a drama directed by Ken Russell! And not for *The Rainbow*!

There is *some* Ken Russell humour in the 1989 film of *The Rainbow*, however: a scene where a nude Anton Skrebensky pulls the cork out of a champagne bottle held between his legs (if it was real champers, I bet Russell led the team in partaking of the champagne afterwards); Miss Harby caricatured as a witch on a blackboard; the painter MacAllister quipping that he's not painting Ursula's face (the paintbrush is on her ass, in close-up); in the church, Skrebensky says he'll buy Ursula a lolly; and some quips in the dialogue about marriage. (But the script is too reverential of the novel, which's uncharacteristic of Russell).

The interlude with the painter MacAllister (Dudley Sutton) is a curious addition to the 1915 novel. Distinctly Oscar Wildean, an artist and model scenario, it features MacAllister painting Ursula Brangwen on a plinth in the nude (naturally), but becomes more suggestive when MacAllister hints at the great British pastime of corporal punishment – a little flagellation and classic Russellian kinkiness (again, this is more like *The Romance of Lust* or *The Secret Diaries of Walter!*). But our Urtler's not having any of this, and leaves in a huff.

THE LOOK AND STYLE.

I don't believe the *mise-en-scène* of *The Rainbow* film at all: it is just too summery, too sunny, too cute, too clean, too plastic. It's one aspect of filmmaking that Ken Russell and his many crews are so adept at: delivering lived-in settings on relatively low budgets. And if a low budget hampers the production a little, Russell and the teams can usually make up for that with *tour-de-force* filmmaking.

That does not occur in *The Rainbow* adaption. the filmmakers' approach needs to be way more moody, brooding, stylized. In short: *cinematic*. Too much of the 1989 *Rainbow* is like filmed theatre. For once, the *tableaux* approach doesn't work, doesn't produce the drama or tension or psychological illumination that the piece requires.

As to the score for *The Rainbow*, Carl Davis (b. 1936) composed a kind of pastiche of Ralph Vaughan Williams, Edward Elgar and William Walton. For a time, Davis seemed to be the composer of the moment in the 1980s,[8] but the score for *The Rainbow* appears a little undistinguished (bet you can't hum any of the cues from it,

---
[8] Carl Davis's credits in the Eighties include *The French Lieutenant's Woman, Oppenheimer, Scandal, King David, Macbeth* and *The Pickwick Papers*.

including the big, orchestral cue that accompanies Ursula Brangwen's climactic rebirth and rush towards the rainbow at the end). Certainly, *The Rainbow* doesn't count among the finest scores to a Ken Russell movie.

## WHAT IS *THE RAINBOW* ABOUT?

Question: *What is The Rainbow the novel about?*

That has to be decided very early on in a film or TV or radio or dramatic adaption. Is it a coming-of-age story? Is it a *Bildungsroman*? Is it about a person finding their place in the world? Is is a spiritual quest, a journey in which they discover themselves? Is it a love story? It could be all of the above and many more.

Certainly, *The Rainbow* is *not* an ordinary novel. There are none of the elements that movie-makers looks for: there is no villain, no grand narrative, no suspense, no jeopardy, no big set-pieces (except the flood), no comic sidekicks, no cliffhangers, no chases or climactic scenes, etc.

And the heroine of *The Rainbow* is impossible to play, and impossible to cast. Who is Ursula Brangwen? Clearly, she is no ordinary heroine of literature. She is not a conventional character in any accepted sense.

So what is the novel *The Rainbow about*? Once you've decided that, many of your decisions in the scripting and production will be easier. But in the 1989 version of *The Rainbow* directed by Ken Russell, and co-written by Russell and Vivian Jolly, it clearly *hasn't* been decided what the novel is about, and what the movie is about.

Compare the film of *The Rainbow* with, say, *Tommy* or *The Music Lovers* or *Delius: Song of Summer* or *The Devils*. Well, you can see Ken Russell and the teams honing in on the subject of those movies like a cruise missile. 'Know what you want' is one of Russell's mantras for good filmmaking. He repeats it many times in his advice to young filmmakers. But in *The Rainbow* it's obvious that Russell and the team had not quite decided what they wanted or what their film is going to be about.

## URSULA BRANGWEN AND INFINITE DESIRE.

Ursula Brangwen is a rebel, an outsider, an eternally-dissatisfied soul. She doesn't fit in *anywhere*. In short, she's a punk rocker: she doesn't know what she wants and doesn't know how to get it. She a hippy, a drop-out, a bohemian, decades before her time.

And Ursula is so clearly a poet or a writer or some kind of artist. But she is *not* an artist⁹ in the 1915 novel. You can see how much easier it would have been for Ken Russell if Ursula had been a painter or sculptor or musician or poet. Then there would have been ways and means of exploring her character and her dilemma.

The key scene in *The Rainbow* is where Ursula Brangwen is prowling in the surf in moonlight on the South Coast like a wolf after making love with Anton Skrebensky. It's one of the greatest moments in English literature:

> She stood on the edge of the water, at the edge of the solid, flashing body of the sea, and the wave rushed over her feet.
> "I want to go," she cried, in a strong, dominant voice. "I want to go."
> He saw the moonlight on her face, so she was like metal, he heard her ringing, metallic voice, like the voice of a harpy to him.
> She prowled, ranging on the edge of the water like a possessed creature, and he followed her. He saw the froth of the wave followed by the hard, bright water swirl over her feet and her ankles, she swung out her arms, to balance, he expected every moment to see her walk into the sea, dressed as she was, and be carried swimming out.
> But she turned, she walked to him.
> "I want go," she cried again, in the high, hard voice, like the scream of gulls.
> "Where?" he asked.
> "I don't know." (531)

That's as profound as you can get, as an expression of total desire and not knowing what the hell to do with all that feeling: *I want to go… Where? I don't know.* That says it all.

The restless, dissatisfied but eternally yearning elements of that scene are simply exquisitely expressed. And that Ursula Brangwen is prowling through the surf by moonlight makes it all the more powerful.

If I was filming *The Rainbow*, it would be a scene I'd want to get absolutely right. It's the money scene, it's the scene you make the whole of the rest of the movie for. Needless to say, the 1989 version of *The Rainbow* doesn't come within a million miles of that scene or the many others like it in the novel.

---

9 Unless she is the artist (architect) of her own life.

But, in fairness, it should be stated that the scene is virtually unfilmable. Despite the magnificent visuals, it is an *internal scene*, a psychological scene.[10]

▼

The first time Anton Skrebensky and Ursula Brangwen make love is upstairs at Uncle Tom's wedding. Reduced from an outdoor nighttime scene for budgetary reasons (it should be in amongst wild nature), it's a deeply disappointing interpretation of D.H. Lawrence's fiction. I could go on and anlayze the scenes in the 1989 picture and the novel, but there's no need to here: you can go back to the novel, and find out in a few seconds that what's on screen is a million miles from Lawrence's 1915 novel.

In the chapter "First Love", there are so many things going in the lovemaking scene in the novel – some subtle, some cruel, some tender, but all intense – that are lost in the movie, which depicts Ursula's first experience of fucking more like the violent deflowering of a virgin out of Victorian porn (nothing wrong with 19th century porn, but this is D.H. Lawrence, supposedly high art and a little more subtle. Maybe Ken Russell and co. should've filmed *Fanny Hill* or *The Romance of Lust* instead).[11]

In the 1989 movie, Anton Skrebensky rams Ursula Brangwen and fucks her until he comes – but she, understandably, wants a little more (and the scene in the novel *isn't* about *his* freakin' orgasm!). How many times have we seen that in movies? The scene plays more like a rape, and is far from what D.H. Lawrence depicts in his novel. (The film introduces the full moon, always such a powerful motif in Lorenzo's writing, but in the movie it's only vaguely suggestive of something other or mysterious, and the flash cuts to the moon, accompanied by a percussive music cue, also don't really evoke what's going on in the 1915 novel. There was apparently more to this scene but according to Joseph Lanza it was deleted by the producers [PF, 286]).

LESBIANISM.

Ursula Brangwen's relationship with Winifred Inger was played as a full-on lesbian affair in the 1980s movie. In the 1910s novel, the author had to be more restrained. It's plainly there, the fascination of the younger woman for the older teacher (and also

---

10 I had a go at using that scene in my theatre production of *The Horse-Dealer's Daughter* in 2006, switching it to a cemetery, where the heroine has come to visit her mother's grave.
11 He tried to make an adaption of *Moll Flanders*.

vice versa). But the 1989 adaption was much more explicit – at least in terms of depicting full nudity, images of the women kissing and caressing, massaging each other in front of the fireplace, and dashing about the countryside naked.

For a mainstream movie, this kind of lesbian imagery and relationship is still very rare (many production companies, film studios and TV broadcasters as well as actors wouldn't go anywhere near this sort of material).[12]

Once again, the 1989 Vestron picture doesn't capture the sense or subtlety or poetry of D.H. Lawrence's writing about Ursula Brangwen's love affair with Winifred Inger in *The Rainbow*. The imagery is halfway there – the underwater shots of the women swimming naked in a pool, for instance, or lounging around nude in front of the fire. But Lawrence's prose needs more than that.

SCHOOL.

In one section *The Rainbow* comes vividly alive, and that is the sequence dealing with Ursula Brangwen's experience as a new school teacher. Ken Russell and the team mount a memorable evocation of the horrific psychological and emotional as well as physical abuse in the educational system. On the movie-movie level, it is pure Charles Dickens – it's Russell & co. doing their version of *Oliver Twist* (though without the Gothic, Expressionist *mise-en-scène* of the classic Dickensian adaptions of the 1940s and 1950s).

But you can clearly see the filmmakers going to town on the pettiness, the meanness, the surliness, the stupidity and the intolerance in being at school. It's everyone's nightmare of school days.

In the school sequence in *The Rainbow*, Ursula Brangwen becomes part of the capitalist machine, just another cog in the social system. And when she is pushed to the limit, and finally explodes and thrashes the schoolboy Williams with a cane, the cost to her soul as well as to poor Williams is plain to see. 'She was as if violated to death', as Bertie Lawrence put it in *The Rainbow* (449), and 'she had paid a great price out of her own soul' (455). (There's a whole scene of fall-out from the beating, when William's mother comes to the school to complain, saying that her

---

[12] There was also a lesbian relationship in *The Boy Friend*, between the characters played by Antonia Ellis and Georgina Hale, but it was cut – it was one sub-plot too many (Bax, 214).

boy has a weak heart and is delicate).[13]

As well as the mindless routine and dull-as-shit conditions of school life, the 1989 film of *The Rainbow* is particularly strong on the power games played out by the teachers – particularly between Ursula and Miss Harby (the always-wonderful Judith Paris), and Ursula and Mr Harby, the headmaster (Jim Carter). Ken Colley's Mr Brunt acts as a kind of hapless, world-weary go-between.

Ken Russell's films have always been highly adept at depicting power games, whether sexual, social or artistic – think of Franz von Liszt and Richard Wagner in *Lisztomania* or Peter Tchaikovsky and Count Chiluvsky in *The Music Lovers*. In *The Rainbow*, Russell and Vivian Jolly add a layer of sexual violence between Ursula Brangwen and the headmaster – the movie has Mr Harby ogling Ursula, and later cornering her in a corridor, and making a pass at her (after he's gone, Ursula cowers down on the floor, weeping. D.H. Lawrence's Ursula wouldn't do that).

※

There is an important theme to *The Rainbow* which doesn't really come out in the 1989 movie – the ugliness and dreariness of modern life, the violence and inhumanity of the mines and mining, and the brutality lying underneath relationships. Yes, there are scenes of Ursula Brangwen berating her Uncle Tom for his exploitation of the working people (in scenes which include scale models of mines in Tom's living room – a budget cut solution to filming outdoors), and a scene where miners detonate the countryside when Ursula and Winifred are out walking the fells, and have their pleasant ramble interrupted with loud explosions – but they don't really get across the many facets to D.H. Lawrence's deconstruction of work and living in the modern era.

ADAPTING *THE RAINBOW*.

A big problem with *The Rainbow* and D.H. Lawrence's fiction in general is that so much of the novel takes place inside the characters: inside, they are experiencing all sorts of feelings and conflicts. At times, Ursula Brangwen is a volcano of emotions and opinions and ideas. It's expressing that in cinematic language that's the challenge.

---

[13] Sammi Davis said she went too far in that scene, and was full of remorse when she accidentally hit the boy on the wrist (J. Caryn, *New York Times*, May 5, 1989).

Here's a simple test for you, dear reader: pick up a copy of *The Rainbow* or *Women In Love* or *The Plumed Serpent* and choose any page and ask yourself: how am I going to dramatize or visualize these words on celluloid or video?

Here's another test for you: try taking just one scene from a D.H. Lawrence book and have a go at turning it into a script that can be filmed.

Not easy. Oh no, not easy at all.

It's funking difficult.

For instance, how would you adapt the following couple of extracts?

> But hard and fierce she had fastened upon him, cold as the moon and burning as a fierce salt. Till gradually his warm, soft iron yielded, yielded, and she was there fierce, corrosive, seething with his destruction, seething like some cruel corrosive salt around the last substance of his being, destroying him, destroying him in the kiss. And her soul crystallised with triumph, and his soul was dissolved with agony and annihilation. (*The Rainbow*, 368)

That's a lovemaking scene from *The Rainbow*. So, in your script all it says is: 'THEY MAKE LOVE'. How do you shoot it? How do you show his 'warm, soft will yielding, yielding'? Or someone's 'being'? Or maybe you will instruct your actress: 'I want to see your soul crystallizing with triumph, honey'. And she might reply: 'how the $$$$ do I do that, boss?'

Or what about this, from the 1915 novel's ending:

> Gradually she began really to sleep. She slept in the confidence of her new reality. She slept breathing with her soul the new air of a new world. The peace was very deep and enriching. She had her root in new ground, she was gradually absorbed into growth.
> When she woke at last it seemed as if a new day had come on the earth. How long, how long had she fought through the dust and obscurity, for this new dawn? (546)

*The Rainbow* is about *rebirth* in large part – how a person can give birth to themselves, how they can find a new life in amongst the old life, how they can nurse themselves through darkness and emerge, healed. So towards the end of *The Rainbow*, Ursula Brangwen is in a chrysalis state, struggling to ascend from a cocoon.

How does the 1989 movie of *The Rainbow* adapt such prose? It depicts a young woman emerging from an illness, conversing with her father, and finally, after seeing a rainbow from her window, deciding to leave – to literally follow the rainbow. In the novel, Bertie Lawrence piles on religious and spiritual imagery and motifs, making Ursula Brangwen's convalescence and healing a religious rebirth, as well as (or much more than) a physical one.

The 1989 filmic adaption only suggests such spiritual themes. In cinematic terms, Ursula Brangwen running out of doors towards the giant rainbow hanging above the sunny fields is only part of the thematic, psychological and emotional impact of the novel's ending.

So the close of *The Rainbow* is disappointing – but that's partly because a film of this kind is very difficult to end satisfactorily. It's *not* an ordinary narrative, after all: no heroes, no villains, no guns, no car chases, no simple goals to achieve.

What is *The Rainbow* about? we have to ask yet again.

As to the *action* climax of *The Rainbow*, which derives in part from Lorenzo's Midlands novel, that isn't wholly convincing or successful either. Ursula, poor dear, has been menaced by men throughout this movie – from the headmaster Mr Hanby trying it on at school to the faceless workmen who seem to threaten her in the finale.

❊

For Pauline Kael, *The Rainbow* was spoilt by Ken Russell's 'staggeringly superficial' treatment of the novel; lacklustre and misguided acting; and a misinterpretation of the central role, played by Sammi Davis, whose Ursula Brangwen Kael called 'a snippy, closed-off brat', 'blank-faced and lightweight', 'an impossibly petulant twerp' (1992, 139-40). Well, Kael had it in for Russell throughout her career, of course, but *The Rainbow* is certainly very wide of the mark in relation to the novel, is miscast, is structurally awkward, has the wrong texture, design and look, is indifferently acted, and, worst of all, doesn't satisfy as a movie on its own (if it were a great movie, many of its flaws could be forgiven or ignored).

The cast of The Rainbow

Ursula Brangwen and her teacher Winifred Inger
in a lesbian idyll in 1989's The Rainbow

Running around the mountains of the Lake District in Britain in an erotic dream sequence from a D.H. Lawrence adaption: it can only be a Ken Russell movie

Sammi Davis in The Rainbow

# 22

# *PRISONER OF HONOR*

*Prisoner of Honor* (1991) was produced by Richard Dreyfuss, Judith Rutherford, Michael Bendix, Colin Callender and Steven Nalevansky for Dreyfuss/ James Productions, Warner Bros. Television and HBO (Home Box Office). Ron Hutchinson wrote the screenplay (easily the single, most significant contribution to this complicated, historical piece), Mia Goldman, Margaret Goodspeed and Brian Tagg were the editors, Michael Jeffrey was costume designer, Ian Whittaker was production designer, music was by Barry Kirsch, and Mike Southon was DP. Some of those were Russell regulars (Whittaker, Tagg, Southon, Jeffrey, and Ronaldo Vasconcellos the line producer). The cast too included many actors who had worked with Russell before: Peter Vaughan, Ken Colley, Judith Paris, Imogen Claire, Paul Dufficey, Christopher Logue, Murray Melvin, and Patrick Ryecart. And Oliver Reed – it was his last collaboration on film with Russell.

*Prisoner of Honor* was a star vehicle for its producer, Richard Dreyfuss (b. October 29, 1947), and Dreyfuss was accordingly in most scenes, and was largely the hero of the piece (playing Colonel Picart). While the subject matter (and *milieu*) was very French, the production was in many respects very British (being populated largely by – mainly male – British character actors), and filmed in English locations (with studio work at Pinewood). But it was a North American production.

If you didn't know that Ken Russell directed *Prisoner of Honor*, you might not have guessed it (aside from the clues in the casting). Because *Prisoner of Honor* had few of the usual Russell flourishes or symbols or techniques of the maestro. That's not a criticism, though, because *Prisoner of Honor* was a very solid piece of directing. Keeping track of this complex story would require plenty of concentration and organization.

However, it was the *writing* and the *editing* that really formed the backbone of *Prisoner of Honor*'s approach to the famous Dreyfuss affair. That's not to belittle Ken Russell's contribution as director, but it's in the screenplay, which takes numerous twists and turns, and how the editors (Goldman, Goodspeed[1] and Tagg) and their assistants have put together this elaborate and intricate narrative, that the meat of this film resides.

The *pace* of *Prisoner of Honor* is rapid – it really does hurtle along. And yet each new revelation or new view or new piece of information which alters the central spine of the story is kept clearly in focus. (Because *Prisoner of Honor* could so easily be a mess of explanations and myriad characters and plot twists).

*Prisoner of Honor* wasn't the first film to be made about the Dreyfus Affair by any means – it had been filmed in 1899 (twice),[2] 1930, 1931, 1937, 1958, and after *Prisoner of Honor* in 1995. And there are bound to be more movies or TV shows about it. It was first dramatized by the grandfather of all fantasy cinema, Georges Méliès (if Méliès represents one tradition of cinema, and the Lumière brothers the other, Ken Russell is definitely an inheritor of Méliès – cinema as magic, as alchemy, as poetry, as fantasy).

*Prisoner of Honor* is a history lesson, on one level, and it's beautifully done. That's always been a key element of Ken Russell's cinema, but too few of his detractors acknowledge it (and some of his fans also ignore it). They are overwhelmed by the density and OTT quality of his imagery. Yet Russell has always stressed the historical accuracy of his movies, and the amount of historical research that's up there on screen.

It's no different in *Prisoner of Honor,* which requires plenty of exposition to outline the era and the politics and concerns and the ethics of the period (the late 19th century and early 20th century – the timescale of *Prisoner of Honor* is roughly from 1894 to 1906). Aside from setting the 1991 picture firmly in its time and place

---

[1] Goodspeed – a terrific name for 99a film editor.
[2] The Dreyfuss affair had been dramatized very early on in the history of cinema – by French master showman Géorges Méliès. Ken Russell is very much of the Méliès school of making cinema – cinema as a show, as magic, as a performance, as fantasy.

(which is always going to take up more screen time in a complex story like this than, say, a love story), *Prisoner of Honor* also has to introduce numerous characters. For *Prisoner of Honor,* Russell and his team (the casting director Susi Bruffin was absolutely vital in this movie), wisely brought in a collection of virtually every character actor in Britain (aside from Russell regulars, there is Peter Firth, Brian Blessed, Jeremy Kemp, Martin Friend, and even director Lindsay Anderson, as the Minister of War).

With so many characters and so much narrative information thrown at the viewer, a movie like *Prisoner of Honor* can easily be derailed or become submerged. But it clocks in at a trim 88 minutes, and makes the spine of the story crystal clear.

However there are *some* Ken Russell flourishes in *Prisoner of Honor* – there's a cabaret skit which depicts Dreyfus as a vampire, a fascist song number performed by Imogen Claire (about 'France the Fatherland'), and there's a little bit of sex between Colonel Picart and his paramour (someone else's wife).

Richard Dreyfuss is solid and watchable as ever as Colonel Georges Picart, who holds onto his ideals and principles right to the end, never giving in to pressure to stand down or recant (a familiar Ken Russell theme, and one which drives one of his greatest movies, *The Devils*). It's a revenge theme, too – so that Picart can say that he was right all along and that Major Esterhazy (Patrick Ryecart) was the real villain. But the costs have been too high (he has to give up his lover, for instance).

*Prisoner of Honor* also confronts themes such as anti-semitism, which Ken Russell had explored previously in movies such as *Mahler* and *Lisztomania*. If the politics of *Prisoner of Honor* is inevitably a bit self-conscious and right-on (actor Richard Dreyfuss is known for being out-spoken politically – which's still highly unusual in the contemporary Hollywood community, when politics is the *last* thing anyone will bring up), it's still a powerful piece.

# 23

# *WHORE*

*Whore* (1991) was based on David Hines' stage play *Bondage* (1989),[3] co-scripted by Ken Russell and Deborah Dalton, and starred Theresa Russell[4] as a prostitute working the streets of a contemporary North American city (the play had been set in King's Cross, London, but was transferred to the U.S.A., partly because the money for the movie came from the North America – from Trimark Pictures). *Whore* thus followed a pattern of Americanization which has been applied to numerous British fictions.

Dan Ireland, Ronaldo Vasconcellos, Mark Amin and Michael Pariser produced; Amir M. Mokri was DP; Brian Tagg edited; Richard B. Lewis was production designer; Leonard Pollack did the wardrobe; and Michael Gibbs provided the music.[5] Also in the cast were Benjamin Mouton, Elizabeth Moorhead, Antonio Fargas ('Huggy Bear' from *Starsky and Hutch*), and Jack Nance (best-known as one of David Lynch's regular actors, and as the star of *Eraserhead*).

The structure of *Whore* mixed Theresa Russell's character Liz delivering monologues to the camera (in the theatrical tradition), her encounters with clients, her run-ins with her pimp Blake (Benjamin Mouton), and flashbacks to her earlier life, including

---

[3] Hines was a London cabby, and had drawn on his experiences driving prostitutes in the capital.
[4] Theresa Russell, wife of Russell's contemporary Nic Roeg, had appeared in *Aria*.
[5] The score for *Whore* is a gloomy affair which seems disconnected from the movie – it also delivers conventional, American TV thriller sounds which seem out of place within the social context of the piece.

numerous clients, her relationship with her pimp, his friendship with a woman, Katie (Elizabeth Moorhead), and her married life (drunk, abusive husband, and a child that's taken away from her).

Theresa Russell, strutting around in white make-up, red lipstick, a short, red jacket, silver bras and a red mini-skirt, was impressive (this was very much a one-woman show),[6] but the film did not add up to much, and seemed pointless.

*Whore* depicts a harsh world of soulless city streets in Los Angeles, hookers being moved on by cops, blowjobs in restrooms, and Liz getting drunk in titty bars. All Liz wants is some peace and quiet. All she wants to do is to sleep.

A movie which takes prostitution as its main topic is almost always going to be a political and social movie, not a sexy or nudie pic (no matter how much distributors or publicists emphasize the titillation angle). There *is* nudity and some sex in *Whore*, but this is as far from porn as possible.

Stylistically, it seemed as if the filmmakers were aiming for something simultaneously 'gritty' and 'realistic' and also theatrical and stylized. It was unusual, perhaps, in seeing a Ken Russell movie which explored the mean streets of a modern city, rather than the breezy heights of the Lake District or a cottage where poets and painters lived.

Talking about the look of *Whore* – budgetary issues are at stake here: as in other Ken Russell pictures, much of *Whore* should really have been filmed at night (especially most o' the street scenes). But maybe the washed-out *mise-en-scène* of drab, American city streets by day suits the desolate subject matter.

The setting of *Whore* was 'realistic', and Ken Russell's treatment couldn't seem to decide between docu-drama and ideological rant. The subject matter – prostitution, sex, sleaze – seemed right up Russell's street – but it was ground he had covered before (and much better) in films such as *Crimes of Passion*. (Indeed, the direction seems rather indifferent at times, and by far the most significant contributors to the 1991 piece are the script and Theresa Russell's performance).

Maybe I've seen too many movies, but pretty much everything in *Whore* was just too predictable: (1) that every john is

---

6 Personally, I find Theresa Russell an odd-looking person, with her squat, chunky legs and strange eyes. I have no idea why she became something of a movie star in the 1980s and early 1990s. Of course, her then-husband Nic Roeg was nuts about being her chief promoter, putting her in movie after movie.

a jerk, for instance; (2) that Liz is just trying to make a buck; (3) that her pimp is an aggressive manipulator;[7] (4) that Liz finds herself in numerous dangerous situations (including being gangbanged in the back of a van and thrown out of the vehicle on a piece of waste land).

What is the theme of *Whore*? That men[8] are shits? Jeez, tell us summat we don't know! That prostitution demeans everyone involved? Come on! That prostitution as an issue and a melodrama highlights inequalities of gender, power, economy and politics?

And what was the point of making *Whore* at all? We've heard all of this polemic about prostitution before. We've had movies that've used prostitution as a way of investigating Western capitalist societies (Jean-Luc Godard has made that ideological approach one of his stand-bys). And feminists such as Andrea Dworkin, Susan Griffin, Robin Morgan and Catherine MacKinnon, among hundreds, have attacked the issue of prostitution and the exploitation of women far more elegantly and angrily than *Whore*.

This being a Ken Russell movie, some dancing is squeezed into *Whore* (where, let's face it, it doesn't really fit!). And some classical music. The dance occurs in a TV show that Liz and Katie are watching (in dry ice, a dancer slinks about a TV studio Isadora Duncan-style – as if Russell had shot a Kate Bush pop promo). The classical music is found in the most interesting segment of *Whore* from a cinematic point-of-view – the montage sequence about an hour into the piece, when the duologue between Liz and Rasta about prostitution (in a movie house) is intercut with the pimp Blake's angle on whoredom, as he drives his car thru the city streets at night and delivers a monologue.

The title *Whore* was problematic for distributors,[9] but worse was when the 1991 movie was given an 'NC-17' rating by the MPAA's Classification and Ratings Administration, which's death at the box office (1990's *Henry and June,* a literary adaption which has affinities with Ken Russell's movies (art and artists, sex, Paris, bohemia), was the first Hollywood studio picture to test the new

---

7 How Blake literally 'brands' Liz like an animal (with a tattoo); how he takes her to a high-class French restaurant in a prolonged scene of nasty power-gaming (with Ken Russell playing a French waiter like something out of a *Carry On* movie).
8 Male punters are continually put down in *Whore* – they're depicted as losers: violent, ugly, boorish, badly-dressed, insensitive, and stupid.
9 It was changed to: *If You Can't Say It, Just See It.*

'NC-17' rating). That, plus bad reviews, helped to damage *Whore* at the box office, as Frank Miller noted in *Censored Hollywood* (249). So an 'R' rated version of *Whore* was released (with five minutes dropped). The distributor, Vidmark, eventually released four versions of *Whore*: the theatrical 'NC-17' cut, the 'R' rated version, and video versions (in 1992), as *Whore,* and using the title *If You Can't Say It, Just See It.* Yet the 'NC-17' rating seemed too severe for a movie that contained little nudity or sex, and was really an anti-porn movie with a rather conventional, conservative character at its heart.

The censorship issue is stuffed with hypocrisies – all of them are obvious, so there's no need to go into 'em here. The most striking one concerns the target market and the financing of the production: a movie such as *Whore* is clearly going to be a niche market from the outset. It was always going to be a limited release movie, a movie with a small audience among adults. (Thus, tho' *Whore* might've been conceived by Ken Russell & co. as an answer to *Pretty Woman,* the Walt Disney movie of the previous year, 1990, it wouldn't attract or play to the same audience as that hugely successful movie starring Richard Gere and Julia Roberts).

By far the more sexually 'explicit' material in *Whore* occurs in the dialogue – where we hear about blowjobs, anal sex, handjobs, shoe fetishists and all the rest (stuff which the movie is desperate to evoke, but can't show). This is a standard ploy in translating graphic sexual material to the screen, turning visuals into words. *Whore* is as coy as a prim maiden aunt at times when it comes to portraying sexual acts on screen (tho' Mary Whitehouse would've hated it). Instead, the movie employs off-screen space and sounds (the old coot who likes to be whipped is heard behind a bathroom door, for example, and the gangbang in the back of the van is played out as sound effects, over a close-up of the young driver jerking off as he listens to the orgy in the back behind him).

As a counter-attack to *Pretty Woman, Whore* achieves its goal – Ken Russell insisted that prostitution was a nasty business in which people got hurt. *Whore* shows that. But the politics of *Whore,* its ideological and social foundation, is just as conservative and even as Disneyfied as *Pretty Woman* was.

As for the finale, it was predictable and cheap and the filmmakers didn't seem that interested in it: yes, Liz is attacked by her pimp Blake (yet again), this time more viciously (Blake sees Liz giving the kiss of life to a punter who's just expired while banging her in a car, and goes nuts). So, yeah, Blake strangles Liz, only to have his throat cut by Rasta, who materializes by magic, out of nowhere.

It's a lame ending to *Whore*, but it doesn't affect the 1991 movie at all – because it's been a series of monologues rather than a story with characters undergoing psychological development. Indeed, Liz isn't altered one iota from the beginning of the movie (that she walks off into the sunset with a smile on her face is just silly – the smile probably means: thank God this horseshit is over!).

*Whore* does seems a case of the filmmakers engaging with only parts of the material, not the whole deal. There is more style and flair from Ken Russell than a 'director for hire' assignment, but somehow it might've been far more enjoyable if David Hines' original play had been ditched entirely, and if Russell and Deborah Dalton had come up with a new screenplay. Too much of *Whore* is predictable, too many of the points it makes are wholly expected, and too much of it doesn't catch fire.

As a 'sequel' of sorts to *Crimes of Passion*, *Whore* disappoints – because *Crimes of Passion* featured that out-there performance from Anthony Perkins, and also a central relationship – between Perkins' Reverend Peter Shayne and the hooker China Blue – that took *Crimes of Passion* into some very strange zones (however, the married couple Bobby and Amy Grady brought the 1984 movie right back down to banal levels again).

By contrast, the people who surround Liz in *Whore* just aren't especially engaging, or they're just too predictable: not a single person here does something unexpected. But *we* expect something more from Ken Russell as a film director! (Compare *Whore* with a 1992 movie about hookers, tough big cities and dodgy punters – *Naked Killer*, a wild, beyond-camp and ultra-trashy, Hong Kong action movie starring Chingmy Yau, Carrie Ng, Simon Yam, Sugawara Madoka, Kelly Yiu and Johnny Lo, and produced and written by the famous (and *very* prolific) director-producer-writer-mogul Wong Jing. *Naked Killer* has no more meaning than a plastic cup, is gloriously, gleefully violent, contains astounding action sequences, and is filled with sleek, super-sexy super-babes and super-bitch, lesbian assassins that make Theresa Russell look like an old spinster).[10]

ADDENDUM.
*HENRY AND JUNE.*

*Henry and June* could not shake the associations between NC-17 films and X-rated films, even though the NC-17 was created to separate 'serious' films with 'X-rated' sex scenes from pornography. *Henry and June* played in only 307 cinemas (In the Land of the Free), and grossed about $11 million. Critics pointed out that other 1990 films, such as *Wild At Heart* and *Total Recall*, combined sex and violence in a much more sinister way than *Henry and June*, while other critics said that other movies, such as *Desert Hearts* (Donna Deitch, 1985) and *Personal Best* (Robert Towne, 1982) had more explicit depictions of lesbianism than *Henry and June*. Observers noted that, over a year after *Henry and June* had been given an 'NC-17' certificate, there had been no studio-financed and studio-distributed 'NC-17' movies. That is, no 'serious', 'adult', non-pornographic films. It seemed that the major studios were not convinced by the creation of the 'NC-17' rating: they still regarded the 'NC-17' label as a different name for an 'X' rating.

ADDENDUM.
*PRETTY WOMAN.*

*Pretty Woman* (directed by Garry Marshall, produced by A. Milchan and S. Reuther, and distributed by Buena Vista), was a giant success. *Pretty Woman* cost $18 million to make (a lot more than *Whore!*), but generated $82 million in rentals in the domestic (U.S.A.) market alone. *Pretty Woman* grossed $177 million in the U.S.A. and over $200 million overseas by the end of its theatrical run (total gross was c. $438.2m). The lead-up marketing to the film had included the re-release of the Roy Orbison title song and other singles.

*Pretty Woman* had echoes of *Cinderella* and *Pygmalion*, a traditional fairy tale modernized. It was popular with female audiences.[11] *Pretty Woman* was an archetypal Walt Disney project: it was a high concept film; easy to market; it appealed to women;

---

10 Yep, Chingmy Yau as Kitty is sensational in thigh-high, black boots and a fitted, red mini-dress (or, as in the publicity photos for *Naked Killer*, leather shorty-shorts and a bandolier covering her tits).
11 J. Gelmis: "A Sexy Cinderella, or 'My Best Hooker'", *Newsday*, Oct 19, 1990; G. Fairikant: "*Pretty Women* Finds Best Friend in Profit", *New York Times*, July 21, 1990.

it was aspirational, glamorous, stylish, funny, romantic, a feel-good movie with a happy ending. It didn't have expensive stars (apart from Richard Gere); it was relatively cheap to make (much of the action takes place on single sets, with two actors); it was blissfully conservative, happily populist, and unashamedly formulaic, predictable and undemanding. It was the perfect movie for the adult brand of the Disney film studio. (Although popular with female audiences, feminists could find much to irritate them in *Pretty Woman,* from the title and the title character on down.)

*Pretty Woman* was definitely a film with 'legs'; it kept on drawing in audiences, so that, by the 17th week, it was still playing in 1,200 theatres in North America, and competing with the Summer blockbusters. Meanwhile, *Whore* was probably seen by about three people (and two of them would've been friends of the publicist).[12] If Ken Russell had had a hit of that magnitude in the 1990s, we might've seen many of his long-cherished projects coming to fruition (*Nijinsky, Beethoven, Evita, Maris Callas,* etc).

---

12 According to Box Office Mojo (online), *Whore* grossed $1 million in the U.S.A., though I can't believe that.

Two movies from the 1990s directed by Ken Russell

# 24

# *THE MYSTERY OF DR MARTINU*

*The Mystery of Dr Martinu* (1992) was another curio in Ken Russell's long (and unique) career of manufacturing curios. Very few television companies (and even fewer commercial ones) would commission and pay for (and broadcast) a drama-documentary-fantasy like *The Mystery of Dr Martinu!* It starred Patrick Ryecart as Boshuslav Martinu, Hannah King as his gorgeous mistress Slava, Amanda Ray-King as his wife Donna, Martin Friend as the doctor, Professor Mirisch, and Tamzin Outhwaite as a girlfriend. Russell's daughter Victoria did the costumes, and his son Xavier was the editor.[1] Also on the team were Reiner Moritz, Josef d'Bache-Kane, Brian King (vfx) and Clive Mackey.

It's one of Ken Russell's collections of wild imaginings inspired by the music of a classical composer. The recipe had been well-established by 1992:

(1) You put on some records;

(2) As the music plays you imagine all sort of crazy stuff;

(3) Which you go out and film (after remembering to write down the visions you had while listening to the music).

Well, you can do that if you're Ken Russell, that is! It's not as simple as that, but that's what *The Mystery of Dr Martinu* amounts

---
[1] Some of the editing in some of Russell's work for television, it has to be said, doesn't quite have the punch, the self-assurance or the invention of the finest editing work in the movies he directed. Also on a technical level, the sound in the later television pieces has that horrible, trebly audio which picks up every rustle of clothing, but actually distracts from the show.

to. Altho' part of *The Mystery of Dr Martinu* comprises a documentary, most of it is staged in a heightened, self-conscious, and highly theatrical manner. One wonders what the audience made of it – if you don't know Bohuslav Martinu's music, or his biography, some of what happens in *The Mystery of Dr Martinu* must appear confusing or crazy (how many people had even heard of Martinu before this TV show?).

Bohuslav Martinu (Dec 8, 1890 - Aug 28, 1959) was a Neo-classical composer and violinist who lived (and studied) in Prague, followed by Paris (in 1924) and the U.S. of A. (in 1941). He produced operas (*The Miracles of Our Lady, Ariadne, The Voice of the Forest*), 6 symphonies, choral works (*The Epic of Gilgamesh*), and chamber pieces.

An actor with a huge amount of work in British television (like many of the actors who appeared in Russell's work), Patrick Ryecart plays Bohuslav Martinu with a suave aloofness that seems out of keeping with the rest of the piece. Ryecart also delivers the dialogue as if he's providing the voiceover for a toothpaste or insurance TV commercial.

*The Mystery of Dr Martinu* contains plenty of self-consciously surreal/ OTT Ken Russell moments: Slava and a German soldier enacting WW2 as a silly game of table football; Slava dancing naked with a flag; Slava giving a guy head while Bohuslav Martinu watches in envious agony (from the other side of a door), only to see the guy now sitting in an electric chair and frying; Martinu watching a movie of his life in North America (as *Donald and Donna*) in a cinema, with popcorn and cola; and some visual effects scenes (Martinu falling onto some rocks, for instance, or some butterflies and flowers forming the backdrop to a sex scene between Slava and her lover).

Many of the ingredients of *The Mystery of Dr Martinu* are regulars in the Ken Russell cosmos: mysterious happenings, dancing, symbolic acts and objects, and filming by the sea on the South Coast of England. Bohuslav Martinu wakes up repeatedly in the sand dunes by the ocean (reminiscent of *A Matter of Life and Death*), and reviews his life. In the distance, atop a lighthouse, his naked mistress Slava calls to him like a siren, while in the foreground events play out in a theatrical style from his life.

Or something like that.

Forget the 'story', forget the aspects of exposition and information² in *The Mystery of Dr Martinu* (about Bohuslav Martinu's life, about his visits to France or the U.S.A., etc), which the filmmakers seem to include merely as sops to the commissioning TV company (who always have an eye on the 'public broadcasting' angle their bosses and investors know they need to stay in business), forget all of that, and enjoy the ditzy, abstract, sexy and over-the-top images and concoctions that Ken Russell and the team deliver in this 1992 TV show.

Give Ken Russell some money for shooting on a beach, rent a lighthouse for a week, hire three or four actors, and this is what he'll come back with! And what hangs it all together? You should know by now! You don't need to ask: THE MUSIC. Yep, it's *the music*, not the visuals, not the Nazis playing table football, not the nudity and sex, not the anguished expressions that Patrick Ryecart pulls as his life goes tits-up, it's *the music* (which plays pretty much all the way thro'). The filmmakers have decided that whatever else they're gonna do, they're gonna make sure that the viewer listens to plenty of classical music.

Take the lighthouse location³ in *The Mystery of Dr Martinu*, for example: it is exploited in the classic Ken Russell manner: no, not for the finale of a science fiction flick like *The Day of the Triffids* (actors vs. man-eating plants! They kill the triffids with sea water and hoses! Gack!), but for the composer to chase his naked mistress Slava up the stairs, all the way to the very tippermost top. Where she appears as the enigmatic, ghostly *anima* figure that haunts all of Russell's hapless, dreaming, horny artists, framed behind the fracturing lens of the lighthouse's lamp. And then she pushes the artist off the top, onto the rocks below. Again and again. (Well, that's what lovers do to you, isn't it?!).

Love and death, sex and death – Slava is one of Ken Russell's funniest incarnations of the artist's muse, of 'woman' as *femme fatale*, sexily hypnotic and hypnotically deadly. She's introduced nude, dancing and waving a flag as she runs over some grass. And soon she's dancing draped with the gauzy flag in the middle of the theatrically-stylized room that Martinu shares with his wife

---

2 There *is* information that's delivered about Bohuslav Martinu, tho', in this 1992 production. We do find out quite a bit about Martinu (particularly in the second half).

3 The locations for *The Mystery of Dr Martinu* were in and around Eastbourne, Sussex, where Russell has filmed many times (notably in *The Debussy Film*). The lighthouse, for example, is at Dungenness (a favourite location with photographers and filmmakers; Derek Jarman had a house down here, with a celebrated garden which you can still visit).

(he plonks away on a piano (at one point it's a toy piano), while his wife churns out money on a Singer sewing machine).

Poor Bohuslav Martinu hurries up the stairs of the lighthouse one too many times, only to find Slava getting jiggy with her many lovers. Impotence and voyeurism, in the classic Alfred Hitchcock manner (*à la Psycho*), are played out for the *n*-th time in Ken Russell's cinema, as Martinu pitifully spies on Slava fucking a guy and blowing another. Hannah King, playing many of her scenes naked, is terrific (with a gorgeous body) in a role that requires plenty of dancing and gestural acting.

*The Mystery of Dr Martinu* is also a send-up of Ken Russell's own musical biographies. By this time, he'd produced so many of them, he knew the form backwards. Yet certain elements still inspired the film director, provoking some kind of reaction in him. Apart from the music (obviously!), there was sexual jealousy: erotic tension is an energy or force or emotion that has powered many of Russell's finest moments in cinema and TV (as with most of the great filmmakers – yes, folks, love and sex are still the major themes of all cinema). War is another *bête noire* that drives Russell to furious rages. Another is the uneasy relation between an artist and his audience. And death. And finally – and always – let's we forget the *real* reason for making *The Mystery of Dr Martinu*, there is music, *music*, MUSIC!

*The Mystery of Dr Martinu* is divided in two parts: the first is the dream, the nightmare and the fantasy section; the second is the explanation. The second section is far less compelling: in it, Bohuslav Martinu recovers in a hospital while his doctor, Professor Mirisch (Martin Friend) visits him. Their conversations, filmed in a simple manner of singles and two-shots (with only the occasional tracking shot or unusual angle), are dully scripted, with the question-and-answer format providing information about Martinu's life. Well, folks, there are many ways to deliver exposition, such as voiceover, captions, inserts, flashbacks, etc, but the solution here of a psychiatrist figure drawing out his patient is too unadorned, too straightforward. But I guess it fulfils the demands of television to 'inform' and 'educate' as well as 'entertain' (British TV is still founded on Reithian ethics). You can see Ken Russell and the teams champing at the bit in many of his documentaries – they would rather be exploring dreams and heightened fantasy, than churning thru page after page of expositional dialogue.

Talky scenes, as we all know, scupper many a filmmaker, even the celebrated ones (Steven Spielberg for instance dislikes filming long, talky scenes, and it shows).[4]

---

[4] Indeed, many Hollywood movies, from any moment in history since the talkies, fall flat on their face during the talky scenes.

The Mystery of Dr Martinu (1992)

# 25

# *LADY CHATTERLEY*

INTRO: IT DOESN'T WORK.

I can sum up my view of *Lady Chatterley* (directed by Ken Russell for the British Broadcasting Corporation and London Film Productions in 1993) in one, simple phrase:

*It doesn't work.*

Now, you know by now that I am a MAJOR FAN of the films of Ken Russell, and have regarded him as the greatest living British director ever since – well, Michael Powell, I guess (and even when he's dead, Russell is still the greatest living film-maker!). Russell is a fantastically amazing film magician, one of the greats without a doubt. He directed *Dante's Inferno*. He directed *The Music Lovers*. He directed *Delius: Song of Summer*. He directed *The Devils*. He directed *Tommy*.

But there are times when, for all sorts of reasons (but very often the script and the concept), it just doesn't work. And *Lady Chatterley* is one of those times.

What a pity. I know, I know: because the ingredients sound very promising: Ken Russell *plus* D.H. Lawrence *plus* Lady Chatt-erley's Lover! How could it fail? But it did. And I *really* wanted this piece to work. Unfortunately, not every outing can be *The Devils* or *Tommy*.

Why doesn't *Lady Chatterley* work?

Chiefly for the same reason that *The Rainbow* didn't work: *the script*. *Lady Chatterley* has a script credit from Michael Haggiag and Ken Russell. And it's because the fiction of D.H. Lawrence is a heap big challenge to adapt for the screen: in short, it demands heightened, abstract, alternative or visionary interpretations.

*Women In Love* is a slightly different case: not only was that movie only part of the novel (as with *The Rainbow*), it worked as a movie in its own terms. But when you compare the 1969 picture with the 1920 novel, oh no, *Women In Love* is not particularly successful at all.

In short – and this is so cruel to say – I don't think any of Ken Russell's adaptions of D.H. Lawrence's novels are successful as adaptions for the screen. He and his production teams have taken on the Three Big Novels by the Midlands Maestro, but if you know (and love) the novels, they are very disappointing.

But if you judge *Women In Love*, *The Rainbow* and *Lady Chatterley* as pieces of cinema or television, you also have to admit that, of the three, only *Women In Love* is truly successful.

The chief flaw in the 1993 BBC *Lady Chatterley* is the script. And it so often is when we're talking about lit'ry adaptions. In short, the script does *not* capture the essence of the three *Lady C* novels – *The First Lady Chatterley*, *John Thomas and Lady Jane* and *Lady Chatterley's Lover* – the atmosphere of the novels, the themes of the novels or even some of the major imagery of the novels. And, disregarding the source material, it does not work on its own, as a TV series.

Ah, at least Ken Russell and the production team will pick up some of the great imagery in the novels, one might imagine, and transfer them into spellbinding cinema (or rather, spellbinding television). But they *don't* in *Lady Chatterley*. They just don't.

If you go back to the 1920s books, you find Lorenzo waxing lyrical, as only he can, about trees and woods and pheasants and daffodils and living things. But the 1990s TV series simply doesn't deliver that.

Too much of the 1993 *Lady Chatterley* TV series is talky, talky, talky, and waaaay too static. It's far too much like run-of-the-mill TV drama and not enough like a Ken Russell piece. With Russell, you expect something special, something out-there.

Oh, the BBC TV series does deliver some typical Russelliana: in the first episode, for instance, there's a lengthy, erotic dream sequence in which Connie Chatterley rides a black stallion (the black stallion of the senses, from Socrates, signposted when Clifford reads aloud to Constance), along a summery, garden path lined with red flowers and draped with topless soldiers. They're all young and sexy with khaki pants and bare chests.[1] The fantasy closes with Constance being unable to rescue Clifford, who's drowning in a pool.

This's one of the places where *Lady Chatterley* becomes cinematic – and very much in the Ken Russell manner. In another scene, Connie answers her husband's ringing of the bell from his bed by appearing naked in his room with a veil over her face (she'd mentioned earlier that it would be nice to see people's bodies, not only their faces). The frustration that Clifford feels bursts into rage.[2]

*Lady Chatterley* is certainly good at hammering home the point that Constance Chatterley must be sexually frustrated because she hasn't got a husband who can satisfy her. The script ensures that *everyone* from here to Timbuktu understands that plot point, even though Connie denies it all the time.[3]

Ken Russell's and Michael Haggiag's *Lady Chatterley* was a co-production between London Films, BBC Films and Global Arts. It was shot on 35mm film and broadcast in four 50-minute episodes, which enabled Russell to make a better job of the three novels, he claimed, than he did with *Women In Love*.

Michael Haggiag should take much of the credit for *Lady Chatterley* – he was not only the co-writer, but also the producer. Johan Eliasch, Robert Haggiag, Tom Donald and Barry Hanson were executive producers. Marina Gefter and Wendy Oberman were associate producers.

Pretty much everybody would agree that a four-part TV series adaption of a long novel can do the source material better justice than a two-hour movie. Well, usually, yes. And if you want to tease out all of the material in D.H. Lawrence's three 1920s versions of *Lady Chatterley*, then, yes, 200 minutes would seem to be better than two hours.

But in the case of 1993's *Lady Chatterley*, I don't agree: I

---

[1] Joseph Lanza identifies the young guys here as a nod to Derek Jarman's movies (307), and I think he may be right.
[2] But, Jeez, hasn't he got hands and a tongue?!
[3] Imaginative viewers might be able to think of erotic experiences Connie and Clifford could enjoy – without the need for a penis or an erection. But in them days, no no no, it had to be the dick and nuttin' else. Or at least, in the world of D.H. Lawrence, it had to be the phallus and nothing else. No clitoris, for instance, in Lorenzo's sexual philosophy: his negative views of clitoral sex, for instance, are well-known.

wonder if *Lady Chatterley* might've fared much better as a two-hour movie. Certainly there were scenes in the TV series which would've been dropped instantly for a feature film version (the excursion for a spot of painting, for instance). A two-hour movie would've been much pacier, for a start, and it would probably have stuck firmer to the central spine of the D.H. Lawrence novels. The TV series was too meandering, too diffuse.

Another problem with *Lady Chatterley* is the casting. Now, the three principals – Joely Richardson,[4] Sean Bean and James Wilby – are all fine actors, who have done some great work. But none of them quite suit their characters, or play their characters in a way that fits the material, and the tone. It's not simply that every reader has their impression of each character, and that the actors don't look like that (but it is true that the actors are not as the characters are described in the book: Connie Chatterley is much fleshier and curvier than Richardson, for instance, and Oliver Mellors is much tougher and gruffer than Bean. Of the three, Wilby's interpretation of Clifford Chatterley comes out best, but is still very different from the Clifford in the three *Lady Chatterley* books).

It's more that the actors don't seem to have embodied the characters – the way that, say, Martin Sheen in *Apocalypse Now* (1979) completely embodies Captain Willard, or Orson Welles in *Chimes At Midnight* (1966) wholly embodies Falstaff.

Or maybe it's just that the performances in some of Ken Russell's other movies – *The Devils*, *The Music Lovers*, *Mahler*, *Tommy* – are so much more successful in comparison.

ON SOME OF THE DELETED CHARACTERS.

Towards the end of the four-part *Lady Chatterley*, the momentum stumbles and wavers. In the 1928 novel, the drama becomes increasingly desperate, with the return of the formidable Bertha Coutts, and Oliver Mellors taking up with his wife again. The 1993 adaption did away with Coutts completely, so she is a shadowy presence referred to in dialogue by other characters (though Mellors' mom appears, played by Pat Keen). Dropping Bertha, though, alters the book a good deal: in the 1993 TV adaption, Mellors, poor dear, gets beaten up by Bertha's brother,

---

4 Ken Russell of course used Joely Richardson's mom, Vanessa Redgrave, in *The Devils*, and her sister, Natasha Richardson, in *Gothic*.

and goes to work in another colliery. In the novel, Bertha moves back in with Mellors. (Bertha Coutts adds plenty of sexual jealousy between her and Connie Chatterley and dramatic tension between her and Mellors, fr'instance, which the TV adaption would've benefitted from.[5] Coutts would thus provide a decent enough obstacle to the lovers, which would've enhanced the melodrama).

It's curious that, although *Lady Chatterley* was stretched over four 50 minute episodes, quite a few of the secondary characters were eliminated. Not only Bertha Coutts, but also figures such as Michaelis, one of Connie's previous boyfriends,[6] Charlie May, and Arnold Hammond. Tommy Dukes (Ben Aris) makes an appearance, but barely makes an impression (in the novel, Dukes has quite a few key lines of dialogue).[7]

In fact, Tommy Dukes is another of the characters that D.H. Lawrence repeats, because he shares traits with Oliver Mellors: both are military men; both live somewhat apart from other people; both espouse a similar life-philosophy; and both exalt the phallus (but what Lawrencean man doesn't?!). Like Mellors, Dukes is clearly partly a Lawrencean mouthpiece; much of what he prates not only prefigures what Mellors says, it is also very familiar, Lawrencean metaphysics. Like Mellors, Dukes is mainly womanless: Dukes admits to the stereotype of the army as a surrogate mother: '"[t]he army leaves me time to think, and saves me from having to face the battle of life"' (33). The narrator emphasizes the connection between Dukes and Mellors for Lady C. during one of the first times Connie meets Mellors (50). The decision to drop or severely limit the character of Dukes in the TV series was probably because of the large amount of repetition: that is, in the novel, Dukes is already spouting much of the Lawrencean philosophy that Mellors later takes up.

ASPECTS OF THE PRODUCTION.

Some of the music (by Michael Garrett) isn't particularly distinctive. For other parts of *Lady Chatterley*, Ken Russell and his team seem to have selected out-of-copyright pieces of (I think

---

5 There's also a suggestion in the novel that Bertha Coutts enjoys anal sex.
6 Donald Forbes (Breffni McKenna) instead stands in for Connie's past suitors, an amalgam of characters such as Michaelis and Charlie May.
7 "Give me the democracy of touch, the resurrection of the body!" yells Dukes in *Lady Chatterley's Lover* (78). Tommy Dukes also complains about women not being fleshy enough for him: "[f]ellows with swaying waists fucking little jazz girls with small boy buttocks" (42).

British) music (or maybe BBC library pieces),[8] which don't quite fit. There's a curiously floaty feeling to the marriage of music and image in *Lady Chatterley*: on most Russell outings, music is foregrounded to the point where the images are sometimes secondary. And the music is usually integrated with immense skill into the piece. That flair for integration in *Lady Chatterley* founders.

You'll recognize some of the locations in *Lady Chatterley* – some of it was filmed at Wrotham Park and Gaddesden Place, which Ken Russell had used in, among others, *Gothic*.[9] The rest of *Lady Chatterley* was shot in Oxfordshire and the Isle of Wight (as well as on the ferry between Southampton and the Isle of Wight). The interiors were filmed at Pinewood Studios, as with so many of Russell's other works.[10]

*Lady Chatterley* contained many of Ken Russell's regular players, including Judith Paris and Ben Aris. *Lady Chatterley* was also something of a family affair: Ken Russell's new wife Hetty Baynes played Connie's sister Hilda, and did the choreography, and Xavier Russell (Russell's son) was one of the editors (along with Mick Audsley, Peter Davies and Alan Mackay). Molly Russell and Rupert Russell (Russell's children) also appeared.

Other credits included costumes by Evangeline Harrison, design by James Merifield, music by Jean Claude Petit, the DP was Robin Vidgeon, and the line producer was Ronaldo Vasconcellos.

Ken Russell turned in a fun cameo in *Lady Chatterley*, as Sir Michael Reid, an artist. A jolly figure with a shock of white hair and ruddy face, Russell looked like he was enjoying himself in front of the camera. It's one of the pleasures of the piece, Russell's cameo.

THE LOOK OF *LADY C.*

As to the look, design and style of *Lady Chatterley*, I think each element is very disappointing – certainly when compared to the best of Ken Russell's work. One of the biggest challenges for the art department was to represent the four seasons. And the seasons

---

[8] The Beeb certainly has one of the largest libraries of music anywhere on Earth.
[9] Wragby in *Lady Chatterley* was probably inspired by the Sitwells' home of Renishaw, with other places drawing on Eastwood, Chesterfield, and Staveley.
[10] The TV series of *Lady Chatterley* opens with a church scene (very Lawrencean – and very Russellian!), in which the lines, 'Ours is essentially a tragic age', etc – the first words of *Lady Chatterley's Lover* – are quoted. It's an amusing spoof on Lawrence the preacher, because the speech is delivered by a priest in a pulpit (and Clifford immediately says 'it's absurd').

are *so much* a part of D.H. Lawrence's three *Lady C* novels. I mean, you've just *got* to have Connie Chatterley with the chicks in Spring, or the new life of the trees in Summer.

Because *Lady Chatterley* was filmed from May 11 to July 25, 1992, three of the seasons – Spring, Autumn and Winter – had to be faked. So, as on so many movies, the Winter scenes were shot when it was hot. It's always the way.

But strewing bagfuls of dried leaves around the sets, plus a few shrivelled or browned bushes, just didn't give the right impression or texture of Autumn. Not when the camera is using so wide a lens, and captures the trees in full leaf a few feet above the actors' heads, ruining the illusion.

OK, this sounds like nit-picking. Yeah, *it is*! And on most movies or TV shows, it wouldn't matter a jot. But *Lady Chatterley's Lover* is one novel where, if you're going to try to do a 'faithful' adaption (OK, that's impossible, I know!), or at least an adaption that comes close to the novel (or captures something of the novel – otherwise, why the fuck bother with the novel at all!), you simply gotta have a *really strong* and *really poetic* sense of the seasons, of nature, of living things. This is a novel which's *all about* nature and the seasons. (In short, you need a much bigger budget for the production design, greens dept, and practical effects than you've got here. Or you need a greater amount of attention paid to the atmospheres and textures).

And that's the ironic thing about *Lady Chatterley*, because Ken Russell is one of the few filmmakers working in the commercial world of movies who has an acute sense of the natural world! Look at the way he films the Lake District! But, somehow, that intimate feeling for nature eluded him in 1992-1993. You can see the camera picking up the images, and the sound team have added birdsong or the swooshing of the breeze, but it just doesn't gel.

The alchemy that should take place isn't ignited. The poetry that Ken Russell is famous for – rightly – isn't there on the screen.

If you look back to the films Ken Russell directed such as *The Devils* or *Tommy*, there's a visceral genius to the camerawork. I don't mean only the famous shock effects like the crash zooms or the dynamic, handheld movements, I mean the way that scenes are staged, the way the camera interacts with the performers.

*Lady Chatterley* is filmed in Ken Russell's later style, with wide angles and often static set-ups, rendering the narrative a series of *tableaux* (Russell is credited as camera operator, using his pseudonym Alf Russell, so he was right there in the thick of things behind the camera, as well as being the director and the co-writer).

The *tableaux* and static approach can work fantastically well – think of the films of Sergei Paradjanov, for example, which took the flattened perspectives of *tableaux* to a level of extraordinary sophistication (it worked for the stage play *Salomé's Last Dance*). But in *Lady Chatterley* it dampens the dynamics of the plot and the themes down to the level of mediocre TV drama. A *tableaux* approach to *Lady C* simply does *not* translate the material into compelling television.

And then you've got the worst kind of cinema or television: *people talking in a room*. Talking heads. Static camera. Like filmed theatre, as Robert Bresson once called it. Or filmed radio (which's what most television is: a camera pointed at someone reading from an autocue. Radio on film).

But when *Lady Chatterley* jettisons the 500-page wedge of paper called the script, and shifts into Ken Russell's favoured images-plus-music approach to cinema, it comes alive. Maybe the whole of *Lady Chatterley* could've been done as a silent movie. I know that Russell might have delivered that brilliantly, but of course the British Brainwashing Corporation and London Films and Global Arts didn't want that. They wanted (and paid for) a TV drama series they could show after the 9 p.m. watershed (and later sell on video, and to other territories).

The lighting, too (courtesy of DP Robin Vidgeon) often appears either flat or too bright, as if the sets were being lit for video in a TV studio rather than celluloid. Why is that? Why does so much of *Lady Chatterley*, and other later productions directed by Ken Russell, have such flat, all-over lighting? (Especially when you consider just how many of the great Russellian outings have been stellar in terms of lighting).

SEX IN *LADY C.*

OK, so what about the love and sex in 1993's *Lady Chatterley*? That's what *Lady Chatterley's Lover* is all about, isn't it? Plenty of tupping? A really *good* fuck?!

Oh dear. Not good. Not good at all. D.H. Lawrence wanted

readers to believe that his story was more than just a Good Fuck – a line that is quoted in the 1993 TV series. Lorenzo wanted a new religion founded on the body, on sensuality, on sex. Unfortunately, the 1993 BBC adaption seemed to reduce the novel again to a 'good fuck' (but the fucking depicted in this version of *Lady Chatterley* doesn't seem particularly good or enjoyable).

The trouble with the 1993 BBC adaption of *Lady Chatterley's Lover* is that the whole enterprise boils down to a young wife being bored and restless and aching for sensuality and companionship and, yes, some sex. For the critics who don't like D.H. Lawrence – and there are plenty of them – *Lady Chatterley's Lover* is a terrible novel because it tries to build a new religion or new spirituality out of sex, and also because it reduces love to sex, and also because it presents a tired and clichéd situation, of a young woman deprived of affection and sex when her husband is wounded in the war (it's the 'bored housewife' scenario of porn).

In other words, for the detractors of D.H. Lawrence's Twenties book, Connie Chatterley is an upper-class woman who fancies a bit of sex and finds it with her gamekeeper. And that's all there is to it. It's Mills & Boon or two-cent romantic fiction. It's *Sleeping Beauty* or *Cinderella* with some rough sex thrown in.

And the 1993 TV series does deliver something of that: it sends up the situation as the same time as wanting to keep it straight. And that is very typical of the cinema of Ken Russell, to simultaneously spoof a topic while also playing it straight (which's partly what irritates some viewers about Russell's movies – they can't take something that's meant to be consumed on two apparently conflicting levels).

But Bertie Lawrence intended *Lady Chatterley's Lover* to be *much* more than that. And that's where the 1993 adaption comes unstuck, and that's where all other adaptions of the novel go to pieces, and it's also where *all* screen adaptions of Lawrence's fiction fall apart.

They can render the melodrama, the conflicts between characters, and even a bit of simulated sex (usually badly), but they can't do the transcendence of sex, the religion of sex, the new spirituality based on touch and the body, which Lorenzo was so passionate about, and which fuelled so much of his art.

And yet, *without* that mysticism of sensuality in a D.H. Lawrence screen adaption, you don't have the full impact of the books. Instead, you have melodrama that looks like any other TV costume drama.

In short: D.H. Lawrence's fiction requires something very special from filmmakers. And no one yet has achieved it. *No one.*

Because what do Russell, Haggiag, Eliasch, Hanson, Gefter, Oberman, Vasconcellos and the rest of the production team give us in the 1993 *Lady Chatterley* adaption? Feebly-staged sex scenes, a real lack of chemistry between the principals (Joely Richardson and Sean Bean), some pontifications upon love and women and men, and so the whole project of Lawrencean sensuality and spirituality falls to bits.

The script of the 1993 *Lady Chatterley* is the main problem, because it simply *does not* render the essence (or even the superficial elements) of D.H. Lawrence's three *Lady C.* novels. Assuredly, at the level of the tro-ings and fro-ings between the country house and the hut in the woods and Oliver Mellors' cottage, at the level of the intrigue and melodrama between the four main characters – Connie, Mellors, Clifford and Mrs Bolton – the 1993 *Lady Chatterley* is solid. The narrative set-up at the Wragby mansion between Connie, Clifford, Bolton and the servants is clearly drawn, and the domestic aspects of life there is convincing (the games of chess, trays of food being brought to Clifford, the meal times, the evening pastimes of Clifford reading aloud and Connie sewing, for instance – all of that is great).[11]

Unfortunately, *Lady Chatterley* is not a Jane Austen or E.M. Forster adaption, where people in pretty frocks sip tea in drawing rooms and discuss the weather with the vicar.

There has to be *more* going on than that. This is *Lady Chatterley's Lover*! This is the great, infamous British novel of spiritual, transformative love-making. Or at the very least, a good fuck! And I do mean a *good fuck*. A *really* good, super-transcendent fuck, where the lovers are coming in mystical bliss.

But aside from the problems with the script, and the casting, you have to acknowledge that the direction must take some of the blame for the disappointment of the 1993 *Lady Chatterley*. Part of the problem here I think is that Ken Russell simply prefers to portray love and sex in unusual or weird or anything-but-straight ways. Oh, Russell can depict regular sex and love when he wants to, but I get the impression that he's bored by that. Rather like

---

[11] Is this a snapshot of Russell's home life?!

Jean-Luc Godard often said that he tried to make a regular film with regular storylines, but he just couldn't, he always found himself disrupting the usual A-B-C logic of traditional narrative.

So, in a film like *Women In Love*, each sexual encounter was staged and shot in a manner that departed (slightly) from the norm. Also, it really grates, and was a mistake, I think, to have Oliver Mellors always be so rough with Connie Chatterley in the TV *Lady Chatterley*. I mean, he was really man-handling her harshly, like a piece of meat. Although Mellors is meant to be working-class, and passionate (i.e., the stereotypical 'bit of rough'), he's also meant to be a fabulous lover, and a tender lover. And Sean Bean grabbing Joely Richardson like an ape didn't convince: you don't believe for a second that Bean could make Richardson come and come (as Connie does in the novel).

However, when the sex in *Lady Chatterley was* filmed in a regular way – such as when Connie C. visits Oliver M. at his cottage and she straddles him – that too didn't capture anything like the transformative sex that the books portrayed. Because the night in the cottage is the famous 'night of sensual passion'! That is, the scene of anal sex.

It's the highpoint of the sexual discourse in *Lady Chatterley's Lover*, on pages 257-8, chapter sixteen, when sex is used to burn out and purify the body and the soul. Connie reaches to 'the very heart of the jungle of herself'. The lovers embrace in a sharp, searing sensuality, which is intended to be more than sentimentality, or mere hedonism – and more than a good ass fuck – but a religious, ontological catharsis. After it, Connie is purified, made whole. After this an 'ultimate nakedness', a poetry of absolutes, of extremes, of totality.

D.H. Lawrence tries to describe going over the edge in sensuality, a breaking-through. The sexual scenes have been building up to this point, in which Connie Chatterley, as in some fierce, painful religious ritual, loses herself, and is purified by sheer sensuality.

The narrator of *Lady Chatterley's Lover* says it is a phallic, not sexual, transformation, on the 'night of sensual passion'. It is this for him because life sears through the lovers, not sex in particular (sex is the means of the 'democracy of touch', but the phallus = life). D.H. Lawrence put life above passion, sex, desire, phallic transformation or whatever else he called it. Passion, sex, desire, and so on, are simply terms for the manifestation of the Lawrencean life-force. The power behind the phallus is life itself. The means are masculine – the phallus is used in a mystical fashion. The phallus is a god, associated with Pan at the end of *Lady Chatterley's Lover* (315).[12] It is an ithyphallic, pagan, burning religion Lawrence proposed.

The scene of ass fucking in the novel of *Lady Chatterley's Lover* has given literary critics plenty to drool about. Some critics suggested that it was D.H. Lawrence's fear of women that prompted him to employ a scene of anal intercourse.[13] Ridiculous, but typical of the way some critics interpret fiction (i.e., always literally, or, even duller, biographically). In *Lady Chatterley's Lover,* there is an element of sadomasochism in the depiction, with Oliver Mellors the active one, with his phallic thrusting, and Connie Chatterley as the passive recipient (again, a hopelessly reductive view of what sex is and how it is experienced).

The anal intercourse in *Lady C.* also appears 'unfeminine' to some critics, bypassing the vulva, an act that perhaps expresses D.H. Lawrence's latent homosexual desire (as if enjoying anal sex means you're gay! *Arrgh!*).[14] Another suggestion is that the gamekeeper, having 'specific and different phobias about female genitalia' (D. Britton, 51), avoids the pussy.

Some commentators[15] criticized D.H. Lawrence for concealing or misrepresenting the anal sex scene in *Lady Chatterley's Lover.* However, Derek Britton points out (in *Lady Chatterley: The Making of the Novel*) that Lawrence was writing in an age in which an explicit depiction of sodomy would be too controversial (1988, 278).

OK, so the 1993 TV adaption of *Lady Chatterley's Lover* probably wouldn't have got away with depictions of ass fucking. But it didn't even (bother to) suggest that this was what was happening (but D.H. Lawrence too is self-consciously vague – remember that *Lady Chatterley's Lover* was published privately first, because Lawrence knew it wouldn't have been published by an establishment firm).

Ken Russell, Michael Haggiag, Johan Eliasch *et al* also chickened out on the worshipping of the phallus scene, too, where Connie Chatterley kneels in front of Oliver Mellors and coos and

---

12 Quotes are from *Lady Chatterley's Lover* unless otherwise stated.
13 W. Ober, 1979, 113.
14 W. Ober, 112; K. Millett, 241; D. Britton, 51.
15 W. Ober, 114, H. Daleski, 308, E. Delavenay, 60.

caws over his prick. For D.H. Lawrence, the erect phallus was a holy male secret, at the base of secular power. It rises out of gold-red hair, again, the Lawrencean colour of phallic, fiery power:

> The sun through the low window sent in a beam, that lit up his thighs and slim belly and the erect phallos, rising darkish and hot-looking from the little cloud of vivid gold-red hair. She was startled and afraid.
> "How strange!" she said slowly. "How strange he stands there! So big! and so dark and so cock-sure! Is he like that?" (218)

Feminists have rightly sprung upon this scene as an example of D.H. Lawrence's misogyny. He is at least honest, artistically, in this scene. But it can't work. It is laughable. Meanwhile Ken Russell has sent up the whole, phallic worship thing often in his movies – think of the mighty dong that Franz Liszt wields in *Lisztomania*, for example (there are numerous other examples).

In sum, the 1993 TV adaption of *Lady Chatterley* had to convince that the love-making that Connie Chatterley and Oliver Mellors was something special, something more than just a tup in a hut or a rut in the rain. Because that's what the novel promises – and, for those who love *Lady Chatterley's Lover*, it delivers.

It might be reductive and misogynist of D.H. Lawrence to elevate sex so much in a novel, but that's what he did. *Lady Chatterley's Lover* is a novel about the rebirth of a woman through sex as well as love, and the author admits that sex is primary in this instance. So a film or TV or radio or theatrical adaption has to be true to that.

Thus, in a way, Ken Russell was *not* the most suitable director for this project, because he is known for subverting sex as well as conventional melodrama. Russell would not do a straight interpretation of the novel, but even as 'A Ken Russell Movie' or 'A Ken Russell TV Series', *Lady Chatterley* still doesn't work.

CHEER US UP, SPIKE!

To counter the seriousness of the *Lady Chatterley* enterprise, and to finish up, it's worth lightening up with a little humour – courtesy of the brilliant Spike Milligan (Ken Russell had produced a documentary about Milligan in 1959). Milligan later in life created marvellous spoofs of famous works – *The Bible, Wuthering Heights* and *Lady Chatterley's Lover*:

After her affair with Paddy, other men meant nothing to her. Tom Loon meanting nothing to her, nor did Dick Squats, Len Lighthower, nor Lord Louis Mountbatten nor Eric Grins, not even Houdini. No, she was married to Clifford, she would stand by him, something he couldn't do for her. She wanted a good deal from life but this poor cuckolded cripple couldn't give it to her, he had tried but it gave him a nose-bleed. She had insured his legs in the event of him walking again. She thought of Paddy and knew that their affair was at an end, she knew he couldn't keep anything up (Eh?). The world was full of possibilities. There was lots of fish in the sea but no chips. The vast masses of fish were mackerel or herring, so reasoned Constance, if you're not mackerel or herring, you're not likely to find good fish in the sea.

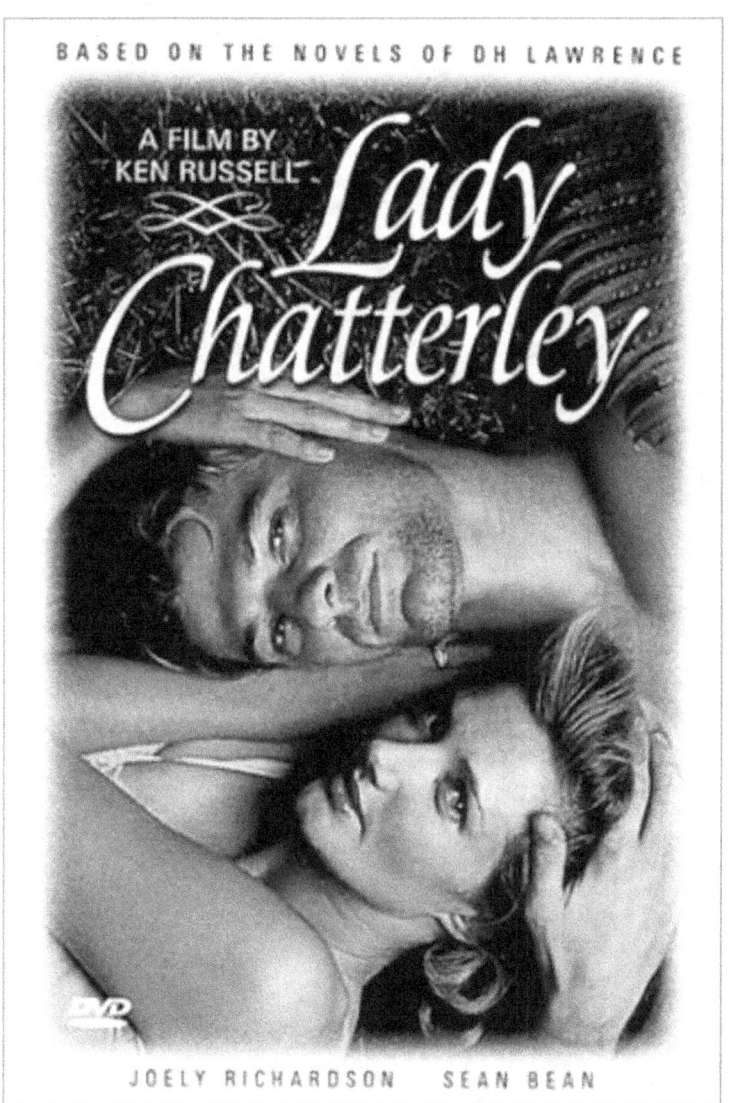

This page and over:
the adaption of D.H. Lawrence's Lady Chatterley novels

Two other adaptions of Lady C, including a dreadful recent French version.

# 26

# *DOGBOYS*

*Dogboys* (a.k.a. *Tracked,* 1998) was certainly an odd movie if you consider it in the context of Ken Russell's career in movies and television. Or put it like this – if you didn't know Ken Russell was the director of *Dogboys*, could you have guessed? With *The Music Lovers* or *Tommy* or *Gothic,* you could've guessed (!), but not from *Dogboys*, which had very few elements which immediately suggested the involvement of Britain's greatest living film director.

*Dogboys* was a TV movie made for Showtime; Hugh Martin, Rob Stork and Christopher Courtney were the producers; Ed Hanna was production designer; Russell's son Xaxier was cutter; Csilla Márki did the costumes; Jamie Thomson was DP; the story and screenplay were by Rob Stork, Dennis Kleinman, Hugh Martin and David Taylor. (Stork seems to be one of the key players in *Dogboys* – he has co-writer and co-executive producer credits).[1]

Among the performers, Dean Cain as the lead and Tia Carrere as the District Attorney officer were both easy on the eye and solid, while Bryan Brown made a suitably nasty piece of work as the psychotic villain Captain Robert Brown (Dean Cain was best-known as Superman in the spin-off TV series). Brown and Ken James (as warden Adam Wakefield) hammed it up wildly, and Sean McCann was low-key but impressive as the go-between and conscience of the piece, Pappy.

---

1 However, producer credits don't mean as much as they used to.

*Dogboys* was a prison drama filmed (like so many recent North American movies and shows, because of the tax incentives) in Canada;[2] however, it was set somewhere in rural America (in the present). The primary locations included the prison, the dog kennels, the D.A.'s office, and the woods where the prisoners help to train the dogs (by trying to run away from them, pursued by the wardens on horseback).

And it was an action movie – yep, here was Ken Russell directing fist fights and face-offs in the American idiom, complete with guns and horses and bullet wounds and squibs and blood. And although Russell had produced many movies, including lots of action, he rarely stages action like this, in this very American TV show manner (I would imagine that stunt co-ordinator John Stoneham had a lot to do with it).

*Dogboys* was solid from every angle, and had a genuine sense of menace in the depiction of prison wardens hunting down convicts for real, stringing them up like deer and collecting their prison numbers and photos (as hunting trophies). But it wasn't much more than that. Those hoping for some of the much-loved Ken Russell flourishes will not find them in *Dogboys*.

There is one scene in *Dogboys* which's typical Ken Russell, though, and that's where the D.A. officer (Tia Carrere) rushes in to Wakefield's (Ken James) workplace to find the prison manager dressed in fetish gear playing strip poker with three buxom, topless women. Here, Russell sneaks some nudity into a run-of-the-mill TV drama (I bet this scene was Russell's idea, and I bet the TV execs hated it!). And the best thing about it is that the D.A. agent, who's a stiff-ass, by-the-rulebook kinda woman, doesn't do the obvious and go ballistic, but barely reacts.

And the bad guy, Captain Brown, listens to classical music (Johann Sebastian Bach) on headphones as he pursues his prison quarry on a big, white horse (vaguely D.H. Lawrencean). And in a brief scene, the D.A. officer's assistant is depicted in a car with a transvestite.

But aside from these minor elements, *Dogboys* is far away from the finest of Ken Russell's cinema – not only in quality and approach, but also in its themes and story. *Dogboys* is the kind of

---

[2] The limitations of the budget of *Dogboys* are apparent: for instance, at least some of those dogs-chasing-convicts scenes should really have been shot at night, to make them more suspenseful and more atmospheric. But night shoots are expensive (a scene in *The Rainbow* was shifted from outside to indoors to cut the budget, for instance).

movie that Sam Peckinpah or John McTiernan or Howard Hawks might've enjoyed directing. It's very much men in a man's world stuff, a testosterone fest, with plenty of macho posturing.

Ken Russell has made movies with a hothouse, interior environment, where a bunch of people are thrown together – *The Devils* and *Delius: Song of Summer*, for instance. But this journey into the darker side of contemporary North America, with its gun culture and hunting culture, and the male penitentiary setting and relationships, just isn't Russell's sort of thing at all.

Ken Russell has turned in some wonderful explorations of the bleaker aspects of American Dream – most notably in *Crimes of Passion*, and also *Altered States*. The problem with *Dogboys* is that the script is too predictable, taking an obvious good guys and bad guys approach (i.e., the typical Hollywood way). Whereas a more ambiguous take would be so much more interesting – in the portrayal of Captain Brown especially, but also the people around him like Wakefield and Pappy who also knows what's going, that prisoners are being hunted and killed like animals.

Or maybe Ken Russell should've been allowed to include some chorus girls in bunny outfits wearing gas masks running through the scenes. *Dogboys/ Tracked* is a director-for-hire gig for Russell: there's no connection to the material, and afterwards you wonder why you watched it (you will never have those ninety minutes back!).

# 27

# OTHER MOVIES AND PROJECTS

*AMELIA AND THE ANGEL.*
*Amelia and the Angel* (1957) was a consciously Roman Catholic-themed movie, starring 9 year-old Mercedes Quadros, daughter of the Ambassador of Uruguay. Seldom seen, it is known mainly from a photograph of a grinning Quadros holding up the angel's wings that feature prominently in the piece (it's included on the British Film Institute release of *The Devils*). Russell had approached the Catholic Film Institute for assistance (but they were broke; Tony Evans offered moral support). The BFI gave him £152.13.0 ($228) to make the movie (Bax, 15).

*Amelia and the Angel* is a charming, quaint and modest piece, which suffers from far too many shots of the heroine doing nothing but walking, walking and more walking (around locations in London) – a mistake that so many students and young filmmakers make (they have the actors, the location, and the camera, but they don't know what *to do* with it all). Yet *Amelia and the Angel* contains numerous elements that crop up later in the Russellian universe: Catholic imagery, dance, handheld camera, silent movie comedy, location shooting, artists and models, art, statues, etc.

POP GOES THE EASEL.

*Pop Goes the Easel* (tx 1962.3.25) is an unusual television documentary about four British Pop artists: Peter Blake, Pauline Boty, Peter Phillips and Derek Boshier (all in their twenties). Altho' Ken Russell had directed about 18 documentaries before *Pop Goes the Easel*, there is still an awkwardness and discomfort with the subject matter: artists. Just what is an artist, what does an artist do, and how do you film artists? Russell got *a lot* better than this! *Pop Goes the Easel* is unusual in only depicting the artists at work at the end of the piece. Instead, they shown are sitting about smoking, drinking tea from stripey mugs (so British!), and talking (tho' their conversations are dispensed with in favour of the artists musing in voiceover about their art). There's no attempt at offering a critical or historical context to the art or the artists, outside of Huw Wheldon's to-camera introduction and his narration (which is soon abandoned).

There are scenes in *Pop Goes the Easel* where the artists dramatize aspects of themselves or their art, tho' only Pauline Boty's dream/ nightmare sequence makes any impression (filmed in the curving corridors of what appears to be the Beeb's Broadcasting House in Londinium).[3] Riding around in a big, American car (still unusual in Britain at the time), visiting a fun fair, making more tea, smoking more cigarettes – *Pop Goes the Easel* comes across as a very studenty sort of TV documentary, where inspiration goes out of the window, and the filmmaking team seems happy to film people doing not much of anything. (Yet by 1965, with *The Debussy Film*, Russell and his cohorts would nail the young, media-oriented, London scene perfectly).

One of the curious aspects of *Pop Goes the Easel* is its laidbackness, its inclusion of a host of casual, inconsequential details. The sound is unusual, too,[4] with the music dipping out many times to be replaced by, for instance, the pings and bells of a pinball machine, which's played with the determination of a 1960s Jean-Luc Godard movie (that is, monotonously and incessantly). Why is a girl with long, blonde hair playing pinball interesting? Well, here it is! Or is it that, the camera, desperately seeking sexiness and summat interesting to shoot, latches on to attractive blondes?!

---

3 The nightmare sequence also employs jump cuts – in a manner which suggests the influence of *Breathless*; there are also rapid dolly shots *à la Breathless*.
4 Allan Tyrer was editor, as often in Russell's *Monitor* work.

(Pauline Boty also shines under the lens).[5]

Because, let's face it, Peter Blake sitting below one of his paintings and drinking tea does not make for fascinating television.

The camera pans over many artworks in *Pop Goes the Easel* – and many of the artists of the period must've griped about the British Broadcasting Corporation being so cheap as to shoot in black-and-white (and 16mm, not 35mm, too!). This is a show about Pop Art! And it's in black-and-white! Oh man – shades of grey do look nice, and might be suited to gritty, kitchen sink dramas of the early 1960s, or a documentary about Ad Reinhardt (five-foot square black canvases), but have you seen any Pop Art? Colour is *utterly fundamental* to it!

Historically, tho', the *Pop Goes the Easel* documentary does have a charm of its own. If you know anything about British culture of the 1960s, you'll know that for young people, America loomed large. The myth and legend of the New World, its music, its movies, its superstars, its rock stars, its bluesmen, informed so much of pop culture in the Sixties. The Rolling Stones, the Who, the Beatles, David Bowie – and, well, *everybody* – has cited the significance of American culture in their formative years in the 1950s and 1960s.

In *Pop Goes the Easel,* Derek Boshier, for instance, discusses the impact of Americanization on England, so that a simple act like eating breakfast means literally consuming Yankee culture in the form of cereal boxes with their free toys and cartoon strips on the back. This is of course one of Ken Russell's pet peeves – the grotesque over-commercialization of British life (which he would send up many times).

And what began in the 1950s and the 1960s in Britain has become today even more widespread – Americanation and globalization is absolutely everywhere in dear, old Blighty. The Allies won World War Two, as Jean-Luc Godard wryly noted, and Amerika filled the cultural vacuum. Amerika won the cultural war.

For the Ken Russell fan, *Pop Goes the Easel* also contains numerous Russellisms, including dancing (a too-long scene of the

---

[5] The sexual aspects of this foursome of three guys and a girl isn't explored in the documentary. There's a suggestive scene, fr'instance, where Boty is depicted waking in her bedsit (where she sleeps and lives alone, of course! Like a good unmarried girl in the early 1960s), and the three guys call for her, hanging around on the street below as she gets dressed inside.

young artists and their chums doing the twist), movie references (clips from a Fred Astaire musical), pinball machines (*Tommy*), and a ton of music (including show tunes, Buddy Holly and Elvis Presley). There is also a visit to a wrestling match, another form of movement, and a precursor of the most famous scene in Russell's entire career, in *Women In Love*.

### FRENCH DRESSING.

*French Dressing* was Ken Russell's troubled entry into feature filmmaking of 1963. Intended to be a comedy about a British seaside town making a bid for glamour and sensation, it had a script written by many hands (including Peter Myers and Johnny Speight) that wasn't particularly funny. And Russell found that this kind of British humour wasn't his strong point, either. It didn't work. There was a terrible press screening which Russell attended, where everybody ignored him. In 1973, Russell said: 'I didn't know how to handle actors at that time. I didn't know one has to be a psychologist and a Dad and Mum as well as a director' (Bax, 148).

### ALWAYS ON SUNDAY.

*Always On Sunday* (tx 1965.6.29), a BBC *Monitor* biopic about French primitive painter Henri Rousseau (1844-1910), also known as the Douanier (the customs officer), was one of the least successful (and least enjoyable) of Ken Russell's collaborations with writer Melvyn Bragg. The problems included: (1) Henri Rousseau wasn't a particularly interesting personality, and neither was his lifestyle;[6] (2) the script didn't find imaginative ways of depicting a painter, what a painter does, and how they work (which other movies have also attempted, and found difficult); (3) the film gave no indication of the artist's inner life, or what made him tick (despite the quiet authority of Oliver Reed reading Bragg's commentary, which contained tons of information but failed to come alight); and finally, (4) the guy that Ken Russell chose to play the Douanier was Yorkshire painter James Lloyd (Russell had filmed a *Monitor* portrait of Lloyd in 1964).

Unfortunately, James Lloyd could not act. At all. Not even a teensy bit. Lloyd's stodgy, gruff and non-actorly interpretation of Henri Rousseau lent *Always On Sunday* a tired, rather hopeless

---

[6] For Russell, *Always On Sunday* was about 'the very ordinary life of that very extraordinary man Henri Rousseau' (Bax, 127).

atmosphere. Of course, that suited the exploration of an artist who struggled for decades b4 achieving even a modest success.[7] It was Vincent van Gogh's story all over again – years of trying to sell a painting, being misunderstood by everyone, including loved ones, etc (there was a recurring motif of Rousseau schlepping his paintings by cart along the River Seine to an annual art exhibition). Except that van Gogh blazes with passion, and Rousseau came across as a bland, unimaginative and very boring, middle-aged man.[8] Russell was insistent, however, that *Always On Sunday* 'proved my great belief in going on instinct with actors' (Bax, 127).

No, it didn't.

The notion of an artist who's stubbornly (but also genuinely) simple or modest or just plain stupid is intriguing. *Always On Sunday* depicted that side of Henri Rousseau, with his friends (such as poet Guillaume Apollinaire) playing pranks on him.

Also, it should be said that Henri Rousseau's art is still an acquired taste – for me, it's preposterous and laughable (just as the gallery-goers laugh at it). Yes, Gotham's MOMA might've valued one of Rousseau's paintings at a million dollars, as the narration mentions right at the end, and Wassily Kandinsky, Robert Delaunay and Pablo Picasso might've been fans of the Douanier, but so what? It's still unappealing, unilluminating art.

There were two moments when *Always On Sunday* took fire, though: one was when Annette Robertson (sensational in *The Debussy Film*), appeared in drag as the pint-size, ultra-bohemian Alfred Jarry. Zinging into *Always On Sunday* and Henri Rousseau's life on a bicycle, with hat and moustache and studiedly dishevelled attire,[9] Robertson's Jarry lifted the energy of the 1965 documentary by a few thousand degrees, and when he (she) was gone, the show deflated like a burst, red balloon. Scenes in Jarry's bohemian garret were terrific, with its ceiling lowered to five feet! Best of all was Jarry's habit of firing pistols at glass bottles, a little bit of the American West.

---

[7] In representing the Douanier as a misunderstood and much-maligned artist, the filmmakers had to ignore a banquet given in his honour in 1908, at which Pablo Picasso, Robert Delaunay, Guillaume Apollinaire and others were guests.

[8] Also, *Always On Sunday* is filmed in a manner that resembles the British 'kitchen sink' movies of the late 1950s and early 1960s – the kind of socialist realist claptrap that Russell railed against (the locations, which look like Newcastle or Manchester standing in for Paris, evoke English fog and cold and dreariness). Rousseau might be a miner soon to be laid off.

[9] It was a pity that Robertson was dubbed (poorly – hopefully intentionally poorly) by a guy with a Yorkshire accent.

What a pity *Always On Sunday* didn't shove Henri Rousseau and his cartload of crappy paintings into the River Seine five minutes into the show, and follow Alfred Jarry instead?

The second enjoyable outing in *Always On Sunday* was the recreation of a performance by *avant garde* guru Père Ubu (played by Ken Russell regular Bryan Pringle). Fun and games with actors on stage pretending to eat shit ladled out of a piss-pot (shit being a favourite theme with 20th century *avant garde* artists).

Ultimately, *Always On Sunday* is a very minor addition to the Ken Russell canon: yes, you can link this portrait of a struggling artist to the film director himself, but why bother? Yes, the key scene where punters in the art gallery laugh at length at Henri Rousseau's paintings, while Rousseau stands to one side, looking forlorn and offering no resistance, is another of Russell's pointed attacks on audiences and critics (yeah, but you know for sure that Ken Russell would *not* stand there while people – critics, punters, artists, presidents, royalty, *anyone* – laughed at his work and say nothing!!).

All well and good. But in the end, Henri Rousseau was no Peter Tchaikovsky or Gustav Mahler or Henri Gaudier-Brzeska. And *Always On Sunday* was no *The Music Lovers*, *Mahler*, or *Savage Messiah*.

ARIA.

*Aria* (Miramax, 1987) was the baby of British producer Don Boyd. Boyd assembled an unlikely group of (mainly British) directors (Nic Roeg, Charles Sturridge, Jean-Luc Godard, Julien Temple, Bruce Beresford, Robert Altman, Franc Roddam, Derek Jarman, Bill Bryden and Ken Russell). Each took part of an opera and filmed it in their own individual style. Russell chose *Nessum Dorma* from *Turandot*, by Giacomo Puccini.

*Nessum Dorma*'s a very famous piece of music, which Ken Russell and his team illustrated with an after-death fantasy, involving a woman (Linzi Drew)[10] who dies in a car crash; the woman imagines or experiences something elaborate, ritualistic and religious, whereas in reality she dies on the operating table (once again, there are echoes of *A Matter of Life and Death*).

---

10 Drew was a topless dance in *Salomé's Last Dance*.

*A BRITISH PICTURE.*

Produced for the British TV arts programme *The South Bank Show*, *A British Picture: Portrait of an Enfant Terrible* (tx 1989.10.15) was Ken Russell's version of his autobiography, *A British Picture* (published the same year). Ronaldo Vasconcellos and Nigel Watts produced; Dick Bush was DP; Russell narrates (and has cameos), his son Rupert appeared as the younger Russell (and other family members were involved, such as Molly, Vivian, and another son, Xavier, edited the film, and his daughter Victoria did the costumes).

In a silly, humorous manner, Ken Russell and co. recreate moments from Russell's life – showing German silent classics during the Blitz; Russell in uniform; visiting Hollywood, etc.

*A British Picture* contains clips from the movies that Ken Russell adored as a child (*Metropolis, Die Niebelungen, Putting On the Ritz*, etc), and clips from his own movies (including *Mahler, Tommy, Dance of the Seven Veils, Clouds of Glory*, etc). At least the clips are worth sitting thru *A British Picture* (they remind you that, yes, Russell is a Great Director).

*A British Picture* is mildly amusing, tho' the childishly satirical approach gets wearying after a while (and Rupert Russell is an appalling child actor, performing gormlessly in a rainbow hued, Hallowe'en wig – *A British Picture* is definitely not one of the great movies featuring child actors!). If you know anything about Ken Russell, *A British Picture* adds little – it's a send-up of the life of Ken Russell filmed in a Ken Russell style.

And if you compare how Woody Allen fictionalized his childhood in movies such as *Annie Hall* (1977) and *Radio Days* (1987), or Ingmar Bergman in *Fanny and Alexander* (1982), *A British Picture* is feeble. And we could cite many filmmakers who have explored their own cinema in documentaries made by themselves (rather than in fiction films): Jean-Luc Godard, Werner Herzog, and Orson Welles (*A British Picture* sure ain't *F For Fake* (Welles) or *Histoir(es) du Cinéma* (Godard)!

*A British Picture* is trying to be funny, but it isn't; it isn't very informative (because the direction is often inept and the narration is unclear – the movie relies too much on the audience already knowing about Russell's film career); and it's not even an 'anti-documentary'.

There are many great stories from Ken Russell's film career

that would benefit from a decent dramatization, but they don't appear in *A British Picture* (for instance, visits to porn merchant Bob Guccione's mansion to discuss *Moll Flanders*, or the lengthy slog and bust-up with Sherry Lansing about *Evita*). Instead, we get the cretinous pantomime of that kid and another kid (Molly) pretending to be the slightly younger Russell and his wife Vivian Jolly, or the real Russell hurrying across the garden to answer the phone, hoping it will be Hollywood calling.[11]

*A British Picture* is further proof (along with the feature films), that Ken Russell lost his way somewhat in the late 1980s (or that he seemed to deliberately subvert his own projects).

❊

*Mindbender* was a 1996 TV movie about the spoon-bender Uri Geller. Produced for Major Motion Pictures, it featured Ishai Golan as Geller, Terence Stamp and Hetty Baynes, and mainly Israeli actors.

### ELGAR: FANTASY ON A COMPOSER ON A BICYCLE.

In 2002 Ken Russell revisited the subject and site of his most famous documentary, on Edward Elgar, for the 25th anniversary season of Britain's *The South Bank Show*. Russell's *Elgar: Fantasy On a Composer On a Bicycle* (tx 2002.9.22) employed the standard Russell structure of exploring an artist's life through their art, he had done so often in the past. In the course of the documentary, Russell visited the famous Elgar sites: his birthplace, his last home, Worcester, Worcester Cathedral, Great Malvern and of course the spectacular Malvern Hills. Russell's narration consisted of brief introductions to extracts from Elgar's greatest hits, which were illustrated by gently dramatized *tableaux* from Elgar's life or general purpose dramatizations. There was little or no local sound: the soundtrack comprised Elgar's music and Russell's short commentaries.[12]

As always, Ken Russell's love of classical music was apparent throughout, his sympathies entirely and uncritically with the composer, whom Russell regarded as the greatest in the modern British era. *Elgar: Fantasy On a Composer On a Bicycle* was one of Russell's most upbeat films: shot in high Summer, it was full of bright, sunny, colourful imagery, a self-consciously nostalgic evoc-

---

11 Melvyn Bragg appears as himself to discuss potential projects.
12 Ken Russell's daughter Victoria did the costumes; and Elize Tribble, Russell's wife, appeared.

ation of the Summers of youth, a world of flowers, thick, long grass, forests, country lanes, the seashore and the serpentine spine of the Malverns.

Unashamedly and unapologetically romantic (as ever), Ken Russell illustrated Edward Elgar's music with images of the composer (James Johnston) and his wife (Caroline Alice Roberts) on their honeymoon by the sea on the Isle of Wight, the composer riding around Worcestershire on a bike, Elgar praying in little churches, playing with his dog by a river, rowing on the River Severn under the shadow of Worcester Cathedral, cycling around Worcester (and into the Cathedral at one point), and so on.

To portray a piece about fairies and giants, the filmmakers shot a group of young girls in blue, fairy costumes prancing about a sunlit glade and a brass band of boys processing through a model village. Along the way, *Elgar* hinted at Elgar's dalliances with several beautiful young women, but in a remarkably (for Russell) discreet fashion (no rutting in the woods here, or the camera emulating the thrusting of copulation; instead, Elgar and an admirer entering a wooden garden hut to shelter from the rain. But the familiar erotic triangles were evoked, with Elgar's wife looking on, decidedly unhappy).

There were flashes of the old Ken Russell, though: one of Edward Elgar's old flames, 'Windflower', was seen dancing in a garden and beside by sea – a scene that might have come out of *Women In Love* or Russell's piece on Isadora Duncan (there was a lot of dancing in *Elgar: Fantasy of a Composer On a Bicycle*). There were many images, too, of the beauty of the landscape, a recurring Russell, pantheistic theme (the first image of *Elgar: Fantasy On a Composer On a Bicycle* was of the composer on a bicycle riding on the Malvern Hills, an obvious reference to one of the most famous Ken Russell images, the boy on the horse on the Hills in his earlier Elgar documentary).

### THE FALL OF THE LOUSE OF USHER.

*The Fall of the Louse of Usher* (2002) was Ken Russell's take on Edgar Allan Poe's famous book. It was a return to classic 19th century literature, and the Gothic and fantastical genres. *The Fall of the House of Usher* had been filmed b4 as *House of Usher* (Roger Corman, 1960)[13] and *House of Usher* (1988, Alan Birkinshaw),

---

[13] The most celebrated version, this starred Vincent Price: the incredible Roger Corman went on to shoot eight more adaptions of Edgar Allan Poe.

among others.[14] Russell had originally planned the project to star Twiggy and Roger Daltrey (PF, 318).

*The Fall of the Louse of Usher* was shot on digital video by a small team of enthusiasts, in and around Ken Russell's home in the New Forest in the South of England (the New Forest is not far from Russell's home-town of Southampton). It was a 'Gorsewood Production' (gorse bushes being found in the area), released through Ken Russell Productions Ltd and Image Entertainment in the U.S.A. A family affair, Russell's daughter Victoria designed the costumes for *The Fall of the Louse of Usher,* his wife Elize Tribble played Usher's sister, and his son Alex was Igor and production designer.

You won't recognize anyone in *The Fall of the Louse of Usher* apart from Ken Russell himself, who plays an eccentric doctor, Dr Calahari[15] (most of Russell's scenes are played opposite the beautiful Nurse ABC Smith, played by 'Tulip Junkie', a.k.a., Marie Findley).[16] Russell camps it up in a parody of a German psychologist, yelling 'achtung!' and 'schnell!' at the cast.

Jack Johnston (from the pop band Gallon Drunk) played the lead and provided the music. Other performers included Elize Tribble, Emma Millions, Peter Mastin, Lesley Nunnerly, Barry Lowe, Sandra Scott and Alex Russell.

*The Fall of the Louse of Usher* is essentially an extended home movie, though distinctly a Ken Russell project, with Russell's customary flourishes. Much of the film pivots around music (including a pop promo, in a graveyard), as in so many Russell productions; unfortunately, the music by Johnston and co. isn't particularly distinctive (and Johnston can't act).

There's not much else to say about *The Fall of the Louse of Usher*: the performances are all high camp, people dicking about, and it's all jolly fun. Lots of sex toys, blow-up animals, tons of masks, wigs and Hallowe'en costumes, references to astrology, Tarot, magicke, etc. You have to take *The Fall of the Louse of Usher* in the spirit it's intended – as a very low budget home movie which isn't meant to be serious at any moment.

But *The Fall of the Louse of Usher* is important in Ken Russell's cinema in two respects: production and distribution. A very low

---

14 The 1988 movie starred Russell regular Oliver Reed as Roderick Usher.
15 Yet another reference to the German Expressionist movie.
16 Marie Findley was an actress and performer, and also screenwriter, and was part of the music act Mediaeval Baebes up until 2007.

budget piece,[17] Russell had complete control over the show, including final cut of course. 'I'm not answerable to anyone but me,' Russell asserted; 'I don't have to get the script approved. I don't have the final cut taken away from me'.[18]

And arranging distribution himself meant he could bypass the multi-national corporations who control much of the distribution of movies globally (and also, presumably, he would take a bigger slice of the returns). The internet was key here, in marketing the new, low budget, digital video movies, and also in distributing them. Finally, home DVD was vital: without a theatrical release, the movies could be sold direct to customers on DVD.

Other movies that Ken Russell produced in this low budget format included *The Lion's Mouth, Boudicca Bites Back, Brave Tart vs. the Loch Ness Monster, A Kitten for Hitler* (2007), and *Hot Pants* (a series of 'sexy shorts'). *The Lion's Mouth* (2000) was a short movie about 'the prostitute's padre', a 1930s rector of Stiffkey (that is, it's sex and religion yet again). The three short films in *Hot Pants* (2006) are *The Revenge of the Elephant Man* (2004, about a guy with an elephantine weenie), *The Mystery of Mata Hari* (2004) and *The Good Ship Venus* (2005).

OPERA.

As well as filmmaking, Ken Russell has also directed[19] opera,[20] as have directors such as Peter Greenaway, Ingmar Bergman, Werner Herzog and Andrei Tarkovsky. Russell directed *Madame Butterfly* by Giacomo Puccini (Spoleto Festival, 1983), *The Italian Woman in Algiers* by Gioacchino Rossini (1984, Geneva), *The Rake's Progress* by Igor Stravinsky (Florence, 1982), *La Bohéme* by Giacomo Puccini (1984, Macreta Festival, Italy), *Die Soldaten* by Bernd-Alois Zimmermann (1984, London), *Méphistophélès* by Arrigo Boito (1989, Genoa), *Salomé* by Richard Strauss (Bonn, 1993), *Princess Ida* by Gilbert & Sullivan (1992, Lyon and London), and *Faust* by Charles Gonoud (1859), staged

---

17 It cost less than $30,000, according to Joseph Lanza (PF, 316).
18 K. Russell, *Reuters*, 2003.
19 In *A British Picture*, Russell claimed that he didn't like opera. Which seems far-fetched from such a classical music buff. But then he was converted
20 Sometimes critics have dubbed Russell's cinema 'operatic', but nobody seems to know what it means. Russell takes it as a compliment: 'in England, the critics always accused me of being operatic. Operatic to them was a dirty word. I took it as a compliment.'

in 1985 in Vienna (available on DVD).[21]

Although there have been attempts to put operas on film, Werner Herzog may be right when he pointed out that the two forms, opera and cinema, have fundamental elements which're incompatible. Ken Russell contributed to the opera anthology *Aria*, and that was one of the better opera movies (but it was still dissatisfying).

---

21 Some of Ken Russell's film collaborators worked on the operas: for instance, artist Paul Dufficey designed the costumes for *Méphistophélès*, and Derek Jarman designed *The Rake's Progress*.

# 28

# UNMADE MOVIES

> What on earth does an out-of-work film director do? He knows all about editing but can't actually join two pieces of film together. He masterminds his sets and costumes and draws like a child. He supervises the light but can't use an exposure meter. He knows how to direct the stars but can't act for toffee himself. Responsible for handling millions of dollars, he can't add up a grocery bill.
>
> Ken Russell, *A British Picture* (146)

I wish Ken Russell had nine lives, so he would be able to produce movies on many more of his favourite topics. Let's see the Nijinsky movie. His Rabelais. His Beethoven film. His version of *Evita*. His *Gerschwin Dream*. And five more musicals. No, ten! And more biopics of classical composers. And, please, some more biographies of poets: Paul Verlaine and Arthur Rimbaud, for a start. Charles Baudelaire. The Brontë sisters. Friedrich Hölderlin. Robert Graves.

And, oh I would *love* to see Ken Russell doing the definitive biography of England's great painter, J.M.W. Turner.[22] The story of Turner has got a few elements that would appeal to Russell, and which we know Russell could run with: the British landscape and the Romantic Sublime; attacks by critics and being misunderstood by his contemporaries; paintings which drew on music; and a passion for making art and the sheer hard work of art. Oh, and

---
[22] J.M.W. Turner crops up in the Tate Gallery sequence in *The Debussy Film*. A film about Turner was released in 2014, with Timothy Spall (*Gothic*) as the artist.

sex.

Because we *need* Ken Russell. Otherwise, we get solidly-made, reverent and ultimately dull portraits of artists, such as the John Keats movie *Bright Star* (Jane Campion, 2009), and the C.S. Lewis weepie *Shadowlands* (Richard Attenborough, 1993).

Every filmmaker has heaps of unmade films, movies that never got made for all sorts of reasons, and Ken Russell is no exception. Following the success of *Women In Love*, Russell was planning a raft of biographical projects, including lives of Edith Piaf, Ludwig II, Sarah Bernhardt, Gustav Mahler, Lytton Strachey and Vaslav Nijinsky. In the end, only the Mahler project came off for Russell (*Nijinsky*, directed by Herbie Ross, was made in the U.K. with Alan Bates as Sergei Diaghilev and George de la Pena as Nijinsky in 1980, and Luchino Visconti directed the Ludwig film in the mid-1970s). Ideas for movies come and go, Russell said, and the old ones recur, but ultimately a choice has to be made, and 'it always seems inevitable' (Bax, 182).

*

In a 2001 *South Bank Show*, Ken Russell explained why he had become 'unbankable': it started with the failure of *Valentino* (Russell blamed Rudolf Nureyev for part of the flop), and backing for personal projects drying up. Then came the call to go to New York to meet Paddy Chayefsky, to direct *Altered States*. Despite the many problems in making the film, *Altered States* was relatively successful (it appeared in the top 25 films for 1980, grossing 25 million green in the U.S.A., putting it at no. 18, ahead of *Caligula, The Fog, The Octagon* and *The Howling*).

After *Altered States*, Ken Russell said he was offered three or so science fiction films and turned them down, not wanting to be typecast as a sci-fi director (the films went on to become successful). It was at this point that Russell became 'unbankable', refusing to play the Hollywood game, to make whatever was offered, to be the director for hire. Indeed, he didn't helm another feature for four years (*Crimes of Passion*, in 1984), and tended to work much more in television than in features from the 1980s onwards (he was also directing opera productions).

*NIJINSKY.*

The Vaslav Nijinsky project had been long cherished by Ken Russell: '[i]t's something I've always been mad about... I think

[Nijinsky] was a mystic genius who danced his philosophy and vision' (Bax, 163). Melvyn Bragg had developed a script for it, and Russell had found his leading man: ballet dancer Christopher Gable. Russell was close to setting up the film in the late 1960s, in the period after *Billion Dollar Brain*. Russell had got producer Harry Saltzman interested, but the *James Bond* producer said he could only obtain backing if Rudolf Nureyev was cast. Tests of Gable in four scenes from *Nijinsky* were shot at Pinewood Studios, Russell scouted locations throughout Europe,[23] met with designers and choreographers, etc. Russell went to see *The Rite of Spring* with Saltzman in Paris, but the producer wasn't impressed. Things turned sour when Russell and Saltzman met with Nureyev for a disastrous dinner in central London, followed by a screening of *Isadora Duncan*, which Nureyev hated, telling Russell that he had would only do the picture if Russell and his entourage left (and Nureyev also wanted the script rewritten: it was too old-hat, he thought).

Ken Russell said that Harry Saltzman had approached him again (acting as if nothing had happened), after Rudolf Nureyev saw *Women In Love* and liked it. By then, some five other directors had been attached to the project, including Tony Richardson. But Russell also said in *An Appalling Talent* that he probably wouldn't have done the movie – it was just pleasurable to see Saltzman and Nureyev jumping through hoops now they were without a director.[24] And the script, now rewritten by Edward Albee, seemed to Russell to be Melvyn Bragg's script but

> with nothing added but an American accent and a couple of new scenes of monumental sentiment and banality. And I thought: well, Harry, you bloody-well got what you deserved. You had all the ingredients to start with and you fucked it up. You've spent a million dollars and ended up with nothing. (Bax, 166)

Ken Russell found it difficult to keep up Harry Saltzman's interest in the *Nijinsky* movie: he would soon be distracted, and move onto other topics. Russell also came to resent being part of Saltzman's court, a bunch of hangers-on who got their dinners and freebies by being Saltzman's coterie of admirers. 'I began to realize that Harry would never make it'; ultimately, *Nijinsky* just

---

[23] Including Vienna, Milan, Holland, Spain and Yugoslavia. Throughout this period of planning, Melvyn Bragg came along with Russell and his wife Shirley (Bax, 164).
[24] Russell did manage to include Nijinsky in a film – dancing with Valentino in the 1977 movie.

wasn't commercial enough for Saltzman (Bax, 163).

The 1980 *Nijinsky*, with Alan Bates as Sergei Diaghilev and American dancer George de la Pena as Vaslav Nijinsky, focussed on the homosexual relationship between the mentor and the pupil, which's presumably what Ken Russell would've concentrated on. It's the kind of ambiguous, potentially obsessive relationship that Russell has explored many times. (There was also a 2002 movie based on the diary of Nijinsky, starring Derek Jacobi).

There are other elements in the story of Vaslav Nijinsky, tho', that were closer to Ken Russell's concerns: music and dance. Nijinsky choreographed performances that outraged Parisian audiences (such as his version of Claude Debussy's *L'Après-midi d'un Faune*), and Andrei Rimsky-Korsakov's *Scheherezade*. The combination of classical music, ballet and public scandal were perfect for Russell (there are links between Nijinsky and Debussy, Rimsky-Korsakov, Peter Tchaikovsky, etc, which also chime with Russell's work). Oh, and there was plenty of sex, too: not only in Nijinsky's gay relationships, but also in his performances (Nijinsky added erotic, phallic elements to his shows).

Other possible projects for Ken Russell of the early Seventies included an adaption of Virginia Woolf's *To the Lighthouse* (later made in the 1980s by the BBC),25 and also *Mrs Dalloway*; *A Handful of Dust* by Evelyn Waugh (later filmed as one of those po-faced, pretty-photography, British heritage period flicks by LWT/ Stagescreen in 1988); Graham Greene's *A Burnt-out Case*; a documentary for the BBC on Ralph Vaughan Williams (this finally surfaced in 1986 – Russell had been planning it for years); *Rachel Lily Rosenbloom* was a pop musical which was to be done on Broadway;26 a remake of *Juliette ou la Clé des Songes* by Georges Neveux, with Mia Farrow;27 and a theatrical production based on black history in America and the slave trade (this was Shirley Kingdon's idea).

---

25 According to Ken Russell in 1973, his version of *To the Lighthouse* would be more Russell than Virginia Woolf, and would evoke his childhood by the sea in Hampshire, England.

26 Russell had to choose between *Rachel Lily Rosenbloom* and *Gargantua*, due to the timing, and found the musical 'all sex and pessimism', while the Rabelais project was 'all love and optimism' (Bax, 230).

27 Mia Farrow had asked producer Harry Benn to find a project on which she could work with Russell. The *Julietta* project would merge into *The Angels*, becoming 'a grotesque reflection of the modern world and Russell's own career' (Bax, 96).

According to Oliver Reed's authorized biographer, Robert Sellers, after *The Debussy Film* he and Ken Russell had planned a horror movie from an H.P. Lovecraft story, *The Shuttered Room*. Carol Lynley and Flora Robson were part of the cast. But on the first day of shooting, Ken Russell didn't show: 'why, I never found out. So we have a crew, money, the actors, everything in place, but no director', recalled Lynley (R. Sellers, 130).

Among Ken Russell's other unmade films were a Western (he said he'd tried to sell it at a time when three Westerns in a row had bombed). And no one wanted to do his film about Percy Grainger, the Australian composer. But then *Shine* had been a big hit with the critics.

*The Gershwin Dream* was a biopic that Ken Russell considered making in the mid-Seventies, but chose to do *Lisztomania* instead. In the 1960s he had been offered *Summer Holiday* by producer Kenneth Harper, the Cliff Richard musical which appeared in 1963 (directed by Peter Yates for Elstree).

*Cleopatra* was set up with HBO, Ken Russell said (BP, 210), but was cancelled when a new regime took over (which's standard practice).

*A CLOCKWORK ORANGE.*

Ken Russell was interested in filming *A Clockwork Orange*; David Puttnam had approached Russell, but the director moved on to *The Devils* instead. Prior to Stanley Kubrick becoming involved in *A Clockwork Orange*, Terry Southern owned the rights, and was to make the film with photographer Michael Cooper. The project was sold to Si Litvinoff, who was approached by Sandy Lieberson, who planned to film it with the Rolling Stones. Russell would later work with Lieberson and Puttnam on *Tommy*. In *An Appalling Talent*, however, Russell said he hadn't been approached to make the Anthony Burgess novella (Bax, 28).

*TAVERNER.*

In the mid-1970s, other unmade projects of Ken Russell's included *Taverner*, Peter Maxwell Davies' opera about the 16th century composer. It would've been a theatrical show in London, at the Royal Opera House in 1972, to be designed by Derek Jarman (i.e., a kind of follow-up to *The Devils*). Taverner (c. 1490-1545) was choir-master and organist in Oxford, and was supposedly involved in heresy and the persecution of Catholics (in the time of Cardinal Wolsey). Music, religion and heretics – it's right up Russell's street.

### SARAH BERNHARDT.

A biopic of the actress Sarah Bernardt (*The Life of Sarah*) was developed in the early 1970s, with Barbara Streisand, no less, in the title role. It might have out-camped Ken Russell's work (up to that point), with a look drawing on the art of Aubrey Beardsley and Oscar Wilde. The combination of Russell and Streisand and Bernardt and the camp approach could have been amazing.[28] Another Might Have Been.

▼

Two projects coalesced in *The Angels* (*Juliette ou la Clé des Songes*, by George Neveux and a piece on race in America employing elements of mime, opera, ballet and musicals, suggested by Ken Russell's wife Shirley), a script that Russell never made, but which he cannibalized for *Tommy*. Elements from *The Angels* that made it into *Tommy* included a satire on religious adulation: in *The Angels*, film director Michael Mann has a star, Poppy Day, who apparently dies, and a shrine's created around her image. Russell took up that idea and replaced Poppy with Marilyn Monroe, a modern-day saint, in *Tommy*'s wonderful *Eyesight To the Blind* sequence starring Eric Clapton.

### *MUSIC, MUSIC, MUSIC.*

Another unmade project was *Music, Music, Music*, a time travel fantasy about the confrontation between music and money. In *Music, Music, Music* a composer, John Fairfax, writes a religious rock opera, *Jesus On Venus*, but has to do the music for TV adverts in order to make money (sound familiar?).

The artist must make art, in Ken Russell's cinematic morality, and must retain her/ his integrity. S/he must not sell out – either to commercialism, or to politics. At its worst, art is perverted by political groups – the Nazis using the music of Richards Strauss and Wagner, for instance – and the artist becomes a political pawn.

Selling out to money is a recurring theme, too – which has a personal link, because of Ken Russell's own work in advertizing.

---

28 This was around the time of Barbara Streisand's success following *Hello Dolly*.

That occurs in *Tommy*, when the Tommy cult becomes all about the money, or when Modeste exploits Peter Tchaikovsky on the concert tours in *The Music Lovers*.

### GARGANTUA.

A version of François Rabelais' *Gargantua* was proposed in the early 1970s, with Italian financing from Produzioni Europe Associati.[29] Warners were also interested, and the producer Alberto Grimaldi. According to Russell, Pier Paolo Pasolini had pulled out of doing *Gargantua*, 'leaving the producer with a script by Alberto Moravia and no director' (Bax, 229). *Gargantua* would also have contained plenty of satire on religion and politics (partly taken from *Music, Music, Music* and *The Angels*). The bawdy, phallic elements of *Gargantua and Pantagruel* would have been part of the mix, as well as the construction of the Abbey of Thélème. Locations were scouted in Italy (BP, 102), and Russell got together with designer Derek Jarman to plan the sets and look, but the project didn't go further.

### ALEISTER CROWLEY.

Aleister Crowley was considered at one time for a movie; a favourite with the *avant garde* and literati, Crowley's crazy life was tailor-made for Ken Russell (of course, only Oliver Reed could have played Crowley – and he did, in the radio play Russell wrote, broadcast in 1995 on the BBC, about Crowley meeting composer Alexander Scriabin in 1914). There still hasn't been a great movie made about Aleister Crowley; certainly one directed by Russell would've been fascinating.[30]

### MARIA CALLAS.

A biopic about the opera diva Maria Callas (1923-77, born in the U.S.A., but of Greek descent) (announced by *Variety* in October, 1982) led to another location trip through Italy for Ken Russell (taking in Venice, Rome and Milan – ah, filmmaking is tough!), and a visit to the star, Sophia Loren, and her husband, the Italian producer Carlo Ponti. However, as Russell recounted

---

29 PEA had also backed *The Decameron* directed by Pier Paolo Pasolini and *Satyricon* by Federico Fellini.

30 Eventually, a movie about Aleister Crowley – *Chemical Wedding* (Julian Doyle, 2009) – did appear: it promised much – a movie about the Beast himself! – but delivered so little. How can you miss, when you've got someone like Crowley as the subject of your movie? Well, *Chemical Wedding* did miss. Oh, if only Ken Russell had directed it!

wryly in his autobiography, Loren wanted a number of changes to the script and the characterization of Callas that Russell and his co-writer and wife, Vivienne Jolly, had created (including intimate details of Callas's marriage with the Italian industrialist G.B. Meneghini, with an accusation from Callas that Meneghini 'couldn't get it up'). When they disagreed, the project foundered: 'bang goes another year's hard labour', as Russell put it (BP, 211).

As intriguing as it was – the combination of Ken Russell and Maria Callas and a movie legend like Sophia Loren – it's hard to see a big star like Loren going along with the irreverent, colourful, and OTT Ken Russell School of Filmmaking.

### DRACULA.

Ken Russell said he pitched a *Dracula* script (BP, 167) when three films with a *Dracula* theme were released at the same time (presumably that was 1979[31] – the year of the Frank Langella *Dracula*, the George Hamilton comedy *Love At First Bite*, and the Klaus Kinski-Werner Herzog remake of *Nosferatu*.)[32] The *Dracula* project was taken up again years later – Russell offered it to Vestron at the same time as *The Rainbow* (but this time there was a problem with the rights to *Dracula* – as many filmmakers have found, right back to the greatest vamp flick of them all, *Nosferatu* in 1922 [BP, 275]).

Ken Russell's take on the King of Vampires would have included a werewolf coachman, a carnival procession, a woman being sacrificed in a ritual, and the Count as a patron of the arts: he would revive great artists, bringing them back from the dead as vampires (PF, 219). Aubrey Beardsley would again form the decor – his illustrations to *Salomé* by Oscar Wilde would adorn the walls of Castle Dracula. In the end, Russell put some of his ideas about vampires into *The Lair of the White Worm*, and Beardsley was an inspiration for *Salomé's Last Dance*. (Russell had already memorably delivered a *Dracula* skit in *Lisztomania*, where Richard Wagner was the Count).

### THE BEETHOVEN SECRET.

This project got 'close, very close' to being made – only days before principal photography, the money collapsed, Ken Russell

---

31 Russell is hazy with dates in his memoirs.
32 Mick Fleetwood, drummer with Fleetwood Mac, was interested in the *Dracula* project, including playing the Count. Err, well, that might've been interesting!

recalled of the early 1980s project (BP, 211). It would have starred Anthony Hopkins, Oliver Reed (as Beethoven), Jodie Foster and Glenda Jackson. The German bank backing the show pulled out near shooting. (A film about Beethoven's personal life, *Immortal Beloved*, appeared in 1994).

### ALL-AMERICAN MURDER.

At the end of the 1980s, Ken Russell was preparing a thriller with Barry Sandler, the writer of *Crimes of Passion*, for Vestron. Set on a campus in America, *All-American Murder* was about copycat murders. Actors such as Linda Grey and Jeff Goldblum were cast (though Russell wanted Ann-Margret). Finding a location proved tricky – the University of Southern California didn't want the film there, but Marymount College said yes. However, the project was dropped because Vestron was in trouble financially.

### MOLL FLANDERS.

An adaption of *Moll Flanders* by Daniel Defoe was set up with Bob Guccione and the Penthouse company. At the time, Guccione and Penthouse had been involved in movies (most infamously, *Caligula*). A Hollywood version of *Moll Flanders* appeared in 1996, directed by Pen Densham, and starring Robin Wright, Morgan Freeman and Stock Channing; there was also a British ITV production in 1996, and previous TV adaptions in 1965 and 1975.

The *Moll Flanders* project has been recounted in Ken Russell's autobiography: there were meetings with porn mogul Bob Guccione in Rome, discussions about the script (and future projects), writing the screenplay, and initial casting (including a lengthy and troubled search for the lead). There were problems with Equity (the British actors' union), who told the production they had to use a union actor. But the actress they picked (one of the *Penthouse* calendar stars) didn't have a union card. When it looked like the production couldn't shoot in England, Ireland was considered (but then Equity brought in the International Federation of Actors to ban the production of *Moll Flanders* everywhere).

In the end, the *Moll Flanders* movie ended up going the way of all flesh. It wound up with Bob Guccione suing Ken Russell for, Russell says, a million dollars (BP, 247). Guccione, for instance, put his own producer on the show, who set about firing Russell's DP, editor, costume designer and assistant (BP, 254). The problems mounted (exacerbated by the decision to shoot in Italy). Meanwhile, Guccione had his own ideas, and was rewriting the script in secret (BP, 254). It ended with legal wrangles.

In 2007 there were rumours that Russell was going to take up *Moll Flanders* again, with Lucinda Rhodes-Flaherty and Barry Humphries to appear.

### CHARGED: THE LIFE OF NIKOLA TESLA.

The battles of early electrical systems would have provided the substance of *Charged*, Ken Russell's biography of the Serb Nikola Tesla, in particular the conflict between Tesla and Thomas Edison. The movie was set up for 2002, but collapsed when the Serbian government withdrew their backing. A previous film about Tesla had been made in 1980 (*The Secret of Nikola Tesla*), plus TV movies, and *The Prestige* (2006), with David Bowie as Tesla.

### EVITA.

Another unmade Ken Russell project was the film version of the celebrated 1978 Broadway musical show by Andrew Lloyd-Weber and Tim Rice, about Eva Perón.[33] The *Evita* project underwent many changes on its journey to the screen, and took a long time to be finally realized; the project had been knocking around Hollywood for years. (It was eventually made by Hollywood Pictures,[34] produced by Robert Stigwood and Alan Parker, and directed Parker[35] in 1996 with Madonna in the title role).

In the late 1980s for instance, Oliver Stone set up the project with Mario Kassar and Andrew Vajna's Carolco and Madonna, but that came to nothing (the Material Girl wanted to change some of the songs). Stone then set up *Evita* with Meryl Streep, but when Streep demanded too much money, she dropped out. It went on and on. (Other directors linked to *Evita* included Francis Coppola, Richard Attenborough, Michael Cimino, Alan Pakula, Hector Babenco, Franco Zeffirelli and Herbie Ross).

The Disney production of *Evita* was well-intentioned and well-made and all that, but it was just *dull* (I think I got halfway

---

[33] A TV movie about Péron appeared in 1981, starring Faye Dunaway, directed by Marivn Chomsky.
[34] Hollywood Pictures was a new company launched by Walt Disney in January, 1989.
[35] Alan Parker had long been associated with musical movies: *Bugsy Malone*, *Fame*, *Pink Floyd: The Wall* and *The Commitments*.

through it then gave up). Alan Parker, like Ken Russell, had a strong musical input in his movies; at the time (mid-1990s), he was more bankable than Russell, having made more hits in Hollywood. But *Evita* was always a *producer's film* – it was the pet project of Lloyd-Weber, Rice and Stigwood. It wouldn't have mattered too much which director made it (though one suspects that Russell would have slipped in some sly – and gross – humour to lighten proceedings, and Oliver Stone would have intensified the political struggle). But Parker delivered precisely the kind of tepid, join-the-dots film that Russell was always keen to avoid.

As well as Madonna, the 1996 *Evita* starred Jonathan Pryce and Antonio Bandieras. *Evita* was a very traditional, musical movie, shot like something out of the 1970s. Alan Parker and co. handled the big scenes well, as he usually did, but *Evita,* while slick and spectacular, was emotionally empty and curiously affectless. While you could admire the photography (which, because Darius Khondji was DP, was always going to be good), or the production design, the story was unengaging. Maybe it was partly the music, which seemed dated and mired in a late 1970s disco/ soft rock mode, or Tim Rice's too obvious and clunky lyrics. On stage, the audience may have forgiven *Evita*'s excesses and deficiencies, but on screen it seemed an unwelcome remnant from another era. And some of the scenes – such as of riots or earthquakes – were tasteless in the context of a Nineties entertainment movie.

In his book *A British Picture*, Ken Russell describes at length his own involvement in the *Evita* project (in 1982), the meeting with music mogul Robert Stigwood (with whom Russell had made *Tommy*), 3 months for writing the screenplay, location scouting around Europe for a month, and 9 months, off and on, for screen tests and the endless search for the lead role. (Russell was happy with David Essex as Che Guevara).

Ken Russell didn't want Elaine Paige in the lead, but the studio (20th Century Fox) and Sherry Lansing (the first female head of a studio), and Stigwood and Lloyd-Weber and Rice did; Russell favoured Liza Minnelli. She turned in an exhilarating screen test, Russell said, in jeans and a T-shirt:

> Liza was giving out a million volts. Here was a woman who could start a revolution and sway a nation... Waves of electricity, waves of

power, swept through the studio, waves of sound, waves of sex. And when she reached her climax with an orgasmic 'I'm coming', so was everyone else in the place, man, woman and dog. At the eleventh hour, it seemed we had found our Evita. (BP, 214)

Barbara Streisand was also considered (Ken Russell met her in London); it seemed that every actress in Hollywood was interested in or considered for the part. But Russell dug his heels in: he would *not* make *Evita* with Elaine Paige in the title role (in his autobiography he relates making more than one screen test with Paige, but she had a face like a potato. Russell met Sherry Lansing, but the meeting was cut short when Russell told Lansing he would not make *Evita* with Paige, and the champagne was put back in the fridge.)

Amelia and the Angel

Pop Goes the Easel (above). Always On Sunday (below).

Ken Russell in The Fall of the Louse of Usher (2001)

Charles Gounod's Faust directed by Ken Russell in 1985

A later Ken Russell book,
based on the lives of famous composers.

# 29

# THE CINEMA OF KEN RUSSELL: SOME CONCLUSIONS

In this study – which I can't finish 'cos there's so much to say about Ken Russell's cinema – I keep emphasizing the *difference* of Russell from all of his contemporary filmmakers, and the uniqueness and brilliance of Russell's talent and vision. None of Russell's contemporaries among British film directors – Ridley Scott, Alan Parker, Mike Newell, Richard Attenborough, John Glen, Lewis Gilbert, Bryan Forbes, Adrian Lyne, Richard Eyre, Bill Forsyth, Clive Donner, Jack Clayton, Alan Bridges, Roy Ward Baker, Terence Fisher, Michael Apted, Ken Annakin, Neil Jordan, Roland Joffé, Mike Leigh, Ken Loach, Michael Lindsay-Hogg, John Madden, Gavin Millar, Anthony Mingella, Ronald Neame, Pat O'Connor, Michael Radford, Karel Reisz, Franc Roddam, Tony Scott, Charles Sturridge, J. Lee Thompson, Michael Winner, Peter Yates, Terence Young, Charles Crichton, Lindsay Anderson and Nic Roeg – would open a savage exploration of religious and political hypocrisy set in plague-ridden 17th century France with a dance number featuring the King of France dressed as the Goddess Venus! None of those contemporary film directors have made a movie about a tortured, gay, classical composer!

I am also exalting Ken Russell's cinema for its unique take on life, its enshrinement of art and artists, its love of the British landscape, and its wild and ceaseless devotion to music, because contemporary cinema coming out of Britain nowadays is so fucking *dull*, and because contemporary culture in Britain now is so fucking *dull*. Conservative, unoriginal, safe, *tame*.

Since the 1990s, I've found culture and society in Britain more conservative than ever – to the point where it's stifling in its banality and unadventurousness, combined with its aggressive consumerism. Ken Russell feels the same: in 2001 he lamented 'the *Daily Mail* mentality' of modern Britain, 'where everything is safe and yet prurient'.

'Passion in British films worries some people', claimed Ken Russell, and adds that British cinema is thin on religion and music biopics (1993, 75). In England, it's embarrassing to talk about art and artists. As Bernardo Bertolucci put it:

> I think the problem in England is embarrassment. People in England keep using the term embarrassment. It's part of English reticence, and the famous English understatement. You find art embarrassing. This is quite unlike the French who have no sense of embarrassment, otherwise they wouldn't use words like *sublime* and *sublimissime*.[1]

Ken Russell was cast in British cinema as a rebel, an outsider, a vulgarian,[2] a wayward talent who hadn't made much of merit since his 'golden age' of the early Seventies (*Women In Love* is routinely regarded as Russell's best film, but certainly not by the director himself, or most of his acolytes). Russell was all contradiction (which he actively encouraged): though regarded as vulgar his films were about intellectuals and artists; his artistic ambitions were continually undercut by camp, over-the-top performances (both in front of and behind the camera); his anti-naturalism did not fit in with the quasi-social realism of much of British cinema (in this he resembled filmmakers such as Peter

---

1 Quoted in I. Halberstadt, *Pix*, 2, BFI, 1997.
2 Viewers who feel assaulted by the imagery and shock tactics probably miss some of the subtlety in Ken Russell's movies, but there is subtlety there: for instance, the level of *detail* in the *mise-en-scène*, or the amount of cultural allusions and references in the films.

Greenaway[3] and Derek Jarman, who also worked on the margins and advocated anti-realism). Russell complained:

> I sometimes think I would fare better in the hands of British critics if I was called Russellini. They may forgive Fellini his excesses, but I am chastised for being theatrical. (1993, 82).

There is some truth in this: somehow, it's OK if European *auteurs* go wildly over-the-top, with exaggerated, flamboyant or plain bizarre movies, such as: Luchino Visconti (in *Ludwig* and *Death in Venice*), Pier Paolo Pasolini (in *Salò* or *Pigsty*), Jean-Luc Godard (in *Weekend*), Volker Schlöndorff (in *The Tin Drum*) or Werner Herzog (in *Nosferatu* or *Fitzcarraldo*), but not a British director. Like the MGM musical, the Western, or the space opera, Ken Russell's kind of cinema was seen as 'un-British', too brash, noisy, lurid, camp, etc. It was over-the-top and sensual like some of the cinemas of Europe. Russell's work had most in common, perhaps, with Italian cinema: with the Italian combination of vulgarity and intellectualism, high camp and high art, sensuality and spirituality, found in the films of Visconti, Fellini and Pasolini. There is also a tradition in Japanese animation for including silly, over-the-top moments of humour right in the middle of 'serious' scenes.

And as the comedies of Mel Brooks, Zucker-Abrahams-Zucker, Woody Allen, the Marx Brothers and many others have demonstrated, you can make all of the serious points you want to make in a movie by using comedy and humour. A movie sure doesn't havta be 'serious' or solemn to explore any issue you fancy. Unfortunately, critics continually under-value comedy movies, and revere 'serious' or drama movies.

Vulgarity and art were part of the same thing for Ken Russell. But the vulgar didn't mean the commercial – that was a vulgarity that Russell despised:

> It's a strange thing that people can't reconcile vulgarity and artistry. They're the same thing to me. But an exuberant over-the-top larger-than-life slightly bad taste red-blooded thing. (Bax, 131)

---

[3] Ken Russell did not like Peter Greenaway at all – maybe because his filmic territory was too similar (mixing art with sex, art with violence, art with philosophizing, and so on). 'What is it about Greenaway's films that makes the flesh crawl?' Russell asked in *Fire Over England*. Remarking on Greenaway's technique of cutting up Michael Nyman's music into 'arbitrary chunks according to his needs', Russell said that 'Greenaway treats the human race in much the same way. And he is more interested in shit than soul' (1993, 168).

But the finest filmmakers have been dubbed too baroque and theatrical: Orson Welles is the classic example. He made the two greatest American films ever – *Citizen Kane* and *The Magnificent Ambersons* (and a clutch of other films which are simply staggeringly spectacular – *The Trial, Chimes At Midnight, The Lady of Shanghai* and *Othello*) – but he was attacked non-stop for being too baroque, too self-conscious and too flamboyant.

Flamboyant, over-the-top, baroque, coarse, vulgar – you can fling the same epithets at Steven Spielberg, Ridley Scott, Gore Verbinski, Alfred Hitchcock, Roger Corman, Werner Herzog, Akira Kurosawa, etc.

Like some other filmmakers, Ken Russell will switch genres and moods from one film to another: after *The Devils*, which left some of the cast and crew exhausted, Russell jumped at the chance of directing a film version of *The Boy Friend*. Unfortunately, the filming of *The Boy Friend* proved to be an unhappy experience, with major fall-outs among the cast and crew, and technical obstacles, such as the sound stages, which weren't tall enough for the sets the production wanted to use.[4]

Ken Russell thinks you can have comedy and satire at the same time in a serious and dramatic film: it's quite OK to have sudden shifts from seriousness to comedy, or from literary dialogue to vaudeville fooling about. Some audiences find this mix confusing, or irritating, or tiring. Russell's films continually play around with the viewer's perceptions. For instance, fantasies are merged with the present tense of a movie, so the audience isn't sure if what they're seeing is meant to be taken straight, or if it's a fantasy (not a *dream* – Russell doesn't use *dreams* nearly so much as *fantasies*).

As well as fantasies, Ken Russell's films also employ a fantastical or exaggerated form of filmmaking – this may be the mode or approach that confuses viewers most, and which critics find particularly annoying. That is, the mode is not the fantasy of a particular character, but is the filmmakers' fantasy. Conventional dramatic modes such as memories and flashbacks are also employed, which further complicate the narratives of Russell's movies. (You could argue that all cinema is dream-like and

---

[4] It also appeared that the British film crew weren't used to staging a musical on this large scale. (But some of 'em must have worked on big musicals – quite a few were made in Britain in the 1960s, the period when the Hollywood studios were investing heavily in the British film scene: *Oliver!, Half a Sixpence* and *Chitty Chitty Bang Bang*).

fantastical – and Russell's works simply draw attention to it, or exaggerate it).

Certainly some of the confusions and irritations that some viewers and critics have with Ken Russell's movies is that they are not sure how to take a particular scene or mode of narration. Is this scene meant to be serious or comic? Is this a fantasy of the main character, or is it the filmmaker fantasizing about the character's state of mind? Is this scene an ironic commentary on the situation? The movies say: yes, all of the above.

And, crucially, Ken Russell and the production teams don't necessarily indicate where one mode of address ends and another begins: they take away the signposts (no dissolves to shaky, black-and-white footage, for instance, to indicate a newsreel-style memory, and no watery, optical effects to indicate a dream).

At their most intense moments, when the montage sustains an apparently chaotic mix of music, images, dances, designs, stunts, looks and visual effects, nothing in a Ken Russell movie seems to be 'real', or is intended to be 'real', or has any link to 'reality'. Of course not! It's a movie! It's a piece of entertainment! Nothing about movies is 'real', was ever 'real', could ever be 'real'. It is movie-making as a mystery play from the Middles Ages, as Russell explained:

> You see, I think of my films as sort of modern mediaeval mystery plays. In the days of mystery plays, they took religion, bashed it over the head, cocked a snook at it, blasphemed it, sent it up, treated it melodramatically, comically... all in one act. And people liked it.[5]

I agree wholeheartedly with Ken Russell when he says that he's not that interested in 'reality', that there's plenty of 'reality' around as it is. No need to add to it.

In a Ken Russell movie, some audiences are not sure where the filmmaker is coming from, or aiming at, nor where the film is headed. And they don't like that: they want to know if what they're watching is a comedy, if it's *meant* to be a comedy, and if it's OK to laugh, or if they are *meant* to laugh (consequently, you can see that Russell's movies would be tough to preview, and why a college audience might be a better bet than a shopping mall audience).

But Ken Russell is clearly a filmmaker who can happily send

---
5 In P. Mezan, 1973

up his subject even as he celebrates it or takes it seriously (and some viewers find that hard to accept). Thus, Russell and his team take Peter Tchaikovsky or Henri Gaudier very seriously, but they also spoof them, in the same movie.[6] As Joseph Gomez noted, sometimes in Russell's films 'the importance of the image outweighs the action' (40). A useful remark, because it means that the *image itself* (maybe the beauty of it, or the compelling nature of it, or just the photographic quality of it) can have more value or more juice in the movie than the *action* or the *narrative*. 'I am eaten up with the image, with the way things look,' Russell has said.

Some critics and some spectators want a film to have *meanings* or *actions* or *characters* or *ideas*, and to have these organized into a logical flow, so that cause leads to effect. But all of that traditional dramaturgy, while valuable, isn't always what a Ken Russell movie is about, or is interested in pursuing.

In other words, in a Ken Russell picture, the question is not: 'what does this mean?', or: 'why did that character do that?', or: 'what is this character saying?', or even: 'what is happening?'. The question is, rather: 'what does it feel like?', or: 'what is the mood of this scene?', or: 'what is the movement within this shot?', or: 'don't ask questions, just look at the costumes! the lighting! the sets! the make-up! and listen to that music!' (Again and again and again: *listen to that music!*).

Ken Russell's cinema simply reminds movie-goers that films are not only about *stories* and *characters* and *themes*, that they are also about the look of things, the sound of things, the links between things, and the stupidity or humour of things.

In this sense, a movie directed by Ken Russell might be usefully thought of in terms of the classic Hollywood musical. When I'm watching a Gene Kelly musical movie or a Vincente Minnelli musical, I'm not always asking questions like: 'what does that line of dialogue mean?', or: 'how will the next scene relate to this one, will the dramatic conflicts be resolved?', or: 'what was that character's motivation in that scene?'

Instead, I am looking at Gene Kelly – what a beautiful, nimble, athletic man! And I'm thinking: 'wow, that is such a fabulous movement!' Or: 'look at the way Kelly dances across the floor and leaps up onto that wall. So graceful!' Or: 'oh man, look at the way the camera glides with Kelly as he spins and ends up

---

[6] Being amongst artists like Tchaikovsky, Shelley and Byron, Ken Russell said, was like being among old friends, his contemporaries (RC, 246).

framed in that doorway!'

And when I'm enjoying a Ken Russell movie, I'm reacting along the lines of: 'isn't it cool the way that Roger Daltrey grinned at that moment?' Or: 'look at the way that Glenda Jackson dances under the trees!' Or: 'look at the colours in that set and those costumes!' Or: 'how does our Ken get away with such apparent simplicity and vulgarity?!' And: 'oh, why oh why isn't Ken Russell being fêted as a genius?'

We do live on a magic island, without doubt, but so far as British films are concerned there is precious little evidence of this. By and large, contemporary filmmakers seem to revel in squalor, glorify ignorance and extol violence. There is another kind of life outside of this which many people in this country would like to celebrate, if only they were given the opportunity and not made to feel guilty about it. It has nothing to do with religion; it is to do with the spirit of the land in which we live, that elusive quality touched on by the music of VW (Vaughan Williams) and his contemporaries such as Arnold Bax, Frank Bridge and John Ireland: music expressing the majesty of nature, forgotten rituals, pagan goddesses and ancient heroes.

Ken Russell, A British Picture (238-8)

# APPENDICES

# A SUMMARY OF KEN RUSSELL'S MOVIE CAREER

'Classic' Ken Russell movies, if there can be such a thing, would include *The Music Lovers, Savage Messiah, Valentino, The Devils, Women In Love, Tommy* and *Mahler*, the films of the late Sixties and early-to-mid-Seventies. These were also the pictures (along with his British Broadcasting Corporation films, such as *Dante's Inferno, Isadora Duncan* and *The Debussy Film*, and the last one, *Dance of the Seven Veils*), that gave Russell his reputation as the *enfant terrible* of British cinema. After the 1960s and his BBC/ *Monitor/ Omnibus* biopics, Russell helmed some genre productions, some as a director for hire (*Billion Dollar Brain* [1967], one of the *Harry Palmer* series, made for producers Harry Saltzman, André de Toth and United Artists), and the Sandy Wilson musical, *The Boy Friend* (1971), starring Twiggy.

The biopics about artists and musicians continued in the Seventies with *Lisztomania, Valentino* and *Mahler*; *Valentino* marks a shift in Ken Russell's career: when he took over the troubled production of *Altered States*, Russell went to Hollywood, to make his first movie in the U.S.A. (much later than one would have supposed; Russell did not follow the usual trail to Hollywood, like so many of his peers – such as John Schlesinger, Peter Yates, Guy Hamilton and Lewis Gilbert). One or two other Hollywood films followed (such as *Crimes of Passion* with Kathleen Turner and Anthony Perkins, and, later, *Whore* with Theresa Russell). But of course, as Russell points out often, his feature movies were all financed bar one by North American money.

In the Eighties, Ken Russell directed a series of smaller-budget movies, in a deal with American mini-studio Vestron (*The Rainbow, Gothic, The Lair of the White Worm* and *Salomé's Last Dance*). These were wayward in quality and substance, but still recognizably Ken Russell films. After the 1980s, Russell directed fewer films that were released theatrically: *Whore* (1991) and *Mindbender* (1995). Russell contributed *The Insatiable Mrs Kirsch* (1993) to *Tales of Erotica* (a.k.a. *Erotic Tales*, 1996), a German-funded film co-directed by Bob Rafelson, Susan Seidelman, Melvin Van Peebles, Paul Cox and Mani Kaul.

Later, Ken Russell made movies for one of the biggest American cable companies, Home Box Office (*Women & Men* and *Prisoner of Honor*), while *Whore* (1991), with Theresa Russell, was produced for Trimark Pictures. Russell also contributed to some anthology films, including *Aria* (1987), produced by Don Boyd for Miramax.

Ken Russell continued to helm many films and documentaries for television from the 1970s onwards: when he wasn't making feature movies, he was often working on TV material, including: the *Clouds of Glory* documentaries on Samuel Taylor Coleridge and William Wordsworth (both 1978),[1] *The Planets* (1983), about Gustav Holst's very famous suite (1914-16), *Vaughan Williams* (1986), *Méphistophélès* (1989), *A British Picture* (1989), *The Strange Affliction of Anton Bruckner* (1990), *Women and Men: Stories of Seduction* (1990), *Prisoner of Honor* (1991), *The Secret Life of Sir Arnold Bax* (1992), *Lady Chatterley* (1993), *The Mystery of Doctor Martinu* (1992), *Alice in Russialand* (1995), *Classic Widows* (1995), *Ken Russell's Treasure Island* (1995), *Tales of Erotica* (1996), *In Search of the English Folk Song* (1998), *Dogboys* (1998), *Brighton Belles* (2001) and *Elgar: Fantasy of a Composer On a Bicycle* (2002). Many of these are quirky, unusual dramas and documentaries which could've been helmed by only one person on Earth, Ken Russell.

Among Ken Russell's regular collaborators were his wife Shirley Kingdon as costume designer, DPs Billy Williams and Dick Bush, editors Mike Bradsell, Stuart Baird and Peter Davies, producers Harry Benn and Roy Baird, production designers Ian Whittaker, Philip Harrison, Lucciana Arrighi, Christopher Hobbs and Derek Jarman, writer Melvyn Bragg, and actors Oliver Reed,

---

1 A third programme, on Robert Southey, was planned, but Granada dropped it. The Coleridge piece, *The Rime of the Ancient Mariner*, wasn't broadcast by PBS in America.

Glenda Jackson, Robert Powell, Georgina Hale, Christopher Gable, Paul Nicholas, Max Adrian, Judith Paris, Andrew Faulds, Murray Melvin and Imogen Claire.

Shirley Kingdon also advised Ken Russell on his films: John Baxter wrote that Kingdon 'sits in on and makes comments about every step of a production' (1973, 56). It's an aspect of many filmmakers that critics tend to ignore. Certainly Kingdon can be regarded as the co-author of some of Russell's films (consider the influence she had on the look and design of *Women In Love*, for instance. And she would suggest casting particular actors, such as James Lloyd for *Always On Sunday*).[2]

Among filmmakers, Ken Russell has cited Orson Welles, Ingmar Bergman, Federico Fellini, Jean Cocteau, Fritz Lang, the Marx Brothers, Sergei Eisenstein, Alfred Hitchcock, Jean-Luc Godard, the French *nouvelle vague* and Charlie Chaplin. It's easy to spot these and many more (Michael Powell, say, or Vincente Minnelli), in Russell's cinema. The intense chamber pieces of Bergman, the King of Film Angst (as well as the crisp black-and-white photography, giant close-ups, and long takes in Bergman's films), can be discerned in *Delius* and *Dante's Inferno*. References to Hitch and *Psycho* crop up in *The Mystery of Dr Martinu* and *Crimes of Passion*. The Marxes're spoofed in *Mahler*. Fritz Lang and *Metropolis* occur in *Lisztomania*. The *rondo* structure of *Citizen Kane* and *Lola Montes* is employed many times. And so on.

Many views have been put forward on Ken Russell's later career, and why he wasn't given the backing for the films he wanted to make: was he both too esoteric and too vulgar? Did he squander his talent on projects way below his potential? Did he find it difficult to select material suited to his genius? Did he deliberately (or unconsciously) sabotage his movies? (as some have suggested). Was it because he hadn't had a hit in ages?

Actually, when *was* the last theatrical movie that Ken Russell directed that was aimed at a *wide* audience? Was it *Altered States*? Because many of the 1980s movies – *Gothic, The Rainbow, Salomé's Last Dance* – were literary, *niche* audience projects (Romantic poets in Switzerland; working class families in 1910s Nottinghamshire – these are not Hollywood blockbuster movie subjects! No super-heroes, car chases, no product placement, no glib one-liners or endless action scenes here!).

---

2 That was a terrible choice, however.

In fact, you have to go back quite a way to find a Russell-directed movie that is definitely aimed at a wide audience. Before *Altered States*, there was: *Tommy*, *The Boy Friend* and *The Devils*. In fact, Russell has rarely gone for the mainstream in his choice of directing jobs. Russell's work isn't esoteric or intellectual without good cause, but it does avoid obviously mainstream material.

# SOME OF THE FINEST MOMENTS IN KEN RUSSELL'S MOVIES

♣ The chase on the frozen lake in *Billion Dollar Brain*.
♣ Strauss as Zarathustra dancing with the nuns in *The Dance of the Seven Veils*.
♣ The Oxford mural sequence in *Dante's Inferno*.
♣ The ending of *Isadora Duncan*.
♣ The water party in *Women In Love*.
♣ The *First Piano Concerto* sequence in *The Music Lovers*.
♣ Tchaikovsky visiting von Meck's home in *The Music Lovers*.
♣ The fireworks party in *The Music Lovers*.
♣ The *1812* fantasy in *The Music Lovers*.
♣ The 'rape of Christ' sequence in *The Devils* (even in its truncated form).
♣ The procession in *The Devils*.
♣ The *Pierrot* dance in *The Boy Friend*.
♣ Gaudier-Brzeska working all night on the sculpture in *Savage Messiah*.
♣ 'The Convert' fantasy sequence in *Mahler*.
♣ The Acid Queen sequence in *Tommy*.
♣ The Pinball Wizard sequence in *Tommy*.
♣ 'Eyesight To the Blind' in *Tommy*.
♣ Richard Wagner's Superman rally in *Lisztomania*.
♣ The phallic dance in *Lisztomania*.
♣ The second hallucination (peyote/ Emily) in *Altered States*.
♣ The nightmares in *Gothic*.

# QUOTES BY KEN RUSSELL

Reality is a dirty word for me, I know it isn't for most people, but I am not interested. There's too much of it about.

It's a strange thing that people can't reconcile vulgarity and artistry. They're the same thing to me. But an exuberant over-the-top larger-than-life slightly bad taste red-blooded thing.

With the first big feature film I made, *Billion Dollar Brain*, I could afford to have an army on an expanse of ice and have the army fall through the ice, well of course you couldn't do that on TV. Feature filmmaking was far freer and pictorially the sky was the limit, but the budgetary limitations of TV didn't bother me, it meant you were forced to use you imagination even more.

I was always fairly lucky with the censors. John Trevelyan [head of the British Board of Film Classification in the late 60s and early 70s] was very good; he stuck his neck out to keep the nude wrestling scene in *Women In Love*. He argued that it wasn't me who put the scene in it was the author D.H. Lawrence, so it wasn't for pure sensationalism; it was an integral part of the novel.

Sacrifice is the central pivot of the Catholic faith and one of the best things about it. It comes into a lot of my films, especially *The Devils*.

The television adman's trick of passing off his dream as an attainable and desirable reality is to my mind the great tragedy of our age.

# VIDEO AND DVD: AVAILABILITY

Here's a reminder about access to Ken Russell's movies and TV work, as listed in the filmography, because it's a fairly fundamental issue: some films are easy to buy or rent on home entertainment formats like video, Blu-ray and DVD, but some are either difficult to track down, or unavailable. Most of Russell's television work of the 1960s, for instance, is not available on DVD or video, and has only the occasional airing on television. And the LWT and *South Bank Show* pieces, which were terrific television, also aren't in print (altho' some *South Bank Shows* have more recently been released on DVD. I would highly recommend the stunning North American release *Ken Russell At the BBC*).

As to showings on television, very occasionally pieces are re-broadcast. But don't expect *Dance of the Seven Veils: A Comic Strip In Seven Episodes On the Life of Richard Strauss, 1864-1949* to be shown after another re-run of *Cheers* or *Friends* or *Letterman* on CBS or ABC or the BBC any time soon.

But some releases feature audio commentaries by Ken Russell, and these are by far and away the most valuable editions of Russell's work on the home entertainment market. I highly recommend the DVDs releases of *Lisztomania* and *Tommy*. *The Devils* came in 2012. *The Music Lovers*, Russell's own favourite movie, has recently been released.

# 'FIGS' BY D.H. LAWRENCE

This is all of the poem 'Figs' by D.H. Lawrence, which's quoted in *Women In Love*:

The proper way to eat a fig, in society,
Is to split it in four, holding it by the stump,
And open it, so that it is a glittering, rosy, moist, honied, heavy-
                            petalled four-petalled flower.

Then you throw away the skin
Which is just like a four-sepalled calyx,
After you have taken off the blossom, with your lips.

But the vulgar way
Is just to put your mouth to the crack, and take out the flesh in one bite.

Every fruit has its secret.

The fig is a very secretive fruit.
As you see it standing growing, you feel at once it is symbolic:
And it seems male.
But when you come to know it better, you agree with the Romans, it is
                            female.

The Italians vulgarly say, it stands for the female part; the fig-fruit:
The fissure, the yoni,
The wonderful moist conductivity towards the centre.

Involved,
Inturned,

The flowering all inward and womb-fibrilled;
And but one orifice.

The fig, the horse-shoe, the squash-blossom.
Symbols.

There was a flower that flowered inward, womb-ward;
Now there is a fruit like a ripe womb.

It was always a secret.
That's how it should be, the female should always be secret.

There never was any standing aloft and unfolded on a bough
Like other flowers, in a revelation of petals;
Silver-pink peach, venetian green glass of medlars and sorb-apples,
Shallow wine-cups on short, bulging stems
Openly pledging heaven:
*Here's to the thorn in flower! Here is to Utterance!*
The brave, adventurous rosaceæ.

Folded upon itself, and secret unutterable,
And milky-sapped, sap that curdles milk and makes *ricotta*,
Sap that smells strange on your fingers, that even goats won't taste it;
Folded upon itself, enclosed like any Mohammedan woman,
Its nakedness all within-walls, its flowering forever unseen,
One small way of access only, and this close-curtained from the light;
Fig, fruit of the female mystery, covert and inward,
Mediterranean fruit, with your covert nakedness,
Where everything happens invisible, flowering and fertilization, and
                                                              fruiting
In the inwardness of your you, that eye will never see
Till it's finished, and you're over-ripe, and you burst to give up your ghost.

Till the drop of ripeness exudes,
And the year is over.

And then the fig has kept her secret long enough.
So it explodes, and you see through the fissure the scarlet.
And the fig is finished, the year is over.

That's how the fig dies, showing her crimson through the purple slit
Like a wound, the exposure of her secret, on the open day.
Like a prostitute, the bursten fig, making a show of her secret.

That's how women die too.

The year is fallen over-ripe,
The year of our women.
The year of our women is fallen over-ripe.
The secret is laid bare.
And rottenness soon sets in.
The year of our women is fallen over-ripe.

When Eve once knew *in her mind* that she was naked
She quickly sewed fig-leaves, and sewed the same for the man.
She'd been naked all her days before,
But till then, till that apple of knowledge, she hadn't had the fact on her mind.

She got the fact on her mind, and quickly sewed fig-leaves.
And women have been sewing ever since.
But now they stitch to adorn the bursten fig, not to cover it.
They have their nakedness more than ever on their mind,
And they won't let us forget it.

Now, the secret
Becomes an affirmation through moist, scarlet lips
That laugh at the Lord's indignation.

*What then, good Lord!* cry the women.
*We have kept our secret long enough.*
*We are a ripe fig.*
*Let us burst into affirmation.*

They forget, ripe figs won't keep.
Ripe figs won't keep.

Honey-white figs of the north, black figs with scarlet inside, of the south.
Ripe figs won't keep, won't keep in any clime.
What then, when women the world over have all bursten into affirmation?
And bursten figs won't keep?

# SALOMÉ'S LAST DANCE

An extract from *Salomé's Last Dance* by Oscar Wilde.
This is Salomé's speech to John the Baptist:

Ah! thou wouldst not suffer me to kiss thy mouth, Iokanaan. Well! I will kiss it now. I will bite it with my teeth as one bites a ripe fruit. Yes, I will kiss thy mouth, Iokanaan. I said it; did I not say it? I said it. Ah! I will kiss it now. But wherefore dost thou not look at me, Iokanaan? Thine eyes that were so terrible, so full of rage and scorn, are shut now. Wherefore are they shut? Open thine eyes! Lift up thine eyelids, Iokanaan! Wherefore dost thou not look at me? Art thou afraid of me, Iokanaan, that thou wilt not look at me? And thy tongue, that was like a red snake darting poison, it moves no more, it speaks no words, Iokanaan, that scarlet viper that spat its venom upon me. It is strange, is it not? How is it that the red viper stirs no longer? Thou wouldst have none of me, Iokanaan. Thou rejectedest me. Thou didst speak evil words against me. Thou didst bear thyself toward me as to a harlot, as to a woman that is a wanton, to me, Salomé, daughter of Herodias, Princess of Judaea! Well, I still live, but thou art dead, and thy head belongs to me. I can do with it what I will. I can throw it to the dogs and to the birds of the air. That which the dogs leave, the birds of the air shall devour. Ah, Iokanaan, Iokanaan, thou wert the man that I loved alone among men! All other men were hateful to me. But thou wert beautiful! Thy body was a column of ivory set upon feet of silver. It was a garden full of doves and lilies of silver. It was a tower of silver decked with shields of ivory. There was nothing in the world so white as thy body. There was nothing in the world so black as thy hair. In the whole world there was nothing so red as thy mouth. Thy voice was a censer that scattered strange perfumes, and when I looked on thee I heard strange music. Ah! wherefore didst thou not look at me, Iokanaan? With the cloak of thine hands, and with the cloak of thy blasphemies thou didst hide thy face. Thou didst put upon thine eyes the covering of him who would see God. Well, thou hast seen thy God, Iokanaan, but me, me, thou didst never see me. If thou hadst seen me thou hadst loved me. I saw thee, and I loved thee. Oh, how I loved thee! I love thee yet, Iokanaan. I love only thee. I am athirst for thy beauty; I am hungry for thy body; and neither wine nor apples can appease my desire. What shall I do now, Iokanaan? Neither the floods nor the great waters can quench my passion. I was a princess, and thou didst scorn me. I was a virgin, and thou didst take my virginity from me. I was chaste, and thou didst fill my veins with fire. Ah! ah! wherefore didst thou not look at me? *[She kisses the head.]* Ah! I have kissed thy mouth, Iokanaan, I have kissed thy mouth. There was a bitter taste on thy lips. Was it the taste of blood? Nay; but perchance it was the taste of love. They say that love hath a bitter taste. But what matter? what matter? I have kissed thy mouth.

# THE WHO

♪

As the Who are such an important ingredient in *Tommy* – it's their story and show, after all – it's worth reminding ourselves who the Who were: they were one of the great British supergroups of the postwar period. Indeed, after the Beatles and the Stones, the Who would likely be in anyone's list of the top five acts in British pop music in the 1960s and 1970s.

By the time of their famous tours of North America and stadium concerts (from the late 1960s to the early 1980s), with the stories of hotel trashing and drug-fuelled antics, the Who were called 'the greatest rock 'n' roll band in the world'. They were one of many supergroups to be routinely described thus (others included Cream, the Rolling Stones, the Eagles, Led Zeppelin, Pink Floyd, Queen, Yes, Emerson, Lake and Palmer, and the Jackson Five). For a while, the Who did seem untouchably good – the period of *Tommy*, the *Life House* project, *Who's Next* and *Live at Leeds* (from the late 1960s to the mid-1970s). The classic Who albums are *Tommy*, *Quadrophenia*, *Who's Next* and *Live at Leeds*.[3]

The Who's origins were in Shepherd's Bush in West London. They started out doing the usual small clubs, back rooms of pubs, and schlepping across the country in vans and trucks, just like thousands of other acts of the era (Pete Townshend (b. May 19, 1945) and John Entwistle (1944-2003) knew each other from school (they both attended Acton Grammar School), where they had undertaken their first forays into music. Townshend and Entwistle were the first Who members to become friends). Roger Daltrey (born on March 1, 1944) had his own band, the Detours, and they were already established when Townshend and Entwistle joined them (thus it was 'Roger's band', at least initially). Keith Moon (1946-78), in one of many legends surrounding the Who, presented himself to the group, cheekily (and typically) claiming that he was a better

---

[3] The Leeds recordings came from a Valentine's Day concert, 1970, at the Leeds University refectory. The original album contained only a few tracks – 'The Seeker', 'Summertime Blues', 'See Me, Feel Me', 'Young Man Blues' (which had been recorded for *Tommy*), 'Substitute', 'Shakin' All Over', 'Magic Bus' and 'My Generation' – but it has come to be recognized as one of the great live records. (Later editions included more of the original recordings).

drummer than the one they had.[4]

The Detours were a party band, Pete Townshend explained, that played 'Hava Nagila', Cliff Richard, the conga, the hokey-cokey, chart hits, and Country & Western songs.[5] By the early 1960s, the Detours were gigging regularly, and developing a reputation beyond the local scene around Shepherd's Bush and West London. They supported the Rolling Stones (in Putney – they were huge Stones fans),[6] the Beatles, the Kinks, Lulu and Dusty Springfield. They gathered a Mod audience, and played at venues such as the Notre Dame Church Hall, Soho, the Glenlyn Ballroom, Forest Hill, the Goldhawk, Shepherd's Bush, the Aquarium, Brighton, the Scene Club, and the Fender Club, Kenton.

The Detours, on the advice of Chris Parmienter, an A & R guy at Fontana Records, ditched their drummer, Doug Sandom (Parmienter thought he was too old). It was a lousy moment: 'one of the actions of my career I most regret', Townshend confessed (67). But it did allow for the entry of Keith Moon, the final ingredient of the four members of the Detours/ Who.

There were four strong personalities[7] in the band; not only a powerful singer and guitarist/ writer team in Roger Daltrey and Pete Townshend, but also John Entwistle's unusual bass playing and musicianship, and Keith Moon's utterly idiosyncratic drumming (Moon beating the hell out of his many Premier drum kits, then demolishing them, is one of the unforgettable sights in rock music. If you invented a personality like Moon, as well as a musician like Moon, nobody would believe you!).[8]

Pete Townshend was for many critics the powerhouse of the Who, an extraordinarily gifted songwriter, lyricist and stage performer (there could be no Who without Townshend – although they carried on after the deaths of Keith Moon and John Entwistle; equally, there could be no Who without Roger Daltrey. Daltrey said he was the straight one, compared to Moon, Townshend and Entwistle, all of whom were alcoholics at some time; Daltrey didn't indulge much in drugs, for instance).

Pete Townshend's songwriting was easily the equal of the finest of any of the other supergroups, including the much-vaunted partnerships of Jagger/ Richards and Lennon/ McCartney. Townshend produced an amazing run of singles and hits in the 1960s and 1970s, including 'My Generation', 'Substitute', 'I'm a Boy', 'I Can See For Miles', 'Happy Jack', 'Pictures of Lily', 'I Don't Mind', 'The Seeker', 'I Can't Explain', 'I'm a Man', 'I'm Free', 'Who Are You', 'Pinball Wizard', 'The Kids Are

---

[4] As Moony bragged, he was the best 'Keith-Moon-type drummer in the world!' Moony was closest to Entwistle at first.

[5] Quotes from Pete Townshend are from his 2012 autobiography (44).

[6] When the Detours supported the Stones in Putney (Dec 15, 1963), it was an epiphany for Townshend.

[7] As Townshend put it, they might think the rest of the people in the band were jerks, but didn't let it bother them: 'deeply written in Who philosophy is the fact that each member thinks the other guy's way is total bullshit but-it's-all-right-by-me'.

[8] But on the 1975 album *Tommy*, the drums are also played by Kenny Jones, Mike Kelly, Tony Newman, Richard Bailey, and Elton John's drummer Nigel Olsson.

Alright', 'Won't Get Fooled Again', 'Baba O'Riley', 'Magic Bus', 'See Me, Feel Me', 'Squeezebox' and 'You Better, You Bet'.[9] Some of these classics were featured in *Tommy,* and many have become enduring pop anthems.[10] (But Townshend also felt the pressure, and sometimes buckled under it, of having to come up with great songs, including chart hits).

The early key song that Pete Townshend wrote for the Who was entitled 'I Can't Explain'. It was a song about music (which Townshend often wrote about, including in *Tommy*): the Who would make music which would express what its audience couldn't verbalize (*you feel it, we'll sing it* might've been their musical slogan). An epiphany occurred for Townshend in the dressing room at a gig, when Jack Lyons and some others visited the band backstage at the Goldhawk in London, and confirmed that 'I Can't Explain' was precisely about that. It was a life-changing realization for Townshend (80).

♪

The Who were associated with the Mod movement early on in their career; these were the mid-Sixties days of singles such as 'Substitute' and 'My Generation', and teen anthem sentiments such as 'hope I die before I get old'.[11] 'My Generation' also contained the memorable line 'why don't you just f-f-fade away', hissed with vitriol by Roger Daltrey.[12] Mod culture features in *Tommy*, of course; though, partly due its production date – the mid-1970s – glam rock is just as prominent.

The Who's early work was r 'n' b, moving into the Mod scene of the mid-1960s. Shifting away from covers of Motown, James Brown, rhythm 'n' blues and rock 'n' roll songs, the Who developed their own heavy, electric sound (along with hard rock bands like Cream, the Yardbirds, Jimi Hendrix, the Kinks *et al*), dominated by Pete Townshend's jangling, feedbacked guitar, and built on Keith Moon's mad percussion, and John Entwistle's nimble, melodic bass lines. Songs such as 'Substitute'[13] and 'I'm a Boy' played around with gender stereotypes ('I'm a boy, I'm a boy, but my Ma won't admit it'; 'I'm just a substitute for another guy'), which would become a big thing in the early Seventies, glam rock era (Ken Russell's cinema has of course loved to play around with gender roles, in particular with reversing gender expectations.)

Peak period Who material – 'My Generation', 'Substitute', 'I'm a Boy', 'I Can See For Miles', 'Baba O'Riley', 'Won't Get Fooled Again', 'Pinball Wizard' – had an anger and viciousness powering it, ever-

---

[9] 'You Better, You Bet' was the lead single from *Face Dances*, the first post-Keith Moon Who album.
[10] Success came early with singles such as 'I Can't Explain' in April, 1964 (it grossed £30,00 ($50,000), and made the band about £250 ($400) each).
[11] Townshend called 'My Generation' his 'folk song single', his 'talking-blues thing'. It drew on blues acts such as Bo Diddley, Jimmy Reed and Mose Allison. And Bob Dylan.
[12] The famous stutter came from bluesmen, Pete Townshend recalled, such as John Lee Hooker (others have said that Kit Lambert suggested it). Everyone wants to take credit for such iconic moments.
[13] 'Substitute' started out as an *hommage* to Smokey Robinson, Pete Townshend recalled, with some Rolling Stones '19th Nervous Breakdown' added (92).

present in Roger Daltrey's vocals, Pete Townshend's lyrics and guitar work, and Keith Moon's frenetic drumming. These weren't simply great pop songs (though that would have been satisfying enough), they had an edge of alienation and danger, presaging the 'fuck you' attitude of punk rock by a decade (the Who's stage act also pre-empted punk. The Who, and other acts of the Sixties, had wrecked stages a long time before the Sex Pistols). It was high energy music ('maximum R and B'), amphetamine and pills music, at times like an assault (the Who were famously *very* loud). 'Rock for me was about catching fire on stage, going the extra mile,' asserted Townshend (281).

The iconography of the Who played with images of British nationalism: the Union Jack and the Mod circular target; there were also Pop Art flags, chevrons and other insignia; the imagery and lyrics evoked West London (their stamping ground) and Brighton.[14] The Who and their music were re-aligned with Pop Art, partly due to Pete Townshend's own art school sensibilities. Pop Art formed the æsthetic basis for concepts like *The Who Sell Out* album, with its bold imagery culled from (radio) advertizing. Songs were mixed in with bursts of real radio jingles (which also handily fleshed out the running time for the album), while the band turned in spoof adverts (for products such as Odorono, Premier Drums, Heinz Baked Beans, Medac spot cream, and used car companies). The Ox and Moony created many of the joky radio ads. *The Who Sell Out* was an early concept album which really worked (although it wasn't such a hit with fans). Again, the send-up of commercials would appeal to Ken Russell, who included an incredible spoof of TV ads in *Tommy*.

Two of the key members of the Who team were managers Kit Lambert (1938-81) and Chris Stamp.[15] Roger Daltrey recalled that Pete Townshend had a close working relationship with Lambert, and valued his opinions highly (*Tommy* was the last record Lambert produced for the Who). Daltrey called Lambert and Stamp the fifth and sixth members of the Who. Stamp (brother of actor Terence) was one of the producers of the film *Tommy*, along with Robert Stigwood. The producers, Ken Russell said, left them alone to get on with it (the ideal situation for a filmmaker).

♫

In the late 1960s, the Who moved, like so many other bands (most famously the Beatles), into more conceptual, hippy territory, with the large-scale 'rock operas' *Tommy*, the Brighton Mod drama *Quadrophenia* (filmed by producers Roy Baird (Russell's regular producer) and Bill Curbishley (the Who's manager), writers David Humphries and Martin Stellman and director Franc Roddam in 1979),[16] and the *Life House* project. An early mini-opera was *A Quick One While He's Away* (it linked together six song fragments: 'Her Man's Been Gone', 'Crying Town', 'We Have a Remedy', 'Ivor the Engine Driver', 'Soon Be Home' and 'You Are

---

14 The Mod look had been encouraged by Peter Meaden, who helped to re-model the Who with Mod fashion.
15 Stamp, nrother of actor Terence Stamp, managed the Who up until 1975.
16 See appendix.

Forgiven'). It shared the theme of erotic betrayal with *Tommy*.

The Who were one of the big rock acts of the 1960s and 1970s era who were connected to not one but two outstanding movies – *Tommy* and *The Kids Are Alright* (some would add *Quadrophenia*). The Who fared better than, say, Led Zeppelin with their disappointing (and in places truly wacky) *Song Remains the Same* movie (1976), or Pink Floyd with the self-loathing, ultra-cynical and bleak *The Wall* (1982). Meanwhile, some rock acts, such as Genesis, Yes, Emerson, Lake and Palmer, King Crimson,[17] Deep Purple, Black Sabbath and Cream have no such famous, myth-making movies.

♪

Wrecking hotels rooms, chucking television sets out of buildings,[18] driving a Rolls Royce into a fish pond – the Who had their fair share of crazy antics (the famous incidents occurred, as with many of the supergroups, in the 1970s). Roger Daltrey flattened Pete Townshend with a punch in a recording studio, for instance, and Townshend chucked a chair thru a glass partition in a studio, causing 1,000s of $$$$$ of damage. Moony driving a Rolls Royce car into a pool was perhaps the most legendary of Moon the Loon's pranks (he also drove Chevrolets into swimming pools,[19] inviting people to look). Moon liked dropping high explosives into toilets and blowing up hotel doors (he used cherry bombs, and famously blew up his drum kit on live TV in the U.S.A.; Townshend said he had been made permanently deaf by Moon's explosion).

PETE TOWNSHEND.

The long-awaited autobiography of Pete Townshend – *Who I Am* – arrived in 2012. It was fascinating. Guilt over relationships with other women while married (to Karen Ashley); mad infatuations with women that went nowhere or led to rejection (such as actress Theresa Russell, star of the Ken Russell movie *Whore*); guilt over abandoning his family, and not being there for his daughters; 'oddly guilty about my professional success' (201); a workaholic who ran away from the present (and the past); indulging in a *ton* of drinking (Rémy Martin) and drug-taking (cocaine); getting drunk but trying to abstain; abstaining but then giving in (sometimes with disastrous consequences); buying houses in Twickenham and Richmond (Townshend has been long associated with West London), and boats for vacations in Cornwall or Greece; hanging out with famous friends like Eric Clapton, Mick Jagger and George Harrison; plenty of jolly japes from Keith Moon during the Who years; and a lot of background information on the Who (including Townshend's numerous dis-

---

17 Pete Townshend was a fan of *In the Court of the Crimson King*: 'an uncanny masterpiece'.
18 Launching TV sets out of hotel windows has all of the hallmarks of Keith Moon – silly, pointless, destructive (and the touch that the TV set had to be switched on – requiring extension cables – was typical of Moon, too).
19 And a Lincoln Continental into a Holiday Inn pool with, Moon insists, himself at the steering wheel (as well as destroying cars and a piano with fire extinguishers. The hotel gave Moon a $36,000 bill).

satisfactions, doubts, and disillusionments).

The early life depicted in the Pete Townshend autobiography included his darkest period, around the age of 7, when he lived with his grandmother Denny. This is the period of sexual abuse (tho' Townshend doesn't go into details). Some of that appears in the musical of *Tommy* (tho' Townshend asked the Ox to pen the songs, finding the material too disturbing).[20]

In his autobiography, Pete Townshend describes many typical activities of being young in Britain after WWII (some of which appear in the movie *Tommy*): his best mate Jimpy (and the trouble they used to get into); anxiety over his parents breaking up (then getting back together again); seeing his father Cliff Townshend (1916-1986) playing live at concerts; visits to seaside towns (again following his father with the swing band); holidays on the Isle of Man; the first fumblings with girls (he was a late developer, he confessed, while his mates, including the rest of the band, seemed to be doing well with girls); being encouraged at school in writing; the early instruments (the first guitars); going to Sunday school at church, and singing in a choir; and playing with his school chums (including John Entwistle) in his first bands (they called themselves the Confederates) in 1958.

Pete Townshend attended Ealing Art College[21] at the same time as he was playing with the Detours (at first the band 'felt like a side project' to Townshend). It got to the point where he had to choose between the band and his studies (the other members of the Detours worked – Townshend was the only student. Roger Daltrey was a metal worker, Entwistle was a tax clerk). By this time, he was earning £30 ($45) a week – very good money in those days (1963-64) – in fact, it was more than his lecturers at art college were making.

Pete Townshend often discusses the effect that music has on him in his autobiography – that alone would endear him to Ken Russell, for whom music was of absolutely primary significance. Townshend often talks about some near-mystical experiences of music when he was outdoors (and often beside water) – when he would hear 'the music of the spheres', so to speak. That is, the sound of nature itself, the flow of the universe, you might say: when he was in the Isle of Man fishing, he recounted:

> I got lost in the sound of the mouth organ, then had the most extraordinary, life-changing experience. Suddenly I was hearing music within the music – rich, complex harmonic beauty that had been locked in the sounds I'd been making. The next day I went fly fishing, and this time the murmuring sound of the river opened up a well-spring of music so enormous that I fell in and out of a trance. (30)

In his autobiography, Pete Townshend describes himself as happiest

---

20 At the time, Pete Townshend saw Tommy's experience of abuse as having a positive attribute. For Townshend, altho' Tommy had been raped by his uncle Ernie, he 'gets an incredible, spiritual push from it', he is 'incredibly elated'. It's not horrific, because for Tommy 'everything is incredible, meaningless beauty'.
21 At Ealing Art College, the typical British art school attitudes and practises prevailed.

when he's noodling about in the recording studio – and sometimes not even playing music, but setting up a new mixing desk, or messing about with his Synclavier, or trying out a new piece of gear. The recording studio is Townshend's 'garden shed', as he admits, a den where cranky, old guys can retreat to play about with their (expensive) toys, whether it's fishing, or motorbikes, or synthesizers.

Critics often talked up Keith Moon the Loon as the craziest performer in the Who, but Pete Townshend was, in a way, far nuttier.[22] He pulled all sorts of strange contortions on stage (including his famous, bird-like pose). It was Townshend, too, who seemed to have the rage and bile in him that fuelled his songwriting. He was the conceptual genius in the Who, the one coming up with the grand schemes, the cosmic themes, and the brilliant music to accompany his ideas.

Certainly there's an undercurrent of anger and resentment in the *Tommy* project, which crops up in the 1975 Columbia movie too, and it goes far beyond being merely teenage angst and social rebellion. Indeed, onto the character of Tommy Pete Townshend projects so much of his anxieties and fears as well as his pet targets, such as organized religion, families, parents, education, the waste of war, and institutions.

The psychological elements of Pete Townshend's personality would emerge throughout the Who's career: at times, Townshend comes across, in interviews and in some of his behaviour, as well as in the Who's lyrics and songs (and in the opinions of others), as an angst-ridden, self-doubting guy, with numerous moments of confusion, lassitude, self-loathing and depression. Townshend's rigorous self-analysis would permeate the Who's output, fuelling many of their greatest moments in music and on stage (and in movies). We have to keep reminding ourselves *pace Tommy* that it was Townshend who devised the concept, story, characters and themes.

For instance, Pete Townshend had an ambivalent attitude towards his audience: he wasn't afraid of criticizing the Who's fans, particularly towards the end of the 1970s (unusual among pop and rock stars, and unheard-of in celebrities – who's gonna criticize the people that buy the tickets, Tee shirts an' records?). Townshend seems to have relied a good deal on (or reacted to) how the Who were perceived, especially by the fans. He criticized fans for living thru the Who, for wanting too much of him, and for expecting too much of rock 'n' roll (even though Townshend was very idealistic about what rock music could do – changing people's perceptions, and even changing the world. And how he often spoke of fans living thru the music).[23]

Pete Townshend veered between the out-and-out idealism of the

---

22 Pete Townshend also got tired of Moon's looning – it might've been funny afterwards, or to other people, but Moon could also 'be a twat', as Townshend put it. 'How amusing it has been to spend my life pretending it was amusing' (128).
23 There seems to be an incident or two behind Townshend's critique of the fans – incidents which aren't mentioned in his autobiography. *Tommy* of course contains a lengthy episode about fans and adulation, starring Ken Russell's daughter Victoria as Sally Simpson.

1960s, with its goals of utopia, nirvana, heaven, a hippy paradise, fuelled by drugs and spiritual gurus such as Meher Baba, and a realistic and cynical recognition that those ideals cannot be achieved, that society and politics are way more complicated than people realize, that the fans don't understand what he's trying to do, and that nothing seems to change in the end.

Meher Baba (1864-1969), the Indian mystic (born in Poona, India, as Merwan Sheheriarji Irani), was a significant influence on Pete Townshend, and on the *Tommy* project, including its religious and messianic themes (Townshend travelled to India, like the Beatles). Baba was 'always a presiding presence over my work on *Tommy*, in whatever form', Townshend admitted (2012, 421). Meher Baba (his name means 'compassionate father') made a vow of silence in July, 1925, and kept to it until his death.

Do your best, then leave the results to me and don't worry – be happy.

This is one of Meher Baba's famous sayings. The theme of silence and of being worshipped as a messiah or religious leader would of course play into *Tommy*. If one wants to see it, there is plenty of Baba's vision in *Tommy*.[24] However, the 1975 movie inevitably leans much more towards Ken Russell's penchant for OTT Catholic imagery and themes, rather than Eastern and Indian religion. If you hire Russell as your director, you have to expect that – this is the guy who directed *The Devils*, *The Music Lovers*, and *Mahler*! Not to mention five of the most incredible television documentaries about dancers, painters and composers: *Dante's Inferno*, *The Debussy Film*, *Delius: Song of Summer*, *Isadora Duncan* and *The Dance of the Seven Veils*.

The ending of *Tommy*, for example, was pure Ken Russell: it depicts Roger Daltrey joyously running, swimming and climbing towards a mountain-top (filmed in Russell's beloved Lake District), greeting the rising sun with raised arms. It was meant to be a mythic finale of rebirth (accompanied by the Who's 'Listening to you I hear the music').

KEITH MOON.

Keith Moon's (1946-78) musical style was unique: no other mainstream rock drummer sounded so cacophonous, so wild, so all-over-the-place. For some, he was *the* rock drummer; he tended to lead the Who, rather be in the background providing the beat. With Pete Townshend, he became the focus of attention in the band. Both Moon and Townshend smashed up their instruments on-stage, Moon kicking over his cymbals and drums, and Townshend hurling his guitar into the speaker stacks. Towards the end, though, he was literally all over the place. By 1978, aged 32, bloated and slow, and looking ten years older, Moon was dead from a drug overdose, ironically from the pills that were supposed to cure

---

24 Pete Townshend later ruefully commented that he'd wished he'd simply let Baba's philosophy speak for itself – 'don't worry, be happy, leave the results to God', instead of wrapping it up in an entertainment package. Townshend decided that audiences wouldn't respond to a direct statement.

him of his alcoholism. (He had gone to live in Los Angeles, which some say encouraged his wild lifestyle; L.A. was certainly a party town for many rock stars in the Seventies; he returned to Blighty in 1977).

Keith Moon was the authentic, over-the-top rock star, whose sensation-seeking excessive antics have become part of popular legend. A perennial party animal, Moon pursued an extravagant rock career fuelled by alcohol, pills, and crazy stunts (as Tony Fletcher noted in his biography). His drug and drink intake was prodigious: champers and half a bottle of Courvusier for breakfast; purple hearts, uppers, downers, cocaine, etc. When it becomes rock myth, it's hilarious, but when it was happening at the time, as John Entwistle said, Keith's Moonery was 'a pain in the arse'.

MORE ON *TOMMY*, THE ALBUM.

1969's album *Tommy*[25] was about a deaf, dumb and blind youth, from a dysfunctional family, living in a dysfunctional society. *Tommy* explored the familiar themes in rock music of alienation, disaffection, loneliness, insanity, spirituality, sexuality and excess. The album contained some Who classics, such as 'Pinball Wizard', 'See Me, Feel Me', 'The Acid Queen' and 'I'm Free'.[26] In the 1975 Columbia movie, the Second World War and its aftermath of Fifties austerity cast a long shadow over *Tommy*; the movie goes back over the pre-war period, and the immediate post-war era, into the 'present' of the 1960s. When *Tommy* was being written (and later filmed), WW2 was still an enormous influence on life in Britain (ah, but it still is – in fact, at times Britain feels as if it's still struggling thru WWII). But for the 1969 album, Tommy is born in 1921, so that Tommy's youth occurs primarily in the 1930s, a quite different era from the 1950s (austere, but with a different kind of austerity).

*Tommy* had a substantial after-life, not only as the 1975 movie, but on stage and in revivals (though it hasn't quite been as successful as the Andrew Lloyd Weber and Tim Rice musicals, such as *Jesus Christ Superstar, Cats* and *Starlight Express*). I saw *Tommy* on stage in London's West End in 1979, at the Queen's Theatre, with my sister Mandie, and loved it (this was a version of the Rainbow Theatre production). *Tommy* on stage was an impressive theatrical experience. It has been revived a number of times, including a Broadway production at the St James Theater in 1993 called *The Who's Tommy* (this was a very successful show that was showered with awards),[27] which was overseen by Pete Townshend. There was also a touring ballet of *Tommy*. *Tommy* was revived in Toronto in 1995; in London's West End in 1996-97; in Gotham

---

25 The first plans for *Tommy* were written in the U.S.A., when the Who were on tour.

26 There is some padding on the album. 'Undertune', for instance, goes on and on with an undistinguished instrumental (running 10m 07s). This noodling about would resurface in live performances (such as at the Isle of Wight).

27 *The Who's Tommy* received 11 Tony Award nominations (winning 5, including one for Peter Townshend, which greatly pleased him). It opened to a box office of $494,897, and ran for 899 performances.

in 2008; and in 2013 in Ontario.

In August, 1989, the Who performed *Tommy* at the Universal Amphitheater, with guests that included Phil Collins, Billy Idol, Steve Winwood and Patti LaBelle. In 1992 *Tommy* was re-staged in San Diego (directed by Des McAnuff). For some of the new versions of *Tommy*, Pete Townshend composed new songs (such as 'I Believe My Own Eyes').

The members of the Who fought with each other legally over *Tommy*: Roger Daltrey and John Entwistle, for example, argued with Pete Townshend over his involvement with the stage show of *Tommy* (one of the bones of contention was the *Tommy* Grand Right document).[28]

Pete Townshend has admitted to feeling possessive about *Tommy*, and has been involved directly in most of its incarnations. Like *Quadrophenia* and *Lifehouse*, *Tommy* is a project close to Townshend's heart, one he can't or won't let go of.

As *Tommy* became more well-known, sometimes punters thought that Tommy was part of the band, or they mistook Roger Daltrey for Tommy, or thought the band were called Tommy the Who.

### *TOMMY* ON STAGE.

As a live show, *Tommy* has been performed in many incarnations. Indeed, it would require a whole book to record all of the productions given to *Tommy*. So this musical, with its unusual and unconventional story, must touch something in audiences, for it to have been revived so many times. It comes way out of leftfield, from a band that wasn't trained or well-versed in musical theatre, that hadn't got a track record of producing musicals, and that crafted a story and a character from somewhere far removed from the usual sources of musicals.

First and foremost must be the performances the Who themselves have given *Tommy* – from the late 1960s up to the present day. Way b4 the 1975 movie production, or subsequent musical theatre performances, the Who had already delivered many shows of *Tommy*,[29] usually played right thru without an interval (remember that *Tommy* was created in the recording studio specifically as something that the Who could perform live as their usual bass-drums-guitar-vox band set-up,[30] without additional musicians or performers: it was a rock opera or a rock cantata,[31] but for four musicians). *Tommy* was performed at the Metropolitan Opera House in Gotham (but only once – on June 7, 1970).

Early stage productions of *Tommy* included a college show at the University of South Carolina, a ballet by Les Grands Ballets Canadiens in Montreal in 1970 (which came to Broadway for 2 weeks and toured the

---

28 There has been some legal dispute over the years about whether Pete Townshend signed the Grand Right document (a type of copyright which is legal in the U.S.A., but not in Britain).
29 The Who had performed *Tommy* over 160 times.
30 Townshend remarked: 'although it was recorded – it was recorded and composed for the stage. It had to work live'.
31 *Jazz & Pop* magazine insisted in its review of the 1969 album that *Tommy* wasn't an opera: it's 'a rock cantata: in other words, a piece of music which is primarily vocal – a sung piece'.

U.S.A.), a stage show in Seattle, another in Hollywood (at the Aquarius Theater), and Lone Mountain College in Frisco.

Another era of performance of *Tommy* was the orchestral outing of 1972, overseen by producer Lou Reizner. Then came the movie – which necessitated a whole new block of recording sessions (and new arrangements, new musicians, new lyrics, and new songs). In the late 1970s, *Tommy* was reconceived for a musical theatre production which went to London's West End and Broadway (in 1979). The musical was revived, and also newly interpreted by subsequent productions (including 1992, 1993, 1995, 1996-97, 2008 and 2013). *Tommy* has also been prod-uced specifically for video.

For the production of the 1990s (directed by Des McAnuff), the ending was changed: now Tommy's family is re-united (Pete Townshend was OK with that change,[32] tho' some found it mawkish. Townshend defended the changed ending with the family re-united: 'the family is a fucking battlefield in which we grow up, and I think that rock and roll is about the moment we leave it and become alone').

When you to add that already long list many amateur and student productions, and tribute bands, and charity gigs, you can see that altho' *Tommy* is known as a movie, and two main recordings by the Who and friends (in 1969 and the movie soundtrack in 1975), it has also flourished in the theatre.

We should also note that *Tommy* changed quite a bit over the years, with new arrangements and new songs being added, as well as old songs being interpreted in new ways. Indeed, *Tommy* would possibly not have been such an enduring piece if it hadn't changed over the years. (The movie version has influenced the subsequent stage productions. For example, producers have followed Ken Russell's structural alteration, changing the timeline to begin in WWII.)

Purist Who fans might regard the original 1969 album and the subsequent live shows by the Who themselves as the *Tommy* project at its height, but each incarnation has its pluses and minuses. For instance, when the Who performed *Tommy* in the early days, it could be somewhat rambling. Listen to one of the Who's stand-out concerts, at the Isle of Wight Festival, and you find the Who meandering a little, with Pete Townshend getting lost in unaccompanied guitar sections.

THE WHO LIVE.

Live,[33] the Who could be extraordinary: they had stunning songs, the requisite supergroup lasers and lightshow, and some charismatic performers: Roger Daltrey was the typical, rock god-type lead singer (though not too tall), with a mane of blond curls, with a trademark

---

32 'In the end the whole story turns to face God. when the people stand up and cheer, even though they may not know it, they're actually praying', Townshend said of this ending (N. Cawthorne, 190).

33 The Who prided themselves on always delivering a show. Very rarely, they would have to abandon a show – as when Moony took three elephant tranquill-izers.

gesture of hurling the mic lead around like a lasso, and stomping his feet in a march; John Entwistle stood off to one side, the stereotype of the quiet, implacable bass player ('the quiet one'), long fingers running up and down the bass neck (Entwistle would complain that he wasn't quiet – it was everyone else who was too loud). Entwistle was known for his unusual approach to bass playing, using it more as a lead instrument to Pete Townshend's rhythm guitar and power chords.

The real spectacle in the Who, though, were Keith Moon and Pete Townshend. Moon had a style of drumming all his own, a frenetic cacophony of sounds generated by his sticks flailing around his Premier drum kit in all directions. Moon was an irrepressible showman, hurling his sticks into the air, grimacing, and finally kicking his drum kit to bits at the end of the set. Another of Moon's favourite ploys was to blow up his drum kit using cherry bombs, or put goldfish in his floor tom.

Pete Townshend, meanwhile, was a dynamic force on stage, with his trademark moves of a propeller or windmill or 'Birdman'[34] arm playing power chords on his Gibson guitar, leaping into the air and scissor-kicking, and long-jumping along the stage, landing on his knees. A gangly, chaotic figure, he was clearly the band leader (or was he? Of the music, yes – but Townshend has also stated: 'Roger was the leader, and always had been' [346]). Townshend also created feedback effects, used the mic stand like a violin bow, and shoved his guitar into the speakers, ruining thousands of pounds worth of guitars.[35] Part of that stage act appears in the film of *Tommy* – particularly the Destroying The Guitar bit, and Moon kicking over his drum kit (it would be crazy not to have some of that in the movie. But in *Tommy*, it doesn't stand out, because this is a picture *stuffed* with crazy moments!).

Among the famous Who live appearances were Woodstock, Monterey,[36] the Isle of Wight, and the Leeds concerts. After Moony's passing, they appeared at Live Aid, tho' 15 fans dying at a Cincinnati concert was probably their lowest point. With the death of John Entwistle in Las Vegas at the age of 58, the Who continued to perform and record. They appeared at the Royal Albert Hall, for instance (a show later released on DVD), in New York City for a post-9/11 concert in 2001, in Las Vegas in 1999, and at *Live 8* in July, 2005 (where their incredible performance stole the show, really, though the reformation of the original members of Pink Floyd was also amazing). The Who were still recording albums into the 2000s – with *Endless Wire* in 2006, for instance (however, *Endless Wire* was their first studio album for some 24 years).

---

34 Pete Townshend stole the windmill move from Keef Richards, when he saw him warming up at a gig in 1963. But while Richards mighta done it once, Townshend made it one of his trademarks: it's not a Who gig unless Townshend is whirling like a madman.
35 Guitar roadies would dutifully try to glue the smashed guitars back together.
36 Jimi Hendrix and the Mamas and the Papas were on the bill.

LIFE HOUSE.

Around the late 1960s, Pete Townshend developed his *Life House* project, which was linked to the themes of *Tommy*, and involved happenings at the Young Vic Theatre in London. *Life House* was another search for spiritual transformation in a materialist world, using the familiar story in rock music of an alienated individual's quest for self-transcendence. Nobody seemed to understand what the *Life House* story was about, except Townshend. The rest of the band were baffled. It had a less easily grasped through-line than *Tommy* (in fact, nobody seemed to quite grasp it). For Townshend, it involved spiritual searching, as with *Tommy*, but with ecological, cosmological elements (there was a journey thru a dystopian Britain). *Life House* was also going to feature an early exploration of virtual reality, with the hero putting on a suit which would enable him to have artificially constructed experiences. So it was partly about brainwashing and indoctrination, about controlling the masses through technology (*A Clockwork Orange* explored similar territory in the same era).

The *Life House* project would be revived a number of times by its author, on stage and in music. Some of the *Life House* songs found their way onto Who albums, most famously *Who's Next*. Pete Townshend was particularly taken with the possibility of music as a transformative experience, especially on a spiritual level. Thus, in the *Life House* project, music would literally change people's thinking, and their lives. You can hear it in the lovely song 'Pure and Easy' (a.k.a. 'The Note'), the signature song of *Life House*:

> There once was a note, pure and easy,
> Playing so free, like a breath, rippling by.
> The note is eternal, I hear it, it sees me,
> Forever we blended, forever we die.

The goal is a single piece of music, or just one note, that would be transcendent, that could change the world, that would bring performers and audience together in union (this faith in the miraculous potential of music recurs throughout Pete Towsnshend's repertoire). 'The core of my idea was that we could all hear music – and compose it – if only we would truly listen', Townshend remarked (204). Yet that super-spiritual note would also be apocalyptic: in 1970, Townshend said that the note would create 'complete devastation. And when everything is destroyed, only the real note, the true note that they have been looking for is left. Of course, there is no one left to hear it'.[37]

Pete Townshend's faith in music as spiritual transformation must've appealed to Ken Russell: both were incredibly passionate about music. Remember Russell's statement: 'music is the most incredible event in human history'.

---

37 Quoted in C. Heylin, 150.

QUADROPHENIA: THE ALBUM.

The album *Quadrophenia* was a hit for the Who, reaching number 2 in the U.K. and U.S.A. For Pete Townshend, *Quadrophenia* was 'about growing up' for its hero, Jimmy the London Mod. It was the Who at their finest for Townshend, but Roger Daltrey got fed up with the project, partly because the recording of it dragged on for so long. Daltrey also wasn't happy at all with the way the vocals had been mixed in the *Quadrophenia* album: due to a technical fault, they are too often buried in the mix, with too much reverb added. (The album was remixed in 1979 for the *Quadrophenia* movie, but that didn't please Daltrey either).

For Pete Townshend, *Quadrophenia* was difficult to realize as a dramatic performance in the form of a stage show because it was largely a psychological story: 'it's an inside view. It's an internal story', Townshend explained. It was about someone forced to work things out for himself: about growing up and forming one's identity in a postwar world in which new ambiguities and uncertainties had shifted the balance of power between the generations. It was a teenage rebellion – but against what? and for what purpose? That was what Jimmy had to find out in the story of *Quadrophenia*. (Townshend and Roger Daltrey disagreed about how to present the story of *Quadrophenia*: Daltrey reckoned it need explaining to the audience, but Townshend didn't think it was very complicated).

The title of the *Quadrophenia* album was about an effect that the *Tommy* movie explored: split personalities (suggested by the mirrors). It also referred to the four members of the Who, and also to the quadraphonic sound system. (Pete Townshend had begun with developing something about the four members of the Who, so that each section would not only express aspects of the Who's personalities as ('extremely eccentric') individuals but also aspects of the central character.[38] Instead of being 'schizophrenic', it would be 'quadroph(r)enic' – that is, it would be, once again, about psychological disturbance, one of *Tommy*'s perennial themes). 'This isn't a direct nostalgic thing, it's more a search for the essence of what makes everything tick,' Townshend asserted.

*Quadrophenia* is an album that's been worked over intensively in the recording studio. The term is 'over-produced', and *Quadrophenia* does sound like that (other acts famous for spending months in the studio in the same obsessive manner included Queen and 10CC). It is full of atmospheric sounds, such as the ocean, the wind, the radio, cars, etc.[39]

The 1979 movie version of *Quadrophenia* was no doubt encouraged by the success of *Tommy* – indeed, Ken Russell's regular producer, Roy Baird, co-produced *Quadrophenia*. Russell said he'd wanted to make *Quadrophenia*, and hadn't liked director Franc Roddam's interpretation

---

38 Townshend wanted to 'to try to stay *inside* my hero for the entire opera', with a 'four-angled approach' that would be '*quadrophenic*' (237).
39 Pete Townshend said he was inspired by Walter (Wendy) Carlos's album *Sonic Seasonings* (248).

(BP, 232).[40] Oh, if only the producers of *Quadrophenia* had given Russell the helm, particularly after seeing what a wonderful job Russell did on *Tommy*.

### THE KIDS ARE ALRIGHT.

The Who also appeared in *The Kids Are Alright* (Jeff Stein, 1979), a documentary on the band, which included some specially staged live performances (such as at Shepperton Studios, which closes the movie with an all-out rendition of 'Won't Get Fooled Again'). *The Kids Are Alright* is an absolute gem of a movie, collecting in one place so many incredible performances by the Who, on TV shows such as *Beat Club*, *Top of the Pops* and *Ready, Steady, Go*, some very early appearances, their outstanding turn on the *Rolling Stones Rock and Roll Circus*, their famous appearance at Woodstock, and also many TV interviews (plus some silliness staged for *The Kid Are Alright* with Keith Moon and Ringo Starr, and John Entwistle). And a famous soundbite from Ken Russell on the significance of the Who.

*The Kids Are Alright* is without doubt one of the great rock 'n' roll movies – even better that it allows the music and the band to speak for themselves, without narration or overloading the viewer with information (there are no captions detailing the TV appearances, for instance). *The Kids Are Alright* also manages to capture some of excitement of the Who's incendiary live performances. Director Jeff Stein offers an illuminating commentary on the DVD release of *The Kids Are Alright*, and reckons that the Who were definitely the greatest live band. He may be right. The excellent recent documentary *The Amazing Journey* (2007) brings together even more performances, with contemporary interviews.

### AFTER THE OFFICIAL SPLIT.

When was the Last Great Who album? Fans and critics differ. For some, it was *Quadropehnia* (1973), for others, it was 1978's *Who Are You*. But the Who soldiered on following Keith Moon's death in 1978, with Kenney Jones as drummer, producing *Faces Dances* in 1981, *It's Hard* in 1982, and a long wait (24 years!) b4 *Endless Wire* in 2006. (Jones had the impossible task of replacing Moon on drums, and no matter what he did, there was no way he could follow that crazy guy, as Jones knew as well as anybody. Fans were split, but at least the Who were carrying on. Roger Daltrey, however, was never convinced that Jones was strong enough for the Who, and publicly criticized the drummer. It was Daltrey who insisted that Jones was eventually dropped).

---

40 While the Who were recording the *Quadrophenia* album, Ken Russell was in the studio from time to time, for meetings about the *Tommy* script.

# QUADROPHENIA

*Quadrophenia*, although directed by Franc Roddam, can be regarded as a Pete Townshend movie (as can *Tommy*): it was Townshend's concept and story, his characters, and his music dominates the movie.[41] The Who's music and imagery is seen throughout *Quadrophenia*: the posters in Jimmy's bedroom, album covers, the video clip of the Who on the TV pop show *Ready, Steady, Go*, the mods dancing to 'My Generation' at a party, and the use of the Who's music all through the film, illustrating the narrative (especially in the largely dialogue-free closing section, where one Who song after another leads and comments on the action).[42]

*Quadrophenia* starred a bunch of young British actors who would appear in many other films and TV shows of the 1980s and later: Phil Daniels (superb as Jimmy Cooper),[43] Sting (as Ace), Phil Davis, Mark Wingett, Leslie Ash[44] (as Steph), Toyah Wilcox (as Monkey), Garry Cooper, Ray Winstone, Gary Shail and Timothy Spall. The surviving members of the Who acted as musical supervisors (that would be inevitable – there's no way that Pete Townshend would have a movie made from his musical without being involved). *Quadrophenia* concerns another of Townshend's disaffected youths, familiar from his *Tommy* rock opera (and many of his songs, including the later ones).

---

41 Writers David Humphries and Martin Stellman were hired to pen the screenplay (Franc Roddam shares the writing credit). Humphries was a TV writer (*Target, The Professionals*), and also worked on *Flame* (1975), Slade's movie, and the Joan Collins/ Jackie Collins movies *The Bitch* (1979), one of the worst movies ever made in Britain, and *The Stud* (which Humphries co-wrote with Christopher Stagg), a piece of s-$-$-t, a truly, God-awful movie.

42 However, there is less Who music than one would expect, and far less of the album *Quadrophenia* than there is of *Tommy* the 1969 album in *Tommy* the movie. In fact, you hanker after more music in *Quadrophenia*.
The soundtrack for the movie also includes 'Louie Louie', 'Green Onions', and 'Be My Baby'. As it's a dramatic story, rather than a musical, the music tends to be supporting the action; in *Tommy*, of course, it leads the action throughout (only the later part of *Quadrophenia* uses the 'operatic' approach of *Tommy*).

43 That Phil Daniels also looked a little like the young Pete Townshend helped – to emphasize this, in the early scene where Jimmy returns to his bedroom (pinning up a news cutting next to his nudie photos), Daniels leans against the wall where there's a prominent b/w photo of Townshend.

44 It was one of the Leslie Ash's first acting jobs – she was 17 at the time she went for the audition at Shepperton Studios.

*Quadrophenia* is set in familiar Who territory – West London, around Shepherd's Bush and Goldhawk's Road, and Brighton[45] (and it was filmed in many locations in West London, as well as Covent Garden). Apart from the narrative of Jimmy's alienation from everyone around him, *Quadrophenia* can be seen as a nostalgic pæan to an aspect of British culture in the 1960s: the mods, the green parka coats and jeans, the scooters, the emphasis on style, the parties, the dancehalls, the cafés, the fights between mods and rockers, and, above all, the music.

A youth-oriented film, like *Tommy*, *Quadrophenia* conjured up very familiar youth themes: hanging out in gangs, sitting around in bars and cafés, rebelling against authority figures (parents, people in the workplace, the police), doing menial jobs (Jimmy is a dogsbody in an advertizing agency), gambling with cards, having a haircut, drug-taking, burglary, drinking, and fighting. The *form*, as far as these teenage pursuits are concerned, is wholly American, no matter how much of the movie appears to be 'British'. *Quadrophenia* demonstrates, once again, that the concept of 'youth' and 'youth culture' was largely manufactured in the U.S.A.

One of the main narrative threads of *Quadrophenia* was a simple love story, concerning Jimmy's attempt to date his dream girl (Steph). It was all stuff seen a million times in the movies. What gave *Quadrophenia* an edge over other coming-of-age youth movies was the fury of Jimmy's character; his anger (directed most of all at himself), and by the end of the film, the total alienation from everyone in his life (there was also a plethora of bad language – *de rigeur* in any youth movie). It was a parallel to Tommy's journey – though Tommy starts with alienation and ends up in a more positive place.

Some of this edge derived from the timing of *Quadrophenia* – it was released in the era just after punk (1979);[46] one can see this in the house party scene, where Jimmy puts on the Who's youth anthem 'My Generation',[47] which sets the mods pogo-ing around the room, like punks at a Clash gig; punk bands acknowledged the influence of bands of the late 1960s, such as the Who, the Small Faces and the Rolling Stones (the Sex Pistols weren't the only punk act who used to play covers of Stones and Faces songs. And much of punk rock anyway sounded like rougher, pumped-up David Bowie, Stones, Kinks and the Who). *Quadrophenia* also employed some of the stars of the punk scene (Sting and Toyah Wilcox). However, the love story was added to Pete Townshend's concept for *Quadrophenia*, and 'doesn't have much to do with the musical journey I mapped out'.

In the end, for Jimmy, the two main areas in his life – Steph, and the mods – combine in an orgiastic manner in *Quadrophenia*: he fucks Steph right in the middle of the battle between the mods and the rockers in

---

45 It filmed in 24 locations in Brighton.
46 The movie might've benefitted from being released two years earlier, at the height of the Sex Pistols and punk rock era.
47 That Jimmy selects the 7-inch single at that moment because his dream girl Steph has just walked out with her boyfriend is the perfect embodiment of using pop music as an emotional catharsis (which's one of Pete Townshend's maxims).

Brighton, literally a climax for him of his life with the mods gang and his romance with Steph.[48] (That would be the perfect day out for many a mod, rocker, skin, hippy, New Ager or metal freak: a fuck and a riot by the seaside). These scenes, filmed on location in Brighton (tho' the long shots of the town are of Eastbourne), are the most famous in the 1979 movie.

Phil Daniels[49] turned in an accomplished performance in *Quadrophenia* as Jimmy, moving from a naïve enjoyment of life to being a complete outsider. For Jimmy, as for so many anti-heroes in youth movies, nothing seems to fit. He loses his girlfriend to his best mate Dave, becomes disaffected with his gang of mods, hankers for the idyll that Brighton represented (and is already, as a teenager, dreaming nostalgically of his past), falls out violently with his parents, leaves home, loses his job, and wanders aimlessly (on the train, in a rather too literal, pop video illustration of the Who song, he's 'out of his brain on the 5.15'). Even the mod he admires, Ace (Sting), who seemed to be so cool, who drove an amazing scooter, turns out to be nothing more than a bellboy at a Brighton hotel.

With nowhere to go, Jimmy ends up stealing Ace's shiny scooter and making for the famous suicide spot of Seven Sisters, near Eastbourne. The 1979 movie inevitably ends with Jimmy apparently driving off the iconic, white, chalk cliffs on the scooter[50] (however, the movie also ambiguously opens with an image of Jimmy on the cliffs walking towards the camera in silhouette – *away* from the ocean behind him. Also, we don't see Jimmy falling, only the totemic scooter: the ending is thus open-ended: many in the cast and crew reckoned that Jimmy was saying goodbye to his former life, breaking free, but he didn't kill himself: it was a symbolic suicide).

The vehemence and self-loathing evoked in the final act of *Quadrophenia* is striking. Jimmy's anger and frustration doesn't really fit in with the rest of the movie, and seems out of balance with the persona created earlier. Suddenly, Jimmy becomes a manic depressive Angry Young Man, screaming at the mail men who run down his scooter accidentally, yelling at his mom (and later his dad), pleading with Steph, telling his boss to shove his job up his ass, and generally ranting at the world which doesn't understand him or want him (*Saturday Night Fever* depicted much of the same teen rebellion two years earlier, but in a far, far more powerful and charismatic way). Jimmy embodies the 'teenage wasteland' of the Who's song, a classic image of a kid who doesn't know what he wants, doesn't know how to get it, who finds everything frustrating or corrupt or dumb

---

48 But probably not a climax for Steph.
49 John Lydon of the Sex Pistols was considered for the role of Jimmy – how cool would that have been! However, Lydon didn't have the acting experience, and neither was he right for the role physically (S. Grantley, 177). Franc Roddam said that Lydon had been auditioned (and did well), but the film's insurers wouldn't insure him (they also didn't believe Lydon would have the professionalism to turn up to a five week shoot – such was the media impact of punk rock. People really did believe punk rockers were like that! Lydon, of course, could be completely professional and focussed when he wanted to be – as his subsequent career showed. Lydon has made TV documentaries). 6
50 The album closes with Jimmy in a suicidal mood, stealing a boat and sailing out to a rock in the ocean.

or not worth his time.

In *Quadrophenia*'s final scenes, Jimmy becomes a rather pathetic, lonely figure – the scenes take 'downbeat' and 'self-loathing' to new levels of depression and desperation: the way that Jimmy heads for Brighton, visiting the site of earlier happiness, like the alley where he schtupped Steph (which's now a mod shrine!), and loons about on the beach, and takes drugs, and wallows in his own hopelessness and helplessness... It's *incredibly* bitter, an attitude that would never appear in a Ken Russell movie![51] (You can see that acute bitterness in other pop movies of the period, such as *Rude Boy, Jubilee, The Wall* and *Breaking Glass*).

*Quadrophenia* was shoddily directed at times (visually, it was sometimes dull, with some lacklustre camerawork and awkward, lengthy takes), and featured some simplistic (but also charming) dramatizations of disaffected youth. For example, there was a very stereotypical scene of Jimmy watching *Ready, Steady, Go* (a TV music show of the 1960s) in the front room of his parents' house, absolutely loving watching the Who, with his father (Michael Elphick) coming in and complaining about the louts making a racket on TV (a stereotype in every respect, yet pop musicians as well as fans have cited exactly this scenario – of irritating parents – as fundamental in their pop culture growth). Other scenes were similarly naïve (such as the house party which the mods crash, with couples having sex in the upstairs rooms – Jimmy, instead of tupping a girl, as his mates're doing, opts to drive his scooter around the lawn to wreck the flowers. No, it isn't *Tommy*!).[52]

*Quadrophenia* was one of a group of youth-oriented and popular music films which aimed to depict the darker, more cynical aspect of growing up in modern Britain (others might include: *Stardust, Backbeat, Sid and Nancy,* and, to a lesser extent, *Trainspotting, The Acid House, Twin Town, The Great Rock 'n' Roll Swindle, Rita, Sue and Bob Too, That'll Be the Day,* and *Naked*). Like *Tommy, Quadrophenia* has had an after-life on stage (though not as often revived as *Tommy*: it was staged as a 'workshop' production in Cardiff, Wales in 2007, and later toured, in 2009. The Who have also revisited the piece).

*Quadrophenia* is crippled by the disease that affects all of British cinema – realism, or attempts at realism, or social-realism, or naturalism, whatever you wanna call it – which stems back way beyond the 'kitchen sink' dramas of the early 1960s (the period of this movie), into the 'Free Cinema' movement of the 1950s and to the documentary tradition of the 1930s.

Consequently, *Quadrophenia* isn't the portrayal of the inner, psychological and spiritual world of Jimmy the West London mod, as the Who's

---

51 On the plus side, the dialogue is sometimes allowed to falter so that the Who's music can take centre stage. And then the movie is imagery accompanying music.
52 Steve Grantley and Alan Parker reckon that *Quadrophenia* has aged better than *Tommy* (2010, 181), but although *Quadrophenia* has a cult following, you can't even put it beside *Tommy*.

album was (and as Pete Townshend definitely intended).⁵³ The 1973 *Quadrophenia* album contains plenty of yearning, searching, quasi-spiritual material and music (interspersed with numerous sound effects sequences),⁵⁴ but the 1979 movie is a social-realist portrait of growing up in England in the 1960s (there is, for instance, a lot of the filmmakers' own memories and ideas about being young in England in the 1960s in *Quadrophenia*. Director Franc Roddam consciously moved in a different direction from the 1975 movie of *Tommy*).

So *Quadrophenia* isn't the movie of the Who's recordings, nor is it the story told in that album, nor is it particularly Who-ish or Townshendian at all. The liveliness of the young cast, tho', keeps the thing entertaining, even tho' as a whole it comes across as a television movie, a cross between stalwarts of British television in the 1970s – such as *The Sweeney*, a 'worthy' left-wing TV play, and something from TV directors such as Alan Clarke, Ken Loach or Mike Leigh (and in that company, Ken Russell stands out as somebody *utterly different in every single respect!*).

---

53 Indeed, Townshend remarked that the interior-looking story of *Quadrophenia* made it harder to perform on stage.
54 Pete Townshend calls *Quadrophenia* 'a kind of distorted dream-view' rather than a 'straight narrative'. The 1979 movie, tho', moved away from late 1960s psychology and exploration to late 1970s, post-punk 'realism'.

# FANS ON KEN RUSSELL

A selection of reviews of Ken Russell's movies on Amazon.com.

(I haven't included film critics on Russell's work – no need to dish out more bile here!).

### ON *WOMEN IN LOVE*

Can you really do better that Alan Bates AND Oliver Reed? I love everything about this movie. It is filmed so beautifully and Glenda Jackson's performance gives me the chills. Many people know about this film because of its treatment of sexuality, but it is not raunchy or tasteless, it is perfect. This is one of my favorite movies to curl up and watch on a rainy afternoon. I suppose it is dated, but give it a chance and as crazy as it sounds, you too will start to fall in love.

- Flipping through cable stations late one night, I came across a bearded Alan Bates intellectually and poetically analogizing a fig to "the female part" before a party of mesmerized and embarrassed picnickers. I, too, was mesmerized, especially by the quiet, deep, limpid restraint of the scene, the little subtle expressions on the faces of the main characters revealing their fundamental natures, Bates's clear, precise voice, his deadly serious playfulness, the rich green English countryside, etc. Oliver Reed's reaction to the monologue was especially impressive for its understated humor and intelligence.

- I think a film can only attempt to show what the book more specifically says so to the mind the book will always be preferred but with a writer like Lawrence film makes perfect sense. In fact Lawrence's flaw is perhaps that he at times uses too many words when an image would suffice. So I love that someone as visually audacious as Ken Russell made this film. I've seen it many times and always love different things about it. Russell is usually equated with excess but here everything exists in just the right amount, nothing is overdone, he finds just the right way to convey literary content without overly revering it and so framing it too neatly.

- This is one of my all time favourite movies and after seeing it again on DVD, it still holds up really well. The photography and location shots are lush, beautiful and sensual, with superb acting by the whole cast.

- There is no need to summarize the story of the two sets of lovers; just see it. The major actors have never been better. They become the complex characters, who while not totally explained are something better: totally present and alive. They pick up a big slice of the private and public aura of the period in their wake. Also, the film has the most incredible punch line at the end which Russell just perfectly transmits.

### ON *THE DEVILS*

Wonderful, visually confrontational film by Ken Russell. This movie takes on: religion, politics, sin, sex, lust, love and (yes, even) honor through compelling performances by an outstanding and outlandish cast, led by Oliver Reed and Vanessa Redgrave.

- I first saw this Ken Russell masterpiece when I was 16, during its original release. Especially in retrospect, I can say that this is a film that changed the way I viewed films. I not only learned what acting and directing were about (from an astounding Oliver Reed and the unique Russell respectively), but also became aware of the impact of editing and, most of all from *The Devils*, what sets could do for a film. And what sets they were! Minimalist fortifications, virgin-white within and without, checkerboard tiling and nuns and their habits (never was black and white starker), claustrophobic yet open to the heavens. And the colour and the contrast, how they could render any scene surreal.

•

Passionately made, *The Devils*, still resonates, morally and politically, 40 years later: it remains a relevant, enduring piece of film making. A searing experience.

•

Aside from the quality of the transfer, this version of *The Devils* is one of the most bizarre films I have seen. I love it for its impact and its grotesque and over-the-top visuals, and it is enjoyable to watch in a twisted sense. It's a nightmare, it's a dream. It's horrifying, it's alienating. Also, it is brilliant! Russell is no doubt the film industry's anti-christ.

### ON *TOMMY*

As the five-star rating would indicate, I've loved TOMMY since the day it opened (and yes, I was there for its premiere). I've also purchased the movie in just about every incarnation that have been released: videotape, laserdisc, and now DVD.

•

Beautifully filmed, unique conception, brilliant use of symbolism, and over the top performances.

•

There are some artworks throughout the course of history that can scarcely be evaluated as either good or bad, because they are so unique... they are so THEMSELVES that they can't be compared to anything else. Such is TOMMY. Of all the incarnations of the TOMMY story (I can think of four now: the original concept album, a preliminary stage adaptation which featured Ringo Starr among others, this Ken Russell film, and the latest stage musical) this movie is by far my favorite.

•

Taken in all at once, *Tommy* the Movie is one bizarre, trippy experience.

•

One of the few movies that I watch over and over again without even for a moment feeling bored.

•

Long a personal favourite of mine, from the minute my brother brought home the soundtrack back in 1975 I knew TOMMY was something new, different & very special. The film fulfilled every expectation.

### ON *THE LAIR OF THE WHITE WORM*

This one was despised by the serious critics, but all that means is that they weren't weird enough to enjoy it. All right, it's trash. But it's great trash. It's my idea of a feelgood movie. It's kinky, erotic, scary, and funny. And bright. Literally. After zillions of creepy, dark, scary scenes in movies, the sunshine and well-lit rooms in this one emphasize the horror scenes. But who cares about the lighting? It's main attraction is an over-the-top performance by Amanda Donohoe as a very bad girl.

•

Ken Russell does it again, flourishing as a genius of mondobizarro cinema! Here he engages us in a game of sorts, pulling us into the action as it writhes around on the screen before us. It draws us in, taking every ounce of Donohoe's performance into our jealously campy hearts. You can't help but completely fall in love with every performace presented here, but Amanda Donohoe is fabulous!!! Complete with monstrous white worms lurking in caves, vampire cults, blood and gore, sword play, Hugh Grant at his campy best (outshining even the likes of Rupert Everett) and a satirical director at the top of his form. *Lair of the White Worm* is a masterpiece, a hidden gem that must be given serious reconsideration!

•

Up front, NOT everyone will like this film. It's a Ken Russell film, after all... Amanda Donohoe turns out a stunning performs as the Lady who is not a lady.

•

I watched it. I liked it. I felt guilty watching it and loving it. I had to buy it. Hugh Grant was okay. Catherine Oxenburg was gorgeous. Sammi Davis was lovable. Amanda Donohoe was outrageous as she stole the show.

•

Stoker could never have envisaged his creation being presented like this, but secretly – in his starched-collar, stoic Victorian way – I think he would've approved.

•

I love this film, I love this film, I love this film!

# KEN RUSSELL
✳
# FILMOGRAPHY

Films as director

Peepshow (1956)
Knights on Bikes (1956)
Amelia and the Angel (1957)
Lourdes (1958)
French Dressing (1964)
Billion Dollar Brain (1967)
Women In Love (1969)
The Music Lovers (1970)
The Devils (1971)
The Boy Friend (1971)
Savage Messiah (1972)
Mahler (1974)
Tommy (1975)
Lisztomania (1975)
Valentino (1977)
Altered States (1980)
Crimes of Passion (1984)
Gothic (1986)
Aria (1987) (Segment: Nessun Dorma)
Salomé's Last Dance (1988)
The Lair of the White Worm (1988)
The Rainbow (1989)
Whore (1991)
Tales of Erotica (1996) (Segment: The Insatiable Mrs. Kirsch)
Mindbender (1996)
The Lion's Mouth (2000)
The Fall of the Louse of Usher (2002)
Trapped Ashes (2006) (Segment: The Girl With Golden Breasts)
Hot Pants (2006)

## Television work as director

Scottish Painters (1959)
Variations on a Mechanical Theme (1959)
Guitar Craze (1959)
Gordon Jacob (1959)
Poet's London (1959)
Portrait of a Goon (1959)
Journey Into a Lost World (1960)
Marie Rambert Remembers (1960)
Cranko at Work (1960)
The Light Fantastic (1960)
Shelagh Delaney's Salford (1960)
A House in Bayswater (1960)
The Miner's Picnic (1960)
Architecture of Entertainment (1960)
London Moods (1961)
Old Battersea House (1961)
Lotte Lenya Sings Kurt Weill (1961)
Antonio Gaudi (1961)
Pop Goes the Easel (1962)
Preservation Man (1962)
Mr. Chesher's Traction Engines (1962)
Elgar (1962)
Prokofiev: Portrait of a Soviet Composer (1963)
Lonely Shore (1964)
The Dotty World of James Lloyd (1964)
Watch the Birdie (1964)
Bartók (1964)
Diary of a Nobody (1964)
The Debussy Film (1965)
Always On Sunday (1965)
Isadora Duncan, the Biggest Dancer in the World (1966)
Don't Shoot the Composer (1966)
Dante's Inferno (1967)
Song of Summer: Frederick Delius (1968)
A House in Bayswater: Prokofiev (1968)
Dance of the Seven Veils (1970)
Clouds of Glory: William and Dorothy (1978)
Clouds of Glory: The Rime of the Ancient Mariner (1978)
The Planets (1983)
The South Bank Show: Vaughan Williams: A Symphonic Portrait (1984)
Faust (1985)
Ken Russell's ABC of British Music (1988)
A British Picture (1989)
Méphistophélès (1989)
Women and Men: Stories of Seduction (1990) (Segment: Dusk Before Fireworks)
The Strange Affliction of Anton Bruckner (1990)
Road To Mandalay (1991)
Prisoner of Honor (1991)
The Secret Life of Arnold Bax (1992)
Lady Chatterley (1993)
The Mystery of Dr Martinu (1993)
Classic Widows (1995)
Alice in Russialand (1995)
Treasure Island (1995)
In Search of the English Folk Song (1997)
Dogboys (1998)
Brighton Belles (2001)
Elgar: Fantasy of a Composer on a Bicycle (2002)

Revenge of the Elephant Man (2004)
A Kitten For Hitler (2007)
Boudicca Bites Back (2009)

# BIBLIOGRAPHY

## KEN RUSSELL

"*The Music Lovers*", *Filmfacts*, 14, 1971
"Conversation With Ken Russell", in T. Fox, *Oui*, June, 1973
"Mahler the Man", *Mahler Brochure*, Sackville Publishing, London, 1974
*A British Picture: An Autobiography*, Heinemann, London, 1989
*Altered States*, Bantam Books, New York, 1991
*Fire Over England: The British Cinema Comes Under Friendly Fire* (a.k.a. *The Lion Roars*), Hutchinson, London, 1993
*Mike and Gaby's Space Gospel*, Little, Brown, 1999
*Violation*, Author House, 2001
*Directing Film*, Brassey's, Washington DC, 2001
*Elgar: The Erotic Variations* and *Delius: A Moment With Venus*, Peter Owen, London, 2007
*Beethoven Confidential* and *Brahms Gets Laid*, Peter Owen, London, 2007
"Ken Russell, the master director", *The Observer*, Aug 30, 2009

## OTHERS

Y. Allom *et al*, eds. *Contemporary British and Irish Film Directors, A Wallflower Critical Guide*, Wallflower, London, 20001
R. Armes. *A Critical History of British Cinema*, Secker & Warburg, London, 1978
J. Ashby & A. Higson, eds. *British Cinema, Past and Present*, Routledge, London, 2000
T. Atkins, ed. *Ken Russell*, Monarch/ Simon & Schuster, New York, 1976
S. Au. *Ballet and Modern Dance*, Thames & Hudson, London, 2012
M. Auty & N. Roddick, eds. *British Cinema Now*, British Film Institute, London, 1985
M. Barker, ed. *The Video Nasties: Freedom and Censorship In the Media*, Pluto Press, London, 1984
—. & J. Petley, eds. *Ill Effects: The Media/ Violence Debate*, Routledge, London, 1997
P. Barnes & P. Townshend. *The Story of Tommy*, Eel Pie Publishing, Twickenham, 1977
J. Baxter. *An Appalling Talent: Ken Russell*, M. Joseph, London, 1973
—. "The Television Films", in T. Atkins, 1976
L. Bawden, ed. *The Oxford Companion To Film*, Oxford University Press, Oxford, 1976
M. Beja. *Film and Literature: An Introduction*, Longman, London, 1979
R. Bell-Metereau: "*Altered States*", *Journal of Popular Film and Television*, 9, 4, 1982
E. Blom, ed. *The New Everyman Dictionary of Music*, J.M. Dent, London, 1988
C. Bloom, ed. *Gothic Horror*, Macmillan, London, 1998
G. Bluestone. *Novels Into Film*, University of California Press, Berkeley, CA, 1961
D. Bordwell & K. Thompson. *Film Art: An Introduction*, McGraw-Hill Publishing Company, New York, NY, 2001
—. *et al. The Classical Hollywood Cinema: Film Style and Mode of Production To 1960*, Routledge, London, 1985

—. *Narration In the Fiction Film*, Routledge, London, 1988
—. *The Way Hollywood Tells It*, University of California Press, Berkeley, CA, 2006
F. Botting. *Making Monstrous: Frankenstein, Criticism, Theory*, Manchester University Press, Manchester, 1991
—. *Gothic*, Routledge, London, 1996
C. Bowen & B. von Meck. *Beloved Friend*, Random House, New York, 1937
J. Brady. *The Craft of the Screenwriter*, Touchstone, New York, 1982
M. Bragg. *The Seventh Seal*, BFI Classics, British Film Institute, London, 1993
A. Britton *et al. American Nightmare: Essays On the Horror Film*, Toronto, 1979
D. Britton. *Lady Chatterley: The Making of the Novel*, Unwin Hyman, London, 1988
H. Brodzky. *Henri Gaudier-Brzeska*, Faber, London, 1933
J. Brosnan. *Primal Screen: A History of Science Fiction Film*, Orbit, London, 1991
P. Buckley. "Savage Saviour", *Films and Filming*, Oct, 1972
S. Bukatman. *Terminal Identity: The Virtual Subject In Postmodern Science Fiction*, Duke University Press, Durham, NC, 1993
G. Burt. *The Art of Film Music*, Northeastern University Press, 1994
I. Butler. *Religion In the Cinema*, A.S. Barnes, New York, NY, 1969
Ross Care, *Film Quarterly*, Spring, 1978
K. Carroll. "The Dark Brilliance of Ken Russell", *Sunday News*, March 30, 1975
M. Carter, ed. *Dracula: The Vampire and the Critics*, UMI Research Press, Ann Arbor, MI, 1988
D. Cavallaro. *The Gothic Vision*, Continuum, New York, NY, 2002
N. Cawthorne. *The Who and the Making of Tommy*, Unanimous, London, 2005
I. Christie. *Arrows of Desire: The Films of Michael Powell and Emeric Pressburger*, Faber, London, 1994
M. Cloonan. *Banned! Censorship In Popular Music In Britain, 1967-92*, Arena, Aldershot, 1996
D.A. Cook. *A History of Narrative Film*, W.W. Norton, New York, NY, 1981, 1990, 1996
P. Cook & M. Bernink, eds. *The Cinema Book*, 2nd ed., British Film Institute, London, 1999
J. Crist, ed. *Take 22: Moviemakers On Moviemaking*, Continuum, New York, NY, 1991
R. Crouse. *Raising Hell*, ECW Press, 2012
J. Curran & V. Porter, eds. *British Cinema History*, Weidenfeld & Nicolson, London, 1983
H.M. Daleski. *The Forked Flame: A Study of D.H. Lawrence*, London, 1968
W. Darby & J. Du Bois. *American Film Music*, McFarland, Jefferson, NC, 1990
E. De Grazia & R.K. Newman. *Banned Films: Movies, Censors and the First Amendment*, Bowker, New York, NY, 1982
E. Delavenay. *D.H. Lawrence: The Man and His Work: The Formative Years, 1885-1919*, tr. K.M. Delavenay, Southern Illinois University Press, Carbondale, 1972
M. Dempsey: "The World of Ken Russell", *Film Quarterly*, 25, 3, 1972
—. "Ken Russell Again", *Film Quarterly*, 31, 2, 1977-78
L. Denham. *The Films of Peter Greenaway*, Minerva Press, London, 1993
R. Serge Denisoff & W. Romanowski. *Risky Business: Rock In Film*, Transaction, 1991
W.W. Dixon, ed. *Re-viewing British Cinema*, State University of New York Press, Albany, NY, 1994
K.J. Donnelly, ed. *Film Music*, Edinburgh University Press, Edinburgh, 2001
O. Doughty. *Dante Gabriel Rossetti*, Yale University Press, New Haven, 1949
S.C. Dubin. *Arresting Images: Impolitic Art and Uncivil Actions*, Routledge, London, 1992
R. Durgnat. *A Mirror For England: British Movies From Austerity To Affluence*, Faber, London, 1970
J. Eberts. *My Indecision Is Final: The Rise and Fall of Goldcrest Films*, Faber, London, 1990
H.S. Ede. *Savage Messiah*, 1931
R. Eder. "The Screen: Ken Russell's *Mahler*", *New York Times*, Apl 5, 1976
J. Eszterhas. *The Devil's Guide To Hollywood*, Duckworth, London, 2006
S. Farber, "Russellmania", *Film Comment*, 11, 6, Nov, 1975
E. Fenby. *Delius As I Knew Him*, Icon Books, London, 1966
J. Finler. *The Movie Director's Story*, Octopus Books, London, 1985
A. Finney. *The Egos Have Landed: The Rise and Fall of Palace Pictures*, Heinemann,

London, 1996
J. Fisher. "Three Masterpieces of Sexuality", in T. Atkins, 1976
Kevin M. Flanagan, ed. *Ken Russell: Re-Viewing England's Last Mannerist*, Scarecrow Press, 2009
G. Flatley. "I'm Surprised My Films Shock People", *New York Times*, Oct, 1972
T. Fletcher. *Dear Boy: The Life of Keith Moon*, Omnibus, London, 1998
G.E. Forshey. *American Religious and Biblical Spectaculars*, Praeger, Westport, CT, 1992
T. Fox. "Conversation With Ken Russell", *Oui*, June, 1973
K. French, ed. *Screen Violence*, Bloomsbury, London, 1996
L. Friedman, ed. *Fires Were Started: British Cinema and Thatcherism*, UCL Press, London, 1993
H. Gal, ed. *The Musician's World*, Thames & Hudson, London, 1965
K. Gelder. *Reading the Vampire*, Routledge, London, 1994
—. ed. *The Horror Reader*, Routledge, London, 2000
—. *New Vampire Cinema*, BFI/ Palgrave Macmillan, London, 2012
J. Gelmis. *The Film Director as Superstar*, Penguin, London, 1974
R. Gentry: "Ken Russell", *Post Script*, 2, 3, 1983
L. Gianetti. *Understanding Movies*, Prentice-Hall, NJ, 1982
R. Giddings et al. *Screening the Novel: The Theory and Practice of Literary Dramatisation*, Macmillan, London, 1990
—. & E. Sheen, eds. *The Classic Novel From Page To Screen*, Manchester University Press, Manchester, 2000
D. Gifford. *The British Film Catalogue, 1895-1985*, David & Charles, London, 1986
H. Mark Glancy. *When Hollywood Loved Britain*, Manchester University Press, Manchester, 1999
J. Gomez. *Ken Russell*, Muller, 1976
—. "Russell's Methods of Adaption", in T. Atkins, 1976
—. "Russell's Images of Lawrence's Vision", in M. Klein, 1981
C. Goodwin. *Evil Spirits*, Virgin Books, 2001
B.K. Grant, ed. *Planks of Reason: Essays on the Horror Film*, Scarecrow Press, Metuchen, NJ, 1984
—. ed. *The Dread of Difference: Gender and the Horror Film*, University of Texas Press, Austin, TX, 1996
S. Grantley & A. Parker. *The Who By Numbers*, Helter Skelter, London, 2010
J. Green. *The Encyclopedia of Censorship*, Facts on File, New York, NY, 1990
L. Greiff. *D.H. Lawrence: 50 Years On Film*, Southern Illinois University Press, Carbondale, IL, 2001
Elizabeth Grosz. *Sexual Subversions*, Allen & Unwin, London, 1989
—. "Lesbian Fetishism?", *differences*, 3, 2, 1991
—. *Volatile Bodies*, Indiana University Press, Bloomington, IN, 1994
—. *Space, Time and Perversion*, Routledge, London, 1995
J. Hacker & D. Price, eds. *Take 10: Contemporary British Film Directors*, Oxford University Press, Oxford, 1991
L. Halliwell. *Halliwell's Filmgoer's Companion*, 7th edition, Granada, London, 1980
—. *Halliwell's Film and Video Guide*, 15th ed, ed. J. Walker, HarperCollins, 2000
K. Hanke. *Ken Russell's Films*, Scarecrow Press, New Jersey, 1984
P. Hardy, ed. *The Aurum Encyclopedia of Science Fiction*, Aurum, London, 1991
S. Harper. *Picturing the Past: The Rise and Fall of the British Costume Film*, British Film Institute, London, 1994
C. Heylin. *All the Madmen*, Constable, London, 2012
G. Hickenlooper. *Reel Conversations: Candid Interviews With Film's Foremost Directors and Critics*, Citadel, New York, NY, 1991
A. Higson. *Waving the Flag: Constructing a National Cinema In Britain*, Oxford University Press, Oxford, 1995
—. *English Heritage, English Cinema: Costume Drama Since 1980*, Oxford University Press, Oxford, 2003
J. Hill et al, eds. *Border Crossing*, British Film Institute, London, 1994
—. *British Cinema In the 1980s*, Oxford University Press, Oxford, 1999
J. Hillier. *The New Hollywood*, Studio Vista, London, 1992
L. Hunt. *British Low Culture: From Safari Suits To Sexploitation*, Routledge, London, 1998
I.Q. Hunter. *British Science Fiction Cinema*, Routledge, London, 1999

A. Huxley. *The Devils of Loudun*, Chatto & Windus, London, 1970
I. Inglis, ed. *Popular Music and Film*, Wallflower Press, London, 2003
G. Jackson. *Esquire*, May, 1972
D. Jarman. *Dancing Ledge*, Quartet, London, 1984
D. Jones, ed. *Meaty Beaty Big & Bouncy! Classic Rock & Pop Writing From Elvis To Oasis*, Hodder & Stoughton, London, 1996
P. Kael, *Kiss Kiss Bang Bang*, Bantam, New York, NY, 1969
—. "Hyperbole and Narcissus", *The New Yorker*, Nov 18, 1972
—. *Taking It All In*, Marion Boyars, 1986
—. *State of the Art*, Marion Boyars, London, 1987
—. *Movie Love*, Marion Boyars, London, 1992
K. Kalinak. *Settling the Score: Music and the Classical Hollywood Film*, University of Wisconsin Press, Madison, WI, 1992
F. Karlin. *Listening To Movies*, Schirmer, New York, NY, 1994
B.F. Kawin. *How Movies Work*, Macmillan, New York, NY, 1987
M. Kermode. "Raising Hell", *Sight & Sound*, 2002
—. *Hatchet Job*, Picador, 2013
P. Keough, ed. *Flesh and Blood: The National Society of Film Critics on Sex, Violence, and Censorship*, Mercury House, San Francisco, CA, 1995
C. Kipps. *Out of Focus: Power, Prejudice: David Puttnam In Hollywood*, Century Hutchinson, London, 1989
M. Klein & G. Parker, eds. *The English Novel and the Movies*, F. Ungar, New York, NY, 1981
P. Kolker. *The Altering Eye: Contemporary International Cinema*, Oxford University Press, New York, NY, 1983
—. *A Cinema of Loneliness: Penn, Stone, Kubrick, Scorsese, Spielberg, Altman*, Oxford University Press, New York, NY, 2000
J. Kristeva. *Powers of Horror: An Essay on Abjection*, tr. Leon S. Roudiez, Columbia University Press, New York, 1982
—. *Tales of Love*, tr. Leon S. Roudiez, Columbia University Press, New York 1987
—. *Black Sun: Depression and Melancholy*, tr. L.S. Roudiez, Columbia University Press, New York, 1989
—. "A Question of Subjectivity: an interview" [with Susan Sellers], *Women's Review*, 12, 1986, in Philip Rice & Patricia Waugh, eds. *Modern Literary Theory: A Reader*, Arnold, 1992
L. Langley, "Ken Russell", *Show*, Oct, 1971.
J. Lanza. *Fragile Geometry: The Films, Philosophy and Misadventures of Nicolas Roeg*, PAJ, New York, NY, 1989
—. *Phallic Frenzy: Ken Russell and His Films*, Aurum Pres, London, 2008
D.H. Lawrence. *The Letters of D.H. Lawrence*, ed. A. Huxley, Heinemann, London, 1934
—. *Selected Essays*, Penguin, 1950
—. *A Selection from Phoenix*, ed. A.A.H. Inglis, Penguin, 1971
—. *The Complete Poems*, ed. Vivian de Sola Pinto & Warren Roberts, 2 vols, Heinemann, London 1972
—. *The Rainbow*, ed. J. Worthen, Penguin, London, 1981/86
—. *Women In Love*, ed. C.L. Ross, Penguin, London, 1982/86
—. *The First Lady Chatterley*, Penguin, London, 1973
—. *John Thomas and Lady Jane*, Penguin, London, 1973
—. *Lady Chatterley's Lover*, Penguin, London, 1960
—. *Lady Chatterley's Lover*, ed. J. Lyon, Penguin, London, 1990
—. *Lady Chatterley's Lover* and *A Propos of Lady Chatterley's Lover*, ed. M. Black, Cambridge University Press, Cambridge, 1993
P. Leprohan. *The Italian Cinema*, tr. R. Greaves & O. Stallybrass, Secker & Warburg, London, 1972
J. Lewis. *The Road To Romance and Ruin: Teen Films and Youth Culture*, Routledge, London, 1992
—. *Hollywood v. Hard Core: How the Struggle Over Censorship Created the Modern Film Industry*, New York University Press, New York, NY, 2000
C. Lyons. *The New Censors*, Temple University Press, Philadelphia, PA, 1997
T.D. Matthews. *Censored*, Chatto & Windus, London, 1994
R. Manvell. *New Cinema In Britain*, Dutton, New York, NY, 1968

G. Mast *et al*, eds. *Film Theory and Criticism: Introductory Readings*, Oxford University Press, New York, NY, 1992a
—. & B. Kawin, *A Short History of the Movies*, Macmillan, New York, NY, 1992b
J.R. May & M. Bird, eds. *Religion In Film*, University of Tennessee Press, Knoxville, 1982
—. *New Image of Religious Film*, Sheed & Ward, London, 1996
S.Y. McDougal. *Made Into Movies: From Literature To Film*, Holt, Rinehart and Winston, New York, NY, 1985
B. McFarlane, ed. *An Autobiography of British Cinema*, Methuen, London, 1997
P. Mezan. "Relax, It's Only a Ken Russell Movie", *Esquire*, May, 1973
M. Miles. *Seeing and Believing: Religion and Values In the Movies*, Beacon, Boston, MA, 1996
F. Miller. *Censored Hollywood: Sex, Sin and Violence On Screen,* Turner Publishing, Atlanta, 1994
H. Miller. *The World of Lawrence: A Passionate Appreciation*, ed. Evelyn J. Hinz & John J. Teunissen, Calder, 1985
K. Millett. *Sexual Politics*, Doubleday, Garden City, 1970
G. Mulholland. *Popcorn: Fifty Years of Rock 'n' Roll Movies*, Orion Books, London, 2011
R. Murphy. *Realism and Tinsel: British Cinema and Society, 1939-48*, London, 1989
—. *Sixties British Cinema*, British Film Institute, London, 1992
—. ed. *British Cinema of the 90s*, British Film Institute, London, 2000
—. ed. *The British Cinema Book*, Palgrave/ Macmillan, London, 2nd edition, 2009
R. Murray. *Images In the Dark: An Encyclopedia of Gay and Lesbian Film and Video*, Titan Books, London, 1998
S. Neale & M. Smith, eds. *Contemporary Hollywood Cinema*, Routledge, London, 1998
K. Newman. *Nightmare Movies*, Harmony, New York, NY, 1988
—. *Millennium Movies*, Titan Books, London, 1999
—. ed. *Science Fiction/ Horror: A Sight & Sound Reader*, British Film Institute, London, 2002
P. Norman. *Mick Jagger,* HarperCollins, 2012
G. Nowell-Smith, ed. *The Oxford History of World Cinema*, Oxford University Press, Oxford, 1996
W. Ober. *Boswell's Clap and Other Essays*, Southern Ilinois University Press, IL, 1979
M. O'Pray, ed. *The British Avant Garde Film, 1926-1995*, University of Luton Press/ John Libbey, London, 1996
J. Orr. *Contemporary Cinema*, Edinburgh University Press, Edinburgh, 1998
C. Paglia. *Sexual Personae: Art and Decadence From Nefertiti To Emily Dickinson*, Penguin, London, 1992
J. Park. *Learning To Dream: The New British Cinema*, Faber, London, 1984
—. *British Cinema*, B.T. Batsford, London, 1990
D. Parkinson. *The Rough Guide To Film Musicals*, Penguin, London, 2007
D. Peary, ed. *Omni's Screen Flights, Screen Fantasies,* Doubleday, New York, NY, 1984
C. Penley, ed. *Feminism and Film Theory*, Routledge, London, 1988
—. *et al*, eds. *Close Encounters: Film, Feminism and Science Fiction*, University of Minnesota Press, Minneapolis, 1991
G. Perry. *Life of Python*, Pavilion, London, 1983
—. *The Great British Picture Show*, Pavilion, London, 1985
D. Petrie. *Creativity and Constraint In the British Film Industry*, Macmillan, London, 1991
—. ed. *New Questions of British Cinema*, British Film Institute, London, 1992
—. *Screening Europe: Image and Identity In Contemporary European Cinema*, British Film Institute, London, 1992
—. *The British Cinematographer*, British Film Institute, London, 1996
G. Phelps. *Film Censorship*, Gollancz, London, 1975
G. Philips. "Ken Russell as Adaptor", *Literature/ Film Quarterly*, 5, 1977
—. *Ken Russell*, Twayne, Boston, MA, 1979
D. Pirie. *A Heritage of Horror: The English Gothic Cinema*, Gordon & Fraser, 1973
E. Pound. *Gaudier-Brzeska*, New Directions, New York, 1970
M. Powell. *A Life In the Movies*, Heinemann, London, 1986, 1992
—. *Million-Dollar Movie*, Heinemann, London, 1992
R. Prendergast. *Film Music*, W.W. Norton, New York, NY, 1992
S. Prince, ed. *Screening Violence*, Athlone Press, London, 2000

D. Puttnam. *The Undeclared War: The Struggle For Control of the World's Film Industry*, HarperCollins, London, 1997
M. Pye & Lynda Myles. *The Movie Brats: How the Film Generation Took Over Hollywood*, Faber, London, 1979
J. Pym. *Film On Four*, British Film Institute, London, 1992
D. Quinlan. *The Illustrated Guide To Film Directors*, B.T. Batsford, London, 1983
T. Reeves. *The Worldwide Guide To Movie Locations*, Titan Books, London, 2003
J. Richards, ed. *Films and British National Identity*, Manchester University Press, Manchester, 1997
M. Richardson. *Surrealism and Cinema*, Berg, New York, NY, 2006
F. Robbins, "The Savage Russell", *Gallery*, May, 1973
J. Robertson. *The British Board of Film Censors*, Croom Helm, 1985
—. *The Hidden Cinema*, Routledge, London, 1989
W.H. Rockett. *Devouring Whirlwind: Terror and Transcendence In the Cinema of Cruelty*, Greenwood Press, New York, NY, 1988
J. Romney & A. Wooton, eds. *Celluloid Juke Box*, British Film Institute, London, 1995
V. Sage. *The Gothick Novel: A Casebook*, Macmillan, London, 1990
L. Sandahl. *Rock Music On Film*, Blandford Press, Poole, 1987
D. Schaefer & L. Salvato, eds. *Masters of Light*, University of California Press, Berkeley, CA, 1984
T. Schatz. *Old Hollywood/ New Hollywood*, UMI Research Press, Ann Arbor, MI, 1983
—. *The Genius of the System: Hollywood Filmmaking In the Studio Era*, Pantheon, New York, NY 1988
R. Sellers. *Oliver Reed*, Constable & Robinson, London, 2013
T. Shaw. *British Cinema and the Cold War*, I.B. Tauris, London, 2001
D. Shipman. *The Story of Cinema*, Hodder & Stoughton, London, 1984
—. *Caught In the Act: Sex and Eroticism In the Movies*, Hamish Hamilton, London, 1986
T. Shone. *Blockbuster: How the Jaws and Jedi Generation Turned Hollywood Into a Boom-Town*, Scribner, London, 2005
L. Sider *et al*, eds. *Soundscapes: The School of Sound Lectures 1998-2001*, Wallflower Press, London, 2003
N. Sinyard. *Filming Literature: The Art of Screen Adaption*, Croom Helm, Beckenham, Kent, 1986
P. Adams Sitney, ed. *The Avant-Garde Film: A Reader of Theory and Criticism*, New York University Press, New York, NY, 1978
—. *Visionary Film: The American Avant-Garde, 1943-1978,* 2nd ed., Oxford University Press, New York, NY, 1979
A. Slide. *'Banned In the USA': British Films In the United States and Their Censorship, 1933-1960*, I.B. Tauris, London, 1998
J. Smith. *Withnail and Us: Cult Films and Film Cults In British Cinema*, Tauris, London, 2010
J. Squire, ed. *The Movie Business Book*, Fireside, New York, NY, 1992
G. Stewart. *Between Film and Screen: Modernism's Photo Synthesis*, University of Chicago Press, Chicago, IL, 1999
S. Street. *British National Cinema*, Routledge, London, 1997/ 2009
D Strerritt, "Whole Film Is 'One Flash' In His Mind", *Christian Science Monitor*, June 2, 1975
J. Stringer, ed. *Movie Blockbusters*, Routledge, London, 2003
P. Swann. *The Hollywood Feature Film In Postwar Britain*, Croom Helm, 1987
K. Thompson & D. Bordwell. *Film History: An Introduction*, McGraw-Hill, New York, NY, 1994
—. *Storytelling In the New Hollywood*, Harvard University Press, Cambridge, MA, 1999
D. Thomson. *A Biographical Dictionary of Film*, Deutsch, London, 1995
C. Tohill & P. Tombs. *Immoral Tales: Sex and Horror Cinema In Europe 1956-1984*, Titan Books, London, 1995
P. Townshend & D. McAnuff. *The Who's Tommy*, Pantheon, London, 1993
—. *Tommy, the Musical*, Vintage, London, 1999
—. *Who I Am*, HarperCollins, London, 2012
G. Tremlett. *Rock Gold: The Music Millionaires*, Unwin Hyman, London, 1990
J. Trevelyan. *What the Censor Saw*, Michael Joseph, London, 1973

P. Tyler. *Screening the Sexes: Homosexuality In the Movies*, Doubleday, New York, NY, 1973
K. Van Gunden. *Fantasy Films*, McFarland, Jefferson, NC 1989
G. Vincendeau, ed. *Encyclopedia of European Cinema*, British Film Institute, London, 1995
—. ed. *Film/ Literature/ Heritage: A Sight & Sound Reader*, British Film Institute, London, 2001
H. Vogel. *Entertainment Industry Economics*, Cambridge University Press, Cambridge, 1995
R. Wakeman. *Grumpy Old Rock Star*, London, 2008
—. *Further Adventures of a Grumpy Old Rock Star*, Arrow, 2010
A. Walker. *National Heroes: British Cinema In the Seventies and Eighties*, Harrap, London, 1985
—. *Hollywood, England: The British Film Industry In the Sixties*, Harrap, London, 1986
J. Walker. *The Observer*, Sept 8, 1974
J. Walker. *The Once and Future Film: British Cinema In the 1970s and 1980s*, Methuen, London, 1985
—. *Art and Artists on Screen*, Manchester University Press, Manchester, 1993
P. Webb. *The Erotic Arts*, Secker & Warburg, London, 1975
E. Weiss. & J. Belton, eds. *Film Sound: Theory and Practice*, Columbia University Press, New York, NY, 1989
O. Welles. *Orson Welles: Interviews,* ed. M. Estrin, University of Mississippi Press, Jackson, 2002
C. Wilson. *Ken Russell*, Intergroup, London, 1974
M. Wolf. *The Entertainment Economy*, Penguin, London, 1999
S. Wolter & K. Kimber. *The Who In Print*, McFarland & Co., Jefferson, NC, 1992
L. Wood, ed. *British Films, 1971-1981*, British Film Institute, London, 1983
J. Wyatt. *High Concept: Movies and Marketing In Hollywood*, University of Texas Press, Austin, TX, 1994
A. Yule. *Fast Forward: David Puttnam, Columbia Pictures and the Battle For Hollywood*, Delacorte, New York, NY, 1989
A.L. Zambrano: "Women In Love", *Literature/ Film Quarterly*, 1, Jan, 1973
J. Zipes, ed. *The Oxford Companion To Fairy Tales*, Oxford University Press, 2000
—. *The Enchanted Screen: The Unknown History of Fairy-tale Films*, Routledge, New York, NY, 2011
—. *The Irresistible Fairy Tale*, Prince University Press, Princeton, NJ, 2012


WEBSITES

Savage Messiah/ Ken Russell: iainfisher.com/Russell

The Who:                thewho.com
Richard Chamberlain:    richardchamberlain.net
D.H. Lawrence:          dh-lawrence.org.uk • lawrenceseastwood.co.uk • dhlsna.com • dhlawrencesocietyaustralia.com.au
Aldous Huxley:          somaweb.org
Dante Gabriel Rossetti: rossettiarchive.org
The *Harry Palmer* movies: keesstam.tripod.com

Jeremy Robinson has written many critical studies, including *Hayao Miyazaki, Walerian Borowczyk, Arthur Rimbaud,* and *The Sacred Cinema of Andrei Tarkovsky,* plus literary monographs on: William Shakespeare; Samuel Beckett; Thomas Hardy; André Gide; Robert Graves; and John Cowper Powys.

It's amazing for me to see my work treated with such passion and respect. There is nothing resembling it in the U.S. in relation to my work.
Andrea Dworkin (on *Andrea Dworkin*)

This model monograph – it is an exemplary job, and I'm very proud that he has accorded me a couple of mentions... The subject matter of his book is beautifully organised and dead on beam.
Lawrence Durrell (on *The Light Eternal: A Study of J.M.W. Turner*)

Jeremy Robinson's poetry is certainly jammed with ideas, and I find it very interesting for that reason. It's certainly a strong imprint of his personality.
Colin Wilson

*Sex-Magic-Poetry-Cornwall* is a very rich essay... It is a very good piece... vastly stimulating and insightful.
Peter Redgrove

# CRESCENT MOON PUBLISHING

web: www.crmoon.com  e-mail: cresmopub@yahoo.co.uk

## ARTS, PAINTING, SCULPTURE

The Art of Andy Goldsworthy
Andy Goldsworthy: Touching Nature
Andy Goldsworthy in Close-Up
Andy Goldsworthy: Pocket Guide
Andy Goldsworthy In America
Land Art: A Complete Guide
The Art of Richard Long
Richard Long: Pocket Guide
Land Art In the UK
Land Art in Close-Up
Land Art In the U.S.A.
Land Art: Pocket Guide
Installation Art in Close-Up
Minimal Art and Artists In the 1960s and After
Colourfield Painting
Land Art DVD, TV documentary
Andy Goldsworthy DVD, TV documentary
The Erotic Object: Sexuality in Sculpture From Prehistory to the Present Day
Sex in Art: Pornography and Pleasure in Painting and Sculpture
Postwar Art
Sacred Gardens: The Garden in Myth, Religion and Art
Glorification: Religious Abstraction in Renaissance and 20th Century Art
Early Netherlandish Painting
Leonardo da Vinci
Piero della Francesca
Giovanni Bellini
Fra Angelico: Art and Religion in the Renaissance
Mark Rothko: The Art of Transcendence
Frank Stella: American Abstract Artist
Jasper Johns
Brice Marden
Alison Wilding: The Embrace of Sculpture
Vincent van Gogh: Visionary Landscapes
Eric Gill: Nuptials of God
Constantin Brancusi: Sculpting the Essence of Things
Max Beckmann
Caravaggio
Gustave Moreau
Egon Schiele: Sex and Death In Purple Stockings
Delizioso Fotografico Fervore: Works In Process 1
Sacro Cuore: Works In Process 2
The Light Eternal: J.M.W. Turner
The Madonna Glorified: Karen Arthurs

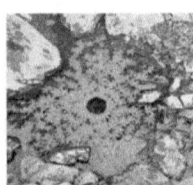

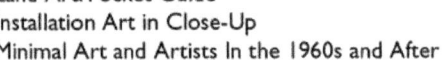

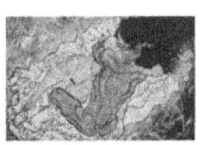

# LITERATURE

J.R.R. Tolkien: The Books, The Films, The Whole Cultural Phenomenon
J.R.R. Tolkien: Pocket Guide
Tolkien's Heroic Quest
The *Earthsea* Books of Ursula Le Guin
Beauties, Beasts and Enchantment: Classic French Fairy Tales
German Popular Stories by the Brothers Grimm
Philip Pullman and *His Dark Materials*
Sexing Hardy: Thomas Hardy and Feminism
Thomas Hardy's *Tess of the d'Urbervilles*
Thomas Hardy's *Jude the Obscure*
Thomas Hardy: The Tragic Novels
Love and Tragedy: Thomas Hardy
The Poetry of Landscape in Hardy
Wessex Revisited: Thomas Hardy and John Cowper Powys
Wolfgang Iser: Essays and Interviews
Petrarch, Dante and the Troubadours
Maurice Sendak and the Art of Children's Book Illustration
Andrea Dworkin
Cixous, Irigaray, Kristeva: The *Jouissance* of French Feminism
Julia Kristeva: Art, Love, Melancholy, Philosophy, Semiotics and Psychoanalysis
Hélène Cixous I Love You: The *Jouissance* of Writing
Luce Irigaray: Lips, Kissing, and the Politics of Sexual Difference
Peter Redgrove: Here Comes the Flood
Peter Redgrove: Sex-Magic-Poetry-Cornwall
Lawrence Durrell: Between Love and Death, East and West
Love, Culture & Poetry: Lawrence Durrell
Cavafy: Anatomy of a Soul
German Romantic Poetry: Goethe, Novalis, Heine, Hölderlin
Feminism and Shakespeare
Shakespeare: Love, Poetry & Magic
The Passion of D.H. Lawrence
D.H. Lawrence: Symbolic Landscapes
D.H. Lawrence: Infinite Sensual Violence
Rimbaud: Arthur Rimbaud and the Magic of Poetry
The Ecstasies of John Cowper Powys
Sensualism and Mythology: The Wessex Novels of John Cowper Powys
Amorous Life: John Cowper Powys and the Manifestation of Affectivity  (H.W. Fawkner)
Postmodern Powys: New Essays on John Cowper Powys (Joe Boulter)
Rethinking Powys: Critical Essays on John Cowper Powys
Paul Bowles & Bernardo Bertolucci
Rainer Maria Rilke
Joseph Conrad: *Heart of Darkness*
In the Dim Void: Samuel Beckett
Samuel Beckett Goes into the Silence
André Gide: Fiction and Fervour
Jackie Collins and the Blockbuster Novel
Blinded By Her Light: The Love-Poetry of Robert Graves
The Passion of Colours: Travels In Mediterranean Lands
Poetic Forms

## POETRY

Ursula Le Guin: Walking In Cornwall
Peter Redgrove: Here Comes The Flood
Peter Redgrove: Sex-Magic-Poetry-Cornwall
Dante: Selections From the Vita Nuova
Petrarch, Dante and the Troubadours
William Shakespeare: Sonnets
William Shakespeare: Complete Poems
Blinded By Her Light: The Love-Poetry of Robert Graves
Emily Dickinson: Selected Poems
Emily Brontë: Poems
Thomas Hardy: Selected Poems
Percy Bysshe Shelley: Poems
John Keats: Selected Poems
Joh n Keats: Poems of 1820
D.H. Lawrence: Selected Poems
Edmund Spenser: Poems
Edmund Spenser: Amoretti
John Donne: Poems
Henry Vaughan: Poems
Sir Thomas Wyatt: Poems
Robert Herrick: Selected Poems
Rilke: Space, Essence and Angels in the Poetry of Rainer Maria Rilke
Rainer Maria Rilke: Selected Poems
Friedrich Hölderlin: Selected Poems
Arseny Tarkovsky: Selected Poems
Arthur Rimbaud: Selected Poems
Arthur Rimbaud: A Season in Hell
Arthur Rimbaud and the Magic of Poetry
Novalis: Hymns To the Night
German Romantic Poetry
Paul Verlaine: Selected Poems
Elizaethan Sonnet Cycles
D.J. Enright: By-Blows
Jeremy Reed: Brigitte's Blue Heart
Jeremy Reed: Claudia Schiffer's Red Shoes
Gorgeous Little Orpheus
Radiance: New Poems
Crescent Moon Book of Nature Poetry
Crescent Moon Book of Love Poetry
Crescent Moon Book of Mystical Poetry
Crescent Moon Book of Elizabethan Love Poetry
Crescent Moon Book of Metaphysical Poetry
Crescent Moon Book of Romantic Poetry
Pagan America: New American Poetry

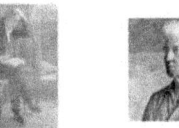

## MEDIA, CINEMA, FEMINISM and CULTURAL STUDIES

J.R.R. Tolkien: The Books, The Films, The Whole Cultural Phenomenon
J.R.R. Tolkien: Pocket Guide
The *Lord of the Rings* Movies: Pocket Guide
The Cinema of Hayao Miyazaki
Hayao Miyazaki: *Princess Mononoke*: Pocket Movie Guide
Hayao Miyazaki: *Spirited Away*: Pocket Movie Guide
Tim Burton : Hallowe'en For Hollywood
Ken Russell
Ken Russell: *Tommy*: Pocket Movie Guide
The Ghost Dance: The Origins of Religion
The Peyote Cult
Cixous, Irigaray, Kristeva: The *Jouissance* of French Feminism
Julia Kristeva: Art, Love, Melancholy, Philosophy, Semiotics and Psychoanalysis
Luce Irigaray: Lips, Kissing, and the Politics of Sexual Difference
Hélène Cixous I Love You: The *Jouissance* of Writing
Andrea Dworkin
'Cosmo Woman': The World of Women's Magazines
Women in Pop Music
HomeGround: The Kate Bush Anthology
Discovering the Goddess (Geoffrey Ashe)
The Poetry of Cinema
The Sacred Cinema of Andrei Tarkovsky
Andrei Tarkovsky: Pocket Guide
Andrei Tarkovsky: *Mirror*: Pocket Movie Guide
Andrei Tarkovsky: *The Sacrifice*: Pocket Movie Guide
Walerian Borowczyk: Cinema of Erotic Dreams
Jean-Luc Godard: The Passion of Cinema
Jean-Luc Godard: *Hail Mary*: Pocket Movie Guide
Jean-Luc Godard: *Contempt*: Pocket Movie Guide
Jean-Luc Godard: *Pierrot le Fou*: Pocket Movie Guide
John Hughes and Eighties Cinema
*Ferris Bueller's Day Off*: Pocket Movie Guide
Jean-Luc Godard: Pocket Guide
The Cinema of Richard Linklater
Liv Tyler: Star In Ascendance
*Blade Runner* and the Films of Philip K. Dick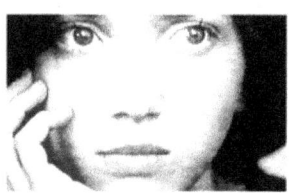
Paul Bowles and Bernardo Bertolucci
Media Hell: Radio, TV and the Press
An Open Letter to the BBC
Detonation Britain: Nuclear War in the UK
Feminism and Shakespeare
Wild Zones: Pornography, Art and Feminism
Sex in Art: Pornography and Pleasure in Painting and Sculpture
Sexing Hardy: Thomas Hardy and Feminism

*The Light Eternal* is a model monograph, an exemplary job. The subject matter of the book is beautifully organised and dead on beam. (Lawrence Durrell)
It is amazing for me to see my work treated with such passion and respect. (Andrea Dworkin)

### CRESCENT MOON PUBLISHING
P.O. Box 1312, Maidstone, Kent, ME14 5XU, Great Britain. www.crmoon.com

cresmopub@yahoo.co.uk    www.crescentmoon.org.uk